O9-AHV-882

The Christian Theology Reader

B

Praise for *Christian Theology: An Introduction*,
by Alister McGrath

"*Christian Theology: An Introduction* is a work of prodigious learning and notable clarity. Alister McGrath here combines a mastery of the history of doctrine with his gift of communication to produce the finest university textbook available in this field. The author introduces the reader to the major Christian teachings, surveys their historical development, examines the landmark disputes, and explores myriad interpretative traditions. McGrath demonstrates throughout a knowledge of classical and contemporary material – from patristics to postmodernism – that matches his well-known expertise in Reformation studies. A glossary of key theological terms further enriches the work as a resource for private study as well as the classroom."

Professor Gabriel Fackre, Abbot Professor of Christian Theology, Andover Newton Theological School

"Dr McGrath appreciates the importance of the diversity of Christianity as well as the excitement and relevance of the key issues today. He has produced a work that can help in teaching yourself theology or can act as a valuable reference work for students in particular courses. It is a genuine introduction, with clear explanations, a full glossary and index, good recommendations for further reading, and also questions for discussion. Above all, the whole range of major doctrines is taken seriously and the reader is introduced to some of the ways they are being thought about today."

Professor David F. Ford, Regius Professor of Divinity, University of Cambridge

"This comprehensive and up-to-date training manual on theologizing as a Christian is outstanding of its kind. Dr McGrath's confident clarity, open orthodoxy, shrewd judgment, and didactic flair should secure for so user-friendly a textbook a long and fruitful life."

Professor James Packer, Sangwoo Youtong Chee Professor of Theology, Regent College, Vancouver

"Dr McGrath's *Christian Theology: An Introduction* admirably provides exactly what its title promises. It offers a clear, eminently readable and perceptive introduction to a vast range of issues and thinkers in historical theology, as well as incorporating a basic philosophical and systematic theology. It judiciously places thinkers and issues in a broad historical and theological context, achieving a due sense of historical perspective as well as theological information. It will kindle engagement on the part of the reader, and I warmly commend it to all students who are beginning a serious study of Christian theology."

Professor Anthony Thiselton, Professor of Christian Theology and Head of Department, University of Nottingham

"This is an excellent introduction to theology. It is very clearly set out and carefully planned to be an educational resource. It provides extremely helpful grounding for any student of theology. It will be invaluable as a clear and unprejudiced guide to the whole discipline of theology."

Professor J. S. K. Ward, Regius Professor of Divinity, University of Oxford

"Alister McGrath's book is a delight to read and immensely instructing. It is well-ordered, systematic, and lucid in its presentation – clearly the work of someone well attuned to the needs of students. It presents insightful analysis of a range of theological opinions without being prescriptive or overly dogmatic. We are introduced to an impressive array of theologians: classical and modern; eastern and western; 'liberal' and 'conservative'; male and female – and yet without being overwhelmed by them all . . . I recommend this book without reservation and am confident that it will become the standard textbook for a generation of theological students."

Dr John W. Pryor, Australian College of Theology, New South Wales

Blackwell books by Alister E. McGrath

Reformation Thought, 2nd edn (1993)
The Genesis of Doctrine (1990)
A Life of John Calvin (1990)
Luther's Theology of the Cross (1987)
The Intellectual Origins of the European Reformation (1987)
The Blackwell Encyclopedia of Modern Christian Thought (editor; 1993)
Christian Theology: An Introduction (1994)

The Christian Theology Reader

EDITED BY

ALISTER E. McGRATH

BLACKWELL
Oxford UK & Cambridge USA

This collection copyright © Blackwell Publishers Ltd, 1995
Editorial matter copyright © Alister E. McGrath, 1995

First published 1995

Blackwell Publishers Inc.
238 Main Street
Cambridge, Massachusetts 02142
USA

Blackwell Publishers Ltd
108 Cowley Road
Oxford OX4 1JF
UK

All rights reserved. Except for the quotation of short passages for the purpose of criticism and review, no part of this publication may be reproduced, stored in a retrieval system, or transmitted, in any form or by any means, electronic, mechanical, photocopying, recording or otherwise, without prior permission of the publisher.

Except in the United States of America, this book is sold subject to the condition that it shall not, by way of trade or otherwise, be lent, resold, hired out, or otherwise circulated without the publisher's prior consent in any form of binding or cover other than that in which it is published and without a similar condition including this condition being imposed on the subsequent purchaser.

Library of Congress Cataloging-in-Publication Data

The Christian theology reader/edited by Alister E. McGrath.
    p.   cm.
  Includes bibliographical references and index.
  ISBN 0–631–19584–X (alk. paper). — ISBN 0–631–19585–8 (pbk.   :
alk. paper)
    1. Theology, Doctrinal.   I. McGrath, Alister E., 1953–   .
  BT77.C47   1995
  230—dc20   94–45500
                                                                             CIP

ISBN 0–631–19584 X; 0–631–19585 8 (pbk.)

British Library Cataloguing in Publication Data

A CIP catalogue record for this book is available from the British Library.

Commissioning editor: Alison Mudditt
Desk editor: Tony Grahame
Production controller: Lisa Eaton
Text designer: Lisa Eaton

Typeset in 10 on 12 pt Palatino
by Graphicraft Typesetters Ltd, Hong Kong
Printed in Great Britain by T.J. Press Ltd, Padstow, Cornwall

EPISCOPAL DIVINITY SCHOOL LIBRARY
99 BRATTLE ST.
CAMBRIDGE, MA 02138

MAR 2 8 1996

BT
77
.C47
1995

Contents

3   The Doctrine of God   90

5 Salvation in Christ   174

6 Human Nature, Sin, and Grace   210

7   The Church   258

8 The Sacraments   288

9   Christianity and Other Religions   318

10   Last Things   352

Study Panels

Preface

Christian theology is one of the most fascinating and rewarding subjects it is possible to study. The rich theological tradition of Christianity has taken root in virtually every part of global culture, and given rise to some of the most creative and important reflection in the history of human thought. To study this is to do more than gain insights into the Christian gospel; it is to understand more about human culture itself. For, as its influence has spread, Christianity has not demanded that cultures should fall into line with its precepts; from the outset, Christianity has taken root in cultures, and set in motion a rich and dynamic process of interaction between the ideas and values of the gospel, and those already present in the culture.

The motives for the study of Christian theology vary enormously. Some wish to study it in order to prepare themselves for some form of Christian ministry. Others undertake it in order to deepen their grasp and appreciation of their faith. Others are curious outsiders, wondering what Christianity has to say on various issues. Yet for every ten people who would like to begin the serious study of theology, there are probably six or seven who find the task to be impossible, due to the lack of a reliable and intelligible introduction to its themes. There are many such introductions available; the problem is that they make what often turns out to be hopelessly unrealistic demands of their readers. They assume too much knowledge on the part of those who use them, and fail to take the trouble to introduce and explain ideas, debates, and terms.

It was the widespread recognition of this need that led to the development of *Christian Theology: An Introduction*, which was first published in 1994. This work evolved over a decade of teaching theology in the United Kingdom, North America and Australia, and was rigorously tested against its intended readership to ensure that it was as comprehensive and intelligible as possible. The widespread adoption of this work suggests that it has achieved at least some of its goals.

Nevertheless, the approach adopted in the *Introduction* placed limits upon the amount of primary source material which could be cited. It is invaluable to have the basic themes, debates, and personalities of Christian theology introduced by a skilled and unbiased commentator. Yet this can only lay a foundation for interacting with these themes, debates, and personalities *by reading original texts*. The idea of adding a reader was considered at an early stage in the planning of the *Introduction* itself, in order that appropriate texts could be identified at an early stage, and the nature and extent of difficulties encountered by students noted so that the correct level of explanation could be established. Indeed, extracts from some of the seminal texts thus identified are incorporated into the *Introduction* itself. However, limitations upon space and the consistent emphasis upon explanation within this earlier work restricted the amount of citation possible.

This *Reader* makes available a series of 280 seminal texts of Christian theology, drawn from 161 different sources, arranged on a broadly thematic basis, to allow its users to engage directly with the intellectual richness of the Christian tradition. (A "source" here means an individual theologian, irrespective of how many of that theologian's writings are excerpted, or confessional document such as the Council of Trent or the Heidelberg Catechism.) Every attempt has been made to ensure that the work is broadly representative, chronologically and intellectually, of the two thousand years of sustained critical reflection within Christianity. With the single exception of the seventh century, readings are provided from every century of Christian thought after the closing of the New Testament. On rare occasions, readings are drawn from non-Christian sources (such as Karl Marx), where the author or current of thought which she or he represents has had a significant impact on Christian theological reflection.

The emphasis upon explanation, characteristic of the *Introduction*, has been carried over into this *Reader*. Within the limits of the space available, every effort has been made to explain the importance of each reading, identify its context and key features, and alert the reader as to what to look out for in reading the text. With one exception, every text published in a language other than English prior to 1800 has been retranslated for this reader, with explanatory notes added where the translation remains difficult or ambiguous. (The sole exception here is Julian of Norwich; as my command of Middle English is not good enough to allow me to undertake a fresh translation of her writings, I have drawn on what is recognized to be the best English translation available.)

To allow easy correlation with the *Introduction*, the *Reader* is divided into ten chapters which reflect the basic structure of the earlier work. However, the *Reader* can be used as a freestanding resource, without any need to consult the *Introduction*.

This *Reader* aims to make available a collection of texts likely to be of interest to those beginning the study of Christian theology. The texts chosen belong to two categories. In the first place, there are seminal texts which represent landmarks in Christian thinking on certain subjects. These texts represent the statement of ideas or the development of arguments which have had a considerable impact, or which illustrate aspects of major debates within the Christian tradition. These texts are often quite brief. I have seen no pressing reason for quoting extended passages simply for the sake of doing so. The reader will thus find regular citation from such landmark writers as Irenaeus, Clement of Alexandria, Origen, Tertullian, Augustine, Thomas Aquinas, Martin Luther, John Calvin, F. D. E. Schleiermacher, Karl Barth and Karl Rahner. Despite this focus on classic texts, however, some 30 percent of the sources for this reader date from the twentieth century, ensuring that classic and modern writings are both fairly and fully represented.

In the second place, texts published after 1950 have often been selected on the basis of the lucidity or convenience of their discussion of highly complex questions. Often, these texts act as surveys of a broad field on the part of an informed writer, or as statements of a general theological position or trend – such as feminism, postliberalism, or evangelicalism. These texts tend to be more extended, in that it is the discussion of the questions under consideration, as much as the ideas that are actually defended, which will be of interest to readers. The discipline of Christian theology includes a substantial commitment to dialogue with the past tradition, as well as with its living representatives. In addition to illustrating approaches and ideas from the recent past and present, these more extended texts allow readers to gain an appreciation of the importance of interaction with the past in theology. They are all included here to allow the reader to sample and appreciate the great richness and diversity of modern Christian theology.

This book is a reader in Christian theology, not in church history. It is not a collection of texts for the church historian. There are many documents of historical importance – such as the Toleration Edict of Galerius (April 311) – which have limited theological relevance. The texts have been chosen on the basis of the known needs of those studying Christian theology at seminary, college, or university level. Church history is a separate discipline, requiring its own collections of texts, many of which are currently available to interested readers. Nor is this book a specialist reader, focusing on one historical period, or a single writer, theological school, or geographical region. The work is intended to act as a general introduction to the great tradition of doing theology within a Christian context, in order to encourage its readers to take matters further.

Sadly, there is not space to include all the texts which one might hope to include in a work of this sort. If it is of any interest, the 280 readings finally selected were chosen from a group of roughly 1,250 possible candidates, identified on the basis of literature searches and discussion with colleagues and students, and evaluated on the basis of first-hand classroom testing. It will therefore be clear that an enormous amount of important material has been omitted. Time and time again, pressure on space has forced me to set to one side texts that many readers will feel ought to have been included, or to give only a brief extract from a text that some will feel to merit fuller citation. I can only apologize for these shortcomings, of which I am only too painfully aware. The omission of a theologian must not in any way be understood to imply that this theologian has made an insignificant contribution to the development of Christian theology; for example, two of the greatest medieval theologians – Bonaventure and Duns Scotus – have had to be omitted from this selection, with the greatest of reluctance. Equally, it has proved necessary to omit many theologians writing since 1950 for the same reason. It is hoped that in future editions of this work, it will prove possible to incorporate a greater selection of more recent writings, in addition to those already included.

It is the firm intention of the author and publisher to make this volume as useful and helpful as possible in the long term. The structure of the work has been designed to make inclusion of additional or alternative texts possible in later editions without major disturbance of its existing form.

Both the author and publisher are committed to responding to end-user evaluation in improving and extending the work in the future. If you have any comments which might be helpful in this ongoing process of revision and improvement of this volume or *Christian Theology: An Introduction*, you are invited to send them in writing to the publisher.

Alister E. McGrath
Oxford

Approaching the Readings

Each text in this reader follows a common pattern, as follows:

The text is identified by a *number*, which allows cross-reference to texts within this reader. This number allows the chapter within which the reading occurs, and the location of that reading within the chapter, to be identified. Thus "4.9" (Gregory of Nazianzen on Apollinarianism) designates the ninth reading within chapter 4, dealing with the person of Jesus Christ.

There then follows a concise statement of the *author and theme* of the reading. For example, the title "Thomas Aquinas on the Principle of Analogy" allows the reader to identify both the author of the piece, and its broad theme. The readings have been grouped thematically over ten chapters, for ease of reference; within groups, they have been arranged chronologically, so that Augustine's views on the church are found before those of Luther. Once more, it must be emphasized that a reading allocated to one chapter may well prove to be of relevance in other contexts. Basic biographical and bibliographical details concerning each author cited will be found in the major section "Details of Authors". Note that the list of authors is cross-referenced to the readings, so that looking up "Augustine" will immediately identify all readings from this author.

There then follows a brief *introduction* to each reading, which provides background information to the text, and allows its importance to be appreciated. In some cases, the introduction will be brief; in others, a more extended introduction is required to ensure that the full significance of the text in question is understood. The introduction may include matters such as the date of writing of the text, as well as its original language, information concerning technical terms, other writers referred to in the text, or points of possible difficulty. A full glossary of theological terms, cross-referenced to the readings, is also provided at the end of the work. The introduction ends by referring the reader to other related readings of interest within this volume.

The *source* of the text is then identified, for the benefit of readers who wish to study the text in its original context or language, or (where material has been omitted: see below) who wish to study the passage intact. Where possible, this reference is given to precise line numbers or page columns; if this is not possible, the page number alone is provided. Where material has been taken from copyright material, appropriate acknowledgement is provided. In the case of classic pieces, care has been taken to ensure that references are given to the best critical edition available.

The *text* itself then follows, in English translation. Extended texts have often been abridged, to allow the exclusion of material which is not of major importance to the point under discussion. The exclusion of material is indicated in the standard manner, using ellipsis: . . . Where the original text is not in English, and the reader might benefit from knowing, for example, the original Latin term or phrase being translated, this term will be included in italic print in parentheses. For example, the reading based on Martin Luther's 1539 treatise *On the Councils and the Church* makes reference to "this holy Christian people" (*dis Christlich heilig Volck*); the reading here includes a contemporary English translation of this significant phrase, with the original early modern German version indicated. Readers not concerned with the original need not worry about material presented in this way.

A series of *study panels* have been incorporated into the introductions to chapters. These 23 panels provide an overview of readings relevant to specific theological themes – including specific doctrines, such as "the Trinity" and more general issues, such as "Faith and History." These panels will give users of this work an idea of the material available, and stimulate them to develop their own panels in relation to the specific themes they wish to explore. Each chapter ends with a series of *questions*, which will allow readers to assess their understanding of the material contained in that section.

How to Use
this Book

Studying by Yourself

If you are studying theology by yourself, please read what follows
carefully.

1 You are strongly recommended to purchase the companion volume
  Christian Theology: An Introduction, which will provide you with substantial background material that will is invaluable in making sense of the
  readings. In particular, you should read the four chapters dealing with
  "landmarks," which will help you understand more about the history of
  Christian theology, and some of the key theologians you will encounter
  at first hand in this reader. You are also recommended to read the specific
  chapter in *Christian Theology: An Introduction* relating to the topic you wish
  to study. It will help you set the reading in the present book in its full
  context.
2 The texts in this reader are arranged *thematically* by chapter, and *chrono-*
  logically within each chapter. It is recommended that you adopt a thematic approach, and work your way through each chapter, noticing the
  way in which later writers often draw on or engage with the ideas of
  their predecessors – even if they do not always admit it!
3 Try using the following approach in relation to each reading.
  (a) Make sure that you can identify the author. When did she live? In
      which part of the world was he based?
  (b) Spend a little time thinking about the work from which the reading
      is taken. What kind of a work is it: for example, is it academic,
      polemical, pastoral, popular? Who is the author writing for?
  (c) Note any points of importance identified in the introduction.

(d) Now read the text itself. This book has generous margins, to encourage and enable you to annotate the readings, and scribble notes in the margins. Note any important phrases used. Try to summarize the passage, noting the flow of the argument and any assumptions which seem to be especially important.

(e) Now close the book, and see if you can summarize the reading. The more information you can retain, the better. In particular, try to recall the main points of any arguments used. Your summary will vary from one reading to another, depending on its length and complexity. However, the kind of summary that you are aiming to produce will take the following forms:

> 1.7 In his *Proslogion*, Anselm of Canterbury argues for the existence of God like this. He defines God as being "that than which nothing greater can be thought." He then points out that the idea of God is not as great as the reality of God. So if we agree on this definition of God, and can think of God, God must exist.

> 8.19 In *The Babylonian Captivity of the Church*, which Luther wrote in 1520, he argues that the Lord's Supper (which he refers to as either "the Mass" or "the sacrament of the altar") is like a testament, for three reasons. First, because it is about an inheritance. Second, because it identifies heirs. And third, because it proclaims the death of the testator.

This kind of exercise will help you test your own understanding of the passage, and also enable you to make the best possible use of the information for yourself. You will also find the questions included at the end of each chapter helpful in allowing you to assess your grasp of the material included in each section.

Some Tips in Locating Readings

1 Use the *Study Panels* (listed on p. xv) to find all major readings relating to the 23 themes treated in this way.
2 Use the *Details of Authors* section (pp. 375–89) to identify every reading by a given author, and the *Details of Conciliar, Creedal, and Confessional Material* (pp. 390–1) to identify other source material.
3 Use the *Theological Timeline* (pp. 415–19) to identify authors by period, so that you can easily identify readings relating to a given century.
4 Use the *Glossary* (pp. 392–407) to find readings illustrating a specific theological term, or relating to a specific movement or school of thought.

Being Taught by Someone Else

If you are using this reader as part of a taught course, whoever is directing the course will explain the way in which you are to use this book. This will generally take the form of directing you to read, summarize, and comment on certain passages. You may find that the explanatory material will thus be unnecessary, on account of the guidance and input that will be provided for you. However, experience suggests that you will benefit considerably from the additional material provided. You may also like to try using the approach recommended for those studying theology by themselves, which may be a helpful supplement to what your instructor recommends.

Preparing Talks?

The book will also be of service to those preparing talks, sermons, or addresses on key themes of Christian theology, who wish to incorporate source material into the lecture, or interact with a leading representative of a position under examination. The 23 Study Panels provide guidance for some themes, and point to how others could be handled. For example, the following topics, among many others, could easily be addressed on the basis of this reader:

- The Place of Icons in the Reformed Tradition (see 1.13 The Heidelberg Catechism on Images of God; 3.33 Jacques Ellul on the Theology of Icons).
- What can we know of God from nature? (see STUDY PANEL 7).
- What does it mean to say that we are "created in the image of God"? (see STUDY PANEL 16).
- Some themes in the theology of Martin Luther (see 1.11; 2.14; 2.15; 4.20; 6.26; 6.27; 6.28; 7.9; 7.10; 8.17; 8.18; 8.19; 8.20).

Acknowledgments

In producing this work, I have incurred debts of many kinds. It is my privilege to be able to acknowledge them.

I owe an enormous debt to my students at Wycliffe Hall, Oxford, and Oxford University in general, on whom much of the material contained in this reader was tested over a period of nearly ten years. They patiently suffered my expositions and explanations of key texts in a series of seminars and lectures, just as I patiently listened to their difficulties and questions. More recently, my students in systematic theology at Regent College, Vancouver, have given me invaluable assistance in assessing the suitability of potential texts for this volume.

I also owe much to discussions with faculty and students at Princeton Theological Seminary, McGill University, Wheaton College, Drew University, Westminster Theological Seminary, Regent College, Vancouver, Moore College, Sydney, and Ridley College, Melbourne. The mutual sharing of experiences, frustrations, and approaches did much to enable me to plan this volume.

I am enormously grateful to Morwenna Ludlow (Trinity College, Oxford), who interrupted her research on early patristic eschatology to track down and copy the best critical editions of the texts cited in this volume.

Copyright holders, who are fully and individually acknowledged at the appropriate points in the work, are thanked for granting permission to reprint extracts from their publications. Every effort has been made to trace and contact copyright holders and properly acknowledge them. In the event of any such acknowledgment not being made fully or properly, the situation will be rectified in subsequent printings of this work.

And finally, Blackwell Publishers, and especially Alison Mudditt, are to be thanked for commissioning this volume, and for their patience in dealing with its compiler.

1 Getting Started: Preliminaries

Starting to study Christian theology involves exploring a whole range of issues. Some of these center on the identity and characteristics of theology itself. For example, what is theology? And how did it develop? How does it relate to other areas of life, such as philosophy or culture? How does our way of talking about God relate to our everyday language? To what extent – and in what ways – can the existence of God be proved?

The present chapter provides readings which explore all of these issues, some in depth. Three issues are here singled out as being of particular importance, and illustrating the way in which this reader may be used thematically: the question of the proofs of God's existence (STUDY PANEL 1); the general relation of philosophy and theology (STUDY PANEL 2); and the nature of theological language and images (STUDY PANEL 3).

STUDY PANEL 1

The Proofs of God's Existence

STUDY PANEL 2

The Relation of Theology and Philosophy

STUDY PANEL 3

Theological Language and Images

1.1   Justin Martyr on Philosophy and Theology

In his two apologies for the Christian faith, written in Greek at Rome at some point during the period 148–61, Justin sets out a vigorous defense of Christianity, in which he seeks to relate the gospel to secular wisdom. A central theme in this defense is the idea that God has scattered "the seeds (*spermata*) of his Logos" throughout the world before the coming of Christ, so that secular wisdom and truth can point, however imperfectly, to Christ. See also 1.2; 1.3; 1.4.

Source: *Apologia* I.xlvi.2–3; II.x.2–3; II.xiii.4–6; in *Saint Justin: Apologies*, ed. A. Wartelle (Paris: Etudes Augustiniennes, 1987), 160.6–9; 210.3–7; 216.11–18.

* * * ──

> We have been taught that Christ is the firstborn of God, and we have proclaimed that he is the Logos, in whom every race of people have shared. And those who live according to the Logos are Christians, even though they may have been counted as atheists – such as Socrates and Heracleitus, and others like them, among the Greeks . . . Whatever either lawyers or philosophers have said well, was articulated by finding and reflecting upon some aspect of the Logos. However, since they did not know the Logos – which is Christ – in its entirety, they often contradicted themselves . . . Whatever all people have said well (*kalōs*) belongs to us Christians. For we worship and love, next to God, the Logos, who comes from the unbegotten and ineffable God, since it was for our sake that he became a human being, in order that he might share in our sufferings and bring us healing. For all writers were able to see the truth darkly, on account of the implanted seed of the Logos which was grafted into them. Now the seed and imitation (*mimēma*) of something which is given on the basis of a person's capacity to receive it is quite different from that thing itself, of which the communication and imitation are received according to the grace of God.

1.2   Clement of Alexandria on Philosophy and Theology

The eight books of Clement's *Stromata* (the word literally means "carpets") deal at length with the relation of the Christian faith to Greek philosophy. In this extract from the *Stromata*, originally written in Greek in the early third century, Clement argues that God gave philosophy to the Greeks as a way of preparing them for the coming of Christ, in more or less exactly the same way as he gave the Jews the law of Moses. While not conceding that philosophy has the status of revelation, Clement goes beyond Justin Martyr's suggestion that the mere seeds of the Logos are to be found in Greek philosophy. See also 1.1; 1.3; 1.4.

Source: *Stromata* I.v.28; in *Die griechischen christlichen Schriftsteller der erste Jahrhunderte*. Clemens Alexandrinus: Zweiter Band. Stromata Buch I–VI, ed. O. Stählin and L. Früchtel (Berlin: Akademie Verlag, 1985), pp. 17.31–18.5.

* * * ──

Thus until the coming (*parousia*) of the Lord, philosophy was necessary to the Greeks for righteousness. And now it assists those who come to faith by way of demonstration, as a kind of preparatory training (*propaideia*) for true religion. For "you will not stumble" (Proverbs 3:23) if you attribute all good things to providence, whether it belongs to the Greeks or to us. For God is the source of all good things, some directly (as with the Old and the New Testaments), and some indirectly (as with philosophy). But it might be that philosophy was given to the Greeks immediately and directly, until such time as the Lord should also call the Greeks. For philosophy acted as a "schoolmaster" (*epaidagōgei*) to bring the Greeks to Christ, just as the law brought the Hebrews. Thus philosophy was by way of a preparation, which prepared the way for its perfection in Christ.

Tertullian on the Relation of Philosophy and Heresy

1.3

Tertullian was noted for his hostility towards the intrusion of philosophy into theology. Philosophy, he argued, was pagan in its outlook, and its use in theology could only lead to heresy within the church. In his *de praescriptione haereticorum* ("On the Rule of the Heretics"), written in Latin in the first years of the third century, Tertullian sets up a celebrated contrast between Athens and Jerusalem, symbolizing the tension between pagan philosophy and the revelation of the Christian faith. Note that the reference to the "Academy" is not a general reference to the academic world, but specifically to the Platonic Academy at Athens. See also 1.1; 1.2; 1.4.

Source: *de praescriptione haereticorum*, 7; in *Sources Chrétiennes, 46*, ed. R. F. Refoulé (Paris: Editions du Cerf, 1957), 96.4–99.3.

* * *

For philosophy provides the material of worldly wisdom, in boldly asserting itself to be the interpreter of the divine nature and dispensation. The heresies themselves receive their weapons from philosophy. It was from this source that Valentinus, who was a disciple of Plato, got his ideas about the "aeons" and the "trinity of humanity". And it was from there that the god of Marcion (much to be preferred, on account of his tranquility) came; Marcion came from the Stoics. To say that the soul is subject to death is to go the way of Epicurus. And the denial of the resurrection of the body is found throughout the writings of all the philosophers. To say that matter is equal with God is to follow the doctrine of Zeno; to speak of a god of fire is to draw on Heracleitus. It is the same subjects which preoccupy both the heretics and the philosophers. Where does evil come from, and why? Where does human nature come from, and how? . . . What is there in common between Athens and Jerusalem? between the Academy and the church? Our system of beliefs (*institutio*) comes from the Porch of Solomon, who himself taught that it was necessary to seek God in the simplicity of the heart. So much the worse for those who talk of a "stoic", "platonic", or "dialectic" Christianity! We have no need for curiosity after Jesus Christ, nor for inquiry (*inquisitio*) after the gospel. When we believe, we desire to believe nothing further. For we need believe nothing more than "there is nothing else which we are obliged to believe."

1.4 Augustine on Philosophy and Theology

In this writing, originally written in Latin around 397, Augustine deals with the relation between Christianity and pagan philosophy. Using the exodus from Egypt as a model, Augustine argues that there is no reason why Christians should not extract all that is good in philosophy, and put it to the service of preaching the gospel. Just as Israel left behind the burdens of Egypt, while carrying off its treasures, so theology can discard what is useless in philosophy, and exploit what is good and useful. See also 1.1; 1.2; 1.3.

Source: *de doctrina Christiana*, II.xl.60–61; in *Florilegium Patristicum*, vol. 29, ed. H. J. Vogels (Bonn: Peter Hanstein, 1930), 46.7–36.

* * * ———————————————————————————————

If those who are called philosophers, particularly the Platonists, have said anything which is true and consistent with our faith, we must not reject it, but claim it for our own use, in the knowledge that they possess it unlawfully. The Egyptians possessed idols and heavy burdens, which the children of Israel hated and from which they fled; however, they also possessed vessels of gold and silver and clothes which our forebears, in leaving Egypt, took for themselves in secret, intending to use them in a better manner (Exodus 3:21–2; 12:35–6) . . . In the same way, pagan learning is not entirely made up of false teachings and superstitions . . . It contains also some excellent teachings, well suited to be used by truth, and excellent moral values. Indeed, some truths are even found among them which relate to the worship of the one God. Now these are, so to speak, their gold and their silver, which they did not invent themselves, but which they dug out of the mines of the providence of God, which are scattered throughout the world, yet which are improperly and unlawfully prostituted to the worship of demons. The Christian, therefore, can separate these truths from their unfortunate associations, take them away, and put them to their proper use for the proclamation of the gospel . . .

What else have many good and faithful people from amongst us done? Look at the wealth of gold and silver and clothes which Cyprian – that eloquent teacher and blessed martyr – brought with him when he left Egypt! And think of all that Lactantius brought with him, not to mention Marius Victorinus, Optatus, and Hilary of Poitiers, and others who are still living! And look at how much the Greeks have borrowed! And before all of these, we find that Moses, that most faithful servant of God, had done the same thing: after all, it is written of him that "he was learned in all the wisdom of the Egyptians" (Acts 7:22).

The Nicene Creed   1.5

The "Nicene Creed" is widely regarded as the basis of orthodox Christianity in both the eastern and western churches. Although its focus is Christological, its importance relates to its function as a "rule of faith" within the churches. As part of its polemic against the Arians, the Council of Nicea (June 325) formulated a short statement of faith, based on a baptismal creed used at Jerusalem. This Creed was intended to affirm the full divinity of Christ against the Arian understanding of his creaturely status, and includes four explicit condemnations of Arian views, as well as its three articles of faith. As the full details of the proceeding of Nicea are now lost, we are obliged to rely on secondary sources (such as ecclesiastical historians, and writers such as Athanasius and Basil of Caesarea) for the text of this creed. Note that the translation provided here is of the Greek original, rather than of the Latin version of Hilary of Poitiers. Note also that the term "Nicene Creed" is often used as a shorter way of referring to the "Niceno-Constantinopolitan Creed", which has a sighificantly longer discussion of the person of Christ, and also makes statements concerning the church, forgiveness, and eternal life. See also 2.7; 2.19; 4.6; 4.7.

Source: H. Denzinger (ed.), *Enchiridion Symbolorum*, 24–5 edn (Barcelona: Herder, 1948), pp. 29–30.

* * *

We believe in one God, the Father, the almighty (*pantocrator*), the maker of all things seen and unseen.

And in one Lord Jesus Christ, the Son of God; begotten from the Father; only-begotten – that is, from the substance of the Father (*ek tēs ousias tou patros*); God from God; light from light; true God from true God; begotten not made; of one substance with the Father (*homoousion tō patri*); through whom all things in heaven and on earth came into being; who on account of us human beings and our salvation came down and took flesh, becoming a human being (*sarkōthenta, enanthrōpēsanta*); he suffered and rose again on the third day, ascended into the heavens; and will come again to judge the living and the dead.

And in the Holy Spirit.

As for those who say that "there was when he was not," and "before being born he was not," and "he came into existence out of nothing," or who declare that the Son of God is of a different substance or nature, or is subject to alteration or change – the catholic and apostolic church condemns these.

The Apostles' Creed   1.6

The document known as the "Apostles' Creed" is widely used in the western church as a succinct summary of the leading themes of the Christian faith. Its historical evolution is complex, with its origins lying in declarations of faith which were required of those who wanted to be baptized. The twelve individual statements of this Creed, which seems to have assumed its final form in the eighth century, are traditionally ascribed to individual apostles, although there is no historical justification for this belief. During the twentieth century, the Apostle's Creed has become widely accepted by most churches, eastern and western, as a binding statement of Christian faith despite the fact that its statements concerning the "descent into hell" and the "communion of saints" (here printed within brackets) are not found in eastern versions of the work. See also 2.7; 2.19.

Source: H. Denzinger (ed.), *Enchiridion Symbolorum*, 24–5 edn (Barcelona: Herder, 1948), p. 6.

* * * ───

1. I believe in God, the Father almighty, creator of the heavens and earth;
2. and in Jesus Christ, his only (*unicus*) Son, our Lord;
3. who was conceived by the Holy Spirit and born of the Virgin Mary;
4. suffered under Pontius Pilate, was crucified, dead and buried; [he descended to hell;]
5. on the third day he was raised from the dead;
6. he ascended into the heavens, and sits at the right hand of God the Father almighty;
7. from where he will come to judge the living and the dead.
8. I believe in the Holy Spirit;
9. in the holy catholic church; [the communion of saints;]
10. the forgiveness of sins;
11. the resurrection of the flesh (*resurrectio carnis*);
12. and eternal life.

1.7 Anselm of Canterbury's Proof for the Existence of God

In his *Proslogion*, written in Latin around 1079, Anselm offers a definition of God as "that than which no greater thing can be thought" (*aliquid quo maius cogitari non potest*). He argues that, if this definition of God is correct, it necessarily implies the existence of God. The reason for this is as follows. If God does not exist, the idea of God remains, yet the reality of God is absent. Yet the reality of God is greater than the idea of God. Therefore, if God is "that than which no greater thing can be thought," the idea of God must lead to accepting the reality of God, in that otherwise the mere idea of God is the greatest thing which can be thought. And this contradicts the definition of God on which the argument is based. Therefore, given the existence of the idea of God, and the acceptance of the definition of God as "that than which no greater thing can be thought," the reality of God necessarily follows. Note that the Latin verb *cogitare* is sometimes translated as "conceive," leading to the definition of God as "that than which no greater thing can be conceived." Both translations are acceptable. See also 1.8; 1.18.

Source: *Proslogion*, 3; in *S. Anselmi Opera Omnia*, vol. 1, ed. F. S. Schmitt (Edinburgh: Nelson, 1946), 102.6–103.9.

* * * ───

This [definition of God] is indeed so true that it cannot be thought of as not being true. For it is quite possible to think of something whose non-existence cannot be thought of. This must be greater than something whose non-existence can be thought of. So if this thing (than which no greater thing can thought) can be thought of as not existing, then, that very thing than which a greater thing cannot be thought is not that than which a greater cannot be thought. This is a contradiction. So it is true that there exists something than which nothing greater can be thought, that it cannot be thought of as not existing.

And you are this thing, O Lord our God! So truly therefore do you exist, O Lord my God, that you cannot be thought of as not existing, and with good reason; for if a human mind could think of anything greater than you, the creature would rise above the Creator and judge you; which is obviously absurd. And in truth whatever else there be beside you may be thought of as not existing. So you alone, most truly of all, and therefore most of all, have existence: because whatever else exists, does not exist as truly as you, and therefore exists to a lesser degree.

Gaunilo's Reply to Anselm's Argument   1.8

In this response to Anselm's argument for the existence of God (see 1.7), written at some point in the late eleventh century, the Benedictine monk Gaunilo argues that the mere idea of something – whether a perfect island or God – does not guarantee its existence. This document is sometimes referred to as "The Reply on behalf of the Fool," a reference to the fool who denied the existence of God in Scripture (Psalm 14:1). See also 1.7; 1.18.

Source: *Responsio Anselmi*, 6; in *S. Anselmi: Opera Omnia*, vol. 1, ed. F. S. Schmitt (Edinburgh: Nelson, 1946), 128.14–32.

* * *

To give an example. People say that somewhere in the ocean there is an island which, because of the difficulty (or rather the impossibility) of finding that which does not exist, some have called the "Lost Island" (*perdita*). And we are told that it is blessed with all manner of priceless riches and delights in abundance, far more than the Happy Isles, and, having no owner or inhabitant, it is superior in every respect in the abundance of its riches to all those other lands that are inhabited by people. Now, if someone were to tell me about this, I shall easily understand what is said, since there is nothing difficult about it. But suppose I am then told, as though it were a direct consequence of this: "You cannot any more doubt that this island that is more excellent than all other lands truly exists somewhere in reality than you can doubt that it is in your mind; and since it is more excellent to exist not just in your mind but in reality as well, therefore it must exist. For if it did not exist, any other land existing in reality would be more excellent than it, and so this island, already conceived by you to be more excellent than others, will not be more excellent." I say that if anyone wanted to persuade me in this way that this island really exists beyond all doubt, I should either think that they were joking, or I should find it hard to decide which of us I ought to think of as the bigger fool: I myself, if I agreed with them, or they, if they thought that they had proved the existence of this island with any certainty, unless they had first persuaded me that its very excellence exists in my mind precisely as a thing existing truly and indubitably and not just as something unreal or doubtfully real.

1.9   Thomas Aquinas on Proofs for the Existence of God

In this famous discussion of whether God's existence can be demonstrated, Aquinas sets out five ways in which the existence of God may be demonstrated. Although not "proofs" in the strict sense of the word, Aquinas regards them as demonstrating the consistency of Christian theology with what is known of the world. The "Five Ways" do not include the argument set out by Anselm earlier (see 1.7). The *Summa Theologiae* ("The Totality of Theology"), which Aquinas began to write in Latin in 1265 and left unfinished at the time of his death, is widely regarded as the greatest work of medieval theology. Note that the Latin term *motus* can be translated "motion" or "change". The first of Aquinas's arguments is normally referred to as the "argument from motion"; however, it is clear that the *motus* in question is actually understood in more general terms, so that the term "change" is more appropriate as a translation. See also 1.7; 1.8; 1.15; 1.16.

Source: *Summa Theologiae*, la, q. 2, aa. 2–3.

* * * ───

2. Whether God's Existence Can Be Demonstrated

There are two types of demonstration. There is demonstration through the cause, or, as we say, "from grounds," which argues from cause to effect. There is also demonstration by means of effects, following the order in which we experience things, arguing from effect to cause. Now when an effect is more apparent to us than its cause, we come to know the cause through its effect. Even though the effect should be better known to us, we can demonstrate from any effect that its cause exists, because effects always depend on some cause, and a cause must exist if its effect exists. We can therefore demonstrate that God exists from what is not evident to us on the basis of effects which are evident to us . . .

3. Whether God Exists

The existence of God can be proved in five ways. The first and most obvious proof is the argument from change (*ex parte motus*). It is clearly the case that some things in this world are in the process of changing. Now everything that is in the process of being changed is changed by something else, since nothing is changed unless it is potentially that towards which it is being changed, whereas that which changes is actual. To change something is nothing else than to bring it from potentiality to actuality, and a thing can be brought from potentiality to actuality only by something which is actual. Thus a fire, which is actually hot, makes wood, which is potentially hot, to be actually hot, thus changing and altering it. Now it is impossible for the same thing to be both actual and potential in the same respect, although it may be so in different respects. What is actually hot cannot at the same time be potentially hot, although it is potentially cold. It is therefore impossible that, in the same manner and in the same way, anything should be both the one which effects a change and the one that is changed, so that it should change itself. Whatever is changed must therefore be changes by something else. If, then, whatever is changing it is itself changed, this also must be changed by something else, and this in turn by something else again. But this cannot go on forever, since there would then be no first cause to this process of change, and consequently no other agent of change, because secondary things which change cannot change unless they are changed by a first cause, in the same way as a stick cannot move unless it is moved by the hand. We are therefore bound to arrive at a first cause of change which is not changed by anything, and everyone understands that this is God.

The second way is based on the nature of an efficient cause. We find that there is a sequence of efficient causes in the observable world. But we do not find that anything is the efficient cause of itself. Nor is this possible, for the thing would then be prior to itself, which is impossible. But neither can the sequence of efficient causes be infinite, for in every sequence the first efficient cause is the cause of an intermediate cause, and an intermediate cause is the cause of the ultimate cause, whether there are many intermediate causes, or just one. Now when a cause is taken away, so is its effect. Hence if there were no first efficient cause, there would be no ultimate cause, and no intermediate cause. But if there was an infinite regression of efficient causes, there would be no first efficient cause. As a result, there would be no ultimate effect, and no intermediate causes. But this is plainly false. We are therefore bound to suppose that there is a first efficient cause. And everyone calls this "God."

The third way is from the nature of possibility and necessity. There are some things which may either exist or not exist, since some things come to be and pass away, and may therefore exist or not exist. Now it is impossible that all of these should exist at all times, because there is at least some time when that which may possibly no exist does not exist. Hence if all things were such that they might not exist, at some time or other there would be nothing. But if this were true there would be nothing in existence now, since what does not exist cannot begin to exist, unless through something which does exist. If nothing had ever existed, it would have been impossible for anything to begin to exist, and there would now be nothing at all. But this is plainly false, and hence not all existence is merely possible. Something in things must be necessary. Now everything which is necessary either derives its necessity from somewhere else or does not. But we cannot go on to infinity with necessary things which have a cause of their necessity, any more than with efficient causes, as we proved. We are therefore bound to suppose something necessary in itself, which does not owe its necessity to anything else, but which is the cause of the necessity of other things. And everyone calls this "God."

The fourth way is from the gradation that occurs in things, which are found to be more good, true, noble and so on, just as others are found to be less so. Things are said to be more and less because they approximate in different degrees to that which is greatest. A thing gets hotter and hotter as it approaches the thing which is the hottest. There is therefore something which is the truest, the best, and the noblest, and which is consequently the greatest in being, since that which has the greatest truth is also greatest in being . . . Now that which most thoroughly possesses the nature of any genus is the cause of all that the genus contains. Thus fire, which is most perfectly hot, is the cause of all not things . . . There is therefore something which is the cause of the being of all things that are, as well as of their goodness and their every perfection. This we call "God."

The fifth way is based on the governance of things. We see how some things, like natural bodies, work for an end even though they have no knowledge. The fact that they nearly always operate in the same way, and so as to achieve the maximum good, makes this obvious, and shows that they attain their end by design, not by chance. Now things which have no knowledge tend towards an end only through the agency of something which knows and also understands, as in the case of an arrow which requires an archer. There is therefore an intelligent being by whom all natural things are directed to their end. This we call "God."

1.10 Thomas Aquinas on the Principle of Analogy

In this major analysis, Aquinas points out that speaking about God involves using words that normally apply to things in the everyday world. So how do these two different uses relate to each other? Aquinas draws a distinction between the "univocal" use of a word (where the word means exactly the same thing whenever it is used) and the "equivocal" use (where the same word is used, but with different meanings). Thus the word "bat" is used univocally when it is used to refer to a vampire bat and a long-eared bat, in that the word refers to a nocturnal flying animal with wings in each case. But the word "bat" is used equivocally when the same word is used to refer to both a nocturnal flying animal with wings, and a piece of wood used to strike a ball in baseball or cricket. The word is the same; the meaning is different.

In this important passage, Aquinas argues that words cannot be used univocally to refer both to God and to humanity. The word "wise" does not mean the same in the statements "God is wise" and "Solomon is wise." The gulf between God and humanity is too great for the word to mean the same. Yet the word is not used equivocally, as if it referred to something totally different. There is a relation between its use to refer to God, and its use in human contexts. The word "wise" is used *analogously*, to mean that divine wisdom is not identical to, nor totally different from, human wisdom. There is "an analogy, that is a certain proportion, between them." See also 1.21; 1.24.

Source: *Summa Theologiae*, 1a, q. 13, aa. 5–6.

* * *

5. Are Words Used Univocally or Equivocally of God and Creatures?

It is impossible to predicate anything univocally of God and creatures. The reason for this is that every effect which is less than its cause does not represent it adequately, in that the effect is thus not the same sort of thing as the cause. So that exists in a variety of divided forms in the effects exists simply and in a unified way in the cause – just as the simple power of the sun produces many different kinds of lesser things. In the same way, as we said earlier, the many and various perfections in creatures pre-exist in God in a single and unified form.

So the words that we use in speaking of creatures differ in meaning, and each of them signifies a perfection which is distinct from all the others. Thus when we say that a man is wise, we signify his wisdom as something distinct from other things about him – such as his essence, his powers, or his existence. But when we use this word in relation to God, we do not intend to signify something distinct from his essence, power, or existence. When "wise" is used in relation to a human being, it so to speak delimits and embraces the aspect of humanity that it signifies (*quodammodo circumscribit et comprehendit rem significatum*). This, however, is not the case when it is used of God; what it signifies in God is not limited by our meaning of the word, but goes beyond it. Hence it is clear that the word "wise" is not used in the same sense of God and of a human being, and the same is true of all other words, so they cannot be used univocally of God and creatures.

Yet although some have said that this is mere equivocation, this is not so. If it were the case, we could never argue from statements about creatures to statements about God – any such argument would be rendered invalid by the fallacy of equivocation. But we know, both from the teachings of the philosophers who prove many things about God and from the teaching of St. Paul, who says, "The invisible things of God are made known by those things that are made" (Romans 1:20), that this does not happen. We must say, therefore, that words are used of God and creatures according to an analogy, that is a certain proportion, between them (*nomina dicuntur de Deo et creaturis secundum analogiam, id est, proportionem*).

We can distinguish two kinds of analogical uses of words. First, there is the case of one word being used of several things because each of them has some proportion to another. Thus we use the word "healthy" in relation to both a diet and a complexion because each of these has some order and proportion to "health" in an animal, the former as its cause, the latter as its symptom. Secondly there is the case of the same word used because of some proportion – just as "healthy" is used in relation to both the diet and the animal because the diet is the cause of the health in the animal.

In this way some words are used neither univocally nor purely equivocally of God and creatures, but analogically (*analogice, et non aequivoce pure neque pure univoce*). We cannot speak of God at all except on the basis of creatures, and so whatever is said both of God and creatures is said in virtue of a certain order that creatures have in relation to God (*ordo creaturae ad Deum*) as their source and cause in which all their perfections pre-exist.

This way of using words lies somewhere between pure equivocation and simple univocity. The word is neither used in the same sense, as in the case of univocation, nor in totally different senses, as with equivocation. The several senses of a word which is used analogically signify different relations to something, just as "health" in a complexion means a symptom of health and in a diet means a cause of that health . . .

6. Are Words Predicated Primarily of God or of Creatures?

. . . All words used metaphorically in relation to God apply primarily to creatures and secondarily to God. When used in relation to God they signify merely a certain likeness between God and the creature (*nihil aliud significant quam similitudines ad tales creaturas*). When we speak of a meadow as "smiling" we only mean that it is seen at its best when it flowers, just as people are seen at their best when they smile, according to a similarity of proportion (*secundum similitudinem proportionis*) between them. In the same way, if we speak of God as a "lion" we only mean that he is mighty in his deeds, like a lion. It is thus clear that, when something is said in relation to God, its meaning is to be determined on the basis of the meaning it has when used in relation to creatures.

This is also the case for words that are not used metaphorically, if they were simply used, as some have supposed, to express God's causality. If, for example, "God is good" meant the same as "God is the cause of goodness in creatures," the word "good" as applied to God would have contained within its meaning the goodness of the creature. "Good" would thus apply primarily to creatures and secondarily to God.

But it has already been shown that words of this sort are said of God not just causally, but also essentially (*causaliter, sed etiam essentialiter*). When we say "God is good" or "God is wise" we do not simply mean that God causes wisdom or goodness, but that these perfections pre-exist supremely in him. We conclude, therefore, that from the point of view of what the word means it is used primarily of God and derivatively of creatures, for what the word means – the perfection it signifies – flows from God to the creature. But from the point of view of our use of the word we apply it first to creatures because we know them first. That, as we have mentioned already, is why it has a way of signifying what is appropriate to creatures.

1.11 Martin Luther on the Theology of the Cross

In 1518, Luther defended a series of theses in a disputation at Heidelberg, in which he set out the basic features of the "theology of the cross." Of particular importance is the idea that theology involves a response to the "rearward parts of God," which are only made known in the cross. The theses allude to Exodus 33:23, which refers to Moses only being allowed to catch a glimpse of God from the rear, as he disappears into the distance. See also 1.17; 3.32.

Source: Heidelberg Disputation, Theses 19–20; in *D. Martin Luthers Werke: Kritische Gesamtausgabe*, vol. 1 (Weimar: Böhlaus, 1911), 354.17–21.

* * *

19. The person who looks on the invisible things of God, as they are seen in visible things, does not deserve to be called a theologian.

20. But the person who looks on the visible rearward parts of God (*visibilia et posteriora Dei*) as seen in suffering and the cross does deserve to be called a theologian.

John Calvin on the Nature of Faith 1.12

In this important analysis of the nature of faith, provided in the 1559 edition of the *Institutes of the Christian Religion*, Calvin establishes a direct relation between faith and the merciful promises of God. Note the emphasis placed upon the role of the Holy Spirit in revealing and sealing this knowledge. Calvin also deals with the question of whether the certainty of faith necessarily implies that doubt is excluded from the Christian life. For Calvin, doubt is a normal part of the Christian life, and is not inconsistent with his emphasis upon the trustworthiness of God's promises. See also 6.27; 6.31.

Source: *Institutes*, III.ii, 7; 17; in *Joannis Calvini: Opera Selecta*, ed. P. Barth and W. Niesel, vol. 4 (Munich: Kaiser, 1931), 16.31–5; 27.25–36.

* * *

Now we shall have a right definition of faith if we say that it is a steady and certain knowledge of the divine benevolence towards us (*divinae erga nos benevolentia firmam certamque cognitionem*), which is founded upon the truth of the gracious promise of God in Christ, and is both revealed to our minds and sealed in our hearts (*revelatur mentibus nostris et cordibus obsignatur*) by the Holy Spirit . . .

When we stress that faith ought to be certain and secure, we do not have in mind a certainty without doubt, or a security without any anxiety. Rather, we affirm that believers have a perpetual struggle with their own lack of faith, and are far from possessing a peaceful conscience, never interrupted by any disturbance. On the other hand, we want to deny that they may fall out of, or depart from, their confindence (*fiducia*) in the divine mercy, no matter how much they may be troubled.

The Heidelberg Catechism on Images of God 1.13

This Catechism, written in German in 1563, was intended to set out the main features of the Reformed faith for a German audience. In this section, the Catechism develops the idea that images of God are neither necessary nor helpful for Christian believers. There is an interesting parallel with Islam here, in that both Islam and Reformed theology are concerned to avoid images of God becoming objects of worship in themselves, instead of being aids to the worship of God. See also 3.33.

Source: Heidelberg Catechism, Questions 96–8; in E. F. K. Müller (ed.), *Die Bekenntnisschriften der reformierten Kirche* (Leipzig: Böhme, 1903), 710.8–27.

* * *

Question 96. What does God require in the next commandment?
Answer: That we should not portray God in any way, nor worship him in any other manner than he has commanded in his Word.

Question 97. So should we not make any use of images?
Answer: God cannot and should not be depicted in any way. As for creatures, although they may indeed be depicted, God forbids making use of or having any likeness of them, in order to worship them or to use them to serve him.

Question 98. But should we allow pictures instead of books in churches, for the benefit of the unlearned?
Answer: No. For we should not presume to be wiser than God, who does not want Christendom to be taught by means of dumb idols, but through the living preaching of his Word.

1.14 John Locke on the Formation of the Concept of God

In this passage from his *Essay Concerning Human Understanding*, which was published in December 1689, Locke argues that the notion of God is derived from experience. The human mind constructs the idea of God by extrapolating ideas already present in the world to infinity, thus leading to the idea of God as a supreme Being. The idea of God thus results from experience, rather than from pure reason. See also 1.19.

Source: John Locke, *An Essay Concerning Human Understanding*, ed. P. H. Nidditch (Oxford: Clarendon Press, 1975), 314.25–315.24. By permission of Oxford University Press.

* * *

For if we examine the idea we have of the incomprehensible supreme Being, we shall find that we come by it the same way; and that the complex ideas we have both of God, and separate Spirits, are made up of the simple ideas we receive from Reflection; v.g., having from what we experiment in our selves, got the ideas of existence and duration; of knowledge and power; of pleasure and happiness; and of several other qualities and powers which it is better to have, than to be without; when we would frame an idea the most suitable we can to the supreme Being, we enlarge every one of these with our idea of Infinity; and so putting them together, make our complex idea of God. For, that the mind has such a power of enlarging some of its ideas, received from sensation, has been already shewed.

If I find, that I know some few things, and some of them, or all, perhaps imperfectly, I can frame an idea of knowing twice as many; which I can double again, as often as I can add to Number, and thus enlarge my idea of Knowledge, by extending its Comprehension to all things existing, or possible. The same I can also do of knowing them more perfectly; i.e., all their Qualities, Powers, Causes, Consequences, and Relations, etc., till all be perfectly known, that is in them, or can any way relate to them, and thus frame the idea of infinite or boundless knowledge. The same may also be done of Power, till we come to that we call infinite; and also of the Duration of Existence, without beginning or end; and so frame the idea of an eternal Being; the Degrees of Extent, wherein we ascribe Existence, Power, Wisdom, and all other Perfection (which we can have any ideas of) to that Sovereign Being, which we call God, being all boundless and infinite, we frame the best idea of him our Minds are capable of; all which is done, I say, by enlarging those simple ideas we have taken from the Operations of our own Minds, by Reflection; or by our Senses, from exterior things, to that vastness, to which Infinity can extend them.

For it is Infinity, which, joined to our ideas of Existence, Power, Knowledge, etc., makes that complex idea, whereby we represent to our selves the best we can, the supreme Being.

René Descartes on the Existence of God   1.15

Descartes's argument for the existence of God, dating from 1642, bears obvious resemblances to that set out in the eleventh century by Anselm (see 1.7). God is a "supremely perfect being". As existence is a perfection, it follows that God must have the perfection of existence, as he would otherwise not be perfect. Descartes supplements this argument with two examples (triangles and mountains). To think of God is to think of his existence, in just the same way as to think of a triangle is to think of its three angles being equal to two right angles, or thinking of a mountain is to think of a valley. See also 1.7; 1.8; 1.14; 1.16; 1.18; 1.19; 1.22.

Source: *Meditations on First Philosophy*; in *Mediationes de Prima Philosophia* (Paris: Librairie Philosophique J. Vrin, 1944), 65.7–15; 66.8–28.

* * *

Having given the matter careful attention, I am convinced that existence can no more be taken away from the divine essence than the magnitude of its three angles taken together being equal to two right angles can be taken away from the essence of a triangle, or than the idea of a valley can be taken away from the idea of a mountain. So it is no less absurd to think (*cogitare*) of God (that is, a supremely perfect being) lacking existence (that is, lacking a certain perfection), than to think of a mountain without a valley . . . I am not free to think of God apart from existence (that is, of a supremely perfect being apart from supreme perfection) in the way that I am free to imagine a horse either with wings or without wings . . . Whenever I choose to think of the First and Supreme Being, and as it were bring this idea out of the treasury of my mind, it is necessary that I ascribe all perfections to him . . . This necessity clearly ensures that, when I subsequently point out that existence is a perfection, I am correct in concluding that the First and Supreme Being exists.

1.16 Blaise Pascal on Proofs for the Existence of God

Pascal's *Pensées* ("Thoughts"), originally written in French during the period 1658–62, represents a collection of jottings and musings which were assembled after his death. In this selection, Pascal stresses the role of the heart, rather than reason, in our knowledge of God, as well as the limitations of reason. He also makes the point that "knowledge of God" is of little use to anyone unless it is accompanied by an awareness of human misery and of the possibility of redemption in Christ. Note that the numeration of the *Pensées* used follows that of the edition of Louis Lafuma, rather than that of the older Braunschweig edition. See also 1.7; 1.8; 1.14; 1.18; 1.19; 1.22.

Source: *Pensées* 110, 188, 190, 449; in Blaise Pascal, *Pensées* (Paris: Editions du Seuil, 1962), pp. 66, 99, 100, 196–7.

* * *

110. We know the truth, not only through our reason (*raison*), but also through our heart (*cœur*). It is through this latter that we know first principles; and reason, which has nothing to do with this, vainly tries to refute them. The sceptics have no intention other than this; and they fail to achieve it. We know that we are not dreaming. Yet however unable we may be to prove this by reason, this inability demonstrates nothing but the weakness of our reason, and not the uncertainty of all our knowledge, as they assert . . . Our inability must therefore do nothing except humble reason – which would like to be the judge of everything – while not confuting our certainty. As if reason could be the only way in which we can learn! . . .

188. The final step which reason can take is to recognize that there are an infinite number of things which are beyond it. It is merely impotent if it cannot get as far as to realize this. And if natural things are beyond it, what are we to say about supernatural things? . . .

190. The metaphysical proofs for the existence of God (*les preuves de Dieu métaphysiques*) are so remote from human reasoning, and so complex, that they have little impact. Even if they were of help to some people, this would only be for the moment during which they observed the demonstration, because an hour later, they would be afraid that they had deceived themselves . . .

449. ... It is equally as dangerous for someone to know God without knowing their misery as it is for someone to know their misery without knowing the Redeemer who can heal them. Only one of these insights (*connaissances*) leads to the pride of the philosophers, who have known God but not their misery, the other to the despair of the atheists, who know their misery without a Redeemer ... Even if someone were to be convinced that the relations between numbers are immaterial and eternal truths, which depend upon a first truth, called God, in which they subsist, I would not think that he or she had made much progress towards being saved.

Blaise Pascal on the Hiddenness of God   1.17

In a series of brief passages, written over the period 1658–1662, Pascal argues that it is both proper and necessary for God to be at least partly concealed. If this is not the case, humanity would become arrogant, trusting in its own ability to discover the full truth. The "obscurity" of God in the world forces humanity to recognize its own limitations, and thus to pay attention to God's self-revelation in Christ. Note that the numeration of the *Pensées* used follows that of the edition of Louis Lafuma, rather than that of the older Braunschweig edition. See also 1.11.

Source: *Pensées* 232, 242, 446, 449; in Blaise Pascal, *Pensée* (Paris: Editions du Seuil, 1962), pp. 117, 120, 195, 198.

* * *

232. We can understand nothing of the works of God unless we accept as a matter of principle that he wished to blind some and enlighten others ...

242. As God is hidden, any religion that does not say that God is hidden is not true, and any religion which does not explain why this is does not educate ...

446. If there was no obscurity, humanity would not be aware of its own corruption. If there was no light, humanity could not hope for a cure. Thus it is not only right for us that God should be partly concealed and partly revealed; it is also useful, in that it is equally dangerous for humanity to know God without knowing its own misery or to know its own misery without knowing God ...

449. What can be seen on earth points to neither the total absence nor the obvious presence of divinity, but to the presence of a hidden God. Everything bears this mark.

Immanuel Kant on Anselm's Ontological Argument   1.18

Kant was unimpressed by the arguments of either Anselm (1.7) or Descartes (1.15) for the existence of God. Kant, who appears to be have been the first person to refer to this approach as the "ontological argument", insists that "being is not a predicate". As a result, conceiving the idea of God cannot in any way be thought to necessarily lead to conceiving the idea "God exists". His analogy of the "hundred dollars" makes more or less the same point made earlier by Gaunilo: having an idea does not imply that its object exists! In the original German, Kant uses the word Thaler as a unity of currency; I have translated this as "dollar" to give a more contemporary feel to the passage, taking advantage of the fact that the word "dollar" derives directly from this original German term. See also 1.7; 1.8; 1.15; 1.16.

Source: Immanuel Kant, *Kritik der reinen Vernunft*, 2nd edn (Riga: Hartknoch, 1787), pp. 626–7.

* * *

Now "Being" is clearly not a genuine predicate; that is, it is not a concept of something which could be added to the concept of a thing. It is merely the positing of a thing, or of certain determinations, as existing in themselves. Logically, it is merely the copula of a judgement. The proposition "God is omnipotent" contains two concepts, each of which has its object – God and omnipotence. The little word "is" adds no new predicate, but only serves to posit the predicate *in its relation* to the subject. Now if we take the subject (God) with all its predicates (among which is omnipotence), and say "God exists" or "There is a God," we do not attach any new predicate to the concept of God; we merely posit the subject in itself with all its predicates. In fact, we posit it as being an object that stands in relation to the concept. The content of both must be one and the same. Nothing can have been added to the concept, which expresses merely what is possible, by my thinking its object (through the expression "it is") as given absolutely. Otherwise stated, the real contains no more than the merely possible. A hundred real dollars would not be worth more than a hundred possible dollars. For as the latter signify the concept, and the former the object and the positing of the object, my concept would not, in that case, express the whole object, and would not therefore be an adequate concept of it. My financial position is, however, affected in a very different manner by a hundred real dollars than it is by the mere concept of a hundred dollars (that is, the concept of their possibility). For the object, as it actually exists, is not analytically contained in my concept, but is added to me concept (which is a determination of my state) synthetically; and yet the conceived hundred dollars are not themselves in the least increased through thus acquiring existence outside my concept.

1.19 John Henry Newman on the Grounds of Faith

Newman here argues that the grounds of assurance of faith rest on a deep-seated intuitive or instinctive knowledge of God, which is not necessarily enhanced by rational arguments or demonstrations. The full logical structures of faith can thus never be fully understood, as religion ultimately depends upon an immediate and spontaneous "feeling" or "revelation" which cannot be adequately grasped or expounded on the basis of reason. There are important parallels here, probably unknown to Newman, with Pscal's emphasis upon the role of the heart in religious knowledge and experience. See also 1.7; 1.8; 1.14; 1.15; 1.18; 1.22.

Source: John Henry Newman, *Essay in Aid of a Grammar of Assent*, 2nd edn (London: Burns & Oates, 1870), pp. 159–60.

———————————————————————————————————— * * *

We know from experience that beliefs may endure without the presence of the inferential acts upon which they were originally elicited. It is plain that, as life goes on, we are not only inwardly formed and changed by the accession of habits, but we are also enriched by a great multitude of beliefs and opinions, and that on a variety of subjects. These, held, as some of them are, almost as first principles, constitutes as it were the furniture and clothing of the mind. Sometimes we are fully conscious of them; sometimes they are implicit, or only now and then come directly before our reflective faculty. Still they are beliefs, and when we first admitted them we had some kind of reason, slight or strong, recognized or not, for doing so. However, whatever those reasons were, even if we ever realized them, we have long since forgotten them. Whether it was the authority of others, or our own observation, or our reading, or our reflections which became the warrant of our belief, anyhow we received the matters in question into our minds, and gave them a place there. We believed them and we still believe, though we have forgotten what the warrant was. At present they are self-sustained in our minds, and have been so for long years. They are in no sense "conclusions," and imply no process of reasoning. Here, then, is the case where belief stands out as distinct from inference.

———

Karl Barth on the Nature and Task of Theology

1.20

Over the period 10–12 April 1934, Karl Barth delivered three lectures on theology to the Free Protestant Theological Faculty at Paris. This extract from Barth's lecture on "Theology" sets out a vision of the inspirational nature of the subject, and mounts a vigorous protest against any temptation to "professionalize" the subject. Theology is a matter for the church, not for some professional elite. In many ways, Barth's ideas can be seen as a theological extension of the Reformation doctrine of the "priesthood of all believers." See also 7.10.

Source: Karl Barth, "Theology," in *God in Action* (Edinburgh: T. & T. Clark, 1936), pp. 39–57. Used with permission of the publisher.

———————————————————————————————————— * * *

Of all the sciences which stir the head and heart, theology is the fairest. It is closest to human reality, and gives us the clearest view of the truth after which all science quests. It best illustrates the time-honored and profound word: "Fakultät." It is a landscape, like the landscape of Umbria or Tuscany, in which distant perspectives are always clear. Theology is a masterpiece, as well-planned and yet as bizarre as the cathedrals of Cologne and Milan. What a miserable lot of theologians – and what miserable periods there have been in the history of theology – when they have not realized this! ...

The task which is laid upon theology, and which it should and can fulfil, is its service in the Church, to the Lord of the Church. It has its definite function in the Church's liturgy, that is, in the various phases of the Church's expression; in every reverend proclamation of the gospel, or in every proclaiming reverence, in which the Church listens and attends to God. Theology does not exist in a vacuum, nor in any arbitrarily selected field, but in that province between baptism and confirmation, in the realm between the Scriptures and their exposition and proclamation. Theology is, like all other functions of the Church, uniquely based upon the fact that God has spoken to humanity and that humanity may hear his Word through grace. Theology is an act of repentant humility, which is presented to humanity through his fact. This act exists in the fact that in theology the Church seeks again and again to examine itself critically as it asks itself what it means and implies to be a Church among humanity . . .

The task of theology consists in again and again reminding the people in the Church, both preachers and congregations, that the life and work of the Church are under the authority of the gospel and the law, that God should be heard . . . It has to be a watchman so as to carefully observe that constant threatening and invasive error to which the life of the Church is in danger, because it is composed of fallible, erring, sinful people . . .

Theology is not a private subject for theologians only. Nor is it a private subject for professors. Fortunately, there have always been pastors who have understood more about theology than most professors. Nor is theology a private subject of study for pastors. Fortunately, there have repeatedly been congregation members, and often whole congregations, who have pursued theology energetically while their pastors were theological infants or barbarians. Theology is a matter for the Church.

1.21 Ludwig Wittgenstein on Analogy

In this passage, originally published in German with an accompanying English translation in 1953, two years after the author's death, Wittgenstein argues that the meaning of words is established by their use in real life. The use of terms in this way allows their "family resemblances" to be established. Wittgenstein's insistence upon the actual usage of words is an important corrective to more ontological approaches to analogy. See also 1.10; 1.14.

Source: Ludwig Wittgenstein, *Philosophical Investigations* (Oxford: Blackwell, 1968), pp. 31–2. Reprinted with the permission of the publishers.

* * *

Consider for example the proceedings that we call "games." I mean board-games, card-games, ball-games, Olympic games, and so on. What is common to them all? Don't say: "There must be something common, or they would not be called "games" – but *look and see* whether there is anything common to them all. – For if you look at them you will not see something that is common to *all*, but similarities, relationships, and a whole series of them at that. To repeat: don't think, but look! – Look for example at board-games with their multifarious relationships. Now pass to card-games; here you find many correspondences with the first group, but many common features drop out, and others appear. When we pass next to ball-games, much that is common is retained, but much is lost. – Are they all "amusing"? Compare chess with noughts and crosses. Or is there always winning and losing, or competition between players? Think of patience. In ball-games there is winning and losing; but when a child thows his ball at the wall and catches it again, this feature has disappeared. Look at the parts played by skill and luck; and at the difference between skill in chess and skill in tennis. Think now of games like ring-a-ring-a-roses; here is the element of amusement, but how many other characteristic features have disappeared! And we can go through the many, many other groups of games in the same way; can see how similarities crop up and disappear.

And the result of this examination is: we see a complicated network of similarities overlapping and criss-crossing: sometimes overall similarities, sometimes similarities of detail.

I can think of no better expression to characterize these similarities than "family resemblances"; for the various resemblances between members of a family: build, features, colour of eyes, gait, temperament, etc. etc. overlap and criss-cross in the same way. – And I shall say: "games" form a family.

Ludwig Wittgenstein on Proofs for the Existence of God   1.22

In this passage, originally written in German and published after his death, Wittgenstein demonstrates the limitations of logical deductions of the existence of God, and stresses the importance of experience and life in bringing about belief in God. See also 1.7; 1.8; 1.14; 1.15; 1.18; 1.19.

Source: *Culture and Value*, ed. G. H. von Wright, translated by Peter Winch (Oxford: Blackwell, 1980), pp. 82–6. Reprinted with permission of the publishers.

* * *

God's essence is supposed to guarantee his existence – what this really means is that what is at issue here is not the existence of something. Couldn't one actually say equally well that the essence of colour guarantees its existence? As opposed, say, to white elephants. Because all that really means is: I cannot explain what "colour" is, what the word "colour" means, except with the help of a colour sample. So in this case there is no such thing as explaining "what it *would* be like if colours were to exist". . . . And now we might say: There can be a description of what it would be like if there were gods on Olympus – but not "what it would be like if there were such a thing as God." And to say this is to determine the concept "God" more precisely . . . How are we taught the word "God" (its use, that is)? I cannot give a full grammatical description of it. But I can, as it were, make some contributions to such a description; I can say a good deal about it and perhaps in time assemble a sort of collection of examples . . .

A proof of God's existence ought really to be something by means of which one could convince oneself that God exists. But I think that what *believers* who have furnished such proofs have wanted to do is to give their "belief" an intellectual analysis and foundation, although they themselves would never have come to believe as a result of such proofs . . . Life can educate one to a belief in God. And *experiences* too are what bring this about: but I don't mean visions and other forms of sense experience which show us the "existence of this being," but, e.g., sufferings of various sorts. These neither show us God in the way a sense impression shows us an object, nor do they give rise to *conjectures* about him. Experiences, thoughts – life can force this concept on us.

1.23 Dietrich Bonhoeffer on God in a Secular World

In this letter from Tegel prison, Bonhoeffer speaks of the new challenge to Christianity in a world in which the existence of God is not taken for granted. He identifies a central theme of Christianity, which distinguishes it from all other religions, in its focus on the sufferings of God in Christ. Bonhoeffer is one of the most vigorous critics of the idea that human "religiosity" is a point of contact for the gospel. The theme of a suffering God is of major importance to Bonhoeffer, as this passage makes clear. Note that the German song title referred to means "If only I knew the way back, the long way to the land of childhood." See also 3.29; 3.32.

Source: Letter to Eberhard Bethge, dated 16 July 1944; in Dietrich Bonhoeffer, *Letters and Papers from Prison*, ed. E. Bethge (New York: Macmillan, and London: SCM Press, 1971), pp. 359–61. Reprinted with the permission of SCM Press and Simon & Schuster from *Letters and Papers from Prison*, revised and enlarged edition, by Dietrich Bonhoeffer, translated from the German by Reginald Fuller et al. Copyright © 1953, 1967, 1971 by SCM Press Ltd.

* * *

Now for a few more thoughts on our theme. I'm only gradually working my way to the non-religious interpretation of biblical concepts; the job is too big for me to finish just yet.

On the historical side: There is one great development that leads to the world's autonomy. In theology one sees it first in Lord Herbert of Cherbury, who maintains that reason is sufficient for religious knowledge. In ethics it appears in Montaigne and Bodin with their substitution of rules of life for the commandments. In politics Machiavelli detaches politics from morality in general and founds the doctrine of "reasons of state." Later, and very differently from Machiavelli, but tending like him towards the autonomy of human society, comes Grotius, setting up his natural law as international law, which is valid *etsi deus non daretur*, "even if there were no God." The philosophers provide the finishing touches: on the one hand we have the deism of Descartes, who holds that the world is a mechanism, running by itself with no interference from God; and on the other hand the pantheism of Spinoza, who says that God is nature. In the last resort, Kant is a deist, and Fichte and Hegel are pantheists. Everywhere the thinking is directed towards the autonomy of man and the world.

(It seems that in the natural sciences the process begins with Nicolas of Cusa and Giordano Bruno and the "heretical" doctrine of the infinity of the universe. The classical *cosmos* was finite, like the created world of the Middle Ages. An infinite universe, however it may be conceived, is self-subsisting, *etsi deus non daretur*. It is true that modern physics is not as sure as it was about the infinity of the universe, but it has not gone back to the earlier conceptiolls of its finitude.)

God as a working hypothesis in morals, politics, or science, has been surmounted and abolished; and the same thing has happened in philosophy and religion (Feuerbach!). For the sake of intellectual honesty, that working hypothesis should be dropped, or as far as possible eliminated. A scientist or phisician who sets out to edify is a hybrid.

Anxious souls will ask what room there is left for God now; and as they know of no answer to the question, they condemn the whole development that has brought them to such straits. I wrote to you before about the various emergency exits that have been contrived; and we ought to add to them the *salto mortale* [death-leap] back into the Middle Ages. But the principle of the Middle Ages is heteronomy in the form of clericalism; a return to that can be a counsel of despair, and it would be at the cost of intellectual honesty. It's a dream that reminds one of the song *O wusst'ich doch den Weg zurück, den weiten Weg ins Kinderland*. There is no such way – at any rate not if it means deliberately abandoning our mental integrity; the only way is that of Matthew 18:3, i.e., through repentance, through *ultimate* honesty.

And we cannot be honest unless we recognize that we have to live in the world *etsi deus non daretur*. And this is just what we do recognize – before God! God himself compels us to recognize it. So our coming of age leads us to a true recognition of our situation before God. God would have us know that we must live as men who manage our lives without him. The God who is with us is the God who forsakes us (Mark 15:34). The God who lets us live in the world without the working hypothesis of God is the God before whom we stand continually. Before God and with God we live without God. God lets himself be pushed out of the world on to the cross. He is weak and powerless in the world, and that is precisely the way, the only way, in which he is with us and helps us. Matt. 8:17 makes it quite dear that Christ helps us, not by virtue of his omnipotence, but by virtue of his weakness and suffering.

Here is the decisive difference between Christianity and all religions. Man's religiosity makes him look in his distress to the power of God in the world: God is the *deus ex machina*. The Bible directs man to God's powerlessness and suffering; only the suffering God can help. To that extent we may say that the development towards the world's coming of age outlined above, which has done away with a false conception of God, opens up a way of seeing the God of the Bible, who wins power and space in the world by his weakness. This will probably be the starting-point for our secular interpretation.

1.24 Paul Tillich on the Method of Correlation

One of Tillich's primary concerns was apologetic. To ensure the continuing credibility of Christianity, he argued, it was necessary to correlate the gospel proclamation with the questions which secular culture raised. For Tillich, culture raised "ultimate questions," to which theology was obliged to respond. In this lengthy and important passage, Tillich explores the general principles of correlating the Christian message with secular culture.

Source: Paul Tillich, *Systematic Theology*, vol. 1 (Chicago: University of Chicago Press, 1951), pp. 59–64. Copyright © 1951 by The University of Chicago. Cited with permission of the University of Chicago Press.

* * *

The principle of methodological rationality implies that, like all scientific approaches to reality, systematic theology follows a method. A method is a tool, literally a way around, which must be adequate to its subject matter. Whether or not a method is adequate cannot be decided a priori; it is continually being decided in the cognitive process itself. Method and system determine each other. Therefore, no method can claim to de adequate for every subject. Methodological imperialism is as dangerous as political imperialism; like the latter, it breaks down when the independent elements of reality revolt against it. A method is not an "indifferent net" in which reality is caught, but the method is an element of the reality itself. In at least one respect the description of a method is a description of a decisive aspect of the object to which it is applied. The cognitive relation itself, quite apart from any special act of cognition, reveals something about the object, as well as about the subject, in the relation. The cognitive relation in physics reveals the mathematical character of objects in space (and time). The cognitive relation in biology reveals the structure (*Gestalt*) and spontaneous character of objects in space and time. The cognitive relation in historiography reveals the individual and value-related character of objects in time (and space). The cognitive relation in theology reveals the existential and transcending character of the ground of objects in time and space. Therefore, no method can be developed without a prior knowledge of the object to which it is applied. For systematic theology this means that its method is derived from a prior knowledge of the system which is to be built by the method.

Systematic theology uses the method of correlation. It has always done so, sometimes more, sometimes less, consciously, and must do so consciously and outspokenly, especially if the apologetic point of view is to prevail. The method of correlation explains the contents of the Christian faith through existential questions and theological answers in mutual interdependence.

The term "correlation" may be used in three ways. It can designate the correspondence of different series of data, as in statistical charts; it can designate the logical interdependence of concepts, as in polar relations; and it can designate the real interdependence of things or events in structural wholes. If the term is used in theology all three meanings have important applications. There is a correlation in the sense of correspondence between religious symbols and that which is symbolized by them. There is a correlation in the logical sense between concepts denoting the human and those denoting the divine. There is a correlation in the factual sense between man's ultimate concern and that about which he is ultimately concerned. The first meaning of correlation refers to the central problem of religious knowledge . . . The second meaning of correlation determines the statements about God and the world; for example, the correlation of the infinite and the finite . . . The third meaning of correlation qualifies the divine–human relationship within religious experience. The third use of correlative thinking in theology has evoked the protest of theologians such as Karl Barth, who are afraid that any kind of divine–human correlation makes God partly dependent on man. But although God in his abysmal nature is in no way dependent on man, God in his self-manifestation to man is dependent on the way man receives his manifestation. This is true even if the doctrine of predestination, namely, that this way is foreordained by God and entirely independent of human freedom, is maintained. The divine–human relation, and therefore God as well as man within this relation, changes with the stages of the history of revelation and with the stages of every personal development. There is a mutual interdependence between "God for us" and "we for God." God's wrath and God's grace are not contrasts in the "heart" of God (Luther), in the depth of his being; but they are contrasts in the divine–human relationship. The divine–human relation is a correlation. The "divine–human encounter" (Emil Brunner) means something real for both sides. It is an actual correlation, in the third sense of the term.

The divine–human relationship is a correlation also in its cognitive side. Symbolically speaking, God answers man's questions, and under the impact of God's answers man asks them. Theology formulates the questions implied in human existence, and theology formulates the answers in divine self-manifestation under the guidance of the questions implied in human existence. This is a circle which drives man to a point where question and answer are not separated. This point, however, is not a moment in time. It belongs to man's essential being, to the unity of his finitude with the infinity in which he was created, and from which he is separated . . . A symptom of both the essential unity and the existential separation of finite man from his infinity is his ability to ask about the infinite to which he belongs: the fact that he must ask about it indicates that he is separated from it.

The answers implied in the event of revelation are meaningful only in so far as they are in correlation with questions concerning the whole of our existence, with existential questions. Only those who have experienced the shock of transitoriness, the anxiety in which they are aware of their finitude, the threat of nonbeing, can understand what the notion of God means. Only those who have experienced the tragic ambiguities of our historical existence and have totally questioned the meaning of existence can understand what the symbol of the Kingdom of God means. Revelation answers questions which have been asked and always will be asked because they are "we ourselves." Man is the question he asks about himself, before any question has been formulated. It is, therefore, not surprising that the basic questions were formulated very early in the history of mankind. Every analysis of the mythological material shows this. Nor is it surprising that the same questions appear in early childhood, as every observation of children shows. Being human means asking the questions of one's own being and living under the impact of the answers given to this question. And, conversely, being human means receiving answers to the questions of one's own being and asking questions under the impact of the answers.

In using the method of correlation, systematic theology proceeds in the following way: it makes an analysis of the human situation out of which the existential questions arise, and it demonstrates that the symbols used in the Christian message are the answers to these questions. The analysis of the human situation is done in terms which today are called "existential." Such analyses are much older than existentialism; they are, indeed, as old as man's thinking about himself, and they have been expressed in various kinds of conceptualization since the beginning of philosophy. Whenever man has looked at his world, he has found himself in it as a part of it. But he also has realized that he is a stranger in the world of objects, unable to penetrate it beyond a certain level of scientific analysis. And then he has become aware of the fact that he himself is the door to the deeper levels of reality, that in his own existence he has the only possible approach to existence itself. This does not mean that man is more approachable than other objects as material for scientific research. The opposite is the case! It does mean that the immediate experience of one's own existing reveals something of the nature of existence generally. Whoever has penetrated into the nature of his own finitude can find the traces of finitude in everything that exists. And he can ask the question implied in his finitude as the question implied in finitude universally. In doing so, he does not formulate a doctrine of man; he expresses a doctrine of existence as experienced in him as man. When Calvin in the opening sentences of the *Institutes* correlates our knowledge of God with our knowledge of man, he does not speak of the doctrine of man as such and of the doctrine of God as such. He speaks of man's misery, which gives the existential basis for his understanding of God's glory, and of God's glory, which gives the essential basis for man's understanding of his misery. Man as existing, representing existence generally and asking the question implied in his existence, is one side of the cognitive correlation to which Calvin points, the other side being the divine majesty. In the initial sentences of his theological system Calvin expresses the essence of the method of correlation.

The analysis of the human situation employs materials made available by man's creative self-interpretation in all realms of culture. Philosophy contributes, but so do poetry, drama, the novel, therapeutic psychology, and sociology. The theologian organizes these materials in relation to the answer given by the Christian message. In the light of this message he may make an analysis of existence which is more penetrating than that of most philosophers. Nevertheless, it remains a philosophical analysis. The analysis of existence, including the development of the questions implicit in existence, is a philosophical task, even if it is performed by a theologian, and even if the theologian is a reformer like Calvin. The difference between the philosopher who is not a theologian and the theologian who works as a philosopher in analyzing human existence is only that the former tries to give an analysis which will be part of a broader philosophical world, while the latter tries to correlate the material of his analysis with the theological concepts he derives from the Christian faith. This does not make the philosophical work of the theologian heteronomous. As a theologian he does not tell himself what is philosophically true. As a philosopher he does not tell himself what is theologically true. But he cannot help seeing human existence and existence generally in such a way that the Christian symbols appear meaningful and understandable to him. His eyes are partially focused by his ultimate concern, which is true of every philosopher. Nevertheless, his act of seeing is autonomous, for it is determined only by the object as it is given in his experience. If he sees something he did not expect to see in the light of his theological answer, he holds fast to what he has seen and reformulates the theological answer. He is certain that nothing he sees can change the substance of his answer, because this substance is the *logos* of being, manifest in Jesus as the Christ. If this were not his presupposition, he would have to sacrifice either his philosophical honesty or his theological concern.

The Christian message provides the answers to the questions implied in human existence. These answers are contained in the revelatory events on which Christianity is based and are taken by systematic theology *from* the sources, *through* the medium, *under* the norm. Their content cannot be derived from the questions, that is, from an analysis of human existence. They are "spoken" to human existence from beyond it. Otherwise they would not be answers, for the question in human existence itself. But the relation is more involved than this, since it is correlation. There is a mutual dependence between question and answer. In respect to content the Christian answers are dependent on the revelatory events in which they appear; in respect to form they are dependent on the structure of the questions which they answer. God is the answer to the question implied in human finitude. This answer cannot be derived from the analysis of existence. However, if the notion of God appears in systematic theology in correlation with the threat of nonbeing which is implied in existence, God must be called the infinite power of being which resists the threat of nonbeing. In classical theology this is being-itself. If anxiety is defined as the awareness of being finite, God must be called the infinite ground of courage. In classical theology this is universal providence. If the notion of the Kingdom of God appears in correlation with the riddle of our historical existence, it must be called the meaning, fulfilment, and unity of history. In this way an interpretation of the traditional symbols of Christianity is achieved which preserves the power of these symbols and which opens them to the questions elaborated by our present analysis of human existence.

1.25 Sallie McFague on Metaphor in Theology

In several of her writings, including *Metaphorical Theology*, Sallie McFague develops the idea that Christian ways of speaking about God are primarily metaphorical in character, drawing attention to the differences between God and humanity as well as the similarities. After making the point that theology needs images or models to stimulate and inform its reflection, she considers the particular role of metaphors, focusing on the metaphor of "God as mother." See also 1.10; 1.21; 3.22; 3.34; 3.35.

Source: Sallie McFague, *Models of God: Theology for an Ecological Nuclear Age* (Philadelphia: Fortress Press, 1987), pp. 32–4. Reprinted from *Models of God* by Sallie McFague. Copyright © 1987 Fortress Press. Used by permission of Augsburg Fortress.

* * *

The first thing to say is that theology, as constructive and metaphorical, does not "demythologize" but "remythologizes." To envision theology as metaphorical means, at the outset, to refuse the attempt to denude religious language of its concrete, poetic, imagistic and hence inevitably anthropomorphic, character, in the search for presumably more enlightened (and usually more abstract) terminology. It is to accept as one of theology's primary tasks remythologizing for our time: identifying and elucidating primary metaphors and models from contemporary experience which will express Christian faith for our day in powerful, illuminating ways. Theologians are not poets, but neither are they philosophers (as, in the Christian tradition, they have often become). Their place, as understood by metaphorical theology, is an anomalous one that partakes of both poetry and philosophy: they are poets insofar as they must be sensitive to the metaphors and models that are at once consonant with the Christian faith and appropriate for expressing that faith in their own time, and they are philosophers insofar as they must elucidate in a coherent, comprehensive, and systematic way the implications of these metaphors and models . . .

A second and more complex issue in regard to theology, as constructive and metaphorical, concerns metaphor and model. What are they, and why call theology metaphorical? A metaphor is a word or phrase used inappropriately. It belongs properly in one context but is being used in another: the arm of the chair, war as a chess game, God the father. From Aristotle until recently, metaphor has been seen mainly as a poetic device to embellish or decorate. The idea was that in metaphor one used a word or phrase inappropriately but one need not have: whatever was being expressed could be said directly without the metaphor. Increasingly, however, the idea of metaphor as unsubstitutable is winning acceptance: what a metaphor expresses cannot be said directly or apart from it, for if it could be, one would have said it directly. Here, metaphor is a strategy of desperation, not decoration; it is an attempt to say something about the unfamiliar in terms of the familiar, an attempt to speak about what we do not know in terms of what we do know. Not all metaphors fit this definition, for many are so enmeshed in conventional language (the arm or the chair) that we do not notice them and some have become so familiar that we do not recognize them as attempting to express the unfamiliar (God the father). But a fresh metaphor, such as in the remark that "war is a chess game," immediately sparks our imaginations to think of war, a very complex phenomenon, as viewed through a concrete grid or screen, the game of chess. Needless to say, war is not a chess game; hence, a description of war in terms of chess is a partial, relative, inadequate account that, in illuminating certain aspects of war (such as strategizing), filters out other aspects (such as violence and death).

Metaphor always has the character of "is" and "is not": an assertion is made but as a likely account rather than a definition. That is, to say, "God is mother," is not to define God as mother, not to assert identity between the terms "God" and "mother," but to suggest that we consider what we do not know how to talk about – relating to God – through the metaphor of mother. The assumption here is that all talk of God is indirect: no words or phrases refer directly to God, for God-language can refer only through the detour of a description that properly belongs elsewhere. To speak of God as mother is to invite us to consider some qualities associated with mothering as one partial but perhaps illuminating way of speaking of certain aspects of God's relationship to us. It also assumes, however, that many other metaphors may qualify as partial but illuminating grids or screens for this purpose.

Gustavo Gutiérrez on Theology as Critical Reflection

1.26

One of the characteristic features of Latin American liberation is its emphasis on practice, rather than theory. This emphasis, whose origins may be traced back to Karl Marx's distinction between theory and praxis, shows itself particularly in the liberationist emphasis on the need for practical social involvement and political commitment, and the implicit criticism of western understandings of theology as a disinterested and detached academic discipline. See also 3.30; 7.21; 9.3.

Source: Gustavo Gutiérrez, A Theology of Liberation, 2nd edn (Maryknoll, NY: Orbis Books, and London: SCM Press, 1978), pp. 9–12. Reprinted with the permission of the publishers.

* * *

Theology must be critical reflection on humankind, on basic human principles. Only with this approach will theology be a serious discourse, aware of itself, in full possession of its conceptual elements. But we are not referring exclusively to this epistemological aspect when we talk about theology as critical reflection. We also refer to a clear and critical attitude regarding economic and socio-cultural issues in the life and reflection of the Christian community. To disregard these is to deceive both oneself and others. But above all, we intend this term to express the theory of a definite practice.

Theological reflection would then necessarily be a criticism of society and
the Church, insofar as they are called and addressed by the Word of God;
it would be a critical theory, worked out in the light of the Word accepted
in faith and inspired by a practical purpose – and therefore indissolubly
linked to historical praxis.

By preaching the Gospel message, by its sacraments, and by the charity
of its members, the Church proclaims and shelters the gift of the Kingdom
of God in the heart of human history. The Christian community professes
a faith which works through charity. It is – at least ought to be – real
charity, action, and commitment to the service of others. Theology is reflection, a critical attitude. *Theology follows*; it is the second step. What Hegel
used to say about philosophy can likewise be applied to theology: it rises
only at sundown. The pastoral activity of the Church does not flow as a
conclusion from theological premises. Theology does not produce pastoral
activity; rather it reflects upon it. Theology must be able to find in pastoral
activity the presence of the Spirit inspiring the action of the Christian community. A privileged *locus theologicus* for understanding the faith will be the
life, preaching, and historical commitment of the Church.

To reflect upon the presence and action of the Christian in the world
means, moreover, to go beyond the visible boundaries of the Church. This
is of prime importance. It implies openness to the world, gathering the
questions it poses, being attentive to its historical transformations. In the
words of Yves Congar, "If the Church wishes to deal with the real questions
of the modern world and to attempt to respond to them, . . . it must open
as it were a new chapter of theologico-pastoral epistemology. Instead of
using only revelation and tradition as starting points, as classical theology
has generally done, it must start with facts and questions derived from the
world and from history." It is precisely this opening to the totality of
human history that allows theology to fulfill its critical function *vis-à-vis*
ecclesial praxis without narrowness.

This critical task is indispensable. Reflection in the light of faith must
constantly accompany the pastoral action of the Church. By keeping historical events in their proper perspective, theology helps safeguard society and
the Church from regarding as permanent what is only temporary. Critical
reflection thus always plays the inverse role of an ideology which rational-
izes and justifies a given social and ecclesial order. On the other hand,
theology, by pointing to the sources of revelation, helps to orient pastoral
activity; it puts it in a wider context and so helps it to avoid activism and
immediatism. Theology as critical reflection thus fulfills a liberating function for humankind and the Christian community, preserving them from
fetishism and idolatry, as well as from a pernicious and belittling narcis-
sism. Understood in this way theology has a necessary and permanent role
in liberation from every form of religious alienation – which is often fos-
tered by the ecclesiastical institution itself when it impedes an authentic
approach to the Word of the Lord.

As critical reflection on society and the Church, theology is an understanding which both grows and, in a certain sense, changes. If the

commitment of the Christian community in fact takes different forms throughout history, the understanding which accompanies the vicissitudes of this commitment will be constantly renewed and will take untrodden paths. A theology which has as its points of reference only "truths" which have been established once and for all – and not the Truth which is also the Way – can be only static and, in the long run, sterile. In this sense the often-quoted and misinterpreted words of Bouillard take on new validity: "A theology which is not up-to-date is a false theology."

Finally, theology thus understood, that is to say as linked to praxis, fulfills a prophetic function insofar as it interprets historical events with the intention of revealing and proclaiming their profound meaning. According to Oscar Cullmann, this is the meaning of the prophetic role: "The prophet does not limit himself as does the fortune-teller to isolated revelations, but his prophecy becomes preaching, proclamation. He explains to the people the true meaning of all events; he informs them of the plan and will of God at the particular moment." But if theology is based on this observation of historical events and contributes to the discovery of their meaning, it is with the purpose of making Christians' commitment within them more radical and clear. Only with the exercise of the prophetic function understood in this way, will the theologian be – to borrow an expression from Antonio Gramsci – a new kind of "organic intellectual." Theologians will be personally and vitally engaged in historical realities with specific times and places. They will be engaged where nations, social classes, and peoples struggle to free themselves from domination and oppression by other nations, classes, and peoples. In the last analysis, the true interpretation of the meaning revealed by theology is achieved only in historical praxis – "The hermeneutics of the Kingdom of God," observed Schillebeeckx, "consists especially in making the world a better place. Only in this way will I be able to discover what the Kingdom of God means." We have here a political hermeneutics of the Gospel.

Theology as a critical reflection on Christian praxis in the light of the Word does not replace the other functions of theology, such as wisdom and rational knowledge; rather it presupposes and needs them. But this is not all. We are not concerned here with a mere juxtaposition. The critical function of theology necessarily leads to redefinition of these other two tasks. Henceforth, wisdom and rational knowledge will more explicitly have ecclesial praxis as their point of departure and their context. It is in reference to this praxis that an understanding of spiritual growth based on Scripture should be developed, and it is through this same praxis that faith encounters the problems posed by human reason. Given the theme of the present work, we will be especially aware of this critical function of theology with the ramifications suggested above. This approach will lead us to pay special attention to the life of the Church and to commitments which Christians, impelled by the Spirit and in communion with others, undertake in history. We will give special consideration to participation in the process of liberation, an outstanding phenomenon of our times, which takes on special meaning in the so-called Third World countries.

This kind of theology, arising from concern with a particular set of issues, will perhaps give us the solid and permanent albeit modest foundation for the *theology in a Latin American perspective* which is both desired and needed. This Latin American focus would not be due to a frivolous desire for originality, but rather to a fundamental sense of historical efficacy and also – why hide it? – to the desire to contribute to the life and reflection of the universal Christian community. But in order to make our contribution, this desire for universality – as well as input from the Christian community as a whole – must be present from the beginning. To concretize this desire would be to overcome particularistic tendencies – provincial and chauvinistic – and produce something *unique*, both particular and universal, and therefore fruitful.

"The only future that theology has, one might say, is to become the theology of the future," Harvey Cox has said. But this theology of the future must necessarily be a critical appraisal of historical praxis, of the historical task in the sense we have attempted to sketch. Jürgen Moltmann says that theological concepts "do not limp after reality . . . They illuminate reality by displaying its future." In our approach, to reflect critically on the praxis of liberation is to "limp after" reality. The present in the praxis of liberation, in its deepest dimension, is pregnant with the future; hope must be an inherent part of our present commitment in history. Theology does not initiate this future which exists in the present. It does not create the vital attitude of hope out of nothing. Its role is more modest. It interprets and explains these as the true underpinnings of history. To reflect upon a forward directed action is not to concentrate on the past. It does not mean being the caboose of the present. Rather it is to penetrate the present reality, the movement of history, that which is driving history toward the future. To reflect on the basis of the historical praxis of liberation is to reflect in the light of the future which is believed in and hoped for. It is to reflect with a view to action which transforms the present. But it does not mean doing this from an armchair; rather it means sinking roots where the pulse of history is beating at this moment and illuminating history with the Word of the Lord of history, who irreversibly committed himself to the present moment of humankind to carry it to its fulfillment.

It is for all these reasons that the theology of liberation offers us not so much a new theme for reflection as a *new way* to do theology. Theology as critical reflection on historical praxis is a liberating theology, a theology of the liberating transformation of the history of humankind and also therefore that part of humankind – gathered into *ecclesia* – which openly confesses Christ. This is a theology which does not stop with reflecting on the world, but rather tries to be part of the process through which the world is transformed. It is a theology which is open – in the protest against trampled human dignity, in the struggle against the plunder of the vast majority of humankind, in liberating love, and in the building of a new, just, and comradely society – to the gift of the Kingdom of God.

Brian A. Gerrish on Accommodation in Calvin's Theology

1.27

For Calvin, divine revelation takes place in a form which is "accommodated" or "adjusted" to human capacities and abilities. In this helpful analysis, Brian A. Gerrish sets out the basic features of Calvin's approach, which has had a considerable influence on Reformed theology in particular. See also 1.10; 1.12; 1.25; 6.31.

Source: Brian A. Gerrish, *The Old Protestantism and the New: Essays on the Reformation Heritage* (Chicago: University of Chicago Press, and Edinburgh: T. & T. Clark, 1982), p. 175. © 1982 by The University of Chicago. Cited with the permission of the publishers.

* * *

According to Calvin, the forms of revelation are adapted in various ways to the nature of man as the recipient. His general term for the several types of adaptation is "accommodation." It is axiomatic for Calvin that God cannot be comprehended by the human mind. What is known of God is known by revelation; and God reveals himself, not as he is in himself, but in forms adapted to man's capacity. Hence in preaching he communicates himself through a man speaking to men, and in the sacraments he adds a mode of communication adapted to man's physical nature. Now in speaking of the Bible, Calvin extends the idea of accommodation beyond the mode to the actual content of revelation, and argues that the very diction of biblical language is often adapted to the finitude of man's mind. God does not merely condescend to human frailty by revealing himself in the prophetic and apostolic word and by causing the Word to be written down in sacred books: he also makes his witnesses employ accommodated expressions. For example, God is represented anthropomorphically as raising his hand, changing his mind, deliberating, being angry, and so on. Calvin admits that this accommodated language has a certain impropriety about it. It bears the same relation to divine truth as does the baby talk of a nurse or mother to the world of adult realities.

George Lindbeck on Postliberal Approaches to Doctrine

1.28

George Lindbeck's *Nature of Doctrine* (1984) is widely regarded as a manifesto of postliberalism. The work sets out a "cultural–linguistic" approach to Christian doctrine, which argues that doctrine regulates the language of the Christian tradition. After considering approaches to doctrine which treat it as making cognitive truth claims or expressing human experience, Lindbeck turns to set out his own position, in which the historical and cultural phenomenon of the Christian tradition is argued to be of central importance.

Source: George Lindbeck, *The Nature of Doctrine* (Philadelphia: Westminster Press, 1984), pp. 32–5. Reprinted from *The Nature of Doctrine: Religion and Theology in a Postliberal Age*, by George A. Lindbeck. © 1984 George A. Lindbeck. Used by permission of Westminster John Knox Press.

* * *

The description of the cultural–linguistic alternative that I shall now sketch is shaped by the ultimately theological concerns of the present inquiry, but it is consonant, I believe, with the anthropological, sociological, and philosophical studies by which it has been for the most part inspired. In the account that I shall give, religions are seen as comprehensive interpretive schemes, usually embodied in myths or narratives and heavily ritualized, which structure human experience and understanding of self and world. Not every telling of one of these cosmic stories is religious, however. It must be told with a particular purpose or interest. It must be used, to adopt a suggestion of William Christian, with a view to identifying and describing what is taken to be "more important than everything else in the universe," and to organizing all of life, including both behavior and beliefs, in relation to this. If the interpretive scheme is used or the story is told without this interest in the maximally important, it ceases to function religiously. To be sure, it may continue to shape in various ways the attitudes, sentiments, and conduct of individuals and of groups. A religion, in other words, may continue to exercise immense influence on the way people experience themselves and their world even when it is no longer explicitly adhered to.

Stated more technically, a religion can be viewed as a kind of cultural and/or linguistic framework or medium that shapes the entirety of life and thought. It functions somewhat like a Kantian a priori although in this case the a priori is a set of acquired skills that could be different. It is not primarily an array of beliefs about the true and the good (though it may involve these), or a symbolism expressive of basic attitudes, feelings, or sentiments (though these will be generated). Rather, it is similar to an idiom that makes possible the description of realities, the formulation of beliefs, and the experiencing of inner attitudes, feelings, and sentiments. Like a culture or language, it is a communal phenomenon that shapes the subjectivities of individuals rather than being primarily a manifestation of those subjectivities. It comprises a vocabulary of discursive and nondiscursive symbols together with a distinctive logic or grammar in terms of which this vocabulary can be meaningfully deployed. Lastly, just as a language (or "language game," to use Wittgenstein's phrase) is correlated with a form of life, and just as a culture has both cognitive and behavioral dimensions, so it is also in the case of a religious tradition. Its doctrines, cosmic stories or myths, and ethical directives are integrally related to the rituals it practices, the sentiments or experiences it evokes, the actions it recommends, and the institutional forms it develops. All this is involved in comparing a religion to a cultural–linguistic system . . .

Thus the linguistic–cultural model is part of an outlook that stresses the degree to which human experience is shaped, molded, and in a sense constituted by cultural and linguistic forms. There are numberless thoughts we cannot think, sentiments we cannot have, and realities we cannot perceive unless we learn to use the appropriate symbol systems. It seems, as the cases of Helen Keller and of supposed wolf children vividly illustrate, that unless we acquire language of some kind, we cannot actualize our specifically human capacities for thought, action, and feeling. Similarly, so the argument goes, to become religious involves becoming skilled in the language, the symbol system of a given religion. To become a Christian involves learning the story of Israel and of Jesus well enough to interpret and experience oneself and one's world in its terms. A religion is above all an external word, a *verbum externum*, that molds and shapes the self and its world, rather than an expression or thematization of a preexisting self or of preconceptual experience. The *verbum internum* (traditionally equated by Christians with the action of the Holy Spirit) is also crucially important, but it would be understood in a theological use of the model as a capacity for hearing and accepting the true religion, the true external word, rather than (as experiential-expressivism would have it) as a common experience diversely articulated in different religions ...

In thus inverting the relation of the internal and external dimensions of religion, linguistic and cultural approaches resemble cognitivist theories for which external (i.e., propositionally statable) beliefs are primary, but without the intellectualism of the latter. A comprehensive scheme or story used to structure all dimensions of existence is not primarily a set of propositions to be believed, but is rather the medium in which one moves, a set of skills that one employs in living one's life. Its vocabulary of symbols and its syntax may be used for many purposes, only one of which is the formulation of statements about reality. Thus while a religion's truth claims are often of the utmost importance to it (as in the case of Christianity), it is, nevertheless, the conceptual vocabulary and the syntax or inner logic which determine the kinds of truth claims the religion can make. The cognitive aspect, while often important, is not primary.

This stress on the code, rather than the (e.g., propositionally) encoded, enables a cultural–linguistic approach to accommodate the experiential-expressive concern for the unreflective dimensions of human existence far better than is possible on a cognitivist outlook. Religion cannot be pictured in the cognitivist (amd voluntarist) manner as primarily a matter of deliberate choosing to believe or follow explicitly known propositions or directives. Rather, to become religious – no less than to become culturally or linguistically competent – is to interiorize a set of skills by practice and training. One learns how to feel, act, and think in conformity with a religious tradition that is, in its inner structure, far richer and more subtle than can be explicitly articulated. The primary knowledge is not about the religion, nor that the religion teaches such and such, but rather how to be religious in such and such ways. Sometimes explicitly formulated statements of the beliefs or behavioral norms of a religion may be helpful in the learning process, but by no means always. Ritual, prayer, and example are normally much more important. Thus – insofar as the experiential-expressive contrast between experience and knowledge is comparable to that between "knowing how" and "knowing that" – cultural–linguistic models, no less than expressive ones, emphasize the experiential or existential side of religion, though in a different way.

Study Questions to Chapter 1

What point is Tertullian making by contrasting Jerusalem with Athens?

What theological point does Augustine make by using the image of Israel plundering the wealth of Egypt?

What point does Gaunilo make by making his readers think of an island "blessed with all manner of priceless riches and delights"?

Why does Pascal suggest that God reveals himself in an occasionally difficult or obscure way?

"Theology formulates the questions implied in human existence, and theology formulates the answers in divine self-manifestation under the guidance of the questions implied in human existence." What does Tillich mean by this?

2 The Sources of Theology

What sources is Christian theology based on? There is widespread agreement within the Christian tradition that the most fundamental source is the collection of texts usually known as "the Bible." One of the most fundamental questions in Christian theology therefore relates to the authority and interpretation of Scripture. (Note that many theological writings tend to use the term "Scripture" or "Holy Scripture" in preference to "the Bible," even though the two terms refer to exactly the same collection of writings.) A substantial section of the readings assembled in this chapter deal directly with this issue (see STUDY PANELS 4 AND 5).

However, from the earliest of times, it was realized that Scripture was open to a series of interpretations which were not even remotely Christian. This insight is especially associated with the Gnostic controversies of the second century, during which Gnostic writers put forward some intensely speculative interpretations of Scripture. In response to this, writers such as Irenaeus emphasized the need to interpret Scripture within the parameters of the living tradition of the church. This led to growing interest in the way in which tradition was to be understood as a source for theology (see STUDY PANEL 6).

Many other questions of importance are touched on in this chapter. For example, what is revelation – the imparting of knowledge, or the establishment of a personal relationship? The different positions associated with Karl Barth, Emil Brunner, and James I. Packer will indicate the importance of this question, as well as allowing readers to sample the answers given. Finally, another debate of interest may be noted. To what extent may God be known from nature? This issue is of perennial importance, in relation to the classical debate over how theology relates to philosophy, and more recently, to the debate over how Christianity relates to other religions. A selection of readings, noted in STUDY PANEL 7, explores this important issue.

STUDY PANEL 4

The Authority of Scripture

2.7   Cyril of Jerusalem on the Role of Creeds
2.9   Jerome on the Role of Scripture
2.15 Martin Luther on Revelation in Christ
2.17 John Calvin on the Relation between Old and New Covenants
2.18 The Gallic Confession on the Canon of Scripture
2.19 The Formula of Concord on Scripture and the Theologians
2.20 Philip Jakob Spener on Scripture and the Christian Life
2.24 Archibald Alexander Hodge on the Inspiration of Scripture
2.28 Karl Rahner on the Authority of Scripture
2.31 James I. Packer on the Nature of Revelation

STUDY PANEL 5

The Interpretation of Scripture

2.3   Clement of Alexandria on the Fourfold Interpretation of Scripture
2.4   Hippolytus on Typological Interpretation of Scripture
2.6   Origen on the Three Ways of Reading Scripture
2.8   Augustine on the Literal and Allegorical Senses of Scripture
2.11 Bernard of Clairvaux on the Allegorical Sense of Scripture
2.12 Stephen Langton on the Moral Sense of Scripture
2.13 Jacques Lefèvre d'Etaples on the Senses of Scripture
2.14 Martin Luther on the Fourfold Sense of Scripture
2.27 Rudolf Bultmann on Demythologization and Biblical Interpretation
2.29 Phyllis Tribble on Feminist Biblical Interpretation
2.30 Donald G. Bloesch on Christological Approaches to Biblical Hermeneutics

STUDY PANEL 6

The Role of Tradition

2.2   Irenaeus on the Role of Tradition
2.5   Tertullian on Tradition and Apostolic Succession
2.7   Cyril of Jerusalem on the Role of Creeds
2.10 Vincent of Lérins on the Role of Tradition
2.23 Johann Adam Möhler on Tradition
2.28 Karl Rahner on the Authority of Scripture

STUDY PANEL 7

Revelation in Nature

6.24 Francis of Assisi on the Creation
2.15 Martin Luther on Revelation in Christ
2.16 John Calvin on the Natural Knowledge of God
2.22 Jonathan Edwards on the Beauty of Creation
2.32 Thomas F. Torrance on Karl Barth's Natural Theology

2.1 The Muratorian Fragment on the New Testament Canon

This writing, discovered by L. A. Muratori in 1740, represents the oldest known listing of the books of the New Testament. Written in appalling Latin, the fragment lists all of the New Testament books, except for Hebrews, James, and both letters of Peter. Although Matthew and Mark are also omitted, this is because the opening lines of the work are missing. Internal evidence suggests that the work was composed around 190. Note that the "conversation with the disciples" (*conuesatio cum decipulis suis*) is almost certainly a reference to the incident on the road to Emmaus. Marcion was a heretic who declared that the Old Testament was an irrelevance to Christians, in that it related to a different God than the New Testament. The reference to "sitting in the chair of the church of the city of Rome" (*sedente cathedra urbis romae aeclesiae*) is a technical term referring to Pius being bishop of the city. See also 2.18.

Source: E. S. Buchanon, "The Codex Muratorianus," *Journal of Theological Studies*, 8 (1907), pp. 540–3.

* * *

The third book of the gospel is according to Luke. This Luke was a physician who Paul had taken after the ascension of Christ to be a legal expert. Yet he had not seen the Lord in the flesh. So, as far as he could, he begins his story with the birth of John. The fourth of the gospels was written by John from the Decapolis, one of the disciples. When urged to do so by his fellow disciples, he said "Fast with me for three days, and we will tell each other of whatever is revealed to any of us." That same night, it was revealed to Andrew, one of the apostles, that John would write everything under his own name, and that they would certify it. And although there are various ideas taught in the main books of the gospel, it makes no difference to the faith of believers, since all things are set out in each of them, by the one Spirit, concerning the birth, passion, resurrection, the conversation with the disciples, and his two comings, one in humility and the other, to be in the future, in royal power. It is therefore a wonder that John so clearly sets out each statement in his letters as well, saying in relation to himself "What we have seen with our eyes and heard with our ears and have touched with our hands, these things we have written to you." He thus declares that he is not just an eyewitness and hearer, but also a writer of all the wonders of the Lord, which are set out in order.

The Acts of all the apostles are written in one book. Luke, writing to the excellent Theophilus, includes events which took place in his own presence. He shows this clearly by leaving out the passion of Peter, and also the departure of Paul from the city as he journeyed to Spain. The letters of Paul themselves make clear to those who wish to understand them which letters were written by him, where they were written from, and why they were written. He wrote at some length first of all to the Corinthians, forbidding the schism of heresy. Next he wrote to the Galatians about circumcision, then to the Romans about the rule of the Scriptures, whose first principle is

Christ, and writing at greater length about other things which it is not necessary for us to discuss.

The blessed apostle Paul, following the order of his predecessor John, writes by name only to seven churches in the following order: the first to the Corinthians, the second to the Ephesians, the third to the Philippians, the fourth to the Colossians, the fifth to the Galatians, the sixth to the Thessalonians, and the seventh to the Romans. It is true, however, that he followed this up, for the sake of correction [with second letters to] the Corinthians and Thessalonians. One church, however, is recognized as being dispersed throughout the world. For John in the Apocalypse also writes to seven churches, while speaking to all. It is true that one [letter] to Philemon, one to Titus and two to Timothy were written out of personal inclination and affection; however, they are to be held in honour throughout the catholic church for the ordering of church discipline. Letters under the name of Paul to the Laodiceans and Alexandrians were also written promoting the heresy of Marcion and others, which cannot be accepted in the catholic church, as it is not fitting that honey should be mixed with gall.

The letter of Jude and the two under the name of John are accepted as sound in the catholic church, as is the wisdom written by the friends of Solomon in his honour. We also accept the Apocalypse of John and [the letters] of Peter, which some of our friends do not wish to be read in our churches. But "the Shepherd" was written by Hermas in our times in the city of Rome, while his brother Pius was sitting in the chair of the church of the city of Rome. Therefore it ought to be read, but should not be read in public to the people of the church, since it is not among the complete number of the prophets nor apostles to the end of time.

Irenaeus on the Role of Tradition   2.2

In his writing "Against all Heresies," originally written in Greek towards the end of the second century, but now known mainly through a Latin translation, Irenaeus insisted that the living Christian community possessed a tradition of interpreting Scripture which was denied to heretics. By their historical succession from the apostles, the bishops ensure that their congregations remain faithful to their teachings and interpretations. See also 2.5; 2.7; 2.10; 2.19; 2.23; 2.28.

Source: adversus haereses, II.ii.1–iv.1; in Sources Chrétiennes, vol. 211, ed. A. Rousseau and L. Doutreleau (Paris: Editions du Cerf, 1974), 24.1–32.29; 44.1–7.

* * *

When [the heretics] are refuted out of the Scriptures, they turn to accusing the Scriptures themselves, as if they were not right or did not possess authority, because the Scriptures contain a variety of statements, and because it is not possible for those who do not know the tradition to find the truth in them. For this has not been handed down by means of writings, but by the "living voice" ... And each one of them claims that this wisdom is something that he has come across by himself, which is clearly a fiction ...

Yet when we appeal once more to that tradition which is from the apostles, safeguarded in the churches by successions of presbyters, we provoke them into becoming the enemies of traditions, claiming to be wiser than those presbyters, and even the apostles themselves, and to have discovered the undefiled truth . . . Thus they end up agreeing with neither the Scriptures not with tradition . . . Everyone who wishes to perceive the truth should consider the apostolic tradition, which has been made known in every church in the entire world. We are able to number those who are bishops appointed by the apostles, and their successors in the churches to the present day, who taught and knew nothing of such things as these people imagine. For if the apostles had known secret mysteries (*recondita mysteria*) which they taught privately and secretly to the perfect, they would have passed them down to those to whom they entrusted the churches. For they would have wanted those who they left as their successors, and to whom they handed over their own office of authority (*locum magisterii*), to be perfect and blameless . . . We point to the greatest, most ancient and most glorious of churches, the church known to everyone, which was founded and established at Rome by the two most glorious apostles, Peter and Paul, through which the apostolic tradition and the faith which is preached to humanity has come down to us through the successions of bishops . . . For every church ought to agree with this church, on account of its powerful position, for in this church the apostolic tradition has always been preserved by the faithful . . .

Therefore, as there are so many demonstrations of this fact, there is no need to look anywhere else for the truth which we can easily obtain from the church. The apostles have, as it were, deposited this truth in all its fullness in this depository, so that whoever wants to may draw from this water of life. This is the gate of life; all others are thieves and robbers.

2.3 Clement of Alexandria on the Fourfold Interpretation of Scripture

The eight books of Clement's *Stromata* (the word literally means "carpets") deal with a variety of questions, including the way in which Scripture is to be interpreted. In this extract from the *stromata*, originally written in Greek in the early third century, Clement clearly sets out the principle that there are four ways of interpreting Scriptures: a literal way, and three spiritual ways. This would later be formalized in what came to be known as the *Quadriga*, which recognized literal, allegorical, moral or tropological, and anagogical senses of Scripture. See also 2.4; 2.6; 2.8; 2.9; 2.11; 2.12; 2.13; 2.14; 2.27; 2.28; 2.30.

Source: *Stromata*, I.xxviii.3; in *Die griechischen christlichen Schriftsteller der erste Jahrhunderte*. Clemens Alexandrinus: Zweiter Band. Stromata Buch I–VI, ed. O. Stählin and L. Früchtel (Berlin: Akademie Verlag, 1985), pp. 17.13–18.5.

* * *

The meaning of the law is to be understood by us in four ways [in addition to the literal sense]: as displaying a sign, as establishing a command for right conduct, or as making known a prophecy.

Hippolytus on Typological Interpretation of Scripture

Typological exegesis involved the forging of links between persons, events or objects mentioned in the Old Testament and corresponding persons, events or doctrines in the New. In this passage, Hippolytus takes the typological interpretation of Scripture to what might seem to be ridiculous lengths. During the course of commenting on Isaiah 18:2, which mentions ships, Hippolytus expands on the typological significance of virtually every aspect of a ships' structure. See also 2.3; 2.6; 2.8; 2.9; 2.11; 2.12; 2.13; 2.14; 2.27; 2.29; 2.30.

Source: *de antichristo*, 59; in J. P. Migne, *Patrologia Graeca*, 10. 777C–779A.

* * *

The oars of the ship are the churches. The sea is the universe (*kosmos*), in which the church, like a boat on the open sea, is shaken but does not sink, because she has Christ on board as an experienced navigator. At the center she has the prize of the passion of Christ, carrying with her his cross. Her prow points towards the east, and her stern to the west. The two steering oars are the two Testaments. The sheets are tight, like the love of Christ which sustains the church. She carries water on board, like the washing of regeneration. Her white sail receives the breath of the Spirit, by which believers are sealed. The sailors stand to port and to starboard, just like our holy guardian angels.

Tertullian on Tradition and Apostolic Succession

In this early second-century analysis of the sources of theology, Tertullian lays considerable emphasis upon the role of tradition and apostolic succession in the defining of Christian theology. Orthodoxy depends upon remaining historically continuous with and theologically dependent upon the apostles. The heretics, in contrast, cannot demonstrate any such continuity. See also 2.2; 2.7; 2.10; 2.19; 2.23; 2.28.

Source: *de praescriptione haereticorum*, xx, 4–xxi, 4; xxxii, 1; in *Sources Chrétiennes*, 46, ed. R. F. Refoulé (Paris: Editions du Cerf, 1957), 112.17–115.15; 130.1–8.

* * *

[The apostles] first bore witness to faith in Jesus Christ throughout Judea, and established churches there, after which they went out into the the world and proclaimed the same doctrine of the same faith to the nations. And they likewise established churches in every city, from which the other churches subsequently derived the origins of faith and the seeds of doctrine, and are still deriving them in order that they may become churches. It is through this that these churches are counted as "apostolic," in that they are the offspring of apostolic churches. It is necessary that every kind of thing is to be classified according to its origins. For this reason, the churches, however many and significant they are, are really the one first [church] which derives from the apostles, from which all have their origins. So all are first (*prima*) and all are apostolic, while all are one. And this unity is demonstrated by their sharing of peace, by their title of "brotherhood," and by their obligation of hospitality. For these laws have no basis other than the one tradition of the same revelation.

It is therefore for this reason that we lay down this ruling (*praescriptio*): if the Lord Jesus Christ sent out the apostles to preach, no preachers other than those which are appointed by Christ are to be received, since "no-one knows the Father except the Son and those to whom the Son has revealed him," and the Son appears to have revealed him to no-one except the apostles who he sent to preach what he had revealed to them. What they preached – that is, what Christ revealed to them – ought, by this ruling, to be established only by those churches which those apostles founded by their preaching and, as they say, by the living voice, and subsequently through their letters. If this is true, all doctrine which is in agreement with those apostolic churches, he sources and originals of the faith, must be accounted as the truth, since it indubitably preserves what the churches received from the apostles, the apostles from Christ, and Christ from God ...

If any of these [heresies] dare to trace their origins back to the apostolic era, so that it might appear that they had been handed down by the apostles because they existed under the apostles, we are able to say: let them therefore show the origins of their churches; let them unfold the order of their bishops, showing that there is a succession from the beginning, so that their first bishop had as his precursor (*auctor*) and predecessor an apostle or some apostolic man who was associated with the apostles.

2.6   Origen on the Three Ways of Reading Scripture

Origen, who wrote extensively in the first half of the third century, is widely regarded as one of the early church's most influential and creative interpreters of Scripture. Origen here uses the imagery of "body, soul, and spirit" to distinguish three different ways in which Scripture may be read, according to the maturity of the reader in question. The distinction between different levels of maturity and advancement on the part of Christians is characteristic of both Clement of Alexandria and Origen. See also 2.3; 2.4; 2.8; 2.9; 2.11; 2.12; 2.13; 2.14; 2.27; 2.29; 2.30.

Source: *de principiis*, IV.ii.4–5; in *Sources Chrétiennes*, vol. 268, ed. H. Crouzel and M. Simonetti (Paris: Cerf, 1980), 310.111–312.125; 316.147–320.176.

* * * ────────────────────────────────────

There are three ways in which the meaning of the Holy Scriptures should be inscribed on the soul of every Christian. First, the simpler sort are edified by what may be called the "body" of scripture. This is the name I give to the immediate acceptance. Secondly, those who have made some progress are edified by, as it were, the "soul." Thirdly, the perfect . . . are edified by the "spiritual" Law, which contains the shadow of the good things to come. Thus just as a human being consists of body, soul, and spirit, so also does the Scripture which is the gift of God designed for human salvation . . .

Some parts of Scripture have no "body." In these parts, we must look only for the "soul" and "spirit." Perhaps this is the point of the description in John's gospel of the water-pots "for the purifying of the Jews, holding two or three measures" (John 2:6). The Word implies by this that the apostle calls the Jews in secret, so that they may be purified through the word of the Scripture which sometimes holds two measures, that is what one may call the "soul" and "spirit"; sometimes three, that is, the "body" as well . . . The usefulness of the "body" is testified by the multitude of simple believers and is quite obvious. Paul gives us many examples of the "soul" . . . The spiritual interpretation belongs to people who are able to explain the way in which the worship of the "Jews after the flesh" (1 Corinthians 10:18) yields images and "shadows of heavenly things" (Hebrews 8:5) and how the "Law had the shadow of good things to come."

Cyril of Jerusalem on the Role of Creeds   2.7

In a series of 24 lectures given around the year 350 to those who were about to be baptized, Cyril explains the various aspects of the Christian faith and its practices. In the section which follows, he explains the origins and role of creeds, noting their importance as summaries of Scripture. See also 2.2; 2.5; 2.10; 2.19; 2.23; 2.28.

Source: *Catechesis*, V, 12; in *Opera quae supersunt omnia*, ed. W. C. Reischl (Munich: Keck, 1849), p. 150.

* * *

This synthesis of faith was not made to be agreeable to human opinions, but to present the one teaching of the faith in its totality, in which what is of greatest importance is gathered together from all the Scriptures. And just as a mustard seed contains a great number of branches in its tiny grain, so also this summary of faith brings together in a few words the entire knowledge of the true religion which is contained in the Old and New [Testaments].

Augustine on the Literal and Allegorical Senses of Scripture   2.8

One of Augustine's earliest and most important controversies related to the Manicheans, a sect which dismissed the Old Testament as an irrelevance, on the basis of an excessively literal approach to its meaning. In this passage, originally written in Latin during the 390s, Augustine draws a distinction between the literal sense of the Old Testament, and its allegorical or spiritual sense. He argues that the spiritual sense has always been present in the Old Testament;

however, it is only seen properly in the light of the New Testament. He compares the reading of the Old Testament in the light of the New to the lifting of the veil which had hitherto covered the true sense of the Old Testament. See also 2.3; 2.4; 2.6; 2.9; 2.11; 2.12; 2.13; 2.14; 2.27; 2.28; 2.30.

Source: de utilitate credendi, III, 9; in Œuvres de Saint Augustin, vol. 8, ed. J. Pegon (Paris: Desclée, 1951), pp. 226–8.

* * *

Now while [the Manicheans] maliciously try to make the Law into an irrelevance, at the same time they force us to approve of these same Scriptures. They pay attention where it is said that those who are under the Law are in bondage, and brandish this decisive passage above all others: "You who are justified by the Law are banished from Christ. You have fallen from grace." (Galatians 5:4). Now we admit that all this is true. We do not say the Law is necessary except for those for whom bondage is a good thing. It was laid down with good reason because human beings, who could not be won from their sins by reason, had to be coerced by threats and terrors of penalties which even fools can understand. When the grace of Christ sets people free from such threats and penalties it does not condemn the Law but invites us now to submit to His love and not to be slaves to fear. Grace is a benefaction conferred by God, which those who wish to continue under the bondage of the Law do not understand. Paul rightly calls such people unbelievers, by way of reproach, who do not believe that they are now set free by our Lord Jesus from a bondage to which they had been subjected by the just judgement of God. This is the form of words used by the Apostle: "The Law was our *paedagogus* to Christ" (Galatians 3:24). God thus gave humanity a pedagogue whom they might fear, and later gave them a master whom they might love. But in these precepts and commands of the Law which Christians may not now lawfully obey, such as the Sabbath, circumcision, sacrifices, and the like, there are contained such mysteries that every religious person may understand there is nothing more dangerous than to take whatever is there literally, and nothing more wholesome than to let the truth be revealed by the Spirit. For this reason: "The letter kills but the Spirit brings life" (2 Corinthians 3:6). And again: "The same veil remains in the reading of the Old Testament and there is no revelation, for in Christ the veil is removed" (2 Corinthians 3:14). It is not the Old Testament that is abolished in Christ but the concealing veil, so that it may be understood through Christ. That which without Christ is obscure and hidden is, as it were, opened up . . . [Paul] does not say: "The Law or the Old Testament is abolished." It is not the case, therefore, that by the grace of the Lord that which was covered has been abolished as useless; rather, the covering which concealed useful truth has been removed. This is what happens to those who earnestly and piously, not proudly and wickedly, seek the sense of the Scriptures. To them is carefully demonstrated the order of events, the reasons for deeds and words, and the agreement of the Old Testament with the New, so that not a single point remains where there is not complete harmony. The secret truths are conveyed in figures that are to be brought to light by interpretation.

Jerome on the Role of Scripture   2.9

Jerome was, along with Origen, the early church's leading expositor and interpreter of Scripture, with a particular concern for biblical translation. Underlying this was a profound conviction of the fundamental importance of Scripture to the life and thought of the church and the individual believer, which is clearly expressed in this letter. See also 2.3; 2.4; 2.6; 2.8; 2.11; 2.12; 2.13; 2.14; 2.27; 2.28; 2.29; 2.30.

Source: *Letter* LIII, 4–6, 10; in *Corpus Scriptorum Ecclesiasticorum Latinorum*, vol. 54, ed. I. Hilberg (Vienna: Tempsky, 1910), 450.4–452.7; 463.13–464.6.

* * *

[Paul] speaks of a "wisdom of God hidden in a mystery, which God ordained before the world" (1 Corinthians 2:7). God's wisdom is Christ, for Christ, we are told, is "the power of God and the wisdom of God" (1 Corinthians 1:30). This wisdom remains hidden in a mystery. It is to this that the title of Psalm 9:1, "for the hidden things of the son" refers. In him are hidden all the treasures of wisdom and knowledge. The one who was hidden in mystery is the same who was predestined before the world, and was foreordained and prefigured in the Law and the Prophets. That is why the prophets were called seers: they saw him whom others did not see. Abraham also saw his day, and was glad (John 8:56). The heavens which were sealed to a rebellious people were opened to Ezekiel (Ezekiel 1:1). "Open my eyes," says David, "so that I may behold the wondrous things of your law" (Psalm 118:18). For the law is spiritual, and in order to understand it we need the veil to be removed and the glory of God to be seen with an uncovered face (2 Corinthians 3:14–18) . . .

In the Acts of the Apostles, the holy eunuch . . . was reading Isaiah, when he was asked by Philip: "Do you understand what you are reading?" "How can I," he replied, "unless someone teaches me?" (Acts 8:30–1). I am no more holy nor more learned than this eunuch, who was from Ethiopia, that is from the ends of the world. He left a royal court and went as far as the temple; and such was his love for divine knowledge that he was reading the Holy Scriptures while in his chariot. Yet even though he was holding a book in his hand and was reflecting on the words of the Lord, even sounding them with his tongue and pronouncing them with his lips (*lingua volveret, labiis personaret*), he did not know who he was worshipping in this book. Then Philip came, and showed him Jesus hidden in the letter (*qui clausus latebat in littera*). What a marvellous teacher! In the same hour the eunuch believed and was baptized. He became one of the faithful and a saint. From being a pupil he became a master. He found more in the desert spring of the church than he had done in the gilded temple of the synagogue . . .

This matter I have dealt with only briefly – I could not manage any more within the limits of a letter – so that you will understand that you cannot advance in the Holy Scriptures unless you have an experienced guide to show you the way . . .

I beg you, my dearest brother, to live among these [sacred books], to meditate on them, to know nothing else, to seek nothing else. Does not this seem to you to be a little bit of heaven here on earth (*in terris regni caelestis habitaculum*)? Do not take offence on account of the simplicity of Holy Scripture or the unsophistication of its words (*quasi vilitate verborum*), for these are either due to translation faults or have some deeper purpose. For Scripture offers itself in such a way that an uneducated congregation can more easily learn from it, some benefit there and both the learned and the unlearned can discover different meanings in the same sentence. I am not so arrogant nor so forward as to claim that I know this, which would be like wanting to pick on earth the fruits of trees whose roots are in heaven. However, I confess that I would like to do so . . . The Lord has said: "ask, and it shall be given; knock, and it shall be opened; seek, and you will find" (Matthew 7:7). So let us study here on earth that knowledge which will continue with us in heaven.

2.10 Vincent of Lérins on the Role of Tradition

Writing in the year 434, in the aftermath of the Pelagian controversy, Vincent expressed his belief that the controversies of that time had given rise to theological innovations. It is clear that he regarded Augustine's doctrine of double predestination as a case in point. But how could such doctrinal innovations be identified? In response to this question, he argues for a triple criterion by which authentic Christian teaching may be established: ecumenicity (being believed everywhere), antiquity (being believed always), and consent (being believed by all people). See also 2.2; 2.5; 2.7; 2.19; 2.23; 2.28.

Source: *Commonitorium* II, 1–3; in *Florilegium Patristicum 5: Vincentii Lerinensis Commonitoria*, ed. G. Rauschen (Bonn: Hanstein, 1906), pp. 10–12.

* * * ⸻

Therefore I have devoted considerable study and much attention to enquiring, from men of outstanding holiness and doctrinal correctness, in what way it might be possible for me to establish a kind of fixed and, as it were, general and guiding principle for distinguishing the truth of the catholic faith from the depraved falsehoods of the heretics. And the answer I receive from all can be put like this: if I or anyone else wish to detect the deceits of the heretics or avoid their traps, and to remain healthy and intact in a sound faith, we ought, with the help of the Lord, to strengthen our faith in two ways; first, by the authority of the divine law, and then by the tradition of the catholic church.

Here someone may ask: since the canon of the scriptures is complete, and is in itself adequate, why is there any need to join to its authority the understanding of the church? Because Holy Scripture, on account of its depth, is not accepted in a universal sense. The same statements are interpreted in one way by one person, in another by someone else, with the result that there seem to be as many opinions as there are people . . . Therefore, on account of the number and variety of errors, there is a need for someone to lay down a rule for the interpretation of the prophets and the apostles in such a way that is directed by the rule of the catholic church.

Now in the catholic church itself the greatest care is taken that we hold that which has been believed everywhere, always, and by all people (*quod ubique, quod semper, quod ab omnibus creditum est*). This is what is truly and properly catholic. This is clear from the force of the word and reason, which understands everything universally. We shall follow "universality" in this way, if we acknowledge this one faith to be true, which the entire church confesses throughout the world. We affirm "antiquity" if we in no way depart from those understandings which it is clear that the greater saints and our fathers proclaimed. And we follow "consensus" if in this antiquity we follow all (or certainly nearly all) the definitions of the bishops and masters.

Bernard of Clairvaux on the Allegorical Sense of Scripture   2.11

In the course of his exposition of Song of Songs 1:16, written in Latin in the first half of the twelfth century, Bernard provides an allegorical interpretation of the phrase "the beams of our houses are of cedar, and our panels are of cypress." This extract is an excellent illustration of the way in which doctrinal or spiritual meaning was "read into" otherwise unpromising passages at this time. See also 2.3; 2.4; 2.6; 2.8; 2.9; 2.12; 2.13; 2.14; 2.27; 2.29; 2.30.

Source: *Sermones super Cantico Canticorum*, XLVI, 2; in *Sancti Bernardi Opera*, ed. J. Leclerc, C. H. Talbot and H. M. Rochais (Rome: Editiones Cistercienses, 1958), 56.22–57.7.

                                                        * * *

By "houses" we are to understand the great mass of the Christian people, who are bound together with those who possess power and dignity, rulers of the church and the state, as "beams." These hold them together by wise and firm laws; otherwise, if each of them were to operate in any way that they pleased, the walls would bend and collapse, and the whole house would fall in ruins. By the "panels" (*laqueria*), which are firmly attached to the beams and which adorn the house in a royal manner, we are to understand the kindly and ordered lives of a properly instructed clergy, and the proper administration of the rites of the church. Yet how can the clergy carry out their work, or the church discharge her duties, unless the princes, like strong and solid beams, sustain them through their goodwill and munificence, and protect them through their power?

2.12 Stephen Langton on the Moral Sense of Scripture

In this twelfth-century commentary on an incident related in Amos 7:10–13, the great medieval biblical commentator and preacher Stephen Langton develops the "moral" or "tropological" sense of the passage. This technique involves the extraction of a moral from a biblical passage. Just as Amasius, the high priest of Bethel, denounced the prophet Amos to Jeroboam in biblical times, so modern priests show just the same weakness. The style adopted is that of "glossing" – in other words, adding extensive interpretative comments to the words of Scripture. In what follows, the text of the biblical passage is printed in italics, with Langton's comments in normal type. See also 2.3; 2.4; 2.6; 2.8; 2.9; 2.11; 2.13; 2.14; 2.27; 2.29; 2.30.

Source: Unpublished manuscript B.II.26, Trinity College, Cambridge, as cited by Beryl Smalley, "Stephen Langton and the Four Senses of Scripture," *Speculum*, 6 (1931), pp. 60–76; Latin text at p. 73, note 1.

* * *

Amasius is to be understood as a type (*typus*) of a bad priest, a bad and evil prelate, who is set in his evil ways and has no interest in good. He is a stranger to the fire of charity. He would be happy to travel two miles or more on a winter's night to visit a prostitute or for financial gain. But he would not even leave his table for a few minutes to hear a dying man's confession . . . When he comes across someone who is correctly preaching the way of truth, which he fears will put an end to his own evil ways, he does not mention this anxiety (even though it is his chief concern) and instead denounces the preacher to his king or prince. He pretends to be worried about the disrespect being shown to the king, and so tries to incite him to take vengeance. But note how Jeroboam dismisses the accusation as groundless. This shows that prelates are far more evil than secular princes. Yet although the prince dismisses the false accusation of this evil priest, he does not stop doing evil. *And Amasius said to Amos: you seer.* You prophet and learned doctor who threatens us so terribly through your preaching *go, run away to the land of Judah.* Leave my bishopric or my parish, and go back to your studies at Paris, *eat bread there and prophesy there.* Restrict your teaching and preaching to Paris! *In Bethel,* that is, in my bishopric, *do not prophesy any more,* that is, stop preaching here. Your remarks are offensive to the king, and as this place belongs to him, he can hire and fire as he likes any person of the church.

2.13 Jacques Lefèvre d'Etaples on the Senses of Scripture

In the preface to his 1508 edition of the Hebrew text of five Psalms, the French humanist writer Jacques Lefèvre d'Etaples sets out his understanding of the way in which the Old Testament is to be interpreted. A distinction is drawn between the "literal–historical" sense of Scripture, which understands the Old Testament as a historical narrative, and the "literal–prophetic" sense ("a literal sense which coincides with the Spirit"), which understands it as a prophecy of the coming of Jesus Christ. He thus argues that there are two "literal" senses of Scripture. Note that the context of this passage requires that the Latin term *litera* should often be translated as "literal sense" rather than simply as "letter". See also 2.3; 2.4; 2.6; 2.8; 2.9; 2.11; 2.12; 2.14; 2.27; 2.29; 2.30.

Source: *Quincuplex Psalterium*, preface; in *Quincuplex Psalterium* (Paris, 1508), α recto–α verso.

---

* * *

Then I began to realize that perhaps this had not really been the true literal sense at all; rather, just like bad pharmacists and their herbs, one thing is substituted for the other – a false sense for the true literal sense. Therefore I went immediately for advice to our first leaders – to the apostles (I mean, Paul) and the prophets, who first entrusted this seed to the furrows of our souls and opened the door of understanding of the letter of Holy Scripture. I then seemed to see another sense of Scripture – the *intention* of the prophet and of the Holy Spirit speaking in him. This I call the "literal" sense – but a literal sense which coincides with the Spirit. The Spirit has conveyed no other literal sense to the prophets or to those who have open eyes, although I do not want to deny the other senses, the allegorical, tropological, and anagogical, especially where the content of the text requires it. To those who do not have open eyes but still think that they have, another literal sense takes its place, which, as the Apostle [Paul] says, kills and opposes the Spirit.

This literal sense is pursued today by the Jews, in whom even now this prophecy is being fulfilled. Their eyes are darkened so that they cannot see, and their whole outlook is seriously distorted. This kind of sense they call "literal," yet not the literal sense of their prophets, but rather of certain of their rabbis. These interpret the divine hymns of David for the most part as applying to David himself, such as his difficulties during his persecution by Saul and the other wars he fought. They do not regard him in these Psalms as a prophet; rather, they regard him as a narrator of what he has seen and done, as if he were writing his own history. But David himself says regarding himself, "The Spirit of the Lord spoke through me, his word is upon my tongue." And Holy Scripture calls him the man in all of Israel to whom it was given to sing about the Christ of the God of Jacob and the true Messiah. And where else does he sing of the Christ of the God of Jacob and the true Messiah other than in the Psalms?

And so I came to believe that there is a twofold literal sense. One is the distorted sense of those who do not have open eyes, and who interpret divine things according to the flesh and in human terms. The proper literal sense is grasped by those who can see and receive insight. The former is the invention of human understanding, the latter is a gift of God's Spirit, which the false sense represses, and the other exalts. Hence there seems to be good reason for the complaint of monks (*religiosi*) that when they went in for "literal" exposition, they came away from it gloomy and miserable. All their religious devotion had suddenly collapsed and disappeared, just as if icy water had been thrown on a burning fire. For just as the healthy body is aware of what is harmful to it, so also the mind is also aware of what mortifies it. Therefore I have good reason to feel that this should be avoided. We should aspire to that sense which is given life by the Spirit, just as colours are given life by light. With this goal in mind, I have tried to write a short exposition of the Psalms with the assistance of Christ, who is the key to the understanding of David. He is the one about whom David spoke, commissioned by the Holy Spirit, in the book of Psalms.

In order that it might be clear how great the difference is between the proper and improper sense, let us consider a few examples which demonstrate this. Psalm 2: "Why do the nations conspire and the peoples plot in vain? The kings of the earth set themselves up and the rulers take counsel together against the Lord and his Christ," and so on. For the Jews, the literal sense of this passage is that the people of Palestine rose up against David, the Messiah of the Lord. But the true literal sense, according to Paul and the other Apostles, refers to Christ the Lord, the true Messiah and true Son of God (which is both true and appropriate). Now take Psalm 18. For the Jews, the literal sense here is that David expresses thanks to God for being liberated from the hands of Saul and his other enemies. Yet Paul takes the literal sense to mean Christ the Lord. The Jews understand Psalm 19 to deal with the first giving of the law. Paul takes it to be not the first but the second giving of the law when it was declared to all nations through the blessed apostles and their successors.

2.14 Martin Luther on the Fourfold Sense of Scripture

The passage, written in manuscript around 1516, sets up a contrast between the "spirit" and "flesh," which Luther regards as two different ways of living, each with their associated ways of understanding the meaning of the Old Testament. Clearly dependent on the works of Jacques Lefèvre d'Etaples (see 2.13), Luther here retains the traditional fourfold scheme for interpreting Scripture (usually referred to as the *Quadriga*), while insisting that each of these four senses may be understood purely historically (relating to the history of Israel) or prophetically (relating to the coming of Jesus Christ). Thus there are two literal senses of the Old Testament, the "literal–historic" and the "literal–prophetic." The passage dates from Luther's earliest period, before his "Reformation breakthrough," and is an important witness to the merging of scholastic and humanist approaches to biblical interpretation in the second decade of the sixteenth century. The eightfold interpretation of "Mount Zion" is here presented in a tabular form, to bring out Luther's meaning more clearly. See also 2.3; 2.4; 2.6; 2.8; 2.9; 2.11; 2.12; 2.13; 2.27; 2.29; 2.30.

Source: *Dictata super Psalterium*, preface; in *D. Martin Luthers Werke: Kritische Gesamtausgabe*, vol. 3, ed. G. Kawerau (Weimar: Böhlau, 1885), 11.3–35.

* * *

"I will sing with the spirit, and I will also sing with the mind" (1 Corinthians 14:15). To "sing with the spirit" is to sing with spiritual devotion and feeling, which contrasts with those who sing only with the flesh . . . Those who have a purely fleshly understanding of the Psalter, such as the Jews, always apply this text to ancient history apart from Christ. But Christ has opened the mind of his people, so that they might understand the Scripture . . .

Mount Zion

The letter which kills	*The spirit which gives life concerning the Babylonian church body*
Historically, the land of Canaan	historically, the people living in Zion
Allegorically, the synagogue, or some person of importance in it	Allegorically, the church, or some doctor, bishop, or person of importance
Tropologically, Pharisaic and legal righteousness	Tropologically, the righteousness of faith or something else excellent
Anagogically, the future glory of the flesh	Anagogically, the eternal glory in the heavens.

. . . In Scripture, therefore, no allegory or tropology or anagogy is valid, unless the same truth is explicitly stated in an historical manner somewhere else. Otherwise, Scripture would become ludicrous.

Martin Luther on Revelation in Christ   2.15

In the course of his major Galatians commentary of 1535, Luther turns to deal with the question of how God may be known. While affirming that God may be known through nature, Luther insists that this is a limited and inadequate knowledge of God which must be supplemented and corrected in the light of Scripture. Note the strongly Christocentric understanding of the knowledge of God which Luther develops in this passage.

Source: *Commentary on Galatians*; in *D. Martin Luthers Werke: Kritische Gesamtausgabe*, vol. 40 (Weimar: Böhlaus, 1911), 602.18–603.13; 607.19–609.14.

* * *

According to John 1:18, God does not want to be known except through Christ; nor can he be known in any other way. Christ is the offspring promised to Abraham; on him God has grounded all his promises. Therefore Christ alone is the means, the life, and the mirror through which we see God and know his will.

Through Christ God declares his favor and mercy to us. In Christ we see that God is not an angry master and judge but a gracious and kind father, who blesses us, that is, who delivers us from the law, sin, death, and every evil, and gives us righteousness and eternal life through Christ. This is a certain and true knowledge of God and divine persuasion, which does not fail, but depicts (*depingit*) God himself in a specific form, apart from which there is no God . . .

Everyone naturally has a general idea that there is a God. This can be seen from Romans 1:19–20: "To the extent that God can be known, he is known to them. For his invisible nature, etc." In any case, the various cults and the religions, past and present, among all nations are abundant evidence that at some time all people have had a general knowledge of God. Whether this was on the basis of nature or from the tradition of their parents, I do not propose to discuss now.

But someone may object: "If all people know God, why does Paul say that before the proclamation of the gospel the Galatians did not know God?" I reply that there is a twofold knowledge of God (*duplex est cognitio Dei*), general and particular. All people have the general knowledge, namely, that God exists, that he has created heaven and earth, that he is righteous, that he punishes the wicked, etc. But people do not know what God proposes concerning us, what he wants to give and to do, so that he might deliver us from sin and death, and to save us – which is the proper and the true knowledge of God (*propria et vera est cognitio Dei*). Thus it can happen that someone's face may be familiar to me but I do not really know him, because I do not know his intentions. So it is that people know naturally that there is a God, but they do not know what he wants and what he does not want. For it is written (Romans 3:11): "No-one understands God"; and elsewhere (John 1:18): "No-one ever seen God," that is, no one knows what the will of God is. Now what good does it do you if you know that God exists, but do not know what his will is for you? Now here others imagine things differently. The Jews imagine that it is the will of God that they should worship God according to the commandment of the Law of Moses; the Turks, that they should observe the Koran; the monk, that he should do what he has been told to do. But all of them are deceived and, as Paul says in Romans 1:21, "become futile in their thinking." Being ignorant of what is pleasing to God and what is displeasing to him, they worship the imaginations of their own heart as though these were true God by nature, when by nature these are nothing at all.

Paul indicates this when he says: "When you did not know God," that is, when you did not know what the will of God is, "you were in bondage to beings that by nature are no gods"; that is, "you were in bondage to the dreams and imaginations of your own hearts, by which you invented the idea that God is to be worshiped with this or that work or ritual." Now, because people accept this as a major premise, "There is a God," all kinds of human idolatry came into being, which would have been unknown in the world without the knowledge of divinity. But because people had this natural knowledge about God, they conceived empty and evil thoughts about God apart from and contrary to his Word; they embraced these as the very truth, and on the basis of them they imagined God otherwise than he is by his own nature. Thus a monk imagines a God who forgives sins and grants grace and eternal life on account of observance of his Rule of Life. This God does not exist anywhere; therefore [the monk] neither serves nor worships the true God; in fact, he serves and worships one who by nature is no God, namely, a figment and idol of his own heart, his own false and empty notion about God, which he supposes to be certain truth. But even reason itself is obliged to admit that human opinion is not God. Therefore whoever wants to worship God or serve him without the Word is serving, not the true God but, as Paul says, "one who by nature is no god."

John Calvin on the Natural Knowledge of God

2.16

Calvin opens the 1559 edition of his *Institutes* with a discussion of how we know anything about God. According to Calvin, a true and full knowledge of God is only available through Scripture. However, Calvin insists that a natural knowledge of God is possible, which prepares the way for the full knowledge of God, and eliminates any human excuse for being ignorant of God's existence or nature. Note especially Calvin's argument for an implanted sense of divinity within human beings. See also 2.22; 2.32.

Source: *Institutes*, I.iii.1, 2; in *Joannis Calvini: Opera Selecta*, ed. P. Barth and W. Niesel, vol. 3 (Munich: Kaiser Verlag, 1928), 37.16–46.11.

* * *

There is within the human mind, and that by natural instinct, a sense of divinity (*divinitatis sensus*). This we take to be beyond controversy. So that no-one might take refuge in the pretext of ignorance, God frequently renews and sometimes increases this awareness, so that all people, recognizing that there is a God and that he is their creator, are condemned by their own testimony because they have failed to worship him and to give their lives to his service. If ignorance of God is to be looked for anywhere, surely one is most likely to find an example of it amongst the more backward peoples and those who are really remote from civilization (*ab humanitatis cultu remotiores*). Yet, in fact (as a pagan has said) there is no nation so barbarous, no people so savage, that they do not have a pervasive belief that there is a God . . . There has been no region since the beginning of the world, no city, no home, that could exist without religion; this fact in itself points to a sense of divinity inscribed in the hearts of all people . . .

There are innumerable witnesses in heaven and on earth that declare the wonders of his wisdom. Not only those more arcane matters for the closer observation of which astronomy, medicine, and all of natural science (*tota physica scientia*) are intended, but also those which force themselves upon the sight of even the most unlearned and ignorant peoples, so that they cannot even open their eyes without being forced to see them.

2.17 John Calvin on the Relation between Old and New Covenants

Martin Luther argued for a sharp distinction between "law" and "gospel." While conceding that the Old Testament contained "gospel" and the New "law," Luther's general line of argument is that the Old Testament belongs to a different category than the New. In contrast, Calvin insists on the continuity between the Old and New Testaments. They are identical in terms of their substance; their difference relates to their administration. Calvin sets out three such points of difference. See also 2.3; 2.4; 2.6; 2.8; 2.9; 2.11; 2.12; 2.13; 2.14; 2.27; 2.29; 2.30.

Source: *Institutes*, II.x.1, 2; in *Joannis Calvini: Opera Selecta*, ed. P. Barth and W. Niesel, vol. 4 (Munich: Kaiser Verlag, 1931), 403.5–404.22.

* * *

Now from what has been said above, we can see clearly that all people who have been adopted by God into the company of his people since the beginning of the world were covenanted (*foederatos*) to him by the same law and by the bond of the same doctrine as remains in force among us ... The covenant made with all the patriarchs is so similar to ours, both in substance and in fact, that the two are really one and the same; what differences there are relate to their administration ... First, we hold that it was not material prosperity and happiness which was the goal set before the Jews, and to which they were to aspire, but the hope of immortality. Faith in this adoption was made certain to them by oracles, by the law, and by the prophets. Second, the covenant (*foedus*) by which they were bound to the Lord did not rest upon their own merits, but solely upon the mercy of the God who called them. Thirdly, they both possessed and knew Christ as mediator, through whom they were joined to God and were to benefit from his promises.

2.18 The Gallic Confession on the Canon of Scripture

This French Confession of Faith, published in French in 1559, sets out clearly the characteristic Protestant understanding of the Canon of Scripture. Note how each book is specified by name, with variants of the name being noted – for example, in the case of Proverbs and Revelation. Note also that the letter to the Hebrews is not ascribed to St. Paul, but is treated as an independent writing. This is followed by an affirmation of the authority of Scripture, in which the authority in question is clearly stated to be inherent to the Bible, rather than something which is imposed by the church. See also 2.1; 2.5; 2.7; 2.9; 2.17; 2.28.

Source: *Confessio Gallicana*, 1559, articles 3–5; in E. F. K. Müller (ed.), *Die Bekenntnisschriften der reformierten Kirche* (Leipzig: Böhme, 1903), 222.5–44.

* * *

3. All of this Holy Scripture is contained in the canonical books of the Old and New Testaments, as follows: the five books of Moses, namely Genesis, Exodus, Leviticus, Numbers, Deuteronomy; then Joshua, Judges, Ruth, the first and second books of Samuel, the first and second books of the Kings, the first and second books of the Chronicles, otherwise called Paralipomenon, the first book of Ezra; then Nehemiah, the book of Esther, Job, the Psalms of David, the Proverbs or Maxims of Solomon; the book of Ecclesiastes, called the Preacher, the Song of Solomon; then the books of Isaiah, Jeremiah, Lamentations of Jeremiah, Ezekiel, Daniel, Hosea, Joel, Amos, Obadiah, Jonah, Micah, Nahum, Habakkuk, Zephaniah, Haggai, Zechariah, Malachi; then the holy gospel according to St. Matthew, according to St. Mark, according to St. Luke, and according to St. John; then the second book of St. Luke, otherwise called the Acts of the Apostles; then the letters of St. Paul: one to the Romans, two to the Corinthians, one to the Galatians, one to the Ephesians, one to the Philippians, one to the Colossians, two to the Thessalonians, two to Timothy, one to Titus, one to Philemon; then the letter to the Hebrews, the letter of St. James, the first and second letters of St. Peter, the first, second, and third letters of St. John, the letter of St. Jude; and then the Apocalypse, or Revelation of St. John.

4. We know these books to be canonical, and the sure rule of our faith, not so much by the common accord and consent of the Church, as by the testimony and inward persuasion of the Holy Spirit (*par les tesmoignage et interieure persuasion du sainct esprit*), which enables us to distinguish them from other ecclesiastical books which, however useful, can never become the basis for any articles of faith.

5. We believe that the Word contained in these books has proceeded from God, and receives its authority from him alone, and not from human beings. And in that it is the rule of all truth, containing all that is necessary for the service of God and for our salvation, it is not lawful for anyone, even for angels, to add to it, to take away from it, or to change it. It therefore follows that no authority, whether of antiquity, or custom, or numbers, or human wisdom, or judgments, or proclamations, or edicts, or decrees, or councils, or visions, or miracles, should be opposed to these Holy Scriptures, but, on the contrary, all things should be examined, regulated, and reformed according to them. And therefore we confess the three creeds as follows: the Apostles', the Nicene, and the Athanasian, because they are in accordance with the Word of God.

The Formula of Concord on Scripture and the Theologians   2.19

The Lutheran Formula of Concord (1577) arose through a series of ten major internal controversies within Lutheranism during the period 1537–77. One of the points which emerged as significant was the individual theological authority of Luther and certain of his followers, such as Philip Melanchthon. Determined to ensure that Lutheranism was based on Scripture, rather than on individual theologians, the Formula asserted that the opinions of all theologians, no matter how venerable, had to be judged in the light of Scripture. See also 1.5; 1.6; 2.2; 2.5; 2.7; 2.10; 2.23; 2.28.

Source: *Epitome*, 1–8; in *Die Bekenntnisschriften der evangelisch-lutherischen Kirche*, 2nd edn (Göttingen: Vandenhoeck & Ruprecht, 1952), 767.14–769.34.

* * *

> We believe, teach and confess that there is only one rule and norm according to which all teachings (*dogmata*) and teachers are to be appraised and judged, which is none other than the prophetic and apostolic writings of the Old and New Testaments . . . Other writings, whether of the fathers or more recent theologians, no matter what their names may be, cannot be regarded as possessing equal status to Holy Scripture, but must all be considered to be subordinate to it, and to witness to the way in which the teaching of the prophets and apostles was preserved in post-apostolic times and in different parts of the world . . . Holy Scripture remains the only judge, rule and norm according to which all doctrines are to be understood and judged, as to which are good or evil, and which are true or truly false. Certain other creeds (*symbola*) and writings . . . do not themselves possess the authority of judges, as in the case of Holy Scripture, but are witnesses of our religion as to how [the Holy Scriptures] were explained and presented.

2.20 Philip Jakob Spener on Scripture and the Christian Life

A major Pietist belief was that the reading of Scripture was of central importance to the shaping of the Christian life. In his *Pia Desideria* ("Pious Longings") of 1675, Spener set out a program for the revitalization of the Christian appreciation of Scripture. This program involved giving Scripture a higher priority than it had hitherto been given, along with the setting up of "church meetings" for the study of the Bible. These are generally regarded as the ancestors of the "bible study groups" which are a widespread feature of many modern churches. See also 2.9; 2.21.

Source: *Pia Desideria* (1675); in P. J. Spener, *Pia Desideria*, edited and translated by T. G. Tappert (Philadelphia: Fortress Press, 1964), pp. 87–9. Reprinted from *Pia Desideria* by T. G. Tappert. Copyright © 1964 Fortress Press. Used by permission of Augsburg Fortress.

* * *

> Thought should be given to the more extensive use of the Word of God among us. We know that by nature we have no good in us. If there is to be any good in us, it must be brought about by God. To this end the Word of God is the powerful means, since faith must be enkindled through the gospel, and the law provides the rules for good works and many wonderful impulses to attain them. The more at home the Word of God is among us, the more we shall bring about faith and its fruits.

It may appear that the Word of God has sufficiently free course among us inasmuch as at various places (as in this city [Frankfurt am Main]) there is daily or frequent preaching from the pulpit. When we reflect further on the matter, however, we shall find that with respect to this first proposal, more is needed. I do not at all disapprove of the preaching of sermons in which a Christian congregation is instructed by the reading and exposition of a certain text, for I myself do this. But I find that this is not enough. In the first place, we know that "all Scripture is inspired by God and profitable for teaching, for reproof, for correction, and for training in righteousness" (2 Timothy 3:16). Accordingly all Scripture, without exception, should be known by the congregation if we are all to receive the necessary benefit. If we put together all the passages of the Bible which in the course of many years are read to a congregation in one place, they will comprise only a very small part of the Scriptures which have been given to us. The remainder is not heard by the congregation at all, or is heard only insofar as one or another verse is quoted or alluded to in sermons, without, however, offering any understanding of the entire context, which is nevertheless of the greatest importance. In the second place, the people have little opportunity to grasp the meaning of the Scriptures except on the basis of those passages which may have been expounded to them, and even less do they have opportunity to become as practiced in them as edification requires. Meanwhile, although solitary reading of the Bible at home is in itself a splendid and praiseworthy thing, it does not accomplish enough for most people.

It should therefore be considered whether the church would not be well advised to introduce the people to Scripture in still other ways than through the customary sermons on the appointed lessons. This might be done, first of all, by diligent reading of the Holy Scriptures, especially of the New Testament. It would not be difficult for every housefather to keep a Bible, or at least a New Testament, handy and read from it every day or, if the cannot read, to have somebody else read . . .

Then a second thing would be desirable in order to encourage people to read privately, namely, that where the practice can be introduced the books of the Bible be read one after another, at specified times in the public service, without further comment (unless one wished to add brief summaries). This would be intended for the edification of all, but especially of those who cannot read at all, or cannot read easily or well, or of those who do not own a copy of the Bible.

For a third thing it would perhaps not be inexpedient (and I set this down for further and more mature reflection) to reintroduce the ancient and apostolic kind of church meetings. In addition to our customary services with preaching, other assemblies would also be held in the manner in which Paul describes them in 1 Corinthians 14:26–40. One person would not rise to preach (although this practice would be continued at other times), but others who have been blessed with gifts and knowledge would also speak and present their pious opinions on the proposed subject to the judgment of the rest, doing all this in such a way as to avoid disorder and strife.

2.21 Nicolas Ludwig von Zinzendorf on Reason and Experience

Pietism revolted against the rationalist insistence that God could be known adequately through reason alone. In this passage, Zinzendorf stresses the importance of the experiential aspects of faith. The experiences of faith cannot be contradicted by reason. See also 1.1; 1.2; 1.3; 1.4; 1.12; 1.16; 2.9; 2.15; 2.20.

Source: *Der deutsche Sokrates* (1732), in *Nicolas Ludwig von Zinzendorf: Hauptschriften*, vol. 1; ed. E. Beureuther and G. Meyer (Hildesheim: Georg Olms Verlagsbuchhandlung, 1962), pp. 289–90.

* * * ─────────────────────────────

1. Religion can be grasped without the conclusions of reason; otherwise no one could have religion except a person of intelligence. As a result the best theologians would be those who have the greatest reason. This cannot be believed and is contradicted by experience.

2. Religion must be a matter which is able to be grasped through experience alone without any concepts. If this were not so, someone born deaf or blind, or a mentally deficient person (*ein wachsinniger Mensch*), or a child, could not have the religion necessary for salvation. The first could not hear the truth, the second would lack the mental ability to think about and understand matters, and the third would lack the ability to grasp concepts to put them together and to test them.

3. There is less at stake in the truth of concepts than in the truth of experience; errors in doctrine are not as bad as errors in methods and an ignorant person is not as bad as a fool.

4. Understanding which arises out of concepts changes with age, education, and other circumstances. Understanding arrived at through experience is not subject to these changes; such understanding becomes better with time and circumstances.

5. If the divinity did not give itself in a recognizable form to a person, it could not desire that this person should recognize it.

6. Revelation is indispensably necessary in human experience; however, it is not so much necessary as useful that revelation should be reduced to comprehensible concepts . . .

11. Religion cannot be grasped by reason, so long as reason sets itself against experience.

12. The experience of something cannot be dismissed on the basis of any conclusion of reason.

Jonathan Edwards on the Beauty of Creation

The text which follows was never intended for publication. It is basically a collection of Edwards's notes and jottings, now on deposit at Yale University Library. In it, Edwards develops the idea that God can be known, to a limited extent, through the created order. Like Calvin, Edwards regards nature as echoing what may be found in Scripture, while maintaining the greater clarity and authority of the latter. In many ways, the approach adopted parallels that of John Calvin; however, it is clear that the issue is of considerably greater importance, both theologically and spiritually, to Edwards, not least on account of the growing challenge to Christian theology posed by the rationalism of the Enlightenment. By stressing the congruence between the "book of nature" and the "book of Scripture," Edwards was attempting to show how a "religion of nature" could only find its fulfillment in the Christian gospel. See also 2.16.

Source: The Images of Divine Things, paras 57, 70, 156, 211; in Jonathan Edwards, The Images of Divine Things, ed. Perry Miller (New Haven: Yale University Press, 1948), pp. 61, 69, 109, 134. Copyright © 1948 by Yale University. Reprinted by permission of the publisher.

* * *

57. It is very fit and becoming of God who is infinitely wise, so to order things that there sbould be a voice of His in His works, instructing those that behold him and painting forth and shewing divine mysteries and things more immediately appertaining to Himself and His spiritual kingdom. The works of God are but a kind of voice or language of God to instruct intelligent beings in things pertaining to Himself. And why should we not think that he would teach and instruct by His works in this way as well as in others, viz., by representing divine things by His works and so painting them forth, especially since we know that God hath so much delighted in this way of instruction . . .

70. If we look on these shadows of divine things as the voice of God purposely by them teaching us these and those spiritual and divine things, to show of what excellent advantage it will be, how agreeably and clearly it will tend to convey instruction to our minds, and to impress things on the mind and to affect the mind, by that we may, as it were, have God speaking to us. Wherever we are, and whatever we are about, we may see divine things excellently represented and held forth. And it will abundantly tend to confirm the Scriptures, for there is an excellent agreement between these things and the holy Scripture . . .

156. The book of Scripture is the interpreter of the book of nature two ways, viz., by declaring to us those spiritual mysteries that are indeed signified and typified in the constitution of the natural world; and secondly, in actually making application of the signs and types in the book of nature as representations of those spiritual mysteries in many instances . . .

211. The immense magnificence of the visible world in inconceivable vastness, the incomprehensible height of the heavens, etc., is but a type of the

infinite magnificence, height and glory of God's world in the spiritual world: the most incomprehensible expression of His power, wisdom, holiness and love in what is wrought and brought to pass in the world, and the exceeding greatness of the moral and natural good, the light, knowledge, holiness and happiness which shall be communicated to it, and therefore to that magnificence of the world, height of heaven. These things are often compared in such expressions: Thy mercy is great above the heavens, thy truth reacheth; thou hast for thy glory above the heavens, etc.

2.23 Johann Adam Möhler on Tradition

In this passage, published in 1832, Johann Adam Möhler, the founder of the Catholic Tübingen school, sets out an understanding of tradition as a living voice within the church, by which the Christian community's interpretation of Scripture is safeguarded from error. Möhler argues that it is of little value to have an infallible Bible, if this is constantly misunderstood or misrepresented by fallible human beings. The church is thus a divinely-appointed means by which the correct interpretation of Scripture is ensured. Note in particular the declaration that "tradition is the living Word, perpetuated in the hearts of believers." See also 2.2; 2.5; 2.7; 2.10; 2.19; 2.28.

Source: Johann Adam Möhler, *Symbolism: or Exposition of the Doctrinal Differences between Catholics and Protestants* (New York: Dunigan, 1844), pp. 349–52 (translation modified at points).

* * *

The main question we must now address is this: how do we come to have possession of the true doctrine of Christ? Or, to express this in a more general and accurate manner, how do we come to a clear knowledge of the foundation of salvation, which is offered to us in Christ Jesus? The Protestant replies: "by searching Holy Scripture, which is infallible." The Catholic, on the other hand, replies: "by the Church, in which alone we arrive at a true understanding of Holy Scripture." To give a more detailed exposition of his or her views, the Catholic continues: "doubtless the Sacred Scriptures contain divine communications, and, consequently, the pure truth: whether they contain *all* the truths, which from a religious and ecclesiastical point of view are necessary, or at least very useful to be known, is a question which does not yet come under consideration. Thus, Scripture is God's unerring Word: but however the predicate of inerrability may belong to it, we ourselves are not exempt from error; indeed, we only become so when we have unerringly received the Word, which is in itself inerrable. In this reception of the Word, human activity, which is fallible, necessarily has a part.

But, in order that, in this transfer of the divine contents of the Holy Scriptures into possession of the human intellect, no gross illusion or general misrepresentation may occur, it is taught, that the Holy Spirit, to which are entrusted the guidance and vivification of the Church, becomes, in its union with the human spirit in the Church, a peculiarly Christian sense, a deep and sure feeling, which, as it abides in truth, leads also into all truth. By a confiding attachment to the perpetuated apostleship, by education in the Church, by hearing, learning, and living within her realm, by the reception of the higher principle, which renders her eternally fruitful, a deep interior sense is formed that alone is fitted for the perception and acceptance of the written word, because it entirely coincides with the sense in which the Holy Scriptures themselves were composed. If, with such a sense acquired in the Church, the sacred volume be perused, then its general essential import is conveyed unaltered to the reader's mind. Indeed, when instruction through the apostleship, and the ecclesiastical education in the way described, takes place in the individual, the Holy Scriptures are not even necessary for our acquisition of their general contents.

This is the ordinary and regular course. But errors and misunderstandings, more or less culpable, will never fail to occur; and, as in the times of the apostles, the Word of God was combated out of the Word of God, so this combat has been renewed at all times. What, under such circumstances, is the course to be pursued? How is the Divine Word to be secured against the erroneous conceptions that have arisen? The general sense decides against particular opinion – the judgment of the Church against that of the individual: the Church interprets the Holy Scriptures. The Church is the body of the Lord: it is, in its universality, his visible form – his permanent, ever-renewed, humanity – his eternal revelation. He dwells in the community; all his promises, all his gifts are bequeathed to the community – but to no individuals, as such, since the time of the apostles. This general sense, this ecclesiastical consciousness is tradition, in the subjective sense of the word. What then is tradition? The peculiar Christian sense existing in the Church, and transmitted by ecclesiastical education; yet this sense is not to be conceived as detached from its subject-matter; indeed, it is formed in and by this matter, so it may be called a full sense. Tradition is the living Word, perpetuated in the hearts of believers. To this sense, as the general sense, the interpretation of Holy Writ is entrusted. The declaration, which it pronounces on any controverted subject, is the judgment of the Church; and, therefore, the Church is judge in matters of faith. Tradition, in the objective sense, is the general faith of the Church through all ages, manifested by outwards historical testimonies; in this sense, tradition is usually termed the norm, the standard of Scriptural interpretation – the rule of faith.

Archibald Alexander Hodge on the Inspiration of Scripture

2.24

The leading Princeton theologian Charles Hodge (1797–1878) set out a view of the authority and inspiration of the Bible which had enormous influence in nineteenth-century America. In this passage, his son sets out the main features of the "Old Princeton Theology" (as it is generally known) on biblical authority and inspiration in a particularly clear and direct way. Note especially how biblical authority is specifically linked with correct biblical interpretation. See also 2.9; 2.18; 2.22; 2.28; 2.30; 2.31.

Source: A. A. Hodge, *Outlines of Theology* (1879; reprinted Grand Rapids: Eerdmans, 1948), pp. 66–9.

* * *

In what sense and to what extent has the Church universally held the Bible to be inspired?
That the sacred writers were so influenced by the Holy Spirit that their writings are as a whole and in every part God's Word to us – an authoritative revelation to us from God, indorsed by him, and sent to us as a rule of faith and practice, the original autographs of which are absolutely infallible when interpreted in the sense intended, and hence are clothed with absolute divine authority.

What is meant by "plenary inspiration"?
A divine influence full and sufficient to secure its end. The end in this case secured is the perfect infallibility of the Scriptures in every part, as a record of fact and doctrine both in thought and verbal expression. So that although they come to us through the instrumentality of the minds, hearts, imaginations, consciences, and wills of men, they are nevertheless in the strictest sense the word of God.

What is meant by the phrase "verbal inspiration," and how can it be proved that the words of the Bible were inspired?
It is meant that the divine influence, of whatever kind it may have been, which accompanied the sacred writers in what they wrote, extends to their expression of their thoughts in language, as well as to the thoughts themselves. The effect being that in the original autograph copies the language expresses the thought God intended to convey with infallible accuracy, so that the words as well as the thoughts are God's revelation to us.

That this influence did extend to the words appears – first, from the very design of inspiration, which is, not to secure the infallible correctness of the opinions of the inspired men themselves . . . but to secure an infallible record of the truth. But a record consists of language. Second, men think in words, and the more definitely they think the more are their thoughts immediately associated with an exactly appropriate verbal expression. Infallibility of thought can not be secured or preserved independently of all infallible verbal rendering. Third, the Scriptures affirm this fact (1 Corinthians 2:13, 1 Thessalonians 2:13. Fourth, the New Testament writers, while quoting from the Old Testament for purposes of argument, often base their argument upon the very words used, thus ascribing authority to the word as well as the thought . . .

By what means does the church hold that God has effected the result above defined?
The Church doctrine recognizes the fact that every part of Scripture is at once a product of God's and of man's agency. The human writers have produced each his part in the free and natural exercise of his personal faculties under his historical conditions. God has also so acted concurrently in and through them that the whole organism of Scripture and every part

thereof is his word to us, infallibly true in the sense intended and absolutely authoritative.

God's agency includes the three following elements:

1. His PROVIDENTIAL agency in producing the Scriptures. The whole course of redemption, of which revelation and inspiration are special functions, was a special providence directing the evolution of a specially providential history. Here the natural and the supernatural continually interpenetrate. But, as is of necessity the case, the natural was always the rule and the supernatural the exception; yet as little subject to accident, and as much the subject of rational design as the natural itself. Thus God providentially produced the very man for the precise occasion, with the faultless qualities, education, and gracious experience needed for the production of the intended writing. Moses, David, Isaiah, Paul, or John, genius and character, nature and grace, peasant, philosopher, or prince, the man, and with him each subtile personal accident, was providentially prepared at the proper moment as the necessary instrumental precondition of the work to be done.

2. REVELATION of truth not otherwise attainable. Whenever the writer was not possessed, or could not naturally become possessed, of the knowledge god intended to communicate, it was supernaturally revealed to him by vision or language. This revelation was supernatural, objective to the recipient, and assured to him to be truth of divine origin by appropriate evidence. This direct revelation applies to a large element of the sacred Scriptures, such as prophecies of future events, the peculiar doctrines of Christianity, the promises and threatenings of God's word, etc., but it applies by no means to all the contents of Scripture.

3. INSPIRATION. The writers were the subjects of a plenary divine influence, called inspiration, which acted upon and through their natural faculties in all they wrote, directing them in the choice of subject and the whole course of thought and verbal expression, so as while not interfering with the natural exercise of their faculties, they freely and spontaneously produce the very writing which God designed, and which thus possesses the attributes of infallibility and authority as above defined.

This inspiration differs, therefore, from revelation, first, in that it was a constant experience of the sacred writers in all they wrote, and it affects the equal infallibility of all the elements of the writings they produced. While, as before said, revelation was supernaturally vouchsafed only when it was needed. Second, in that revelation communicated objectively to the mind of the writer truth otherwise unknown. While inspiration was a divine influence flowing into the sacred writer subjectively, communicating nothing, but guiding their faculties in their natural exercise to the producing an infallible record of the matters of history, doctrine, prophecy, etc., which God designed to send through them to his Church.

2.25   Karl Barth on Revelation as God's Self-Disclosure

In this important passage from the first half-volume of the *Church Dogmatics*, written in German in 1932, Barth sets out his understanding of the relationship between "revelation," "the Word of God," and Jesus Christ. It is a complex and nuanced account, which places emphasis on the necessity of divine revelation if human beings are to know anything of God. The German word *Mensch*, here translated as "man," is actually common gender, and should be translated as "a human person." See also 2.26; 2.31; 2.32.

Source: Karl Barth, *Church Dogmatics*, I/1 (Edinburgh: T. & T. Clark, 1975), pp. 191, 193–4. Used with permission of the publisher.

* * *

Primarily and originally the Word of God is undoubtedly the Word that God speaks by and to himself in eternal concealment. We shall have to return to this great and inalienable truth when we develop the concept of revelation in the context of the doctrine of the Trinity. But undoubtedly, too, it is the Word that is spoken to men in revelation, Scripture, and preaching. Hence we cannot speak or think of it at all without remembering at once the man who hears and knows it. The Word of God, Jesus Christ, as the being of the Church, sets us ineluctably before the realization that it was and will be men who are intended and addressed and therefore characterized as recipients but as also themselves bearers of this Word. The Word of God thus sets us before the so-to-speak anthropological problem. How then can men be this? Before the "so-to-speak" anthropological problem, I said, and I indicated thereby that it can be called this only with some reserve. Or is this not so? Shall we say unreservedly that the question of the possibility of the knowledge of God's Word is a question of anthropology? Shall we ask what man generally and as such, in addition to all else he can do, can or cannot do in this regard? Is there a general truth about man which can be made generally perceptible and which includes within it man's ability to know the Word of God? We must put this question because an almost invincible development in the history of Protestant theology since the Reformation has led to an impressive affirmative answer to this question in the whole wing of the Church that we have called Modernist . . .

The question is whether this event ranks with the other events that might enter man's reality in such a way that to be able to enter it actually requires on man's part a potentiality which is bought by man as such, which consists in a disposition native to him as man, in an organ, in a positive or even a negative property that can be reached and discovered by self-reflection, by anthropological analysis of his existence, in short, in what philosophy of the Kantian type calls a faculty.

It might also be that this event did not so much presuppose the corresponding possibility on man's part as bring it with it and confer it on man by being event, so that it is man's possibility without ceasing (as such) to be wholly and utterly the possibility proper to the Word of God and to it alone. We might also be dealing with a possibility of knowledge which can be made intelligible as a possibility of man, but, in contrast to all others, only in terms of the object of knowledge or the reality of knowledge and not at all in terms of the subject of knowledge, i.e., man as such. In the light of the nature of God's Word, and especially of what we said above about its purposiveness or pertinence, its being aimed at man, its character as an address to man, we must decide against the first view and in favour of the second. From this standpoint, the same that concerns us here, we had to understand the Word of God as the act of God's free love and not as if the addressed and hearing man were in any way essential to the concept of the Word of God. That man is the recipient of God's Word is, to the extent that it is true, a fact, and it cannot be deduced from anything we might previously know about God's nature. Even less, of course, can it be deduced from anything we previously knew about the nature of man. God's Word is no longer grace, and grace itself is no longer grace, if we ascribe to man a predisposition towards this Word, a possibility of knowledge regarding it that is intrinsically and independently native to him. But the same results from what was said in the same passage about the content of the Word of God addressed to man.

We then made the assertion that this content, whatever it might be *in concretissimo* for this man or that man, will always be an authentic and definitive encounter with the Lord of man, a revelation which man cannot achieve himself, the revelation of something new which can only be told him. It will also be the limitation of his existence by the absolute "out there" of his Creator, a limitation on the basis of which he can understand himself only as created out of nothing and upheld over nothing. It will also be a radical renewal and therewith an obviously radical criticism of the whole of his present existence, a renewal and a criticism on the basis of which he can understand himself only as created out of nothing and upheld over nothing. It will also be a radical renewal and therewith an obviously radical criticism of the whole of his present existence, a renewal and a criticism on the basis of which he can understand himself only as a sinner living by grace and therefore as a lost sinner closed up against God on his side. Finally it will be the presence of God as the One who comes, the Future One in the strict sense, the Eternal Lord and Redeemer of man, a presence on the basis of which he can understand himself only as hastening towards this future of the Lord and expecting him. To be sure, it is not these formulae which describe the real content of the Word of God, but the content of the Word which God himself speaks and which he does so always as these formulae indicate, the real content of the real Word of God, that tells man also that there can be no question of any ability to hear or understand or know on his part, of any capability that he the creature, the sinner, the one who waits, has to bring to this Word, but that the possibility of knowledge corresponding to the real Word of God that it represents an inconceivable novum compared to all his ability and capability, and that it is to be understood as a pure fact, in exactly the same way as the real Word of God itself.

2.26 Emil Brunner on the Personal Nature of Revelation

During the 1930s, a growing alienation developed between Emil Brunner and Karl Barth. Although both writers were initially regarded as "dialectical theologians," stressing the "otherness" of God over and against humanity, Brunner came increasingly to place emphasis upon the personal disclosure of God to humanity, with this latter being the "conversation-partner of God." In this passage, Brunner stresses the personal nature of divine revelation, which is an integral aspect of his notion of this divine–human dialog. See also 2.25; 2.31.

Source: Emil Brunner, *Truth as Encounter*, 2nd edn (London: SCM Press, 1964), p. 109. Reprinted with the permission of the publisher.

* * *

The self-revelation of God is no object, but wholly the doing and self-giving of a subject – or, better expressed, a Person. A Person who is revealing himself, a Person who demands and offers Lordship and fellowship with himself, is the most radical antithesis to everything that could be called object or objective. Likewise, the personal act of trust is something quite other than subjectivity – that subjectivity which can become actual only when it is over against an object, that subjectivity which appropriates what is foreign to it. If we were to speak of appropriation in this context, it could be only of such a kind as when man gives himself to God to be owned by him. But if we know as believers, we recognize what is meant here, that that which happens in revelation and faith cannot be pushed into the framework of truth and knowledge of truth without its becoming in that way something quite different. Yet in the Bible what we have been talking about is just what is called truth . . . This Biblical "truth" is as different from what otherwise is called truth as this personal encounter and the double-sided self-giving and its resulting fellowship are different from the comprehension of facts by means of reasoning. This is not to say that there do not also exist between both this Biblical and the general rational conception of truth positive relations outside of these differences . . . The concern of the Bible is personal correspondence as it is realized in the correlation between the Word of God and faith; and, contrariwise, such an understanding of the concept of the Word of God and faith as is yielded by reflection about the fundamental Biblical category of personal correspondence. Through it the Biblical conception of truth is determined and differentiated from every other understanding of truth.

Rudolf Bultmann on Demythologization and Biblical Interpretation

On 4 June 1941, Rudolf Bultmann delivered a lecture which introduced the phrase "the demythologization of the New Testament." The basic contention of this controversial lecture was that the New Testament proclamation or *kerygma* concerning Christ is stated and understood in mythological terms (which Bultmann attempted to derive from existing Jewish apocalyptic and Gnostic redemption myths, borrowing ideas deriving from the "history of religions school") which, although perfectly legitimate and intelligible in the first century, cannot be taken seriously today. It is therefore the task of New Testament interpretation to eliminate this mythological cosmology, and extract the existential truths which lie beneath it. See also 2.3; 2.4; 2.6; 2.8; 2.9; 2.11; 2.12; 2.13; 2.14; 2.29; 2.30.

Source: Rudolf Bultmann, "New Testament and Mythology," in H. W. Bartsch (ed.), *Kerygma and Myth* (London: SPCK, 1953), pp. 1–16. Used by permission of the publisher.

* * *

The cosmology of the New Testament is essentially mythical in character. The world is viewed as a three-storied structure with the earth in the center, the heaven above, and the underworld beneath . . . History does not follow a smooth unbroken course; it is set in motion and controlled by supernatural forces. This aeon is held in bondage by Satan, sin and death . . . and hastens towards its end. That end will come very soon, and will take the form of a cosmic catastrophe. It will be inaugurated by the "woes" of the last time. Then the Judge will come from heaven, the dead will rise, the last judgement will take place, and people will enter into eternal salvation or damnation. This, then, is the mythical view of the world which the New Testament presupposes when it presents the event of redemption which is the subject of its preaching . . .

Can Christian preaching expect modern people who accept the mythical view of the world as true? To do so would be both senseless and impossible. It would be senseless, because there is nothing specifically Christian in the mythical view of the world as such. It is simply the cosmology of a pre-scientific age. Again, it would be impossible, because nobody can adopt a view of the world as a matter of choice; it has already been determined by our place in history . . . It is impossible to use electric light and the wireless and to avail ourselves of modern medical and surgical discoveries, and at the same time to believe in the New Testament world of spirits and miracles . . .

The real purpose of myth is not to present an objective picture of the world as it is, but to express human understandings of themselves in the world in which they live. Myth should be interpreted not cosmologically, but anthropologically, or better still, existentially . . . Hence the importance of New Testament mythology lies not in its imagery but in the understanding of existence which it enshrines. The real question is whether this understanding of existence is true. Faith claims that it is, and faith ought not to be tied down to the imagery of New Testament mythology . . . Our task is to produce an existentialist interpretation of the dualistic mythology of the New Testament . . . We have to discover whether the New Testament offers us an understanding of ourselves which will challenge us to a genuine existential decision.

2.28   Karl Rahner on the Authority of Scripture

Karl Rahner, one of the most influential Catholic theologians of the twentieth century, here explores the issue of biblical authority from a Catholic perspective. Note in particular the constant emphasis on the mutually interrelated character of church and Scripture. Rahner also explores two other issues of considerable importance to the theme of the authority of Scripture: the manner in which Scripture relates to Jesus Christ, and the hermeneutical issues associated with the interpretation of Scripture. See also 2.2; 2.5; 2.7; 2.10; 2.19; 2.23; 2.24; 2.25.

Source: Karl Rahner, *Foundations of the Christian Faith: An Introduction to the Idea of Christianity* (New York: Crossroad, and London: Darton, Longman and Todd, 1978), pp. 371, 373–7. Originally published as *Grundkurs des Glaubens: Einführung in den Begriff des Christentums.* Copyright © 1976 by Verlag Herder, Freiburg im Breisgau. English translation copyright © by The Crossroad Publishing Co., New York. Reprinted by permission of The Crossroad Publishing Co., New York, and Darton, Longman and Todd, London.

* * *

We regard [Holy Scripture] as the church's book, the book in which the church of the beginning always remains tangible as a norm for us in the concrete. Indeed it is norm which is already distinguished from those things which are found in the original church but which cannot have a normative character for our faith and for the life of the later church. If the church in every age remains bound to its origins in its faith and in its life; if the church as the community of faith in the crucified and risen Jesus is itself to be in its faith and in its life the eschatological and irreversible sign of God's definitive turning to the world in Jesus Christ, a sign without which Jesus Christ himself would not signify God's irreversible coming into the world and would not be the absolute savior; and if this church of the beginning objectifies itself in scriptural documents at least in fact, and also does so necessarily given the historical and cultural presuppositions in which the church came to be, then in all of this together we have a point of departure for understanding the essence of scripture.

It is also a point of departure from whose perspective we can arrive at an adequate and at the same time a critical understanding of what is really meant by the inspiration of scripture and by a binding canon of scripture. Since scripture is something derivative, it must be understood from the essential nature of the church, which is the eschatological and irreversible permanence of Jesus Christ in history. It is to be understood from this perspective as something normative in the church . . .

During the apostolic age the real theological essence of the church is constituted in a historical process in which the church comes to the fullness of this essence and to the possession of this essence in faith. This self-constitution of the essence of the church until it reaches its full historical existence (and it is not until then that it can fully be the norm for the future church) implies written objectifications. Therefore this process is *also*, but not exclusively, the process of the formation of the canon: the church objectifies its faith and its life in written documents, and it recognizes these objectifications as so pure and so successful that they are able to hand on the apostolic church as a norm for future ages. From this perspective there is no insuperable difficulty with the fact that the formation of these writings and the knowledge that they are representative as objectifications of the apostolic church do not simply coincide in time, and that the formation of the canon was not finished until the post-apostolic age. In this understanding the canonicity of scripture is established by God insofar as he constitutes the church through the cross and the resurrection as an irreversible event of salvation, and the pure objectifications of its beginning are constitutive for this church . . .

From this perspective, or so it seems to us, we can also clarify what is called "inspiration" in the church's doctrine on scripture. In the documents of the church it is said again and again that God is the *auctor* (author) of the Old and New Testaments as scripture. The school theology, which is at work in the encyclicals of Leo XIII and up to those of Pius XII, tried time and time again to clarify by means of psychological theories how God himself is the literary author or the writer of Holy Scripture. And it tried to formulate and to clarify the doctrine of inspiration in such a way that it becomes clear that God is the literary author of scripture. This, however, did not deny (and the Second Vatican Council affirmed it explicitly) that this understanding of God's authorship and of inspiration may not reduce the human authors of these writings merely to God's secretaries, but rather it grants them the character of a genuine literary authorship of their own.

This interpretation of the inspired nature of scripture which we have done no more than sketch can of course be understood in such a way that even today one does not necessarily have to accuse it of being mythological. We would have to recall in this connection what we said in the fifth chapter about the unity between transcendental revelation and its historical objectification in word and in writing, and about the knowledge of the success of these objectifications. In any case it cannot be denied in the Catholic church that God is the author of the Old and New Testaments. But he does not therefore have to be understood as the literary author of these writings. He can be understood in a variety of other ways as the author of scripture, and indeed in such a way that in union with grace and the light of faith scripture can truly be called the word of God. This is true especially because, as we said elsewhere, even if a word about God is causes by God, it would not by this very fact be a word of God in which God offers himself. It would not be such a word of God if this word did not take place as an objectification of God's self-expression which is effected by God and is borne by grace, and which comes to us without being reduced to our level because the process of hearing it is borne by God's Spirit.

If the church was founded by God himself through his Spirit and in Jesus Christ, if the *original* church as the norm for the future church is the object of God's activity in a qualitatively unique way which is different from his preservation of the church in the course of history, and if scripture is a constitutive element of this original church as the norm for future ages, then this already means quite adequately and in both a positive and an exclusive sense that God is the author of scripture and that he inspired it. Nor at *this* point can some special psychological theory of inspiration be appealed to for help. Rather we can simply take cognizance of the actual origins of scripture which follow for the impartial observer from the very different characteristics of the individual books of scripture. The human authors of Holy Scripture work exactly like other human authors, nor do they have to know anything about their being inspired in reflexive knowledge. If God wills the original church as an indefectible sign of salvation for all ages, and wills it with an absolute, formally pre-defining and eschatological will within salvation history, and hence if he wills with this quite definite will everything which is constitutive for this church, and this includes in certain circumstances scripture in a preeminent way, then he is the inspirer and the author of scripture, although the inspiration of scripture is "only" a moment within God's primordial authorship of the church.

From the doctrine that Holy Scripture is inspired theology and the official doctrine of the church derive the thesis that scripture is inerrant. We can certainly say with the Second Vatican Council (*Dei Verbum*, art. 11): "Therefore, since everything asserted by the inspired authors or sacred writers must be considered to be asserted by the Holy Spirit, we must profess of the books of scripture that they teach with certainty, with fidelity and without error the truth which God wanted recorded in the sacred writings for the sake of our salvation." But if because of the very nature of scripture as the message of salvation we acknowledge the inerrancy of scripture first of all in this global sense, we are still far from having solved all of the problems and settled all of the difficulties about the meaning and the limits of this statement which can be raised because of the actual state of the scriptural texts. The inerrancy of scripture was certainly understood earlier in too narrow a sense, especially when inspiration was interpreted in the sense of verbal inspiration, and the sacred writers were only regarded as God's secretaries and not as independent and also historically conditioned literary authors. That difficulties still exist here in the understanding and in the exact interpretation of the church's doctrine on the inerrancy of scripture is shown even by the history on the conciliar text just cited. It follows from this history that the Council evidently wanted to leave open the question whether the phrase about the truth which God wanted to have recorded for the sake of our salvation is supposed to restrict or to explicate the meaning of the sentence . . .

We only want to say here very briefly: scripture in its unity and totality is the objectification of God's irreversible and victorious offer of salvation to the world in Jesus Christ, and therefore in its unity and totality it cannot lead one away from God's truth in some binding way. We must read every individual text within the context of this single whole in order to understand its true meaning correctly. Only then can it be understood in its real meaning, and only then can it really be grasped as "true." The very different literary genre of the individual books must be seen more clearly than before and be evaluated in establishing the real meaning of individual statements . . . Scriptural statements were expressed within historically and culturally conditioned conceptual horizons, and this must be taken into account if the question of what is "really" being said in a particular text is to be answered correctly. In certain circumstances it can be completely legitimate to distinguish between the "correctness" and the "truth" of a statement. Nor may we overlook the question whether the really binding meaning of a scriptural statement does not change if a particular book has its origins outside the canon as the work of some individual, and then is taken into the totality of the canonical scriptures.

Just as by the very nature of the case there is an analogy of faith which is a hermeneutical principle for the correct interpretation of individual statements in the official teaching of the church, so that the individual statement can only be understood correctly within the unity of the church's total consciousness of the faith, so too and in an analogous sense, or as a particular instance of this principle, there is also an *analogia scripturae* or an analogy of scripture which is a hermeneutical principle for interpreting individual texts of scripture. If there is a "hierarchy of truths," that is, if a particular statement does not always have the same objective and existential weight which another statement has, then this has to be taken into account in interpreting individual scriptural statements. This does not mean that the statement which is "less important" in relation to another statement has to be qualified as incorrect or as false.

If we grant the validity of and apply these similar principles, which follow from the very nature of the case and from the nature of human speech and are not the principles of a cheap "arrangement" or a cowardly attempt to cover up difficulties, then we certainly do not inevitably have to get into the difficulty of having to hold that particular statements of scripture are "true" in the meaning which is really intended and is intended in a binding way, although a sober and honest exegesis might declare that they are incorrect and erroneous in the sense of a negation of the "truth."

Phyllis Tribble on Feminist Biblical Interpretation   2.29

Phyllis Tribble, one of North America's most respected feminist biblical scholars, here provides an excellent example of the way in which a feminist theological agenda leads to the re-reading of Scripture, in order to gain insights which have been overlooked or suppressed by previous generations of (mainly male) interpreters. The passage represents an excellent and clearly worked example of modern feminist biblical interpretation. See also 2.3; 2.4; 2.6; 2.8; 2.9; 2.11; 2.12; 2.13; 2.14; 2.27; 2.30; 3.22; 3.34; 3.35; 6.45; 6.46.

Source: Phyllis Tribble, "Feminist Hermeneutics and Biblical Studies", *Christian Century*, 3–10 February 1982, pp. 116–18. Copyright © 1982 Christian Century Foundation. Reprinted by permission from the February 3–10, 1982 issue of *The Christian Century*.

* * * ───

Born and bred in a land of patriarchy, the Bible abounds in male imagery and language. For centuries interpreters have explored and exploited this male language to articulate theology: to shape the contours and content of the Church, synagogue and academy; and to instruct human beings – female and male – in who they are, what rules they should play, and how they should behave. So harmonious has seemed this association of Scripture with sexism, of faith with culture, that only a few have even questioned it.

Within the past decade, however, challenges have come in the name of feminism, and they refuse to go away. As a critique of culture in light of misogyny, feminism is a prophetic movement, examining the status quo, pronouncing judgement and calling for repentance. In various ways this hermeneutical pursuit interacts with the Bible in its remoteness, complexity, diversity and contemporaneity to yield new understandings of both text and interpreter. Accordingly, I shall survey three approaches to the study of women in Scripture. Though these perspectives may also apply to "intertestamental" and New Testament literature, my focus is the Hebrew Scriptures.

When feminists first examined the Bible, emphasis fell upon documenting the case against women. Commentators observed the plight of the female in Israel. Less desirable in the eyes of her parents than a male child, a girl stayed close to her mother, but her father controlled her life until he relinquished her to another man for marriage. If either of these male authorities permitted her to be mistreated, even abused, she had to submit without recourse. Thus, Lot offered his daughters to the men of Sodom to protect a male guest (Genesis 19:8); Jephthah sacrificed his daughter to remain faithful to a foolish vow (Judges 11:29–40); Amnon raped his half-sister Tamar (2 Samuel 13); and the Levite from the hill country of Ephraim participated with other males to bring about the betrayal, rape, murder and dismemberment of his own concubine (Judges 19). Although not every story involving female and male is so terrifying, the narrative literature nevertheless makes clear that from birth to death the Hebrew woman belonged to men.

What such narratives show, the legal corpus amplifies. Defined as the property of men (Exodus 20:17; Deuteronomy 5:21), women did not control their own bodies. A man expected to marry a virgin, though his own virginity need not be intact. A wife guilty of earlier fornication violated the honour and power of both her father and husband. Death by stoning was the penalty (Deuteronomy 22:13–21). Moreover, a woman had no right to divorce (Deuteronomy 24:1–4) and most often, no right to own property. Excluded from the priesthood, she was considered far more unclean than the male (Leviticus 15). Even her monetary value was less (Leviticus 27:1–7).

Clearly, this feminist perspective has uncovered abundant evidence for the inferiority, subordination and abuse of women in Scripture. Yet the approach has led to different conclusions. Some people denounce biblical faith as hopelessly misogynous, although this judgement usually fails to evaluate the evidence in terms of Israelite culture. Some reprehensibly use these data to support anti-Semitic sentiments. Some read the Bible as a historical document devoid of any continuing authority and hence worthy of dismissal. The "Who cares?" question often comes at this point.

Others succumb to despair about the ever-present male power that the Bible and its commentators hold over women. And still others, unwilling to let the case against women be the determining word, insist that text and interpreters provide more excellent ways.

The second approach, then, grows out of the first while modifying it. Discerning within Scripture a critique of patriarchy, certain feminists concentrate upon discovering and recovering traditions that challenge the culture. This task involves highlighting neglected texts and reinterpreting familiar ones.

Prominent among neglected passages are portrayals of deity as female. A psalmist declares that God is midwife (Psalm 22:9–10): "Yet thou art the one who took me from the womb; thou didst keep me safe upon my mother', breast." In turn, God becomes mother, the one upon whom the child is cast from birth: "Upon thee was I cast from my birth, and since my mother bore me thou hast been my God." Although this poem stops short of an exact equation, in it female imagery mirrors divine activity. What the psalmist suggests, Deuteronomy 32:18 makes explicit: "You were unmindful of the Rock that begot you and you forgot the God who gave you birth."

Though the Revised Standard Version translates accurately "The God who gave you birth," the rendering is tame. We need to accent the striking portrayal of God as a woman in labour pains, for the Hebrew verb has exclusively this meaning. (How scandalous, then, is the totally incorrect translation in the Jerusalem Bible, "You forgot the God who fathered you.") Yet another instance of female imagery is the metaphor of the womb as given in the Hebrew radicals *rhm*. In its singular form the word denotes the physical organ unique to the female. In the plural, it connotes the compassion of both human beings and God. God the merciful (*rahum*) is God the mother. (See, for example, Jeremiah 31:15–22.) Over centuries, however, translators and commentators have ignored such female imagery, with disastrous results for God, man and woman. To reclaim the image of God female is to become aware of the male idolatry that has long infested faith.

If traditional interpretations have neglected female imagery for God, they have also neglected females, especially women who counter patriarchal culture. By contrast, feminist hermeneutics accents these figures. A collage of women in Exodus illustrates the emphasis. So eager have scholars been to get Moses born that they pass quickly over the stories that lead to his advent (Exodus 1:8–2:10). Two female slaves are the first to oppose the Pharaoh; they refuse to kill newborn sons. Acting alone, without advice or assistance from males, they thwart the will of the oppressor. Tellingly, memory has preserved the names of these women, Shiprah and Puah, while obliterating the identity of the king so successfully that he has become the burden of innumerable doctoral dissertations. What these two females begin, other Hebrew women continue:

> A woman conceived and bore a son and when she saw that he was a goodly child she hid him three months. And when she could hide him no longer, she took for him a basket made of bulrushes ... and she put the child in it and placed it among the reeds at the river's bank. And his sister stood at a distance to know what would be done to him. (Exodus 2:2–4)

In quiet and secret ways the defiance resumes as a mother and daughter scheme to save their baby son and brother, and this action enlarges when the daughter of Pharaoh appears at the riverbank. Instructing her maid to fetch the basket, the princess opens it, sees a crying baby, and takes him to her heart even as she recognizes his Hebrew identity. The daughter of Pharaoh aligns herself with the daughters of Israel. Filial allegiance is broken; class lines crossed; racial and political difference transcended. The sister, seeing it all from a distance, dares to suggest the perfect arrangement: a Hebrew nurse for the baby boy; in reality, the child's own mother. From the human side, then, Exodus faith originates as a feminist act. The women who are ignored by theologians are the first to challenge oppressive structures.

Not only does this second approach recover neglected women but also it reinterprets familiar ones beginning with the primal woman in the creation story of Genesis 2–3. Contrary to tradition, she is not created the assistant or subordinate of the man. In fact, most often the Hebrew word 'ezer ("helper") connotes superiority ... thereby posing a rather different problem about this woman. Yet the accompanying phrase "fit for" or "corresponding to" ("a helper corresponding to") tempers the connotation of superiority to specify the mutuality of woman and man.

Further, when the serpent talks with the woman (Genesis 3.1–5), he uses plural verb forms, making her the spokesperson for the human couple – hardly the pattern of a patriarchal culture. She discusses theology intelligently, stating the case for obedience even more strongly than did God: "From the fruit of the tree that is in the midst of the garden, God said: 'You shall not eat from it, and you shall not touch it, lest you die.'" If the tree is not touched, then its fruit cannot be eaten. Here the woman builds "a fence around the Torah," a procedure that her rabbinical successors developed fully to protect divine law and ensure obedience.

Speaking with clarity and authority, the first woman is theologian, ethicist, hermeneut and rabbi. Defying the stereotypes of patriarchy, she reverses what the Church, synagogue and academy have preached about women. By the same token, the man "who was with her" (many translations omit this crucial phrase) throughout the temptation is not morally superior but rather belly-oriented. Clearly this story presents a couple alien to traditional interpretations. In reclaiming the woman, feminist hermeneutics gives new life to the image of God female.

These and other exciting discoveries of a counter literature that pertains to women do not, however, eliminate the male bias of Scripture. In other words, this second perspective neither disavows nor neglects the evidence of the first. Instead, it functions as a remnant theology.

The third approach retells biblical stories of terror *in memoriam*, offering sympathetic readings of abused women. If the first perspective documents misogyny historically and sociologically, this one appropriates such evidence poetically and theologically. At the same time, it continues to look for the remnant in unlikely places.

The betrayal, rape, murder and dismemberment of the concubine in Judges 19 is a striking example. When wicked men of the tribe of Benjamin demand to "know" her master, he instead throws the concubine to them. All night they ravish her; in the morning she returns to her master. Showing no pity, he orders her to get up and go. She does not answer, and the reader is left to wonder if she is dead or alive. At any rate, the master puts her body on a donkey and continues the journey. When the couple arrive home, the master cuts the concubine in pieces, sending them to the tribes of Israel as a call to war against the wrong done to him by the men of Benjamin.

At the conclusion of this story, Israel is instructed to "consider, take counsel and speak" (Judges 19:30). Indeed, Israel does reply – with unrestrained violence. Mass slaughter follows; the rape, murder and dismemberment of one woman condones similar crimes against hundreds and hundreds of women. The narrator (or editor) responds differently, however, suggesting the political solution of kingship instead of the anarchy of the judges (Judges 12:25). This solution fails. In the days of David there is a king in Israel, and yet Amnon rapes Tamar. How, then, do we today hear this ancient tale of terror as the imperatives "consider, take counsel and speak" address us? A feminist approach, with attention to reader response, interprets the story on behalf of the concubine as it calls to remembrance her suffering and death.

Similarly, the sacrifice of the daughter of Jephthah documents the powerlessness and abuse of a child in the days of the judges (Judges 11). No interpretation can save her from the holocaust or mitigate the foolish vow of her father. But we can move through the indictment of the father to claim sisterhood with the daughter. Retelling her story, we emphasize the daughters of Israel to whom she reaches out in the last days of her life (Judges 11.37). Thus, we underscore the postscript, discovering in the process an alternative translation.

Traditionally, the ending has read, "She [the daughter] had never known man. And it became a custom in Israel that the daughters of Israel went year by year to lament the daughter of Jephthah the Gileadite four days in the year" (11:40). Since the verb *become*, however, is a feminine form (Hebrew has no neuter), another reading is likely: "Although she had never known a man, nevertheless she became a tradition [custom] in Israel. From year to year the daughters of Israel went to mourn the daughter of Jephthah the Gileadite, four days in the year." By virtue of this translation, we can understand the ancient story in a new way. The unnamed virgin child becomes a tradition in Israel because the women with whom she chooses to spend her last days do not let her pass into oblivion; they establish a living memorial. Interpreting such stories of terror on behalf of women is surely, then, another way of challenging the patriarchy of Scripture.

I have surveyed three feminist approaches to the study of women in Scripture. The first explores the inferiority, subordination and abuse of women in ancient Israel. Within this context, the second pursues the counter-literature that is itself a critique of patriarchy. Utilizing both of these approaches, the third retells sympathetically the stories of terror about women. Though intertwined, these perspectives are distinguishable. The one stressed depends on the occasion and the talents and interests of the interpreter. Moreover, in its work, feminist hermeneutics embraces a variety of methodologies and disciplines. Archaeology, linguistics, anthropology and literary and historical criticism all have contributions to make. Thereby understanding of the past increases and deepens as it informs the present.

Finally, there are more perspectives on the subject of women in Scripture than are dreamt of in the hermeneutics of this essay. For instance I have barely mentioned the problem of sexist translations which, in fact, is receiving thoughtful attention from many scholars, male and female. But perhaps I have said enough to show that in various and sundry ways feminist hermeneutics is challenging interpretations old and new. In time, perhaps, it will yield a biblical theology of womanhood (not to be subsumed under the label humanity) with roots in the goodness of creation female and male. Meanwhile, the faith of Sarah and Hagar, Naomi and Ruth, the two Tamars and a cloud of other witnesses empowers and sobers the endeavour.

2.30 Donald G. Bloesch on Christological Approaches to Biblical Hermeneutics

In this passage Donald Bloesch, one of North America's leading evangelical theologians, sets out a series of options for biblical interpretation, indicating his anxieties concerning each. The passage provides a summary of available options, along with a critique from an evangelical perspective. Later in the article, in a section not reprinted here, Bloesch sets out his own approach, which involves a strongly Christological approach to the issues, avoiding some of the difficulties he here identifies. See also 2.3; 2.4; 2.6; 2.8; 2.9; 2.11; 2.12; 2.13; 2.14; 2.27; 2.29.

Source: Donald G. Bloesch, "A Christological Hermeneutic: Crisis and Conflict in Hermeneutics", in R. K. Johnson (ed.), *The Use of the Bible in Theology: Evangelical Options* (Atlanta: John Knox Press, 1985), pp. 78–84. Reprinted by permission of the author.

* * *

The discipline of biblical hermeneutics, which deals with the principles governing the interpretation of Scripture, is presently in crisis. For some time it has been obvious in the academic world that the scriptural texts cannot simply be taken at face value but presuppose a thought world that is alien to our own. In an attempt to bring some degree of coherence to the interpretation of Scripture, scholars have appealed to current philosophies or sociologies of knowledge. Their aim has been to come to an understanding of what is essential and what is peripheral in the Bible, but too often in the process they have lost contact with the biblical message. It is fashionable among both theologians and biblical scholars today to contend that there is no one biblical view or message but instead a plurality of viewpoints that stand at considerable variance with one another as well as with the modern world-view.

There are a number of academically viable options today concerning biblical interpretation, some of which I shall consider in this essay. These options represent competing theologies embracing the whole of the theological spectrum.

First, there is the hermeneutic of Protestant scholastic orthodoxy, which allows for grammatical–historical exegesis, the kind that deals with the linguistic history of the text but is loathe to give due recognition to the cultural or historical conditioning of the perspective of the author of the text. Scripture is said to have one primary author, the Holy Spirit, with the prophets and Apostles as the secondary authors. For this reason Scripture is believed to contain an underlying theological and philosophical unity. It is therefore proper to speak of a uniquely biblical life- and world-view. Every text, it is supposed, can be harmonized not only with the whole of Scripture but also with the findings of secular history and natural science. The meaning of most texts is thought to be obvious even to an unbeliever. The end result of such a treatment of Scripture is a coherent, systematic theological system, presumably reflecting the very mind of God. This approach has been represented in Reformed circles by the so called Princeton School of Theology associated with Charles Hodge, Archibald Alexander Hodge, and Benjamin Warfield.

In this perspective, hermeneutics is considered a scientific discipline abiding by the rules that govern other disciplines of knowledge. Scripture, it is said, yields its meaning to a systematic, inductive analysis and does not necessarily presuppose a faith commitment to be understood. Some proponents of the old orthodoxy (such as Gordon Clark and Carl Henry) favor a metaphysical–deductive over an empirical–inductive approach, seeking to deduce the concrete meanings of Scripture from first principles given in Scripture.

A second basic approach to biblical studies is historicism in which Scripture is treated in the same way as any worthy literature of a given cultural tradition. The tools of higher criticism are applied to Scripture to find out what the author intended to say in that particular historical cultural context. Higher criticism includes an analysis of the literary genre of the text, its historical background, the history of the oral tradition behind the text and the cultural and psychological factors at work on the author and editor (or editors) of the text. With its appeal to the so-called historical–critical method for gaining an insight into the meaning of the text, this approach is to be associated with the liberal theology stemming from the Enlightenment.

Historicism is based on the view that the historicity of a phenomenon affords the means of comprehending its essence and reality (H. Martin Rumscheidt). It is assumed that meaning is to be found only in the historical web of things. The aim is the historical reconstruction of the text, in other words, seeing the text in its historical and cultural context (*Sitz im Leben*). Historical research, it is supposed, can procure for us the meaning of the Word of God.

Ernst Troeltsch articulated the basic principles of historicism, but this general approach has been conspicuous in J. S. Semler, David Friedrich Strauss, Ferdinand Christian Baur, Adolf von Harnack, and, in our day, Willi Marxsen and Krister Stendahl. A historicist bent was apparent in Rudolf Bultmann and Gerhard Ebeling, especially in their earlier years, though other quite different influences were also at work on them.

It was out of this perspective that the quest for the historical Jesus emerged, since it was believed that only by ascertaining by historical science what Jesus really believed in terms of his own culture and historical period can we find a sure foundation for faith. Albert Schweitzer broke with historicism when he discovered that the historical Jesus indisputably subscribed to an apocalyptic vision of the kingdom of God. Finding this incredible to the modern mind, he sought a new anchor for faith in the mystical Christ.

A third option in hermeneutics is the existentialist one, popularized by Rudolf Bultmann, Ernst Fuchs, Gerhard Ebeling, and Fritz Buri, among others. This approach does not deny the role of historical research but considers it incapable of giving us the significance of the salvific events for human existence. It can tell us much about the thought-world and language of the authors, but it cannot communicate to us the interiority of their faith. Demonstrating an affinity with the Romanticist tradition of Schleiermacher and Dilthey, these men seek to uncover the seminal experience or creative insight of the authors of the texts in question, the experience that was objectified in words. Only by sharing this same kind of experience of entering into the same type of vision do we rightly understand the meaning of the text. Drawing upon both Hegel and Heidegger, these scholars affirm that real knowledge is self-knowledge and that the role of the text is to aid us in self-understanding.

In existentialist hermeneutics history is dissolved into the historicity of existence. The Word becomes formative power rather than informative statement. The message of faith becomes the breakthrough into freedom. Jesus is seen as a witness to faith or the historical occasion for faith rather than the object of faith. It is contended that we should come to Scripture with the presuppositions of existentialist anthropology so that the creative questions of our time can be answered.

In contradistinction to the above approaches I propose a christological hermeneutic by which we seek to move beyond historical criticism to the christological, as opposed to the existential, significance of the text. The text's christological meaning can in fact be shown to carry tremendous import for human existence. I believe that I am here being true to the intent of the scriptural authors themselves and even more to the Spirit who guided them, since they frequently made an effort to relate their revelatory insights to the future acts of cosmic deliverance wrought by the God of Israel (in the case of the Old Testament) or to God's self-revelation in Jesus Christ (in the case of the New Testament). This approach, which is associated with Karl Barth, Jacques Ellul, and Wilhelm Vischer, among others, and which also has certain affinities with the confessional stances of Gerhard von Rad and Brevard Childs, seeks to supplement the historical–critical method by theological exegesis in which the innermost intentions of the author are related to the center and culmination of sacred history mirrored in the Bible, namely, the advent of Jesus Christ. It is believed that the fragmentary insights of both Old and New Testament writers are fulfilled in God's dramatic incursion into human history which we see in the incarnation and atoning sacrifice of Jesus Christ, in his life, death, and resurrection.

Here the aim is to come to Scripture without any overt presuppositions or at least holding these presuppositions in abeyance so that we can hear God's Word anew speaking to us in and through the written text. According to this view, the Word of God is not procured by historical–grammatical examination of the text, nor by historical–critical research, nor by existential analysis, but is instead received in a commitment of faith.

This position has much in common with historical orthodoxy, but one major difference is that it welcomes a historical investigation of the text. Such investigation, however, can only throw light on the cultural and literary background of the text; it does not give us its divinely intended meaning. Another difference is that we seek to understand the text not simply in relation to other texts but in relation to the Christ revelation. Some of the theologians of the older orthodoxy would agree, but others would say that what the Bible tells us about creation, for example, can be adequately understood on its own apart from a reference to the incarnation. With the theology of the Reformation and Protestant orthodoxy, I hold that we should begin by ascertaining the literal sense of the text – what was in the mind of the author – and we can do this only by seeing the passage in question in its immediate context. But then we should press on to discern its christological significance – how it relates to the message of the cross of Jesus Christ.

In opposition to liberalism, I believe that the text should be seen not simply against its immediate historical environment but also against the background of Eternity. To do this, we need to go beyond authorial motivation to theological relation. Moreover, it is neither the faith of Jesus (as in Ebeling) nor the Christ of faith (as in Bultmann and Tillich) but the Jesus Christ of sacred history that is our ultimate norm in faith and conduct.

According to this approach, God reveals himself fully and definitively only in one time and place, viz., in the life history of Jesus Christ. The Bible is the primary witness to this event or series of events. This revelation was anticipated in the Old Testament and remembered and proclaimed in the New Testament . . .

The christological hermeneutic that I propose is in accord with the deepest insights of both Luther and Calvin. Both Reformers saw Christ as the ground and center of Scripture. Both sought to relate the Old Testament, as well as the New, to the person and work of Christ. Their position, which was basically reaffirmed by Barth and Vischer, was that the hidden Christ is in the Old Testament and the manifest Christ in the New Testament.

Luther likened Christ to the "star and kernel" of Scripture, describing him as "the center part of the circle" about which everything else revolves. On one occasion he compared certain texts to "hard nuts" which resisted cracking and confessed that he had to throw these texts against the rock (Christ) so that they would yield their "delicious kernel."

2.31 James I. Packer on the Nature of Revelation

In this passage, first published in 1964, the noted evangelical writer James I. Packer responds to the idea of revelation as God's self-disclosure. This approach was particularly associated with Emil Brunner (see 2.26), but was popularized in England by writers such as William Temple (1881–1944), who wrote of revelation simply in terms of "divine presence". Packer here argues for the impossibility of such a personal self-disclosure without an accompanying informational or verbal element. See also 2.15; 2.24; 2.25; 2.26.

Source: J. I. Packer, *God has Spoken*, 2nd edn (London: Hodder & Stoughton, 1979), pp. 80–2. North American edition published by InterVarsity Press. Reprinted with permission of Hodder & Stoughton.

* * *

What is revelation? From one standpoint it is God's act, from another His gift. From both standpoints it is correlative to man's knowledge of God, as on the one hand an experience and on the other a possession. As God's act, revelation is the personal self-disclosure whereby He brings us actively and experimentally to know Him as our own God and Saviour. As God's gift, revelation is the knowledge about Himself which He gives us as a means to this end. Revelation as God's act takes place through the bestowing of revelation as God's gift; the first sense of the word thus comprehends the second. Accordingly, revelation in the narrower sense ought always to be studied in the setting of revelation in the broader sense.

How does God reveal what has to be revealed in order that we may know Him? By verbal communication from Himself. Without this, revelation in the full and saving sense cannot take place at all. For no public historical happening, as such (an exodus, a conquest, a captivity, a crucifixion, an empty tomb), can reveal God apart from an accompanying word from God to explain it, or a prior promise which it is seen to confirm or fulfil. Revelation in its basic form is thus of necessity propositional; God reveals Himself by telling us about Himself, and what He is doing in His world. The statement in Hebrews 1:1, that in Old Testament days God spoke "in divers manners," reminds us of the remarkable variety of means whereby, according to the record, God's communications were on occasion given: theophanies, angelic announcements, an audible voice from heaven

(Exodus 19:9; Matthew 3:17, 2 Peter 1:17), visions, dreams, signs . . . as well as the more organic type of inspiration, whereby the Spirit of God so controlled the reflective operations of men's minds as to lead them to a right judgment in all things. But in every case the disclosures introduced, or conveyed, or confirmed, by these means were propositional in substance and verbal in form.

Why does God reveal Himself to us? Because, as we saw, He who made us rational beings wants, in His love, to have us as His friends; and He addresses His words to us – statements, commands, promises – as a means of sharing His thoughts with us, and so of making that personal self-disclosure which friendship presupposes, and without which it cannot exist.

What is the content of God's revelation? This is determined primarily by our present plight as sinners. Though we have lapsed into ignorance of God and a godless way of life, God has not abandoned His purpose to have us as His friends; instead, He has resolved in His love to rescue us from sin and restore us to Himself. His plan for doing this was to make Himself known to us as our Redeemer and Re-creator, through the incarnation, death, resurrection and reign of His Son. The working out of this plan required a long series of preparatory events, starting with the promise to the woman's seed (Genesis 3:15) and spanning the whole of Old Testament history. Also, it required a mass of concurrent verbal instruction, predicting each item in the series before it came and applying its lessons in retrospect, so that at each stage men might understand the unfolding history of salvation, hope in the promise of its full accomplishment, and learn what manner of persons they, as objects of grace, ought to be. Thus the history of salvation (the acts of God) took place in the context of the history of revelation (the oracles of God).

Thomas F. Torrance on Karl Barth's Natural Theology

2.32

Thomas F. Torrance, widely regarded as the most important British theologian of the twentieth century, was noted both as an interpreter and translator of Karl Barth. In this important passage, which formed part of the Page-Barbour and James W. Richard Lectures at the University of Virginia, Torrance sets out clearly Karl Barth's fundamental objections to natural theology. See also 2.16; 2.22; 2.25.

Source: Thomas F. Torrance, *The Ground and Grammar of Theology* (Charlottesville: University Press of Virginia, 1980), pp. 87–91. Used by permission of the University Press of Virginia.

* * *

How are we, in the light of all this, to understand Karl Barth's objections to natural theology? They certainly have nothing at all to do with some kind of deistic dualism between God and the world implying no active relation between God and the world, or with some form of Marcionite dualism between redemption and creation implying a depreciation of the creature, as so many of Barth's critics have averred; nor have they to do with a skepticism coupled with a false fideism, such as was condemned by the First Vatican Council. On the contrary, Barth's position rests upon an immense stress on the concrete activity of God in space and time, in creation as in redemption, and upon his refusal to accept that God's power is limited by the weakness of human capacity or that the so-called natural reason can set any limits to God's self-revelation to mankind. The failure to understand Barth at this point is highly revealing, for it indicates that his critics themselves still think within the dualist modes of thought that Barth had himself long left behind, in his restoration of an interactionist understanding of the relation between God and the world in which he operated with an ontological and cognitive bridge between the world and God, which God himself has already established. Thus Barth's objections to traditional natural theology are on grounds precisely the opposite of those attributed to him!

Barth's thought, it must be understood, moves within the orbit of the Reformation's restored emphasis on the creation of the world out of nothing and thus upon its utter contingence, in which the natural is once again allowed to be natural, for nature is set free from the hidden divinzation imposed upon it when it was considered to be impregnated with final causes – the notion of *deus sive natura*. That is the way nature is treated if God is actually thought of as deistically detached from it, so that nature can in some measure substitute for God by providing out of itself a bridge to the divine. Hence Barth attacked the kind of Augustinian metaphysics advocated by Erich Przywara, in which the Aristotelian notion of a divine entelechy embedded in nature was reinforced with a neoplatonic notion of infused grace and enlightenment. Thus it could be claimed that all being is intrinsically analogical to the divine and that man endowed with grace is inherently capable of participating in God. Barth understood the immanentism latent in this theology to be the other side of the deism he found so unacceptable, and in contrast he emphasized all the more the Godness of God and the humanity of man, substituting for an illicit divinity inherent in man – which could easily be made the ground for a synthesis between God and the world – the Judeo-Christian understanding of God's creative, revelatory, and redemptive activity in space and time, as it had come to formulated expression in the theology of the early church, when Christians thought out the interrelation between the incarnation and the creation.

Barth's particularly sharp opposition to Przywara's thought was due to his conviction that this was, from the Roman Catholic side, a new version of the immanentist philosophy that lay behind German romantic idealist thought, within the thought-forms of which Protestant theology in Germany had been so imprisoned that it had lost the ground for any effective opposition to the demonic natural theology of the Nazis. This was also the reason for his no-less-sharp rejection of Emil Brunner's attempt to provide a basis for a Protestant natural theology on the double ground of nature and grace, without coming to grips with the fundamental issues at stake. Apart from these polemics, however, Barth's real objection to traditional natural theology rested on theological and scientific grounds. It is the actual content of our knowledge of God, together with the scientific method that inheres in it, that excludes any movement of thought that arises on some other, independent ground as ultimately irrelevant and as an inevitable source of confusion when it is adduced as a second or co-ordinate basis for positive theology.

So far as theological content is concerned, Barth's argument runs like this. If the God whom we have actually come to know through Jesus Christ really is Father, Son, and Holy Spirit in his own eternal and undivided Being, then what are we to make of an independent natural theology that terminates, not upon the Being of the triune God – i.e., upon God as he really is in himself – but upon some Being of God in general? Natural theology by its very operation abstracts the existence of God from his act, so that if it does not begin with deism, it imposes deism upon theology. If really to know God through his saving activity in our world is to know him as triune, then the doctrine of the Trinity belongs to the very groundwork of knowledge of God from the very start, which calls in question any doctrine of God as the one God gained apart from his trinitarian activity – but that is the kind of knowledge of God that is yielded in natural theology of the traditional kind.

So far as scientific method is concerned, Barth demands a rigorous mode of inquiry in which form and content, method and subject-matter are inseparably joined together, and he rejects any notion that we can establish how we know apart from our actual knowledge and its material content. Thus Barth stands squarely on the same grounds as rigorous science when he insists on the freedom to develop a scientific method appropriate to the field of theological inquiry and to elaborate epistemological structures under the compulsion of the nature of the object as it becomes disclosed in the progress of the inquiry, quite untrammelled by a priori assumptions of any kind or by any preconceptions deriving from some other field of investigation. As an a posteriori science, theology involves the questioning of all presuppositions and all structures of thought independent of or antecedent to its own operations. This is why Barth makes so much of the epistemological implications of justification by grace alone, for it forces upon us relentless questioning of all we thought we knew beforehand, or of all prejudgments and external authorities, philosophical or ecclesiastical, in such a way that in the last resort theology is thrown back wholly upon the nature and activity of God for the justification or verification of our concepts and statements about him. It is here in the doctrine of justification that we can see clearly how form and content, method and subject-matter, in theological inquiry coincide.

Epistemologically, then, what Barth objects to in traditional natural theology is not any invalidity in its argumentation, nor even its rational structure, as such, but its *independent* character – i.e., the autonomous rational structure that natural theology develops on the ground of "nature alone," in abstraction from the active self-disclosure of the living and Triune God – for that can only split the knowledge of God into two parts, natural knowledge of the One God and revealed knowledge of the triune God, which is scientifically as well as theologically intolerable. This is not to reject the place of a proper rational structure in knowledge of God, such as natural theology strives for, but to insist that unless that rational structure is intrinsically bound up with the actual content of knowledge of God, it is a distorting abstraction. That is why Barth claims that, properly understood, natural theology is included within revealed theology, where we have to do with actual knowledge of God as it is grounded in the intelligible relations in God himself, for it is there under the compulsion of God's self-disclosure in Being and Act that the rational structure appropriate to him arises in our understanding of him. But in the nature of the case it is not a rational structure that can be abstracted from the actual knowledge of God with which it is integrated, and made to stand on its own as an independent or autonomous system of thought, for then it would be meaningless, like something that is complete and consistent in itself but without any ontological reference beyond itself: it becomes merely a game to be enjoyed like chess – which Barth is as ready to enjoy as much as anyone else, although he cannot take it seriously.

Study Questions to Chapter 2

Why is the idea of "tradition" so important to Irenaeus?

In the view of Augustine, has the New Testament rendered the Old Testament obsolete?

Which late patristic writer affirmed the importance of universality, antiquity and consensus in matters of doctrine? And what did he mean by this?

What three points of continuity between the Old and New Testaments does Calvin identify?

"The Bible is only infallible if interpreted properly." Assess the different approaches of Johann Adam Möhler and Archibald Alexander Hodge to this statement.

According to T. F. Torrance, why was Karl Barth so critical of any attempt to find knowledge of God in nature?

3 The Doctrine of God

The term theology literally means "talk about God." Although the modern understanding of the word now goes beyond this, meaning something like "the study of the distinctive ideas of a religion," this point reminds us of the centrality of God to Christian theology. The collection of readings assembled in this chapter surveys a range of issues concerning the doctrine of God.

A major issue in recent theological discussion has been whether God can be said to suffer. STUDY PANEL 8 brings together a selection of texts which address this issue, which has become of particular importance since the First World War, partly in response to a perceived need to relate God to the suffering of the human situation. As the texts will indicate, there was discussion of the relation of God and human suffering within the Christian tradition long before the First World War focused attention on this issue.

One of the most important themes to note here is that of the Trinity – the distinctively Christian understanding of the nature of God. The readings noted in STUDY PANEL 9 focus on this theme, dealing with the reasons for conceiving of God in this way, and with ways of making sense of what is generally conceded to be a difficult doctrine to understand.

However, the theme of the Trinity by no means exhausts any Christian discussion of the nature of God. Several classic debates are touched on in this collection of readings, including the way in which God can be considered to have created the world, what it means to speak of God as all-powerful, and the distinctive character of the Holy Spirit.

One other theme dealt with in this collection has emerged as particularly important in more recent times. An increased awareness of the past tendency of male theologians to treat women as invisible has led to increased interest in whether God is to be thought of as "male." This debate is reflected both in the discussion of God, and also in discussions concerning the identity and significance of Jesus Christ.

STUDY PANEL 8

Does God Suffer?

STUDY PANEL 9

The Trinity

3.1   Athenagoras of Athens on the Christian God

In this defense of the Christian faith against pagan criticisms, written in Greek around 177 and addressed to the Roman emperors Marcus Aurelius Antonius and Lucius Aurelius Commodus, Athenagoras sets out the main features of the gospel in a lucid and reasoned manner. The early Christians were accused of atheism on account of their refusal to worship the emperor. In this extract, in which Athenagoras explains what Christians believe about God, important anticipations of later thinking on the Trinity can be detected. The work is known by various names, including *Apologia*, *Legatio* (as in this edition), and *Supplicatio pro Christianis*. See also 1.1; 1.2; 1.3; 1.4.

Source: *Apologia*, X, 1–4; in *Athenagoras: Legatio and De Resurrectionem* ed. W. R. Schoedel (Oxford: Clarendon Press, 1972), pp. 20–2.

* * * ──

So we are not atheists, in that we acknowledge one God, who is uncreated, eternal, invisible, impassible, incomprehensible, and without limit. He is apprehended only by the intellect and the mind, and is surrounded by light, beauty, spirit, and indescribable power. The universe was created and ordered, and is presently sustained, through his Logos . . . For we acknowledge also a "Son of God." Nobody should think it ridiculous that God should have a son. Although the pagan poets, in their fictions, represent the gods as being no better than human beings, we do not think in the same way as they do concerning either God the Father or God the Son. For the Son of God is the Logos of the Father, both in thought and in reality. It was through his action, and after his pattern, that all things were made, in that the Father and Son are one . . . [The Son] is the first creation of the Father – not meaning that he was brought into existence, in that, from the beginning, God, who is the eternal mind (*nous*), had the Logos within himself, being eternally of the character of the Logos (*logikos*). Rather, it is meant that he came forth to be the pattern and motivating power of all physical things . . . We affirm that the Holy Spirit, who was active in the prophets, is an effluence of God, who flows from him and returns to him, like a beam of the sun.

3.2   Irenaeus on the Origin of Evil

This second-century work, originally written in Greek but now known only in an Armenian translation, sets out the view that the origin of evil lies in human frailty. God did not create humanity in perfection, but with the capacity for this perfection through a process of growth. The initial vulnerability of humanity thus led directly to its seduction. See also 3.6; 3.13; 6.1.

Source: *Demonstration of the Apostolic Preaching*, 12; in *Sources Chrétiennes*, vol. 62, ed. L. M. Froidevaux (Paris: Cerf, 1965), pp. 50–2.

* * * ──

God made humanity to be master of the earth and of all which was there
... Yet this could only take place when humanity had attained its adult
stage ... Yet humanity was little, being but a child. It had to grow and reach
full maturity ... God prepared a place for humanity which was better than
this world ... a paradise of such beauty and goodness that the Word of
God constantly walked in it, and talked with humanity; prefiguring that
future time when he would live with human beings and talk with them,
associating with human beings and teaching the n righteousness. But
humanity was a child; and its mind was not yet fully mature; and thus
humanity was easily led astray by the deceiver.

Irenaeus on the Trinity   3.3

This important statement of the basic elements of the doctrine of the Trinity is set out in a
creedal form, presumably to allow its readers to relate the passage to any of the creeds then
in circulation. The importance of the passage lies in the way in which it clearly assigns distinct
functions to each person of the Trinity, and links the three persons together as a "rule of faith,"
which expresses the distinctively Christian understanding of the nature of God. See also 3.10;
3.11; 3.12; 3.14; 3.15; 3.19; 3.30; 3.31; 3.34.

Source: *Demonstration of the Apostolic Preaching*, 6; in *Sources Chrétiennes*, vol. 62, ed. L. M. Froidevaux
(Paris: Cerf, 1965), pp. 39–40.

---
                                                                    * * *

This is the rule of our faith, the foundation of the building, and what gives
support to our behaviour.

God the Father uncreated, who is uncontained, invisible, one God, creator
of the universe; this is the first article of our faith. And the second is:

The *Word of God*, the Son of God, our Lord Jesus Christ, who appeared
to the prophets according to their way of prophesying, and according to the
dispensation of the Father. Through him all things were created. Furthermore, in the fulness of time, in order to gather all things to himself, he
became a human being amongst human beings, capable of being seen and
touched, to destroy death, bring life, and restore fellowship betwe. n God
and humanity. And the third article is:

The *Holy Spirit*, through whom the prophets prophesied, and our forebears learned of God and the righteous were led in the paths of justice, and
who, in the fulness of time, was poured out in a new way on our human
nature in order to renew humanity throughout the entire world in the sight
of God.

3.4   Tertullian on Creation from Pre-Existent Matter

In this controversial work, written to refute the views of his opponent Hermogenes, Tertullian deals with Hermogenes' idea that God created the world out of pre-existing matter. How can God be Lord, he asked, unless there has always been something – such as pre-existent matter – to rule? Tertullian argues that a distinction may be drawn between the terms "God" and "Lord." God has always been "God"; he only became "Lord" when there was something to be Lord over – in other words, once the creation had been brought into being. Tertullian's views should be compared with those of Origen (3.5) at this point.

Source: *adversus Hermogenem*, 2–3; in *Stromata Patristica et Medievalia*, ed. C. Mohrmann and J. Quasten. *Quinti Septimi Florentis Tertulliani adversus Hermogenem Liber*, ed. J. H. Waszink (Utrecht: Spectrum, 1956), 16.10–18.7.

* * *

[Hermogenes] argues that God made everything either out of himself, or out of nothing, or out of something. His intention here is to refute the first two of these possibilities, and to establish the third, namely, that God created out of something, and that the "something" was matter (*materia*). He argues that God could not have created anything out of himself, because whatever he created would then have been part of himself. But God cannot be reduced to parts in this way, in that he is indivisible and unchangeable, and always the same, in that he is Lord. Further, anything made of himself would have been something of himself. His creation and his creating would then have to be accounted as being imperfect, so that they are only a partial creation and a partial creating. Or if God completely made a complete creation, then God must have been at one and the same time complete and incomplete; complete, that he might make himself, and incomplete, that he might be made of himself. There is a further serious difficulty; if he existed he could not be created, if he did not exist, he could not create. Again he who always exists cannot become, but is for everlasting. Therefore he did not create out of himself; that would be inconsistent with his nature. Similarly, he argues that he could not have created out of nothing. He defines God as good, totally good, and therefore wishing to make all things good, just as totally good as he is himself ... but evil is found in his creation, and this is certainly not according to his will ... therefore we must assume it came into being as a result of a fault in something, and that something is undoubtedly matter.

He adds another argument; God has always been God, and always Lord. Now he could not be regarded as always Lord, as he is always God, if there had not been something already existing over which he could be accounted Lord. Therefore matter always existed for God to be always Lord over it ... We maintain that he always has the title of God, but not always that of Lord; for the nature of these two titles is different. God is the title of the substance, the divine nature: Lord the title of power ... He became Lord and acquired that name from the time when things came into being over which the power of the Lord was exercised: the position and the title come through the accession of power. God is father and judge: but it does not follow that he is father and judge eternally because he is always God. He could not be father before he had a son; nor a judge before sin was committed.

Origen on Creation from Pre-Existent Matter 3.5

In this work, written in the first half of the third century, Origen argues that God created the world from pre-existing matter. This matter is understood to be formless, so that the act of creation consists in fashioning this material into its proper form. Origen's views on this matter should be compared with those of Tertullian (3.4).

Source: de principiis, II.i.4; in Sources Chrétiennes, vol. 252, ed. H. Crouzel and M. Simonetti (Paris: Editions du Cerf, 1978), 242.118–244.156.

* * *

For this material is so considerable and of such a nature that it is enough for the creation of all the bodies of the world, to whom God wishes to give existence, and can serve the creator in any way which he wishes in making all the forms and species, and in providing them with the qualities which he wished to impose upon them. I do not understand how so many distinguished people have thought that it was uncreated, that is to say, that it was not made by God, the creator of the world; or how they thought that its nature and action were the result of chance. I am astonished that these people blame those who deny that God is the creator and sustainer of the world, accusing them of impious thoughts, because they hold that the work (opus) of the world endures without a creator or someone to tend it, when they themselves are just as guilty of impiety when they say that matter is uncreated (ingenitus) and co-eternal with the uncreated God. According to this line of thought, God would have had nothing to do, not having any matter with which he could have begun his work; for they allege that he could not make anything out of nothing, and that matter was present by chance rather than by God's design. They thus believe that something which came into being by chance could be good enough for the mighty work of creation . . . This seems to me to be absurd, the result of people who ignore the power and the intelligence of the uncreated nature. But, in order to be able to consider the arguments at stake here, let us suppose provisionally that matter did not exist, and that God, at a point at which nothing existed, gave existence to whatever he wished. What follows? That this material which God was obliged to create, and to bring into existence through his power and wisdom, could have been better or superior to, or something very different from, what these people call "uncreated"? Or, on the contrary, that it could have been inferior or worse, or even similar or identical?

I think that it is clear that neither a better material, nor a worse material, could have taken on the forms and species which are in the world; it would have had to be the kind of matter which, in fact, actually did assume them. Therefore it must be considered impious to call something "uncreated" which, if it is believed to have been created by God, would undoubtedly be found to be of the same type as that which is called "uncreated."

3.6 Origen on the Relation of God and Evil

This passage develops the idea of "necessary evil," which, within God's providence, can lead to the fulfillment of his purposes. It is not God's intention or will that evil should exist in the world. However, given that it does exist, God is able to direct it in such a way that good comes out of it. Origen illustrates this by pointing out how the treachery of Judas led to the redemption of the world through the death of Christ. See also 3.2; 3.13.

Source: *Homilia in Numeros*, XIV, 2; in J. P. Migne, *Patrologia Graeca*, 12.677D–678A; 678C–679A.

* * *

God does not create evil; still, he does not prevent it when it is shown by others, although he could do so. But he uses both evil and those who show it for necessary purposes. For through those in whom there is evil, he brings distinction and testing to those who strive for the glory of virtue. Virtue, if unopposed, would not shine out nor become more glorious by being tested. Virtue is not virtue if it be untested and unexamined . . . If you remove the wickedness of Judas and cancel his treachery you take away likewise the cross of Christ and his passion: and if there were no cross then principalities and powers have not been stripped nor triumphed over by the wood of the cross. Had there been no death of Christ, there would certainly have been no resurrection and there would have been no "firstborn from the dead" (Colossians 1:18) and then there would have been no hope of resurrection for us. Similarly concerning the devil himself, if we suppose, for the sake of argument, that he had been forcibly prevented from sinning, or that the will to do evil had been taken away from him after his sin; then at the same time there would have been taken from us the struggle against the wiles of the devil, and there would be no crown of victory in store for those who struggled.

3.7 Origen on the Suffering of God

This remarkable third-century passage suggests that God was understood to experience suffering, on account of the incarnation. This runs counter to the prevailing consensus of the early patristic period, which insisted that Christ suffered only in his human nature, leaving his divinity immune from such suffering. Although originally written in Greek, this text survives only in the Latin translation of Rufinus of Aquilea. It is possible that a slight distortion in Origen's meaning may have resulted in translation. Note the different view found in 3.8. See also 3.18; 3.20; 3.26; 3.29; 3.32.

Source: *Homilia in Ezechiel*, VI, 6; in *Sources Chrétiennes*, vol. 352, ed. Marcel Borret (Paris: Editions du Cerf, 1989), 228.35–230.49.

* * *

[The savior] descended to earth to grieve for the human race, and took our sufferings on himself before he endured the cross and deigned to assume our flesh. If he had not suffered, he would not have come to share in human life. What is this suffering which he suffered for us beforehand? It is the suffering of love. For the Father himself, the God of the universe, who is "long-suffering and full of mercy" (cf. Psalm 102:8) and merciful, does he not suffer in some way (*nonne quodammodo patitur*)? Or do you now know that, when he deals with humanity, he suffers human suffering (*passionem patitur humanam*)? "For the Lord your God has taken your ways upon him as a man bears his son" (cf. Deuteronomy 1:31). Therefore God has taken our ways upon himself, just as the Son of God bore our sufferings. The Father himself is not impassible (*Ipse Pater non est impassibilis*).

Origen on the Changelessness of God 3.8

In this passage, Origen argues that the Word of God is not changed in any temporal way by the Incarnation. The Word therefore does not suffer human pain, whether physical or mental. This suggests that Origen upholds the traditional view of the *apatheia* of God. Compare this passage with the different view expressed in 3.7. See also 3.18; 3.20; 3.26; 3.29; 3.32.

Source: *Contra Celsum*, IV, 15; in *Sources Chrétiennes*, vol. 136, ed. M. Borret (Paris: Cerf, 1968), 220.18–27.

* * *

It seems to Celsus that the assumption by the immortal divine Word of a mortal body and a human soul means a temporal change and alteration. He ought to learn that the Word remains the Word in his essential being and does not suffer what the body or soul suffers; that he comes down at a certain time to be with him who cannot behold the splendour and brightness of his godhead, and as it were becomes flesh, or to use physical terms, until he who has received him in this shape, being gradually raised to a higher level by the Word, may be able to gaze upon what I may call his primary form.

Basil of Caesarea on the Work of the Holy Spirit 3.9

After reflecting on the biblical terms used for the Holy Spirit, Basil turns to deal with the particular roles of the Spirit. After an initial discussion of the role of the Spirit in sanctification, Basil notes the work of the Spirit in relation to "being made like God" and "being made God." The close connection between the Spirit and deification is a distinctive feature of much eastern Greek thought of this period. See also 3.3; 3.10; 3.14; 3.16; 3.17; 4.19; 5.25.

Source: *de spiritu sancto*, IX, 22–3; in *The Book of Saint Basil the Great on the Holy Spirit*, ed. C. F. H. Johnston (Oxford: Clarendon Press, 1892), pp. 51–4.

* * *

He is called "Spirit of God" (Matthew 12:28), "Spirit of truth which proceeds from the Father" (John 15:26), "right Spirit" (Psalm 51:12), "Lord Spirit" (Psalm 50:14). His proper and peculiar title is 'Holy Spirit', which is a name specially appropriate to all that is not physical, purely immaterial and indivisible. That is why the Lord, when teaching the woman who thought God was an object of local worship that what is not physical cannot be limited, said, "God is Spirit" (John 4:24). So it is not possible when one hears this name of Spirit to conceive of a limited nature, which is subject to change and variation, or at all like any creature. On the contrary, we have to raise our thought to the highest level and think of a substance endowed with intelligence, of infinite power, of a greatness which knows no limit, which cannot be measured in times or ages, and which lavishes its good gifts.

All who are in need of sanctification turn to the Spirit; all those seek him who live by virtue, for his breath refreshes them and comes to their aid in the pursuit of their natural and proper end. Capable of perfecting others, the Spirit himself lacks nothing. He is not a being who needs to restore his strength, but himself supplies life; he does not grow by additions, but possesses abundant fullness; he abides in himself, but is also present everywhere. The source of sanctification, a light perceptible to the mind, he supplies through himself illumination to every force of reason searching for the truth. By nature inaccessible, he can be understood by reason of his goodness; filling all things with his power, he communicates himself only to those who are worthy of him, not by sharing himself according to a unique measure but by distributing his energy in proportion to faith. Simple in essence, varied in his miracles, he is wholly present to everyone and wholly everywhere at the same time. He is shared without being affected; he remains whole and yet gives himself in the sharing, like a sunbeam whose warming light shines on the one who enjoys it as though it shone for him alone, yet lights land and sea and mingles with the air. Similarly, the Spirit is present to all who are capable of receiving him as though given to them alone, and yet he sends forth full and sufficient grace for all humanity, and is enjoyed by all who share in him, according to the capacity, not of his power but of their nature. Souls in which the Spirit dwells, illuminated by the Spirit, themselves become spiritual and send forth their grace to others. From here comes foreknowledge of the future, understanding of mysteries, apprehension of what is hidden, the sharing of the gifts of grace, heavenly citizenship, a place in the chorus of angels, joy without end, abiding in God, being made like God and – the greatest of them all – being made divine.

Gregory of Nazianzen on the Gradual Revelation of the Trinity 3.10

In this work, written around 380, Gregory sets out the main features of the Christian faith. In this section, he explains why the doctrine of the Trinity is not explicitly stated in Scripture. Note especially his understanding of the gradual revelation of the doctrine, through the guidance of the Holy Spirit within the church. Note also that the "theological orations" are generally distinguished from the "orations" as a whole, of which they are part. "Theological Oration 1" is "Oration 27," "Theological Oration 5" is "Oration 31," and so forth. See also 3.3; 3.11; 3.12; 3.14; 3.15; 3.19; 3.30; 3.31; 3.34.

Source: *Oratio theologica*, V, 26 [= *Oratio XXXI*, 26]; in *Sources Chrétiennes* vol. 250, ed. Paul Gallay and Maurice Jourjon (Paris: Cerf, 1978), 326.4–16.

* * *

The Old Testament preached the Father openly and the Son more obscurely. The New Testament revealed the Son, and hinted at the divinity of the Holy Spirit. Now the Spirit dwells in us, and is revealed more clearly to us. It was not proper to preach the Son openly, while the divinity of the Father had not yet been admitted. Nor was it proper to accept the Holy Spirit before [the divinity of] the Son had been acknowledged ... Instead, by gradual advances and ... partial ascents, we should move forward and increase in clarity, so that the light of the Trinity (*Trias*) should shine.

Hilary of Poitiers on the Trinity 3.11

In this important witness to the role of the Trinitarian formula in baptism, and more specifically the relation of the Spirit to the Father and Son, Hilary emphasizes that the Christian faith rests upon revelation, rather than reason. The most important section of the passage sets out an understanding of the relation of the Spirit to the Father and the Son: the Spirit is "from the Father" and "through the Son." See also 3.3; 3.10; 3.12; 3.14; 3.15; 3.19; 3.30; 3.31; 3.34.

Source: *de Trinitate*, XII, 52, 57; in *Corpus Christianorum: Series Latina*, vol. 62A, ed. P. Smulders (Turnholt: Brepols, 1980), 622.1–9; 627.1–11.

* * *

For as long as I enjoy the life which you have given me by your Spirit, O Holy Father, Omnipotent God, I shall proclaim you as the eternal God and also as the eternal Father. Nor shall I ever show such folly and impiety as to make myself judge of your omnipotence and mysteries, and put the feeble understanding of my weakness above a true understanding of your infinity and faith in your eternity. I shall never declare that you could have existed without your wisdom, your virtue, your word: the only-begotten God, my Lord Jesus Christ ...

Preserve, I ask of you, this piety of my faith without any contamination, and to the end of my life give me this awareness of my knowledge, that I always may hold fast to what I possess, that is, what I professed in the creed of my regeneration when I was baptized in the name of the Father, and of the Son, and of the Holy Spirit. Grant that I may adore you, our Father, and your Son together with you, and that I may be worthy of the Holy Spirit who is from you through your only-begotten (*sanctum Spiritum tuum qui ex te per unigenitum tuum est*). He bears witness to my faith who says, "Father, all things that are mine are yours, and yours are mine" – my Lord Jesus Christ, who for ever abides as God in you, from you and with you, who is blessed for ever and ever. Amen.

3.12 Augustine on the Trinity

In this important discussion, originally written over the period 400–416, Augustine sets out a distinctive approach to the Trinity which would have a major impact on western Trinitarian thought. The passage is notable on account of its detailed analysis of the concept of "love," in which it is argued that this concept necessarily implies a lover, a beloved, and their mutual love. On the basis of this psychological analogy, Augustine argues for a threefold understanding of the Godhead, in terms of Father, Son and Holy Spirit. See also 3.3; 3.10; 3.11; 3.14; 3.15; 3.19; 3.30; 3.31; 3.34.

Source: *de Trinitate*, IX.i.1–v.8; in *Corpus Christianorum: Series Latina*, vol. 50, ed. W. J. Mountain (Turnholt: Brepols, 1968), 293.33–301.31.

* * *

We believe that Father, Son and Holy Spirit are one God, maker and ruler of every creature, and that "Father" is not "Son," nor "Holy Spirit" "Father" or "Son"; but a Trinity of mutually related persons, and a unity of equal essence. So let us attempt to understand this truth, praying that he who we wish to understand would help us in doing so, so that we can set out whatever we thus understand with such careful reverence that nothing unworthy is said (even if we sometimes say one thing instead of another). In this way, if we say something about the Father which is not properly appropriate to him, it may be appropriate to the Son or to the Holy Spirit, or to the whole Trinity; or if we say something about the Son which does not properly apply to the Son, it may at least apply to the Father, or to the Holy Spirit, or to the whole Trinity; or if we say something about the Holy Spirit which is not proper in his case, then it may not be incorrect in the case of the Father or the Son, or the one God which is the Trinity itself. Now we want to see whether that most excellent gift of love is properly the Holy Spirit. If this is not the case, then either the Father is love, or the Son is, or the whole Trinity is (since we may not oppose the certainty of faith and most valid authority of the Scripture which says "God is love" (1 John 4:8, 16). But we must never allow any error to lead us astray in such a way that we say something about the Trinity which relates to the *creature* rather than the *Creator*, or results from wild speculation.

In view of all this let us consider those three things which we wish to discover more about. We are not yet talking about things in heaven, nor about God, Father, Son, and Holy Spirit; but about this flawed image (but an image none the less), that is, humanity, which is so much more familiar and less difficult for the weakness of our mind to study.

Now when I, who am asking about this, love anything, there are three things present: I myself, what I love, and love itself. For I cannot love love unless I love a lover (*non enim amo amorem nisi amantem*); for there is no love where nothing is loved. So there are three things: the lover, the loved, and love (*amans et quod amatur et amor*). Yet if the object of my love is myself, then the three become two – the object of love, and love. For when the lover loves himself, subject and object are the same; just as loving and being loved are in the love of self the same thing. So there would be no difference between saying "he loves himself," and "he is loved by himself." In that case, "to love" and "to be loved" are not two things, any more than the lover and the loved are two persons. But still the love and what is loved remain two. For the one who loves himself can be identical with love only if love itself is what is loved. It is one thing to love oneself and another to love one's love, since love which is loved must love something, because when nothing is loved, there is no love. So there are two things present when someone loves themselves, love and what is loved (the lover and the loved being one). From this it seems that three things are not understood to be present wherever there is love.

Let us remove from this discussion all the other things of which human nature is composed, so that we may find what we are looking for in as clear a form as possible. So let us take the mind alone. In the love of the mind for itself, two things are shown – mind and love. Now what is love of oneself other than the will to be at one's own disposal for self-enjoyment? If the mind wills itself to be what it is, then "will" corresponds to "mind" and "love" to "lover." If love is some kind of substance, it is not body but spirit, just as the mind is not body but spirit. Yet the mind and its love are not two spirits, but one spirit, not two essences but one. In other words, the two are as one, "lover" and "love," or (as you might say) "love" and "that which is loved." And these two are mutually related terms; "lover" being related to "love" and "love" to "lover"; for the lover loves in virtue of a particular love and love is the activity of a particular lover. Mind and spirit, on the other hand, are not relative terms but refer to essence in itself. It is not the fact that mind and spirit belong to a particular human being that determines that they are mind and spirit. Remove whatever it is that, being added, constitutes a human being (that is, the body), and mind and spirit will still remain. But remove the lover and there will be no love; remove the love and there will be no lover. Thus these two terms are mutually related: in themselves, each is spirit, and both together are one spirit; each is mind, and both together are one mind. Where then is there a trinity? Let us consider this as best we are able, asking the everlasting Light to lighten our darkness, that we may see in ourselves *the image of God*.

The mind cannot love itself unless it also knows itself. How can it love something it does not know? The suggestion that the mind forms either a general or a specific knowledge (*notitia*) from its experience of other minds, and believes itself to belong to the same class of being and on that basis loves itself, is to be regarded as absurd. How can a mind know any other mind, if it does not know itself?. . . We may say then that the mind acquires knowledge of physical things by the bodily senses, and of things that are not physical through the fact that it is not physical. It must know itself by itself: if it does not know itself, it cannot love itself.

Now just as there are two things (the mind and its love) present when it loves itself, so there are also two things present, the mind and its knowledge, when it knows itself. So there are three things – the mind, its love, and its knowledge (*mens et amor et notitia eius*) – which are one, and when perfect they are equal. If it loves itself less than the word implies – as, for example, if the human mind, which is greater than the human body, loves itself only with the love due to the human body – then it sins, and its love is not perfect. Again, if it loves itself more than it should – as, for example, if the human mind loves itself with the love due to God, to whom it is incomparably inferior – then it also sins greatly, and its love is not perfect. It sins in a particularly perverse and iniquitous manner when it loves the body to the extent that God is to be loved. Similarly a knowledge which falls short of its object, where full knowledge is possible, is not perfect. A knowledge which is greater than its object implies a superiority in the nature of the knower to that of the known: the knowledge of a body is greater than the body which is the object of the knowledge. For knowledge is a mode of life in the knowing mind, whereas the body is not life; and any life is greater, not in extent but in power, than any body. But when the mind knows itself, the knowledge does not exceed the self, for the self is both subject and object of the knowledge. If it knows the whole of itself, without anything else being added from outside, the knowing corresponds to the mind; for it is no less apparent that in this knowledge of itself the knowing is not dependent on any other source. And when this knowledge takes in the whole self and nothing more, it is neither less nor greater than the self. Thus it is true to say that when each member of these three is perfect, it follows that all three are equal.

Now we are challenged to see how these [three things] are present in the soul . . . The mind knows not only itself but many other things as well. Therefore love and knowledge (*cognitio*) are not present in the mind simply as aspects of their subject: their existence is as substantive as that of the mind itself. They are to be understood as mutually related things, each of which are distinctive substances. As mutually related things they cannot be compared to "color" and "that which is colored" (*color et coloratum*), in that the color possesses no substance proper to itself: the substance is the colored body; the color is in the substance. It is like two friends, who are both men and are therefore substances. While "men" is not a relative term, whereas "friends" is.

"Lover" and "knower," "knowledge" and "love" are all substances. But while "lover" and "love," "knower" and "knowledge" are – like "friends" – relative terms, "mind" and "spirit" – like "men" – are not. Now men who are friends can exist apart from each another. Yet this is not the case with "lover" and "love," "knower" and "knowledge." It may seem that friends can be separated in body only and not in soul. But it is possible for a friend to begin to hate his friend and thereby cease to be his friend, though the other may not know it and may continue to love him. On the other hand, if the love with which the mind loves itself ceases to exist, the mind will also cease to be a lover. Similarly, if the knowledge with which the mind knows itself ceases to exist, the mind will cease to know itself . . .

If any bodies exist which cannot be severed or divided in any way, they must still consist of their parts or they would not be bodies. "Part" and "whole" are related terms, since every part belongs to some whole, and the whole is whole on account of its totality of parts. But since the body is both "part" and "whole," these exist not only as mutually related terms but as substances. It may thus be said that the mind is a whole, and that the love with which it loves itself and the knowledge with which it knows itself are like two parts composing the whole; or that they and the mind itself are equal parts making up the one whole . . . Wine, water, and honey make a single, in which each of these will extend throughout the whole, and yet they remain three. There would be no part of the drink which does not contain all three – not side by side as in the case of oil and water, but completely mixed. All are substances, and the whole fluid is one definite substance made out of the three. Can we suppose that the three things – mind, love and knowledge – exist together in the same sort of way? Yet water, wine and honey do not derive from a single substance, though one single substance of drink results from that mixture. But I do not see how these three are not the same essence, since the mind loves itself and knows itself, without being loved or known by anything else. The three must then necessarily have one and the same essence, so that if they were to be inter-mingled in such a way as to be confused, they would not be three things nor could they be said to be in a mutual relation. It would be like three similar rings made out of the same gold, which are mutually related on the basis of their similarity, since everything that is similar is similar to some-thing else, and there would be a trinity of rings (*trinitas anulorum*) and one gold. However, if they were mixed together to form a single lump, this trinity would be destroyed. We could still speak of "one gold" as in these three rings, but no longer of three golden objects.

In the case of the three things by which the mind knows and loves itself, the trinity of mind, love, and knowledge remains (*manet trinitas, mens, amor, notitia*). There is no intermingling or loss of identity . . . The mind is distinct in itself, and is itself called "mind," even though it is termed "knowing," "known," or "knowable" in relation to its knowledge, and "loving," "loved," or "lovable" in relation to the love with which it loves itself. Knowledge is indeed related to the mind which knows or is known, but it is still properly termed "known" and "knowing" in itself, for the knowledge by which the mind knows itself is not unknown to the knowledge itself. Similarly love, though related to the loving mind to which it belongs, still remains distinct by itself and in itself; for love is loved, and that can only be by the love itself. This shows that each of the three is distinct in itself. Again, they are

alternately in one another: the loving mind is in the love, love is in the
lover's knowledge, and knowledge in the knowing mind ... In a wonderful
way, the three are inseparable from one another, and yet each one of them
is a distinct substance, and all together are one substance or essence, even
though they are said to be mutually related to each another.

3.13 Augustine on the Relation of God and Evil

In his early period, Augustine was attracted to Manicheism, partly because it provided a simple
explanation of the origin of evil. According to this movement, evil had its origins in an evil or
defective deity, who was opposed to the true and righteous God. On becoming a Christian,
Augustine rejected this dualism, and was therefore obliged to give an alternative explanation
of the origins of evil. In this passage, written in Latin during the period 388–95, he argues that
evil represents a free turning away from God, rather than a positive entity in its own right.
However, he is unable to provide a convincing explanation of why someone should wish to turn
away from God in this manner. See also 3.2; 3.4; 3.5.

Source: de libero arbitrio, II.xx.54; in Corpus Scriptorum Ecclesiasticorum Latinorum, vol. 74, ed. W. M.
Green (Vienna: Hoelder–Pichler–Tempsky, 1961), 87.18–88.20.

* * *

If there is a movement, that is a turning away (aversio) of the human will
from the Lord God, which without doubt is sin, can we then say that God
is the author of sin? God, then, will not be the cause of that movement. But
what will its cause be? If you ask this question, I will have to answer that
I do not know. While this will sadden you, it is nevertheless a true answer.
For that which is nothing cannot be known. But hold to your pious opinion
that no good thing can happen to you, to your senses or to your intelligence
or to your way of thinking which does not come from God. Nothing of any
kind can happen which is not of God ... For all good is from God. Hence
there is no nature which is not from God. The movement of turning away,
which we admit is sin, is a defective movement; and all defect comes from
nothing. Once you have understood where it belongs, you will have no
doubt that it does not belong to God. Because that defective movement is
voluntary, it is placed within our power. If you fear it, all you have to do
is simply not to will it. If you do not will it, it will not exist. What can be
safer than to live a life where nothing can happen to you which you do not
will? But since we cannot rise by our own free will as we once fell by our
own free will spontaneously, let us hold with steadfast faith the right hand
of God stretched out to us from above, even our Lord Jesus Christ, and look
forward to receiving the certain hope and love which we greatly long for.

Augustine on the Holy Spirit

The text deals with the distinctive role and identiy of the Holy Spirit within the Trinity, and especially the manner in which the Holy Spirit can be thought of as "love." In this discussion, originally written in Latin over the period 400–416, Augustine develops an argument for it being especially appropriate to think of the Holy Spirit in terms of "lover," while at the same time recognizing the involvement of the entire Trinity in the process. The major difficulty which Augustine is obliged to face is that there is no biblical text which explicitly affirms that the "Holy Spirit is love." For this reason, Augustine is obliged to enter into a complex – and, to some of his critics, somewhat unconvincing – argument to show that this is implied by the texts in question. See also 3.3; 3.9; 3.10; 3.11; 3.12; 3.15; 3.19; 3.30; 3.31; 3.34.

Source: de Trinitate, XV.xvii.27–xviii, 32; in Corpus Christianorum: Series Latina, vol. 50A, ed. W. J. Mountain (Turnholt: Brepols, 1968), 501.34–508.32.

* * *

We have now said as much concerning the Father and the Son as we have found possible to discern by means of this dark mirror (1 Corinthians 13:12) of the human mind. Now we must consider, with such insight as God's gift may grant us, the Holy Spirit. Scripture teaches us that he is the Spirit neither of the Father alone nor of the Son alone, but of both; and this suggests to us the mutual love (caritas) by which the Father and the Son love one another . . . Yet Scripture does not say: "the Holy Spirit is love." If it did, much of our inquiry would have been rendered unnecessary. Scripture does indeed say: "God is love" (1 John 4:8, 16); and so has left us to ask whether it is God the Father, or God the Son, or God the Holy Spirit, or God the Trinity itself, who is love. Now it is no use to say that love is called "God" because it is a gift of God and that therefore it is not a substantive reality worthy to be named God. There are, it is true, passages in Scripture where God is addressed in such terms as "you are my patience" (Psalm 71:5), and there the meaning is not that our patience is the substance of God, but that it comes to us from him, as indeed we read elsewhere: "from him is my patience" (Psalm 62:5). But in the case of love any such interpretation is at once refuted by the actual language of the Scriptures. "You are my patience" is like "You, Lord, are my hope" (Psalm 91:9), and "My God is my compassion" (Psalm 59:17) and many expressions of the kind; but we do not read: "the Lord is my love," or "You are my love," or "God is my love." Instead, we read: "God is love" – just as "God is spirit" (John 4:24). Anyone who cannot see the difference should ask for understanding from the Lord, rather than explanation from us; for words cannot make this point clearer.

God, then, is love. The question is whether this refers to Father, or Son, or Holy Spirit, or the Trinity itself (which is not three gods, but one God). I have argued earlier in the present book that the divine Trinity must not be so conceived, from the likeness or the three members [that is, memory, understanding, love] displayed in our mental trinity, as to make the Father "memory" or all three, the Son "understanding" or all three, and the Holy Spirit "love" or all three. It is not as if the Father neither understood nor loved for himself, but the Son understood for him and the Holy Spirit loved for him, while he himself did nothing but "remember," both for himself and for them. Nor is it as if the Son neither remembered nor loved for himself, but the Father remembered for him and the Holy Spirit loved for him, while he himself did nothing but understand both for himself and for them. Nor is it as if the Holy Spirit neither remembered nor understood for himself, but the Father remembered for him and the Son understood for him, while he himself loved both for himself and for them. Rather must we think that all and each of them possess all three powers in their proper nature; and that in them, the three are not separate (whereas in ourselves, memory is one thing, understanding another, and love another). Rather, there is one single power whose capacity is sufficient for all, such as wisdom itself, which is so to be found in the nature of each individual person that he who possesses it is that which he possesses, in that he is a changeless and incomposite substance. If this be understood and its truth is clear, so far as we may be allowed to see or to conjecture in these great matters, I see no reason why, just as Father, Son and Holy Spirit are each called "wisdom," and all together are not three wisdoms but one, so Father, Son, and Holy Spirit may not each be called "love," and all together one charity. In the same way the Father is God, the Son is God, and the Holy Spirit God; and all together are one God.

Yet there is good reason why in this Trinity we speak of the Son alone as Word of God, of the Holy Spirit alone as Gift of God, and of God the Father alone as the one of whom the Word is begotten and from whom the Holy Spirit principally proceeds (*nec de quo genitum est verbum et de quo procedit principaliter spiritus sanctus nisi Deus pater*). I add the word "principally," because we learn that the Holy Spirit proceeds also from the Son. But this is again something given by the Father to the Son – not that he ever existed without it, for all that the Father gives to his only-begotten Word he gives in the act of begetting him. He is begotten in such a manner that the common gift proceeds from him as well, and the Holy Spirit is Spirit of both. And this distinction within the indivisible Trinity is not of minor importance, but to be noted carefully. For it is especially appropriate that the Word of God is also called the "wisdom of God," though both Father and Holy Spirit are wisdom. Now if it is especially appropriate that one of the three is to be called "love," this name is most appropriately given to the Holy Spirit. And this means that in the indivisible and supreme being of God, substance is not to be distinguished from love, but substance is itself love, and love itself is substance, whether in the Father or in the Son or in the Holy Spirit, and yet it is especially appropriate that the Holy Spirit is named "love". . . .

We may say, then, that just as it is especially appropriate for us to give the name of "wisdom" to the one Word of God, though in general both the Holy Spirit and the Father himself are wisdom, so it is especially appropriate that the Spirit be called "love," though both Father and Son are love in general. The Word of God, God's only-begotten Son, is explicity named as the "wisdom of God" in the apostle's own phrase, "Christ the power of God and the wisdom of God" (1 Corinthians 1:24). But we can also find authority for calling the Holy Spirit "love," by a careful examination of the apostle John's language (1 John 4:7, 19). After saying "Beloved, let us love one another, for love is of God," he goes on to add, "and everyone who loves is born of God; he who does not love has not known God, for God is love." This makes it plain that the love which he calls "God" is the same love which he has said to be "*of* God." Love, then, is God of (or from) God (*Deus ergo ex deo est dilectio*). But since the Son is begotten from God the Father and the Spirit proceeds from God the Father, we must ask to which of them we should apply this saying that God is love. Only the Father is God without being "of God"; so that the love which is God and "of God" must be either the Son or the Holy Spirit. Now in what follows the writer refers to the love of God – not that by which we love him, but that by which "he loved us, and sent his Son as expiator for our sins" (1 John 4:10); and on this he bases his exhortation to us to love one another, that so God may dwell in us, since God (as he has said) is love. And there follows at once, designed to express the matter more plainly, the saying: "hereby we know that we dwell in him, and he in us, because he has given us of his Spirit." Thus it is the Holy Spirit, of whom he has given us, who makes us dwell in God, and God in us. But that is the effect of love. The Holy Spirit himself therefore is the God who is love. A little further on, after repeating his statement that "God is love," John adds immediately, "he who abides in love abides in God, and God abides in him": which corresponds to the earlier saying, "hereby we know that we abide in him and he in us, because he has given us of his Spirit." It is the Spirit therefore who is signified in the text "God is love." God the Holy Spirit who proceeds from God is the one who, when given to us, set us on fire with the love of God and of our neighbour, and is himself love. For we have no means of loving God, unless it comes of God: that is why John says a little later on "let us love because he first loved us." It is the same in the apostle Paul: "the love of God is shed abroad in our hearts through the Holy Spirit which is given to us" (Romans 5:5).

There is no more excellent gift of God than this. It alone distinguishes between the sons of the eternal kingdom and the sons of eternal damnation. Other favours also are given through the Spirit, but without love they are of no use. Unless the Holy Spirit is bestowed on us to such an extent that we are made to be lovers of God and of our neighbour, we cannot pass from the left hand to the right. The name of Gift belongs specially to the Spirit, only on account of love . . . Thus the love which is of God and is God is specially the Holy Spirit, through whom is spread abroad in our hearts the love of God by which the whole Trinity will make its habitation within us. And therefore the Holy Spirit, God though he is, is most rightly called also the "gift of God." What gift is more proper than love, which brings us to God, and without which no other gift of God, whatever it may be, can bring us to God?

3.15 Epiphanius of Constantia on Sabellianism

In his *Panarion*, written in Greek in the late fourth century, Epiphanius provided a vigorous defense of Christian orthodoxy against every heresy which had emerged by this stage. In the course of this survey and exposition, he deals with Sabellianism. See also 3.3; 3.10; 3.11; 3.12; 3.14; 3.19; 3.30; 3.31; 3.34.

Source: *Panarion*, lxii, 1; in *Epiphanii Episcopi Constantiae Opera*, ed. W. Dindorf (Leipzig: Weigel, 1860), vol. 2, 572.20–573.17.

* * *

A certain Sabellius arose not long ago (in fact, quite recently); it is from him that the Sabellians take their name. His opinions, with a few unimportant exceptions, are the same as those of the Noetians. Most of his followers are to be found in Mesopotamia and the region of Rome . . .

Their doctrine is that Father, Son and Holy Spirit are one and the same being, in the sense that three names are attached to one substance (*hypostasis*). It is just like the body, soul and spirit in a human being. The body is as it were the Father; the soul is the Son; while the Spirit is to the Godhead as his spirit is to a human being. Or it is like the sun, being one substance (*hypostasis*), but having three manifestations (*energia*): light, heat, and the orb itself. The heat . . . is analogous to the Spirit; the light to the Son; while the Father himself is represented by the essence of each substance (*to eidos tēs pasēs hypostaseōs*). The Son was at one time emitted, like a ray of light; he accomplished in the world all that related to the dispensation of the gospel and the salvation of humanity, and was then taken back into heaven, as a ray is emitted by the sun and then withdrawn again into the sun. The Holy Spirit is still being sent forth into the world and into those individuals who are worthy to receive it.

3.16 Cyril of Alexandria on the Role of the Holy Spirit

In this early fifth-century work, Cyril focuses on the role of the Spirit as the bringer of unity within the church. Note especially how the unifying role of the Spirit within the church is explicitly linked to a comparable role for the flesh in the incarnation of Christ; just as the humanity of Christ unites him with believers, so the Spirit bonds believers together. See also 3.9; 3.10; 3.14; 3.17.

Source: in *Joannis evangelium*, XVI, 20; in *In D. Joannis evangelium*, ed. P. E. Pusey (Oxford: Clarendon Press, 1872), 736.23–737.4.

* * *

All of us who have received the one and the same Spirit, that is, the Holy Spirit, are in a sense merged together with one another and with God. For if Christ, together with the Spirit of the Father and himself, comes to dwell in each one of us, even though there are many of us, then it follows that the Spirit is still one and undivided. He binds together the spirit of each and every one of us . . . and makes us all appear as one in him. For just as the power of the holy flesh of Christ unites those in whom it dwells into one body, I think that, in much the same way, the one and undivided Spirit of God, who dwells in us all, leads us all into spiritual unity.

Fulgentius of Ruspe on the Holy Spirit and Eucharist   3.17

This work, which dates from the early sixth century, develops the idea that receiving the Holy Spirit is equivalent to receiving the gift of God's love. The text refers to the moment in the eucharist when the Holy Spirit is invoked (usually referred to as the *epiklēsis*). See also 3.12; 3.14; 3.16; 8.1; 8.9.

Source: *contra Fabianum*, XXVIII, 16–19; in *Corpus Christianorum*, vol. 91A, ed. J. Fraipont (Turnhout: Brepols, 1968), 813.264–814.274.

* * *

Since Christ died for us out of love, when we celebrate the memorial of his death, at the moment of sacrifice we ask that love may be granted to us by the coming of the Holy Spirit. We humbly pray that, in the strength of this love, by which Christ willed to die for us, we may be able to regard the world as being crucified to us, and ourselves as being crucified to the world, by receiving the gift of the Holy Spirit . . . Having received this gift of love, let us die to sin and live to God.

Anselm of Canterbury on the Compassion of God   3.18

Anselm here argues that God may be said to be compassionate in terms of his behavior towards us, but not in terms of his own experience. God responds positively towards suffering, without himself experiencing suffering. It is clear that Anselm regards it as axiomatic that God cannot be affected in any way by human suffering. See also 3.7; 3.8; 3.20; 3.26; 3.29; 3.32.

Source: *Proslogion*, 8; in *S. Anselmi: Opera Omnia*, vol. 1, ed. F. S. Schmitt (Edinburgh: Nelson, 1946), 106.5–14.

* * *

But how are you compassionate (*misericors*), yet at the same time impassible (*impassibilis*)? For if you are impassible, you do not feel sympathy (*non compateris*). And if you do not feel sympathy, your heart is not miserable on account of its sympathy for the miserable. Yet this is what compassion is. Yet if you are not compassionate, where does such great comfort for the miserable come from?

So how, O Lord, are you both compassionate and not compassionate, unless it is because you are compassionate in terms of our experience, and not in terms of your own being (*secundum te*). You are truly compassionate in terms of our experience. Yet you are not so in terms of your own. For when you see us in our misery, we experience the effect of compassion; you, however, do not experience this feeling (*non sentis affectum*). Therefore you are compassionate, in that you save the miserable and spare those who sin against you; and you are not compassionate, in that you are not affected by any sympathy for misery.

3.19 Richard of St. Victor on Love within the Trinity

In this sustained analysis of the nature of love within the Godhead, dating from the second half of the twelfth century, Richard argues that the idea of the "sharing of love" can only be sustained if there are three persons within the Godhead. See also 3.3; 3.10; 3.11; 3.12; 3.14; 3.15; 3.30; 3.31; 3.34.

de Trinitate, III, 14; in *Richard de Saint Victor: De Trinitate*, ed. J. Ribaillier (Paris: Librairie Philosophique J. Vrin, 1958), 149.4–150.35.

* * *

If we concede that there exists in the true divinity some one person of such great benevolence that he wishes to have no riches or delights that he does not wish to share with others, and if he is of such great power that nothing is impossible for him, and of such great happiness that nothing is difficult for him, then it is necessary to acknowledge that a Trinity of divine persons must exist. In order that the reasons for this may be clear, let us draw together all our arguments at this point.

If there was only one person in the divinity, that one person would certainly not have anyone with whom he could share the riches of his greatness. But on the other hand, the abundance of delights and sweetness, which would have been able to increase for him on account of intimate love, would lack any eternal dimension. But the fulness of goodness does not permit the supremely good One to keep those riches for himself, nor does his fulness of blessedness allow him to be without a full abundance of delights and sweetness. And on account of the greatness of his honour, he rejoices at sharing his riches as much as he glories over enjoying the abundance of delights and sweetness. On the basis of these considerations, it is clearly impossible that any one person in the divinity could lack the fellowship of association. If he were to have only one partner, he would not be without anyone with whom he could share the riches of his greatness. However, he would not have anyone with whom he could share the delights of love. There is nothing which gives more pleasure or which delights the soul more than the sweetness of loving. Only someone who has a partner and a loved one in that love that has been shown to him possesses the sweetness of such delights.

So it follows that such a sharing of love cannot exist except among less than three persons. As we said earlier, there is nothing more glorious and nothing more magnificent than sharing in common whatever is useful and pleasant. This fact can hardly be unknown to the supreme wisdom, nor can it fail to please the supreme benevolence. And as the happiness of the supremely powerful One cannot be lacking in what pleases him, so in the divinity it is impossible for two persons not to be united to a third.

Alexander of Hales on the Suffering of God in Christ

3.20

In this important early thirteenth-century work, this English Franciscan theologian argues that God, who was not obliged to suffer, chose to suffer in Christ. The work carefully avoids an explicit statement to the effect that God experienced suffering in his own person. Note that the passage in question may not be due to Alexander himself, but may have been compiled by William of Melitona, who completed the work after Alexander's death in 1245. See also 3.7; 3.8; 3.18; 3.26; 3.29; 3.32.

Source: *Summa Theologica*, vol. 4 (Ad Claras Aquas: Collegii S. Bonaventurae, 1948), p. 197.

* * *

In our case, the possibility [of suffering] is linked to the necessity of suffering, and the will not to suffer (which, however, cannot prevent suffering from taking place). In the case of Adam, there was the possibility of being in the state of innocence without any necessity or disposition towards suffering, and the will to suffer or not to suffer, as he wished. In the case of the Lord, however, this possibility (which was not merely remote, as in the case of Adam) is not linked with the necessity of suffering, as in our case. Rather, it is linked with an inclination to suffer, and a will which would have had the power to prevent that suffering.

Thomas Aquinas on Divine Omnipotence

3.21

This passage includes Aquinas's discussion of the question: "can God sin?" At first sight, it might seem that the suggestion that "God cannot sin" amounts to a denial of his omnipotence. However, Aquinas argues that sin is a defect, and is therefore inconsistent with the idea of God as a perfect being. God cannot sin, because it is not in his nature to be deficient. The *Summa Theologiae* ("The Totality of Theology"), which Aquinas began to write in Latin in 1265 and left unfinished at the time of his death, is widely regarded as the greatest work of medieval theology. See also 3.23; 3.25.

Source: *Summa Theologiae*, 1a, q. 25, aa. 3–4.

* * *

It is commonly said that God is almighty. Yet it seems difficult to understand the reason for this, on account of the doubt about what is meant when it is said that "God can do 'everything'" ... If it is said that God is

omnipotent because he can do everything possible to his power, the understanding of omnipotence is circular, doing nothing more than saying that
God is omnipotent because he can do everything that he can do ... To sin
is to fall short of a perfect action. Hence to be able to sin is to be able to be
deficient in relation to an action, which cannot be reconciled with omnipotence. It is because God is omnipotent that he cannot sin ... Anything
that implies a contradiction does not relate to the omnipotence of God. For
the past not to have existed implies a contradiction. Thus to say that Socrates is and is not seated is contradictory, and so also to say that he had and
had not been seated. To affirm that he had been seated is to affirm a past
event; to affirm that he had not been seated is thus to affirm what was not
the case.

3.22 Julian of Norwich on God as our Mother

The *Revelation of Divine Love* is an account of sixteen visions which appeared to the English
recluse Julian of Norwich in May 1373. The visions are notable for their constant emphasis
upon the love and kindness of God, even to the most frail of sinners. The sections which follow,
all of which are drawn from the fourteenth revelation, show Julian's distinctive tendency to refer
to both God and Jesus Christ in strongly maternal terms, paralleling her regular use of
"mother" to refer to the church. See also 1.25; 3.35; 4.31.

Source: Julian of Norwich, *Revelations of Divine Love*, 52, 62, 63; in Julian of Norwich, *Revelations of
Divine Love*, translated by Clifton Wolters (Harmondsworth: Penguin, 1958), pp. 151, 174, 176. Copyright
© Clifton Wolters 1958. Reproduced by permission of Penguin Books Ltd.

* * * ─────────────────────────────

In this way, I saw that God rejoices to be our Father, and also that he
rejoices to be our Mother; and yet again, that he rejoices to be our true
Husband, with our soul as his beloved bride. And Christ rejoices to be both
our Brother and our Saviour ...

[God's] love never allows us to lag behind. All this is due to God's innate
goodness, and comes to us by the operation of his grace. God is kind because it is his nature. Goodness-by-nature implies God. He is the foundation, substance and the thing itself, what it is by nature. He is the true
Father and Mother of what things are by nature. Every kind of "nature"
that he has caused to flow out of himself to fulfil his purpose will be brought
back and restored to him when we are saved by the work of grace ...

We need have no fear of this, unless it is the kind of fear that urges us
on. But we make our humble complaint to our beloved Mother, and he
sprinkles us with his precious blood, and makes our soul pliable and
tender, and restores us to our full beauty in the course of time ... Thus
in Jesus, our true Mother, has our life been grounded, through his own
uncreated foresight, and the Father's almight power, and the exalted and
sovereign goodness of the Holy Spirit ... Beautiful and sweet is our heavenly Mother in the sight of our souls; and, in the sight of our heavenly

Mother, dear and lovely are the gracious children; gentle and humble, with all the lovely natural qualities of children. The natural child does not despair of its mother's love . . . There is no higher state in this life than that of childhood, because of our inadequate and feeble capacity and intellect, until such time as our gracious Mother shall bring us up to our Father's bliss.

William of Ockham on the Two Powers of God   3.23

In this dense passage, Ockham draws a distinction between two modes of divine action. God must originally have been able to act in any manner, providing it did not involve contradiction. Ockham designates this as the "absolute power of God." Ockham notes that God has now chosen to act in a specified and reliable way, by which he has limited his freedom to act. This is referred to as his "ordained power." See also 3.21; 3.25.

Source: Quodlibetal Questions, VI, q. 1; *Opera Philosophica et Theologica*, vol. 9 (New York: St. Bonaventure Publications, 1966), 585.14–586.24.

* * *

Concerning the first point, it must be said that God is able to do some things by his ordained power (*de potentia ordinata*) and others by his absolute power (*de potentia absoluta*). This distinction should not be understood to mean that there are actually in God two powers, one of which is "ordained" and the other of which is "absolute," because there is only one power of God directed towards the external world, the exercise of which is in all respects God himself. Nor should this be understood to mean that God can do some things by his ordained power, and others by his absolute, not his ordained, power, in that God does nothing without having first ordained it. But it should be understood in this way: God can do something in a manner which is established by laws which were ordained and established by God. In this respect, God acts according to his ordained power.

Thomas à Kempis on the Limits of Trinitarian Speculation   3.24

The noted late medieval spiritual writer Thomas à Kempis here sets out a strongly anti-speculative approach to the Christian faith, which rests firmly on the need to obey Christ rather than indulge in flights of intellectual fancy. Speculation concerning the Trinity is singled out as a case of such speculation, which he urges his readers to avoid. See also 3.3; 3.10; 3.11; 3.12; 3.14; 3.15; 3.19; 3.30; 3.31; 3.34.

Source: *de imitatione Christi*, I, 1–2; in *De imitatione Christi libri quatuor*, ed. T. Lupo (Vatican City: Libreria Editrice Vaticana, 1982), 4.7–8.8.

* * *

What good does it do you if you dispute loftily about the Trinity, but lack humility and therefore displease the Trinity? It is not lofty words that make you righteous or holy or dear to God, but a virtuous life. I would much rather experience contrition (*compuctio*) than be able to give a definition of it. If you knew the whole of the Bible by heart, along with all the definitions of the philosophers, what good would this be without grace and love? "Vanity of vanities, and all is vanity" (Ecclesiastes 1:2) – except, that is, loving God and serving him alone. For this is supreme wisdom: to draw nearer to the heavenly kingdom through contempt for the world . . .

Naturally, everyone wants knowledge. But what use is that knowledge without the fear of God? A humble peasant who serves God is much more pleasing to him than an arrogant academic (*superbus philosophus*) who neglects his own soul to consider the course of the stars . . . If I were to possess all the knowledge in the world, and yet lacked love, what good would this be in the sight of God, who will judge me by what I have done? So restrain an extravagant longing for knowledge, which leads to considerable anxiety and deception. Learned people always want their wisdom to be noticed and recognized. But there are many things, knowledge of which leads to little or no benefit to the soul. In fact, people are foolish if they concern themselves with anything other than those things which lead to their salvation.

3.25 John Owen on the Sovereignty of God

During the course of his exposition of Psalm 130:5–6, which was first published in 1668, Owen set out the characteristic Reformed emphasis on the total sovereignty of God as creation, by which every aspect of the creation has been ordered by God. Despite the disruptive effects of the Fall, Owen insists that every aspect of the creation remains under God's sovereign authority, by which God is able to determine his will for every aspect of his creatures. For Owen, and the Reformed tradition in general, the doctrine of the sovereignty of God finds a special application in the area of election; whether an individual is saved or not depends solely upon the will and good pleasure of God. Here, Owen explores related insights, focusing on the creation in general. See also 3.21; 3.23.

Source: *Exposition of Psalm 130*; in *The Works of John Owen*, vol. 6, ed. W. Goold (Edinburgh: Johnson and Hunter, 1851), pp. 626–7.

* * * ———

[God] made all this world of nothing, and could have made another, more, or all things, quite otherwise than they are. It would not subsist one moment without his omnipotent supportment. Nothing would be continued in its place, course, use, without his effectual influence and countenance. If any thing can be, live, or act a moment without him, we may take free leave to dispute its disposal with him, and to haste unto the accomplishment of our desires. But from the angels in heaven to the worms of the earth and the grass of the field, all depend on him and his power continually. Why was this part of the creation an angel, that a worm; this a man, that a brute beast? Is it from their own choice, designing or contrivance, or brought about by their own wisdom? or is it merely from the sovereign pleasure and will of God? And what a madness it is to repine against what he doth, seeing all things are as he makes them and disposeth them, nor can be otherwise! Even the repiner himself hath his being and subsistence upon his mere pleasure . . . All is one; whatever God doth, and towards whomsoever, be they many or few, a whole nation, or city, or one single person, be they high or low, rich or poor, good or bad, all are the works of his hands, and he may deal with them as seems good unto him.

Benedict Spinoza on the Impassibility of God   3.26

In this important philosophical argument, which had some considerable influence on Christian theology in the eighteenth century, Spinoza reasons that any passion on the part of God involves a change in his being. Either he moves to a greater perfection, or to a lesser. In either case, the perfection of God is compromised, in that God either becomes more perfect (in which case he was not perfect to start with), or less perfect (in which case, suffering leads to him ceasing to be perfect). As a result, Spinoza argues, it is not possible to speak of God loving anyone, as this proves to be inconsistent with the idea of a perfect God. Note that Spinoza's original text is littered with cross-references to earlier sections of the work, making it somewhat difficult to follow the argument. These have been omitted for the purposes of this reader, to allow for easier reading. The sense of the argument is not altered nor distorted by these omissions. See also 3.7; 3.8; 3.18; 3.20; 3.29; 3.32.

Source: *Ethics*, V, 17; in *Opera: Lateinisch und Deutsch*, vol. 2, ed. Konrad Blumenstock (Darmstadt: Wissenschaftliche Buchgesellschaft, 1980), 526.31–528.6.

* * *

Proposition 17. God is without passions, nor is he affected with any experience of joy (*laetitia*) or sadness (*tristitia*).

Demonstration. All ideas, in so far as they have reference to God, are true, that is, they are adequate: and therefore God is without passions (*Deus expers est passionum*). Again, God cannot pass to a higher or a lower perfection: and therefore he is affected with no emotion of joy or sadness. Q.E.D.

Corollary: God, strictly speaking, loves no one nor hates any one. For God is affected with no emotion of joy or sadness, and consequently loves no one (*neminem etiam amat*) nor hates any one.

F. D. E. Schleiermacher on the Trinity   3.27

Schleiermacher's discussion of the doctrine of the Trinity comes right at the end of his *Christian Faith*, and represents the "last word" of theology on the doctrine of God. In this passage, Schleiermacher sets out his understanding of the distinctive place and function of the doctrine as the "coping stone" of Christian theology. See also 3.3; 3.10; 3.11; 3.12; 3.14; 3.15; 3.19; 3.30; 3.31; 3.34.

Source: Friedrich Schleiermacher, *The Christian Faith* (Edinburgh: T. & T. Clark, 1928), pp. 738–9.

* * *

An essential element of our exposition in this Part has been the doctrine of the union of the Divine Essence with human nature, both in the personality of Christ and in the common Spirit of the Church; therewith the whole view of Christianity set forth in our Church teaching stands and falls. For unless the being of God in Christ is assumed, the idea of redemption could not be thus concentrated in His Person. And unless there were such a union also in the common Spirit of the Church, the Church could not thus be the Bearer and Perpetuator of the redemption through Christ. Now these exactly are the essential elements in the doctrine of the Trinity, which, it is clear, only established itself in defence of the position that in Christ there was present nothing less than the Divine Essence, which also indwells the Christian Church as its common Spirit, and that we take these expressions in no reduced or sheerly artificial sense, and know nothing of any special higher essences, subordinate deities (as it were) present in Christ and the Holy Spirit. The doctrine of the Trinity has no origin but this; and at first it had no other aim than to equate as definitely as possible the Divine Essence considered as thus united to human nature with the Divine Essence in itself. This is the less doubtful that those Christian sects which interpret the doctrine of redemption differently are also necessarily without the doctrine of the Trinity – they have no point of belief to which it could be attached – which could not possibly be the case if even in Catholic doctrine there existed at least some other points than this to which the attachment could be made. It is equally clear from this why those divergent sects which are chiefly distinguishable by their denial of the Trinity are not thereby forced into still other divergences in the doctrine of God and the divine attributes, as must have been the case if the doctrine of the Trinity were rooted in a special view of the nature of the Supreme Being as such. But on the other hand, they are forced to set up a different theory of the person of Christ, and hence also of the human need for redemption and of the value of redemption. In virtue of this connexion, we rightly regard the doctrine of the Trinity, in so far as it is a deposit of these elements, as the coping-stone of Christian doctrine (*als den Schlußstein der christlichen Lehre*), and this equating with each other of the divine in each of these two unions, as also of both with the Divine Essence in itself, as what is essential in the doctrine of the Trinity.

3.28 Karl Barth on the "Otherness" of God

Karl Barth's Romans commentary, which first appeared in German in 1918, caused a sensation on account of its vision of a dialectic between God and humanity. There is a total gulf between God and the world, which can never be bridged from our side. The fact that we know anything about God is itself the result of God's self-revelation, not human activity or insight. God is totally distinct from human thought and civilization. This relentless emphasis on the "total qualitative distinction" between God and humanity established Barth as a radical voice in the theology of the period immediately after the First World War. See also 2.25; 2.32; 9.4.

Source: Karl Barth, *The Epistle to the Romans* (Oxford: Oxford University Press, 1933), pp. 28–9. By permission of Oxford University Press.

—— * * *

[Paul] appeals only to the authority of God. This is the ground of his authority. There is no other.

Paul is authorized to deliver – *the Gospel of God.* He is commissioned to hand over to humanity something quite new and unprecedented, joyful and good – the truth of God. Yes, precisely – *of God!* The Gospel is not a religious message to inform humanity of their divinity, or to tell them how they may become divine. The Gospel proclaims a God utterly distinct from humanity. Salvation comes to them from him, and because they are, as human beings, incapable of knowing him, they have no right to claim anything from him. The Gospel is not one thing in the midst of other things, to be directly apprehended and comprehended. The Gospel is the Word of the Primal Origin of all things, the Word which, since it is ever new, must ever be received with renewed fear and trembling...

Jesus Christ our Lord. This is the Gospel and the meaning of history. In this name two worlds meet and go apart, two planes intersect, the one known and the other unknown. The known plane is God's creation, fallen out of its union with him, and therefore the world of the "flesh" needing redemption. The world of human beings, and of time, and of things – our world. This known plane is intersected by another plane that is unknown – the world of the Father, of the Primal Creation, and of the final Redemption. The relation between us and God, between this world and his world, presses for recognition, but the line of intersection is not self-evident. The point on the line of intersection at which the relation becomes observable and observed is Jesus, Jesus of Nazareth, the historical Jesus.

———

Jürgen Moltmann on the Suffering of God   3.29

Jürgen Moltmann is widely regarded as one of the most important contemporary exponents of a "theology of the cross." This is especially evident in his major work *The Crucified God*, which sets out an understanding of the doctrine of God which takes the cross of Christ as foundational to an authentically Christian understanding of God. The present extract provides a lucid overview of the themes of this work. Note especially the radical emphasis upon the cross, and the criticism of philosophical ideas of God, such as those found in the patristic period. Note also the way in which Moltmann distinguishes his approach from Patripassianism and Theopaschitism, and the manner in which he uses this approach to lay the foundations for a doctrine of the Trinity. See also 1.11; 3.7; 3.8; 3.18; 3.20; 3.26; 3.32.

Source: Jürgen Moltmann, "The 'Crucified God': God and the Trinity Today," in *New Questions on God*, ed. J. B. Metz (New York: Herder & Herder, 1972), pp. 31–5. Reprinted with the permission of the author.

—— * * *

The Council of Nicaea rightly declared, in opposition to Arius, that God was not so changeable as his creature. This is not an absolute statement about God, but a comparative statement. God is not subject to compulsion by what is not divine. This does not mean, however, that God is not free to change himself or to be changed by something else. We cannot deduce from the relative statement of Nicaea that God is unchangeable that he is absolutely unchangeable.

The early Fathers insisted on God's inability to suffer in opposition to the Syrian Monophysite heresy. An essential inability to suffer was the only contrast to passive suffering recognized in the early Church. There is, however, a third form of suffering – active suffering, the suffering of love, a voluntary openness to the possibility of being affected by outside influences. If God were really incapable of suffering, he would also be as incapable of loving as the God of Aristotle, who was loved by all, but could not love. Whoever is capable of love is also capable of suffering, because he is open to the suffering that love brings with it, although he is always able to surmount that suffering because of love. God does not suffer, like his creature, because his being is incomplete. He loves from the fullness of his being and suffers because of his full and free love.

The distinctions that have been made in theology between God's and man's being are externally important, but they tell us nothing about the inner relationship between God the Father and God the Son and therefore cannot be applied to the event of the cross which took place between God and God. Christian humanists also find this a profound *aporia*. In regarding Jesus as God's perfect man, and in taking his exemplary sinlessness as proof of his "permanently powerful consciousness of God," they interpret Jesus' death as the fulfilment of his obedience or faith, not as his being abandoned by God. God's incapacity, because of his divine nature, to suffer (*apatheia*) is replaced by the unshakeable steadfastness (*ataraxia*) of Jesus' consciousness of God. The ancient teaching that God is unchangeable is thus transferred to Jesus' "inner life," but the *aporia* is not overcome. Finally, atheistic humanists who are interested in Jesus but do not accept the existence of God find it impossible to think of Jesus as dying abandoned by God and therefore regard his cry to God from the cross as superfluous.

All Christian theologians of every period and inclination try to answer the question of Jesus' cry from the cross and to say, consciously or unconsciously, why God abandoned him. Atheists also attempt to answer this question in such a way that, by depriving it of its foundation, they can easily dismiss it. But Jesus' cry from the cross is greater than even the most convincing Christian answer. Theologians can only point to the coming of God, who is the only answer to this question.

Christians have to speak about God in the presence of Jesus' abandonment by God on the cross, which can provide the only complete justification of their theology. The cross is either the Christian end of all theology or it is the beginning of a specifically Christian theology. When theologians speak about God on the cross of Christ, this inevitably becomes a trinitarian debate about the "story of God" which is quite distinct from all monotheism, polytheism or pantheism. The central position occupied by the crucified Christ is the specifically Christian element in the history of the world and the doctrine of the Trinity is the specifically Christian element in the doctrine of God. Both are very closely connected. It is not the bare trinitarian formulas in the New Testament, but the constant testimony of the cross which provides the basis for Christian faith in the Trinity. The most concise expression of the Trinity is God's action on the cross, in which God allowed the Son to sacrifice himself through the Spirit (B. Steffen).

It is informative to examine Paul's statements about Jesus' abandonment on the cross in this context. The Greek word for "abandon" (*paradidomi*) has a decidedly negative connotation in the gospel stories of the passion, meaning betray, deliver, give up, and even kill. In Paul (Romans 1:18–21), this negative meaning of *paredoken* is apparent in his presentation of God's abandonment of ungodly men. Guilt and punishment are closely connected and men who abandon God are abandoned by him and "given" up to the way they have chosen for themselves – Jews to their law, Gentiles to the worship of their idols and both to death. Paul introduced a new meaning into the term *paredoken* when he presented Jesus' abandonment by God not in the historical context of his life, but in the eschatological context of faith. God "did not spare his own Son, but gave him up for us all; will he not also give us all things with him?" (Romans 8:32). In the historical abandonment of the crucified Christ by the Father, Paul perceived the eschatological abandonment or "giving up" of the Son by the Father for the sake of "ungodly" men who had abandoned and been abandoned by God. In stressing that God had given up "his own Son," Paul extended the abandonment of the Son to the Father, although not in the same way, as the Patripassian heretics had done, insisting that the Son's sufferings could be predicated of the Father. In the Pauline view, Jesus suffered death abandoned by God. The Father, on the other hand, suffered the death of his Son in the pain of his love. The Son was "given up" by the Father and the Father suffered his abandonment from the Son. Kazoh Kitamori has called this "the pain of God."

The death of the Son is different from this "pain of God" the Farther, and for this reason it is not possible to speak, as the Theopaschites did, of the "death of God." If we are to understand the story of Jesus' death abandoned by God as an event taking place between the Father and the Son, we must speak in terms of the Trinity and leave the universal concept of God aside, at least to begin with. In Galatians 2:20, the word *paredoken* appears with Christ as the subject: "... the Son of God, who loved me and gave himself for me." According to this statement, then, it is not only the Father who gives the Son up, but the Son who gives himself up. This indicates that Jesus' will and that of the Father were the same at the point where Jesus was abandoned on the cross and they were completely separated. Paul himself interpreted Christ's being abandoned by God as love, and the same interpretation is found in John (John 3:16). The author of 1 John regarded this event of love on the cross as the very existence of God himself; "God is love" (1 John 4:16). This is why it was possible at a later period to speak, with reference to the cross, of *homoousia*, the Son and the Father being of one substance. In the cross, Jesus and his God are in the deepest sense separated by the Son's abandonment by the Father, yet at the same time they are in the most intimate sense united in this abandonment or "giving up." This is because this "giving up" proceeds from the event of the cross that takes place between the Father who abandons and the Son who is abandoned, and this "giving up" is none other than the Holy Spirit.

Any attempt to interpret the event of Jesus' crucifixion according to the doctrine of the two natures would result in a paradox, because of the concept of the one God and the one nature of God. On the cross, God calls to God and dies to God. Only in this place is God "dead" and yet not dead. If all we have is the concept of one God, we are inevitably inclined to apply it to the Father and to relate the death exclusively to the human person of Jesus, so that the cross is "emptied" of its divinity. If, on the other hand, this concept of God is left aside, we have at once to speak of persons in the special relationship of this particular event, the Father as the one who abandons and "gives up" the Son, and the Son who is abandoned by the Father and who gives himself up. What proceeds from this event is the Spirit of abandonment and self-giving love who raises up abandoned men.

My interpretation of the death of Christ, then, is not as an event between God and man, but primarily as an event within the Trinity between Jesus and his Father, an event from which the Spirit proceeds. This interpretation opens up a number of perspectives. In the first place, it is possible to understand the crucifixion of Christ non-theistically. Secondly, the old dichotomy between the universal nature of God and the inner triune nature of God is overcome and, thirdly, the distinction between the immanent and the "economic" Trinity becomes superfluous. It makes it necessary to speak about the Trinity in the context of the cross, and re-establishes it as a traditional doctrine. Seen in this light, this doctrine no longer has to be regarded as a divine mystery which is better venerated with silent respect than investigated too closely. It can be seen as the tersest way of expressing the story of Christ's passion. It preserves faith from monotheism and from atheism, because it keeps it close to the crucified Christ. It reveals the cross in God's being and God's being in the cross. The material principle of the trinitarian doctrine is the cross; the formal principle of the theology of the cross is the trinitarian doctrine. The unity of the Father, the Son and the Holy Spirit can be designated as "God." If we are to speak as Christians about God, then, we have to tell the story of Jesus as the story of God and to proclaim it as the historical event which took place between the Father, the Son and the Holy Spirit and which revealed who and what God is, not only for man, but in his very existence. This also means that God's being is historical and that he exists in history. The "story of God" then is the story of the history of man.

Leonardo Boff on the Trinity as Good News for the Poor

The Brazilian writer Leonardo Boff, one of the most noted exponents of Latin American liberation theology, here provides an exploration of the manner in which the Trinity itself can provide a model for social living, arguing that the mutual relationship of Father, Son, and Holy Spirit acts as a basis for Christian social theory and practice. See also 1.26; 3.3; 3.10; 3.11; 3.12; 3.14; 3.15; 3.19; 3.31; 3.34; 7.21.

Source: Leonardo Boff, *Trinity and Society* (Tunbridge Wells: Burns & Oates, Maryknoll, NY: Orbis Books, 1988), pp. 156–8. Reprinted with the permission of the publishers.

* * *

In what sense can the Trinity be called "gospel," good news, to people, especially to the poor and oppressed? For many Christians it is simply a mystery in logic: how can the one God exist in three Persons? How can a Trinity of Persons form the unity of the one God? Any Christian coming into contact with debates on the Trinity for the first time might well form this impression: the Christian faith developed intellectually in the Hellenic world; Christians had to translate their doxology into a theology appropriate to that world in order to assert the truth of their faith. So they used expressions accessible to the critical reasoning of that time, such as substance, person, relation, perichoresis, procession. This was a most difficult path to follow, as we saw in earlier chapters; it has left its mark even today, even though the mystery defies all human categories and calls for new approaches, springing from an encounter between biblical revelation and dominant cultures. We should never forget that the New Testament never uses the expressions "trinity of persons" and "unity of nature." To say that God is Father, Son and Holy Spirit is revelation; to say that God is "one substance and three Persons" is theology, a human endeavour to fit the revelation of God within the limitations of reason.

The same thing happens when Christians read the pronouncements of the magisterium. These are statements of great pithiness and logical coherence, designed to curb the speculative exuberance of theologians. Dogmatic progress virtually came to an end with the Council of Florence (1439–45); from then to the present (with some noted exceptions, as we have seen) theological works have generally confined themselves to commenting on the terms defined and investigating historical questions of detail of the system already constructed.

It is not easy to explain to Christians caught up in the "logical mystery" of the Trinity that the number "three" in the Trinity (*Trias* and *Trinitas,* words established by Theophilus of Antioch and Tertullian at the end of the second century) does not signify anything that can be counted and has nothing to do with arithmetical processes of addition and subtraction. The scriptures count nothing in God; they know only one divine number – the number "one": one God, one Lord, one Spirit. This "one" is not a number, nor the number "one" in the sense of first in a series; it is rather the negation of all numbers, simply "the only." The Father is "an only," as are the Son and the Holy Spirit; these "onlies" cannot be added together. As we have tried to explain earlier, it is the eternal communion between these Onlies that forms the divine oneness in the power of life and love (the divine nature). Nevertheless, by reason of the communion and relationship revealed to us between the Father, Son and Holy Spirit, there is an order to the divine names. Though each Person is co-eternal with the others and, therefore, none can exist before the others, we must, nevertheless, affirm that the Father who begets is logically "before" the Son who is begotten, as is the Son "before" the Spirit, breathed out by the Father with and through the Son. This is the explanation for the order of the divine names, and from this comes the human convention of speaking of three "Persons." But theology has never been satisfied with the expression "three Persons," as the continuous debates have shown.

We need to go beyond the understanding of Trinity as logical mystery and see it as saving mystery. The Trinity has to do with the lives of each of us, our daily experiences, our struggles to follow our conscience, our love and joy, our bearing the sufferings of the world and the tragedies of human existence; it also has to do with the struggle against social injustice, with efforts at building a more human form of society, with the sacrifices and martyrdoms that these endeavours so often bring. If we fail to include the Trinity in our personal and social odyssey, we shall have failed to show the saving mystery, failed in evangelization. If oppressed believers come to appreciate the fact that their struggles for life and liberty are also those of the Father, Son and Holy Spirit, working for the Kingdom of glory and eternal life, then they will have further motives for struggling and resisting; the meaning of their efforts will break out of the restricting framework of history and be inscribed in eternity, in the heart of the absolute Mystery itself. We are not condemned to live alone, cut off from one another; we are called to live together and to enter into the communion of the Trinity. Society is not ultimately set in its unjust and unequal relationships, but summoned to transform itself in the light of the open and egalitarian relationships that obtain in the communion of the Trinity, the goal of social and historical progress. If the Trinity is good news, then it is so particularly for the oppressed and those condemned to solitude.

3.31 Robert Jenson on the Trinity

The American Lutheran writer Robert Jenson here argues that the Trinity is the distinctively Christian means of identifying or naming God. The Trinity can be thought of in terms of the proper name of the Christian God, which establishes the identity of God on the basis of an affirmation and identification of God's redemptive acts in history. See also 3.3; 3.10; 3.11; 3.12; 3.14; 3.15; 3.19; 3.30; 3.34.

Source: Robert Jenson, "The Triune God," in C. E. Braaten and R. W. Jenson (eds), *Christian Dogmatics*, vol. 1 (Philadelphia: Fortress Press, 1984), pp. 87–92. Reprinted from *Christian Dogmatics*, edited by C. E. Braaten and R. W. Jenson. Copyright © 1984 Fortress Press. Used by permission of Augsburg Fortress.

* * *

Meditating on the foundation of biblical faith, the exodus, Israel's first theologians made Moses' decisive question be: "If I come to the people of Israel and say to them, 'The God of your fathers has sent me to you': and they ask me, 'What is his name?' what shall I say to them?" If Israel was to risk the future of this God, to leave secure nonexistence in Egypt and venture on God's promises, Israel had first and fundamentally to know which future this was. The God answered, "Say this to the people of Israel, [Yahweh], the God of your fathers, the God of Abraham, the God of Isaac, and the God of Jacob, has sent me to you, this is my name for ever, and thus I am to be remembered throughout all generations" (Exodus 3:13–15)!

The answer provides a proper name, "Yahweh." It also provides what logicians now call an identifying description, a descriptive phrase or clause, or set of them, that fits just the one individual thing to be identified. Here the description is "the God whom Abraham and Isaac and Jacob worshipped." The more usual description is that found in a parallel account a few chapters later: God said to Moses, "Say . . . to the people of Israel, 'I am [Yahweh], and I will bring you out from under the burdens of the Egyptians . . .; and you shall know that I am [Yahweh] your God, *who* has brought you out . . . I am [Yahweh]'" (Exodus 6:2–7; emphasis added).

In general, proper names work only if such identifying descriptions are at hand. We may say, "Mary is coming to dinner" and be answered with, "Who is Mary?" Then we must be able to say, "Mary is the one who lives in apartment 2C, and is always so cheerful, and . . ." continuing until the questioner says, "Oh, *that* one!" We may say, "Yahweh always forgives:" and be answered with, "Do you mean the Inner Self?" Then we must be able to say, "No. We mean the one who rescued Israel from Egypt, and . . ."

. . . Trinitarian discourse is Christianity's effort to identify the God who has claimed us. The doctrine of the Trinity comprises both a proper name, "Father, Son, and Holy Spirit," in several grammatical variants, and an elaborate development and analysis of corresponding identifying descriptions . . .

The gospel of the New Testament is the provision of a new identifying description for this same God [as that of Israel]. The coming-to-apply of this new description is the event, the witness to which is the whole point of the New Testament. God, in the gospel, is "whoever raised Jesus from the dead." Identification of God by the resurrection did not replace identification by the exodus; it is essential to the God who raised Jesus that he is the same one who freed Israel. But the new thing that is the content of the gospel is that God has now identified himself also as "him that raised from the dead Jesus our Lord" (Romans 4:24). In the New Testament such phrases become the standard way of referring to God.

To go with this new identifying description there are not so much new names as new kinds of naming. "Yahweh" does not reappear as a name in use. The habit of saying "Lord" instead has buried it too deeply under the appellative. But in the church's missionary situation, actual use of a proper name in speaking of God is again necessary in a variety of contexts. It is the naming of Jesus that occurs for all such functions. Exorcism, healing, and indeed good works generally are accomplished "in Jesus' name" (e.g., Mark 9:37ff). Church discipline and quasi-discipline are carried out by sentences pronounced in Jesus' name (e.g., 1 Corinthians 1:10), and forgiveness is pronounced in the same way (e.g., 1 John 1 2:12). Baptism is described as into Jesus' name (e.g., Acts 2:38), whether or not it was ever actually performed with this formula. Undergoing such baptism is equated with that calling on the name "Yahweh" by which, according to Joel 3:5, Israel is to be saved (Acts 2:21, 38). Above all, perhaps, prayer is "in Jesus' name" (e.g., John 14:13–14), in consequence of which the name can be posited as the very object of faith (e.g., John 1:12). Believers are those "who call on the name of our Lord Jesus Christ" (e.g., Acts 9:14).

So dominant was the use of the name "Jesus" in the religious life of the apostolic church that the whole mission can be described as proclamation "in his name" (Luke 24:47), "preaching good news about the kingdom of God and the name of Jesus Christ" (Acts 8:12), indeed, as "carrying" Jesus' name to the people (e.g., Acts 9:15). The gatherings of the congregations can be described as "giving thanks . . . in the name of our Lord Jesus Christ" (Ephesians 5:20), indeed, simply as meetings in his name (Matthew 18:20). Where faith must be confessed over against the hostility of society, this is "confession of the name" (e.g., Mark 13:13). The theological conclusion was drawn in such praises as the hymn preserved in Philippians in which God's own eschatological triumph is evoked as cosmic obeisance to the name "Jesus" (Philippians 1:10), or in such formulas as that in Acts which makes Jesus' name the agent of salvation (Acts 4:12). However various groups in the primal church may have conceived Jesus' relation to God, "Jesus" was the way they all invoked God.

One other new naming appears in the New Testament, the triune name: "Father, Son, and Holy Spirit." Its appearance is undoubtedly dependent on naming God by naming Jesus, as just discussed, but the causal connections are no longer recoverable. It is of course toward this name that we have been steering. That the biblical God must have a proper name, we have seen in the Hebrew Scriptures. In the life of the primal church, God is named by uses that involve the name of Jesus. "Father, Son, and Spirit" is the naming of this sort that historically triumphed.

That "Father, Son, and Holy Spirit" in fact occupies in the church the place occupied in Israel by "Yahweh" or, later, "Lord" even hasty observation of the church's life must discover . . . Our services begin and are punctuated with "In the name of the Father, Son, and Holy Spirit." Our prayers conclude, "In his name who with you and the Holy Spirit is . . .' Above all, the act by which people are brought both into the fellowship of believers and into their fellowship with God is an initiation "into the name 'Father, Son, and Holy Spirit.'"

The habit of trinitarian naming is universal through the life of the church. How far back it goes, we cannot tell. It certainly goes further back than even the faintest traces of trinitarian reflection, and it appears to have been an immediate expression of believers' experience of God. It is in liturgy, when we talk not *about* God but to and for him, that we need and use God's name, and that is where the trinitarian formulas appear, both initially and to this day. In the immediately postapostolic literature there is on use of a trinitarian formula as a piece of theology or in such fashion as to depend on antecedent development in theology, yet the formula is there. Its home is in the liturgy, in baptism and the eucharist. There its use was regularly seen as the heart of the matter.

Eberhard Jüngel on the Crucified God 3.32

The German theologian Eberhard Jüngel is widely regarded as one of the most articulate contemporary representatives of a "theology of the cross" – that is, a theology which argues that the Christian knowledge of God is uniquely grounded in and is decisively shaped by the cross of Christ. Jüngel argues that the theology of the Enlightenment has been deeply shaped by Cartesian assumptions, and that a return to a "theology of the cross" provides the means of liberation from this Cartesian framework. In this brief extract, Jüngel stresses the need to be told what God is like, and that the cross of Christ provides both a locus and focus for this process of "being told." Note that the German original of the phrase "we *must have said to us* what the word 'God' should be thought to mean" would more naturally be translated as "we *need to be told* what the word 'God' should be understood to mean". See also 1.11; 1.17; 2.25; 2.31; 2.32.

Source: Eberhard Jüngel, *God as the Mystery of the World* (Edinburgh: T. & T. Clark, 1983), p. 13. Used with permission of the publishers.

* * *

Since Christian theology understands God himself, for the sake of Jesus, in this sense as the one who speaks, as the word, it ascribes to the word "God" a function of announcing God himself, but solely on the basis of the word of God. The traditional language of Christianity (*die christliche Sprachüberlieferung*) insists, therefore, on the fact that we *must have said to us* what the word "God" should be thought to mean. The presupposition is that ultimately only the speaking God himself can say what the word "God" should provide us to think about. Theology comprehends this whole subject with the category of revelation.

We have understood that God is one who speaks and as such one who expresses himself as an assertion which is inseparably tied to faith in Jesus. Hebrews, like Romans 1:2, relates Old Testament talk about God (as God speaking through prophets) to Jesus. This expresses the fact that in the person Jesus is revealed what God as the one who speaks is all about. The humanity of this person is extremely relevant to the meaning of the word "God," according to the New Testament view. This is true not just of the life but especially of the death of this person. Therefore, when we attempt to think of God as the one who communicates and expresses himself in the person Jesus, it must be remembered that, in fact, this man was *crucified*, that he was killed in the name of God's law. For responsible Christian usage of the word "God," the Crucified One is virtually the real definition of what is meant with the word "God." Christianity is thus fundamentally the "theology of the Crucified One (*Theologie der Gekreuzigten*)."

3.33 Jacques Ellul on the Theology of Icons

In this critique of the use of idols, based on an interaction with Paul Evdokimov's *L'art de l'icône: théologie de la beauté* (Paris: Desclée, 1970), Ellul argues for the need for an understanding of the divine nature which is based primarily upon the word of God, rather than on images. The critique offers some characteristic Reformed perspectives on the nature and origins of the knowledge of God, and especially the type of knowledge of God available through Christ. See also 1.13; 2.15; 4.18.

Source: Jacques Ellul, *The Humiliation of the Word* (Grand Rapids: Eerdmans, 1985), pp. 102–6. Reprinted with the permission of the publisher.

* * *

The icon, of course, is not worshipped for itself; in itself, it has no value. It is not a work of art . . . The object is not venerated; Beauty is by means of the resemblance mysteriously conveyed by the icon. It irradiates "the ineffable reflections of divine Beauty." The image is clearly superior to the word: "the image shows what the word says" . . . The word is not sufficient. The icon is a symbol, but must be surpassed; though nothing in itself, it is indispensable in mystical contemplation. As a kind of sacrament that makes transcendent communion possible, in itself it is transcendent. The icon *alone* enables a person to participate in the indescribable . . .

All of this is closely linked to a theology of the Incarnation understood as "sanctification of matter and transfiguration of the flesh." The Incarnation enables us to *see* both spiritual bodies and nature as transformed by Christ. In other words, the Incarnation of Jesus has transformed the entire human species and all of nature; it is a completely finished work, and this transformed nature enables us to contemplate the divine through "indirect thought." Human beings are (already) deified.

This symbolic knowledge needs a material vehicle. But, starting from the symbol, by means of the contemplation and true imagination with its evocative power, such knowledge grasps the figurative presence as an epiphany of the transcendent. This presence is symbolized, but *very real*. The icon guides our *gaze* towards the Highest – toward the Most High, toward the only necessity . . .

The icon of Christ, of course, is certainly not Christ. It is only an image, not a prototype. But it bears witness to a well-defined presence, and permits prayerful communion (which is not eucharistic communion, because it permits spiritual communion with the *Person* of Christ). "The presence of the icon is a circle whose center is found in the icon, but whose circumference is nowhere. As a material point in the world, the icon opens a breach through which the Transcendent bursts" . . . Coming back to the Incarnation, Evdokimov concludes: "A hypostasis in two natures signifies an image in two modes: visible and invisible. The divine is invisible, but it is reflected by the visible human object. The icon of Christ is possible, *true and real*, because his image in the human mode is identical to the invisible image in the divine mode."

Fundamentally, the theology of icons involves first a switch from signs to symbols, because the icon is essentially symbolic. Then, the icon is inserted into an entire liturgy. It implies a theology of the concrete presence of the spiritual realm, and of divine light, which can be symbolically retranscribed and which is the image of glory itself . . .

[This theology of icons] rests on a certain conception of the Incarnation that utterly fails to take into account its unfulfilled aspect: the waiting and the hope. "Having *reestablished* the tarnished image in its former dignity, the Word unites it with divine Beauty." Everything is already accomplished.

Furthermore, this theology rests on a conception of the image of God in the creation that makes of it a concrete resemblance: "the image of God" *is* the materiality of visible humanity. This concept tries to place humanity permanently on Tabor, the mount of Transfiguration . . . That corresponds exactly to the error of the disciples who accompanied Jesus and who wanted to set up tents in order to remain permanently in the Transfiguration.

We must not try to find humanity's deification in God's humanization, as if God became human so that humanity might become God. Humanity goes from being a microcosm to being a micro-theos in this case. This is applied very concretely: to material, corporeal, visual humanity. The human being in himself, as we see him, is the face of God. One wonders then why the Gospels find it necessary to say of Jesus: "Behold the man." He is the *only*, the *unique*, case of a human being as the image of God. But he is God's image precisely in the visible image of the condemned, scourged, individual . . .

One more matter before we leave the controversy over iconoclasm in Orthodox belief. The iconoclasts, whose beliefs were judged in the seventh council, refused to admit the symbolic character of the icon. Consequently, they did not believe in "a mysterious presence of the Model in the image." "They could not seem to understand that besides the visible representation of a visible reality (the portrait) there is a completely different art in which the image presents what is visible of the invisible." In reality, this was not a problem of "understanding"; the iconoclasts simply did not believe this doctrine! They were accused of being docetics, of having a purely realistic view of art, since they refused to ascribe a sacred character to the icon. They denied that a representation of Christ or the Virgin Mary could be anything other than a representation. They denied that even symbolically the icon could have any sacramental value at all.

But the argument against the iconoclasts is utterly fallacious: it is denied that one can have an idolatrous attitude towards an icon, since an idol is the expression of something that does not exist – a fiction, a semblance, a

nothing ... This argument is false because, in many of the religions condemned in the Bible, the idol was a visible representation of an invisible
religious reality, to which it referred ... As for the argument that the iconoclasts were docetics who denied the reality of the Incarnation, this rests on
a cosmic conception of a realized Incarnation. This concept eliminates both
the period of promise and history itself, since Jesus as crucified is considered already to be fully the glorious Christ. This "heresy" is the exact
counterpart of the real docetic heresy (of which the iconoclasts were falsely
accused), but it is no better.

3.34 Paul Jewett on Non-Inclusive Language and the Trinity

In recent years, the issue of whether God must necessarily be referred to using male language
has become significant. The question has particular relevance in connection with the doctrine
of the Trinity, where the traditional language of "Father, Son and Holy Spirit" includes reference
to two apparently male entities. So what options are available here? How can Christian integrity
be maintained alongside a sensitivity towards the proper sensitivities of women? In this reading,
Paul Jewett explores some options. See also 3.3; 3.10; 3.11; 3.12; 3.14; 3.15; 3.19; 3.22;
3.30; 3.31; 3.35.

Source: Paul Jewett, *God, Creation and Revelation* (Grand Rapids: Eerdmans, 1991), pp. 323–5. Reprinted
with the permission of the publisher.

* * *

We have already addressed the question of the analogical character of theological language, including the language used in the trinitarian name: Father, Son, and Holy Spirit. Now that we have finished our treatment of the
nature of God and are about to turn to the question of the divine attributes,
it is fitting that we make a few added comments on our speech about God,
as that speech in its traditional form reflects a use of language that many
regard as sexist. We say it is fitting because, at this juncture, we shall turn
not only from the subject of the divine nature to the divine attributes, but
also from the traditional male use of language about God to the use of
female language. In speaking of the attributes, God will be likened not to
a father (Psalms 103:13) but to a mother (Isaiah 66:13).

Analogical language, to be meaningful, must of course rest upon some
univocal element between the human reality from which it is taken and the
divine reality to which it refers. In our exposition of the doctrine of the
Trinity, so far as God's name – Father, Son, and Spirit – is concerned, we
have identified the univocal element in the concept of origins. The second
and third persons in the Godhead originate, as persons, with the first person, who is therefore called "Father." The Father "begets" the Son and
"breathes" ("spirates") the Spirit. But obviously in using such terms as
"begetting" and "breathing" to describe how the second and third persons
of the Godhead have their origin in the first, we speak analogically, not

univocally. And since this is so, feminine figures could as well be used without altering the substance of our thought about God. If the woman, like the man, is created in the image of God (Genesis 1:27) and is therefore as much like God as the man, then female imagery is just as capable as is male imagery of bearing the truth that God is a trinitarian fellowship of holy love. After all, women have as much to do with origins, at the human level, as men – unless one subscribes to the discredited biological theory that our essential humanity is carried from generation to generation by the sperm lodged in the womb.

If we describe the relationship between the first and second persons of the Godhead analogically as a "begetting" and a "being begotten," may we not as well, still speaking analogically, describe it as a "bearing" and a "being born"? Since God is like a woman as well as a man, may God not be likened to a mother who eternally bears a daughter as well as to a father who eternally begets a son? And may not a mother also breathe the Spirit as well as a father? Do not women have breath as well as men? Are they not alive? We are, it is granted, speaking in a purely hypothetical way, since, as a matter of fact, in the Incarnation God assumed male humanity. But there is nothing either in the concept of God, or in the concept of Incarnation, that leads by logical entailment to masculinity. Given the patriarchal society of Israel, the revelation of God naturally takes a patriarchal form. (We say "naturally" rather than "necessarily" because even in patriarchal cultures female gods were known and worshipped.) It is not surprising, then, that God reveals himself to Israel as the "Father" of "his" people. Being disclosed as the Father of Israel, it is likewise natural that God should send one called a "son" who naturally assumes male humanity. Here an element of necessity does come into the picture; but it is a necessity of a secondary sort. It is due not to the essential, masculine nature of God but to the sexual polarity in which the Creator has given us our humanity. As a result of the way in which we are given our individual humanity, we describe ourselves, not analogically but literally, as male or female. This is why God, in becoming one with us, must of necessity become a man or a woman. Neither the gospels, however, nor the Chalcedonian Christology of the church, lays any emphasis on the maleness of Jesus. In the Incarnation he who is *vere Dei* becomes *vere homo,* not *vere masculus.* Of course, once "the matchless deed's achieved, determined, dared, and done" (Smart), there is a kind of finality, though not ultimacy, in the form of God's self-disclosure that is normative for the church. Christ Jesus is the one mediator between God and humankind (1 Timothy 2:5), and this Christ Jesus is the *man* Christ Jesus.

Nonetheless, to speak of God as a mother who discloses herself to us in a daughter, though it is a hypothetical way of speaking, is not a heretical way of speaking. Given the realities of salvation history, we grant that it is a way of speaking with no prospects of being other than hypothetical. God the Creator, as we have observed, has given us our humanity in a sexual polarity and God the Savior has assumed that humanity as a male rather than a female. Yet the need to speak in this hypothetical way comes from the fact that women are justified in their complaint that the traditional understanding of our traditional language about God has made them second-class citizens both as members of the human race and as members of the family of God.

3.35   Anne Carr on Feminism and the Maleness of God

The use of predominantly male language to refer to God within the Christian tradition has been the subject of attention by many feminist writers. In this lucid survey of some responses to this situation, Anne Carr focuses on the contributions of Sallie McFague, Rosemary Radford Ruether, and Judith Plaskow. In particular, she notes the importance of "metaphorical" approaches (see 1.25) to male imagery for God, and the development of metaphors such as "God as friend." See also 1.25; 3.22; 3.34; 4.31.

Source: Anne Carr, "Feminist Theology," in A. E. McGrath (ed.), *Blackwell Encyclopaedia of Modern Christian Thought* (Oxford: Blackwell, 1993), pp. 223–4. Reprinted with the permission of the publisher.

* * *

The fundamental feminist question about the maleness of God in the imagery, symbolism and concepts of traditional Christian thought and prayer leads to new reflection on the doctrine of God. In spite of theological denials of sexuality (or any materiality) in God, the persistent use of masculine pronouns for God and the reaction of many Christians against reference to God as "she" would appear to affirm the "maleness" attributed to God. Yet it is also logical that "she" is not only as appropriate as "he," but is perhaps necessary to reorient Christian imagination from the idolatrous implications of exclusively masculine God-language and the dominant effects of the father image in the churches and Christian practice. A new theory of the thoroughly metaphorical character of religious language has emerged in the light of feminist discussion of the doctrine of God. This theory argues that traditional analogical understanding has tended to stress the similarity between human concepts and God's own selfhood while a metaphorical theology should focus rather on the God–human relationship and on the unlikeness of all religious language in reference to God even as it affirms some similarity (McFague 1982).

There have been proposals for referring to God as "parent" or as "father and mother" or for the balancing use of feminine language for the Spirit since the Hebrew word for Spirit is grammatically feminine. On the other hand some feminist scholars have urged the move away from parental images entirely since these are suggestive of childish rather than adult religious dependence. While parental images express compassion, acceptance, guidance and discipline, they do not express the mutuality, maturity, cooperation, responsibility and reciprocity required by contemporary personal and political experience. One feminist theologian argues that there is no adequate name for God at present, given the overwhelming bias of traditional Christian thought about God and suggests the designation "God/ess" for the matrix and source of all life (Radford Ruether 1983).

Some feminist theologians call for the use of multiple metaphors and models for God and for the divine–human relationship, since none alone is adequate. The Bible itself uses many different human and cosmic designations, while in fact one metaphor (father) has become the dominant model in Christian thought and practice. One suggestion is the metaphor of God as "friend" (McFague, 1982, 1987). There is a biblical basis for this in Jesus' saying about laying down one's life for one's friends (John 15:13) and his reference to the Son of Man as friend of tax collectors and sinners (Matthew 11:19); Jesus *is* the parable of God's friendship with people. This friendship is shown in his parables of the lost sheep, the prodigal son, the good Samaritan, and the "enacted parable" of Jesus' inclusive table fellowship. The Gospels describe Jesus as critical of views of familial ties that failed to recognize the inclusive significance of his new community. They depict his presence as transforming the lives of his friends. Friendship to the stranger, both as individual and as nation or culture, is a model "on our increasingly small and beleaguered planet where, if people do not become friends, they will not survive" (McFague, 1982).

The metaphor of God as friend corresponds to the feminist ideal of "communal personhood," an ideal that entails non-competitive relationships among persons and groups that are characterized by mutuality and reciprocity rather than dualism and hierarchy. It responds to feminist concerns for expressions of divine–human relation that overcome the images of religious self-denial that have shaped women's experience in patterns of low self esteem, passivity and irresponsibility. It suggests the ideas of mutuality, self-creation in community, and the creation of ever wider communities with other persons and the world (Plaskow, 1980). The theme of God's friendship is intensified in the life and death of Jesus, who reveals a God who suffers for, with, and in people and invites them into a community of suffering with God and for others (Moltmann, [1980] 1981). The theme unites theology with feminist spirituality in its emphasis on women's friendship and interdependence as these are related to the reciprocal interdependence of the whole of creation. There are limitations to the metaphor of God as friend, as there are to any metaphor, and these limitations point to the importance of the use of many different metaphors to suggest the unfathomable character of the divine–human relationship.

Study Questions to Chapter 3

To what does Irenaeus attribute the origin of evil?

On what grounds does Augustine justify his identification of "love" and "the Holy Spirit"?

Summarize Richard of St. Victor's argument for the Trinity on the basis of the "love of God."

Can God sin? How does Thomas Aquinas justify his negative reply to this question?

"God cannot suffer." Assess the way in which this statement is reflected in the writings of Anselm and Spinoza.

Why does Schleiermacher place his discussion of the Trinity right at the end of his *Christian Faith*?

According to Robert Jenson, how does the Trinity "name" God?

4 The Person of Christ

Christology – that is, the section of Christian theology which focuses on the identity of Jesus Christ – has long been recognized as being of central importance to Christian theology. This collection includes readings relating directly to the classic debates of patristic Christology – such as Docetism, Gnosticism, Arianism, Apollinarianism, Nestorianism, Patripassianism, and the Monophysite controversy. In view of the importance of the patristic debates to subsequent theological reflection, STUDY PANEL 10 identifies those readings which focus on this formative period of Christological discussion.

However, Christological debate did not end with the closing of the patristic period. Although Christology was not of fundamental importance to the debates of the Reformation, it became of major importance once more at the dawn of the Enlightenment. One of the most important debates in modern Christology focuses on the historical aspects of the question, in particular the issue of "faith and history." The readings noted at STUDY PANEL 11 deal with the important modern question of how a past historical event can be of foundational importance to Christianity, and particularly the debate over whether Christian theology may have misunderstood Jesus. Other issues have subsequently emerged as important, perhaps most significantly the question of whether the maleness of Jesus compromises his significance for women (see 4.31).

STUDY PANEL 10

The Patristic Christological Debates

STUDY PANEL 11

Faith and History

4.1 Ignatius of Antioch on Docetism

This text, written several years before Ignatius's martyrdom around 107, is an important witness to an early form of the Docetist heresy, which declared that Christ did not suffer in reality, but suffered only in appearance, and was thus not truly human. See also 4.2; 4.12.

Source: Letter to the Trallians, 9–10; in *Sources Chrétiennes*, vol. 10, second edition, ed. P. Th. Camelot (Paris: Cerf, 1951), pp. 118–20.

* * * ───────────────────────────────

So do not pay attention when anyone speaks to you apart from (*chōris*) Jesus Christ, who was of the family of David, the child of Mary, who was truly born, who ate and drank, who was truly persecuted under Pontius Pilate, was truly crucified and truly died, in full view of heaven, earth and hell, and who was truly raised from the dead. It was his Father who raised him again, and it is him [i.e., the Father] who will likewise raise us in Jesus Christ, we who believe in him, apart from whom we have no true life. But if, as some godless people (*atheoi*), that is, unbelievers, say, he suffered in mere appearance (*to dokein peponthenai*) – being themselves mere appearances – why am I in bonds?

4.2 Irenaeus of Lyons on Gnosticism in Christology

In this account of the impact of Gnosticism, dating from the second half of the second century, Irenaeus sets out a list of various Christological heresies which are due to Gnostic influence. Of particular importance is his reference to the Docetic view that Christ was a human being in appearance only. See also 4.1; 4.3.

Source: *adversus haereses*, I.xxiv.1–2; in *Sources Chrétiennes*, vol. 264, ed. A. Rousseau and L. Doutreleau (Paris: Cerf, 1979), pp. 320–4.

* * * ───────────────────────────────

Among these, Saturninus came from Antioch . . . like Menander, he taught that there is one unknown Father (*unum patrem incognitum*), who made angels, archangels, virtues, powers; and that the world, and everything in it, was made by seven angels. Humanity was also created by these angels . . .

He also declared that the Saviour was unborn, incorporeal and without form, asserting that he was seen as a human being in appearance only (*putative autem visum hominem*). The God of the Jews, he declares, was one of the angels; and because the Father wished to destroy all the rulers (*principes*), Christ came to destroy the God of the Jews, and to save all who believed in him, and these are they who have a spark of life (*scintillam vitae eius*). He was the first to say that two kinds of human beings were fashioned by the angels, one bad and the other good. And because the demons assist the worst, the Saviour came to destroy evil human beings and the demons and to save the good. But marriage and procreation, they declare, is of Satan. The majority of his disciples abstain from meat, and by this false temperance have led many people astray. As far as prophecies go, they say that some were made by the angels who created the world, and others by Satan. This last, according to Saturninus, is himself an angel, but an angel who is opposed to the creators of the world and, above all, to the God of the Jews.

Tertullian on Patripassianism   4.3

Patripassianism was a theological heresy which arose during the third century, associated with writers such as Noetus, Praxeas and Sabellius, focusing on the belief that the Father suffered as the Son. In other words, the suffering of Christ on the cross is to be regarded as the suffering of the Father. In this attack on his opponent Praxeas, Tertullian identifies the main features of this teaching. See also 3.15.

Source: *adversus Praxean*, 1; in *Tertullian's Treatise against Praxeas*, ed. E. Evans (London: SPCK, 1948), 89.4–33.

* * *

The devil is opposed to the truth in many ways. He has sometimes even attempted to destroy it by defending it. He declares that there is only one God, the omnipotent creator of the world, only to make a heresy out of that uniqueness. He says that the Father himself descended into the virgin, was himself born of her, himself suffered; in fact that he himself was Jesus Christ . . . It was [Praxeas], a restless foreigner, who first brought this kind of perversity from Asia to Rome . . . he put the Holy Spirit to flight and crucified the Father.

Tertullian on the Incarnation   4.4

In this polemical passage, directed against the teachings of Praxeas, Tertullian insists upon the unity of the person of Christ, while distinguishing the proper functions of the humanity and divinity of Christ. Note especially Tertullian's rejection of the incarnational model of an "amalgam," in which two metals are fused together in such a way as to lose their distinctive characteristics. "Electrum," to which he refers in this context, is a naturally-occurring amalgam of gold and silver. See also 4.7; 4.10; 4.11; 4.12; 4.18.

Source: *adversus Praxean*, 27; in *Tertullian's Treatise against Praxeas*, ed. E. Evans (London: SPCK, 1948), 123.24–125.3.

* * *

. . . others attempt to distinguish two beings in one person, the Father and the Son, saying that the Son is the flesh, that is, the human being that is

Jesus; while the Father is the spirit, that is, God that is Christ. Thus those who are trying to demonstrate the identity of the Father and Son seem to end up dividing them, rather than uniting them . . . Maybe they heard about this kind of "monarchy" (*talem monarchiam*), which distinguishes Jesus from Christ, from Valentinus. But . . . their "Father" is described as Word *of* God, Spirit *of* God . . . Who was the God born in flesh? The Word, and the Spirit, who was born with the Word in accordance with the Father's will. Therefore the Word was in flesh; but we must ask *how* the Word "was made flesh," whether by transformation into flesh or by being clothed with that flesh. The latter is surely the case. We must believe that God's eternal nature precludes change or transformation. Transformation involves the destruction of what originally existed: what is transformed ceases to be what it was and begins to be something else. But God does not cease to be, nor can he be other than what he is: and the Word is God, and "the Word of the Lord remains for ever," that is, it continues in the same form . . . It follows that his incarnation means that he comes to be in flesh and through flesh is revealed, seen, and touched. Other things also support this interpretation. For if he was incarnate by transformation and change of substance, Jesus would then be one substance made of two, of flesh and spirit, a kind of mixture, as electrum is an amalgam of gold and silver. Thus he would come to be neither gold (i.e., spirit) nor silver (i.e., flesh), since the one element is changed by the other and a third thing is produced. Then Jesus will not be God, since he ceases to be the Word, which was made flesh; nor will he be flesh, that is, a human being; for that which was the Word is not flesh in the true sense. Thus out of the two a thing is produced which is neither one nor the other, but a third something, very different from either . . . We see a twofold mode of being, not confused but conjoined in one person, Jesus, who is God and human . . . And the proper quality of each substance remains so intact that the spirit carried out in him his own activities – the powers and works and signs – while the flesh underwent the experiences proper to it: hunger, when it met the devil, thirst, when with the Samaritan woman; weeping, for Lazarus; troubled even unto death; and, in the end, the flesh died.

4.5   Origen on the Two Natures of Christ

Origen here sets out the case for the necessity of a mediator between God and humanity, noting the respective importance of both Christ's divine and his human natures in relation to his work. See also 4.4; 4.8; 4.15.

Source: *de Principiis*, II.vi.3; in *Sources Chrétiennes*, vol. 252, ed. H. Crouzel and M. Simonetti (Paris: Cerf, 1978), 314.106–316.128.

* * * ─────────────────────────────────

Therefore with this soul acting as a mediator between God and flesh – for it was not possible for the nature of God to be mingled with flesh without a mediator – there was born the God-man (*deus-homo*), that "substance" (*substantia*) being the connecting link which could assume a body without denying its own nature . . . The Son of God by whom all things were created is called Jesus Christ, the Son of man. For the Son of God is said to have died in respect of that nature which was certainly capable of death; and he is called the Son of man who is proclaimed about to come "in the glory of God the Father with the holy angels." And for this reason through the whole of Scripture the divine nature is spoken of in human terms, and at the same time the human nature is accorded the distinctive epithets proper to the divine. In this case more than any other, one could say, as it is written, "The two shall be in one flesh, and they are now not two but one flesh" (Matthew 19:6).

Arius on the Status of Christ   4.6

This letter, written in Greek around 321, is one of the few extant documents relating to Arius's Christological views which is written by Arius himself. His views tend to be found primarily in the writings of his opponents, such as Athanasius. Arius's characteristic emphasis is upon the Son having a beginning. Note the connection between this axiom and Arius's firm insistence upon the unchangeability of God. For Arius, the fact that God cannot change is itself a powerful argument against the incarnation. See also 1.5; 4.4; 4.7; 4.15; 4.16; 4.29.

Source: A letter of Arius to Eusebius, Bishop of Nicomedia (*c*.321). This letter is known, with slight variations, in two major sources, as follows: Theodoret of Cyrus, *Ecclesiastical History*, I.v.1–4; in *Die griechischen christlichen Schriftsteller der ersten Jahrhunderte*: *Theodoret Kirchengeschichte*, ed. L. Parmentier and F. Schweiweiler (Berlin: Akademie Verlag, 1954), 26.1–27.6; and Epiphanius of Constantia, *Pararion*, lxix, 6; *Epiphanii Episcopi Constantiae Opera*, ed. G. Dindorfius (Leipzig: Weigel, 1861), 148.10–149.16.

* * *

Since my father Ammonius is coming to Nicomedia, I thought it right to send you my greetings by him, and at the same time to tell you . . . how desperately the bishop attacks, persecutes and pursues us, so that he drives us from the city as if we were atheists because we do not agree with him when he publicly preaches: "God always, the Son always; at the same time the Father, at the same time the Son; the Son co-exists with God, unbegotten; he is ever-begotten, he is not born-by-begetting; neither by thought nor by any moment of time does God precede the Son; God always, Son always, the Son exists from God himself." And Eusebius, your brother, Bishop of Caesarea, Theodotus, Paulinus, Athanasius, Gregory, Aetius, and all the other bishops of the East, have been condemned for saying that God existed, without beginning, before the Son; except Philogonius, Hellanicus and Macarius, men who are heretics and unlearned in the faith; some of whom say that the Son is an effluence, others a projection, others that he is co-unbegotten. We cannot even listen to these faithless things, even though the heretics threaten us with a thousand deaths. But what we say and think we both have taught and continue to teach; that the Son is not unbegotten, nor part of the unbegotten in any way, nor is he derived from any substance;

but that by his own will and counsel he existed before times and ages fully God, only-begotten, unchangeable. And before he was begotten or created or appointed or established, he did not exist; for he was not unbegotten. We are persecuted because we say: "the Son has a beginning, but God is without beginning." For that reason we are persecuted, and because we say that he is from what is not. And this we say because he is neither part of God nor derived from any substance. For this we are persecuted; the rest you know.

4.7   Athanasius on the Two Natures of Christ

In this letter, written in Greek around 350, Athanasius argues for the divinity of Christ on soteriological grounds, while affirming the full humanity of Christ. See also 1.5; 4.4; 4.5; 4.12; 4.15; 4.16; 5.4; 5.5; 5.22.

Source: *Epistulae ad Serapionem*, IV, 14; in J. P. Migne, *Patrologia Graeca*, 26.656C–657B.

* * *

Being God, he became a human being: and then as God he raised the dead, healed all by a word, and also changed water into wine. These were not the acts of a human being. But as a human being, he felt thirst and tiredness, and he suffered pain. These experiences are not appropriate to deity. As God he said, "I in the Father, the Father in me"; as a human being, he criticized the Jews, thus: "Why do you seek to kill me, when I am a man who has told you the truth, which I heard from my Father?" And yet these are not events occurring without any connection, distinguished according to their quality, so that one class may be ascribed to the body, apart from the divinity, and the other to the divinity, apart from the body. They all occurred in such a way that they were joined together; and the Lord, who marvellously performed those acts by his grace, was one. He spat in human fashion; but his spittle had divine power, for by it he restored sight to the eyes of the man blind from birth. When he willed to make himself known as God, he used his human tongue to signify this, when he said, "I and the Father are one." He cured by his mere will. Yet it was by extending his human hand that he raised Peter's mother-in-law when she had a fever, and raised from the dead the daughter of the ruler of the synagogue, when she had already died.

4.8   Apollinarius of Laodicea on the Person of Christ

This passage, taken from a letter written to the bishops at Diocaesarea, sets out the leading features of Apollinarius's Christology. The most important is the unequivocal assertion that the Word did not assume a "changeable" human mind in the incarnation, which would have led to the Word being trapped in human sin. Rather, it assumed "an immutable and heavenly divine mind." As a result, Christ cannot be said to be totally human. See also 4.1; 4.4; 4.5; 4.9; 4.12; 4.15; 4.16.

Source: Letter 2; in H. Lietzmann, *Apollinaris von Laodicea und seine Schule* (Tübingen: Mohr, 1904), 256.3–7.

* * *

We confess that the Word of God has not descended upon a holy man, which was what happened in the case of the prophets. Rather, the Word himself has become flesh without having assumed a human mind – that is, a changeable mind, which is enslaved to filthy thoughts – but which exists as an immutable and heavenly divine mind.

Gregory of Nazianzen on Apollinarianism   4.9

In this letter, written in Greek at some point in 380 or 381, Gregory mounts a frontal assault on the central thesis of Apollinarianism: that Christ was not fully human, in that he possessed "an immutable and heavenly divine mind," rather than a human mind. For Gregory, this amounts to a denial of the possibility of redemption. Only what is assumed by the Word in the incarnation can be redeemed. If Christ did not possess a human mind, humanity is not redeemed. Note the use of the term *Theotokos* or "God-bearer" as a term for Mary. See also 4.8; 4.10; 4.11; 4.12; 4.13; 4.14; 4.15; 4.16.

Source: Letter 101; in J. P. Migne, *Patrologia Graeca*, 37.177B–180A; 181C–184A.

* * *

Do not let people deceive themselves and others by saying that the "Man of the Lord," which is the title they give to him who is rather "Our Lord and God," is without a human mind. We do not separate the humanity from the divinity; in fact, we assert the dogma of the unity and identity of the Person, who aforetime was not just human but God, the only Son before all ages, who in these last days has assumed human nature also for our salvation; in his flesh passible, in his Deity impassible; in the body subject to limitation, yet unlimited in the Spirit; at one and the same time earthly and heavenly, tangible and intangible, comprehensible and incomprehensible; that by one and the same person, a perfect human being and perfect God, the whole humanity, fallen through sin, might be recreated.

If any one does not believe that holy Mary is *Theotokos*, they will be cut off from the Deity . . . If anyone asserts that humanity was created and only afterwards endued with divinity, they also are to be condemned . . . If anyone brings in the idea of two sons, one of God the Father, the other of the mother, may they lose their share in the adoption . . . For the Godhead and the humanity are two natures, as are soul and body, but there are not two Sons or two Gods . . . For both natures are one by the combination, the Godhead made man or the manhood deified, or whatever be the right expression . . .

If anyone has put their trust in him as a human being lacking a human mind, they are themselves mindless and not worthy of salvation. For what has not been assumed has not been healed; it is what is united to his divinity that is saved . . . Let them not grudge us our total salvation, or endue the Saviour only with the bones and nerves and mere appearance (*zōgraphia*) of humanity.

4.10 Nestorius on the Term "Theotokos"

What follows is an extract from a history of the church compiled by Socrates, also known as "Scholasticus." While there is probably a degree of bias in the reporting of Nestorius's actions and words, what is found in this passage corresponds well with what is known of the situation at this time. Notice how the controversy focuses on whether Mary, the mother of Jesus Christ, may properly be referred to as "*Theotokos* (God-bearer)." Nestorius is here depicted as confused about whether to use the term or not, hesitant as to what its use affirmed, yet fearful as to what its denial might imply. See also 4.8; 4.9; 4.11; 4.12; 4.13; 4.14; 4.15; 4.20.

Source: Socrates, *Historia Ecclesiastica*, VII, 32; in *Socratis Scholastica: Ecclesiastica Historia*, ed. R. Hussey (Oxford: Clarendon Press, 1853), vol. 2, pp. 804–7.

* * *

Now [Nestorius] had as a colleague the presbyter Anastasius, who he had brought from Antioch. He had high regard for him, and consulted him over many matters. Anastasius was preaching one day in church, and said, "Let no one call Mary the Mother of God (*Theotokos*): for Mary was only a human being, and it is impossible that God should be born of a human being." This caused a great scandal, and caused distress to both the clergy and the laity, as they had been taught up to this point to acknowledge Christ as God, and not to separate his humanity from his divinity on account of the economy [of salvation] . . . While great offence was taken in the church at what was proclaimed in this way, Nestorius, who was eager to establish Anastasius' proposition – for he did not wish to have someone who he so highly esteemed found guilty of blasphemy – continually kept on giving instruction in church on this subject. He adopted a controversial attitude, and totally rejected the term *Theotokos*. The controversy on the matter was taken one way by some and another way by others, with the result that the ensuing discussion divided the church, and began to look like people fighting in the dark, with everyone coming out with the most confused and contradictory assertions. Nestorius acquired the popular reputation of asserting that the Lord was nothing more than a human being, and attempting to impose the teaching of Paul of Samosata and Photinus on the church. This led to such a great outcry that it was thought necessary to convene a general council to rule on the matter in dispute. Having myself studied the writings of Nestorius, I have found him to be an unlearned man and shall express quite frankly my own views about him . . . I cannot concede that he was a follower of either Paul of Samosata or of Photinus, or that he ever said that the Lord was nothing more than a human being. However, he seemed scared of the term *Theotokos*, as though it were some terrible phantom. The fact is, the groundless alarm he showed on this subject just showed up his extreme ignorance: for being a man of natural ability as a speaker, he was considered well educated, but in reality he was disgracefully illiterate. In fact he had no time for the hard work which an accurate examination of the ancient expositors would have involved and, made arrogant on account of his readiness of expression, he did not give his attention to the ancients, but thought himself above them.

Cyril of Alexandria on Nestorius's Christology 4.11

In an important section of this letter, written around 430, Cyril condemns twelve propositions associated with the Antiochene school of Christology. Although Cyril regards these views as heretical, there are points at which it seems that his primary concern is to establish the supremacy of the Alexandrian over the Antiochene position. Of the twelve propositions, the following are particularly significant theologically. See also 4.8; 4.9; 4.10; 4.12; 4.13; 4.14; 4.15; 4.20.

Source: Letter XVII, 12 (Third Letter to Nestorius); in *Oxford Early Christian Texts*: Cyril of Alexandria: Select Letters, ed. L. R. Wickham (Oxford: Clarendon Press, 1983), 28.17–32.16.

* * *

1. If anyone does not acknowledge that Emmanuel is truly God, and that the holy Virgin is, in consequence, "Theotokos," for she gave birth in the flesh to the Word of God who has become flesh, let them be condemned.
2. If anyone does not acknowledge that the Word of God the Father was substantially (*kath' hypostasin*) united with flesh, and with his own flesh is one Christ, that is, one and the same God and human being together, let them be condemned.
3. If anyone divides the persons in the one Christ after their union, joining them together in a mere conjunction in accordance with their rank, or a conjunction effected by authority or power, instead of a combination according to a union of natures, let them be condemned.
4. If anyone distributes between two characters or persons the expressions used about Christ in the gospels, and apostolic writings . . . applying some to the human being, conceived of separately, apart from the Word, . . . and others exclusively to the Word, let them be condemned.
5. If anyone dares to call Christ a "God-bearing human being" (*theophoros anthrōpos*) . . . , let them be anathema.
6. If anyone says that the Word of God the Father is the god or master of Christ, instead of confessing that this Christ is both God and a human being . . . , let them be condemned.
7. If anyone says that Jesus as a human being was controlled by God the Word, and that the "glory of the only-begotten" was attached to him, as something existing apart from himself, let them be condemned.

8. If anyone dares to say that "the human being who was assumed is to be worshipped together with the Divine Word" . . . , let them be condemned.

9. If anyone says that the one Lord Jesus Christ was glorified by the Spirit, as if Christ used a power alien to himself which came to him through the Spirit . . . , let them be condemned . . .

12. If anyone does not confess that the Word of God suffered in the flesh, and was crucified in the flesh, and tasted death in the flesh . . . , let them be condemned.

4.12 Cyril of Alexandria on the Incarnation

In this letter, written in February 430, Cyril sets out his understanding of the mechanics of the incarnation. Note the emphasis upon the totality of the union between the divinity and humanity of Christ, without in any way allowing that a change occurred in the divinity as a result. Note also Cyril's rejection of the idea of a "union of good pleasure," an approach especially associated with Antiochene theologians such as Theodore of Mopsuestia, who argued that the divinity and humanity were not really united, but merely agreed to coexist in a specific manner. For Cyril, a real union took place. See also 4.8; 4.9; 4.10; 4.11; 4.13; 4.14; 4.15.

Source: Letter IV, 3–5 (Second Letter to Nestorius); in Oxford Early Christian Texts: Cyril of Alexandria: Select Letters, ed. L. R. Wickham (Oxford: Clarendon Press, 1983), 4.22–6.28.

* * *

. . . In declaring that the Word was made to "be incarnate" and "made human," we do not assert that there was any change in the nature of the Word when it became flesh, or that it was transformed into an entire human being, consisting of soul and body; but we say that the Word, in an indescribable and inconceivable manner, united personally to himself flesh endowed with a rational soul, and thus became a human being and was called the Son of man. And this was not by a mere act of will or favour, nor simply adopting a role or taking to himself a person. The natures which were brought together to form a true unity were different; but out of both is one Christ and one Son. We do not mean that the difference of the natures is annihilated by reason of this union; but rather that the divinity and humanity, by their inexpressible and inexplicable concurrence into unity, have produced for us the one Lord and Son Jesus Christ. It is in this sense that he is said to have been born also of a woman after the flesh, though he existed and was begotten from the Father before all ages . . . It was not that an ordinary human being was first born of the holy Virgin, and that afterwards the Word descended upon him. He was united with the flesh in the womb itself, and thus is said to have undergone a birth after the flesh, inasmuch as he made his own the birth of his own flesh.

In the same way we say that he "suffered and rose again." We do not mean that God the Word suffered blows or the piercing of nails or other wounds in his own nature, in that the divine is impassible because it is not physical. But the body which had become his own body suffered these things, and therefore he himself is said to have suffered them for us. The impassible was in the body which suffered.

Cyril of Alexandria on Mary as Mother of God   4.13

At the Council of Ephesus (431), the term "Theotokos" (literally, "bearer of God") was formally endorsed as an appropriate title for Mary, as mother of Jesus Christ. Cyril's homily celebrates the dignity of Mary as a result of her bearing Jesus Christ. The homily is known by various titles; in this edition, it is referred to as "Homily 4." See also 4.8; 4.9; 4.10; 4.11; 4.12; 4.14; 4.15.

Source: *Homily at the Council of Ephesus*; in J. P. Migne, *Patrologia Graeca*, 77.991A–D; 996C.

* * *

I see here a joyful assembly of holy bishops who, at the invitation of the blessed Mother of God (*Theotokos*), Mary, forever a virgin, have gathered enthusiastically. And although I am sad, the presence of these holy Fathers fills me with joy. Among us are fulfilled the sweet words of the psalmist David: "Behold how good and sweet it is, brethren, to dwell together in unity." So we hail you, mysterious holy Trinity, who have brought us all together in this church of holy Mary Mother of God. We hail you, Mary, Mother of God, sacred treasure of all the universe, star who never sets, crown of virginity, sceptre of the orthodox law, indestructible temple, dwelling-place of the incommensurable, Mother and Virgin, for the sake of the one who is called "blessed" in the holy Gospels, the one who "comes in the name of the Lord." We hail you, who held in your virginal womb him whom the heavens cannot contain, through whom the Trinity is glorified and worshipped throughout the world; through whom the heavens exult; through whom the angels and archangels rejoice; through whom the demons are put to flight; through whom the tempter fell from heaven; through whom the fallen creation is raised to the heavens; through whom the whole world, held captive by idolatry, has come to know the truth; through whom holy baptism is given to those who believe, with "the oil of gladness"; through whom churches have been founded throughout the world; through whom pagan nations have been led to conversion. What more shall I say? It is through you that the light of the only-begotten Son of God has shone "for those who dwelt in darkness and in the shadow of death"; it is through you that the prophets proclaimed the future, that the apostles preach salvation to the nations, that the dead are raised and that kings reign, in the name of the holy Trinity. Is there a single person who can worthily celebrate the praises of Mary? She is both mother and virgin. What a marvellous thing! It is a marvel which overwhelms me! Has anyone ever heard it said that the builder was prevented from dwelling in the temple which he himself built? Has anyone the right to speak ill of the one who gave his own servant the title of mother? Thus everyone rejoices! . . .

May it be given us to worship and adore the unity, to worship and honour the indivisible Trinity, by singing the praises of Mary ever virgin, that is the holy church, and those of her Son and immaculate Spouse, to whom be glory for ever and ever, Amen.

4.14 Leo the Great on the Two Natures

This letter, written in Latin from Pope Leo I to Flavian, patriarch of Constantinople, on 13 June 449, is usually referred to as the "Tome of Leo." Leo here sets out the prevailing Christological consensus within the Latin church. The letter was later elevated to a position of authority by the Council of Chalcedon (451), which recognized it as a classic statement of Christological orthodoxy. The letter is primarily a critique of the views of Eutyches, especially his rejection of the true humanity of Christ. For Leo, the formula *totus in suis, totus in nostris* sums up the correct position on this matter. See also 4.4; 4.5; 4.8; 4.9; 4.10; 4.11; 4.12; 4.13; 4.15; 4.29.

Source: Letter 28 to Flavian (13 June 449); in J. P. Migne, *Patrologia Latina*, 54.758B–760A; 764A–768B.

* * *

[Eutyches] did not realize what he ought to believe concerning the incarnation of the Word of God, and did not want to seek out the light of understanding by careful study throughout Holy Scripture in all its breadth. But he might at least have received with careful attention that common and universal confession, in which the whole body of the faithful confess their faith in God the Father almighty and in Jesus Christ his only son our Lord who was born of the Holy Spirit and the Virgin Mary. For by these three statements the strategies of almost all the heretics are overthrown. God is believed to be both Almighty and Father; as a result, the Son is seen to be co-eternal with God, differing in no respect from the Father. For Christ was born God of God, Almighty of Almighty, co-eternal of eternal; not later in time, not inferior in power, not different in glory, not divided in essence. The same only-begotten, eternal Son of the eternal Father was born of the Holy Spirit and the Virgin Mary. But this birth in time has taken nothing from, and added nothing to, that divine eternal nativity, but has bestowed itself wholly on the restoration of humanity, which had been deceived: that it might overcome death and by its own virtue overthrow the devil who had the power of death. For we could not overcome the author of sin and death, unless he had taken our nature and made it his own, whom sin could not defile nor death retain, since he was conceived of the Holy Spirit, in the womb of his Virgin Mother, whose virginity remained entire in his birth as in his conception ... That birth, uniquely marvellous and marvellously unique, ought not to be understood in such a way as to preclude the distinctive properties of the kind [i.e. of humanity] through the new mode of creation. For it is true that the Holy Spirit gave fruitfulness to the Virgin, but the reality of his body was received from her body ...

Thus the properties of each nature and substance were preserved in their totality, and came together to form one person. Humility was assumed by majesty, weakness by strength, mortality by eternity; and to pay the debt that we had incurred, an inviolable nature was united to a nature that can suffer. And so, to fulfil the conditions of our healing, the human being Jesus Christ, one and the same mediator between God and humanity, was able to die in respect of the one, yet unable to die in respect of the other. Thus there was born true God in the entire and perfect nature of true humanity, complete in his own properties, complete in ours (*totus in suis, totus in nostris*). By "ours" we mean those things which the Creator formed in us at the beginning, which he assumed in order to restore; for in the Saviour there was no trace of the properties which the deceiver brought in, and which humanity, being deceived, allowed to enter. Christ did not become partaker of our sins because he entered into fellowship with human infirmities. He assumed the form of a servant without the stain of sin, making the human properties greater, but not detracting from the divine. For that "emptying of himself," by which the invisible God chose to become visible, and the Creator and Lord of all willed to be a mortal, was an inclination of compassion, not a failure of power (*inclinatio fuit miserationis, non defectio potestatis*). Accordingly, the one who created humanity, while remaining in the form of God, was made a human being in the form of a servant. Each nature preserves its own characteristics without diminution, so that the form of a servant does not detract from the form of God. Now the devil boasted that humanity, deceived by his guile, had been deprived of the divine gifts and, stripped of the dower of immortality, had incurred the stern sentence of death; that he himself had found some consolation in his plight from having a companion in sin. He boasted too that God, because justice required it, had changed his purpose in respect of humanity, which God had created in such honour. Therefore there was need for a dispensation by which God might carry out God's hidden plan, that the unchangeable God, whose will cannot be deprived of its own mercy, might accomplish the first design of God's affection towards us by a more secret mystery; and that humanity, driven into sin by the devil's wicked craftiness, should not perish contrary to the purpose of God.

The son of God therefore came down from his throne in heaven without withdrawing from his Father's glory, and entered this world, born after a new order, by a new mode of birth. After a new order, inasmuch as he is invisible in his own nature, and he became visible in ours . . . From his mother the Lord took nature, not sin. Jesus Christ was born from a virgin's womb, by a miraculous birth. And yet his nature is not on that account unlike to ours, for he that is true God is also truly human. There is no unreality in this unity since the humility of the manhood and the majesty of the deity exist in reciprocity. For just as the divinity is not changed by his compassion, so the humanity is not swallowed up by the dignity. Each nature performs its proper functions in communion with the other; the Word performs what pertains to the Word, the flesh what pertains to the flesh. The one is resplendent with miracles, the other submits to insults. The Word withdraws not from his equality with the Father's glory; the flesh does not desert the nature of our kind.

4.15 The Chalcedonian Definition of the Christian Faith (451)

The Council of Chalcedon (451) laid down an understanding of the relation of the humanity and divinity of Jesus Christ which became normative for the Christian churches, both east and west. Notice how the Council is adamant that Christ must be accepted to be truly divine and truly human, without specifying precisely how this is to be understood. In other words, a number of Christological models are legitimated, providing they uphold this essential Christological affirmation. See also 1.5; 4.8; 4.9; 4.10; 4.11; 4.12; 4.13; 4.14; 4.20; 2.30.

Source: H. Denzinger (ed.), *Enchiridion Symbolorum*, 24–5 edn (Barcelona: Herder, 1948), pp. 70–1.

* * *

> Following the holy Fathers, we all with one voice confess our Lord Jesus Christ to be one and the same Son, perfect in divinity and humanity, truly God and truly human, consisting of a rational soul and a body, being of one substance with the Father in relation to his divinity, and being of one substance with us in relation to his humanity, and is like us in all things apart from sin (Hebrews 4:15). He was begotten of the Father before time in relation to his divinity, and in these recent days, was born from the Virgin Mary, the *Theotokos*, for us and for our salvation. In relation to the humanity, he is one and the same Christ, the Son, the Lord, the Only-begotten, who is to be acknowledged in two natures, without confusion, without change, without division, and without separation. This distinction of natures is in no way abolished on account of this union, but rather the characteristic property of each nature is preserved, and concurring into one Person and one subsistence, not as if Christ were parted or divided into two persons, for he remains one and the same Son and only-begotten God, Word, Lord, Jesus Christ; even as the Prophets from the beginning spoke concerning him, and our Lord Jesus Christ instructed us, and the Creed of the Fathers was handed down to us.

4.16 The Emperor Zeno on the Natures of Christ

This important document, which dates from 482, attempted to resolve the differences which were opening up within the church over the "monophysite" controversy. Unfortunately, the document served to make divisions even worse, leading to growing division between eastern and western Christians. The document's affirmations concerning the divinity and humanity of Christ are an important witness to the tensions in Christology at this period. See also 4.15; 4.17.

Source: The *Henoticon*, cited by Evagrius, *Ecclesiastical History*, III, 14; in *The Ecclesiastical History of Evagrius*, ed. J. Bidez and L. Parmentier (London: Methuen, 1898), 113.2–15.

* * *

We confess that our Lord Jesus Christ, the only begotten Son of God, the same God who himself truly assumed human nature, is consubstantial with the Father in respect of the Godhead, and consubstantial with us in respect of his humanity. He descended [from heaven] and become incarnate of the Holy Spirit and Mary, the Virgin and *Theotokos*. He is one, not two, for we affirm that both his miracles and the sufferings which he voluntarily endured in his flesh are those of a single person. In no way do we agree with those who make a division on confusion, or introduce a phantom. For his truly sinless incarnation from the *Theotokos* did not produce an additional son, because the Trinity (*Trias*) contained a Trinity even when one member of the Trinity (that is, God the Word) became incarnate.

The Monophysites on the Natures of Christ 4.17

This petition, which dates from 532, rejects the Chalcedonian definition of "two natures" in Christ, and vigorously upholds the Monophysite view that there is only one nature in Christ. The document stresses the orthodoxy of this position, and is particularly critical of the views of Apollinarius. See also 4.15; 4.16.

Source: *The Petition of the Monophysites to the Emperor Justinian*; text according to Michael the Syrian, *Chronicle*, ed. J. B. Chabot, 3 vols (Paris: Leroux, 1899–1910), vol. 2, pp. 199–200, 202–3.

———————————————————————————————— * * *

We confess a holy Trinity, worthy of adoration, of one nature, power and honour, which is made known in three persons. We worship the Father and his only Son, the Word, who was begotten of him eternally before all ages, and who is of the nature of the Father and of the Son. We declare that one of the persons of this holy Trinity, that is, God the Word, by the will of the Father and for the salvation of humanity took flesh of the Holy Spirit and of the holy Virgin and *Theotokos* Mary, in a body which was endowed with a rational and intellectual soul, passible like our natures, and became a human being without being changed from what he was. And so we confess that while in the Godhead he was of the nature of the Father, he was also of our nature in his state of humanity. So he who is the perfect Word, the unchangeable Son of God, became a perfect human being, and left nothing wanting for us in respect of our salvation. This is what the foolish Apollinaris said, when he declared that God the Word did not become human in a perfect manner, and deprives us of things that are of major importance in relation to our salvation. For, if our intellect was not united with him, as Apollinaris maintained, then we are not saved, and in the matter of salvation we have fallen short of what was of the greatest importance for us. However, he is wrong: the perfect God became a perfect human being without change for our sake, and in this becoming human, God the Word did not omit anything. Nor was it a phantom, as the impious Mani and the erring Eutyches suggested.

Now Christ is truth, and, because he is God, does not know how to lie or to deceive, it may be said that God the Word truly became incarnate, in truth and not merely in appearance, with natural and innocent feelings . . . And just as God the Word left nothing missing, and did not become a phantom in his incarnation and becoming human, so he did not divide it into two persons and two natures, according to the teaching introduced by Nestorius . . .

If, as according to our holy Fathers (which your Serenity also acknowledges) God the Word, who was previously simple and not composite, became incarnate of the Virgin and *Theotokos* Mary, and united an intellectual flesh, possessing a soul, to himself personally, and made it his own and was joined together with it in the incarnation, it is clear that . . . we ought to confess one nature of God the Word, who took flesh and perfectly became a human being. For this reason, God the Word, who was previously simple, cannot be considered to have become composite in a body, if division results after this union through his having two natures. But just as an ordin-ary human being, who is made up of various natures (such as soul, body and so on) is not divided into two natures on account of a soul being joined by composition with a body to make up the one nature and person of a human being, so also God the Word, who was personally united to and joined by composition with a flesh which possesses a soul cannot be "in two natures" on account of his union or composition with a body . . .

For this reason, we do not accept either the Tome [of Leo] or the definition of Chalcedon, because we maintain the canon and law of our fathers who gathered together at Ephesus, and condemned and deprived Nestorius and excommunicated any who were bold enough to lay down any other definition of faith apart from that of Nicea, which was correctly and faithfully laid down by the Holy Spirit.

4.18 John of Damascus on the Incarnation and Icons

In this treatise, originally written is Greek in the first half of the eighth century, John of Damascus argues that the theological fact of the incarnation of Christ provides a solid foundation for the use of icons in devotion. An "icon" (*eikōn*) is a religious painting or picture, which is understood to act as a window through which the worshipper may catch a closer glimpse of the divine than would otherwise be possible. The text from which this citation is taken has no generally agreed title; it can also be found referred to as *pro sacris imaginibus orationes tres*, as, for example, in the Migne edition. See also 1.13; 3.33; 4.8; 4.9; 4.10; 4.11; 4.12; 4.13; 4.14; 4.15.

Source: *contra imaginum calumniatores*, I, 16; in *Patristische Texte und Studien*, vol. 17, ed. P. Bonifatius Kotter O.S.B. (Berlin/New York: de Gruyter, 1979), 89.1–4; 92.90–91.

* * *

Previously there was absolutely no way in which God, who has neither a body nor a face, could be represented by any image. But now that he has made himself visible in the flesh and has lived with people, I can make an image of what I have seen of God ... and contemplate the glory of the Lord, his face having been unveiled.

Gregory Palamas on the Divine Condescension in the Incarnation   4.19

In the course of commenting on Matthew 16:28, "there are some here who will not taste death before they have seen the kingdom of God coming with power," this noted Byzantine theologian deals with the manner in which God descends to his people in Christ. The text, written in Greek around 1335, stresses the importance of the divine descent (*katabasis*) to humanity, and the resulting ascent (*anabasis*) of humanity to God. See also 4.7; 5.5; 5.25.

Source: *Homilia*, 34; in J. P. Migne, *Patrologia Graeca*, 151.428D–429A.

———————————————————————————— * * *

The king of all is everywhere, and his kingdom is everywhere. This means that the coming of the kingdom cannot mean that it is transfered from this place here to that place there, but that it is revealed in the power of the divine Spirit. This is why [Christ] said "coming with power." And this power does not come upon everyone, but upon "those who have stood with the Lord," that is, those who are firmly grounded in the faith, such as Peter, James and John, who were first brought by the Word to this high mountain, in order to symbolize those who are thus able to rise above their humble natures. For this reason, Scripture shows us God descending from his supreme dwelling place and raising us up from our humble condition on a mountain, so that the one who is infinite may be surely but within limits encompassed by created nature.

Martin Luther's Critique of Nestorianism   4.20

Although Christology was not an issue of major controversy at the time of the Reformation, its leading representatives dealt with this aspect of theology in some depth. In this important section of this reforming treatise of 1539, Luther digresses from his analysis of the history and authority of Councils to focus on the Christology of Nestorius. Luther develops his characteristic position concerning the relation of the distinctive attributes (or *idiomata*, to use the technical term which recurs throughout the passage) of God and humanity in Christ. For Luther, the incarnation means that everything that can be said about God is also true of humanity in the specific case of Christ. This leads to his startling assertion that, since Jesus was crucified, suffered, and died, it must follow that God was crucified, suffered and died. See also 4.8; 4.9; 4.10; 4.11; 4.12; 4.13; 4.14; 4.15.

Source: *On the Councils and the Church* (1539); in *D. Martin Luthers Werke: Kritische Gesamtausgabe*, vol. 50 (Weimar: Böhlau, 1914), 587.29–590.4.

———————————————————————————— * * *

So Nestorius' error was not that he thought that Christ was simply a human being, or that he made him into two persons. On the contrary, he confesses that there are two natures, God and humanity, in one person. He does not, however, concede the *communicatio idiomatum*, something which I cannot put into a single word. "Idioma" means something which is inherent in a nature, or is its attribute, such as dying, suffering, crying, speaking, laughing, eating, drinking, sleeping, being sad, being happy, being born . . . [Luther provides a long list here] . . . and other things like these, which are called *idiomata naturae humanae*, that is, qualities which belong to human nature, which humanity can and must do or have done to it . . . Again, an *idioma deitatis* – that is, an attribute of the divine nature – is that it is immortal, all-powerful and infinite; it is not born, it does not eat, drink, sleep, stand, walk, become sad, or cry. So what more can be said? To be God is clearly something completely different to being human. So the *idiomata* of both these two natures cannot coincide. And this is the opinion of Nestorius.

Now suppose I were to preach like this: "Jesus the carpenter of Nazareth (for that is what the gospels call him) is walking down the street over there, fetching a jug of water and a pennyworth of bread for his mother, so that he could eat and drink with her. And this same Jesus the carpenter is the true son of God in one person." Now Nestorius would agree with this, and say that it is true. But now suppose that I say: "there is God going down the street, fetching some water and bread so that he could eat and drink with his mother." Nestorius would not agree with this, but would say: "Fetching water, buying bread, having a mother, and eating and drinking with her, are *idiomata* of a human, not a divine, nature." So if I were to say: "Jesus the carpenter was crucified by the Jews. And this same Jesus is really God." Nestorius would say to me that this is true. But if I were to say: "God was crucified by the Jews," he would say: "No! For to suffer the cross and to die are not divine, but human, *idiomata* or attributes." . . .

So we Christians must allow the *idiomata* of the two natures of Christ, the persons, equally and totally. As a result, Christ is God and a human being in one person because whatever is said about him as a human being must also be said of him as God, namely, "Christ has died," and, as Christ is God, it follows that "God has died" – not God in isolation (*der abgesonderte Gott*), but God united with humanity. For neither of the statements "Christ is God" and "God has died" are true in the case of God in isolation; both are false, for then God is not a human being. If it seems strange to Nestorius that God should die, he should find it just as strange that God becomes a human being; for by doing so, the immortal God becomes that which must die and suffer, and have all the human *idiomata*. If this was not the case, what kind of human being would God have become united to, if it did not have truly human *idiomata*? It would be a phantom (*gespenst*), as the Manichaeans taught earlier. On the other hand, whatever is said of God must also be attributed to the human being. Thus "God created the world and is almighty," and the human being Christ is God; therefore, the human being Christ created the world and is almighty. The reason for this is that since God and the human being have become one person, this person bears the *idiomata* of both natures in consequence.

François Turrettini on the Threefold Office of Christ   4.21

The writings of John Calvin, especially his *Institutes of the Christian Religion* (1559), established a pattern which would become widespread within Reformed Christology. The significance of Christ was explored using the model of the "threefold office," which depicted him as prophet, priest and king. As a prophet, Christ declared the will of God; as a priest, he made atonement for sins; and as king, he rules over his people. The noted seventeenth-century Genevan theologian François Turrettini, a major exponent of the Reformed tradition, here sets out this understanding more fully, in a text originally published in Latin in 1679. See also 5.15; 5.16.

Source: *Institutio theologiae elencticae*, topic 14, q. 5; in *Institutio theologiae elencticae*, 3 vols (Rome: Trajecti, 1734), vol. 2, pp. 424–7.

---

* * *

The office of Christ is nothing other than a mediation between God and humanity, which he was sent into the world by the Father and anointed by the Holy Spirit to carry out. It embraces all that Christ was required to achieve during his mission and calling in relation to an offended God and offending humanity (*erga Deus offensum et homines offendentes*), reconciling and uniting them to each other . . . This mediatorial office of Christ is distributed among three functions, which are individual parts of it: the prophetic, priestly and kingly. Christ sustained these together rather than separately, something which he alone was able to do. For what would, in the case of other people, be divided on account of their weakness (as no mortal could discharge them alone, so great are their dignity and responsibility) are united in Christ on account of his supreme perfection. There could indeed be people who were both kings and priests (such as Melchizedek) or kings and prophets (such as David), or priests and prophets (as in the case of some high priests) – but there is no other who perfectly fulfilled all three. This was reserved for Christ alone, in that he was able to uphold the truth which is embodied in these types . . . The threefold misery of humanity resulting from sin (that is, ignorance, guilt, and the oppression and bondage of sin) required this threefold office. Ignorance is healed through the prophetic office, guilt through the priestly, and the oppression and bondage of sin through the kingly. The prophetic light scatters the darkness of error; the merit of the priest removes guilt and obtains reconciliation for us; the power of the king takes away the bondage of sin and death. The prophet shows God to us; the priest leads us to God; and the king joins us together with God, and glorifies us with him. The prophet illuminates the mind by the spirit of enlightenment; the priest soothes the heart and conscience by the spirit of consolation; the king subdues rebellious inclinations by the spirit of sanctification.

4.22   Gotthold Ephraim Lessing on the Ditch of History

In this important discussion, published in German in 1777, Lessing argued that there was no connection between the "accidental truths of history" and the "necessary truths of reason." As a result, the total history of Jesus of Nazareth – including his resurrection – can have no metaphysical significance. Even if this history could be known with total accuracy and certainty (which Lessing doubts in any case), it could not serve as the basis of a philosophical or theological system. The title of the work, "On the Proof of Spirit and Power," refers to a phrase in the writings of Origen, with which Lessing takes issue. See also 4.24; 4.25; 4.26; 4.27; 4.28; 4.30.

Source: "Über den Beweis des Geistes und der Kraft," in *Gotthold Ephraim Lessings sämtlichen Schriften*, vol. 13, ed. Karl Lachmann (Berlin: Göschen'sche Verlagshandlung, 1897), 4.11–8.20.

* * *

Origen was quite right when he declared that the Christian religion, on account of its spirit and power, was able to provide a demonstration which was far more divine than anything that Greek dialectic had to offer. For in his period, there was still a continuing power do do miracles among those who lived by Christ's precepts . . . But I am no longer in the same situation as Origen. I live in the eighteenth century, in which no more miracles happen . . . The problem is that this demonstration of the "spirit and power" no longer possesses any spirit or power, but has degenerated to human reports of spirit and power . . .

If no historical truth can be demonstrated, then nothing can be demonstrated by means of historical truths. That is: the accidental truths of history can never become the proof of necessary truths of reason . . . If I have no objection, on historical grounds, to the statement "Christ raised a dead man to life," must I therefore accept as true "God has a Son who is of the same essence as himself?" What is the connection between not having any objection to the former, and being obliged to believe something against which my reason revolts? . . . I gladly and heartily believe that Christ (against whose resurrection I can raise no significant historical objection) declared himself to be the Son of God, and that his disciples believed him in this matter. For these truths, which are truths of one and the same class, follow naturally on from each other. But to move on from that historical truth to a totally different class of truth, and to ask me to formulate all my metaphysical and moral ideas on its basis, or to expect me to change all my basic ideas about God because I cannot raise any credible argument against the resurrection of Christ – well, if that is not a *metabasis eis allo genos*, then I don't know what Aristotle meant by the phrase.

That, then, is the ugly great ditch (*der garstige breite Graben*) which I cannot cross, however often and however earnestly I have tried to make this leap. If anyone can help me to cross it, I implore him to do so. And so I repeat what I said earlier. I do not for one moment deny that Christ performed miracles. But since the truth of these miracles has completely ceased to be demonstrable by miracles happening in the present, they are no more than reports of miracles ... I deny that they could and should bind me to have even the smallest faith in the other teachings of Jesus.

So what does bind me? Nothing but the teachings themselves. Eighteen hundred years ago, they were so new, so strange and so foreign to the entire mass of truth recognized in that period, that nothing less than miracles and fulfilled prophecies would have been needed if people were to take them seriously ... But what does it matter to me whether this story (*Sage*) is false or true? Its fruits are excellent.

F. D. E. Schleiermacher on the "Natural Heresies" of Christianity   4.23

Schleiermacher here argues that the "four natural heresies of Christianity" – which he argues to be Docetism and Ebionitism on the Christological side, and Pelagianism and Manicheism on the soteriological – arise from inadequate understandings of the person and work of Christ. In the section reprinted here, Schleiermacher demonstrates the importance of maintaining a critical degree of commonality between Christ and believers, while at the same time acknowledging a fundamental distinction between them. Although the precise historical forms taken by these two heresies differ from Schleiermacher's presentation, the basic thrust of his argument has found wide acceptance. See also 4.1; 4.7; 4.12; 4.20.

Source: Friedrich Schleiermacher, *The Christian Faith* (Edinburgh: T. & T. Clark, 1928), pp. 98–9.

* * *

Now, if the distinctive essence of Christianity consists in the fact that in it all religious emotions are related to the redemption wrought by Jesus of Nazareth, there will be two ways in which heresy can arise. That is to say: this fundamental formula will be retained in general (for otherwise the contradiction would be manifest and complete, so that participation in Christian communion could not even be desired), but *either* human nature will be so defined that a redemption in the strict sense cannot be accomplished, *or* the Redeemer will be defined in such a way that He cannot accomplish redemption. But each of these two cases, again, can appear in two different ways. As regards the former: if people are to be redeemed, they must both be in need of redemption and be capable of receiving it. Now, if one of these conditions is openly stated, but the other implicitly denied, the contradiction at the same time touches the fundamental formula itself, only this is not directly apparent. If, then, in the first place, the need of redemption in human nature, i.e., its inability to bring the feeling of absolute dependence into all human states of consciousness, is stated in such an absolute way that the ability to receive redeeming influences is made actually to disappear, so that human nature is not simultaneously in need of redemption and capable of receiving it, but only becomes capable of receiving it after a complete transformation, this is equivalent to an annulling of our fundamental formula. Now this is the unfailing consequence, if we suppose an Evil-in-itself as being original and opposed to God, and think of human nature as suffering from that inability by reason of a dominion which this original Evil exercises over it; and therefore we call this deviation the Manichean. But, on the other hand, suppose the ability to receive redemption is assumed so absolutely, and consequently any hindrance to the entry of the God-consciousness becomes so utterly infinitesimal, that at each particular moment in each individual it can be satisfactorily counterbalanced by an infinitesimal overweight. Then the need of redemption is reduced to zero, at least in the sense that it is no longer the need of one single Redeemer, but merely, for each person in one of their weak moments, the need of some other individual who, if only for the moment, is stronger as regards the eliciting of the God-consciousness. Thus redemption would not need to be the work of one particular person, but would be a common work of all for all, in which at most, some would only have a greater share than others; amd this aberration we may with good reason call, as above, the Pelagian.

Turn now to the other kind of heresy. If Christ is to be the Redeemer, i.e., the real origin of constant living unhindered evocation of the God-consciousness, so that the participation of all others in it is mediated through Him alone, it is, on the one hand, necessary that He should enjoy an exclusive and peculiar superiority over all others, and, on the other hand, there must also be an essential likeness between Him and all people, because otherwise what He has to impart could not be the same as what they need. Therefore on this side also the general formula can be contradicted in two different ways, because each of these two requisites may be conceived so unlimitedly that the other no longer remains co-posited, but disappears. If the difference between Christ and those who are in need of redemption is made so unlimited that an essential likeness is incompatible with it, then His participation in human nature vanishes into a mere appearance; and consequently our God-consciousness, being something essentially different, cannot be derived from His, and redemption also is only an appearance. Now though the Docetics, properly so called, directly denied only the reality of the body of Christ, yet this likewise excludes the reality of human nature in His person generally, since we never find body and soul given in separation from each other; and therefore we may fitly call this aberration the Docetic. Finally, if on the other hand the likeness of the Redeemer to those who are to be redeemed is made so unlimited that no room is left for a distinctive superiority as a constituent of His being, which must then be conceived under the same form as that of all other people, then there must ultimately be posited in Him also a need of redemption, however absolutely small, and the fundamental relationship is likewise essentially annulled. This aberration we call by the name given to those who are supposed first to have regarded Jesus entirely as an ordinary human being, the Nazarean or Ebionitic.

Martin Kähler on the Historical Jesus   4.24

In this work, which represents the expanded form of a lecture originally given in 1892, Kähler argues that it is the "Christ who is preached" rather than the "historical Jesus" which is of decisive importance to Christian faith. In doing so, he unleashed a theological critique of the "life of Jesus movement" which had a profound influence on writers such as Barth and Bultmann. See also 4.22; 4.25; 4.26; 4.27; 4.28; 4.30.

Source: Martin Kähler, Der sogenannte historische Jesus und der geschichtliche, biblische Christus, ed. E. Wolf (Munich: Kaiser Verlag, 1953), pp. 40–5.

* * *

"Christ is Lord." Neither flesh nor blood can attain, sustain, or impart this certainty. Jesus himself said this to Peter after his confession (Matthew 16:17), and he said it also as he reproached the unbelieving Jews (John 6:43–4); it was confirmed by Peter's denial in the outer court of the High Priest; later, it was said by Paul to his congregations in full expectation of their assent (1 Corinthians 12:3). Yet, wherever this certainty has arisen and exercised influence, it has clearly been linked to another conviction – that Jesus is the crucified, risen, and living Lord. And when we ask at what point in their discussions the historians deal with this certainty, we find that they do not begin with the much disputed and disconnected final narratives of the evangelists, but with the experience of Paul. They determine the constant faith of the early church, to the extent that they can, on the basis of the testimonies and traces left by those early witnesses. The risen Lord is not the historical Jesus behind the Gospels, but the Christ of the apostolic preaching, of the entire New Testament. And if this Lord is called "Christ" (Messiah), it is to confess his historical mission, or as we say today, his vocation, or as our forebears said, meaning the same thing, his "threefold office," that is to say: to confess his unique, supra-historical significance for the whole of humanity (das Bekenntnis zu seiner einzigarten, übergeschichtlichen Bedeutung für die ganze Menschheit). Christians became certain that Jesus was the Messiah, the Christ, in total opposition to public opinion, not just in relation to the idea of the Messiah (that is, the way the Messiah was understood and what one expected of him), but also with regard to the person of this Jesus of Nazareth. This was as true then as it is today. When Christians tried to make the Messiahship of Jesus credible in their sermons and then in the letters and gospels, they always made use of two kinds of evidence: personal testimony to his resurrection, based on experience, and the witness of the Scriptures. As the living Lord, he was for them the Messiah of the Old Covenant.

And so we speak of the historic Christ of the Bible (von dem geschichtlichen Christus der Bibel). The historical Jesus (historische Jesus), as we see him in his earthly ministry, certainly did not win from his disciples a faith capable of witnessing to him, but only a very shaky loyalty, easily prone to panic and betrayal. It is clear that they were all born again, like Peter, into a living hope only through the resurrection of Jesus from the dead (1 Peter 1:3) and that they needed the gift of the Spirit to "bring to remembrance" what Jesus had said, before they were able to understand what he had already given them and to grasp what they had been unable to bear (John 14:26; 16:12, 13). It is clear that they did not subsequently go out into the world to make Jesus the head of a "school" by propagating his teachings, but to witness to his person and his eternal significance for every person, in the same way that it is certain that his first followers could understand his person and mission, his deeds and his word as the offer of God's grace and faithfulness only after he appeared to them in his state of fulfillment – in which he was himself the fruit and the eternal bearer of his own work of universal and lasting significance, a work (to be exact) whose most difficult and decisive part was the *end* of the historical Jesus. Even though we once knew the Messiah according to the flesh, now we no longer see him in this way (2 Corinthians 5:16).

This is the first characteristic of his influence, that he won faith from his disciples. And the second characteristic is, and continues to be, that this faith was confessed. His promise depends upon this (Romans 10:9–10), as does our own decision (*Entscheidung*) of faith and the history of Christianity. The real Christ, that is, the influential Christ, with whom millions in history have had fellowship in a childlike faith, along with the great witnesses of faith as they struggled, gained, triumphed, and proclaimed for this relationship – the real Christ is the preached Christ (*Der wirkliche Christus ist der gepredigte Christus*). The preached Christ, however, is precisely the one who is believed in. He is the Jesus whom the eyes of faith see in every step he takes and through every syllable he utters – the Jesus whose image we impress upon our minds because we both would and do have fellowship with him, as the ascended and living one. From the features of that portrait, which has deeply impressed itself upon the memory of his own people, the person of our living Savior, the person of the Word incarnate, of God revealed (*die Person unsres lebendigen Heilandes an, die Person des fleischgewordenen Wortes, des offenbaren Gottes*), gazes upon us.

4.25 George Tyrrell on the Christ of Liberal Protestantism

Tyrrell here argues for the futility of the Liberal Protestant approach to the "historical Jesus," pointing out that it simply involves projecting the views and values of modern scholars onto the distant historical figure of Jesus. His comment about Adolf von Harnack and the "deep well" is particularly well known. See also 4.22; 4.24; 4.26; 4.27; 4.28; 4.30.

Source: George Tyrrell, *Christianity at the Cross-Roads* (London: Longmans Green, 1909), pp. 46–9.

* * *

The Jesus of the school of critics represented today by Harnack and Bousset, was a Divine Man because He was full of the Spirit of God; full of Righteousness. He came (it is assumed rather than proved) at a time when the

Jews were full of apocalyptic expectations as to the coming of the Messiah, who was to avenge them of their enemies and establish a more or less miraculous and material Kingdom of God upon earth. He Himself seems to have shared this view in a spiritual form, translating it from material to ethical terms. As destined by a Divine vocation to inaugurate a reign of Righteousness, a Kingship of God over men's hearts and consciences, He felt Himself to be the true, because the spiritual, Messiah. With difficulty He trained a few of His followers to this conception of the Kingdom and the Christ. He went about doing good (even working cures which He supposed to be miraculous) and teaching goodness. The essence of His Gospel was the Fatherhood of God and the Brotherhood of man; or else the two great Commandments of the law – the love of God and of one's neighbour; or else the Kingdom of God that is within us. True, these were platitudes of contemporary Jewish piety, and even of pagan philosophy. But Jesus drove them home to the heart by the force of personal example and greatness of character – above all, by dying for His friends and for these ethical principles. Of course He was, to some extent, of His time. He believed in miracles, in diabolic possession; above all, He believed in the immediate end of the world; and a great deal of His ethics, coloured by that belief, was the ethics of a crisis. But these were but accidents of His central idea and interest, in regard to which we may say He was essentially modern, so far as our rediscovery of the equation Religion = Righteousness is modern, not to say Western and Teutonic.

For this almost miraculous modernity the first century was not prepared. No sooner was the Light of the World kindled than it was put under a bushel. The Pearl of Great Price fell into the dustheap of Catholicism, not without the wise permission of Providence, desirous to preserve it till the day when Germany should rediscover it and separate it from its useful but deplorable accretions. Thus between Christ and early Catholicism there is not a bridge but a chasm. Christianity did not cross the bridge; it fell into the chasm and remained there, stunned, for nineteen centuries. The explanation of this sudden fall – more sudden because they have pushed Catholicism back to the threshold of the Apostolic age – is the crux of Liberal Protestant critics . . .

It was to the credit of their hearts, if to the prejudice of their scientific indifference, that these critics were more or less avowedly actuated by apologetic interests. They desired to strip Jesus of His medieval regalia, and to make Him acceptable to a generation that had lost faith in the miraculous and any conception of another life that was not merely a complement, sanction and justification of this life. They wanted to bring Jesus into the nineteenth century as the Incarnation of its ideal of Divine Righteousness, i.e. of all the highest principles and aspirations that ensure the healthy progress of civilization. They wanted to acquit Him of that exclusive and earth-scorning otherworldliness, which had led men to look on His religion as the foe of progress and energy, and which came from confusing the accidental form with the essential substance of His Gospel. With eyes thus preoccupied they could only find the German in the Jew; a moralist in a visionary; a professor in a prophet; the nineteenth century in the first; the natural in the supernatural. Christ was the ideal man; the Kingdom of Heaven, the ideal humanity. As the rationalistic presupposition had strained out, as spurious, the miraculous elements of the Gospel, so the moralistic presupposition strained out everything but modern morality. That alone was the substance, the essence, of Christianity – *das Wesen des Christentums*. If God remained, it was only the God of moralism and rationalism – the correlative of the Brotherhood of man; not the God of Moses, of Abraham, Isaac and Jacob; of David and the prophets.

... [Yet] here the Liberal Protestant critics failed no less than the positively anti-Christian critics. Their hypothesis was an article of faith, not an instrument of inquiry. If they have been beaten off the field we need not, perhaps, set it down to the severer detachment of their conquerors, but to the stricter application of that critical method which they invoked.

It is by that method that Johannes Weiss and his followers have been forced back, very unwillingly in most cases, to the eschatological and apocalyptic interpretation of the Gospel. Very unwillingly, because it destroys the hope of smoothing away the friction between Christianity and the present age; because, in closing the chasm between the Gospel and early Catholicism, it makes the Christianity of Christ, in all essentials, as unacceptable as that of Catholicism.

Of this state of things Loisy was not slow to take advantage in *L'Evangile et l'Eglise*, directed against the Liberal Protestantism of Harnack's *Wesen des Christentums*. The Christ that Harnack sees, looking back through nineteen centuries of Catholic darkness, is only the reflection of a Liberal Protestant face, seen at the bottom of a deep well.

4.26   Albert Schweitzer on the Failure of the "Quest for the Historical Jesus"

In this work, better known by its English title *The Quest of the Historical Jesus*, Schweitzer argues that the "Jesus of history" movement has failed. Jesus remains partly unknown, a distant and strange figure, who cannot be reconstructed on the basis of the methods and approaches offered by the nineteenth century. See also 4.22; 4.24; 4.25; 4.27; 4.28; 4.30.

Source: Albert Schweitzer, *Von Reimarus zu Wrede: Eine Geschichte der Leben–Jesu–Forschung* (Tübingen: Mohr, 1906), pp. 396–401.

* * *

Anyone who wants to talk about negative theology, will not find it difficult to do so here. For there is nothing more negative than the result of the "Life of Jesus movement" (*Leben–Jesu–Forschung*).

The Jesus of Nazareth who came forward as the Messiah, who preached the ethic of the Kingdom of God, who Founded the Kingdom of Heaven upon earth, and died to give His work its dignity, never existed. He is a figure who was thrown up by rationalism, brought to life by liberalism, and clothed by modern theology using the historical method.

This portrait (*Bild*) has not been destroyed from the outside. It has fallen to pieces internally, having been shattered, disintegrated through the actual historical problems which came to the surface one after another. Despite all the ingenuity, skill, inspiration and force which was applied to them, they refused to fit the pattern on the basis of which the Jesus of the theology of the last hundred and thirty years had been constructed. As soon had they been laid to rest, they appeared again in a new form. Thoroughgoing skepticism and the thoroughgoing eschatology (*Der konsequente Skeptizismus und die konzequente Eschatologie*) have just brought this work of destruction to completion by connecting the problems together so that they form a system and so making an end of the "divide and rule" of modern theology, which undertook to solve each of them separately, that is, in a less difficult form. Henceforth it is no longer acceptable to take one problem out of the series and dispose of it by itself, since the weight of the whole hangs upon each.

Whatever the definitive solution of this may be, this can be said: the historical Jesus (*historische Jesus*) of future criticism, which takes as its starting-point the problems which have been recognized and conceded, can never render modern theology the services which it claimed from its own half-historical, half-modern, Jesus. He will be a Jesus, who was Messiah, and lived as such, either on the basis of a literary fiction of the earliest Evangelist, or on the basis of a purely eschatological–messianic conception.

In both cases, he will not be a Jesus Christ to whom the religious present can relate in any recognizable manner, in terms of its customs, thoughts and ideas, as it did with the Jesus of its own making. He is also not a figure which can be created by a historical treatment as sympathetic and universally intelligible to people in general. The historical Jesus will be a stranger and a riddle to our time.

The "Life of Jesus Movement" has a remarkable history. It set out to find the historical Jesus, believing that when it had found him, it could bring him straight into our time as a teacher and Saviour. It loosed the bands by which He had been fettered for centuries to the rock of ecclesiastical doctrine, and was delighted to see life and movement returned to his figure again, and the historical Jesus coming to meet it. But he did not remain there, but passed by our time and returned to his own. What startled and dismayed the theology of the last forty years was that, despite all of its forced and arbitrary interpretations, it could not keep him in our time, but had to let him go. He returned to his own time, not through any historical ingenuity, but by the same inevitable necessity by which a pendulum, once let go, returns to its original position.

The historical foundation of Christianity as set out by rationalism, liberalism, and modern theology, no longer exists. But this does not mean that Christianity has lost its historical foundation. The work which historical theology felt itself obliged to carry out, and which fell to pieces just as it was nearing completion, was only the facade of the real and unshakeable historical foundation which is independent of any historical confirmation or justification.

Jesus means something to our world because a powerful spiritual force (*gewaltige geistige Strömung*) derives from him and flows through our time also. This fact can neither be disproved or confirmed by any historical discovery. It is the solid foundation (*Realgrund*) of Christianity.

Only some thought that Jesus could come to mean more to our time if he were to enter it, living as a human being just like ourselves (*als ein Mensch unser Menscheit*). That is not possible. In the first place, because this Jesus never existed. But also, although historical knowledge can no doubt bring greater clarity to a spiritual existence which is already present, it cannot create such a spiritual life in the first place. History (*Geschichte*) can destroy the present, or reconcile the present to the past. It can even, at least to a certain extent, allow the present to project itself into the past. But it cannot construct the present . . .

We are experiencing what Paul experienced. In the very moment when we were coming so close to the historical Jesus – closer than ever before – and were already stretching out our hands to draw him into our own time, we have been obliged to give up the attempt and acknowledge our failure in that paradoxical saying: "If we have known Christ after the flesh yet henceforth we know him no more." And further we must be prepared to find that the historical knowledge of the personality and life of Jesus will not be helpful to, but perhaps even a nuisance to religion.

But it is not the historically known (*historisch erkannte*) Jesus, but Jesus as one who is spiritually resurrected within humanity, who can mean something for our time and be of use to it. It is not the historical Jesus, but the spirit which goes forth from him and which strives for new influence and rule in the spirits of people, which overcomes the world.

It is not given to history to distinguish what is of lasting and eternal importance in the being of Jesus from the historical forms in which it worked itself out, and to introduce this as a living influence into our world. It has labored in vain at this undertaking. Just as a water-plant flowers beautifully so long as it is growing in the water, but once torn from its roots, withers and becomes unrecognizable, so it is with the historical Jesus when he is torn from the soil of eschatology, and the attempt is made to conceive him "historically" as someone who belongs nowhere in time. What is of lasting and eternal importance in Jesus is absolutely independent of historical knowledge and can only be understood by contact with his spirit, which is still at work in the world. We possess true knowledge of Jesus only to the extent that we possess the spirit of Jesus.

Jesus as a total historical personality remains a stranger to our time. However, his spirit, which lies hidden in his words, is known simply and directly. Every saying contains in its own way the whole Jesus. The very strangeness and absoluteness in which He stands before us makes it easier for individuals to find their own personal standpoint in relation to Him.

It was feared that admitting the claims of eschatology would abolish the significance of his words for our time, and there was great enthusiasm to discover in them any elements that could be considered as not eschatologically conditioned. So there was great rejoicing when any sayings were found, the wording of which did not absolutely imply an eschatological connexion. Something of value in them had been saved from future destruction . . .

The modern "Lives of Jesus" are too general in their scope. They aim to give the total impression of the life of Jesus on an entire community. But the historical Jesus, as he is depicted in the Gospels, influenced individuals by the individual word. They understood Him so far as it was necessary for them to understand, without forming any conception of his life as a whole, since this in its ultimate aims remained a mystery even for the disciples . . .

It is a good thing that the historical Jesus should overthrow the modern Jesus, and that it should revolt against the modern spirit and send upon earth, not peace, but a sword. He was not a teacher or a disputer, but someone who commands and rules (*Gebieter und Herrscher*). It was because he was so in his inner being that he could think of himself as the "Son of Man." That was only the temporally conditioned expression (*zeitlich bedingte Ausdruck*) of the fact that he was someone who commands and rules. The names in which men expressed their recognition of him as such – "Messiah," "Son of Man," "Son of God" – have become for us historical parables. We can find no way of expressing what he means for us.

He comes to us as someone who is unknown and nameless, just as he came to those by the lake-side, who did not know who he was. He speaks to us the same word: "Follow me!", and directs us to the tasks which he has to fulfil for our time. He commands. And to those who obey Him, whether they are wise or simple, he will reveal himself in whatever they must do, struggle and suffer in his fellowship. And they shall experience who he is as an inexpressible mystery . . .

Peter Taylor Forsyth on the Person of Christi

4.27

The Christology of liberal Protestantism placed an emphasis upon the humanity of Jesus, which was occasionally expressed in terms of sharing the faith of Jesus, rather than having faith in Christ. In this critique of such trends, Forsyth argues that this approach is without historical foundation or justification. See also 4.22; 4.24; 4.25; 4.26; 4.28; 4.30.

Source: P. T. Forsyth, *The Person and Place of Jesus Christ* (London: Independent Press, 1909), pp. 35, 41, 44.

* * *

There is nothing we are told more often than those who would discard an evangelical faith than this – that we must now do what scholarship has only just enabled us to do, and return to the religion of Jesus. We are bidden to go back to practise Jesus' own personal religion, as distinct from the Gospel of Christ, from a gospel which calls him its faith's object, and not its subject, founder or classic only. We must learn to believe not *in* Christ, but *with* Christ, we are told . . .

Let us observe what is the effect of the most recent views about the origin of Christianity upon this point, upon the plea that the first form of Christianity was the so-called religion of Jesus. I refer to the new religious–historical school of Germany . . . There is one great service which this religious–historical school has rendered. It has destroyed the fiction of the nineteenth century that there was ever a time in the earliest history of the Church when it cultivated the religion of Jesus as distinct from the Gospel of Christ. The school, of course, may believe itself able to insulate that religion of Jesus and cultivate it, to disengage it from the gospels by a critical process, and preach it to a world pining for a simple creed rescued from the Apostles. That is another matter which I do not here discuss. But it is a great thing to have it settled that, as far as the face value of our record goes, and apart from elaborate critical constructions of them, such imitation of the faith of Jesus never existed in the very first Church; but that, as far back as we can go, we find only the belief and worship of a risen, redeeming, and glorified Christ, whom they could wholly trust but only very poorly imitate; and in his relation to God could not imitate at all.

4.28   Ernst Troeltsch on Faith and History

In this essay, which was first published in German in 1910, Ernst Troeltsch sets out the new questions dealing with "faith and history" which Christian theology needed to address. The issues explored here have been of considerable importance in relation to understanding the way in which the historical event of Jesus Christ has been, and continues to be, of central importance to Christian life and thought. See also 4.22; 4.24; 4.25; 4.26; 4.27; 4.30.

Source: "Faith and History"; in Ernst Troeltsch, *Religion in History*, translated by James Luther Adams and Walter F. Bense (Edinburgh: T. & T. Clark, 1991), pp. 134–45; extract at pp. 134–9. Reprinted with the permission of the publisher.

* * *

A. The Historical Connections of Christian Faith

A particularly difficult problem for current religious thought is posed by the connection of faith with historical matters. Religion is understood and experienced as a *present* religion, as a certainty about God and the eternal world which is apprehended now through inner experience. It is felt to be a difficulty that this experience of God is supposed to depend on the mediation of historical personages and forces, and to include a religious appreciation of historical matters. When the problem is posed in this manner, the first question that arises is what historical connections are actually asserted and how these connections relate to the essential aspects of the Christian faith. From the standpoint of the psychology of religion the following points come to mind:

(a) Faith is always faith in a concrete thought-content. This thought-content never originates solely from the individual subject. On the contrary, the richer and stronger it is, the more it is the communal work of great epochs of intellectual history and of whole generations, or of outstanding personalities that have profited from these communal achievements. Faith feels a need to gather up this whole world of ideas in its starting point and to embody it in an archetype, in order always to be able to rectify and to revitalize itself. This archetype is naturally the personality of the founding prophet or revealer. On the higher levels of religion, moreover, faith becomes increasingly the appropriation of outstanding personages. As its requirements increase, its need for support from personalities that supply direction and impetus increases also. Faith therefore depends upon history, but not only for sustenance and information; its own self-understanding depends upon history, and within history upon the embodiment of revelation to which it looks. Without a conscious relationship to Christ the Christian faith is unthinkable, even though one's faith in God may be regarded as resting upon its own inner evidence and power. The Christian faith originated in the historical disclosure of the life of God, and for the sake of clarity and power it must be constantly referred back to this foundation, which is vitally present to the imagination. Even though some individuals may be able to forego this historical referral because they are carried along by the power of the community, the community as a whole cannot forego it if the community is to retain its vital force.

(b) Christian faith is a redemption through faith in the God who reveals himself in Christ. Through the powers of faith communicated to us by Christ, the Christian faith raises men to a higher level of intellectual, moral, and religious strength, where confidence of victory prevails and where worldly sorrow (*Weltleid*) and the consciousness of guilt are overcome. This means the individual experiences something that elevates and liberates him, something that is not merely a product of his own efforts but that approaches him from the outside with a superior power. Of course, only his own living, actual faith in God himself redeems the individual, but he does not puzzle his way to this faith on his own. He receives it as a liberating and uplifting force through religious impressions that impinge upon him and that essentially have Christ as their starting point and authentication. Even in its redemptive aspect, faith must cling to the historical connection with the sources from which it derives this liberating impulse, the power to provide certainty – in short, the whole wealth of these ideas.

(c) The Christian faith has its goal in the creation of a great community of humanity which strengthened and elevated through faith, is at the same time united in a common recognition of the divine will to which it owes its existence and by which it is directed to mutual works of love. Such an ethical community requires means of solidarity and demarcation. These means can lie only in the realization and common recognition of the historical powers that have brought it into being. At any rate, such means are necessary so long as this community has to broaden itself through conflict. The situation might be different if this community were a victorious power naturally present in all and carrying all before it. Such a state of affairs, however, is unthinkable on earth. Even the ethical community of faith necessitates a conscious historical connection with the foundation that keeps the community together.

(d) Christian faith at the same time maintains, for its propagation and consolidation, a Christian cultus. This is unavoidable if religion is to stay alive. As a means of illustration and edification, and as a classical arche-type, this cultus is bound, in the first instance, to cultivate the memory of the origin and personality of the founder, the revealer, the hero. However else the cultus may utilize forces of the present day, it always remains bound to the historical foundations and their realization.

(e) The faith of Christianity regards itself as the completion of revelation and redemption, and hence must take a stand regarding the faith of other circles of religious belief, which, on their higher levels, likewise depend on revelatory personalities and a content of redemptive faith. The doctrine of the church has taken such a stand by regarding the Christian revelation and redemption as the supernatural restoration of the perfect beginning of his-tory; and by designating the non-Christian religions, insofar as they contain elements of truth, as postulates and products of vestigial reason, and inso-far as they contain elements of untruth, as products of sinful human nature left to its own devices. Even when this Christian philosophy of history is abandoned, some sort of philosophy of history must be taken into account; it remains necessary to relate the Christian faith in revelation and redemp-tion to the non-Christian religions in such a way that Christianity can maintain the conviction of its supreme validity.

All these arguments entail the essential and inseparable connection of faith with history and the necessity of a religious view of history. From time to time it may well be necessary to relax these historical connections and to make room for one's own religious creativity. But, basically, innovations will hardly be more than new positions regarding history and new fruitful applications of what was already given. To abandon history would be tan-tamount to faith's abandoning itself and settling for the fleeting and trivial religious stirrings produced by a subjectivity left to its own resources. The earliest Christian era established these historical connections by setting off Jesus, the church, and the Bible from the natural course of ordinary history; and secured the permanence of the connection by making these historical elements divine. The connection with history, then, was forced by psycho-logical requirement's immanent in faith itself.

B. Objections to Such Historical Relationships

Until modern times, the Christian faith was content to bear these historical connections. While interpretations differed, faith always found its strongest support in them. Even when the content of faith was transformed into a pure religion of the "now" (*Gegenwartsreligion*), the historical connections were not abolished. The modern world first raised fundamental objections. They are the following:

(a) In every area the modern world is the world of individual autonomy. In every field, and hence in religion, compelling personal insight into the universal validity of judgements is the means by which the modern world attains certainty. Religious autonomy can lead to universal judgements and unanimous conviction only when religious truth is contained in the nature of reason itself, and hence shares the universal validity of the latter; that is, if it can be derived from reason as such. This attitude implies a departure from the historical authority: faith is put on its own. It further implies that the content of faith is a universally valid conceptual necessity that follows from the general nature of reason. If autonomous assent to that content is to be possible, faith must be a present self-apprehension of the religious content of reason. Otherwise faith would be formally an unworthy belief in authority and materially a mere attachment to accidental historical occurrences whose spheres of influence we have simply been born into. The age of autonomy and science emancipates itself from mere positive authority and from the historical accident of birth.

(b) The analysis supplied by the psychology of religion, which tries to view faith from a scientific, psychological viewpoint, shows us that in reality faith can be connected only with what is present and eternal, and never with what is merely past and transitory. Whenever faith adheres to historical facts, it alters these into non-historical realities, into miracles that proclaim the eternal purposes of God or into human incarnations of the divine, into transfigurations or resurrections of the historical in which the historical is only the veiling or revealing of the eternal. In addition to establishing historical connections, dogma pertaining to Christ, the church, and the Bible constitutes above all an abrogation of the historicity of these entities and their transformation into timeless metaphysical potencies. This procedure can be continued, however, only so long as the ostensible historical bases do not become the object of real historical research, which would show them to be, like all historical data, relative and conditioned. As soon as historical research is thus employed, the historical and the present separate. Only the latter can be a direct object of faith.

(c) A truly historical consideration of historical matters, such as was unknown to the ancient church and to the Middle Ages, not only shows that such data are relative and conditioned but even makes them objects of criticism. We do not possess the facts themselves but only the traditions concerning the facts. The task is critically to reconstruct from these traditions what probably happened in reality. But the picture of what happened becomes uncertain and shifting as a result of this critical treatment. The upshot can be an utterly unrecognizable opinion or a denial of the alleged facts themselves. A decision can be reached only through scholarly examination, which by its nature is accessible to few, and whose results are by no means assured, since it depends on religious traditions passed on from uncritical ages and social classes. Faith, however, cannot tolerate any uncertainty or dependence on erudition. Faith, therefore, retreats to positions that are not subject to historical criticism.

(d) Furthermore, modern Christianity with its various intermingled denominations is itself historically segmented. The Catholic doctrine of the sole truth of Catholicism and the Old Protestant doctrine of the sole truth of its Bible-Christianity no longer have a place in the general consciousness. They have been replaced by the demand for toleration and, consequently, by a certain relativization of all the historical forms of Christianity. In this toleration and the relativism connected with it, there is implicit a standpoint above all these particular historical forms. This standpoint lies above these particular forms only because it does not itself lie in history, but in present conviction on the basis of which relative values can be assessed and tolerated. Modern tolerance and relativism may also be due to a complete absence of conviction, which gives full play to the different historical forms because there is no fixed standard by which they might be measured. At any rate, there is a tendency toward emancipation from history in the modern idea of tolerance.

(e) Difficulties arise not merely from the relation of Christianity to its own historical elements, but also from its relation to the other historical religions. Christianity appears more and more as one religion among many. This results either in complete skeptical relativism or in the attainment of a general concept of religious truth by which the different historical manifestations are measured. Such a concept derives its validity not from any historical foundation or authority, but from its own inner necessity and correctness. Here again there is a liberation of religion from history.

(f) All these difficulties, which grow out of religious thought itself, coincide with a general frame of mind that is sensitive to the oppressiveness of history and historical erudition. This historical erudition will not allow us direct, ingenuous, and living creativity; instead, it stifles every such innovation with historical comparisons and relations. As a result, the desire for freedom from history characterizes the temper of the times, in reaction to an excess of historical thought and scholarship. Add to this the effects of the temporal and spatial expansion of the historical horizon, which knows a stay of humanity on earth for more than a hundred thousand years and the prospect of a future stay of indefinite length, presumably lasting till the earth becomes uninhabitable. Christianity now appears as only another wave in the ebb and flow of the largely unknown history of mankind. Religious conviction cannot permanently attach itself to a particular historical phenomenon of this sort.

For all these reasons the problem of history is almost more difficult for faith than the problem of modern metaphysics and the modern natural sciences. History presents modern life with a truly serious and grave problem that, like both the others, works for a manifold transformation of our religious thought. The old attitude toward history can no longer be maintained. That the history of humanity reaches through immeasurable stretches of time, that all historical occurrences are alike conditioned and temporal, and that the principles of historical criticism are universally dominant – all these points must be admitted. Amid such concessions the question comes very much to the fore how the historical connections of faith are to stand their ground.

Dorothy L. Sayers on Christology   4.29

In this analysis of the relation of the divinity and humanity of Christ, originally delivered as a lecture in England in 1940, Dorothy L. Sayers argued for their mutual importance in relation to our knowledge of God. Using the rise of Nazism in Germany under Adolf Hitler as an example, she argues that claims to moral or cultural authority must be grounded in something intrinsic to the person of Christ. Otherwise, Christ is judged by moral and cultural principles, instead of acting as their basis. See also 1.5; 4.4; 4.7; 4.15; 5.22.

Source: Dorothy L. Sayers, *Creed or Chaos?* (London: Methuen, 1947), pp. 32–5. Cited with permission of the publisher.

* * *

That you cannot have Christian principles without Christ is becoming increasingly clear, because their validity as principles depends on Christ's authority; and as we have seen, the Totalitarian States, having ceased to believe in Christ's authority, are logically quite justified in repudiating Christian principles. If "the average man" is required to "believe in Christ" and accept His authority for "Christian principles," it is surely relevant to inquire who or what Christ is, and why His authority should be accepted. But the question, "What think ye of Christ?" lands the average man at once in the very knottiest kind of dogmatic riddle. It is quite useless to say that it doesn't matter particularly who or what Christ was or by what authority He did those things, and that even if He was only a man, He was a very nice man and we ought to live by His principles: for that is merely Humanism, and if the "average man" in Germany chooses to think that Hitler is a nicer sort of man with still more attractive principles, the Christian Humanist has no answer to make.

It is not true at all that dogma is "hopelessly irrelevant" to the life and thought of the average man. What is true is that ministers of the Christian religion often assert that it is, present it for consideration as though it were, and, in fact, by their faulty exposition of it make it so. The central dogma of the Incarnation is that by which relevance stands or falls. If Christ was only man, then He is entirely irrelevant to any thought about God; if He is only God, then He is entirely irrelevant to any experience of human life. It is, in the strictest sense, necessary to the salvation of relevance that a man should believe rightly the Incarnation of Our Lord Jesus Christ. Unless he believes rightly, there is not the faintest reason why he should believe at all. And in that case, it is wholly irrelevant to chatter about "Christian principles."

... If the "average man" is going to be interested in Christ at all, it is the dogma that will provide the interest. The trouble is that, in nine cases out of ten, he has never been offered the dogma. What he has been offered is a set of technical theological terms which nobody has taken the trouble to translate into language relevant to ordinary life ... Teachers and preachers never, I think, make it sufficiently clear that dogmas are not a set of arbitrary regulations invented a priori by a committee of theologians enjoying a bout of all-in dialectical wrestling. Most of them were hammered out under pressure of urgent practical necessity to provide an answer to heresy.

4.30 Paul Tillich on the Dispensability of the Historical Jesus

Tillich's existential approach to theology often leads him to treat the specifically historical aspects of the Christian faith with a degree of disinterest. Christianity is about universal existential possibilities, an idea which Tillich discussed with particular reference to the idea of "New Being." But how does this "New Being" relate to Jesus Christ? In this extract, Tillich indicates that he believes that the historical existence of Jesus is not of decisive importance. See also 4.22; 4.24; 4.25; 4.26; 4.27; 4.28.

Source: *Systematic Theology*, 3 vols (Chicago: University of Chicago Press, 1978), vol. 2, pp. 113–14. Copyright © 1957 by The University of Chicago. Cited with permission of the University of Chicago Press.

* * * _____

The preceding evaluation of the historical approach to the biblical records led to a negative and a positive assertion. The negative assertion is that historical research can neither give nor take away the foundation of the Christian faith. The positive assertion is that historical research has influenced and must influence Christian theology, first, by giving an analysis of the three different semantic levels of biblical literature (and, analogously, of Christian preaching in all periods); second, by showing in several steps the development of the christological symbols (as well as the other systematically important symbols); and, finally, by providing a precise philological and historical understanding of the biblical literature by means of the best methods developed in all historical work.

But it is necessary systematically to raise once more a question which is continuously being asked with considerable religious anxiety. Does not the acceptance of the historical method for dealing with the source documents of the Christian faith introduce a dangerous insecurity into the thought and life of the church and of every individual Christian? Could not historical research lead to a complete skepticism about the biblical records? Is it not imaginable that historical criticism could come to the judgment that the man Jesus of Nazareth never lived? Did not some scholars, though only a few and not very important ones, make just this statement? And even if such a statement can never be made with certainty, is it not destructive for the Christian faith if the non-existence of Jesus can somehow be made probable, no matter how low the degree of probability? In reply, let us first reject some insufficient and misleading answers. It is inadequate to point out that historical research has not yet given any evidence to support such skepticism. Certainly, it has not yet! But the anxious question remains of whether it could not do so sometime in the future! Faith cannot rest on such unsure ground. The answer, taken from the "not-yet" of skeptical evidence, is insufficient. There is another possible answer, which, though not false, is misleading. This is to say that the historical foundation of Christianity is an essential element of the Christian faith itself and that this faith, through its own power, can overrule skeptical possibilities within historical criticism. It can, it is maintained, guarantee the existence of Jesus of Nazareth and at least the essentials in the biblical picture. But we must analyze this answer carefully, for it is ambiguous. The problem is: Exactly what can faith guarantee? And the inevitable answer is that faith can guarantee only its own foundation, namely, the appearance of the reality which has created the faith. This reality is the New Being, who conquers existential estrangement and thereby makes faith possible. This alone faith is able to guarantee – and that because its own existence is identical with the presence of the New Being. Faith itself is the immediate (not mediated by conclusions) evidence of the New Being within and under the conditions of existence. Precisely that is guaranteed by the very nature of the Christian faith. No historical criticism can question the immediate awareness of those who find themselves transformed into the state of faith. One is reminded of the Augustinian–Cartesian refutation of radical skepticism. That tradition pointed to the immediacy of a self-consciousness which guaranteed itself by its participation in being. By analogy, one must say that participation, not historical argument, guarantees the reality of the event upon which Christianity is based. It guarantees a personal life in which the New Being has conquered the old being. But it does not guarantee his name to be Jesus of Nazareth. Historical doubt concerning the existence and the life of someone with this name cannot be overruled. He might have had another name. (This is a historically absurd, but logically necessary, consequence of the historical method.) Whatever his name, the New Being was and is actual in this man.

Daphne Hampson on the Possibility of a Feminist Christology

4.31

Jesus Christ was male. What relevance does this observation have on the theological discussion of his significance for humanity? In this important analysis, written from a feminist perspective, Daphne Hampson argues that a series of vital issues are raised by this question, and explores several of them. Although Hampson does not regard herself as a Christian, the line of thought reflected in this extract has had considerable impact within Christian feminist circles since about 1975. See also 2.29; 3.34; 3.35; 6.45; 6.46.

Source: Daphne Hampson, *Theology and Feminism* (Oxford: Blackwell Publishing, 1990), pp. 50–2.

* * *

The nub of the question as to whether feminism is compatible with Christianity is that of whether a Christology can be found of which it may be said that at least it is not incompatible with feminism. By Christology is meant the portrayal of Jesus as the Christ. I have suggested that a meaningful way to set the limits as to what may rightly be called a Christian position, is that Christians are those who proclaim Jesus to have been unique. Such a definition does not only include those Christians who construe their belief in orthodox terms; who proclaim of Christ (following the definition of the Council of Chalcedon) that he was fully God and fully human, these two natures existing in one person. It includes also those who wish to speak of uniqueness in some other way. For example I shall later consider Bultmann, who has no classical two-nature Christology, but who says of Jesus, as of no other, that this was the man whom God raised from the dead; so that for him this man's resurrection becomes the pivot of history. I do not intend to have a restrictive but rather an expansive definition. To say of persons however who simply believe of Jesus that he had a very fine moral teaching, but who wish to say nothing of Jesus himself, that they are Christian surely does not make sense theologically – whatever they may say of themselves. Such a position should rightly be called humanist. Christians have always proclaimed not simply Jesus' teaching, but something about Jesus. There can rightly be no Christianity without a Christology.

The question of the compatibility of feminism and Christianity then is that of whether there can be a way of speaking of Christ's uniqueness which is not incompatible with feminism. (Let us take also a minimalist definition of feminism, as meaning the proclaimed equality of women and men.) The problem of course with Christology for feminists is that Jesus was a male human being and that thus as a symbol, as the Christ, or as the Second Person of the trinity, it would seem that "God" becomes in some way "male." It should be noted at the outset what is the nature of the problem with which we are concerned. It is not a question of whether feminists have something against "men." Whether or not that is the case, the problem here is not that Jesus was a man, but that this man has been considered unique, symbolic of God, God Himself – or whatever else may be the case within Christianity. The Godhead, or at least Christology, then appears to be biased against women. Feminists have been very aware of the power of symbolism and ideology. It is no small matter then to suggest that western religious thought, which has been so fundamental to western culture, has been ideologically loaded against women.

Before we proceed to consider the question as to whether there can be a Christology which is not incompatible with feminism, I should like to point to the significance of this question for Christians. It is not simply that it is a vital matter for some small group of people (as some may think them to be) called "Christian feminists" who would reconcile their feminism with their Christian faith. For Christianity has always proclaimed Christ to be an inclusive concept. In him, it is said, there is no East nor West, he is the new Adam, the first-born of all humanity; there is in Christ no Jew nor Greek, no more male and female. The question which feminists are raising then strikes at the very core of Christology. For it is being questioned whether a symbol which would appear to be necessarily male can be said to be inclusive of all humanity. Does it not give male human beings privilege within the religion? As far as women who would be Christian are concerned, how may they see in the Godhead an image of themselves? The contention that Christology is not inclusive represents the undoing of what, classically, has been claimed of Christ.

Why has this question now come upon the scene? What has changed in human relations between men and women, or how is it that women sense themselves differently, such that this matter has become urgent? It would be difficult to give a definitive answer, but we may have some clue. In other ages, the female seemed in some sense to be "included" in the male, in a way in which this is no longer the case. This made Christology seem natural. Men were normally held to represent women also. Humanity could then as a whole be thought to be summed up in Christ. Mistaken biological beliefs, such that the male alone was thought to be a full human being, underlay western culture, making this seem the more plausible. Today men are not in the same way held to represent women: there are two sexes and women represent themselves.

It may then be that today situations where men alone are priests, or equally the fact that Christ is a male symbol and God is conceptualized using male metaphors, may make God appear to be "male" in a way in which this was not earlier the case. If we see a procession of only men we ask "where are the women?". As we have said, in an age when men alone filled the professions, it appeared only natural that those who led the church were likewise male. When this is no longer so, the fact of a male priesthood makes God appear to be in some way peculiarly male, such that He needs a male priesthood to represent Him. The belief that men alone represent humanity, whereas a woman is an individual who only represents herself, never absolute, does not wash any longer. A symbol which is a male symbol appears in our culture to represent maleness, in a way in which earlier this may not necessarily have been the case. Hence the urgency of the question as to whether Christ is an inclusive symbol, and the feeling of many women that it is not.

Study Questions to Chapter 4

On the basis of the texts provided, give brief descriptions of the following: Docetism; Patripassianism; Apollinarianism.

What does the term *Theotokos* mean? And why was it so important to theologians of the fifth century?

Show how Luther's Christology, expressed in his critique of Nestorianism, leads him to affirm that God suffers.

How does Schleiermacher arrive at his conclusion that Docetism and Ebionitism are the "natural" Christological heresies? Would Dorothy L. Sayers have agreed?

Assess the reasons why Martin Kähler, George Tyrrell and Albert Schweitzer had misgivings concerning the "Quest for the Historical Jesus."

For what reasons do some feminist theologians have difficulties with the maleness of Jesus?

5 Salvation in Christ

Soteriology – that is, the section of Christian theology which deals with the question of what salvation (Greek: *sōteria*) is, and how it is acquired – has always been of central importance to Christian thought, particularly in relation to evangelism and mission. The present collection of readings explores the ways in which salvation is conceived, and especially the manner in which it is connected with the death and resurrection of Jesus Christ.

Several themes are of particular importance. The relation of Christology and soteriology has been of continuing debate within the Christian tradition. It is clear that there is a close connection between the identity and the significance, between the person and the work, of Christ. But how is this to be understood? The positions outlined by Athanasius, F. D. E. Schleiermacher, Charles Gore, and Wolfhart Pannenberg illustrate both the importance of this point, as well as the different approaches to the issue.

In the early church, the idea of Christ gaining a cosmic victory over sin, death, and Satan through his death and resurrection became very influential. This theme has found new importance in the twentieth century, largely through the writings of Gustaf Aulén. STUDY PANEL 12 identifies the readings which will be of especial importance to any wishing to study this theme in detail. However, other themes are also of considerable importance. Amongst these, particular attention should be paid to the theme of the death of Christ providing a "satisfaction" by which the redemption of humanity was made possible. This is especially associated with Anselm of Canterbury. STUDY PANEL 13 will allow this theme to be followed through from its first formal statement, through the medieval debate over the issue, to its emphatic rejection by Socianism in the sixteenth century, and its more recent criticism by liberal and modernist writers, such as Hastings Rashdall. Other themes of importance include the idea, especially associated with the Greek churches, of salvation as deification, and approaches to the death of Christ which focus on its demonstrating the love of God for humanity.

STUDY PANEL 12

Salvation as Victory

STUDY PANEL 13

Salvation and Satisfaction

5.1   Irenaeus on the "Ransom" Theory of the Atonement

In this extract from *adversus haereses* ("Against the Heresies"), written in the second half of the second century, Irenaeus argues that the death of Christ is to be regarded as a ransom, by which God justly liberated humanity from satanic captivity. Irenaeus avoids any suggestion that the redemption of humanity took place by force, insisting that only persuasion was used. Note: the Latin terms such as "redimens" and "redemptio" here have the more technical sense of "ransom" rather than "redemption," and I have translated them as such to bring out this point clearly. See also 5.4; 5.6; 5.7; 5.8.

Source: *adversus haereses*, V.i.1; in *Sources Chrétiennes*, vol. 153, ed. A. Rousseau, L. Doutreleau, and C. Mercier (Paris: Cerf, 1979), 18.19–20.20.

* * *

Thus the powerful Word and true human being, ransoming us by his own blood in a rational manner, gave himself as a ransom for those who have been led into captivity. The apostate one unjustly held sway over us, and though we were by nature the possession of Almighty God, we had been alienated from our proper nature, making us instead his own disciples. Therefore the almighty Word of God, who did not lack justice, acted justly even in the encounter with the apostate one, ransoming from him the things which were his own, not by force, in the way in which [the apostate one] secured his dominion over us at the beginning, by greedily snatching what was not his own. Rather, it was appropriate that God should obtain what he wished through persuasion, not by the use of force, so that the principles of justice might not be infringed, and, at the same time, that God's original creation might not perish. The Lord therefore ransomed us by his own blood, and gave his life for our life, his flesh for our flesh; and he poured out the Spirit of the Father to bring about the union and fellowship of God and humanity, bringing God down to humanity through the Spirit while raising humanity to God through his incarnation, and in his coming surely and truly giving us incorruption through the fellowship which we have with him.

5.2   Irenaeus on "Recapitulation" in Christ

In this section, Irenaeus explores his distinctive idea of "recapitulation." For Irenaeus, this term means something like "going over again." Christ "recapitulates" the history of Adam, except he succeeds at every point at which Adam failed. Thus Adam's disobedience is matched by Christ's obedience. Thus the salvation of humanity, which was lost in Adam, was regained in Christ. See also 5.1; 5.9; 5.25.

Source: *adversus haereses*, III.xviii.1; in *Sources Chrétiennes*, vol. 211, ed. A. Rousseau and L. Doutreleau (Paris: Cerf, 1974), 342.1–344.13.

* * *

Now it has been clearly shown that the Word which exists from the beginning with God, through whom all things were made, who was also always present with the human race, has in these last times, according to the time appointed by the Father, been united to his own creation and has been made a human being capable of suffering (*passibilem hominem factum*). This disposes of the objection of those who say, "If he was born at that time, it follows that Christ did not exist before then." For we have shown that the Son of God did not begin to exist at that point, because he had always existed with the Father. But when he was incarnate and became a human being, he recapitulated in himself (*in seipso recapitulavit*) the long history of the human race, obtaining salvation for us, so that we might regain in Jesus Christ what we had lost in Adam, that is, being in the image and likeness of God (*secundum imaginem et similitudinem esse Dei*).

Clement of Alexandria on Christ's Death as an Example of Love

5.3

Clement of Alexandria wrote a much-admired exposition of Mark 10:17–31, in which he extends the passage to include the apostle John converting the young man "who wished to be saved." In the course of this exposition, which probably dates from the first decade of the third century, Clement deals with the manner in which Christ can be said to demonstrate the love of God for humanity. See also 5.14; 5.23.

Source: *Quis Dives Salvetur*, 37; in *Clement of Alexandria: The Exhortation to the Greeks; The Rich Man's Salvation*, Loeb Classical Library edition, ed. G. W. Butterworth (Cambridge, Mass.: Harvard University Press, 1960), P. 346.

* * *

Consider the mysteries of love, and you will then have a vision of the bosom of the Father, whom the only-begotten God alone has declared. God himself is love, and for the sake of this love he made himself known. And while the unutterable nature of God is Father, his sympathy with us is Mother. It was in his love that the Father became the nature which derives from woman, and the great proof of this is the Son whom he begot from himself, and the love that was the fruit produced from his love. For this he came down, for this he assumed human nature, for this he willingly endured the sufferings of humanity, that by being reduced to the measure of our weakness, he might raise us to the measure of his power. And just before he poured out his offering, when he gave himself as a ransom, he left us a new testament: "I give you my love" (John 13:34). What is the nature and extent of this love? For each of us he laid down his life, the life which was worth the whole universe, and he requires in return that we should do the same for each other.

5.4   Athanasius on the Death of Christ

Athanasius was one of the most vigorous defenders of the doctrine of the incarnation of the Word against its Arian critics. At some point before 318, while still a young man, Athanasius wrote de incarnatione ("On the Incarnation"), which is now regarded as a classic statement of orthodoxy on this matter. In the passage below, Athanasius argues that human redemption is dependent upon the incarnation. It is only by taking on a real human body, capable of dying, that God was able to redeem fallen human nature. This passage indicates the close connection between Christology and soteriology. See also 4.7; 4.29; 5.5; 5.21; 5.22.

Source: de incarnatione, VIII, 4–IX, 1; in Sources Chrétiennes, vol. 199, ed. C. Kannengiesser (Paris: Cerf, 1973), 292.30–296.17.

* * *

Therefore, assuming a body like ours, because all people were liable to the corruption of death, [the Word] surrendered it to death for all humanity, and offered it to the Father. He presented it to the Father as an act of pure love for humanity, so that by all dying in him the law concerning the corruption of humanity might be abolished (inasmuch as its power was fulfilled in the Lord's body, and no longer has capacity against human beings who are like him), and that he might turn back to a state of incorruption those who had fallen into a state of corruption, and bring them to life by the fact of his death, by the body which he made his own, and by the grace of his resurrection . . . The Word thus takes on a body capable of death, in order that, by partaking in the Word that is above all, this body might be worthy to die instead for all humanity, and remain incorruptible through the indwelling Word, and thus put an end to corruption through the grace of his resurrection . . . Hence he did away with death for all who are like him by the offering of the body which he had taken on himself. The Word, who is above all, offered his own temple and bodily instrument as a ransom for all, and paid their debt through his death. Thus the incorruptible Son of God, being united with all humanity by likeness to them, naturally clothed all humanity with incorruption, according to the promise of the resurrection.

5.5   Athanasius on the Relation of Christology and Soteriology

Athanasius defended the doctrine of the incarnation of Christ on a number of grounds, including the soteriological argument that humanity could only be redeemed by God himself. Therefore unless Christ was God, the redemption of humanity through Christ was an impossibility. In this passage, Athanasius stresses the close link between the person and work of Christ, noting in particular the soteriological aspects of the incarnation. See also 5.4; 5.21; 5.22; 5.26.

Source: contra Arianos, III, 33; in J. P. Migne, Patrologia Graeca 26:393A–C.

* * *

If the works of the divinity of the Word had not taken place through a body, humanity would not have been made divine. And again, if the properties of the flesh had not been ascribed to the Word, humanity would not have been thoroughly freed from them ... But now the Word became human and took as his own the properties of the flesh. Thus, because of the Word which has come in humanity, these attributes [death and corruption] no longer pertain to the flesh, but have been destroyed in the body by the Word. Henceforth people no longer remain sinful and dead according to their own attributes, but they rise in accordance with the Word's power, and remain immortal and incorruptible. And just as the flesh is said to have been begotten from Mary the *Theotokos*, he himself is said to have been begotten, he who brings to birth all others so that they come into being. This is in order that he may transfer our birth to himself, that we may no longer return as earth to earth, but, being joined with the Word from heaven, we may be carried up with him into heaven.

Pseudo-Hippolytus on the Cosmic Dimensions of the Cross

5.6

The means in which the death of Christ on the cross enabled humanity to be redeemed was the subject of considerable speculation in the early patristic period. This writing, which cannot be dated with certainty, views the cross against a cosmic background, arguing that the redemption achieved by Christ affected every aspect of the universe. The term "pseudo-Hippolytus" designates the unknown writer of this piece, who has clearly modelled his style on that of Hippolytus. Note in particular the way in which the cross is seen as of central importance to the wellbeing of the cosmos. See also 5.1; 5.7; 5.8; 5.9.

Source: An anonymous paschal homily inspired by the Treatise on the Passion of Hippolytus; in *Sources Chrétiennes: Homélies paschales*, vol. 1, ed. P. Nautin (Paris: Cerf, 1950), 177.8–179.9.

* * *

This tree is for me a plant of eternal salvation. By it I am nourished, by it I am fed. By its roots, I am firmly planted. By its branches, I am spread out, its perfume is a delight to me, and its spirit refreshes me like a delightful wind. I have pitched my tent in its shadow, and during the heat I find it to be a haven full of perfume ... This tree of heavenly proportions rises up from the earth to heaven. It is fixed, as an eternal growth, at the midpoint of heaven and earth. It sustains all things, the support of the universe, the base of the whole inhabited world, and the axis of the earth. Established by the invisible pegs of the Spirit, it holds together the various aspects of human nature in such a way that, divinely guided, its nature may never again become separated from God. By its peak which touches the height of the heavens, by its base which supports the earth, and by its immense arms subduing the many spirits of the air on every side, it exists in its totality in every thing and in every place.

5.7   Rufinus of Aquileia on the "Mousetrap" Theory of the Atonement

This passage, which dates from around the year 400, represents a classic statement of the "mousetrap" or "fish-hook" theory of the atonement, which held that Christ's death on the cross was an elaborate trap laid for Satan. Satan, it was argued, held humanity so securely captive that God was unable to liberate them by any legitimate means, and thus resorted to divine deception. The humanity of Christ was the bait, and his divinity the hook. Unaware of Christ's divinity, Satan was trapped through his humanity. The highly questionable morality of this theory was the subject of intense criticism by many medieval writers. See also 5.1; 5.10.

Source: *Expositio Symboli*, 14; in *Corpus Christianorum: Series Latina*, vol. 20, ed. M. Simonetti (Turnholt: Brepols, 1961), 151.9–152.22.

* * *

> [The purpose of the Incarnation] was that the divine virtue of the Son of God might be like a kind of hook hidden beneath the form of human flesh . . . to lure on the prince of this world to a contest; that the Son might offer him his human flesh as a bait and that the divinity which lay underneath might catch him and hold him fast with its hook . . . Then, just as a fish when it seizes a baited hook not only fails to drag off the bait but is itself dragged out of the water to serve as food for others; so he that had the power of death seized the body of Jesus in death, unaware of the hook of divinity which lay hidden inside. Having swallowed it, he was immediately caught. The gates of hell were broken, and he was, as it were, drawn up from the pit, to become food for others.

5.8   An Ancient Liturgy on Christ's Descent into Hell

This homily (or sermon) was probably written towards the end of the fourth century. The identity of the author is unknown, although some traditions suggest that it was Epiphanius of Constantia. The homily pictures the cosmic dimensions of the cross, particularly the impact which Christ had upon those who were held prisoner in hell. The liberation of the imprisoned dead is described in vivid and realistic terms. The homily was intended to be preached on Holy Saturday – that is, the day which separates the commemoration of the crucifixion (Good Friday) and resurrection (Easter Day) of Christ. See also 5.2; 5.7; 5.9.

Source: Homily for Holy Saturday, ascribed to Epiphanius of Constantia, but of uncertain authorship; in J. P. Migne, *Patrologia Graeca*, 43:440A; 452B–C; 461B.

* * *

> Today, there is a great silence on earth – a great silence and a great stillness. There is a great silence because the king is sleeping. The earth trembled and is still because God has fallen asleep in the flesh, and he has raised up all

who have fallen asleep ever since the beginning of the world. God has appeared in the flesh, and Hades has swallowed him. God will sleep for a short time, and then raise those who are in Hades . . . He has gone to search out Adam, our first father, as if he were a lost sheep. Earnestly longing to visit those who live in darkness and the shadow of death, he – who is both their God and the son of Eve – has gone to liberate Adam from his bonds, and Eve who is held captive along with him . . . "I am your God. For your sake I have become your son . . . I order you, O sleeper, to awake. I did not create you to be a prisoner in hell. Rise from the dead, for I am the life of the dead! Arise, my seed! Arise, my form (*morphē*), who has been made in my image (*eikōn*)!"

Simeon the New Theologian on Salvation as Deification   5.9

Simeon the New Theologian is one of the more important early Byzantine theologians, noted for his emphasis upon the divinization of humanity through Christ. In this poem, which dates from around the year 1000, Simeon sets out the full implications of the believer being united with Christ. It represents a classic statement of a Byzantine approach to divinization in particular, and soteriology in general. The final line of this extract is difficult to render adequately: the Greek conveys the idea of a unity of extremes. See also 4.19; 5.25.

Source: *Hymns of Divine Love, 7; in Supplementa Byzantina: Texte und Untersuchungen*, ed. H. G. Beck, A. Kambylis, and R. Keydell (Berlin/New York, 1976), 71.29–42.

⁎ ⁎ ⁎

> But your nature is your essence, and your essence your nature.
> So uniting with your body, I share in your nature,
> and I truly take as mine what is yours,
> uniting with your divinity, and thus becoming an heir,
> superior in my body to those who have no body.
> As you have said, I have become a son' of God,
> not for the angels, but for us, who you have called gods.
> I have said: "You are gods and are all sons of the Most High."
> Glory be to your kindness and to the plan (*oikonomia*),
> by which you became human, you who by nature are God,
> without change or confusion, remaining the same,
> and that you have made me a god, a mortal by my nature,
> a god by your grace, by the power of your Spirit,
> bringing together as god a unity of opposites.

5.10 Anselm of Canterbury on the Atonement

In this classic text, originally written in Latin in 1098, Anselm sets out his understanding of the reason why God became human. The text as printed here is basically a series of short extracts from the work, which sum up its central themes. The most important point to note is its emphasis that, on account of sin, humanity has an obligation to offer God an infinite satisfaction, which only God can meet. Therefore a God-man would have both the ability (as God) and obligation (as a human) to pay this satisfaction, and thus obtain forgiveness of sins. See also 5.11; 5.12; 5.13; 5.15; 5.16; 5.27.

Source: Extracts from *Cur Deus homo*, I. xi–xxi; II.iv–xx; in *S. Anselmi Opera Omnia*, ed. F. S. Schmitt, vol. 2 (Edinburgh: Nelson, 1946), 68.3–89.32; 99.3–132.6.

* * *

The problem is, how can God forgive human sin? To clear our thoughts let us first consider what sin is, and what satisfaction for sin is . . . To sin is to fail to render to God what God is entitled to. What is God entitled to? Righteousness, or rectitude of will. Anyone who fails to render this honour to God, robs God of that which belongs to God, and thus dishonours God. And what is satisfaction? It is not enough simply to restore what has been taken away; but, in consideration of the insult offered, more than what was taken away must be rendered back. Let us consider whether God could properly remit sin by mercy alone without satisfaction. So to remit sin would be simply to abstain from punishing it. And since the only possible way of correcting sin, for which no satisfaction has been made, is to punish it; not to punish it, is to leave it uncorrected. But God cannot properly leave anything uncorrected in His kingdom. Furthermore, to leave sin unpunished would be tantamount to treating the sinful and the sinless alike, which would be inconsistent with God's nature. And this inconsistency is injustice. It is necessary, therefore, that either the honour taken away should be repaid, or punishment should be inflicted. Otherwise one of two things follows: either God is not just to his own nature; or God is powerless to do what ought to be done, which is a blasphemous supposition. The satisfaction ought to be in proportion to the sin.

Yet you have not yet duly estimated the gravity of sin. Suppose that you were standing in God's presence, and some one said to you "look over there." And God said, "I am altogether unwilling that you should look." Ask yourself whether there could be anything in the whole universe for the sake of which you would allow yourself that one look against the will of God. You should not act against the will of God, not even to prevent the whole creation from perishing. And if you were to act in this way, what could you pay for this sin? You could not make satisfaction for it, unless you were to pay something greater than the whole creation. All that is created, that is, all that is not God, cannot compensate for the sin in question.

It is necessary that God should fulfil His purpose respecting human nature. And this cannot be except there be a complete satisfaction made for sin; and this no sinner can make. Satisfaction cannot be made unless there is someone who is able to pay to God for the sin of humanity. This payment must be something greater than all that is beside God . . . Now nothing is greater than all that is not God, except God. So nobody can make this satisfaction except God. And nobody ought to make it except human beings themselves. If, then, it is necessary that the kingdom of heaven should be fulfilled by the admission of humanity, and if we cannot be admitted unless this satisfaction for sin is first made, and if God only *can*, and only humanity *ought* to make this satisfaction, then it is necessary that someone must make it who is both God and a human being.

This person must have something to offer to God which is greater than all that is lower than God, and something that can be given to God voluntarily, and not as a matter of obligation. Mere obedience would not be a gift of this kind; for every rational creature owes this obedience as a duty to God. But Christ was in no way under any obligation to suffer death, in that Christ never sinned. So death was an offering that he could make as a matter of free will, rather than of debt.

Now anyone who could freely offer so great a gift to God, clearly ought to be rewarded in some way . . . But what reward could be given to someone who needed nothing, someone who demanded neither a gift nor needed a pardon? . . . If the Son chose to make over the claim he had on God to humanity, could the Father justly forbid Him doing so, or refuse to humanity what the Son willed to give him? What greater mercy can be conceived than that God the Father should say to sinners, condemned to eternal torment and unable to redeem themselves: "Receive my only Son, and offer him for yourselves," while the Son himself said: "Take me, and redeem yourselves"? And what greater justice than that One who receives a payment far exceeding the amount due, should, if it be paid with a right intention, remit all that is due?

Peter Abelard on the Love of Christ in Redemption

5.11

Abelard was one of Anselm's earliest critics. In his Commentary on Romans, dating from the early decades of the twelfth century, Abelard argued that one of the chief consequences of the death of Christ was its demonstration of the love of God for humanity. It is through our response of love to Christ that we are joined to him, and benefit from his passion. See also 5.3; 5.10; 5.12; 5.13; 5.15; 5.16; 5.23; 5.27.

Source: *Expositio in Epistolam ad Romanos*, 2; in J. P. Migne, *Patrologia Latina*, 178.832C–D; 836A–B.

* * *

Love is increased by the faith which we have concerning Christ because, on account of the belief that God in Christ has united our human nature to himself, and by suffering in that same nature has demonstrated to us that supreme love (*in ipsa patiendo summam illam charitatem nobis exhibuisse*) of which Christ himself speaks: "Greater love has no-one than this" (John

15:13). We are thus joined through his grace to him and our neighbour by an unbreakable bond of love ... Just as all have sinned, so they are justified without respect of person (*indifferenter*) by this supreme grace which has been made known to us by God. And this is what [Paul] declares: "For all have sinned, and all need the grace of God" (Romans 3:23), that is, they need to glorify the Lord as a matter of obligation ... Now it seems to us that we have been justified by the blood of Christ and reconciled to God in this way: through this singular act of grace made known in us (in that his Son has taken our nature on himself, and persevered in this nature, and taught us by both his word and his example, even to the point of death) he has more fully bound us to himself by love. As a result, our hearts should be set on fire by such a gift of divine grace, and true love should not hold back from suffering anything for his sake ... Therefore, our redemption through the suffering of Christ is that deeper love within us which not only frees us from slavery to sin, but also secures for us the true liberty of the children of God, in order that we might do all things out of love rather than out of fear – love for him who has shown us such grace that no greater can be found.

5.12 Hugh of St. Victor on the Death of Christ

This important passage, written in Latin in the first decades of the twelfth century, represents a development of the theology of atonement associated with Anselm. Anselmian ideas are here mingled with other motifs, including some of an explicitly sacrificial nature. Note in particular the explicit declaration that God could have redeemed humanity in another manner. See also 5.10; 5.11; 5.13; 5.15; 5.16; 5.27.

Source: *de sacramentis*, I.viii.6–7; 10; in J. P. Migne, *Patrologia Latina*, 176.310.B–D; 311D.

* * *

God became a human being so that he might liberate the humanity which he had created, in order that he might be both the creator and redeemer of humanity ... From our nature, he took a victim for our nature, so that the whole burnt offering which was offered up might come from that which is ours. He did this so that the redemption to be offered might have a connection with us, through its being taken from what is ours. We are truly made to be partakers in this redemption is we are united through faith to the redeemer who has entered into fellowship with us through his flesh. Now human nature had become corrupted by sin, and had thus become liable to condemnation on its account. But grace came, and chose some from the mass of humanity (*massa universitis*) through mercy for salvation, while it allowed others to remain for condemnation through justice. Those who grace saved through mercy were not saved without justice, in that it was in its power to do this justly; yet even if it had not saved them, it would still have acted justly, in that in terms of their merit, it would not have been unjust to have acted in this way ...

God, however, would have been able to achieve the redemption of humanity in a totally different manner, if he had wanted to. It was, however, more appropriate to our weakness that God should become a human being, and that he should transform humanity for the hope of immortality by taking its mortality upon himself. In this way, humanity might have the hope of ascending to the good things of the one who descended to bear its evils, and the humanity which has been glorified in God might be an example of glorification to us.

Thomas Aquinas on the Satisfaction of Christ 5.13

The *Summa Theologiae* ("The Totality of Theology"), which Aquinas began to write in Latin in 1265 and left unfinished at the time of his death, is widely regarded as the greatest work of medieval theology. In this important and influential analysis, Aquinas develops the Anselmian theme of satisfaction, dealing with a number of objections which had been raised against it. Note in particular his response to the criticism that the dignity of Christ was not sufficient to obtain God's forgiveness of human sin. See also 5.10; 5.11; 5.12; 5.15; 5.16; 5.27.

Source: *Summa Theologiae*, IIIa, q. 48, a. 2.

* * *

1. It seems that the passion of Christ did not effect our salvation by way of satisfaction. For it seems that to make satisfaction is the responsibility of the one who sins, as is clear from other aspects of penance, in that the one who sins is the one who must repent and confess. But Christ did not sin. As St Peter says, "he committed no sin" (1 Peter 2:22). He therefore did not make satisfaction through his passion.

2. Furthermore, satisfaction can never be made by means of a greater offence. But the greatest offence was perpetrated in the passion of Christ, since those who put him to death committed the most grievous of sins. For this reason, satisfaction could not be made to God through the passion of Christ.

3. Furthermore, satisfaction implies a certain equality with the fault, since it is an act of justice. But the passion of Christ does not seem to be equal to all the sins of the human race, since Christ suffered according to the flesh, not according to his divinity. As St Peter says, "Christ has suffered in the flesh" (1 Peter 4:1) . . . Christ therefore did not make satisfaction for our sins by his passion . . .

I reply that a proper satisfaction comes about when someone offers to the person offended something which gives him a delight greater than his hatred of the offence. Now Christ by suffering as a result of love and obedience offered to God something greater than what might be exacted in compensation for the whole offence of humanity; firstly, because of the greatness of the love, as a result of which he suffered; secondly, because of the worth of the life which he laid down for a satisfaction, which was the life of God and of a human being; thirdly, because of the comprehensiveness of his passion and the greatness of the sorrow which he took upon himself . . . And therefore the passion of Christ was not only sufficient but a superabundant satisfaction for the sins of the human race. As John says, "he is a propitiation for our sins, not only for ours, but also for those of the whole world" (1 John 2:2).

Hence, in reply to the first point, the head and the members are as it were one mystical person; and thus the satisfaction of Christ belongs to all the faithful as to his members . . .

In reply to the second, the love of Christ in his suffering outweighed the malice of them that crucified him . . . In reply to the third, the worth of Christ's flesh is to be reckoned, not just according to the nature of flesh (*solum secundum carnis naturam*), but according to the person who assumed it (*secundum personam assumentem*), in that it was the flesh of God, from whom it gained an infinite worth.

5.14 Nicholas Cabasilas on the Death of Christ

This fourteenth-century work, which represents some of the major strands of Byzantine theology, deals with the purpose of Christ's death. The passage argues that Christ's death took place in such a way that he was able to deal with each of the three afflictions of sinful humanity. See also 5.4; 5.9; 5.25.

Source: *de vita in Christo*, 3; in J. P. Migne, *Patrologia Graeca*, 150:572C–D.

* * *

Just as humanity was cut off from God in three ways – by nature, sin, and death – so the Saviour operated in such a way that it might come to him directly, without any obstacles. He did this by successively removing everything which stood in its way; the first, by sharing in human nature; the second, by undergoing death on the cross; and finally, the third dividing barrier by rising from the dead, and banishing the tyranny of death totally from our nature.

5.15 John Calvin on the Grounds of Redemption

In this letter, Calvin provides a very brief summary of his general position concerning the doctrine of redemption. A fuller treatment may be found in his *Institutes of the Christian Religion*, book 2, chapters 1–17. The style used by Calvin in his brief "letter of advice" (*consilium*) is much lighter and simpler than that adopted in the *Institutes*, making this extract unusually easy to follow and understand. See also 5.10; 5.11; 5.12; 5.13; 5.16; 5.27.

Source: *Consilium de peccato et redemptione; in Corpus Reformatorum*, vol. 10, part 1, ed. G. Baum, E. Cunitz, and E. Reuss (Braunschweig: Schwetschke, 1871), pp. 156–7.

* * *

The first man of all was created by God with an immortal soul and a mortal body. God adorned him with his own likeness (*similitudo*), so that he was free from any evil, and he commanded him to enjoy all that was in his pleasant garden, with the exception of the tree in which all life was hidden. He was so concerned that he should keep his hand away from this tree that he told him that he would die when he first touched its fruit. However, he did touch it. As a result, he died and was no longer like God. This was the primary origin of death. That this is true is proved by the following words: "As often as you eat of it, you will die" . . . Man was therefore driven into exile, along with his descendants, in order that, having lost "the horn of plenty," he should be miserable and experience all kinds of work and every ill, seeking food, sweating and suffering cold, often hungry, often thirsty, always wretched (*famelicus saepe, saepe sitiens, semper miser*). Finally, God took pity upon this unfortunate and thoroughly unhappy man. Although the sentence which he passed upon him was correct, he nevertheless gave his only and much-loved Son as a sacrificial victim for such sins. By reason of this amazing and unexpected mercy (*admirabili et inusitata misericordiae ratione*), God commended his own love towards us more greatly than if he had rescinded this sentence. Therefore Christ, the Son of God, was both conceived through the overshadowing of the Holy Spirit and born of the virgin. He was finally raised up on the cross, and through his own death delivered the human race from eternal death.

The Socinian Critique of the Idea of Satisfaction

5.16

The Socinian critique of the idea of satisfaction gained influence during the sixteenth century. The Racovian Catechism, published in Polish in 1605 at the city of Racow (from which it takes its name), argued that God was perfectly capable of forgiving human sin without the need for the death of Christ, and vigorously opposed the idea of Christ's death representing any form of satisfaction. This extract is taken from the English translation by Thomas Rees, first published at London in 1818. See also 5.10; 5.11; 5.12; 5.13; 5.15; 5.27.

Source: The Racovian Catechism, V, 8; in The Racovian Catechism (London: Longman, 1818), p. 303.

---

* * *

But did not Christ die also, in order, properly speaking, to purchase our salvation, and literally to pay the debt of our sins? Although Christians at this time commonly so believe, yet this notion is false, erroneous, and exceedingly pernicious; since they conceive that Christ suffered an equivalent punishment for our sins, and by the price of his obedience exactly compensated our disobedience. There is no doubt, however, but that Christ so satisfied God by his obedience, as that he completely fulfilled the whole of his will, and by his obedience obtained, through the grace of God, for all of us who believe in him, the remission of our sins, and eternal salvation.

How do you make it appear that the common notion is false and erroneous?

Not only because the Scriptures are silent concerning it, but also because it is repugnant to the scriptures and to right reason ... They who maintain this opinion never adduce explicit texts of Scripture in proof of it, but string together certain inferences by which they endeavour to maintain their assertions. But, besides that a matter of this kind, whereon they themselves conceive the whole business of salvation to turn, ought certainly to be demonstrated not by inferences alone but by clear testimonies of scripture, it might easily be shown that these inferences have no force whatever ... The Scriptures every where testify that God forgives men their sins freely, and especially under the New Covenant (2 Cor. 5:19; Rom. 3:24, 25; Matt. 18:23; etc.). But to a free forgiveness nothing is more opposite than such a satisfaction as they contend for, and the payment of an equivalent price. For where a creditor is satisfied, either by the debtor himself, or by another person on the debtor's behalf, it cannot with truth be said of him that he freely forgives the debt ... It would follow that Christ, if he has satisfied God for our sins, has submitted to eternal death; since it appears that the penalty which men had incurred by their offences was eternal death; not to say that one death, though it were eternal in duration, – much less one so short, – could not of itself be equal to innumerable eternal deaths. For if you say that the death of Christ, because he was a God infinite in nature, was equal to the infinite deaths of the infinite race of men, – besides that I have already refuted this opinion concerning the nature of Christ, – it would follow that God's infinite nature itself suffered death. But as death cannot any way belong to the infinity of the divine nature, so neither, literally speaking (as must necessarily be done here where we are treating of a real compensation and payment), can the infinity of the divine nature any way belong to death. In the next place, it would follow that there was no necessity that Christ should endure such sufferings, and so dreadful a death; and that God – be it spoken without offence, – was unjust, who, when he might well have been contented with one drop (as they say) of the blood of Christ, would have him so severely tormented. Lastly, it would follow that we were more obliged to Christ than to God, and owed him more, indeed owed him every thing; since he, by this satisfaction, showed us much kindness; whereas God, by exacting his debt, showed us no kindness at all ...

They endeavour to [maintain this] first by a certain reason, and then by the authority of Scripture ... They say that there are in God, by nature, justice and mercy: that as it is the property of mercy to forgive sins, so is it, they state, the property of justice to punish every sin whatever. But since God willed that both his mercy and justice should be satisfied together, he devised this plan, that Christ should suffer death in our stead, and thus satisfy God's justice in the human nature, by which he had been offended; and that his mercy should at the same time be displayed in forgiving sin ... This reason bears the appearance of plausibility, but in reality has in it nothing of truth or solidity; and indeed involves a self-contradiction. For although we confess, and hence exceedingly rejoice, that our God is wonderfully merciful and just, nevertheless we deny that there are in him the mercy and justice which our adversaries imagine, since the one would wholly annihilate the other. For, according to them, the one requires that God should punish no sin; the other, that he should leave no sin unpunished. If then it were naturally a property of God to punish no sin, he could not act against his nature in order that he might punish sin: in like manner also, if it were naturally a property of God to leave no sin unpunished, he could not, any more, contrary to his nature, refrain from punishing every sin. For God can never do any thing repugnant to those properties which pertain to him by nature. For instance, since wisdom belongs naturally to God, he can never do any thing contrary to it, but whatever he does he does wisely. But as it is evident that God forgives and punishes sins whenever he deems fit it appears that the mercy which commands to spare, and the justice which commands to destroy, do so exist in him as that both are tempered by his will, and by the wisdom, the benignity, and holiness of his nature. Besides, the scriptures are not wont to designate the justice, which is opposed to mercy, and is discernible in punishments inflicted in wrath, by this term, but style it the *severity*, the *anger*, and *wrath* of God . . . Since I have shown that the mercy and justice which our adversaries conceive to pertain to God by nature, certainly do not belong to him, there was no need of that plan whereby he might satisfy such mercy and justice, and by which they might, as it were by a certain tempering, be reconciled to each other: which tempering nevertheless is such that it satisfies neither, and indeed destroys both; – For what is that justice, and what too that mercy, which punishes the innocent, and absolves the guilty? I do not, indeed, deny that there is a natural justice in God, which is called rectitude, and is opposed to wickedness: this shines in all his works, and hence they all appear just and right and perfect; and that, no less when he forgives than when he punishes our transgressions.

John Donne on the Work of Christ 5.17

This poem indicates the approaches to the incarnation and atonement which were prevalent in the high noon of Anglican theology, just before the period of the English Civil War. In this early edition, the Sonnet appears as the eleventh in a collection of twelve; later editions treat it as the fifteenth in a collection of nineteen. The original orthography has been retained. See also 5.10; 5.11; 5.12; 5.13; 5.15; 5.16; 5.27.

Source: Holy Sonnet XI; in *Poems by John Donne with Elegies on the Authors Death* (London: John Marriot, 1633), p. 39.

* * *

Wilt thou love God, as he thee! then digest,
My Soule, this wholsome meditoation,
How God the Spirit, by Angels waited on
In heaven, doth make his Temple in thy brest.
The Father having begot a Sonne most blest,

And still begetting, (for he ne'r begonne)
Hath deign'd to choose thee by adoption,
Coheire to his glory, and Sabbaths endlesse rest;
And as a robb'd man, which by search doth finde
His stolne stuffe sold, must lose or buy it again:
The Sonne of glory came downe, and was slaine,
Us whom he had made, and Satan stolne, to unbind.
Twas much, that man was made like God before,
But, that God should be made like man, much more.

5.18 George Herbert on the Death of Christ and Redemption

In this poem, which forms part of the collection known as "The Temple," composed around 1633, the poet explores the associations of the term "redemption." Alluding to the Old Testament notion of "redeeming land," Herbert develops the idea of the death of Christ as the price by which God takes legitimate possession of a precious piece of land. While also exploring the idea of the shame and humility of the cross, Herbert is able to bring out the legal and financial dimensions of redemption. See also 5.10; 5.11; 5.12; 5.13; 5.15; 5.16; 5.27.

Source: "Redemption"; in *The Works of George Herbert*, ed. F. E. Hutchinson (Oxford: Clarendon Press, 1941), p. 40.

* * *

Having been tenant long to a rich Lord,
　　Not thriving, I resolved to be bold,
　　And make a suit unto him, to afford
A new small-rented lease, and cancell th'old,
In heaven at his manour I him sought:
　　They told me there, that he was lately gone
　　About some land, which he had dearly bought,
Long since on earth, to take possession.
I straight return'd, and knowing his great birth,
　　Sought him accordingly in great resorts;
　　In cities, theatres, gardens, parks, and courts:
At length I heard a ragged noise and mirth
　　Of theeves and murderers: there I him espied,
　　Who straight, *Your suit is granted*, said, & died.

5.19 Charles Wesley on Salvation in Christ

On 21 May 1738, Charles Wesley underwent a profound conversion experience through the ministry of the Moravian Peter Böhler. In this hymn, written a year after this experience, Wesley put into verse his understanding of the significance of the death of Christ for Christian believers. Note the way in which the hymn brings together a range of images relating to salvation, including liberation and enlightenment. The hymn, originally entitled "Free Grace," can be seen as a summary of the "economy of salvation," placing considerable emphasis upon the self-humiliation of Christ. Notice also the explicit references to the suffering and death of God, most notably in the exclamation "th' Immortal dies"! The original English text (which differs significantly from later versions) is here reproduced without any alterations. Note that the theologically significant fifth verse, which deals with the subjective assurance of salvation and the experiential aspects of Christian existence, is omitted in modern versions. Two points should be noted about Wesley's English: *'Tis* is an archaic version of "It is"; "quickning" is an archaic form of "life-giving." See also 5.3; 5.4; 5.10; 5.11; 5.12; 5.13; 5.15; 5.16; 5.27.

Source: John Wesley and Charles Wesley, *Hymns and Sacred Poems* (London: William Strahan, 1739), pp. 117–19.

                                                 * * *

And can it be that I should gain
    An int'rest in the Saviour's blood!
Dy'd he for me? – who caus'd his pain?
    For me? – who Him to Death pursued?
Amazing love! How can it be
That Thou, my God, shouldst die for me?

'Tis mystery all! th'Immortal dies!
    Who can explore his strange Design?
In vain the first-born Seraph tries
    To sound the Depths of Love divine.
'Tis mercy all! Let earth adore;
Let Angel Minds inquire no more.

He left his Fathers throne above
    (So free, so infinite his grace!)
Empty'd himself of All but Love,
    And bled for *Adam's* helpless Race.
'Tis Mercy all, immense and free,
For, O my God! it found out Me!

Long my imprison'd Spirit lay,
    Fast bound in Sin and Nature's Night
Thine Eye diffus'd a quickning Ray;
    I woke; the Dungeon flam'd with Light.
My Chains fell off, my Heart was free,
I rose, went forth, and follow'd Thee.

Still the small inward Voice I hear,
    That whispers all my Sins forgiv'n;
Still the atoning Blood is near,
    That quench'd the Wrath of hostile Heav'n:
I feel the Life his Wounds impart;
    I feel my Saviour in my Heart.

No Condemnation now I dread,
    Jesus, and all in Him, is mine.
Alive in Him, my Living Head,
    And clothed in Righteousness Divine,
Bold I approach th'Eternal Throne,
And claim the Crown, thro' CHRIST my own.

5.20 F. D. E. Schleiermacher on Christ as a Charismatic Leader

Schleiermacher locates the significance of Jesus of Nazareth in terms of the impact which he has upon the church, or "community of faith." Reacting against the rationalism and moralism of the Enlightenment, Schleiermacher stressed the importance of religious feeling, particularly a "feeling of absolute dependence" on God. This feeling, he argued, is brought about by Jesus Christ. But how? In this passage, Schleiermacher suggests that Jesus of Nazareth relates to the church in mush the same way as a charismatic leader relates to his or her people. Note in particular the emphasis placed upon the role of the community, and the criticism of the traditional language of "satisfaction," which Schleiermacher here refers to as 'magical." See also 4.23; 5.21.

Source: Friedrich Schleiermacher, *The Christian Faith* (Edinburgh: T. & T. Clark, 1928), pp. 429–31.

* * *

An analogy to this relation may be pointed out in a sphere which is universally familiar. As contrasted with the condition of things existing before there was any law, the civil community within a defined area is a higher vital potency. Let us now suppose that some person for the first time combines a naturally cohesive group into a civil community (legend tells of such cases in plenty); what happens is that the idea of the state first comes to consciousness in him, and takes possession of his personality as its immediate dwelling-place. Then he assumes the rest into the living fellowship of the idea. He does so by making them clearly conscious of the unsatisfactoriness of their present condition by effective speech. The power remains with the founder of forming in them the idea which is the innermost principle of his own life, and of assuming them into the fellowship of that life. The result is, not only that there arises among them a new corporate life, in complete contrast to the old, but also that each of them becomes in themselves new persons – that is to say, citizens. And everything resulting from this is the corporate life – developing variously with the process of time, yet remaining essentially the same – of this idea which emerged at that particular point of time, but was always predestined in the nature of that particular racial stock. The analogy might be pushed even further, to points of which we shall speak later. But even this presentation of it will seem mystical to those who admit only a meagre and inferior conception of the civic state.

Let us be content, then, that our view of the matter should be called mystical in this sense; naturally everything to be derived from this main point will be called mystical too. But just as this mystical view can substantiate its claim to be the original one, so too it claims to be the true mean between two others, of which I shall call the one the magical way, and the other the empirical. The former admits, of course, that the activity of Christ is redemptive, but denies that the communication of His perfection is dependent on the founding of a community; it results, they maintain, from

His immediate influence upon the individual: and for this some take the written word to be a necessary means, others do not. The latter show themselves the more consistent, but the more completely they cut themselves loose from everything originating in the community the more obvious becomes the magical character of their view. This magical character lies in an influence not mediated by anything natural, yet attributed to a person. This is completely at variance with the maxim everywhere underlying our presentation, that the beginning of the Kingdom of God is a supernatural thing, which, however, becomes natural as soon as it emerges into manifestation; for this other view makes every significant moment a supernatural one. Further, this view is completely separatist in type, for it makes the corporate life a purely accidental thing; and it comes very near being docetic as well. For if Christ exerted influence in any such way as this – as a person, it is true, but only as a heavenly person without earthly presence, though in a truly personal way – then it would have been possible for Him to work in just the same way at any time, and His real personal appearance in history was only a superfluous adjunct. But those who likewise assume an immediate personal influence, but mediate it through the word and the fellowship, are less magical only if they attribute to these the power of evoking a mood in which the individual becomes susceptible to that personal influence. They are more magical still, if these natural elements have the power of disposing Christ to exert His influence; for then their efficacy is exactly like that attributed to magic spells. The contrary empirical view also, it is true, admits a redemptive activity on the part of Christ, but one which is held to consist only in bringing about an increasing perfection in us; and this cannot properly occur otherwise than in the forms of teaching and example. These forms are general; there is nothing distinctive in them. Even suppose it admitted that Christ is distinguished from others who contribute in the same way to our improvement, by the pure perfection of His teaching and His example, yet if all that is achieved in us is something imperfect, there remains nothing but to forgo the idea of redemption in the proper sense – that is, as the removal of sin – and, in view of the consciousness of sin still remaining even in our growing perfection, to pacify ourselves with a general appeal to the divine compassion. Now, teaching and example effect no more than such a growing perfection, and this appeal to the divine compassion occurs even apart from Christ. It must therefore be admitted that His appearance, in so far as intended to be something special, would in that case be in vain. At most it might be said that by His teaching He brought people to the point of giving up the effort, previously universal, to offer God substitutes for the perfection they lacked. But since the uselessness of this effort can be demonstrated, already in our natural intelligence we have the divine certainty of this, and had no need to obtain it elsewhere. And probably this view is chiefly to blame for the claim of philosophy to set itself above faith and to treat faith as merely a transitional stage. But we cannot rest satisfied with the consciousness of growing perfection, for that belongs just as much to the consciousness of sin as to that of grace, and hence cannot contain what is peculiarly Christian. But, for the Christian, nothing belongs to the consciousness of grace unless it is traced to the Redeemer as its cause, and therefore it must always be a different thing in His case from what it is in the case of others – naturally, since it is bound up with something else, namely, the peculiar redemptive activity of Christ.

5.21 F. D. E. Schleiermacher on Christology and Soteriology

In this highly influential discussion of the relation of Christology and soteriology, Schleiermacher argues that the doctrines of the person and work of Christ are inseparable. The "activity" and "dignity" of Christ are mutually related concepts, which cannot be discussed in isolation from each other. Previously, dogmatic textbooks had tended to regard these two areas of theology as distinct; since Schleiermacher, they have generally been discussed together. See also 4.23; 5.5; 5.20; 5.22; 5.26.

Source: Friedrich Schleiermacher, *The Christian Faith* (Edinburgh: T. & T. Clark, 1928), pp. 374–5.

* * *

The peculiar activity and the exclusive dignity of the Redeemer imply each other, and are inseparably one in the self consciousness of believers.

1. Whether we prefer to call Christ the Redeemer, or to regard Him as the one in whom the creation of human nature, which up to this point had existed only in a provisional state, was perfected, each of these points of view means only that we ascribe to Him a peculiar activity, and that in connexion with a peculiar spiritual content of His person. For if His influence is only of the same kind as that of others, even if it is ever so much more complete and inclusive, then its result also, that is, the salvation of humanity, would be a work common to Him and the others, although His share might be the greater; and there would be, not one Redeemer over against the redeemed, but many, of whom one would only be the first among those like Him. Nor would the human creation then be completed through Him, but through all of those redeemers together, who, in so far as their work implies in them a peculiar quality of nature, are all alike distinguished from the rest of humanity. It would be just the same, if His activity were indeed peculiar to Himself, but this less in virtue of an inner quality belonging to Him than of a peculiar position in which He had been put. The second form of expression, that the human creation had been completed in Him, would then be altogether without content, since it would be more natural to suppose that there are many like Him, only they did not happen to occupy the same position. In that case He would not even be properly Redeemer, even though it could be said that humanity had been redeemed through His act or His suffering, as the case might be. For the result, namely, salvation, could not be something communicated from Him (since He had nothing peculiar to Himself); it could only have been occasioned or released by Him.

Just as little could the approximation to the condition of blessedness be traced to Him, if He had indeed had an exclusive dignity, but had remained passive in it, and had exercised no influence corresponding to it. For (apart from the fact that it is incomprehensible how His contemporaries, and we after them, should ever have come to attribute such an influence to Him, especially when the manner of His appearance was what it was), supposing that the blessedness could have been communicated merely through people observing this dignity, although there were united with it no influence acting on others, then in the observers there must have been something more than receptivity; His appearance would have to be regarded rather as merely the occasion for this idea, spontaneously produced by themselves.

2. Thus the approximation to blessedness, out of the state of misery, cannot be explained as a fact mediated through Jesus, by reference to either of these elements without the other. It follows, therefore, that they must be most intimately related and mutually determined. So that it is vain to attribute to the Redeemer a higher dignity than the activity at the same time ascribed to Him demands, since nothing is explained by this surplus of dignity. It is equally vain to attribute to Him a greater activity than follows naturally from the dignity which one is ready to allow to Him, since whatever results from this surplus of activity cannot be traced to Him in the same sense as the rest. Therefore every doctrine of Christ is inconsistent, in which this equality (of dignity and activity) is not essential, whether it seeks to disguise the detraction from the dignity by praising in Him great but really alien activities, or, conversely, seeks to compensate for the lesser influence which it allows Him by highly exalting Him, yet in a fashion which leads to no result.

3. If we hold fast to this rule, we could treat the whole doctrine of Christ either as that of His activity, for then the dignity must naturally follow from that, or as that of His dignity, for the activity must then result of itself. This is indicated by the two general formulae above. For that the creation of human nature has been completed in His person is in and by itself only a description of His dignity, greater or less, according as the difference between the condition before and after is regarded as greater or less; but the activity follows of itself, if indeed the creation is to continue to exist. Again, that He is the Redeemer similarly describes His activity, but the dignity follows of itself to just the same degree.

Charles Gore on the Relation of Christology and Soteriology

5.22

In this 1883 review of a series of somewhat mediocre English works dealing with aspects of Christology, Gore turns to discuss the relation between what human nature requires and the identity of Jesus Christ. Gore was writing at a time when "Nestorianism" was widely equated with a view of the person of Jesus Christ which stressed his moral example. After an analysis of the weaknesses of moral understandings of the person of Christ, Gore famously declares that "The Nestorian Christ is the fitting Saviour of the Pelagian man." See also 5.5; 5.21.

Source: Charles Gore, "Our Lord's Human Example," *Church Quarterly Review*, 16 (1883), pp. 282–313; quote at p. 298.

* * *

Inadequate conceptions of Christ's person go hand in hand with inadequate conceptions of what human nature wants. The Nestorian conception of Christ ... qualifies Christ for being an example of what man can do, and into what wonderful union with God he can be assumed if he is holy enough; but Christ remains one man among many, shut in within the limits of a single human personality, and influencing man only from outside. He can be a Redeemer of man if man can be saved from outside by bright example, but not otherwise. The Nestorian Christ is logically associated with the Pelagian man ... The Nestorian Christ is the fitting Saviour of the Pelagian man.

5.23 Hastings Rashdall on Christ as a Moral Example

In this sermon, preached at Oxford in 1892, Rashdall argued that Matthew 20:28 ("For the Son of Man came not to be served, but to serve, and to give his life as a ransom for many") had been grossly misunderstood during the patristic period. The patristic *Christus Victor* theory is thus little more than an over-elaboration of a metaphor. Rashdall finds a more acceptable approach in the writings of Abelard, who he misunderstands to teach a purely exemplarist doctrine of the Atonement, in which Christ is nothing more than an outstanding moral example. This idea would receive more substantial exposition in his later work, *The Idea of Atonement in Christian Thought* (London: Macmillan, 1921). See also 5.3; 5.11.

Source: Hastings Rashdall, "The Abelardian Doctrine of the Atonement," in *Doctrine and Development: University Sermons* (London: Methuen, 1898), pp. 128–45; extract at pp. 130–43.

* * *

The history of the interpretation of this text is indeed a melancholy example of the theological tendency to make systems out of metaphors ... In Origen, and still more clearly in later Fathers, it appears that Satan was deliberately deceived by God. He was somehow or other induced to believe that in bringing about the death of Christ he would get possession of his soul. But there he over-reached himself; he found that there was one soul which could not be held in Hades. The very device by which he had hoped to complete his triumph became the means of his own ruin, and the whole body of his ancient subjects escaped his wrath.

Such, in brief outline, was the theory of the Atonement which on the whole held possession of Christian Theology throughout the patristic period ... I wish to call attention to the work of the great men to whom Christendom owes its emancipation from this grotesque absurdity. Among all the enormous services of Scholasticism to human progress, none is greater than this; none supplies better evidence that in very many respects the scholastic age was intellectually in advance of the patristic. The demolition of this time-honoured theory was effected principally by two men ... the attack on the received theology was begun by St Anselm; the decisive victory was won be Abelard ...

[After citing from Abelard's comments on Romans 2, noting his emphasis upon the arousal of God's love within us, Rashdall continues:] Three points may be noted in this Abelardian view of the Atonement.

1. There is no notion of vicarious punishment, and equally little of any vicarious expiation or satisfaction, or objectively valid sacrifice, an idea which is indeed free from some of the coarse immorality of the idea of vicarious punishment, but is somewhat difficult to distinguish from it.

2. The atoning efficacy of Christ's work is not limited to his death ... The whole life of Christ, the whole revelation of God which is constituted by that life, excites the love of man, moves his gratitude, shows him what God would have him be, enables him to be in his imperfect way what Christ alone was perfectly, and so makes at-one-ment, restores between God and man the union which sin has destroyed.

3. And it follows from this view of the Atonement that the justifying effect of Christ's work is a real effect, not a mere legal fiction. Christ's work really does make men better, instead of supplying the ground why they should be considered good or be excused the punishment of sin, without being really made any better than before ...

Even from the slight specimen that I have given you of Abelard's teaching you may be struck with the modernness of his tone. Abelard, in the twelfth century, seems to stretch out his hands to F. D. Maurice and Charles Kingsley and Frederick Robertson in the nineteenth. At least, I know not where to look for the same spirit of reverent Christian rationalism in the intervening ages, unless it be in the Cambridge Platonists.

Gustaf Aulén on the Classic Theory of the Atonement   5.24

In this seminal and highly influential study, originally published as an article in German in 1930, the Swedish Lutheran theologian Gustaf Aulén rehabilitated what he termed the "classic" or *Christus Victor* ("Christ the Victor") approach to the atonement. This approach, he argued, avoided the weaknesses of the approaches associated with Anselm and Abelard. In the section here reprinted, he sets out his anxieties concerning traditional approaches to the atonement. See also 5.10; 5.11; 5.12; 5.13; 5.28.

Source: Gustaf Aulén, *Christus Victor: An Historical Study of the Three Main Types of the Idea of the Atonement* (London: SPCK, 1931), pp. 17–22. Translation © Society of the Sacred Mission. Used by permission of the publisher.

* * *

My work on the history of Christian doctrine has led me to an ever-deepening conviction that the traditional account of the history of the idea of the Atonement is in need of thorough revision. The subject has, indeed, received a large share of attention at the hands of theologians; yet it has been in many important respects seriously misinterpreted. It is in the hope of making some contribution to this urgently needed revision that this work has been undertaken.

The Traditional Account

Let us first take a rapid survey of the history of the idea of the Atonement, according to the generally accepted view. The early church had, it is said, no developed doctrine of the Atonement, properly so called. The contributions of the patristic period to theology lie in another direction, being chiefly concerned with Christology and the doctrine of the Trinity; in regard to the Atonement, only hesitating efforts were made along a variety of lines, and the ideas which found expression were usually clothed in a fantastic mythological dress. The real beginnings of a thought-out doctrine of the Atonement are found in Anselm of Canterbury, who thus comes to hold a position of first-rate importance in the history of dogma. By the theory of satisfaction developed in the *Cur Deus homo?* he repressed, even if he could not entirely overcome, the old mythological account of Christ's work as a victory over the devil; in place of the older and more "physical" idea of salvation he put forward his teaching of a deliverance from the guilt of sin; and, above all, he clearly taught an "objective" Atonement, according to which God is the object of Christ's atoning work, and is reconciled through the satisfaction made to His justice. Needless to say, it is not implied that Anselm's teaching was wholly original. The stones lay ready to hand; but it was he who erected them into a monumental building.

A typical expression of the view which we have described is that of Ritschl, in *The Christian Doctrine of Justification and Reconciliation*. The very full historical section of this book begins with an introductory chapter on certain aspects of "the doctrine of salvation in the Greek church"; the use of the term "salvation," indicates that, in his view, the history of the doctrine of the Atonement proper had not yet begun. This chapter is immediately followed by one entitled "The Idea of Atonement through Christ in Anselm and Abelard."

Typical again is the collocation of the names of Anselm and Abelard. These two are commonly contrasted as the authors respectively of the "objective" and "subjective" doctrines of the Atonement; the latter term is used to describe a doctrine which explains the Atonement as consisting essentially in a change taking place in men rather than a changed attitude on the part of God.

In the subsequent history of the doctrine, it is held that a continuous line may be traced from Anselm, through medieval scholasticism, and through the Reformation, to the Protestant Orthodoxy of the seventeenth century. It is not implied that the teaching of Anselm was merely repeated, for differences of view are noted in Thomas Aquinas and in the Nominalists, and the post-Reformation statements of the doctrine have a character of their own; nevertheless, there is a continuity of tradition, and the basis of it is that which Anselm laid. It must specially be noted that the Reformation is included in this summary, and that it is treated as self evident that Luther had no special contribution to make, but followed in all essentials the Anselmian tradition. Those writers, however, who are opposed to that tradition readily allow an unsolved contradiction in Luther's world of ideas, between the medieval doctrine of Atonement which he left unchanged, and the religious outlook which inspired his reforming work and his teaching of justification by faith.

Finally, according to the traditional account, the last two centuries have been marked by the coexistence of these two types, the "objective" and the "subjective," and by the controversies between them. The subjective type has connections with Abelard, and with a few other movements here and there, such as Socinianism; but its rise to power came during the period of the Enlightenment. The nineteenth century is characterised by the conflict of this view with what was left of the "objective" doctrine, as well as by a variety of compromises; Ritschl regards the period of the Enlightenment as that of the disintegration of the "objective" doctrine, and gives as a chapter heading "The Revival of the Abelardian type of Doctrine by Schleiermacher and his Disciples." Naturally, both sides found support for their respective views in the New Testament. Those who sought to uphold, with or without modifications, the tradition of Protestant Orthodoxy, contended vigorously for the "biblical basis" of this type of Atonement-theory; the other side sought to show that the New Testament could not possibly be made to cover the teaching which was readily allowed the name of "the church doctrine." In this controversy the exegesis of Scripture suffered cruelly and long. Such is the common account of the history of the doctrine of the Atonement. But we may well question whether it is satisfactory.

The Classic Idea of the Atonement

There is a form of the idea of the Atonement which this account of the matter either ignores altogether or treats with very much less than justice, but whose suppression falsifies the whole perspective, and produces a version of the history which is seriously misleading. This type of view may be described provisionally as the "dramatic." Its central theme is the idea of the Atonement as a Divine conflict and victory; Christ – *Christus Victor* – fights against and triumphs over the evil powers of the world, the "tyrants" under which mankind is in bondage and suffering, and in Him God reconciles the world to Himself. Two points here require to be pressed with special emphasis: first, that this is a doctrine of Atonement in the full and proper sense, and second, that this idea of the Atonement has a clear and distinct character of its own, quite different from the other two types.

First, then, it must not be taken for granted that this idea may rightly be called only a doctrine of salvation, in contrast with the later development of a doctrine of Atonement properly so called. Certainly it describes a work of salvation, a drama of salvation; but this salvation is at the same time an atonement in the full sense of the word, for it is a work wherein God reconciles the world to Himself, and is at the same time reconciled. The background of the idea is dualistic; God is pictured as in Christ carrying through a victorious conflict against powers of evil which are hostile to His will. This constitutes Atonement, because the drama is a cosmic drama, and the victory over the hostile powers brings to pass a new relation, a relation of reconciliation, between God and the world; and, still more, because in a measure the hostile powers are regarded as in the service of the will of God the Judge of all, and the executants of His judgment. Seen from this side, the triumph over the opposing powers is regarded as a reconciling of God Himself; He is reconciled by the very act in which He reconciles the world to Himself.

Secondly, it is to be affirmed that this "dramatic" view of the Atonement is a special type, sharply distinct from both the other types. We shall illustrate its character fully in the course of these lectures; for the present a preliminary sketch must suffice.

The most marked difference between the "dramatic" type and the so-called "objective" type lies in the fact that it represents the work of Atonement or reconciliation as from first to last a work of God Himself, a continuous Divine work; while according to the other view, the act of Atonement has indeed its origin in God's will, but is, in its carrying-out, an offering made to God by Christ as man and on man's behalf, and may therefore be called a discontinuous Divine work.

On the other hand, it scarcely needs to be said that this "dramatic" type stands in sharp contrast with the "subjective" type of view. It does not set forth only or chiefly a change taking place in men; it describes a complete change in the situation, a change in the relation between God and the world, and a change also in God's own attitude. The idea is, indeed, thoroughly "objective"; and its objectivity is further emphasised by the fact that the Atonement is not regarded as affecting men primarily as individuals, but is set forth as a drama of a world's salvation.

Since, then, the objective character of the "dramatic" type is definite and emphatic, it can hardly help to a clear understanding of the history of the idea of Atonement to reserve the term "objective Atonement" for the type of view which commonly bears that name. The result can only be a confusion of two views of the Atonement which need to be clearly distinguished. I shall therefore refer to the type of view commonly called objective as the "Latin" type, because it arose and was developed on Western, Latin soil, and to the dualistic–dramatic view as "the classic idea" of the Atonement.

The classic idea has in reality held a place in the history of Christian doctrine whose importance it would not be easy to exaggerate. Though it is expressed in a variety of forms, not all of which are equally fruitful, there can be no dispute that it is the dominant idea of the Atonement throughout the early church period. It is also in reality, as I hope to show, the dominant idea in the New Testament; for it did not suddenly spring into being in the early church, or arrive as an importation from some outside source. It was, in fact, the ruling idea of the Atonement for the first thousand years of Christian history. In the Middle Ages it was gradually ousted from its place in the theological teaching of the church, but it survived still in her devotional language and in her art. It confronts us again, more vigorously and profoundly expressed than ever before, in Martin Luther, and it constitutes an important part of his expression of the Christian faith. It has therefore every right to claim the title of the *classic Christian idea of the Atonement*. But if this be the case, any account of the history of the doctrine which does not give full consideration to this type of view cannot fail to be seriously misleading.

Vladimir Lossky on Redemption as Deification

5.25

In this passage, originally published in French in 1953, this Russian émigré theologian sets out the fundamental importance of the notion of deification to Orthodox theology. Lossky sets out the characteristic Orthodox emphasis upon the redemptive descent (*katabasis*) of God in the incarnation, and the resulting ascent (*anabasis*) of humanity into God, as a result of its being enabled to share in the divine nature. Lossky is particularly critical of the tendency in western theology, which he traces back to Anselm of Canterbury, to treat redemption as a single aspect of theology, rather than its unifying theme. See also 4.19; 5.4; 5.5; 5.9; 5.10.

Source: Vladimir Lossky, "Redemption and Deification," in *In the Image and Likeness of God* (New York: St. Vladimir's Seminary Press, 1974), pp. 97–8. Reprinted by permission of St. Vladimir's Seminary Press, 575 Scarsdale Road, Crestwood, New York, 10707.

*　*　*

"God made Himself man, that man might become God." These powerful words, which are found for the first time in St. Irenaeus, can be found again in the writings of St. Athanasius, St. Gregory of Nazianzen and St. Gregory of Nyssa. The Fathers and Orthodox theologians have repeated them with this same emphasis in every century, wishing to sum up in this striking sentence the very essence of Christianity – an ineffable descent of God to the ultimate limit of our fallen human condition, even unto death – a descent of God which opens to men a path of ascent to the unlimited vision of the union of created beings with the divinity.

The descent (*katabasis*) of the divine person of Christ makes human persons capable of an ascent (*anabasis*) in the Holy Spirit. It was necessary that the voluntary humiliation, the redemptive self-emptying (*kenōsis*) of the Son of God should take place, so that fallen men might accomplish their vocation of *theōsis*, the deification of created beings by uncreated grace. Thus the redeeming work of Christ – or rather, more generally speaking, the Incarnation of the Word – is seen as directly related to the ultimate goal of creatures: to know union with God. If this union has been accomplished in the divine person of the Son, who is God become man, it is necessary that each human person should in turn become god by grace, or become "a partaker in the divine nature," according to St. Peter's expression (2 Peter 1:4) . . . The Son of God came down from heaven to accomplish the work of our salvation, to liberate us from the captivity of the devil, to destroy the dominion of sin in our nature, and to undo with death, which is the wages of sin. The Passion, Death, and Resurrection of Christ, by which his redemptive work was accomplished, thus occupy a central place in the divine dispensation for the fallen world. From this point of view it is easy to understand why the doctrine of the redemption has such a great importance in the theological thought of the Church.

Nevertheless, when the dogma of the redemption is treated in isolation from the general body of Christian teaching, there is always a risk of limiting the tradition by interpreting it exclusively in terms of the work of the Redeemer. Then theological reflection develops in three directions: original sin, its reparation on the cross, and the appropriation of the saving results of the work of Christ to Christians. In these constricting perspectives of a theology dominated by the idea of "redemption," the patristic sentence "God made Himself man, that man might become God" seems to be strange and abnormal. The thought of union with God is forgotten because of our preoccupation solely with our own salvation; or rather, union with God is seen only negatively, in contrast with our present wretchedness.

5.26 Wolfhart Pannenberg on Soteriological Approaches to Christology

In this influential 1964 essay on Christological method originally entitled *Grundzüge der Christologie* ("Foundations of Christology"), Wolfhart Pannenberg set out the case for returning to history in order to establish the foundations of Christology. He expressed a particular concern about the soteriological approach to Christology – in other words, the approach which determines the identity of Jesus on the basis of his saving significance for humanity. For Pannenberg, the identity of Jesus must be established on the basis of the history of Jesus of Nazareth. See also 5.5; 5.21; 5.22; 9.2.

Source: Wolfhart Pannenberg, *Jesus – God and Man* (Philadelphia: Westminster Press, 1968), pp. 38–9; 47–8. Used by permission of the publisher.

* * *

The two designations "God" and "Savior" form the content of the basic confession of the World Council of Churches, which was formulated at Amsterdam in 1948. The divinity of Jesus and his freeing and redeeming significance for us are related in the closest possible way. To this extent, Melanchthon's famous sentence is appropriate: "Who Jesus Christ is becomes known in his saving action." Nevertheless, the divinity of Jesus does not consist in his saving significance for him. Divinity and saving significance are interrelated as distinct things. The divinity of Jesus remains the *presupposition* of his saving significance for us, and, conversely, the saving significance of his divinity is the reason why we take *interest* in the question of his divinity. Since Schleiermacher the close tie between Christology and soteriology has won general acceptance in theology. This is particularly to be seen in one characteristic feature of modern Christology. One no longer separates the divine–human person and the redemptive work of Jesus Christ, as was done in medieval Scholastic theology and, in its wake, in the dogmatics of sixteenth- and seventeenth-century Protestant orthodoxy, but rather, with Schleiermacher, both are conceived as two sides of the same thing ...

A separation between Christology and soteriology is not possible, because in general the soteriological interest, the interest in salvation, in the *beneficia Christi*, is what causes us to ask about the figure of Jesus ... However, the danger that is involved in this connection between Christology and soteriology has emerged at the same time. Has one really spoken there about Jesus himself at all? Does it not perhaps involve projections onto Jesus' figure of the human desire for salvation and deification, of human striving after similarity to God, of the human duty to bring satisfaction for sins committed, of the human experience of bondage in failure, in the knowledge of one's own guilt, and, most clearly in neo-Protestantism, projections of the idea of perfect religiosity, of perfect morality, of pure personality, of radical trust? Do not human desires only become projected upon the figure of Jesus, personified in him? ...

The danger that Christology will be *constructed* out of the soteriological interest ought to be clear. Not everywhere is this so unreservedly expressed as by Tillich: "Christology is a function of soteriology." However, the tendency that is expressed here plays a part, more or less consciously and to a greater or lesser extent, in all the types of Christological thought considered here. The danger becomes acute when this procedure is elevated to a program, as by Melanchthon and later by Schleiermacher, who constructed his Christology by inference from the experience of salvation ...

Therefore Christology, the question about Jesus himself, about his person, as he lived on earth in the time of the Emperor Tiberius, must remain prior to all questions about his significance, to all soteriology. Soteriology must follow from Christology, not vice versa. Otherwise, faith in salvation loses any real foundation.

James I. Packer on Penal Substitution 5.27

In this published lecture, originally given at Tyndale House, Cambridge, in 1973, James I. Packer, one of the most widely read evangelical theologians, argues for an Anselmian approach to the atonement which lays an emphasis upon the substitutionary character of Christ's death. In arguing his case, he deals with the way in which "substitution" is to be understood. See also 5.10; 5.11; 5.12; 5.13; 5.15; 5.16.

Source: J. I. Packer, "What did the Cross Achieve? The Logic of Penal Substitution," *Tyndale Bulletin*, 25 (1974), pp. 3–45; extract taken from pp. 16–22.

* * *

The first thing to say about penal substitution has been said already. It is a Christian theological model, based on biblical exegesis, formed to focus a particular awareness of what Jesus did at Calvary to bring us to God. If we wish to speak of the "doctrine" of penal substitution, we should remember that this model is a dramatic, kerygmatic picturing of divine action, much more like Aulén's "classic idea" of divine victory (though Aulén never saw this) than it is like the defensive formula-models which we call the Nicene "doctrine" of the Trinity and the Chalcedonian "doctrine" of the person of Christ. Logically, the model is put together in two stages: first, the death of Christ is declared to have been *substitutionary*; then the substitution is characterized and given a specific frame of reference by adding the word *penal*. We shall examine the two stages separately.

Stage one is to declare Christ's death *substitutionary*. What does this mean? The *Oxford English Dictionary* defines substitution as "the putting of one person or thing in the place of another." One oddity of contemporary Christian talk is that many who affirm that Jesus' death was vicarious and representative deny that it was substitutionary; for the *Dictionary* defines both words in substitutionary terms! Representation is said to mean "the fact of standing for, or in place of, some other thing or person, esp. with a right or authority to act on their account; *substitution* of one thing or person for another." And vicarious is defined as "that takes or supplies the place of another thing or person; *substituted* instead of the proper thing or person." So here, it seems, is a distinction without a difference. Substitution is, in fact, a broad idea that applies whenever one person acts to supply another's need, or to discharge his obligation, so that the other no longer has to carry the load himself. As Pannenberg says, "in social life, substitution is a universal phenomenon . . . Even the structure of vocation, the division of labour, has substitutionary character. One who has a vocation performs this function for those whom he serves." For "every service has vicarious character by recognizing a need in the person served that apart from the service that person would have to satisfy for himself." In this broad sense, nobody who wishes to say with Paul that there is a true sense in which "Christ died for us" (once, on our behalf, for our benefit), and "Christ redeemed us from the curse of the law, having become a curse for us" . . . and who accepts Christ's assurance that he came "to give his life a ransom for many" . . . should hesitate to say that Christ's death was substitutionary. Indeed, if he describes Christ's death as vicarious he is actually saying it . . .

Broadly speaking, there have been three ways in which Christ's death has been explained in the church. Each reflects a particular view of the nature of God and our plight in sin, and of what is needed to bring us to God in the fellowship of acceptance on his side and faith and love on ours. It is worth glancing at them to see how the idea of substitution fits in with each.

There is, first, the type of account which sees the cross as having its effect entirely on men, whether by revealing God's love to us, or by bringing home to us how much God hates our sins, or by setting us a supreme example of godliness, or by blazing a trail to God which we may now follow, or by so involving mankind in his redemptive obedience that the life of God now flows into us, or by all these modes together. It is assumed that our basic need is lack of motivation Godward and of openness to the inflow of divine life; all that is needed to set us in a right relationship with God is a change in us at these two points, and this Christ's death brings about. The forgiveness of our sins is not a separate problem; as soon as we are changed we become forgivable, and are then forgiven at once. This view has little or no room for any thought of substitution, since it goes so far in equating what Christ did for us with what he does to us.

A second type of account sees Christ's death as having its effect primarily on hostile spiritual forces external to us which are held to be imprisoning us in a captivity of which our inveterate moral twistedness is one sign and symptom. The cross is seen as the work of God going forth to battle as our champion, just as David went forth as Israel's champion to fight Goliath. Through the cross these hostile forces, however conceived – whether as sin and death, Satan and his hosts, the demonic in society and its structures, the powers of God's wrath and curse, or anything else – are overcome and nullified, so that Christians are not in bondage to them, but share Christ's triumph over them. The assumption here is that man's plight is created entirely by hostile cosmic forces distinct from God; yet, seeing Jesus as our champion, exponents of this view could still properly call him our substitute, just as all the Israelites who declined Goliath's challenge in 1 Samuel 17:8–11 could properly call David their substitute. Just as a substitute who involves others in the consequences of his action as if they had done it themselves is their representative, so a representative discharging the obligations of those whom he represents is their substitute. What this type of account of the cross affirms (though it is not usually put in these terms) is that the conquering Christ, whose victory secured our release, was our representative substitute.

The third type of account denies nothing asserted by the other two views save their assumption that they are complete. It agrees that there is biblical support for all they say, but it goes further. It grounds man's plight as a victim of sin and Satan in the fact that, for all God's daily goodness to him, as a sinner he stands under divine judgment, and his bondage to evil is the start of his sentence, and unless God's rejection of him is turned into acceptance he is lost for ever. On this view, Christ's death had its effect first on God, who was hereby *propitiated* (or, better, who hereby propitiated himself), and only because it had this effect did it become an overthrowing of the powers of darkness and a revealing of God's seeking and saving love. The thought here is that by dying Christ offered to God what the West has called *satisfaction* for sins, satisfaction which God's own character dictated as the only means whereby his "no" to us could become a "yes." Whether this Godward satisfaction is understood as the homage of death itself, or death as the perfecting of holy obedience, or an undergoing of the God-forsakenness of hell, which is God's final judgment on sin, or a perfect confession of man's sins combined with entry into their bitterness by sympathetic identification, or all these things together (and nothing stops us combining them together), the shape of this view remains the same – that by under-going the cross Jesus expiated our sins, propitiated our Maker, turned God's "no" to us into a "yes," and so saved us. All forms of this view see Jesus as our representative substitute in fact, whether or not they call him that, but only certain versions of it represent his substitution as penal. [Packer then makes three points, of which the first two are of especial relevance here:]

First, it should be noted that though the two former views regularly set themselves in antithesis to the third, the third takes up into itself all the positive assertions that they make; which raises the question whether any more is at issue here than the impropriety of treating half-truths as the whole truth, and of rejecting a more comprehensive account on the basis of speculative negations about what God's holiness requires as a basis for forgiving sins. Were it allowed that the first two views might be misunder-standing and distorting themselves in this way, the much-disputed claim that a broadly substitutionary view of the cross has always been the main-stream Christian opinion might be seen to have substance in it after all. It is a pity that books on the atonement so often take it for granted that accounts of the cross which have appeared as rivals in historical debate must be treated as intrinsically exclusive. This is always arbitrary, and some-times quite perverse.

Second, it should be noted that our analysis was simply of views about the death of Christ, so nothing was said about his resurrection. All three types of view usually agree in affirming that the resurrection is an integral part of the gospel; that the gospel proclaims a living, vindicated Saviour whose resurrection as the firstfruits of the new humanity is the basis as well as the pattern for ours is not a matter of dispute between them. It is some-times pointed out that the second view represents the resurrection of Jesus as an organic element in his victory over the powers of death, whereas the third view does not, and hardly could, represent it as an organic element in the bearing of sin's penalty or the tasting and confessing of its vileness (however the work of Calvary is conceived); and on this basis the third view is sometimes criticized as making the resurrection unnecessary. But this criticism may be met in two ways. The first reply is that Christ's saving work has two parts, his dealing with his Father on our behalf by offering himself in substitutionary satisfaction for our sins and his dealing with us on his Father's behalf by bestowing on us through faith the forgiveness which his death secured, and it is as important to distinguish these two parts as it is to hold them together. For a demonstration that part two is now possible because part one is finished, and for the actual implementing of part two, Jesus' resurrection is indeed essential, and so appears as an organic element in his work as a whole. The second reply is that these two ways of viewing the cross should in any case be synthesized, following the example of Paul in Colossians 2:13–15, as being complementary models expressing different elements in the single complex reality which is the mystery of the cross.

Colin E. Gunton on the Language of Atonement   5.28

In this important study of the atonement, the British theologian Colin Gunton argues that a proper appreciation of the *status* of the language used in relation to the cross of Christ is fundamental to a correct understanding of its meaning. He illustrates this point by considering some aspects of the *Christus Victor* theory, especially associated with Gustaf Aulén (see 5.24), noting its metaphorical status.

Source: Colin E. Gunton, *The Actuality of Atonement* (Edinburgh: T. & T. Clark, 1988), pp. 62–5. Used with permission of the publisher.

* * *

As the Christian tradition took shape during the early centuries, the way in which Satan and the demonic realm came to be understood underwent some changes. In particular, there was a tendency to personify the devil as an individual being defeated by Christ on the cross. On the whole, as time passes, there is rather less restraint shown in the way in which the devil is depicted. As Aulén has noticed, there is a real contrast between Paul's treatment of the matter and that of later thinkers, in that he makes considerably less mention of the devil than most of the Fathers. This relative lack of restraint in the later period is revealed also in a tendency to picture the defeat of the devil as a kind of deceit, in which the devil, believing that Jesus is merely a human victim, swallows him, only to be impaled on the hidden hook of his divinity. Gregory of Nyssa is clearly uncomfortable, though not uncomfortable enough, with such a conception . . . But the problem with Gregory's way of putting the matter is revealed by . . . its tendency to be what has come to be called mythological. The battle is to be conceived to be fought in a sphere outside the course of concrete divine–human relations. We can contrast here two features of the gospel narratives we have noted: both the temptations and the healings are actual human encounters with evil, theologically conceived. In Gregory, on the other hand, the metaphorical dimension has fallen into the background, the victory is understood too literally, and the result is that *too much* is known about what is supposed to have happened.

The reference to the tendency of the tradition to become mythological brings us to a distinction of immense importance: that between metaphor and myth. Those who spoke too *literally* of the devil having obtained rights over mankind of which he was deprived by deceit had, in effect, failed to appreciate the metaphorical nature of the language they were using. It is as if, when Mark reports Jesus as saying that he had come to give his life as a ransom for many, we were to speculate about how much money was to be handed over, and to whom (Mark 10:45). We have here an example of what some thinkers have claimed to happen when a metaphor is taken too literally: it becomes a myth . . .

What, then, is to be made of biblical and other theological language which uses language of this kind? G. B. Caird speaks as follows about the principalities and powers in the New Testament:

> They stand, as their names imply, for the political, social, economic and religious structures of power . . . of the old world order which Paul believed to be obsolescent. When therefore he claims that on the cross Christ has disarmed the powers and triumphed over them, he is talking about earthly realities, about the impact of the crucifixion on the corporate life of men and nations. He is using mythical language of great antiquity and continuing vitality to interpret the historic event of the cross.

On such an account we can understand Paul to be using mythical language in a non-mythological way. If Caird is right, we have discovered another qualification of Aulén's account. The victory is not over forces which inhabit a transcendent world, separate from ours, and intervene from outside, as Aulén's account might appear to suggest. Paul is speaking about "earthly realities . . . the corporate life of men and nations." But they are not forces which can adequately be described in everyday empirical terms. The forces are "cosmic" in the sense that they *as a matter of fact affect the way things are on earth*, but not simply as aspects, but as qualifications of them. These biblical metaphors, then, are ways of describing realistically what can be described only in the indirect manner of this kind of language. But an indirect description is still a description of what is really there.

Study Questions to Chapter 5

How do understandings of the person and work of Christ interrelate?

Why does Gustaf Aulén argue for the rediscovery of a "classic" theory of the Atonement? And what modifications to it does Colin Gunton suggest may be required?

What, according to Wolfhart Pannenberg, are the dangers of developing a Christology solely on the basis of an understanding of what Christ has done for us?

What reasons may be given for suggesting that Christ's death was a "satisfaction" for sin? And what objections may be raised against it? (Use 5.10; 5.11; 5.15; 5.16; 5.23 and 5.27 in answering.

From the readings provided in this chapter, illustrate the following aspects of a Christian understanding of the work of Christ: liberation from sin or oppression; being made divine.

6 Human Nature, Sin, and Grace

This chapter brings together a substantial body of material which focuses on human nature, and the means by which it is restored to fellowship with God. These issues were of considerable importance in relation to two major controversies within the Christian tradition. The *Pelagian controversy* of the early fifth century, which featured Pelagius of Rome and Augustine of Hippo as the chief protagonists, focused on the question of grace and sin. The *Reformation* of the sixteenth century also focused on the issue of grace, but with particular reference to the doctrine of justification by faith.

As illustrations of the ways in which this material can be used, four study panels explore themes which run throughout this section of Christian theology, and one the theological aspects of a specific historical debate. The reader is reminded that these panels are simply intended to illustrate the kinds of things that can be done with these readings; it is up to the reader to follow up the cross-references, and devise other such study panels, or expand or otherwise improve on those which are suggested here.

STUDY PANEL 14

The Nature and Effects of Grace

STUDY PANEL 15

Justification and Predestination

6.8   Ambrose on the Unmerited Character of Salvation
6.10   Augustine on the Divine Election
6.11   Augustine on the Nature of Predestination
6.15   Augustine on Irresistible Grace and Perseverance
6.26   Martin Luther's Discovery of the "Righteousness of God"
6.27   Martin Luther on Justifying Faith
6.28   Martin Luther on Sin and Grace
6.29   Philip Melanchthon on Justification by Faith
6.30   John Calvin on Predestination
6.32   John Calvin on the Concept of Justification
6.34   Theodore Beza on the Causes of Predestination
6.36   The Westminster Confession of Faith on Predestination
6.40   John Wesley on Justification
6.42   Karl Barth on Election in Christ
6.43   Emil Brunner on Barth's Doctrine of Election

STUDY PANEL 16

Humanity in the Image and Likeness of God

6.4   Tertullian on the Image of God
6.5   Origen on the Image of God
6.7   Lactantius on Political Aspects of the Image of God
6.41   Emil Brunner on the Image of God
6.46   Mary Hayter on Human Sexuality and the Image of God

STUDY PANEL 17

The Nature and Origin of Sin

6.2   Tertullian on the Origin of Sin
6.3   Tertullian on Inherited Guilt
6.6   Origen on Inherited Sin
6.9   Ambrosiaster on Original Sin
6.12   Augustine on the "Mass of Perdition"
6.13   Augustine on Fallen Human Nature
6.14   Augustine on Human Freedom
6.20   Pelagius's Rejection of Original Sin
6.21   The Council of Carthage (418) on Grace
6.28   Martin Luther on Sin and Grace
6.39   Jonathan Edwards on Original Sin
6.44   Reinhold Niebuhr on Original sin
6.45   Daphne Hampson on Feminist Approaches to Sin

STUDY PANEL 18

The Pelagian Controversy

6.10   Augustine on the Divine Election
6.11   Augustine on the Nature of Predestination
6.12   Augustine on the "Mass of Perdition"
6.13   Augustine on Fallen Human Nature
6.14   Augustine on Human Freedom
6.15   Augustine on Irresistible Grace and Perseverance
6.16   Augustine on Freedom and Grace
6.17   Augustine's Saying which Alarmed Pelagius
6.18   Pelagius on Human Responsibility
6.19   Pelagius on Human Freedom
6.20   Pelagius's Rejection of Original Sin
6.21   The Council of Carthage (418) on Grace
6.22   The Synod of Arles on Pelagianism

6.1   Irenaeus on Human Progress

In this passage, which dates from the later part of the second century, Irenaeus develops the idea that humanity was created with the potential for perfection. Humanity was not created perfect; that perfection had to take place through a process of moral and spiritual growth. Irenaeus thus locates the origin of evil in human weakness and frailty, rather than in any defect on the part of God. See also 3.2.

Source: *adversus haereses*, IV.xxxviii.1; in *Sources Chrétiennes*, vol. 100, ed. A. Rousseau (Paris: Cerf, 1965), 942.1–946.17.

* * *

Here, someone may raise an objection. "Could not God have made humanity perfect from the beginning?" Yet one must know that all things are possible for God, who is always the same and uncreated. But created beings, and all who have their beginning of being in the course of time, are necessarily inferior to the one who created them. Things which have recently come into being cannot be eternal; and, not being eternal, they fall short of perfection for that very reason. And being newly created they are therefore childish and immature, and not yet fully prepared for an adult way of life. And so, just as a mother is able to offer food to an infant, but the infant is not yet able to receive food unsuited to its age, in the same way, God, for his part, could have offered perfection to humanity at the beginning, but humanity was not capable of receiving it. It was nothing more than an infant.

6.2   Tertullian on the Origin of Sin

In this passage, originally written in Latin in the first decade of the third century, Tertullian locates the origin of sin in satanic temptation of humanity. Note the emphasis placed on the notion of "discontent," which Tertullian regards as underlying all rebellion against God. See also 3.2; 3.6; 6.6.

Source: *de patientia*, V, 5–14; *Sources Chrétiennes*, vol. 310, ed. J.-C. Fredouille (Paris: Cerf, 1984), 72.15–76.49.

* * *

I find the origin of discontent (*impatientia*) in the devil himself since from the beginning he was discontented and annoyed that the Lord God had subjected the whole of the world to the one who he had created in his own image, that is to humanity. Now if the devil had tolerated that patiently, he would not have grieved; had he not grieved he would not have envied man: and envy was the cause of his deceiving the man . . . Then when [the devil] met the woman, I may say with good reason that as a result of their conversation she was filled with a spirit infected with discontent; for it is certain that she would never have sinned, had she contentedly persisted in obedience to the divine command! Furthermore, she did not stop there, after her meeting with the devil, but she was too discontented to keep silence in the presence of Adam, though he was not yet her husband and therefore not bound to listen: but she passed on to him what she had learned from the evil one. Thus another human perishes through the discontent of the one; and [Adam] himself soon perished through his own discontent . . . Here is the primal source of judgement and of sin; God was aroused to anger and man is induced to sin . . . What offence is ascribed to humanity before the sin of discontent? Humanity was blameless, the intimate friend of God and the steward of paradise (*Deo de proximo amicus et paradisi colonus*). But when he succumbed to discontent he ceased to care for the God, and ceased to have the power to be content with heavenly things. From that moment, humanity was sent out on the earth, and cast out from God's sight. As a result, discontent had no difficulty in gaining the upper hand over humanity, and causing it to do things which were offensive to God.

Tertullian on Inherited Guilt   6.3

Tertullian here warns his readers against thinking of sin or redemption in purely individualist terms. Both sin and grace relate to the whole body of humanity. Tertullian points out that sin is inherited from our forebears, and passed down from one generation to another. Although he does not develop a doctrine of original sin in the strict sense of the phrase, some of the foundational ideas of this doctrine may be found in this passage. See also 6.6; 6.9; 6.12.

Source: *adversus Marcionem*, II.xv.2–3; in *Sources Chrétiennes*, vol. 368, ed. R. Braun (Paris: Cerf, 1991), 96.10–98.25.

* * *

But if the blessing of the fathers was destined to be transmitted to their posterity, without any merit on their part, why should not the guilt of the fathers be passed on to their sons, so that the transgression as well as the grace should spread through the whole human race? (Except for the point, which was to be made known later, that men shall not say, "The fathers have eaten a sour grape and the children's teeth have been set on edge" (Jeremiah 31:29) that is, the father shall not take upon himself the transgression of his son, nor the son the transgression of his father, but each shall be guilty of their own transgression.) This means that after the hardness of the people and the hardness of the law had been overcome, God's justice should then judge individuals and not the whole race. If you would receive the gospel of truth you would discover to whom that saying refers which speaks of bringing home to the sons the transgressions of their fathers. It applies to all those who of their own accord applied to themselves the saying: "may his blood be on our heads and on the heads of our sons" (Matthew 27:25). That is why the providence of God, having already heard this, established it [i.e., the gospel of truth] for them.

6.4   Tertullian on the Image of God

In this important treatise, written in Latin in the first decade of the third century, Tertullian draws a distinction between the "image" and "likeness" of God. Note how Tertullian regards the fall as involving the loss of the indwelling presence of the Holy Spirit, which is restored through baptism. See also 6.5; 6.7; 6.41.

Source: de baptismo, 5; in Quinti Septimi Florentis Tertulliani: de baptismo, ed. B. Luiselli (Turin: Paraviam, 1960), 12.166–72.

* * *

[In Baptism] death is abolished by the washing away of sins: for the removal of guilt also removes the penalty. Thus humanity is restored to God into "his likeness," for he had originally been "in his image." The state of being "in the image of God" relates to his form; "in the likeness" refers to his eternity: for humanity receives back that Spirit of God which at the beginning was received from God's inbreathing, but which was afterwards lost through falling away.

6.5   Origen on the Image of God

Origen here draws a distinction between the "image" and "likeness" of God, arguing that the image refers to the status of humanity, and the likeness to the final perfection of the human race at the resurrection. See also 6.4; 6.7; 6.41; 10.6.

Source: de principiis, III.iv.1; in Sources Chrétiennes, vol. 268, ed. H. Crouzel and M. Simonetti (Paris: Cerf, 1980), 236.14–29.

* * *

"And God said, 'Let us make man in our image and likeness'" (Genesis 1:26). He then adds: "In the image of God he made him" (Genesis 1:27), and is silent about the likeness. This indicates that in his first creation man received the dignity of the image of God, but the fulfilment of the likeness is reserved for the final consummation; that is, that he himself should obtain it by his own effort, through the imitation of God. The possibility of perfection given to him at the beginning by the dignity of the image, and then in the end, through the fulfilment of his works, should bring to perfect consummation the likeness of God. The Apostle John defines this state of things more clearly when he declares: "My little children, we do not yet know what we shall be but if it shall be revealed to us concerning the Saviour, without doubt you will say: We shall be like him" (1 John 3:2).

Origen on Inherited Sin   6.6

Origen here argues that humanity is contaminated by sin from the moment of its entry into the world, with the sole exception of Jesus Christ. Note how Origen sees a link between the virginity of Mary as the mother of Christ and the sinlessness of Christ. See also 6.3; 6.9.

Source: *Homilia in Leviticum* xii, 4; in *Sources Chrétiennes*, vol. 287, ed. M. Borret (Paris: Cerf, 1981), 178.5–23.

———————————————————————————— * * *

Everyone who enters the world may be said to be affected by a kind of contamination (*in quadam contaminatione effici dicitur*) . . . By the very fact that humanity is placed in its mother's womb, and that it takes the material of its body from the source of the father's seed, it may be said to be contaminated in respect of both father and mother . . . Thus everyone is polluted in father and mother. Only Jesus my Lord was born without stain. He was not polluted in respect of his mother, for he entered a body which was not contaminated . . . For Joseph played no part in his birth other than his devotion and his affection, and it is on account of his faithful devotion that Scripture allows him the name "father."

Lactantius on Political Aspects of the   6.7
Image of God

In this passage from his *Divine Institutes*, Lactantius develops the political and ethical aspects of the doctrine of creation. As all human beings are made by the same God, bear his image, and were created from the same original human being – a reference to Adam – they must hold each other in respect. Lactantius uses the Latin term *simulacrum* for "image" instead of the more customary *imago*. This term is often used to refer to idols or statues of Gods, and emphasizes the degree of likeness between the image and its object. See also 6.4; 6.5; 6.41.

Source: *Divinae Institutiones*, VI, 10–11; in *Corpus Scriptorum Ecclesiasticorum Latinorum*, vol. 19, ed. Samuel Brandt and George Laubmann (Prague/Vienna/Leipzig, 1980), 514.6–515.8; 519.3–6.

———————————————————————————— * * *

I have spoken about what is due to God; now I shall speak about what is due to other people, although what is due to people still equally relates to God, since humanity is the image of God (*homo dei simulacrum est*). The first duty of justice concerns God and binds us to him; the second concerns humanity. The name of the first is religion; the name of the second is mercy or humanity. Religion is a characteristic of the righteous and those who worship God. It alone is life. God made us naked and fragile in order to teach us wisdom. In particular he gave us this affection of piety in order that we might protect our fellow human beings, love them, cherish them, defend them against all dangers and give them help. The strongest bond which unites us is humanity. Anyone who breaks it is a criminal and a parricide. Now it was from the one human being that God created us all, so that we are all of the same blood, with the result that the greatest crime is to hate humanity or do them harm. That is why we are forbidden to develop or to encourage hatred. So if we are the work of the same God, what else are we but brothers and sisters? The bond which unites our souls is therefore stronger than that which unites our bodies. So Lucretius does not err when he declares:

> Finally, we are all the offspring of heavenly seed.
> To everyone that same one is Father.

. . . We must therefore show humanity if we want to deserve the name of human beings. And showing humanity means loving our fellow human beings because they are human beings, just as we are ourselves.

6.8   Ambrose on the Unmerited Character of Salvation

In this fourth-century commentary on the opening words of the Lord's Prayer (Matthew 6:9), Ambrose stresses the unmerited nature of the privilege of being able to address and approach God in this way. See also 6.10; 6.11; 6.25; 6.28.

Source: *de sacramentis*, V.iv.19; in *Corpus Scriptorum Ecclesiasticorum Latinorum*, vol. 73, ed. O. Faller, S.J. (Vienna: Hoelder–Pichler–Tempsky, 1955), 66.11–24.

* * * ───────────────────────────────────

O man, you did not dare to raise your face to heaven; you lowered your eyes to the earth – and suddenly you have received the grace of Christ, and all your sins have been forgiven! From being a wicked servant, you have become a good son! And don't suppose that this is due to any action on your part; it is due to the grace of Christ . . . So raise your eyes to the Father who has redeemed you through his Son, and say: "Our Father . . .". But do not claim any privilege. He is the Father in a special way only of Christ; he is the common Father of us all, in that although he has created all of us, he has begotten none but Christ. Then also say by his grace, "Our Father," so that you may merit being his son.

6.9   Ambrosiaster on Original Sin

The Old Latin translation of Romans 5:12, on which Ambrosiaster here depends, mistranslates Paul's Greek, interpreting a reference to "in that all have sinned" to mean "in whom (that is, Adam) all have sinned." On the basis of this misunderstanding, Ambrosiaster develops a notion of original sin which had a considerable impact on Augustine's teaching on the matter. See also 6.12; 6.28; 6.39; 6.44.

Source: *Commentaria in Epistolam ad Romanos* v, 12; in *Corpus Scriptorum Ecclesiasticorum Latinorum*, vol. 81, ed. H. J. Vogels (Vienna: Hoelder–Pichler–Tempsky, 1966), 165.9–15.

* * *

"In whom – that is, in Adam – all have sinned" (Romans 5:12). Notice that he uses the masculine (*in quo*) though he is speaking about the woman, because his reference was not to the sex, but to the race. So it is clear that all have sinned in Adam collectively, as it were (*quasi in massa*). He was himself corrupted by sin, and all that were born were therefore all born under sin. From him therefore all are sinners, because we are all produced from him.

Augustine on the Divine Election 6.10

Augustine here argues that all humanity are contaminated by sin, with the result that salvation is a human impossibility. In his grace, God chose to save some from this "mass of perdition." Note the appeal to the analogy of the potter and the clay (Romans 9:21), which becomes a frequent element in Augustinian and Reformed discussions of election and predestination. See also 6.11; 6.30; 6.34; 6.42; 6.43.

Source: *Sermo 26*, xii, 13; in J. P. Migne, *Patrologia Latina*, 38:177A–B.

* * *

There was one lump of perdition (*massa perditionis*) out of Adam to which only punishment was due; from this same lump, vessels were made which are destined for honour. For the potter has authority over the same lump of clay (Romans 9:21). What lump? The lump that had already perished, and whose just damnation was already assured. So be thankful that you have escaped! You have escaped the death certainly due to you, and found life, which was not due to you. The potter has authority over the clay from the same lump to make one vessel for honour and another for contempt. But, you say, why has He made me to honour and another to contempt? What shall I answer? Will you listen to Augustine, if you will not listen to the Apostle [Paul] when he says "O man, who art you who argues with God?" (Romans 11:33). Two little children are born. If you ask what is due to them, the answer is that they both belong to the lump of perdition. But why does its mother carry the one to grace, while the other is suffocated by its mother in her sleep? Will you tell me what was deserved by the one which was carried to grace, and what was deserved by the one whom its sleeping mother suffocated? Both have deserved nothing good; but the potter has authority over the clay, of the same lump to make one vessel for honour, and the other for contempt.

6.11 Augustine on the Nature of Predestination

Augustine here develops the idea that predestination involves God withholding or making available, according to the divine will, the means by which salvation is possible. Augustine stresses that the divine judgement which determines who will be allowed to be saved in this manner is beyond human understanding. See also 6.10; 6.30; 6.34; 6.42; 6.43.

Source: *de dono perseverantiae*, XIV, 35; in *Oeuvres de Saint Augustin*, ed. J. Chéné and J. Pintard (Paris: de Brouwer, 1962), pp. 680–2.

* * *

This is the predestination of the saints, and nothing else: the foreknowledge and preparation of the benefits of God, whereby whoever are set free are most certainly set free. And where are the rest left by the just judgement of God, except in that mass of perdition, in which the inhabitants of Tyre and Sidon were left? Now they would have believed, if they had seen the wonderful signs of Christ. However, because it was not given to them to believe, they were not given the means to believe (*quoniam ut crederent, non erat eis datum, etiam unde crederent est negatum*). From this, it seems that certain people have naturally in their minds a divine gift of understanding, by which they may be moved to faith, if they hear the words or see the signs which are adapted to their minds (*si congrua suis mentibus*). But if, by virtue of a divine judgement which is beyond us, these people have not been predestined by grace and separated from the mass of perdition, then they must remain without contact with either these divine words or deeds which, if heard or seen by them, would have allowed them to believe.

6.12 Augustine on the "Mass of Perdition"

Augustine here develops the idea that all of humanity constitute a single mass of sin. Note again the use of the image of the potter and the clay to emphasize God's sovereignty in election. See also 6.2; 6.3; 6.6; 6.9.

Source: *de diversibus quaestionibus ad Simplicianum*, I.ii.12; in *Corpus Christianorum: Series Latina*, vol. 44, ed. A. Mutzenbecher (Turnholt: Brepols, 1970), 48. 620–7.

* * *

From Adam has sprung one mass of sinners and godless people (*massa peccatorum et impiorum*), in which both Jews and Gentiles belong to one lump, apart from the grace of God. If the potter out of one lump of clay makes one vessel for honour and another for contempt, it is obvious that God has made some vessels for honour and others for contempt out of the Jews, and similarly out of the Gentiles. It follows that all must be understood to belong to one lump.

Augustine on Fallen Human Nature 6.13

In this important discussion of fallen human nature, originally written in Latin in 415, Augustine identifies the consequences of the fall upon human nature. Originally created without any fault, it is now contaminated by sin, and can only be redeemed through grace. See also 6.2; 6.3; 6.4; 6.6; 6.9; 6.10; 6.11; 6.44.

Source: de natura et gratia, iii, 3–iv, 4; in Corpus Scriptorum Ecclesiasticorum Latinorum, vol. 60, ed. C. F. Urba and J. Zycha (Vienna: Tempsky, 1913), 235.8–236.6

* * *

Human nature was certainly originally created blameless and without any fault (*vitium*); but the human nature by which each one of us is now born of Adam requires a physician, because it is not healthy. All the good things, which it has by its conception, life, senses, and mind, it has from God, its creator and maker. But the weakness which darkens and disables these good natural qualities, as a result of which that nature needs enlightenment and healing, did not come from the blameless maker but from original sin (*ex originali peccato*), which was committed by free will (*liberum arbitrium*). For this reason our guilty nature is liable to a just penalty. For if we are now a new creature in Chirst, we were still children of wrath by nature, like everyone else. But God, who is rich in mercy, on account of the great love with which He loved us, even when we were dead through our sins, raised us up to life with Christ, by whose grace we are saved. But this grace of Christ, without which neither infants nor grown persons can be saved, is not bestowed as a reward for merits, but is given freely (*gratis*), which is why it is called grace (*gratia*)... For this reason, it is those who are not made free by that blood (whether because they have not been able to hear, or because they were not willing to obey, or were not able to hear on account of their youth, and have not received the bath of regeneration which they might have done and through which they might have been saved) who are most justly condemned because they are not without sin, whether they derived from their origins or were acquired by evil actions. For all have sinned, whether in Adam or in themselves, and have fallen short of the glory of God (Romans 3:23).

Augustine on Human Freedom 6.14

Augustine's emphasis on grace occasionally seems to suggest that he denies human freedom. In this passage, originally written in Latin at some point during the period 413–26, Augustine discusses the relation of sin, grace and free will in some detail, noting the various types of freedom which humanity possesses, from the freedom enjoyed by Adam to that which will be enjoyed by those who finally inhabit the heavenly Jerusalem. See also 6.13; 6.16.

Source: de civitate Dei, XXII, 30; in The City of God against the Pagans, Loeb Classical Library, ed. W. M. Green (Cambridge, Mass.: Harvard University Press, 1972), vol. 7, pp. 376–8.

* * *

Nor will they not have free choice because sins will have no power to attract them. Far from it; it will be more truly free, when it has been set free from the delight of sinning, to enjoy the steadfast delight of not sinning. For the first free will (*liberum arbitrium*) which was given to humanity when it was created upright (*rectus*), gave not just the ability not to sin, but also the ability to sin. This new freedom is all the more powerful precisely because it will not have power to sin; and this, not by its unaided natural ability, but by the gift of God. It is one thing to be God, and another to share in God. God is unable to sin; anyone who shares in God has received from God the inability to sin . . . The first immortality, which Adam lost by sinning, was the ability not to die (*posse non mori*), the new immortality will be the inability to die (*non posse mori*). In the same way, the first freedom of choice conferred the ability not to sin (*posse non peccare*); the new freedom will confer the inability to sin (*non posse peccare*) . . . It surely cannot be said that God does not have any freedom of choice, just because God is unable to sin?

Thus the freedom of that city will be one single will present in everyone, freed from all evil and filled with every good, enjoying continually the delight of eternal joy. Although sins and punishments will be forgotten, this will not lead to forgetting its liberation, or being ungrateful to its liberator.

6.15 Augustine on Irresistible Grace and Perseverance

Augustine here argues that God bestows a gift of perseverance on those who he has elected to this end. The nature of this gift is such that it is irresistable, and will ensure that its recipient remains in grace. The distinction Augustine draws between different types of divine assistance would have a considerable impact on medieval thinking on this issue. See also 6.18; 6.30; 6.34; 6.42; 6.43.

Source: *de correptione et gratia*, XII, 34; in J. P. Migne, *Patrologia Latina*, 44:936D–937B.

* * *

Now two kinds of assistance are to be distinguished. On the one hand, there is an assistance without which something does not come about (*adiutorium sine quo non fit*), and on the other there is the assistance by which something does come about (*adiutorium quo fit*). We cannot live without food, but the fact that food is available will not keep people alive if they want to die . . . But in the case of blessedness, when it is bestowed on people who are without it, they become perpetually blessed . . . Thus this is an assistance both *sine quo non* and *quo* . . . Now Adam was created upright, in a state of good; he was given the possibility of not sinning (*posse non peccare*), the possibility of not dying (*posse non mori*), the possibility of not losing that state of good: and in addition he was given the assistance of perseverance, not so that by this assistance it might come about that he should in fact persevere, but because without it he could not persevere through his own free will. Now in the case of the saints who are predestined to the kingdom of God by the grace of God, the assistance of perseverance which is given is not that [granted to the first man], but that kind which brings the gift of actual perseverance. It is not just that they cannot persevere without this gift; once they have received this gift, they can do nothing except persevere.

Augustine on Freedom and Grace   6.16

In this passage, written in 412 at the height of the Pelagian controversy, Augustine stresses that true human freedom is a divine gift, rather than something which naturally occurs within fallen humanity. It is only when the human will has been liberated that it longs to be united with God, and is enabled to achieve this end. See also 6.13; 6.14; 6.44.

Source: de spiritu et littera, 5; in Corpus Scriptorum Ecclesiasticorum Latinorum, vol. 60, ed. C. F. Urba and J. Zycha (Vienna: Tempsky, 1913), 157.10–24.

* * *

But we say that the human will is so divinely aided towards the doing of righteousness that, besides humanity having being created with the free choice of God's will, and besides the teaching which instructs us how to live, it receives also the Holy Spirit, through which there arises in the heart a delight in and a love of that supreme and unchangeable good which is God. This takes place even now, while we still walk by faith and not by sight. Now on account of this free gift, humanity longs to be united to its maker, and be inflamed to be allowed to share in his true light, so that humanity may also derive its blessedness from the one who created it. A person's free choice will only serve to lead them to sin, if the way of truth is hidden from them. And when it is plain to them what they should do and to what they should aspire, even then unless they feel delight and love in doing so, they will not perform their duty, nor undertake it, nor attain to the good life. But in order that we may feel this affection "the love of God is shed abroad in our hearts" not "through the free choice which springs from ourselves" but "through the Holy Spirit which has been given to us" (Romans 5:5).

Augustine's Saying which alarmed Pelagius   6.17

This text, written in Latin in 400, is of both historical and theological importance. Theologically, it demonstrates Augustine's characteristic emphasis on the priority of God in the life of the believer. Historically, it was the public reading of this text at Rome which alarmed Pelagius, and led to the Pelagian controversy. See also 6.13; 6.18; 6.19; 6.20.

Source: Confessions, X, 40; in St Augustine's Confessions, Loeb Classical Library, ed. W. Watts (Cambridge, Mass.: Harvard University Press, 1961), pp. 148–50.

* * *

I have no hope at all but in your great mercy. Grant what you command and command what you will (*da quod iubes et iube quod vis*). You ask us to be continent. "And when I knew," someone said, "that nobody could be continent, unless God gave it, this also was itself a part of wisdom, to know whose gift it was." Truly by continence we are bound together and brought back into that unity from which we were dissipated into a plurality. For anyone who loves anything along with you (unless they love it for your sake), loves you too little. O love that burns for ever and is never quenched! O Charity, my God, set me on fire! You ask us to be continent. Grant what you command and command what you will.

6.18 Pelagius on Human Responsibility

In this letter written to Demetrias, a Roman lady of high social status who eventually became a nun, Pelagius argues that the divine commands are unconditionally binding upon Christians. God knows the abilities of humanity, and the commands reflect the ability with which God endowed humanity at creation. There is no defect in human nature which prevents them from achieving what God commands people to do. See also 6.14; 6.19; 6.20.

Source: *Letter to Demetrias*, 16; in J. P. Migne, *Patrologia Latina*, 33:1110A–B.

* * *

[Instead of regarding God's commands as a privilege] . . . we cry out at God and say, "This is too hard! This is too difficult! We cannot do it! We are only human, and hindered by the weakness of the flesh!" What blind madness! What blatant presumption! By doing this, we accuse the God of knowledge of a twofold ignorance – ignorance of God's own creation and of God's own commands. It would be as if, forgetting the weakness of humanity – his own creation – God had laid upon us commands which we were unable to bear. And at the same time – may God forgive us! – we ascribe to the righteous One unrighteousness, and cruelty to the Holy One; first, by complaining that God has commanded the impossible, second, by imagining that some will be condemned by God for what they could not help; so that – the blasphemy of it! – God is thought of as seeking our punishment rather than our salvation . . . No one knows the extent of our strength better than the God who gave us that strength . . . God has not willed to command anything impossible, for God is righteous; and will not condemn anyone for what they could not help, for God is holy.

6.19 Pelagius on Human Freedom

This extract is taken from what remains of an otherwise lost writing of Pelagius, which is cited by Augustine in order to criticize Pelagius's views. For this reason, it cannot be regarded as totally reliable. The Pelagian idea to which Augustine takes particular exception is that humanity can exist without sin. However, he also criticizes Pelagius for ascribing the will to perform good works to human nature; for Augustine, such a will can only be a divine gift, in that fallen human nature inclines to do evil rather than good. See also 6.13; 6.14; 6.18; 6.20.

Source: Pelagius, *pro libero arbitrio*, as reported by Augustine, *De gratia Christi*, IV, 5; in *Corpus Scriptorum Ecclesiasticorum Latinorum*, vol. 42, ed. C. F. Urba and J. Zycha (Vienna: Tempsky, 1902), 128.1–29.

— — — * * *

We distinguish three things and arrange them in a certain order. We put in the first place "possibility" (*posse*); in the second, "will" (*velle*); in the third, "being" (*esse*). The *posse* we assign to nature, the *velle* to will, the *esse* to actual realization. The first of these, *posse, is* properly ascribed to God, who conferred it on his creatures; while the other two, *velle* and *esse*, are to be referred to the human agent, since they have their source in the divine will. Therefore human praise lies in being willing and in doing a good work; or rather this praise belongs both to humanity and to the God who has granted to possibility of willing and working, and who by the help of grace assists (*gratiae suae adiuvat semper auxilio*) exactly this possibility. The fact that someone has this possibility of willing and doing any good work is due to God alone ... Therefore (and this must be often repeated because of your foolishness), when we say that it is possible for someone to be without sin, we are even then praising God by acknowledging the gift of possibility which we have received. It is God who has bestowed this *posse* on us, and there is no occasion for praising the human agent when we are treating of God alone; for the question is not about *velle* or *esse*, but solely about what is possible (*potest esse*).

Pelagius's Rejection of Original Sin   6.20

Once more, this passage from a lost work of Pelagius derives from a work of Augustine, who cites it in order to discredit it. Note the distinctive Pelagian idea that humanity is born with a capacity for good or evil, rather than intrinsically evil. For Augustine, original sin contaminates humanity from its moment of conception, so that humanity is born sinful. See also 6.2; 6.3; 6.6; 6.9; 6.12; 6.18; 6.19.

Source: Pelagius, *pro libero arbitrio*, as reported by Augustine, *de peccato originale*, XIII, 14; in *Corpus Scriptorum Ecclesiasticorum Latinorum*, vol. 42, ed. C. F. Urba and J. Zycha (Vienna: Tempsky, 1902), 175.22–7.

— — — * * *

"Everything," he says, "good and evil, concerning which we are either worthy of praise or of blame, is done by us, not born with us (*non nobiscum oritur sed agitur a nobis*). We are not born in our full development, but with a capacity for good and evil; we are begotten without virtue as much as without fault (*sine virtute ita et sine vitio*), and before the activity of the individual will there is nothing in humans other than what God has placed in them."

6.21 The Council of Carthage (418) on Grace

The Pelagian controversy was officially ended by the Council of Carthage, which laid down a series of propositions which it defined as the teaching of the catholic church on this matter. It explicitly condemned as heretical a series of eight teachings, as set out below. See also 6.13; 6.14; 6.16; 6.18; 6.19; 6.20.

Source: H. Denziger (ed.), *Enchiridion Symbolum*, 24–5 edn (Barcelona: Herder, 1948), pp. 51–4.

* * *

1. That Adam, the first human being, was created mortal, so that, whether he sinned or not, he would have died from natural causes, and not as the wages of sin;
2. That new-born children need not be baptized, or that they are baptized for the remission of sins, but that no original sin is derived from Adam to be washed away in the laver of regeneration, so that in their case the baptismal formula "for the remission of sins" is understood in a false rather than in its true sense (*non vera sed falsa intelligatur*) . . .
3. That the grace of God, by which we are justified through Jesus Christ our Lord, avails only for the remission of sins already committed, and not for assistance to prevent the sins being committed . . .
4. That this grace . . . only helps us to avoid sin in this way; that by it we are given by revelation an understanding of God's commands that we may learn what we ought to strive for and what we ought to avoid, but that it does not give us also the delight in doing, and the power to do, what we have recognized as being good . . .
5. That the grace of justification is given to us so that we may more easily perform by means of grace that which we are commanded to do by means of our free will (*per liberum arbitrium*); as if we could fulfil those commands even without the gift of grace, though not so easily . . .
6. That the words of the Apostle John, "If we say that we have no sin, etc." (1 John 1:8) are to be taken as meaning that we should say that we have sin not because it is true, but on account of humility on our part . . .
7. That in the Lord's Prayer the saints say "Forgive us our trespasses" not for themselves, because for them this prayer is unnecessary, but for others among their people who are sinners . . .
8. That in the Lord's Prayer the saints say "Forgive us our trespasses" out of humility and not because they are true . . .

6.22 The Synod of Arles on Pelagianism

The condemnation of Pelagianism continued in the fifth century, with southern France emerging as a region in which the issue was of particular importance. The southern French city of Arles was the venue for a synod which confirmed a series of condemnations of Pelagianism. The precise date of this synod is not known; however, it is referred to in a letter of Faustus of Regium to Lucidus, dated 473, suggesting that the synod met shortly before the letter was written. The Synod condemned a series of Pelagian statements, while offering positive statements of its own. A representative selection is printed below. See 6.18; 6.29; 6.20; 6.21.

Source: Letter of Faustus of Rhegium to Lucidus (473); in *Corpus Scriptorum Ecclesiasticorum Latinorum*, vol. 20, ed. A. Engelbrecht (Vienna: Tempsky, 1891), 165.20–166.2; 16–20.

———————————————————————————————— * * *

[The following statements are condemned:]

1. That after the fall of Adam, human free choice (*arbitrium voluntatis*) was extinguished;
2. That Christ, our Lord and Saviour, did not die for the salvation of all people;
3. That the foreknowledge of God forces people violently towards death, or that those who perish, perish on account of the will of God;

[The following statements are affirmed:]

1. Human effort and endeavour is to be united with the grace of God;
2. Human freedom of will (*libertas voluntatis*) is not extinct but attenuated and weakened (*non extinctam sed adtenuatam et infirmatam esse*);
3. Those who are saved could still be lost, and those that have perished could have been saved.

John Scotus Eriugena on the Nature of Paradise

6.23

In this passage, Eriugena spiritualizes the notion of paradise, denying that it is a place. An important part of his argument rests on an appeal to the specific tenses associated with the verbs found in Scripture. Unlike writers such as Augustine, who understood paradise as a specific location in place and time, Eriugena argues that paradise is perfect human nature. A similar line of thought can be found in writers such as Origen, Gregory of Nyssa, and Maximus. See also 10.1; 10.6; 10.13.

Source: *Periphyseon*, IV, 15; in J. P. Migne, *Patrologia Latina*, 122:809B–D.

———————————————————————————————— * * *

[Therefore] the praise of the life of humanity in paradise must refer to the future life that would have been ours if Adam had remained obedient, rather than to the life which he had only just begun, and in which he did not continue. For if he had continued in it for even a brief period, he must have achieved some degree of perfection, and in that case perhaps his master would not have said, "He began to live (*vivebat*)" but "He lived (*vixit*)," or "He had lived (*vixerat*)." However, if he had used the past or pluperfect tenses in this way, or if he used them like this somewhere else, I would have thought that he was using the past tense to refer to the future, rather than meaning that Adam had continued for a space of time in the blessedness of paradise before the Fall. My reason for doing so is that he was giving expression to the predestined and foreordained blessedness, which was to be ours if Adam had not sinned, as though it had already happened – when, as a matter of fact, it was still among the things which were predestined to be perfect in the future, and which have yet to take place. Now I say this because often when he is writing about Paradise, he does not use the past and pluperfect tenses . . . This is not surprising, in that the most wise divine authority often speaks of the future as though it had already taken place.

6.24 Francis of Assisi on the Creation

The *Canticle of the Sun* represents an important affirmation of a positive attitude towards the creation, typical of Franciscan spirituality. Note especially the underlying theology of providence, in which the benefit of each aspect of creation for humanity is identified. The most famous feature of the canticle is its use of the terms "brother" and "sister" to refer to various aspects of the created order. Traditional English translations of this familiar poem have been heavily influenced by the need to ensure rhyming. This prose translation of the original Italian ignores such considerations in order to convey the sense of the poem. The lines of the original have been retained. See also 2.16; 2.31.

Source: *Canticle of the Sun*; in H. Goad, *Greyfriars: The Story of St. Francis and his Followers* (London: John Westhouse, 1947), pp. 137–8.

* * *

The Praises of the Creatures

Most high, all-powerful and good Lord!
To you are due the praises, the glory, the honor and every blessing,
To you only, O highest one, are they due
and no human being is worthy to speak of you.

Be praised, my Lord, with all your creatures
especially by brother sun
by whom we are lightened every day
for he is fair and radiant with great splendor
and bears your likeness, O highest one.

Be praised, my Lord, for sister moon and the stars
you have set them in heaven, precious, fair and bright.

Be praised, my Lord, by brother wind
and by air and cloud and sky and every weather
through whom you give life to all your creatures.

Be praised, my Lord, by sister water
for she is useful and humble and precious and chaste.

By praised, my Lord, by brother fire
by him we are lightened at night
and he is fair and cheerful and sturdy and strong.

Be praised, my Lord, by our sister, mother earth
she sustains and governs us
and brings forth many fruits and coloured flowers and plants.

Be praised, my Lord, by those who have been pardoned by your love
and who bear infirmity and tribulation;
blessed are those who suffer them in peace
for by you, O highest one, they shall be crowned.

Be praised, my Lord, by our sister, physical death
From whom no one who lives can escape
woe to those who die in mortal sin
but blessed are those who are found in your most holy will
for the second death can do them no harm.

May I bless and praise you, my Lord, and give you thanks and serve
you with great humility.

Thomas Aquinas on Grace

6.25

The *Summa Theologiae* ("The Totality of Theology"), which Aquinas began to write in Latin in 1265 and left unfinished at the time of his death, is widely regarded as the greatest work of medieval theology. In this section, Aquinas deals with various ways in which the word "grace" may be understood, while affirming that in its proper sense, grace designates something supernatural implanted by God within the human soul. See also 6.13; 6.16; 6.28; 6.29.

Source: *Summa Theologiae*, IaIIae, q. 110, a. 1.

* * *

As used in everyday language, "grace" is commonly understood to mean three things. First, it can mean someone's love, as when it is said that a soldier has the king's favor – that is, that the king holds him in favor. Secondly, it can mean a gift which is freely given, as when it is said: "I do you this favor." Thirdly, it can mean the response to a gift which is freely given, as when we are said to give thanks for benefits which we have received. Now the second of these depends upon the first, as someone freely bestows a gift on someone else on account of their love for them. And the third depends upon the second, since thankfulness is appropriate to gifts which are freely given.

Now if "grace" is understood in either the second or third sense of the word, it will be clear that it leaves something in the one who receives it – whether it is the gift which is freely given, or the acknowledgement of that gift ... To say that someone has the grace of God is to say that there is something supernatural in the soul, coming forth from God (*quiddam supernaturale in homine a Deo proveniens*).

6.26 Martin Luther's Discovery of the "Righteousness of God"

In this passage, originally written in 1545, the year before his death, Luther reflects on his early life, and particularly a major theological difficulty which he experienced as a young man. What was "good news" about the proclamation of the righteousness of God? For Luther, this could only mean the condemnation of sinners, himself included. Luther here relates how, after wrestling with the meaning of Romans 1:17, he finally came to understand the "righteousness of God (*iustitia Dei*)" in a different way, thus opening the door to his theological reformation. See also 6.27; 6.28.

Source: Preface to the Latin Works (1545); *D. Martin Luthers Werke: Kritische Gesamtausgabe*, vol. 54 (Weimar: Böhlau, 1938), 185.12–186.21.

* * *

Meanwhile in that year [1519], I had returned to interpreting the Psalter again, confident that I was better equipped after I had expounded in the schools the letters of St. Paul to the Romans and the Galatians, and the letter to the Hebrews. I had certainly been overcome with a great desire to understand St. Paul in his letter to the Romans, but what had hindered me thus far was not any "coldness of the blood" so much as that one phrase in the first chapter: "The righteousness of God is revealed in it." For I had hated the phrase "the righteousness of God" which, according to the use and custom of all the doctors, I had been taught to understand philosophically, in the sense of the formal or active righteousness (as they termed it), by which God is righteous, and punishes unrighteous sinners.

Although I lived an irreproachable life as a monk, I felt that I was a sinner with an uneasy conscience before God; nor was I able to believe that I had pleased him with my satisfaction. I did not love (in fact, I hated) that righteous God who punished sinners, if not with silent blasphemy, then certainly with great murmuring. I was angry with God, saying "As if it were not enough that miserable sinners should be eternally damned through original sin, with all kinds of misfortunes laid upon them by the Old Testament law, and yet God adds sorrow upon sorrow through the gospel, and even brings wrath and righteousness to bear through it!" Thus I drove myself mad, with a desperate disturbed conscience, persistently pounding upon Paul in this passage, thirsting most ardently to know what he meant.

At last, God being merciful, as I meditated day and night on he connection of the words "the righteousness of God is revealed in it, as it is written: the righteous shall live by faith," I began to understand that "righteousness of God" as that by which the righteous lives by the gift of God, namely by faith, and this sentence, "the righteousness of God is revealed," to refer to a passive righteousness, by which the merciful God justifies us by faith, as it is written, "The righteous lives by faith." This immediately made me feel as though I had been born again, and as though I had entered through open gates into paradise itself. From that moment, the whole face of Scripture appeared to me in a different light. Afterwards, I ran through the Scriptures, as from memory, and found the same analogy in other phrases such as the "work of God" (that which God works within us), the "power of God" (by which he makes us strong), the "wisdom of God" (by which he makes us wise), the "strength of God," the "salvation of God" and the "glory of God."

And now, where I had once hated the phrase "the righteousness of God," so much I began to love and extoll it as the sweetest of words, so that this passage in Paul became the very gate of paradise for me. Afterwards, I read Augustine, *On the Spirit and the Letter*, where I found that he too, beyond my expectation, interpreted "the righteousness of God" in the same way – as that which God bestows upon us, when he justifies us. And although this is expressed somewhat imperfectly, and he does not explain everything about imputation clearly, it was nevertheless pleasing to find that he taught that the "righteousness of God" is that, by which we are justified.

Martin Luther on Justifying Faith   6.27

In this passage, originally published in German in 1520, Luther develops the idea that faith unites the believer to Christ, in much the same way as marriage unites a bride and bridegroom. The soul is thus made "single and free" from its sin on account of being married to Christ; Luther's language here suggests the image of being "divorced from sin" in order to be "united with Christ." Through this union, the believer shares in all Christ's riches, while Christ swallows up the believer's sin. The passage serves to emphasize that Luther sees faith as far more than intellectual assent to propositions. Faith establishes a living personal relationship between Christ and the believer. See also 1.12; 6.28; 6.31.

Source: *The Freedom of a Christian*; in *D. Martin Luthers Werke: Kritische Gesamtausgabe*, vol. 7 (Weimar: Böhlaus, 1897), 25.26–26.9.

---

     * * *

In the twelfth place, faith does not merely mean that the soul realizes that the divine word is full of all grace, free and holy; it also unites the soul with Christ (*voreynigt auch die seele mit Christo*), as a bride is united with her bridegroom. From such a marriage, as St. Paul says (Ephesians 5:31–2), it follows that Christ and the soul become one body, so that they hold all things in common, whether for better or worse. This means that what Christ possesses belongs to the believing soul; and what the soul possesses, belongs to Christ. Thus Christ possesses all good things and holiness; these now belong to the soul. The soul possesses lots of vices and sin; these now belong to Christ. Here we have a happy exchange (*froelich wechtzel*) and struggle. Christ is God and a human being, who has never sinned and whose holiness is unconquerable, eternal and almighty. So he makes the sin of the believing soul his own through its wedding ring (*braudtring*), which is faith, and acts as if he had done it [i.e., sin] himself, so that sin could be swallowed up in him. For his unconquerable righteousness is too strong for all sin, so that it is made single and free (*leding und frei*) from all its sins on account of its pledge, that is its faith, and can turn to the eternal righteousness of its bridegroom, Christ. Now is not this a happy business (*ein froehliche wirtschafft*)? Christ, the rich, noble, and holy bridegroom, takes in marriage this poor, contemptible and sinful little prostitute (*das arm vorachte boetzes huerlein*), takes away all her evil, and bestows all his goodness upon her! It is no longer possible for sin to overwhelm her, for she is now found in Christ and is swallowed up by him, so that she possesses a rich righteousness in her bridegroom.

6.28 Martin Luther on Sin and Grace

During the academic year 1515–16, Luther delivered a course of lectures in Latin at the University of Wittenberg on Paul's letter to the Romans. A copy of these lectures has survived, allowing insights into Luther's theology at this early stage in his career. In the course of analyzing Romans 4:7, Luther opens up a discussion of the relation of sin and grace in the life of the believer. His basic argument is that sin and righteousness coexist in the existence of believers, so that they are at one and the same time sinners and righteous people. See also 6.12; 6.13.

Source: Lectures on Romans (1515–16); in *D. Martin Luthers Werke: Kritische Gesamtausgabe*, vol. 56 (Weimar: Böhlau, 1938), 269.25–30; 272.3–21.

* * *

Since the saints are always conscious of their sin, and seek righteousness from God in accordance with his mercy, they are always reckoned as righteous by God (*semper quoque iusti a Deo reputantur*). Thus in their own eyes, and as a matter of fact, they are unrighteous. But God reckons them as righteous on account of their confession of their sin. In fact, they are sinners; however, they are righteous by the reckoning of a merciful God (*Re vera peccatores, sed reputatione miserentis Dei iusti*). Without knowing it, they are righteous; knowing it, they are unrighteous. They are sinners in fact, but righteous in hope (*peccatores in re, iusti autem in spe*) . . .

It is like the case of a man who is ill, who trusts the doctor who promises him a certain recovery and in the meantime obeys the doctor's instructions, abstaining from what has been forbidden to him, in the hope of the promised recovery (*in spe promissae sanitatis*), so that he does not do anything to hinder this promised recovery . . . Now this man who is ill, is he healthy? The fact is that he is a man who is both ill and healthy at the same time (*immo aegrotus simul et sanus*). As a matter of fact, he is ill; but he is healthy on account of the certain promise of the doctor, who he trusts and who reckons him as healthy already, because he is sure that he will cure him. Indeed, he has already begun to cure him, and no longer regards him as having a terminal illness. In the same way, our Samaritan, Christ, has brought this ill man to the inn to be cared for, and has begun to cure him, having promised him the most certain cure leading to eternal life . . . Now is this man perfectly righteous? No. But he is at one and the same time a sinner and a righteous person (*simul iustus et peccator*). He is a sinner in fact, but a righteous person by the sure reckoning and promise of God that he will continue to deliver him from sin until he has completely cured him. And so he is totally healthy in hope, but is a sinner in fact (*sanus perfecte est in spe, in re autem peccator*). He has the beginning of righteousness, and so always continues more and more to seek it, while realizing that he is always unrighteous.

Philip Melanchthon on Justification by Faith

6.29

In the first edition of his *Loci Communes* ("Commonplaces"), published in Latin in 1521, Melanchthon set out his understanding of justification by faith. The dominant theme of the passage is the relation between faith and works, and especially Melanchthon's response to the suggestion that his approach leaves no place for good works and invalidates the New Testament references to "rewards" for the Christian life. See also 6.26; 6.27; 6.32; 6.33; 6.40.

Source: *Loci Communes* (1521); in *Melancthons Werke in Auswahl*, ed. H. Engelland (Gütersloh: Bertelsmann Verlag, 1953), vol. 2, 106.22–110.11.

* * *

For what cause is justification attributed to faith alone? I answer that since we are justified by the mercy of God alone, and faith is clearly the recognition of that mercy by whatever promise you apprehend it, justification is attributed to faith alone. Let those who marvel that justification is attributed to faith alone marvel also that justification is attributed only to the mercy of God, and not rather to human merits. For to trust in divine mercy is to have no confidence in any of our own works. Anyone who denies that the saints are justified by faith insults the mercy of God. For since our justification is a work of divine mercy alone and is not a merit based on our own works, as Paul clearly teaches in Romans 11, justification must be attributed to faith alone: faith is that through which alone we receive the promised mercy.

So what about works that precede justification, works of the free will? All those who are of the cursed tree are cursed fruits. Although they are examples of the most beautiful virtues, comparable to the righteousness of Paul before his conversion, yet they are nothing but deceit and treachery on account of their having their source in an impure heart. Impurity of heart consists of ignorance of God, not fearing God, not trusting God, and not seeking after God, as we have shown above. For the flesh knows nothing but fleshly things, as it says in Romans 8:5: "Those who live according to the flesh set their minds on the things of the flesh." . . . The philosophers list many such things in their definitions of the goal of what is good: one suggests "happiness," and another "lack of pain." It is clear that by nature human beings care nothing for the divine. They are neither terrified by the word of God, nor brought to life in faith. And what are the fruits of such a tree but sin?

But although the works that follow justification have their source in the Spirit of God who has taken hold of the hearts of those who are justified, because they are performed in a still impure flesh, the works themselves are also impure. Although justification has begun, it has not yet been brought to its conclusion. We have the firstfruits of the Spirit (Romans 8:23), but not yet the whole harvest. We are still awaiting with groaning the redemption of our bodies, as we read in Romans 8:26. Therefore, because there is something unclean even in these works, they do not deserve the name of righteousness, and wherever you turn, whether to the works preceding justification, or to those which follow, there is no room for our merit. Therefore, justification must be a work of the mercy of God alone. This is what Paul says in Galatians 2:20: "And the life I now live in the flesh I live by faith in the Son of God, who loved me and gave himself for me." He does not say: "I live now in my good works," but "I live by faith in the mercy of God." Moreover, faith is the reason that those works which follow justification are not imputed as sin. This we shall discuss a little later.

Therefore, when justification is attributed to faith, it is attributed to the mercy of God; it is set apart from human efforts, works, and merits. The beginning and growth of righteousness are linked to the mercy of God so that the righteousness of the entire life is nothing else than faith. That is why the prophet Isaiah calls the Kingdom of Christ a kingdom of mercy: "And a throne will be established in steadfast love," etc. (Isaiah 16:5). For if we were justified by our own works, the kingdom would not be that of Christ, nor of mercy, but it would be our own – a kingdom of our own works . . .

You will say: "So do we then merit nothing? For what reason, then, does Scripture use the word 'reward' throughout?" I answer that there is a reward, and it is not because of any merit of ours; but because the Father promised, he has now laid himself under obligation to us and made himself a debtor to those who had deserved nothing at all . . . Paul says in Romans 6:23: "For the wages of sin is death, but the free gift of God is eternal life." He calls eternal life a "gift," not a "debt" – although as a matter of fact it is a debt because the Father has promised it and he has pledged it in faith.

6.30 John Calvin on Predestination

The doctrine of predestination is of major importance to Calvin. In this mature statement of his views, Calvin declares that some people are predestined to eternal life, and others to eternal death. This doctrine, known as "double predestination," affirms that only those who are elected to salvation will, in fact, be saved. Notice how Calvin draws a clear distinction between "predestination" and "foreknowledge." See also 6.15; 6.22; 6.34; 6.36; 6.42; 6.43.

Source: Institutes, III.xxi.1, 5; in Joannis Calvini: Opera Selecta, ed. P. Barth and W. Niesel, vol. 4 (Munich: Kaiser, 1931), 368.33–369.14; 373.33–374.17.

* * *

The covenant of life is not preached equally to all people, and amongst those to whom it is preached, it does not meet with the same acceptance either constantly or in equal degree. In this diversity the unsearchable depths of God's judgement are made known. For there is no doubt that this variety is subordinate to the will of God's eternal election. If it is clear that salvation is freely offered to some while others are barred from access to it, on account of God's pleasure, this raises some major and difficult questions. They can be explained only when election and predestination are rightly understood. Many find this a puzzling subject, in that it seems to be nothing less than capricious, that out of the human community some should be predestined to salvation, others to destruction. But it will become clear in the following discussion that such confusion is needless. In any case, the complexity of this matter makes known both the usefulness of this doctrine and also the very sweet fruit which it brings. We shall never be clearly persuaded, as we ought to be, that our salvation flows from God's free mercy until we come to know his eternal election, which casts light on God's grace by this comparison: he does not indiscriminately adopt all to the hope of salvation but gives to some what he denies to others . . .

Predestination, by which God adopts some to the hope of life, and sentences others to eternal death, is denied by no-one who wishes to be thought of as pious. But there are many, especially those who make foreknowledge its cause, who surround it with all kinds of petty objections. Both doctrines are indeed to be located within God, but subjecting one to the other is absurd. In attributing foreknowledge to God, we mean that all things always have been, and always will be, under his eyes, so that there is nothing future or past to his knowledge, but all things are present – present in such a way that he not only conceives them through ideas, as we have before us those things which our minds remember, but he truly looks upon them and discerns them as things placed before him. And this foreknowledge is extended throughout the universe to every creature. We call predestination God's eternal decree, by which he determined with himself what he willed to become of each human being. For all are not created in equal condition (*non enim pari conditione creantur omnes*); but eternal life is foreordained for some, and eternal damnation for others. Therefore, as any person has been directed (*conditus*) to one or the other of these ends, we speak of him or her as predestined to life or to death.

John Calvin on Faith and the Promises of God 6.31

In this passage, taken from the 1559 *Institutes of the Christian Religion*, Calvin emphasizes the way in which faith is grounded specifically in the promises of God. Faith is not based on the word of God in general, but more specifically, in the promises of God which offer salvation. Calvin also stresses that it is not faith in itself, but being united to Christ through faith, which is of decisive importance. See also 1.12; 6.27.

Source: *Institutes*, III.ii.29, 30; in *Joannis Calvini: Opera Selecta*, ed. P. Barth and W. Niesel, vol. 3 (Munich: Kaiser, 1928), 39.1–40.12.

* * *

We make the foundation of faith the gracious promise, because faith properly consists of this. [Faith] is certain that God is true in everything, whether he commands something or forbids it, whether he promises something or threatens it. Faith also obediently receives his commandments, observes his prohibitions, and heeds his threats. Nevertheless, [faith] properly begins with the promise, consists of it, and ends in it. For in God faith seeks life; a life that is not found in commandments or edicts of penalties, but in the promise of mercy, and a promise which is nothing if it is not gracious . . . When we say that faith must rest upon a gracious promise, we do not deny that believers embrace and grasp the Word of God in every respect; but we identify the promise of mercy as the proper object of faith . . .

It is our intention to make only these two points. First, that faith does not stand firm unless a believer attains to the gracious promise; second, that faith does not reconcile us to God by itself, unless it joins us to Christ. Both points are worth noting. We seek a faith which distinguishes the children of God from the wicked, and believers from unbelievers. If people believe that God justly commands all that he both commands and threatens, can they be called believers for that reason? Certainly not. Therefore, there can be no firm foundation of faith unless it rests upon God's mercy.

6.32 John Calvin on the Concept of Justification

Up to about the year 1500, the term "justification" was widely understood to mean "to be made righteous." This interpretation, which had its origins in the writings of Augustine, saw justification as both an event and a process. The Reformation, however, saw justification defined exclusively in forensic terms – that is, as an event, in which sinners are declared to be righteous before God. Justification is then followed by sanctification, a process in which believers are made righteous. In this passage, Calvin provides a classic articulation of this forensic notion of justification. See also 6.28; 6.33; 6.40.

Source: *Institutes*, III.xi.2, 23; in *Joannis Calvini: Opera Selecta*, ed. P. Barth and W. Niesel, vol. 4 (Munich: Kaiser, 1931), 182.25–183.10; 206.17–32.

* * *

To be justified in God's sight is to be reckoned as righteous in God's judgement, and to be accepted on account of that righteousness . . . The person who is justified by faith is someone who, apart from the righteousness of works, has taken hold of the righteousness of Christ through faith, and having been clothed with it, appears in the sight of God not as a sinner, but as a righteous person. Therefore justification is to be understood simply as the acceptance by which God receives us into his favour as righteous people. We say that it consists of the remission of sins and the imputation of the righteousness of Christ . . .

There is no doubt that we obtain justification in the sight of God only by the intercession of the righteousness of Christ. This is equivalent to saying that believers are not righteous in themselves, but on account of the communication of the righteousness of Christ through imputation, something to be noted carefully . . . Our righteousness is not in us, but in Christ. We possess it only because we participate in Christ; in fact, with him, we possess all his riches.

The Council of Trent on Justification 6.33

During its sixth session, which ended on 13 January 1547, the Council of Trent set out a definitive statement on the Roman Catholic church's teaching on justification. Of particular interest is its definition of justification in terms of both an event and a process, embracing both the act of God by which the Christian life is begun and the process by which God renews the believer. See also 6.29; 6.32; 6.39.

Source: Council of Trent, Session VI, chapter 4; in H. Denzinger (ed.), *Enchiridion Symbolorum*, 24–5 edn (Barcelona: Herder, 1948), pp. 285–6.

* * *

The justification of the sinner may be briefly defined as a translation from that state in which a human being is born a child of the first Adam (*translatio ab eo statu in quo homo nascitur filius primi Adae*), to the state of grace and of the adoption of the sons of God through the second Adam, Jesus Christ our Saviour (*in statum gratiae et adotionis filiorum Dei per secundum Adam Iesum Christum Salvatore nostrum*). According to the gospel, this translation cannot come about except through the cleansing of regeneration, or a desire for this, as it is written, "Unless someone is born again of water and the Holy Spirit, he or she cannot enter into the Kingdom of God" (John 3:5).

Theodore Beza on the Causes of Predestination 6.34

Theodore Beza was one of Calvin's followers in Geneva, who achieved considerable fame as a leading exponent of Calvinist ideas. In this letter to Calvin, written at a time at which the issue of predestination was fiercely debated within Geneva, Beza locates the ultimate ground of predestination as lying totally within the sovereign will of God. See also 6.10; 6.11; 6.30; 6.36; 6.42; 6.43.

Source: Letter to John Calvin, 29 July 1555; in *Correspondence de Théodore de Bèze*, ed. H. Aubert (Geneva: Droz, 1960), vol. 1, p. 171.

* * *

So if someone asks concerning the cause by which God should have decided from all eternity to elect some and to condemn others, I think that we must reply by saying that this is in order that God's immense power may be made known better. Buf if they then ask about the "material cause" (as they call it) of this eternal decree, then I have nothing to point to other than the will of God, who has just as much freedom [over his creation] as the potter, by which he can produce one vessel for honour, and the other for disgrace. If someone should ask why God should have predestined some people instead of others to salvation or destruction, I again point to the will of God, in whose power it lies not merely to produce some vessels for honour and others to disgrace from the same mass of clay, but also to express his own unique judgement in that distinction. So, in responding to these questions, I would not appeal to "secondary causes," among which number are included Christ and Adam, but rather to what follows on from this. The question does not concern the degree of election or reprobation, but their *execution*. There are ordained secondary causes for the execution of the divine counsel. A reason can be brought forward as to why and how we are elect – namely, that God, on account of his enormous love and as he sees us in Christ (to whome he determined to give us before all ages), was not able not to love us (*non potuit nos non amare*), so that we might be righteous and holy in him. But if it is asked what caused God to condemn some, I shall reply that the cause is to be located in the people themselves, in that they persist in corruption and sin, which merit the righteous hatred of God. Such people are thus rightly rejected and renounced by God . . . So when we are said to be "elect in Christ before the creation of the world" (Ephesians 1:4), I understand this . . . to mean: God, when he predestined us to election from all eternity, at the same time subordinated Christ to this decree (*simul huic decreto substravisse Christum*), in whom he might elect us, and call, justify, and glorify the elect. On the other hand, when he predestined some to destruction, he at the same time appointed Adam, in whom those who had been corrupted might be hardened, so that God might declare his supreme power in them.

6.35 James Ussher on the Grounds of Assurance

In this important analysis of the grounds of assurance, the seventeenth-century archbishop of Armagh James Ussher argues that assurance is the result, not the precondition, of justification. He sets out with particular clarity what has come to be known as the *syllogismus practicus* ("practical syllogism"), which argues that anyone who shows the results of justification may be regarded as being justified. See also 6.30; 6.31; 6.34; 6.36.

Source: James Ussher, A Body of Divinity, 3rd edn (London: M.F., 1663), pp. 197–200.

* * *

But is it not necessary to justification, to be assured that my sins are pardoned, and that I am justified? No: that is no act of faith as it justifyeth, but an effect and fruit that followeth after justification. For no man is justified by believing that he is justified; for he must be justified before he can believe it . . . But faith as it justifyeth, is a resting upon Christ to obtain pardon the acknowledging him to be the onely Saviour, and the hanging upon him for salvation . . . It is the direct act of faith that justifyeth; that whereby I do believe; it is the reflect act of faith that assures; that whereby I do believe, and it comes by way of argumentation thus.

Major: Whosoever relyeth upon Christ the Saviour of the world for justification and pardon . . . is actually justified and pardoned.

Minor: But I do truly rely upon Christ for justification and pardon.

Conclusion: Therefore I undoubtedly believe that I am justified and pardoned. But many times both the former propositions may be granted to be true, and yet a weak Christian want strength to draw the conclusion.

The Westminster Confession of Faith on Predestination

6.36

This leading Reformed confession of faith, formulated at London in 1643 during the period of the Puritan Commonwealth, reaffirms the strongly predestinarian teaching of Calvin and Beza. Predestination is totally grounded in the will of God, and owes nothing to anything in human nature. See also 6.10; 6.11; 6.30; 6.34; 6.42; 6.43.

Source: Westminster Confession, x.1–2; in E. F. K. Müller (ed.), *Die Bekenntnisschriften der reformierten Kirche* (Leipzig: Böhme, 1903), 565.12–566.3

* * *

All those whom God had predestinated unto life, and those only, he is pleased, in his appointed and accepted time, effectually to call, by his word and Spirit, out of that state of sin and death in which they are by nature, to grace and salvation by Jesus Christ: enlightening their minds, spiritually and savingly, to understand the things of God, taking away their heart of stone and giving unto them a heart of flesh; renewing their wills, and by his almighty power determining them to than which is good; and effectually drawing them to Jesus Christ; yet so as they come most freely, being made willing by his grace.

This effectual call is of God's free and special grace alone, not from anything at all foreseen in man, who is altogether passive therein until, being quickened and renewed by the Holy Spirit, he is thereby enabled to answer this call, and to embrace the grace offered and conveyed in it.

Nicolas Ludwig von Zinzendorf on Saving Faith

6.37

In September 1746, Zinzendorf delivered nine lectures on various aspects of the Christian faith at the Brethren Chapel, London. The first of these, entitled "Concerning Saving Faith," develops the characteristic Pietist notion of a personally assimilated faith, leading to personal conversion. See also 1.11; 6.27; 6.31.

Source: Nicolas Ludwig von Zinzendorf, *Nine Public Lectures on Important Subjects in Religion* (Iowa City: University of Iowa Press, 1973), pp. 40–1. Reprinted from Zinzendorf: *Nine Public Lectures on Important Subjects in Religion*, edited by George W. Forell, by permission of the University of Iowa Press. Copyright © 1987 by University of Iowa Press.

* * *

No man can create faith in himself. Something must happen to him which Luther calls "the divine work in us," which changes us, gives us new birth, and makes us completely different people in heart, spirit, mind, and all our powers. This is *fides*, faith properly speaking. If this is to begin in us, then it must be preceded by distress, without which men have no ears for faith and trust.

The distress which we feel is the distress of our soul when we become poor, when we see we have no Savior, when we become palpably aware of our misery. We see our corruption on all sides and are really anxious because of it. Then afterward it happens as with patients who have reached the point of crisis; they watch for help, for someone who can help them out of their distress, and accept the first offer of aid without making an exact examination or investigation of the person who helps them. That is the way it went once with the woman whom the Savior healed. For twelve years she had gone to see all kinds of physicians and had endured much from them. And finally she came upon him too and said, "If only I would touch that man's clothes, it would help me; even if I could not get to the man himself, if I could only get hold of a bit of his garment, then I would be helped" (Matthew 9:21).

This is faith-in-distress. And here I can never wonder enough at the blindness and ignorance of those people who are supposed to handle the divine Word and convert men, for example the Jews and heathen, those abortive so-called Christians (who are indeed as blind as Jews and heathen) who think that if they have them memorize the catechism or get a book of sermons into their heads or, at the most, present all sorts of well-reasoned demonstrations concerning the divine being and attributes, thus funneling the truths and knowledge into their heads, that this is the sovereign means to their conversion. But this is such a preposterous method that if one wanted to convert people that way, reciting demonstrations to them, then it is just as if one wanted to go against wind and current with full sails, or as if one, on the contrary, would run one's boat into an inlet so that one could not find one's way out again.

For that same knowledge of divine things which is taken to be faith, although it appears only, other things being equal, as an adjunct of faith, puffs up and nothing comes of it. And if one has all of that together, says Paul, and does not also have love, and even if one can preach about it to others, still it is nothing more than if a bell in the church rings. As little as the bell gets out of it, as little as it is benefited by the fact that it hangs there and rings, just so little does the fact that a teacher makes the most cogent demonstrations benefit him as far as his own salvation is concerned.

But what results from this faith-in-distress, from this blind faith which one has out of love for one's own salvation? What comes of a bold trust in the physician that he can and shall help, without knowing what his name is and who he is, without having known and seen him before, without having clearly sensed what sort and nature of man he is? Thankful love results from it, as long ago with Manoah and his wife, who so loved the man who came to them; they did not know him, though, for they said, "What is your name? We do not know you, but we love you. We should like to know who you are, that we may praise you when what you have said to us comes true" (Judges 13:17). So it is exactly with the faith-in-distress: It has to do completely with an unknown man, yet with a man of whom one's heart says, "He likes to help, he likes to comfort, and he can and will help." My heart tells me that it is he of whom I have heard in my youth, of whom I have heard on this or that occasion. They called him the Savior, the Son of God, the Lord Jesus, or however else one has heard him named and however anyone in anxiety and distress thinks of him. In short: "He must help me; oh, if he would only come to my aid! If he would only take my soul into his care, so that it would not perish! Kyrie Eleison! Lord have mercy!"

Friedrich Christoph Oetinger on Conversion

6.38

In this extract from this dictionary of central biblical terms, as understood within Pietism, originally published in 1776, Oetinger stresses the importance of the notion of conversion (which had been marginalized within German Lutheranism), and draws out its significance for the renewal of the believer. Note the strong defense of the role of the law, both in convicting people of their sin and also of indicating the extent of internal and external renewal that is required of them. The element of legalism which often crept into Pietism was regarded with some horror by its Lutheran critics, who accused it of distorting Luther's doctrine of justification by faith. See also 6.37.

Source: F. C. Oetinger, *Biblisches Wörterbuch*, ed. J. Hamberger (Stuttgart: Steinkopf, 1849), pp. 55–6.

* * *

What is conversion? Answer: If you turn away from false intentions and customs, and if you turn to the Word and law of God, you will learn as its chief purpose the directions of Psalm 1. If you see how you have been blinded to the way in which you were in darkness and under the power of Satan even though you were learned, then you are on the path of blessedness. All preaching has the intention of showing that people who from their youth upwards have clung to many false intentions and cover up their hearts, so that they might look to Jesus as the highest law to love above all and that in this way they might be free of the hardness of their understanding and the whole web of sinfulness (*Sündengewebe*) with its hundred excuses, and turn about completely toward the righteousness to which they have been called internally and externally. They are to do so, indeed, in such a way that they remain directed with all which they have, with all the powers and impulses of God, toward that which is preserved as beautiful and divine in righteousness. They are to do so until the Word comes fully into them from the kingdom and is a judge of hidden inclinations and revealed thoughts. For this reason, the proverbs of Solomon and Psalm 119 note that you are not only to be converted generally to the Lord, but also through your whole heart, soul, mind, and powers toward everything which the law testifies of Christ in particular.

6.39 Jonathan Edwards on Original Sin

The eighteenth-century writer Jonathan Edwards was a leading exponent of Puritan ideas in North America. One of the themes to which he paid particular attention was the doctrine of original sin, which he regarded as being under threat, due to the pressure of Enlightenment rationalism. The treatise from which this extract is taken was published in 1758, shortly after Edwards's death. See also 6.3; 6.6; 6.9; 6.13; 6.20.

Source: *Christian Doctrine of Original Sin Defended*: in *The Works of President Edwards*, ed. S. B. Wright 10 vols (New Haven: Yale University Press, 1929–30), vol. 2, pp. 309–16.

* * *

By *Original* Sin as the phrase has been most commonly used by divines, is meant the innate sinful depravity of the heart. But yet when the doctrine of original sin is spoken of, it is vulgarly understood in that latitude, which includes not only the depravity of nature, but the imputation of Adam's first sin; or, in other words, the liableness or exposedness of Adam's posterity, in the divine judgment, to partake of the punishment of that sin. So far as I know, most of those who have held one of these, have maintained the other; and most of those who have opposed one, have opposed the other: both are opposed by the Author chiefly attended to in the following discourse, in his book against original sin. And it may perhaps appear in our future consideration of the subject, that they are closely connected; that the arguments which prove the one establish the other, and that there are no more difficulties attending the allowing of one, than the other.

I shall in the first place, consider this doctrine more especially with regard to the corruption of nature; and as we treat of this the other will naturally come into consideration, in the prosecution of the discourse, as connected with it. As all moral qualities, all principles either of virtue or vice, lie in the disposition of the heart, I shall consider whether we have any evidence that the heart of man is naturally of a corrupt and evil disposition. This is strenuously denied by many late writers who are enemies to the doctrine of original sin; and particularly by Dr. TAYLOR . . .

Here I would first consider the *truth* of the proposition; and then would shew the certainty of the *consequences* which I infer from it. If both can be clearly and certainly proved, then I trust none will deny but that the doctrine of original depravity is evident, and so the falseness of Dr. TAYLOR's scheme demonstrated; the greatest part of whose book called *The Scripture Doctrine of Original Sin, &c.* is against the doctrine of *innate depravity*. On p. 107, he speaks of the conveyance of a corrupt and sinful nature to *Adam's* posterity as the *grand point* to be proved by the maintainers of the doctrine of original sin.

In order to demonstrate what is asserted in the proposition laid down, there is need only that these two things should be made manifest: *one* is this fact, that all mankind come into the world in such a state as without fail comes to this issue, namely, the universal commission of sin; or that every one who comes to act in the world as a moral agent, is, in a greater or less degree, guilty of sin. The *other* is, that all sin deserves and exposes to utter and eternal destruction under God's wrath and curse; and would end in it, were it not for the interposition of divine grace to prevent the effect. Both which can be abundantly demonstrated to be agreeable to the word of God, and to Dr. TAYLOR's own doctrine.

That every one of mankind, at least such as are capable of acting as moral agents, are guilty of sin (not now taking it for granted that they come guilty into the world) is most clearly and abundantly evident from the holy scriptures: 1 Kings 8:46. If any man sin against thee: for there is no man that sinneth not. Ecclesiastes 7:20. There is not a just man upon earth that doeth good and sinneth not. Job. 9:2–3. I know it is so of a truth, (i.e., as Bildad had just before said, that God would not cast away a perfect man, &c.) but how should man be just with God? If he will contend with him, he cannot answer him one of a thousand. To the like purpose. Psalm 118:2. Enter not into judgment with thy servant; for in thy sight shall no man living be justified. So the words of the apostle (in which he has apparent reference to those of the Psalmist). Romans 3:19, 20. "That every mouth may be stopped, and all the world become guilty before God. Therefore by the deeds of the law there shall no flesh be justified in his sight: for by the law is the knowledge of SIN" . . . In this, and innumerable other places, confession and repentance of sin are spoken of as duties proper for ALL; as also prayer to God for pardon of sin: also forgiveness of those that injure us, from that motive, that we hope to be forgiven of God. Universal guilt of sin might also be demonstrated from the appointment, and the declared use and end of the ancient sacrifices; and also from the ransom which every one that was numbered in Israel was directed to pay, to make atonement for his soul . . . All are represented, not only as being sinful, but as having great and manifold iniquity . . .

There are many Scriptures which both declare the universal sinfulness of mankind, and also that all sin deserves and justly exposes to everlasting destruction, under the wrath and curse of God; and so demonstrate both parts of the proposition I have laid down. To which purpose that passage in Galatians 3:10 is exceeding full: For as many as are of the works of the law are under the curse; for it *is* written, cursed is every one that continueth not in all things which are written in the book of the law, to do them. How manifestly is it implied in the apostle's meaning here, that there is no man but what fails in some instances of doing all things that are written in the book of the law, and therefore as many as have their dependence on their fulfilling the law, are under that curse which is pronounced on them that fail of it? And hence the apostle infers in the next verse, that NO MAN is justified by the law in the sight of *God*.

6.40 John Wesley on Justification

John Wesley's sermon on justification was first published in 1746. The sermon is notable for its vigorous attack on the idea of "forensic justification," associated with Melanchthon and Calvin. Wesley regards the idea of the "imputed righteousness of Christ" as morally and theologically untenable. It suggests that God is deceived when he justifies individuals, or pretends that we are in reality someone else (in this case, Christ). In this exposition of parts of Paul's letter to the Romans, Wesley argues for a move away from forensic ideas of justification to a more biblical understanding of justification simply as "pardon and forgiveness." The scriptural allusion towards the end of the extract is to Romans 3:25. See also 6.29; 6.32; 6.33.

Source: Sermon V, "Justification by Faith," in John Wesley, *Sermons on Several Occasions*, vol. 1 (London: G. Whitfield, 1746), pp. 81–101.

* * *

4. Least of all does Justification imply that God is deceived in those whom he justifies; that he thinks them to be what in fact, they are not, that he accounts them to be otherwise than they are. It does by no means imply, that God judges concerning us contrary to the real nature of things, that he esteems us better than we really are, or believes us righteous, when we are unrighteous. Surely no. The judgement of the all-wise God, is always according to truth. Neither can it ever consist with his unerring wisdom to think that I am innocent, to judge that I am righteous or holy, because another is so. He can no more in this manner confound me with Christ than with David or Abraham. Let any man to whom God hath given understanding weigh this without prejudice and he cannot but perceive, that such a notion of Justification is neither reconcilable to Reason or Scripture.

5. The plain scriptural notion of Justification is pardon – the forgiveness of sins. It is that act of God the Father, whereby for the sake of the Propitiation made by the blood of his Son, he "showeth forth his righteousness (or mercy) by the remission of sins that are past." This is the easy, natural account of it given by St. Paul throughout this whole Epistle.

6.41 Emil Brunner on the Image of God

In his later period, the Swiss Reformed theologian Emil Brunner developed a theology which focused on a dialogue or partnership between God and humanity. Thus Brunner understood revelation to involve a "dialogue" between God and his people. In the passage reprinted here, Brunner develops the idea of an "I–Thou" relationship, grounded in the fact that humanity is created in the image of God (*imago Dei*). See also 6.4; 6.5.

Source: Emil Brunner, *The Christian Doctrine of Creation and Redemption: Dogmatics*, vol. 2 (London: Lutterworth Press, 1952), pp. 55–8. Reprinted with the permission of the publishers.

* * *

God is the One who wills to have from me a free response to His love, a response which gives back love for love, a loving echo, a loving reflection of His glory. I cannot meet the holy loving God in Christ without knowing this about myself. Once more, both are correlated and connected; to be aware of the holy loving God, and to be aware of the fact that my nature is created by God, comes to the same thing. It is thus, and not otherwise, that I am intended to be by the Creator. This generous will which claims me, of the God who wills to glorify Himself, and to impart Himself, is the cause of my being, and the fundamental reason for my being what I am, and as I am. Now we must go into some particular points in greater detail.

(a) God, who wills to glorify Himself and to impart Himself, wills humanity to be a creature who responds to His call of love with a grateful, responsive love. God wills to possess humanity as a free being. God wills a creature which is not only, like other creatures, a mere object of His will, as if it were a reflector of His glory as Creator. He desires from us an active and spontaneous response in our "reflecting"; He who creates through the Word, who as Spirit creates in freedom, wills to have a "reflex" which is more than a "reflex," which is an answer to His Word, a free spiritual act, a correspondence to His speaking. Only thus can His love really impart itself as love. For love can only impart itself where it is received in love. Hence the heart of the creaturely existence of humanity is freedom, selfhood, to be an "I," a person. Only an "I" can answer a "Thou," only a Self which is self-determining can freely answer God. An automaton does not respond; an animal, in contradistinction from an automaton, may indeed react, but it cannot respond. It is not capable of speech, of free self-determination, it cannot stand at a distance from itself, and is therefore not responsible.

The free Self, capable of self-determination, belongs to the original constitution of humanity as created by God. But from the very outset this freedom is limited. It is not primary but secondary. Indeed, it does not posit itself – like the Self of Idealism – but it is posited; it is not *a se* but *a Deo*. Hence although humanity's answer is free, it is also limited. God wills my freedom, it is true, because He wills to glorify Himself, and to give Himself. He wills my freedom in order to make this answer possible; my freedom is therefore, from the outset, a responsible one. Responsibility is restricted freedom, which distinguishes human from divine freedom; and it is a restriction which is also *free* and this distinguishes our human limited freedom from that of the rest of creation. The animals, and God, have no responsibility – the animals because they are below the level of responsibility, and God, because He is above it; the animals because they have no freedom, and God because He has absolute freedom. Humanity, however, has a limited freedom. This is the heart of his being as humanity, and it is the condition on which humanity possesses freedom. In other words, this limited human freedom is the very purpose for which humanity has been created: humanity possesses this "freedom" in order that it may respond to God, in such a way that through this response God may glorify Himself, and give Himself to His creature.

(b) Now, however, it is of the essence of this responsible freedom that its purpose may or may not be fulfilled. This open question is the consequence of freedom. Thus it is part of the divinely created nature of humanity that it should have both a formal and a material aspect. The fact that humanity must respond, that it is responsible, is fixed; no amount of human freedom, nor of the sinful misuse of freedom, can alter this fact. Humanity is, and remains, responsible, whatever its personal attitude to its Creator may be. Humanity may deny its responsibility, and may misuse its freedom, but it cannot get rid of its responsibility. Responsibility is part of the unchangeable structure of human being. That is: the actual existence of humanity – of every human being, not only those who believe in Christ – consists in the positive fact that they have been made to respond to God.

Whatever kind of response humanity may make to the call of the Creator – in any case it does respond, even if the reply is: "I do not know any Creator, and I will not obey any God." Even this answer is an answer, and it comes under the inherent law of responsibility. This formal essential structure cannot be lost. It is identical with human existence as such, and indeed with the quality of being which all human beings possess equally; it only ceases where true human living ceases – on the borderline of imbecility or madness.

In the Old Testament, the Bible describes this formal aspect of human nature by the concept of "being made in the image of God." In the thought of the Old Testament the fact that humanity has been "made in the Image of God" means something which humanity can never lose; even when they sin, they cannot lose it. This conception is therefore unaffected by the contrast between sin and grace, or sin and obedience, precisely because it describes the "formal" or "structural," and not the "material" aspect of human nature. Then how is it possible to perceive reflected similarity in this formal likeness to God? The similarity consists in being "subject," being "person," freedom. Certainly, humanity has only a limited freedom, because it is responsible, but it *has* freedom; only so *can* it be responsible. Thus the formal aspect of human nature, as beings "made in the image of God," denotes being as Subject, or freedom; it is this which differentiates humanity from the lower creation; this constitutes its specifically *human* quality; it is this which is given to humanity – and to humanity alone – and under all circumstances by Divine appointment.

The New Testament simply presupposes this fact that humanity – in its very nature – has been "made in the image of God"; it does not develop this any further. To the Apostles what matters most is the "material" realization of this God-given quality; that is, that humanity should really give *the* answer which the Creator intends, the response in which God is honoured, and in which He fully imparts Himself, the response of reverent, grateful love, given not only in words, but in its whole life. The New Testament, in its doctrine of the *Imago Dei*, tells us that this right answer has not been given; that a quite different one has been given instead, in which the glory is not given to God, but to human beings and to creatures, in which humanity does not live in the love of God, but seeks itself. Secondly, the New Testament is the proclamation of what God has done in order that he may turn this false answer into the true one.

Here, therefore, the fact that humanity has been "made in the image of God" is spoken of as having been lost, and indeed as wholly, and not partially lost. Humanity no longer possesses this *Imago Dei*; but it is restored through Him, through whom God glorifies and gives Himself: through Jesus Christ. The restoration of the *Imago Dei*, the new creation of the original image of God in humanity, is identical with the gift of God in Jesus Christ received by faith.

The *Imago Dei* in the New Testament, in the "material" sense of the word, is identical with "being-in-the-Word" of God. This means that humanity does not possess its true being in itself, but in God. Thus it is not a fact which can be discovered in humanity, something which can be found through introspection. It is not the "Thou" of Idealistic philosophy, but it is the "I" derived from the "Thou." Hence it cannot be understood by looking at humanity, but only by looking at God, or, more exactly, by looking at the Word of God. To be true humanity, humanity must not be itself, and in order to understand his true being it must not look at itself. Our true being is *extra nos et alienum nobis* (Luther); it is "eccentric" and "ecstatic"; humanity is only truly human when it is in God. Then, and then only, is humanity truly itself.

From the standpoint of sinful humanity, the *Imago Dei* is existence in Jesus Christ, the Word made flesh. Jesus Christ is the true *Imago Dei*, which humanity regains when through faith it is "in Jesus Christ." Faith in Jesus Christ is therefore the *restauratio imaginis*, because He restores to us that existence in the Word of God which we had lost through sin. When humanity enters into the love of God revealed in Christ it becomes truly human. True human existence is existence in the love of God. Thus also the true freedom of humanity is complete dependence upon God. *Deo servire libertas* (Augustine). The words "Whose service is perfect freedom" express the essence of Christian faith. True humanity is not genius but love, that love which humanity does not possess from or in itself but which is received from God, who is love. True humanity does not spring from the full development of human potentialities, but it arises through the reception, the perception, and the acceptance of the love of God, and it develops and is preserved by "abiding" in communion with the God who reveals Himself as Love. Hence separation from God, sin, is the loss of the true human quality, and the destruction of the quality of "being made in the Image of God." When the human heart no longer reflects the love of God, but itself and the world, humanity no longer bears the "Image of God," which simply consists in the fact that God's love is reflected in the human heart.

Since through faith in Jesus Christ humanity once more receives God's Primal Word of love, once more the divine Image (*Urbild*) *is* reflected in it, the lost *Imago Dei* is restored. The *Imago Dei*, in the sense of true humanity – not in the sense of formal or structural humanity – is thus identical with the true attitude of humanity in relation to God, in accordance with God's purpose in Creation. Your attitude to God determines what you are. If your attitude towards God is "right," in harmony with the purpose of Creation, that is, if in faith you receive the love of God, then you *are* right; if your attitude to God is wrong, then you are wrong, as a whole.

It is evident that our thought will become terribly muddled if the two ideas of the *imago Dei* – the "formal" and "structural" one of the Old Testament, and the "material" one of the New Testament – are either confused with one another, or treated as identical. The result will be either that we must deny that the sinner possesses the quality of humanity at all; or, that which makes the sinner a human being must be severed from the *imago Dei*; or, the loss of the *imago* in the material sense *must* be regarded merely as an obscuring, or a *partial* corruption of the *imago*, which lessens the seriousness of sin. All these three false solutions disappear once the distinction is rightly made.

6.42 Karl Barth on Election in Christ

In this passage from his *Church Dogmatics*, Karl Barth reinterprets the classic Reformed doctrine of predestination. Noting that the doctrine takes the form of God's pronouncement of "Yes" and "No," Barth argues that the negative aspects of the doctrine relate to Christ, and Christ alone. By taking the negative aspects of predestination upon himself, Christ thus converts predestination into a totally positive and affirming doctrine. See also 6.10; 6.11; 6.30; 6.34; 6.36; 6.43.

Source: Karl Barth, *Church Dogmatics*, II/2 (Edinburgh: T. & T. Clark, 1957), pp. 103; 161; 164; 166–7. Used with permission of the publisher.

* * *

In its simplest and most comprehensive form the dogma of predestination consists, then, in the assertion that the divine predestination is the election of Jesus Christ. But the concept of election has a double reference – to the elector and the elected. And so, too, the name of Jesus Christ has within itself the double reference: the One called by this name is both very God and very man. Thus the simplest form of the dogma may be divided at once into the two assertions that Jesus Christ is the electing God, and that He is also elected man.

In so far as He is the electing God, we must obviously – and above all – ascribe to Him the active determination of electing. It is not that He does not elect as man; i.e., elect God in faith. But this election can only follow His prior election, and that means that it follows the divine electing which is the basic and proper determination of His existence.

In so far as He is man, the passive determination of election is also and necessarily proper to Him. It is true, of course, that even as God he is elected: the Elected of His Father. But because as the Son of the Father, he has no need of any special election, we must add at once that He is the Son of God elected in His oneness with man, and in fulfilment of God's covenant with man. Primarily, then, electing is the divine determination of the existence of Jesus Christ, and election (being elected) the human . . .

The eternal will of God in the election of Jesus Christ is His will to give Himself for the sake of man as created by Him and fallen from Him. According to the Bible this was what took place in the incarnation of the Son of God, in His death and passion, in His resurrection from the dead. We must think of this as the content of the eternal divine predestination. The election of grace in the beginning of all things is God's self-giving in His eternal purpose. His self-giving: God gave – not only as an actual event but as something eternally foreordained – God gave His only begotten Son. God sent forth his own Word. And in so doing, He gave Himself. He gave Himself up. He hazarded himself. He did not do this for nothing, but for man as created by Him and fallen away from Him. This is God's eternal will. And our next task is to arrive at a radical understanding of the fact and extent that this will, as recognized and expressed in the history of doctrine, is a twofold will, containing within itself both a Yes and a No. We must consider how and how far the eternal predestination is a quality, a *praedestinatio gemina* . . .

For if God Himself became man, this man, what else can this mean but that He declared himself guilty of the contradiction against Himself in which man was involved; that He submitted Himself to the law of creation by which such a contradiction could be accompanied only by loss and destruction; that He made Himself the object of the wrath and judgment to which man had brought himself; that He took upon Himself the rejection which man had deserved; that he tasted Himself the damnation, death and hell which ought to have been the portion of fallen man? . . .

When we say that God elected as His own portion the negative side of the divine predestination, the reckoning with man's weakness and sin and inevitable punishment, we say implicitly that this portion is not man's portion. In so far, then, as predestination does contain a No, it is not a No spoken against man. In so far as it is directed to perdition and death, it is not directed to the perdition and death of man . . . Rejection cannot again become the portion or affair of man. The exchange which took place at Golgotha, when God chose as His throne the malefactor's cross, when the Son of God bore what the son of man ought to have borne, took place once and for all in fulfilment of God's eternal will, and it can never be reversed. There is no condemnation – literally none – for those that are in Christ Jesus. For this reason, faith in the divine election as such as *per se* means faith in the non-rejection of man, or disbelief in his rejection. Man is not rejected. In God's eternal purpose it is God Himself who is rejected in His Son. The self-giving of God consists, the giving and sending of His Son is fulfilled, in the fact that He is rejected in order that we might not be rejected. Predestination means that from all eternity God has determined upon man's acquital at His own cost.

6.43 Emil Brunner on Barth's Doctrine of Election

Brunner here reacts against Barth's doctrine of election, by declaring that it amounts to an irresistable imposition of salvation upon humanity. Note especially his analogy of the people in a boat in shallow water. The people in that boat may think that they are in danger of drowning; in reality, they are in no danger at all. See also 6.10; 6.11; 6.30; 6.34; 6.36; 6.42.

Source: Emil Brunner, *The Christian Doctrine of God: Dogmatics*, Vol. 1 (London: Lutterworth Press, 1949), pp. 346–51. Reprinted with the permission of the publisher.

* * *

The monumental presentation of the doctrine of predestination, and that of election in particular, which we find in Karl Barth's *Church Dogmatics*, justifies us in making our own critical estimation of it, in part because it is the most comprehensive discussion of the question in modern theology, but especially because some totally new ideas have been introduced into the discussion of the whole question . . .

The second main article of his doctrine can be expressed as follows: Jesus Christ is the only elect human being. In order to develop this statement further, Barth is obliged to make a third statement: Jesus is "the eternally elect human being," "the pre-existing God–man who, as such, is the eternal ground of all election."

No special proof is required to show that the Bible contains no such doctrine, or that no theologian has ever formulated any theory of this kind. If the eternal pre-existence of the God–man were a fact, then the incarnation could no longer be an *event*. It would no longer be the great miracle of Christmas. In the New Testament, what is new is that the eternal Son of God *became* a human being, and that thereafter, through his resurrection and ascension, humanity has *received* a share of his heavenly glory. Yet according to Barth, all of this is now anticipated, as it were; it is torn out of the sphere of history and set within the pre-temporal sphere, in the pre-existence of the Logos . . .

Karl Barth has been charged with teaching universalism. When he denies this, he is not actually wrong. He knows too much about the not especially illustrious theologians who have maintained this doctrine of *Apokatastasis* in Christian history to be prepared to have himself counted among their number . . . Rather, Barth goes much further. For none of them dared to maintain that through Jesus Christ, everyone – whether believer or non-believer – are saved from the wrath of God and share in redemption through Jesus Christ. But this is precisely what Barth teaches . . . Hell has been blotted out, and condemnation and judgement eliminated. This is not a conclusion *I* have drawn from Barth's statements, but something he has stated himself . . .

There is no doubt that many people today will be gald to hear such a doctrine, and will rejoice that a theologian has finally dared to consign the idea of a final divine judgement, or that someone would finally be "lost," to the rubbish tip. But they cannot dispute one point: that Barth, in making this statement, is in total opposition to the Christian tradition, as well as – and this is of decisive importance – to the clear teaching of the New Testament . . .

Karl Barth, in his transference of the salvation offered to faith to unbelievers, departs from the ground of the biblical revelation, in order to draw a logical conclusion which he finds illuminating. But what is the result? First of all, the result is that the real decision takes place in the objective sphere alone, and not in the subjective sphere. The decision has thus been taken in Jesus Christ – for everyone. It does not matter whether they know it or not, or believe it or not. The main point is that they are saved. They resemble people who seem to be about to sink in a stormy sea. Yet in reality, they are not in a sea in which sinking is a possibility, but in shallow waters in which it is impossible to drown. Only they do not know this. Hence the transition from unbelief to faith is not a transition from "being lost" to "being saved." This transition cannot happen, as it is no longer possible to be lost.

Reinhold Niebuhr on Original Sin   6.44

In his 1939 Gifford Lectures at Edinburgh University, Niebuhr set out his views on the nature and destiny of humanity. By this stage in his career, Niebuhr had gained a reputation as a strong defender of the reality of sin. In the passage reprinted below, Niebuhr explores the notion of original sin, focusing particularly on the issue of how sin can be inevitable, yet still be the responsibility of the individual who sins. See also 6.2; 6.3; 6.12; 6.13; 6.20; 6.39.

Source: Reinhold Niebuhr, The Nature and Destiny of Man, 2 vols (New York: Macmillan, 1941), vol. 1, pp. 256–9; 266–7. Reprinted with the permission of Macmillan College Publishing Company from The Nature and Destiny of Man, vol. 1, by Reinhold Niebuhr. Copyright 1941, © 1964 Charles Scriber's Sons: copyright renewed 1969 Reinhold Niebuhr.

* * *

The Christian doctrine of sin in its classical form offends both rationalists and moralists by maintaining the seemingly absurd position that man sins inevitably and by a fateful necessity, but that he is nevertheless responsible for actions which are prompted by an ineluctable fate. The explicit Scriptural foundation for the doctrine is given in Pauline teaching. On the one hand, St. Paul insists that man's sinful glorification of himself is without excuse . . . and on the other hand, he regards human sin as an inevitable defect, involved in or derived from the sin of the first man . . .

Here is the absurdity in a nutshell. Original sin, which is by definition an inherited corruption, or at least an inevitable one, is nevertheless not to be regarded as belonging to his essential nature and therefore is not outside the realm of human responsibility. Sin is natural for man in the sense that it is universal but not in the sense that it is necessary. Calvin makes this distinction very carefully . . .

Sin is to be regarded as neither a necessity of man's nature nor yet as a pure caprice of his will. It proceeds rather from a defect of the will, for which reason it is not completely deliberate: but since it is the will in which the defect is found, and the will presupposes freedom, the defect cannot be attributed to a taint in man's nature. Here again Calvin is most precise: "Wherefore, as Plato has been deservedly censured for imputing all sins to ignorance, so also we must reject the opinion of those who maintain that all sins proceed from deliberate malice and pravity. For we too much experience how frequently we fall into error even when our intentions are good. Our reason is overwhelmed with deceptions in so many forms." The doctrine of original sin never escapes the logical absurdities in which these words of Calvin abound. Calvin remains within speaking terms of logic by insisting that sin is "an adventitious quality or accident" rather than a necessity. But if this were true it could not be as inevitable as Calvin's own doctrine assumes. Kierkegaard is more correct in his assertion that "sin comes as neither necessity nor accident." Naturally a position which seems so untenable from a logical standpoint has been derided and scorned not only by non-Christian philosophers but by many Christian theologians.

The whole crux of the doctrine of original sin lies in the seeming absurdity of the conception of free-will which underlies it. The Pauline doctrine, as elaborated by Augustine and the Reformers, insists on the one hand that the will of man is enslaved to sin and is incapable of fulfilling God's law. It may be free, declares Augustine, only it is not free to do good . . . Yet on the other hand the same Augustine insists upon the reality of free-will whenever he has cause to fear that the concept of original sin might threaten the idea of human responsibility . . . One could multiply examples in the thought of theologians of the Pauline tradition in which logical consistency is sacrificed in order to maintain on the one hand that the will is free in the sense that man is responsible for his sin, and on the other hand is not free in the sense that he can, of his own will, do nothing but evil . . .

The full complexity of the psychological facts which validate the doctrine of original sin must be analysed, first in terms of the relation of temptation to the inevitability of sin. Such an analysis may make it plain why man sins inevitably, yet without escaping responsibility for his sin. The temptation to sin, as observed previously, lies in the human situation itself. This situation is that man as spirit transcends the temporal and natural process in which he is involved, and also transcends himself. Thus his freedom is the basis of his creativity but it is also his temptation. Since he is involved in the contingencies and necessities of the natural process on the one hand, and since, on the other, he stands outside of them and foresees their caprices and perils, he is anxious. In his anxiety, he seeks to transmute his finiteness into infinity, his weakness into strength, his dependence into independence. He seeks in other words to escape finiteness and weakness by a quantitative rather than qualitative development of his life. The quantitative antithesis of finiteness is infinity. The qualitative possibility of human life is its obedient subjection to the will of God. This possibility is expressed in the words of Jesus: "he that loseth his life for my sake shall find it" (Matthew 10:39).

Daphne Hampson on Feminist Approaches to Sin   6.45

In this perceptive analysis of the nature of sin, the feminist writer Daphne Hampson argues that traditional expositions of sin, such as that found in the writings of Reinhold Niebuhr, are heavily influenced by male understandings of sin. She argues for the need to reconceive the concept of sin in the light of the experience of women, particularly in relation to its individualism and its emphasis on pride. In its place, she proposes approaches to sin which are more faithful to the experience of women. Although Daphne Hampson does not regard herself as a Christian writer, this extract brings together a number of themes which have been of influence within Christian feminist circles since about 1980. See also 2.29; 3.35; 6.44; 6.46.

Source: Daphne Hampson, *Theology and Feminism* (Oxford: Blackwell, 1990), pp. 121–4.

* * *

The doctrine of sin has always been fundamental to theological anthropology. That this is the case may in itself be significant. Human beings have been seen as in apposition to God. God is considered good; humans, by contrast with God, sinful . . . It has also affected . . . the way in which women have been conceived in relation to men. Sin is connected with what is "below" and with our bodily nature; and woman comes to be associated with sexuality. However the primary understanding of sin in the tradition (which has been a male tradition, for theology has been male) has been that sin is in the first instance not sensuality but rather pride. Here again we may think the conceptualization to have fitted a male dynamic; for men have been the ones who have been in a position to be proud.

In my consideration of sin, I shall look at feminist responses to the conceptualization of sin articulated by Reinhold Niebuhr. I turn to the feminist critique of Niebuhr for two reasons. In the first place there has been a concentration of feminist work here. And secondly, Niebuhr's analysis of sin, particularly as developed in his Gifford lectures *The Nature and Destiny of Man*, is arguably the most profound that there has been. The women who have taken issue with Niebuhr (and this includes myself) have trained in theology in the United States where his thought has been influential. The argument is not that Niebuhr's analysis is false, but that it is inapplicable to the situation of all of humanity , while failing to recognize that this is the case.

The setting for Niebuhr's Gifford lectures was Scotland at the outbreak of the Second World War. Europe was faced, in National Socialist Germany, with the most overweening pride (or hubris) of a people in their desire for expansion and their submission of others, which the western world has experienced. Niebuhr's is a multi-faceted analysis, brilliantly interweaving theology with historical, social and psychological insights. Sin he sees in its basic form to be pride, showing convincingly that this has been the major understanding in the western tradition. Sin comes to be, not necessarily but inevitably, in a situation of *Angst*; that anxiety which, having no definite object, consists in a basic disease. In their anxiety human beings are faced with two possibilities. Either they can trust in God; which is what the creator intended – for indeed the anxiety has only arisen through a lack of such trust. Or they fall into sin. Sin can be of two kinds: pride, in which human beings attempt to set themselves up in the place of God, to be gods themselves, subjecting others to their will; or sensuality, in which (rather than having an egotistical sense of self) human beings try to get rid of any sense of themselves and bury themselves in others or the things of this world – for example through the misuse of sexuality.

That Niebuhr's analysis contains deep insights is not in dispute. Indeed feminists might well say that Niebuhr has put his finger on what they find to be so worrying about the male world. He describes a situation in which a man, or a nation, would try to be free of the web of humanity (perhaps through insecurity) and then comes to dominate others. (Again the discussion of the misuse of sexuality as an attempt to escape from self rings true.) But the problem is that of the isolated male who would be free of others. He attempts self-sufficiency at the expense of other life. Women's criticism has thus been twofold. In the first place it is said that this is not a good analysis of the situation in which women find themselves; moreover that women's failings are typically other. Secondly, it is pointed out that Niebuhr (for all that he is concerned with social analysis) has an extraordinarily individuated concept of the human being, who finds himself essentially caught up in competitive relationships.

That Niebuhr (and Tillich also) do not describe what is typically woman's predicament was first elucidated by Valerie Saiving in an article published in 1960, the article which is often taken to mark the beginning of the current wave of feminist theological writing. Saiving writes:

> It is clear that many of the characteristic emphases of contemporary theology . . . its identification of sin with pride, will-to-power, exploitation, self-assertiveness, and the treatment of others as objects rather than persons . . . it is clear that such an analysis of man's dilemma was profoundly responsive and relevant to the concrete facts of modern man's existence . . . As a matter of fact, however, this theology is not adequate to the universal human situation . . . For the temptations of woman *as woman* are not the same as the temptations of man *as man*, and the specifically feminine forms of sin – "feminine" not because they are confined to women or because women are incapable of sinning in other ways but because they are outgrowths of the basic feminine character structure – have a quality which can never be encompassed by such terms as "pride" and "will-to-power." They are better suggested by such items as triviality, distractability, and diffuseness; lack of an organizing center or focus; dependence on others for one's own self-definition; . . . in short, underdevelopment or negation of the self.

One may remark on the fact that Niebuhr, who follows closely the Danish nineteenth-century thinker Søren Kierkegaard in his understanding of the relationship of insecurity, pride and sensuality, does not however take up Kierkegaard's dual articulation of the typically "manly" and "womanly" ways of sinning. Man, says Kierkegaard, would try to be Caesar, whereas woman would be rid of herself. That Kierkegaard's (and Saiving's) analysis is an analysis of women as women are living under patriarchy is of course the case.

Consequently some women have wanted to say that woman's "sin" is – to quote an effective phrase of Judith Plaskow's – "the failure to take responsibility for self-actualization." To name such behaviour "sin" is (as I have discovered when working with groups of women) very effective. For women to hear that it is their right and duty to take themselves seriously, that it matters who they are and what they think, is to turn Christian theology as they have imbibed it upside-down. For it is women largely who have been expected by society to take on board the Christian admonition to be self-effacing. This suggests that the fact that women have had preached to them that self-sacrifice is the message of the gospel has been wholly inappropriate in the situation in which they found themselves. Whether "the failure to take responsibility for self-actualization" should however be called "sin" is another question – as Helen Percy in particular has pointed out to me. If we think of women's typical "failing," as Saiving names them, they can hardly be said (in the way in which this is true of male pride) to be actively destructive of others. Rather have women been destructive of themselves and their own potentialities.

But the feminist criticism is not simply that Niebuhr has described what have been behaviour patterns of men rather than of women. It has seemed to feminist theologians, that in his sense of the individual as highly individuated and "atomic" rather than in relationship to others, Niebuhr has described what is peculiarly a male propensity. When (as I have discovered) it is said by feminists that Niebuhr fails to have a social conception of the human, this may well be misunderstood. For – the response comes back – no theologian more than he has considered the human in society. Of course this is the case. What is being referred to here however is a different level of the word social. Niebuhr sees the human being as monadic rather than as having an essential relationality. In this he is very different from much feminist thought. Very fine work here has been accomplished by Judith Vaughan. Vaughan, in work originally undertaken with Rosemary Ruether, compares Niebuhr's ethics with Ruether's ethics. She shows that their different ethical and political stance relates to a different understanding of the human being. Vaughan, and Ruether, hold what I earlier designated a Marxist–Hegelian perspective. They see persons as caught up in social relationships and believe that the external relations of the self form the understanding which a person has of him or herself. It is from such a position that Vaughan mounts a critique of Niebuhr.

6.46 Mary Hayter on Human Sexuality and the Image of God

The English theologian and writer Mary Hayter here considers the way in which the biblical doctrine of humanity being created in the "image of God" relates to issues of sexuality and gender. In particular, she deals with the issue of the correct relationship between men and women, in the light of the doctrine of creation. See also 3.35; 6.4; 6.5; 6.41; 6.45.

Source: Mary Hayter, The New Eve in Christ (London: SPCK, 1987), pp. 87–92. Used by permission of the publisher.

* * *

We are now in a position to examine specific issues regarding the relation of male and female in God's image. In the past, several deductions have been made from the Genesis passages which seem to me to be based upon misinterpretations of the text. There is need, therefore, for a reappraisal of the biblical material if it is to be used correctly by modern doctrinal scholars in the debate about the role of women in the Church.

First, there has been a persistent tradition which declares that while the "whole man" as male is in God's image, *woman does not participate* in the *Imago Dei*, or that woman is only in the divine image in a *secondary sense*. Diodore of Tarsus, for instance, in his commentary on Genesis, states that woman is not in God's image but is under man's dominion. Again, by "the image of God" in man, John Chrysostom understands Adam's sovereignty over the rest of creation, including woman . . . An unbiased exegesis of Genesis 1:26–27 and 5:1–2 provides no grounds for holding that woman participates in the image of God in a different way from man. It is as false to say that only the male is created in the divine image as it would be to make the same claim for the female . . .

Second, it has been suggested that *originally humanity was sexless or androgynous* and that *the fact of the two sexes was a result of the Fall*. Sexuality in general, and femininity in particular, came to be regarded with fear and suspicion by many Christians. This tallied with some of the motives behind ascetic and monastic movements and the effort to bring man to the level of an angelic, sexless life. Through subversive influences from Gnosticism and Platonic Hellenistic mysticism large sections of the early Church were permeated with the idea that the sex element is something low and unworthy of intelligent man – an idea which, as Emil Brunner points out, has "more or less unconsciously and secretly . . . determined the thought of Christendom down to the present day." A notable twentieth-century spokesman for the view that man's sexual duality is an expression of fallen nature is N. Berdyaev, who refers with approval to the androgynous ideal which he finds in Plato's *Symposium*. As with most supporters of the androgynous ideal, in the end it is not sexuality as such that Berdyaev despises, but femininity. For example, more than a hint of misogyny characterizes the remark that "Man's slavery to sex is slavery to the feminine element, going back to the image of Eve."

I believe that Genesis 1.26–28 provides no evidence to support such views. The subject of this passage, "man," 'adam, is referred to by the collective Hebrew noun for "mankind." Genesis 5:2 confirms that male and female together were named Adam, man, when they were created. In Genesis 5:3, "Adam" is used as a proper name; but this is not the case in Chapter 1, nor in 5:1–2. Therefore, efforts to harmonize the first Creation narrative with the ancient Greek myth of the androgyne or hermaphrodite cannot be sustained . . .

This has important implications for our thinking about the role of women, and their relative position to men in the created order, since it stresses both the unity and the differentiation of the sexes. First, the singular word 'adam with its singular pronoun, "him," 'oto (Genesis 1:27), indicates God's intention for the harmony and community of males and females in their shared humanity and joint participation in the image and likeness of God. Second, sexuality is presented as fundamental to what it means to be human and procreation is the subject of a positive command (Genesis 1:28); the differentiation between the sexes and the means of procreation were not retrograde steps away from an ideal androgyny. This accords with the positive value ascribed to marriage and sexual love in other parts of the Old Testament. For the Hebrews reproduction, and so sexual life, too, are a special gift to all living creatures. Third, since man and woman were created together, with no hint of temporal or ontological superiority, the difference between the sexes cannot be said to affect their equal standing before God and before one another. Sexual differentiation does not mean hierarchy. There is no sexual stereotyping of roles regarding procreation and dominion here; male and female are blessed together and together are commanded to "fill the earth and subdue it" (Genesis 1:28); neither sex is given dominion over the other. If there is any relationship between the image of God and dominion it must be noted that the record ascribes the image of God to man and woman indiscriminately.

Thus, Genesis 1:26–28 does away with any justification for the view that sexuality resulted from sinfulness. Furthermore, by stating that men and women were together created after God's image, the passage forbids us to hold the female half of the human race in contempt as inferior, or in some way closer to the animals, or as needing redemption in the form of a transformation of feminine nature into the "more noble" spirituality of the masculine or the asexual.

Partly in reaction against the low view of sexuality and theories of divine androgyny, and partly as a result of a distinctive exegesis of the Genesis material, a *third* approach to the relation of male and female in God's image has been to say that human *sexuality is part of what it means to be like God.* It must now be asked, therefore, whether or not the fact of the two sexes in humankind tells us anything about the deity . . . Some people have asserted that the use of divine plurals in Genesis 1 . . . and the subsequent creation of mankind as male and female indicate the presence of sexuality in the Godhead. It has been maintained that, in common with the Canaanite divinization of sex, the Hebrew believed that the human capacity for reproduction was a means by which man could become aware of kinship with

God and gain access to divine power. The employment of divine plurals by
Old Testament writers poses a problem with which exegetes have frequently
wrestled. It is beyond the scope of this study to evaluate each of the possible interpretations, but the one which bears directly upon the subject of
divine and human sexuality must be taken into account here. Is it possible
that the divine plural expresses a Hebrew belief in the sexual duality of the
Godhead? And is it true to say that the *Imago Dei* resides in human sexual
polarity?

According to Karl Barth, the basis of the *Imago Dei* doctrine is to be found
in the relationship between man and woman, particularly in the marriage
relationship: "By the divine likeness of man in Genesis 1:27–28 there is
understood the fact that God created them male and female, corresponding
to the fact that God himself exists in relationship and not in isolation." This
definition has been much criticized by other scholars ... To such scholars it
is preferable to see the *Imago* as in some sense finding its existential expression in the interrelatedness of man with others, regardless of whether the
"other" is male or female. The seat of the image is then the "person" as
distinguished from the solipsist individual.

Again, it may be said that Barth's stress upon the importance of marriage
as the "crucial expression" of human I – Thou relationships is more the
result of a reading into the text of his own ideas than of objective Old
Testament exegesis. Although it was probably against Barth's intentions,
his hypothesis can lead to the view that *only* in marriage or at least through
sexual experience does a person become fully human. Vital as marriage
might be in Barthian doctrinal schemata, Genesis 1 itself treats of sexuality
in general and is not concerned first and foremost with the institution of
marriage.

It may be justifiable to say that the use of divine plurals for God, such as
the term *'elohim*, shows that the fullness of deity is comprehended in Yahweh.
Whatever the origin of this practice, the Old Testament usage may be interpreted in an inclusive sense: Yahweh, as *'elohim*, embraces the whole range
of divinity, including any facets of masculinity or femininity which may
legitimately be predicated of deity. Above and beyond the feminist term
God/Goddess, the term *'elohim* as applied to Yahweh can denote that the
God of Israel incorporates and transcends masculinity and femininity. Thus,
John Macquarrie believes that if the image of God is represented by male
and female, then:

> This implies that already in the divine Being there must be, though in an
> eminent way beyond what we can conceive, whatever is affirmative in sexual-
> ity and sociality, in masculinity and femininity ... God transcends the distinc-
> tion of sex, but he does this not by sheer exclusion, but by prefiguring whatever
> is of value in sexuality on an altogether higher level.

Such a sensitive and carefully worded statement marks the limit to which
we may go in making deductions about sexuality in God from Genesis
1:26–27 and 5:1–2. By contrast, when Frazer declares that we gather from

Genesis 1 "that the distinction of the sexes, which is characteristic of humanity, is shared also by the divinity," he seems to be reading back human male- and female-ness on to God. As James Barr reminds us, the question behind Genesis 1:26–28 is not so such "What is God like?" but "What is man like?" The Priestly theologian "is saying not primarily that God's likeness is man, but that man is in a relation of likeness to God." It is incorrect therefore, to state bluntly that the *Imago* concept and the divine plurals in Genesis are illustrative of a sexual distinction in God.

Study Questions to Chapter 6

What does it mean to say that we are "made in the image of God"?

On the basis of the readings provided, what are the main features of Pelagianism?

In what way do Luther and Calvin link faith to the promises of God?

In what way does Karl Barth's doctrine of predestination differ from that of John Calvin? And for what reasons did Emil Brunner criticize Barth's understanding of the issue?

What is meant by "grace"?

Would John Wesley have agreed with John Calvin's understanding of the nature of justification? Or would he have been more sympathetic to the view of the Council of Trent?

7 The Church

Ecclesiology is the section of Christian theology dealing with the nature and tasks of the church (Greek: *ekklēsia*). Once more, major debates on the issue erupted in the patristic and Reformation period. A landmark debate concerning the church broke out in the fourth century, centering on the churches of North Africa. Both Augustine and his Donatist opponents saw themselves as safeguarding the heritage of the martyr Cyprian of Carthage. However, they chose to emphasize different aspects of that heritage. Augustine stressed the priority of Christ as redeemer over his church and its ministers, while the Donatists emphasized the need for personal purity of church members and ministers. At the time of the Reformation, a related debate broke out. However, the main debate associated with the Reformation centered on the identifying characteristics of a church.

The two Study Panels for this chapter focus on themes which have been dominant within the Christian tradition: the nature of catholicity; and the distinguishing marks of a truly Christian church.

STUDY PANEL 19

The Catholicity of the Church

7.3   Cyprian of Carthage on the Unity of the Church
7.5   Cyril of Jerusalem on the Catholicity of the Church
7.7   Thomas Aquinas on the Catholicity of the Church
7.8   Jan Hus on the Church
7.9   Martin Luther on the Marks of the Church
7.11   Philip Melanchthon on the Nature of Catholicity
7.14   John Calvin on the Marks of the Church
7.16   The Westminster Confession of Faith on the Church
7.20   John D. Zizoulas on Local and Universal Churches
7.22   Avery Dulles on the Meanings of "Catholicity"

STUDY PANEL 20

The Marks of the Church

7.2   Origen on the Church and Salvation
7.3   Cyprian of Carthage on the Unity of the Church
7.5   Cyril of Jerusalem on the Catholicity of the Church
7.9   Martin Luther on the Marks of the Church
7.14   John Calvin on the Marks of the Church
7.15   Richard Hooker on the Purity of the Church
7.19   The Barmen Confession on the Identity of the Church
7.20   John D. Zizoulas on Local and Universal Churches
7.21   Leonardo Boff on the Nature of Local Churches

The doctrine of the church continues to be an area of discussion today, with particular emphasis being placed upon the role and tasks of local churches.

7.1 Irenaeus on the Function of the Church

In this passage, which dates from the late second century, Irenaeus stresses the importance of the church as the living body which has been entrusted with the Christian tradition and proclamation. Note the emphasis placed upon the historic institution of the church, which is seen as a living body within which the proper interpretation of Scripture is kept alive. See also 2.2; 2.5.

Source: *adversus haereses*, IV.xxxiii.8; in *Sources Chrétiennes*, vol. 100, ed. A. Rousseau (Paris: Cerf, 1965), 818.137–820.148.

* * *

True knowledge is the teaching of the Apostles, the order of the Church as established from the earliest times throughout the world, and the distinctive stamp (*character*) of the body of Christ, passed down through the succession of bishops in charge of the church in each place, which has come down to our own time, safeguarded without any spurious writings by the most complete exposition [i.e., the Creed], received without addition or subtraction; the reading of the Scriptures without falsification; and their consistent and careful exposition, avoiding danger and blasphemy; and the special gift of love, which is more precious than knowledge, more glorious than prophecy, and which surpasses all other spiritual gifts.

7.2 Origen on the Church and Salvation

In what follows, Origen comments on the reference to Rahab at Joshua 2, seeing in the promise that those inside her house would be saved a prophecy or type of the Christian church. Only those inside the house of God will be saved. The scarlet thread hung in the window of the prostitute Rahab's house, by which it was identified, is seen as anticipating the identification of the house of God by the scarlet sign of the blood of Christ. See also 2.3; 2.8; 2.11; 7.3; 8.7.

Source: *Homilia in Iesu Nave*, III, 5; in J. P. Migne, *Patrologia Graeca* 12.841B–842B.

* * *

If anyone wishes to be saved, let them come to this house, just as they once came to that of the prostitute. If anyone of that people wished to be saved, they could come to that house, and they could have salvation as a result. Let them come to this house where the blood of Christ is a sign of redemption. For that blood was for condemnation among those who said, "His blood be on us and on our children" (Matthew 27:25). Jesus was "for the fall and resurrection of many" (Luke 2:34) and therefore in respect of those who "speak against his sign" his blood is effective for punishment, but effective for salvation in the case of believers. Let no one therefore be persuaded or deceived: outside this house, that is, outside the Church, no one is saved (*extra hanc domum, id est extra ecclesiam nemo salvatur*) . . . The sign of salvation was given through the window because Christ by his incarnation gave us the sight of the light of godhead as it were through a window; that all may attain salvation by that sign who shall be found in the house of her who once was a harlot, being made clean by water and the Holy Spirit, and by the blood of our Lord and Saviour Jesus Christ, to whom be glory and power for ever.

Cyprian of Carthage on the Unity of the Church

7.3

In this discussion of the unity of the church, written in 251, Cyprian stresses the indivisibility of the catholic church, and its essential role in obtaining salvation. Salvation is not possible outside the church. It is not possible to have God as a father unless you also have the church as your mother. See also 7.2; 8.3; 8.7; 8.8.

Source: *de catholicae ecclesiae unitate*, 5–7; in *Corpus Christianorum: Series Latina*, vol. 3, ed. M. Bévenot (Turnholt: Brepols, 1972), 252.117–254.176.

* * *

This unity we ought to hold and preserve, especially the bishops who preside in the Church, so that we may demonstrate that the episcopate itself is united and undivided. Let no one deceive the brotherhood (*fraternitas*) with falsehood or corrupt our faith in the truth by faithless transgression. The episcopate is one, and each [individual member] has a part in the whole. The Church is one, and by her fertility she has extended by degree into many. In the same way, the sun has many rays, but a single light; a tree has many branches but a single trunk resting on a deep root; and many streams flow out from a single source. However many may spread out from the source, it retains its unity. Cut off a ray from the orb of the sun; the unity of light cannot be divided. Break off a branch from the tree, and the broken branch cannot come into bud. Sever the stream from its source, and the severed section will dry up. So it is also with the Church. She is flooded with the light of the Lord, and extends her rays over all the globe. Yet it is the one light which is diffused everywhere, without breaking up the unity of the body. She stretches forth her branches over the whole earth in rich abundance; she spreads widely her flowing streams. Yet there is but one head, one source, one mother, abounding in the increase of her fruitfulness. We are born of her womb, we are nourished by her milk, and we are given life from her breath.

The bride of Christ cannot be made an adulteress; she is undefiled and chaste. She has one home, and guards with virtuous chastity the sanctity of one chamber. She serves us for God, who enrols into his Kingdom the children to whom she gives birth. Anyone who cuts themselves off from the Church and is joined to an adulteress is separated from the promises of the Church, and anyone who leaves the Church of Christ behind cannot benefit from the rewards of Christ. Such people are strangers, outcasts, and enemies. You cannot have God as father unless you have the Church as mother (*Habere iam non potest Deum patrem qui ecclesiam non habet matrem*) . . .

This sacrament of unity, this inseparable bond of peace, is shown in the gospel when the robe of the Lord Jesus Christ was neither divided at all or torn, but they cast lots for the clothing of Christ . . . so the clothing was received whole and the robe was taken unspoilt and undivided . . . That garment signifies the unity which comes "from the part above," that is, from heaven and from the Father, a unity which could not be torn at all by those who received and possessed it, but it was taken individed in its unbreakable entirety. Anyone who rends and divides the Church of Christ cannot possess the clothing of Christ (*possidere non potest indumentum Christi qui scindit et dividit ecclesiam Christi*).

7.4   Petilian of Citra on the Purity of Ministers

Petilian, the Donatist bishop of Citra, circulated a letter to his priests warning against the moral impurity and doctrinal errors of the catholic church. Augustine's reply, dated 401, led Petilian to write against Augustine in more detail. In this letter, dating from 402, from which Augustine quotes extracts, Petilian sets out fully the Donatist insistence that the validity of the sacraments is totally dependent upon the moral worthiness of those who administer them. Petilian's words are included within citation marks within Augustine's text. See also 7.15.

Source: Letter to Augustine; in Augustine, *contra litteras Petiliani*, III.lii.64; in *Corpus Scriptorum Ecclesiasticorum Latinorum*, vol. 52, ed. M. Petschenig (Vienna: Tempsky, 1909), pp. 462–3.

* * *

"What we look for is the conscience" [Petilian] says, "of the one who gives [the sacraments], giving in holiness, to cleanse the conscience of the one who receives. For anyone who knowingly receives 'faith' from the faithless does not receive faith, but guilt." And he will then go on to say: "So how do you test this? For everything consists of an origin" he says, "and a root; if it does not possess something as its head, it is nothing. Nor can anything truly receive a second birth, unless it is born again (*reneneretur*) from good seed."

7.5   Cyril of Jerusalem on the Catholicity of the Church

In this lecture, Cyril argues that the church may be referred to as "catholic" on account of the universality of its teaching and relevance, and also to distinguish it from the sectarian gatherings of heretics. See also 7.7; 7.11; 7.22.

Source: *Catechetical Lecture* XVIII, 23, 26; in J. P. Migne, *Patrologia Graeca*, 33.1044B; 1048A–B.

* * *

The church is thus called "catholic" because it is spread throughout the entire inhabited world (*oikoumenē*), from one end to the other, and because it teaches in its totality (*katholikōs*) and without leaving anything out every doctrine which people need to know relating to things visible and invisible, whether in heaven and earth. It is also called "catholic" because it brings to obedience every sort of person – whether rulers or their subjects, the educated and the unlearned. It also makes available a universal (*katholikōs*) remedy and cure to every kind of sin, whether in body or in soul, and contains within itself every kind of virtue . . . Now the word "church" has different senses. It can refer to the crowd which filled the theatre at Ephesus (Acts 19:41) . . . or to gatherings of heretics . . . And because of this variation in the use of the word "church," the article of faith "and in one holy catholic church" has been given to you, so that you can steer clear of [the heretics'] meetings and remain within the holy catholic church within which you have been born again. If you ever have cause to visit a strange town, do not ask simply . . . "Where is the church?" Instead, ask: "Where is the *catholic* church?" This is the distinctive name of this, the holy church and mother of us all. She is the bride of our Lord Jesus Christ, the only-begotten Son of God.

Leo the Great on Ministry within the Church

7.6

Writing at the middle of the fifth century, Leo I affirms that all Christian believers are sharers in the priestly office of Christ, anticipating aspects of the Reformation doctrine of the priesthood of all believers. See also 7.10.

Source: *Sermo* 95, de *natali ipsius*; in *Sources Chrétiennes*, vol. 200, ed. Dom René Dolle (Paris: Cerf, 1973), p. 266. Note that this sermon is numbered IV.1 in the Migne edition.

* * *

The sign of the cross makes all those who are born again in Christ kings, and the anointing of the Holy Spirit consecrates them all as priests. As a result, apart from the particular service of our ministry, all spiritual and rational Christians are recognized as members of this royal people and sharers in the priestly office [of Christ]. What is there that is as royal for a soul as to govern the body in obedience to God? And what is there that is as priestly as to dedicate a pure conscience to the Lord, and to offer the unstained offerings of devotion (*immaculatas pietatis hostias*) on the altar of the heart?

7.7   Thomas Aquinas on the Catholicity of the Church

In the course of his exposition of the articles of the Apostles' Creed, Aquinas deals with the concept of "catholicity," identifying three key elements of the notion. See also 7.5; 7.11; 7.22.

Source: In Symbolum Apostolorum, 9; in S. Thomae Aquinitatis Opera Omnia, vol. 6., ed. R. Busa (Holzboog: Frommann, 1980), p. 20.

* * *

Concerning the third point, it is known that the church is catholic, i.e., universal, first with respect to place, because it is throughout the entire world (*per totum mundum*), against the Donatists. See Romans 1:8: "Your faith is proclaimed in all the world"; Mark 16:15: "Go into all the world and preach the gospel to the whole creation." In ancient times, God was known only in Judea, but now throughout the entire world. This church, moreover, has three parts. One is on earth, another is in heaven, and the third is in purgatory. Secondly, the church is universal with respect to the condition of people, because no one is rejected, whether master or slave, male or female. See Galatians 3:28: "There is neither male nor female." Thirdly, it is universal with respect to time. For some have said that the church should last until a certain time, but this is false, because this church began from the time of Abel and will last to the end of the world. See Matthew 28:20: "And I am with you always, to the close of the age." And after the close of the age it will remain in heaven.

7.8   Jan Hus on the Church

In his treatise on the church, written in Latin in 1413, Hus offers three definitions of the church. The first corresponds to the Donatist idea of the church as a body of perfect saints, the second to Augustine's concept of a "mixed body" of saints and sinners, and the third to a concept of the church as it will be when it is purified by God on the last day. Hus, who clearly prefers this third approach, appears to have derived it from the writings of John Wycliffe, from which this section borrows heavily. See also 7.15; 7.16; 7.17.

Source: Tractatus de ecclesia, 7; in Tractatus de ecclesia, ed. S. Harison Thomson (Cambridge: Heffer, 1956), pp. 44–5.

* * *

[In response to what has just been said], we may go beyond what is normally reckoned to be the church, and say that the church may be defined in three ways. First, the church is defined as the congregation or convocation of the faithful (*congregacio vel convocacio fidelium*), the faithful, understood as those who are faithful in the sense of being righteous for the present. According to this definition those who are reprobate, yet who possess grace for the present, do belong in the church. But such a church is not the mystical body of Christ nor the holy catholic church nor any part of it. The second definition understands the church to contain a mixture of those who are reprobate, who possess grace and righteousness only for the present, and those who are truly predestined. This church coincides partially but not totally with the holy church of God. It is called "mixed" (*mixtim*) because it contains both grain and chaff, wheat and weeds, just as the kingdom of heaven is like a net cast into the sea which gathers up fish of all kinds, and the kingdom of heaven is like the ten virgins, five of whom were foolish and five of whom were wise ...

But the third definition understands the church as the whole convocation of those who are predestined, regardless of whether or not they are in grace or righteousness for the present. This was the definition used by the Apostle Paul when he said, "Christ loved the Church and gave Himself up for her that he might sanctify her by the washing of water with the word, that the Church might be presented before him without spot or wrinkle or any such thing, that she might be holy and without blemish" (Ephesians 5:25–7).

Martin Luther on the Marks of the Church 7.9

In this treatise, first published in early modern German in 1539, Luther lays down seven distinguishing marks of a true Christian church, including the preaching and hearing of the word of God; the true Christian sacraments of baptism and the sacrament of the altar; the office of the keys and ministry; proper public worship; and the bearing of the cross. The first of these is clearly the most important, and is here explored in some detail. See also 7.8; 7.12; 7.14.

Source: *On the Councils and the Church (1539)*; in *D. Martin Luthers Werke: Kritische Gesamtausgabe*, vol. 50 (Weimar: Böhlau, 1914), 628.29–630.2.

* * *

First, this holy Christian people (*dis Christlich heilig Volck*) is to be recognized as having possession of the holy word of God, even if all do not possess it in equal measure, as St. Paul says (1 Corinthians 3:12–14). Some possess it completely purely, others not so purely. Those who possess it purely are called those who "build on the foundation with gold, silver, and precious stones"; those who do not possess it purely are those who "build on the foundation with wood, hay, and straw," and yet will be saved through fire. More than enough was said about this above. This is the main thing, and the most holy thing of all, by reason of which the Christian people are called holy; for God's word is holy and sanctifies everything it connects with; it is indeed the very holiness of God (Romans 1:16), "It is the power of God for salvation to every one who has faith," and 1 Timothy 4:5, "Everything is consecrated by the word of God and prayer." For the Holy Spirit himself administers it and anoints or sanctifies the Christian church with it, and not with the pope's chrism, with which he anoints or consecrates fingers, clothes, cloaks, chalices, and stones. These objects will never teach one to love God, to believe, to praise, or to be pious. They may adorn this bag of maggots (*madensack*), but afterward they fall apart and decay, along with the chrism and whatever holiness it contains, and the bag of maggots itself.

Yet this holy thing (*heiligthum*) is the true holy thing, the true anointing that anoints with eternal life, even though you may not have a papal crown or a bishop's hat, but will die bare and naked, just like children (as we all are), who are baptized naked and without any such adornment. But we are speaking of the external word, preached orally by people like you and me, for this is what Christ left behind as an external sign (*eusserlich zeichen*), by which his church, or his Christian people in the world, should be recognized. We also speak of this external word as it is sincerely believed and openly confessed before the world, as Christ says, "Every one who acknowledges me before people, I also will acknowledge before my Father and his angels" (Matthew 10:32). There are many who know it in their hearts, but will not profess it openly. Many possess it, but do not believe in it or act on it, for the number of those who believe in and act on it is small. The parable of the seed (Matthew 13:4–8) says that three sections of the field receive and contain the seed, but only the fourth section, the fine and good soil, bears fruit with patience.

Now, anywhere you hear or see such a word preached, believed, confessed, and acted upon (*Wo du nu solch wort hoerest odder sihest predigen, gleuben, bekennen und darnach thun*), do not doubt that the true *ecclesia sancta catholica*, a "holy Christian people" must be there, even though there are very few of them. For God's word "shall not return empty," (Isaiah 55:11), but must possess at least a fourth or a part of the field. And even if there were no other sign than this alone, it would be enough to prove that a holy Christian people must exist there, for God's word cannot be without God's people and conversely, God's people cannot be without God's word. For who would preach the word, or hear it preached, if there were no people of God? And what could or would God's people believe, if there were no word of God?

7.10 Martin Luther on Priests and Laity

In this major reforming treatise, written in early modern German in 1520, Luther argues that there is no fundamental distinction in status between priests and laity. All Christians are priests by virtue of their baptism, faith, and the gospel – a doctrine which is often referred to as the "priesthood of all believers." The only distinction that can be recognized between them relates to the different "office" or "function" (*ampt*) and "work" or "responsibility" (*werck*) with which they are entrusted. Notice that Luther is quite clear that, once priests retire or are dismissed, they revert to the role of lay people. See also 7.6.

Source: *Appeal to the German Nobility* (1520); in *D. Martin Luthers Werke: Kritische Gesamtausgabe*, vol. 6 (Weimar: Böhlau, 1888), 406.21–408.30.

* * *

The Romanists have very cunningly built three walls around themselves, preventing any reformation. As a result, the whole of Christianity has fallen grievously. In the first place, when they have been pressed by the secular authorities, they have laid down laws which declare that the secular authority (*weltlicher gewalt*) has no rights over them; in fact, quite the reverse – the spiritual power has authority over the secular. In the second place, when someone tries to correct them on the basis of Holy Scripture, they lay down that nobody except the Pope can interpret Scripture. And in the third place, when someone threatens them with a Council, they protest that nobody can convene a Council, except the Pope . . .

Let us first assault the first wall. It is an invention that the Pope, bishop, priests and monks are called "the spiritual estate" (*geistlich stand*), while princes, lords, craftsmen and farmers are called "the secular estate" (*weltlich stand*). This is a spurious idea, and nobody should fear it for the following reason. All Christians truly belong to the spiritual estate, and there is no difference among them apart from their office (*ampt*) . . . We all have one baptism, one gospel, one faith, and are all alike Christians, in that it is baptism, gospel, and faith which alone make us spiritual and a Christian people . . . We are all consecrated priests through baptism, as St. Peter says: "You are a royal priesthood and a priestly kingdom" (1 Peter 2:9) . . .

So a bishop's consecration is nothing other than this: in the place and stead of the whole congregation (*der gantzen samlung*), who all alike have the same power, he takes a person and authorizes him to exercise this power on behalf of the others . . .

Since the secular power has been baptized with this same baptism, and has the same faith and the same gospel as the remainder of us, we must concede that they are priests and bishops, and most accept their office as one which has a lawful and useful place in the Christian community (*gemeyne*) . . . Therefore someone who bears the status of a priest (*ein priester stand*) is nothing other than an officeholder (*amptman*). He takes priority for as long as he holds this office; when he is deposed, he becomes a peasant or citizen like all the others. It is thus most true that a priest is never a priest when he has been deposed. But now the Romanists have invented the idea of *characteres indelebiles*, and prattle on about a deposed priest being different from an ordinary lay person . . .

It follows from this that there is no basic true difference between lay people, priests, princes and bishops, between the spiritual and the secular, except for their office and work (*den des ampts odder wercks halben*) and not on the basis of their status (*stand*). All are of the spiritual estate, and all are truly priests, bishops, and popes, although they are not the same in terms of their individual work.

7.11 Philip Melanchthon on the Nature of Catholicity

In this treatise on the use of the word "catholic," Melanchthon emphasizes the importance of doctrinal correctness as its defining element. Although the church may be dispersed throughout the world, it nevertheless remains universally faithful to the same teaching. See also 7.5; 7.7; 7.22.

Source: de appellatione ecclesiae catholicae; in Corpus Reformatorum, vol. 24, ed. G. Baum, E. Cunitz, and E. Reuss (Braunschweig: Schwetschke, 1871), cols 397–9.

* * *

What does "catholic" mean? It means the same as universal. *Kath'holou* means "universally" and "in general" ... Why is this term added in the article of the creed, so that the church is called catholic? Because it is an assembly dispersed throughout the whole world and because its members, wherever they are, and however separated in place, accept and externally profess one and the same utterance or true doctrine throughout all ages from the beginning until the very end ... It is one thing to be called catholic, something else to be catholic in reality. Those are truly called catholic who accept the doctrine of the truly catholic church, i.e., that which is supported by the witness of all time, of all ages, which believes what the prophets and apostles taught, and which does not tolerate factions, heresies, and heretical assemblies. We must all be catholic, i.e., accept this word which the rightly-thinking church holds, separate from, and unentangled with, those sects which oppose that word.

7.12 Sebastian Franck on the True Church

This letter was originally written in Latin in 1531; only fragments of the Latin original remain. This translation is based on the original Latin text, rather than the later German or Dutch translations. In this letter, Franck sets out the characteristic radical view that the true church ceased to exist after the apostles. His frequent reference to "external things (*externa*)" is a reference to external ceremonies, including the sacraments, which he regards as being "fallen (*lapsus*)." The true church will only come into being at the end of time, when Christ returns in glory to gather the scattered people of his church into his kingdom. Until then, the true church will remain concealed. See also 7.4; 7.9; 7.13; 7.14; 7.16; 7.17.

Source: Letter to John Campanus, 1531; in B. Becker, "Fragment van Francks latijnse brief aan Campanus," *Nederlands Archief voor Kerkgeschiedenis*, 46 (1964–5), pp. 197–205; extract cited at pp. 201–4. Only part of this letter exists in its original Latin; for the complete letter in German and Dutch translation, see *Quellen zur Geschichte der Täufer*, vol. 7, ed. M. Krebs and H. G. Rott (Gütersloh: Mohn, 1959), pp. 301–25.

* * *

I maintain, against all the doctors, that all external things which were in use in the church of the apostles have been abolished (*abrogata*), and none of them are to be restored or reinstituted, even though they have gone beyond their authorization or calling and attempted to restore these fallen sacraments (*lapsa sacramenta*). For the church will remain scattered among the heathen until the end of the world. Indeed, the Antichrist and his church will only be defeated and swept away at the coming of Christ, who will gather together in his kingdom Israel, which has been scattered to the four corners of the world . . . The works [of those who understood this] have been suppressed as godless heresies and rantings, and pride of place has instead been given to foolish Ambrose, Augustine, Jerome, Gregory – of whom not even one knew Christ, nor was sent by God to teach. But rather all were and shall remain the apostles of Antichrist . . . Since experience teaches us that the power of the churches and all external things have fallen into decay, and that this church is dispersed among the heathen, it is my definite opinion that no persons on earth (unless they have received a personal divine call to do so) can gather this dispersed church together again or bring its concealed rites (*obruta symbola*) back into the light again . . . The external things of the church ought not to be reestablished unless Christ himself commands it.

The First Helvetic Confession on the Nature of the Church

7.13

The First Helvetic Confession, which was written in Swiss-German in 1536, set out an early Reformed view of the church, which placed emphasis on the importance of outward signs of church ordering and government. See also 7.14; 7.16; 7.17.

Source: The First Helvetic Confession, 1536, article 14; in E. F. K. Müller (ed.), *Die Bekenntnisschriften der reformierten Kirche* (Leipzig: Böhme, 1903), 101.25–37.

* * *

A holy, universal Church (*ein heylige allgemeine kilchen*) is, we affirm, built and gathered together from living stones built upon this living rock [Christ]. It is the fellowship and congregation of all saints which is Christ's bride and spouse, and which He washes with His blood and finally presents to the Father without blemish or any stain. And although this Church and congregation of Christ (*dise kilchen und samlung Christi*) is only open and known to God's eyes, yet it is not only known but also gathered and built up by visible signs, rites and ordinances, which Christ himself has instituted and appointed by the Word of God as a universal, public and orderly discipline. Without these marks (speaking generally and without a special permission revealed by God) no one is numbered with this Church.

7.14 John Calvin on the Marks of the Church

Calvin here defines the essential features, or "marks," of the true church as the preaching of the Word of God, and the proper administration of the sacraments. A degree of failure or diversity on other matters may be permitted, providing that these two essential features are present. See also 7.15; 7.16; 7.17.

Source: *Institutes*, IV.i.9–10; in *Joannis Calvini: Opera Selecta*, ed. P. Barth and W. Niesel, vol. 5 (Munich: Kaiser Verlag, 1936), 13.24–16.31.

* * *

Wherever we see the Word of God purely preached and listened to, and the sacraments administered according to Christ's institution, it is in no way to be doubted that a church of God exists. For his promise cannot fail: "Wherever two or three are gathered in my name, there I am in the midst of them" (Matthew 18:20) . . . If the ministry has the Word and honors it, if it has the administration of the sacraments, it deserves without doubt to be held and considered a church. For it is certain that such things are not without fruit. In this way the unity of the universal church is preserved, which diabolical spirits have always tried to tear apart; and we do not deny authority to those lawful assemblies which have been set up in accordance with the opportunities of different places in mind (*pro locorum opportunitate distributi sunt*).

We have identified that the distinguishing marks of the church are the preaching of the Word and the observance of the sacraments. These can never happen without bringing forth fruit and prospering through God's blessing. I do not say that wherever the Word is preached there will be immediate results, but that wherever it is received and takes root (*statam habere sedem*), it shows its effectiveness. When the preaching of the gospel is reverently heard and the sacraments are not neglected, there for the time being no false or ambiguous form (*facies*) of the church is seen; and no one is permitted to ignore its authority, flout its warnings, resist its counsels, or make light of its chastisements – much less to break away from it and wreck its unity. For the Lord values the fellowship of his church so highly that all those who arrogantly leave any Christian society (provided that it holds fast to the true ministry of Word and sacraments) are regarded by him as deserters. He so values the authority of the church that when it is violated he believes that his own authority has been diminished . . .

When we say that the pure ministry of the Word and pure mode of celebrating the sacraments are a sufficient pledge and guarantee by which we may recognize as a church any society, we mean where both these marks exist, it is not to be rejected, even if it is riddled with faults in other respects (*etiamsi multis alioqui vitiis scateat*). What is more, some shortcoming may find its way into the administration of either doctrine or sacraments, but this ought not to estrange us from communion with this church. For not all articles of true doctrine are of equal weight. Some are so necessary to know that they should be certain and unquestioned by everyone as proper to religion, such as: God is one; Christ is God and the Son of God; our salvation rests in God's mercy; and the like. There are other [articles of doctrine] disputed among the churches which still do not break the unity of faith . . . I am not condoning error, no matter how insignificant it may be, nor do I wish to encourage it. But I am saying that we should not desert a church on account of some minor disagreement (*dissensiuncula*), if it upholds sound doctrine over the essentials of piety, and maintains the use of the sacraments established by the Lord.

Richard Hooker on the Purity of the Church

7.15

In this passage, published in 1594, the English writer Richard Hooker defends an Augustinian view of the visible church, which he distinguished from the "mystical" or invisible church. Hooker adopts a series of biblical images used originally by Augustine (such as the net with a variety of fish, and the field in which both wheat and "tares" (an older English word for "weeds") grew, to bring out the mixed character of the visible church. For this reason, Hooker insists that perfect holiness of life is not a "mark" or defining characteristic of the church, which is defined instead by its doctrine and sacraments. See also 7.4; 7.9; 7.14.

Source: *Laws of Ecclesiastical Polity*. III.i.7–8; in Richard Hooker, *Works*, ed. J. Keble, vol. 1, 3rd edn (Oxford: Oxford University Press, 1845), pp. 342–3.

* * *

7. . . . We speak now of the visible Church, whose children are signed with this mark, "One Lord, one Faith, one Baptism." In whomsoever these things are, the Church doth acknowledge them for her children; them only she holdeth for aliens and strangers, in whom these things are not found. For want of these it is that Saracens, Jews and Infidels are excluded out of the bounds of the Church. Others we may not deny to be of the visible Church, as long as these things are not wanting in them. For apparent it is, that all men are of necessity either Christians or not Christians. If by external profession they be Christians, then are they of the visible Church of Christ: and Christians by external profession they are all, whose mark of recognizance hath in it those things which we have mentioned, yea, although they be impious idolaters, wicked heretics, persons excommunicable, yea, and cast out for notious improbity. Such withal we deny not to be the imps and limbs of Satan, even as long as they continue such.

8. Is it then possible, that the selfsame men should belong to the synagogue of Satan and to the Church of Jesus Christ? Unto that Church which is his mystical body, not possible; because that body consisteth of none but ony true Israelites, true sons of Abraham, true servants and saints of God. Howbeit of the visible body and Church of Jesus Christ those may be and oftentimes are, in respect of the main parts of their outward profession,

who in regard of their inward disposition of mind, yea, of external conversation, yea, even of some parts of their very profession, are most worthily hateful in the sight of God himself, and in the eyes of the sounder part of the visible Church most execrable. Our Saviour therefore compareth the kingdom of heaven to a net, whereunto all which cometh neither is nor seemeth fish (Matthew 13:47): his Church he compareth to a field, where tares manifestly known and seen by all men do grow intermingled with good corn (Matthew 13:24), and even so shall continue till the final consummation of the world. God hath ever and ever shall have some Church visible upon earth. When the people of God worshipped the calf in the wilderness, when they adored the brazen serpent (2 Kings 18:4), when they bowed their knees to Baal, when they burned incense and offered sacrifice unto idols . . . Howbeit retaining the law of God and the holy seal of his covenant, and sheep of his visible flock they continued even in the depth of their disobedience and rebellion.

7.16 The Westminster Confession of Faith on the Church

This important Reformed Confession of Faith, drawn up in London in 1643, sets out a Reformed view of the church, which makes a distinction between the "invisible" and "visible" church. Note how the individual "particular churches" are to be judged in terms of their doctrine and sacraments, rather than the morals of their members. See also 7.4; 7.9; 7.14; 7.15; 7.17.

Source: Westminster Confession, XXV, 1–5; in E. F. K. Müller (ed.), *Die Bekenntnisschriften der reformierten Kirche* (Leipzig: Böhme, 1903), 597.28–599.4.

* * *

The catholic or universal church, which is invisible, consists of the whole number of the elect, that have been, are, or shall be gathered into one, under Christ the head thereof . . . The visible church, which is also catholic or universal under the gospel (not confined to one nation as before under the law), consists of all those throughout the world that profess the true religion, together with their children . . . Unto this catholic visible church, Christ hath given the ministry, oracles, and ordinances of God, for the gathering and perfecting of the saints in this life, to the end of the world; and doth by his own presence and Spirit, according to his promise, make them effectual thereunto . . . Particular churches, which are members [of this catholic church] are more or less pure, according as the doctrine of the gospel is taught and embraced, ordinances administered, and public worship performed more or less purely in them. The purest churches under heaven are subject both to mixture and error; and some have so degenerated as to become apparently no churches of Christ. Nevertheless, there shall always be a church on earth, to worship God according to his will.

John Owen on the Nature of a Gospel Church

In this statement on the "nature of a gospel church," which had considerable influence within contemporary Puritanism, Owen sets out the distinguishing characteristics of such a church, which gained widespread assent within English and American Puritanism. Note how the church is understood to be a body which has separated from the world, and whose members are distinguished by their explicit public profession of faith, and their holiness of life. See also 7.4; 7.9; 7.12; 7.14; 7.15; 7.16.

Source: *The True Nature of a Gospel Church*; in *Works*, ed. William H. Goold, vol. 16 (London: Johnstone & Hunter, 1853), pp. 11–15.

* * *

The church may be considered either as unto its *essence*, constitution and being, or as unto its *power* and *order*, when it is organized. As unto its essence and being, its constituent parts are its *matter* and *form*. These we must inquire into.

By the matter of the church, we understand the persons whereof the church doth consist, with their qualifications; and by its form, the reason, cause, and way of that kind of relation among them which gives them the being of a church, and therewithal an interest in all that belongs unto a church, either privilege or power, as such.

Our first inquiry being concerning what sort of persons our Lord Jesus Christ requireth and admitteth to be the visible subjects of his kingdom, we are to be regulated in our determination by respect unto his honour, glory, and the holiness of his rule. To reckon such persons to be subjects of Christ, members of his body, such as he requires and owns (for others are not so), who would not be tolerated, at least not approved, in a well-governed kingdom or commonwealth of the world, is highly dishonourable unto him . . . But it is so come to pass, that let men be never so notoriously and flagitiously wicked, until they become pests of the earth, yet are they esteemed to belong to the church of Christ; and not only so, but it is thought little less than schism to forbid them the communion of the church in all its sacred privileges. Howbeit, the Scripture doth in general represent the kingdom or church of Christ to consist of persons called *saints*, separated from the world, with many other things of an alike nature, as we shall see immediately. And if the honour of Christ were of such weight with us as it ought to be – if we understood aright the nature and ends of his kingdom, and that the peculiar glory of it above all the kingdoms in the world consists in the holiness of its subjects, such a holiness as the world in its wisdom knoweth not – we would duly consider whom we avow to belong thereunto. Those who know aught of these things will not profess that persons openly profane, vicious, sensual, wicked, and ignorant, are approved and owned of Christ as the subjects of his kingdom, or that it is his will that we should receive them into the communion of the church, 2 Timothy 3:1–5. But an old opinion of the unlawfulness of separation from a church on the account of the mixture of wicked men in it is made a scarecrow to frighten men from attempting the reformation of the greatest evils, and a covert for the composing churches of such members only.

Some things, therefore, are to be premised unto what shall be offered unto the right stating of this inquiry; as –

1. That if there be no more required of any, as unto *personal qualifications*, in a visible, uncontrollable profession, to constitute them subjects of Christ's kingdom and members of his church, Ezekiel 22:26, but what is required by the most righteous and severe laws of men to constitute a good subject or citizen, the distinction between his visible kingdom and the kingdoms of the world, as unto the principal causes of it, is utterly lost. Now, all negative qualifications, as, that men are not oppressors, drunkards, revilers, swearers, adulterers, etc., are required hereunto; but yet it is so fallen out that generally more is required to constitute such a citizen as shall represent the righteous laws he liveth under that to constitute a member of the church of Christ.

2. That whereas *regeneration* is expressly required in the gospel to give a right and privilege unto an entrance into the church or kingdom of Christ, John 3:3, Titus 3:3–5, whereby that kingdom of his is distinguished from all other kingdoms in and of the world, unto an interest wherein never any such thing was required, it must of necessity be something better, more excellent and sublime, than any thing the laws and polities of men pretend unto or prescribe. Wherefore it cannot consist in any outward rite, easy to be observed by the worst and vilest of men. Besides, the Scripture gives us a description of it in opposition unto its consisting in any such rite, 1 Peter 3:21; and many things required unto good citizens are far better than the mere observation of snch a rite.

3. Of this regeneration baptism is the symbol, the sign, the expression, and representation, John 3:5; Acts 2:38; 1 Peter 3:21. Wherefore, unto those who are in a due manner partakers of it, it giveth all the external rights and privileges which belong unto them that are regenerate, until they come unto such seasons wherein the personal performance of those duties whereon the continuation of the estate of visible regeneration doth depend is required of them. Herein if they fail, they lose all privilege and benefit by their baptism . . . Verily it profiteth, if a man stand unto the terms of the covenant which is tendered therein between God and his soul, for it will give him a right unto all the outward privileges of a regenerate state; but if he do not, as in the sight of God, his baptism is no baptism, as unto the real communication of grace and acceptance with him, Philippians 3:18–19; Titus 1:15–16. So, in the sight of the church, it is no baptism, as unto a participation of the external rights and privileges of a regenerate state.

4. God alone is judge concerning this regeneration, as unto its *internal, real principle and state* in the souls of men, Acts 15:8, Revelation 2:23, whereon the participation of all the spiritual advantages of the covenant of grace doth depend. The church is judge of its evidences and fruits in their external demonstration, as unto a participation of *the outward privileges of a regenerate*

state, and no farther, Acts 8:13. And we shall hereon briefly declare what belongs unto the forming of a right judgment herein, and who are to be esteemed fit members of any gospel church-state, or have a right so to be:

1. Such as from whom we are obliged to *withdraw or withhold communion* can be no part of the matter constituent of a church, or are not meet members for the first constitution of it . . . But such are all habitual sinners, those who, having prevalent habits and inclinations unto sins of any kind unmortified, do walk according unto them. Such are profane swearers, drunkards, fornicators, covetors, oppressors, and the like, "who shall not inherit the kingdom of God," 1 Corinthians 6:9–11 . . . As a man living and dying in any known sin, that is, habitually, without repentance, cannot be saved, so a man known to live in sin cannot regularly be received into any church. To compose churches of habitual sinners, and that either as unto sins of commission or sins of omission, is not to erect temples to Christ, but chapels unto the devil.

2. Such as, being in the fellowship of the church, are to be *admonished of any scandalous sin*, which if they repent not of they are to be cast out of the church, are not meet members for the original constitution of a church, Mattew 18:15–18; 1 Corinthians 5:11. This is the state of them who abide obstinate in any known sin, whereby they have given offence unto others, without a professed repentance thereof, although they have not lived in it habitually.

3. They are to be such as *visibly answer* the description given of gospel churches in the Scripture, so as the titles assigned therein unto the members of such churches may on good grounds be appropriated unto them. To compose churches of such persons as do not visibly answer the character given of what they were of old, and what they were always to be by virtue of the law of Christ or gospel constitution, is not church edification but destruction. And those who look on the things spoken of all church-members of old, as that they were saints by calling, lively stones in the house of God, justified and sanctified, separated from the world, etc., as those which were in them, and did indeed belong unto them, but even deride the necessity of the same things in present church-members, or the application of them unto those who are so, are themselves no small part of that woeful degeneracy which Christian religion is fallen under. Let it then be considered what is spoken of the church of the Jews in their dedication unto God, as unto their typical holiness, with the application of it unto Christian churches in real holiness, 1 Peter 2:5, 9, with the description given of them constantly in the Scripture, as faithful, holy, believing, as the house of God, as his temple wherein he dwells by his Spirit, as the body of Christ united and compacted by the communication of the Spirit unto them, as also what is said concerning their ways, walkings, and duties, and it will be uncontrollably evident of what sort our church-members ought to be . . .

4. They must be such as do *make an open profession of the subjection of their souls and consciences unto the authority of Christ in the gospel, and their readiness to yield obedience unto all his commands*, Romans 10:10; 2 Corinthians 8:5 . . . This, I suppose, will not be denied; for not only doth the Scripture

make this profession necessary unto the participation of any benefit or privilege of the gospel, but the nature of the things themselves requires indispensably that so it should be: for nothing can be more unreasonable than that men should be taken into the privileges attending obedience unto the laws and commands of Christ, without avowing or professing that obedience.

7.18 F. D. E. Schleiermacher on the Church as a Fellowship of Believers

In this analysis of the nature and function of the church, originally published in German in 1834, Schleiermacher explores the relation between those who are regenerate and the community of faith. See also 7.9; 7.14.

Source: Friedrich Schleiermacher, *The Christian Faith* (Edinburgh: T. & T. Clark, 1928), pp. 525–8.

* * *

All that comes to exist in the world through redemption is embraced in the fellowship of believers, within which all regenerate people are always found. This section, therefore, contains the doctrine of the Christian Church.

In reckoning the two expressions – the fellowship of believers and the Christian Church – as equivalent, our proposition seems to be in opposition to the Roman Symbol; but neither earlier versions of the latter nor the Nicene Creed know anything of using the two side by side yet with a distinction. What is evident is that fellowship may be taken in a narrower or a wider sense. For, if the regenerate find themselves already within it, they must have belonged to it even before regeneration, though obviously in a different sense from actual believers.

If this were not so, no accession to or extension of the Church could be imagined except by an absolute breach of continuity – that is, in a way unknown to history. But the truth is that the new life of each individual springs from that of the community, while the life of the community springs from no other individual life than that of the Redeemer. We must therefore hold that the totality of those who live in the state of sanctification is the inner fellowship; the totality of those on whom preparatory grace is at work is the outer fellowship, from which by regeneration members pass to the inner, and then keep helping to extend the wider circle. It would, however, be quite a novel and merely confusing use of terms to try to assign the two expressions in question respectively to the two forms of fellowship.

Further, no particular form of fellowship is here definitely asserted or excluded; every form, perfect and imperfect, that has ever been or that may yet appear, is included. This, and this only, is assumed, that wherever regenerate persons are within reach of each other, some kind of fellowship between them is bound to arise. For if they are in contact, their witness to the faith must in part overlap, and must necessarily involve mutual recognition and a common understanding as to their operation within the common area. What was stated at the beginning of our treatment of the consciousness of grace, namely, that it always proceeds from a common life, was meant exclusively in this far-reaching sense; but now that very statement finds for the first time its full explanation. For if, when regenerate, we did not find ourselves already within a common life, but had to set out to discover or constitute it, that would mean that just the most decisive of all the works of grace was not based on a life in common . . .

The Christian self-consciousness expressed in our proposition is the general form, determined by our faith in Christ, taken by our fellow-feeling with human things and circumstances. This becomes all the clearer if we combine with it the corresponding negative expression. For if, leaving redemption out of account, the world is, relatively to humanity, the place of original perfection of men and things which yet has become the place of sin and evil; and if, with the appearance of Christ a new thing has entered the world, the antithesis of the old; it follows that only that part of the world which is united to the Christian Church is for us the place of attained perfection, or of the good, and – relatively to quiescent self-consciousness – the place of blessedness. This is so, not in virtue of the original perfection of human nature and the natural order, though of course it is thus conditioned, but in virtue solely of the sinless perfection and blessedness which has come in with Christ and communicates itself through him. With this goes the converse; that the world, so far as it is outside this fellowship of Christ, is always, in spite of that original perfection, the place of evil and sin. No one, therefore, can be surprised to find at this point the proposition that salvation or blessedness cannot enter from without, but can be found within the Church only by being brought into existence there, the Church alone saves. For the rest, it is self-evident that the antithesis between what is realized in the world by redemption and all the rest of the world is acute in proportion to the completeness with which the peculiar dignity of Christ and the full content of redemption is apprehended. It disappears of loses itself in a vague distinction between better and worse only where the contrast between Christ and sinful man is similarly obliterated or toned down.

This, too, affords the best proof that our proposition is simply an utterance of the Christian self-consciousness. For if the Christian Church were in its essential nature an object of outward perception, that perception might be passed on without involving attachment to the fellowship. But the fact is that those who do not share our faith in Christ do not recognize the Christian fellowship in its antithesis to the world. Wherever the feeling of need of redemption is entirely suppressed, the Christian Church is misconstrued all round; and the two attitudes develop pari passu. With the first stirrings of preparatory grace in consciousness, there comes a presentiment of the divine origin of the Christian Church; and with a living faith in Christ awakens also a belief that the Kingdom of God is actually present in the fellowship of believers. On the other hand, an unalterable hostility to the Christian Church is symptomatic of the highest stage of insusceptibility to redemption; and this hostility hardly admits even of outward reverence for the person of Christ. But faith in the Christian Church as the Kingdom of God not only implies that it will ever endure in antithesis to the world, but also – the fellowship having grown to such dimensions out of small beginnings, and being inconceivable except as ever at work – contains the hope that the Church will increase and the world opposed to it decrease. For the incarnation of Christ means for human nature in general what regeneration is for the individual. And just as sanctification is the progressive domination of the various functions, coming with time to consist less and less of fragmentary details and more and more to be a whole, with all its parts integrally connected and lending mutual support, so too the fellowship organizes itself here also out of the separate redemptive activities and becomes more and more co-operative and interactive. This organization must increasingly overpower the unorganized mass to which it is opposed.

7.19 The Barmen Confession on the Identity of the Church

This historically and theologically important document, first published in 1934 at the height of the "German Church crisis," insists upon the distinctiveness of the church in relation to the state. At a time at which a Nazi government seemed poised to take over the church and subvert it for its own ends, theologians and church leaders (including Karl Barth) insisted that the church found its identity and purpose only in relation to Jesus Christ. See also 2.25; 7.9; 7.14.

Source: "The Theological Clarification of the Present State of the German Evangelical Churches" (1934), 1–5; in *Bekenntnisschriften und Kirchenordnungen der nach Gottes Wort reformierten Kirche*, ed. W. Niesel (Zurich: Evangelischer Verlag, 1938), 335.25–31; 335.46–336.10; 336.21–38.

* * *

1. Jesus Christ, as he is attested for us in Holy Scripture, is the one Word of God which we have to hear and which we have to trust and obey in life and in death. We reject the false teaching, that the church could and should acknowledge any other events and powers, figures and truths, as God's revelation, or as a source of its proclamation, apart from and besides this one Word of God. . . .

3. The Christian church is the congregation of brothers and sisters in which Jesus Christ acts presently as the Lord in Word and sacrament, through the Holy Spirit. As the church of forgiven sinners, it has to bear witness in the midst of a sinful world, with both its faith and its obedience, with its proclamation as well as its order, that it is the possession of him alone, and that it lives and wills to live only from his comfort and his guidance in the expectation of his appearance. We reject the false teaching, that the church is free to abandon the form of its proclamation and order in favour of anything it pleases, or in response to prevailing ideological or political beliefs (*der jeweils herrschenden weltanschaulichen und politischen Überzeugungen*) . . .

5. Scripture declares that the state has, by divine appointment (*nach göttlicher Anordnung*) the task of providing for justice and peace in the as yet unredeemed world in which the church also exists, by means of the threat and exercise of force, according to the measure of human judgement and ability. The church acknowledges before God the benefit of this divine appointment in gratitude and reverence. It recalls the Kingdom of God, God's command and his righteousness, and through this, the responsibilities both of those who rule and those who are ruled. It trusts and obeys the power of the Word of God, by which God upholds all things. We reject the false teaching, that the state, over and beyond its special commission, should or could become the sole and supreme authority in human life, thus fulfilling the vocation of the church as well as its own. We reject the false teaching, that the church, over and beyond its special commission, could or should appropriate the distinctive features, tasks or authority of the state, thus becoming itself an organ of the state.

John D. Zizoulas on Local and Universal Churches   7.20

John D. Zizoulas, a leading contemporary Orthodox theologian, here sets out an understanding of "catholicity," and explores its relevance for local churches. In the course of his discussion, he identifies a number of characteristics which determine whether a local congregation can be said to be a part of the catholic church as a whole. See also 7.21.

Source: John D. Zizoulas, *Being as Communion: Studies in Personhood and the Church* (New York: St. Vladimir's Seminary Press, 1985), pp. 257–9. Reprinted by permission of St. Vladimir's Seminary Press, 575 Scarsdale Road, Crestwood, New York, 10707.

* * *

From what has just been said it follows that the "catholicity" of the Church is not to be juxtaposed to locality: it is rather an indispensable aspect *of the local Church*, the ultimate criterion of ecclesiality for any local body. Universality, however, is a different notion and can certainly be contrasted with locality. How does the concept of universality affect our understanding of the local Church?

It is in the nature of the eucharist to transcend not only divisions occurring within a local situation but also the very division which is inherent in the concept of geography: the division of the world into local places. Just as a eucharist which is not a transcendence of divisions within a certain locality is a false eucharist, equally a eucharist which takes place in conscious and intentional isolation and separation from other local communities in the world is not a true eucharist. From that it follows inevitably that a local Church, in order to be not just local but also Church, must be in full communion with the rest of the local Churches in the world.

For a local Church to be in full communion with the rest of local Churches the following elements are involved:

(a) That the problems and concerns of all local Churches should be the objects of prayer and active care by a particular local Church. If a local Church falls into indifference as to what is going on in the rest of the world, it is certainly not a Church.

(b) That a certain common basis of the vision and understanding of the Gospel and the eschatological nature of the Church exist between a local Church and the rest of the local Churches. This requires a constant vigilance concerning the true faith in all local Churches by every single local Church.

(c) That certain structures be provided which will facilitate this communion. On this point some further explanations become necessary.

If the locality of the Church is not to be absorbed and in fact negated by the element of universality, the utmost care must be taken so that the structures of ministries which are aimed at facilitating communion among the local Churches do not become a superstructure over the local Church. It is extremely significant that in the entire course of church history there has never been an attempt at establishing a super-local eucharist or a super-local bishop. All eucharists and all bishops are local in character – at least in their primary sense. In a eucharistic view of the Church this means that the local Church, as defined earlier here, is the only form of ecclesial existence which can be properly called Church. All structures aiming at facilitating the universality of the Church create a *network of communion of Churches, not a new form of Church*. This is not only supported by history, but rests also upon sound theological and existential ground. Any structural universalization of the Church to the point of creating an ecclesial entity called "universal Church" as something parallel to or above that of the local Church would inevitably introduce into the concept of the Church cultural and other dimensions which are foreign to a particular local context. Culture cannot be a monolithically universal phenomenon without some kind of demonic imposition of one culture over the rest of cultures. Nor is it possible to dream of a universal "Christian culture" without denying the dialectic between history and eschatology which is so central, among other things, to the eucharist itself. Thus, if there is a transcendence of cultural divisions on a universal level – which indeed must be constantly aimed at by the Church – it can only take place *via* the local situations expressed in and through the particular local Churches and not through universalistic structures which imply a universal Church. For a universal Church as an entity besides the local Church would be either a culturally disincarnated Church – since there is no such a thing as universal culture – or alternatively it would be culturally incarnated in a demonic way, if it either blesses or directly or indirectly imposes on the world a particular culture.

In conclusion, all church structures aiming at facilitating communion between local Churches (e.g., synods, councils of all forms etc.) do possess ecclesiological significance and must be always viewed in the light of ecclesiology. But they cannot be regarded as forms of *Church* without the serious dangers I have just referred to.

Leonardo Boff on the Nature of Local Churches

This major discussion of the identity and role of the church brings together a number of insights characteristic of Latin American liberation theology. Notice the importance attached to the "base communities" and the "bottom-upwards" model of authority which they embody. The passage raises the question of whether an ordained ministry, or any form of properly-constituted sacramental worship, is essential if such a community can be regarded as a church. The issues addressed in this passage call into question some of the more conservative understandings of church and ministry which were typical of Latin American catholicism until recently. Note that "Medellín" refers to a conference of bishops of 1968, which was concerned to apply the outlook of Vatican II to Latin America, and which is widely regarded as marking the birth of liberation theology. See also 1.26; 3.30; 7.20; 7.22.

Source: Leonardo Boff, *Ecclesiogenesis: The Base Communities Reinvent the Church* (Maryknoll, NY: Orbis Books, 1986), pp. 11–15. Published in the Philippines by Claretian Communications Inc. Used with permission of the publisher.

* * *

The church comes into being as church when people become aware of the call to salvation in Jesus Christ, come together in community, profess the same faith, celebrate the same eschatological liberation, and seek to live the discipleship of Jesus Christ. We can speak of church *in the proper sense* only when there is question of this ecclesial consciousness. Hence the crucial importance of explicit Christian motivation. We are united and we pursue our social objectives of liberation *because* we react to the call of Christ, and the call of other communities that transmit his call to us and that have preceded us in the living experience of this same community faith. We can speak of a *church* community, therefore, only when a given community has this explicit religious and Christian character. Otherwise it will be some other kind of community, however it may actualize the same values as the church pursues. For an authentic, contemplative Christian, this other community indeed verifies the essential definition of church in its ontic reality. But the presence of the ontic ecclesial reality is not enough. In order formally to be church, the *consciousness* of this reality must be there, the profession of explicit faith in Jesus Christ who died and was raised again.

Having clarified this point, we are now in a position to move on to the next – once more, one of special importance.

Differing Opinions

We speak of "basic church communities." Are these communities themselves actually church, or do they merely contain elements of church?

Many different answers are proposed to this question, but this scarcely deprives it of its importance either for ecclesiology or for the actual members of the basic communities. Opinions tend to vary with the position their subjects occupy in the church structure, or with the model of church they adopt as key to the interpretation of total church reality. Thus those within the actual basic communities will tend to consider these communities as church, while those whose orientation is toward the historically established churches will reserve the minimum requirement for church to the parish community. The hierarchy, as we see from Vatican Council II, will define "a church" in terms of diocesan reality, with bishop and Eucharist. Let us consider each of these opinions in turn, and attempt to establish the theological value of each.

First, we shall examine what the basic church community itself says. There is a study carried out by the Centro de Estatística Religiosa e Investigações Sociais (CERIS), in which Father Alfonso Gregory catalogues various responses to the question of the ecclesiality of various experiences. When he comes to the basic communities, he records the following reasons explaining why the basic church community is properly denominated "church":

1. "Because it is founded on the common faith, and its objectives bear on a deepening and an increase of this faith, with all that this implies."
2. "Because there is a direct connection with the ecclesiastical framework, a sense of church-of-the-people." Or, as another respondent put it: "Because it feels its oneness with the parish, diocese, and church universal."
3. "Because in religious activities only Catholics participate, while other activities are ecumenical" – that is, socioeconomic activities. Here we may add what another respondent said: "When you consider yourselves a church community, you can't work when your religious motives are different, or opposite."
4. "Because the strictly religious activities are basic, while all the others are as a consequence of accepting God's word." Or again: "Christianity is the activating of integral humanism."
5. "Because we are working at the grassroots for a communion in faith, through humanization."

But Gregory also documents the contrary view: The basic communities "are not churches (or, as some would say, they are churches only *juxta modum*), because, though there may be priests and nuns here, these communities are just beginning. In other cases, their activities are oriented consciously and mainly to the social area."

The vast majority of those responsible for these experiments – the respondents in this research project – feel that they are in contact with actual, genuine church, and not just with ecclesial elements or parachurch communities. Jose Marins, who is in the front line of defense of the basic communities, puts it well in his reformulation of the thinking of the communities:

> For us, the basic church community is the church itself, the universal sacrament of salvation, as it continues the mission of Christ – Prophet, Priest, and Pastor. This is what makes it a community of faith, worship, and love. Its mission is explicitly expressed on all levels – the universal, the diocesan, and the local, or basic.

Elsewhere we read that the basic community is genuine church because it has "the same goals" as the universal church: "to lead all men and women to the full communion of life with the Father and one another, through Jesus Christ, in the gift of the Holy Spirit, by means of the mediating activity of the church." These few citations are representative of the thinking of the great majority of pastoral leaders and theologians directly involved with the basic communities, particularly in Latin America. Most of them consider that the basic church communities constitute the true and authentic presence of the Catholic Church.

Once upon a time the populations in the interior of the Latin American countries, cut off by thick rain forests or other wild territory and scattered over the vast expanses of these empty lands, met together only when the priest came to them – once a year, perhaps, or every six months. Only for this brief moment did they feel themselves to be living church united by the word, together with their ordained minister, around the same altar, celebrating and offering the same sacred Victim. Then came the basic communities, and these same people began to meet every week – or twice a week or every day – to celebrate the presence of the risen One and of his Spirit, to hear and meditate on his word, and to renew their commitment to liberation, together with their community leaders who are the principle of unity and communion with other basic communities and with the parish and diocesan community. Are we now going to tell these people that they are not church, that they have certain "ecclesial elements," but that these do not actually constitute the essence of church?

We must ask ourselves: Are they not baptized? Do they not possess the same faith as the church universal? The same love? The same hope? Do they not read the same Scriptures? Do they not live the same Christian praxis? Are they not fully united to Christ, and are they not the body of Christ? We are not dealing with some mere point of sentimentality here. Let us face the actual ecclesiological problem, and face it objectively. If we are to develop a new ecclesiology, we shall need more than just theological perspicacity and historico-dogmatic erudition. We must face the new experiences of church in our midst. We in Brazil and Latin America are confronted with a new concretization of church, without the presence of consecrated ministers and without the eucharistic celebration. It is not that this absence is not felt, is not painful. It is, rather, that these ministers do not exist in sufficient numbers. This historical situation does not cause the church to disappear. The church abides in the people of God as they continue to come together, convoked by the word and discipleship of Jesus Christ. Something is new under the sun: a new church of Christ.

As a result, even those theologians who restrict the definition of church to a community presenting constitutive, essential elements of church such as word, sacrament, the presence of the bishop, and communion with all the other churches – and who therefore pronounce the basic community "not fully church" – are forced nonetheless to conclude: "From the pastoral viewpoint, these basic groups or communities must be considered authentic ecclesial reality – needing development, doubtless, but surely integrated into the one communion of the Father, in Christ, through the Holy Spirit."

The theological problem of the ecclesial character of the basic community must be seen within a context of the recovery by these communities of a true ecclesiological dimension. This is the process now under way in many places. We know that the ninth century saw the rise of papal supremacy. The absolutist ideology of the Gregorian reform two centuries later served to reinforce this development. Then came conciliarism, Gallicanism, and episcopalism, with their attendant polemics. Finally, with the development of the ultramontane ecclesiology and its triumph under Pius IX, the church acquired a unitarian organization, as if it were one great, worldwide diocese, with one sole liturgy, one visible head, one embodiment . . . Vatican II transcended this state of affairs, recognizing the local or particular church as genuine church, but without developing a complete theology of the local church. An important step has been taken, then, in the process of defining what it is to be a particular or local church, and restoring to it its proper evaluation. Vatican II defined the particular church as

> that portion of God's people which is entrusted to a bishop to be shepherded by him with the cooperation of the presbytery. Adhering thus to its pastor and gathered together by him in the Holy Spirit through the gospel and the Eucharist, this portion constitutes a particular church in which the one, holy, catholic, and apostolic church of Christ is truly present and operative.

The particular church, then, is defined in diocesan terms. Unity is secured through the presence of the bishop and the celebration of the Eucharist. The capacity to represent the church universal is not, however, reserved to the diocese gathered around the bishop in the celebration of the Eucharist. *Lumen Gentium* says:

> This church of Christ is truly present in all legitimate local congregations of the faithful . . . united with their pastors . . . In them the faithful are gathered together by the preaching of the gospel of Christ, and the mystery of the Lord's Supper is celebrated, "that by the flesh and blood of the Lord's body the whole brotherhood may be joined together" . . . In these communities, though frequently small and poor, or living far from any other, Christ is present. By virtue of Him the one, holy, catholic, and apostolic Church gathers together.

In all cases, then, the essential constitutive element of a particular church as church, for Vatican Council II, is always the gospel, the Eucharist, and the presence of the apostolic succession in the person of the bishop.

Medellín, in 1968, could already testify to an evolution in the ecclesial experience of the postconciliar era, with the rise of basic communities all over the South American continent:

> Thus the Christian base community is *the first and fundamental ecclesiastical nucleus*, which on its own level must make itself responsible for the richness

and expansion of the faith, as well as of the cult which is its expression. This community becomes then the *initial cell* of the ecclesiastical structures and the focus of evangelization, and it currently serves as the most important source of human advancement and development. The essential element for the existence of Christian base communities are their leaders or directors. These can be priests, deacons, men or women, religious, or laymen.

There is no mention here of the elements of bishop and Eucharist. The church is not being thought of from the top down, but from the bottom up, from the grassroots, from the "base." The church – "God's family" – takes form by "means of a nucleus, although it be small, which creates a community of faith, hope and charity." Truly another step has been taken in a grasp of the church dimension of the basic communities.

Avery Dulles on the Meanings of "Catholicity" 7.22

At the conclusion of a detailed analysis of the notion of the "catholicity" of the church, the American Catholic theologian Avery Dulles sets out five general ways in which the term "catholic" has been used in Christian history. See also 7.5; 7.7; 7.11; 7.20.

Source: Avery Dulles, *The Catholicity of the Church* (Oxford: Clarendon Press, 1985), p. 185. By permission of Oxford University Press.

* * *

The term "catholic," with or without an initial capital, has various levels of meaning ... The following five usages may now be enumerated:

1. The adjectival form of "catholicity" ... To be catholic in this sense is to share in the universal community, rooted in cosmic nature, that transcends the barriers of time and place and has its source in God's self-communication. The opposite of "catholic" in this sense is sectarian.

2. Universal as opposed to local or particular. This seems to be the primary meaning of "catholic" as used in a number of important texts from the early Fathers of the Church, notably Ignatius of Antioch and the Martyrdom of Polycarp, though there is some disagreement about the precise interpretation of these texts.

3. True or authentic as contrasted with false or heretical. This polemical use of the term is found in many church Fathers, especially after AD 150, and is much in use among Greek Orthodox theologians of our own time.

4. The type of Christianity that attaches particular importance to visible continuity in space and time and visible mediation through social and institutional structures, such as creeds, sacraments, and the historic episcopate. This sense of the word "Catholic" (with a capital C) was prominent at the Amsterdam Assembly of the World Council of Churches (1948). The opposite was taken to be "Protestant," although a good case could be made for regarding "charismatic" or "mystical" as the opposite.

5. The title of the church which, organized in the world as a society, is governed by the bishop of Rome, as successor of Peter, and by the bishops in communion with him. In ecumenical circles it has become common to use the term "Roman Catholic" to designate this sociological group, partly because the term "Catholic" has the various other meanings listed above.

Study Questions to Chapter 7

What does it mean to say that the church is "catholic"? Does the existence of "local churches" call this into question?

The Reformation witnessed some disagreements over the nature of the church. In what way do Luther, Calvin, and Franck differ over this issue?

Is there salvation outside the church? (Note in particular the views of Origen and Cyprian.)

Is moral purity an essential feature of a Christian church? (The positions of Petilian of Citra and Richard Hooker are good starting points for this discussion. Note also how neither Luther or Calvin include moral purity in their list of "marks of the church.")

Luther argues that all believers are priests. Is this inconsistent with a professional ministry? And what would happen if this doctrine of the "priesthood of all believers" were extended to include the idea that all believers are theologians? (See the position of Karl Barth outlined at 1.20.)

8 The Sacraments

The theology of the sacraments represents an area of Christian thought in which there is substantial divergence between the various Christian traditions. Whereas the Roman Catholic and the Orthodox churches recognize seven sacraments, and generally regard them as causing what they signify, Protestant churches generally accept only two sacraments (baptism and the Lord's Supper), often regarding them as signifying – but not necessarily causing – grace.

The readings presented in this chapter allow the reader to gain an impression of the considerable differences within the Christian tradition over these issues, and assess their importance. Two Study Panels focus on two particularly important questions: the definition of a sacrament, and the way in which Christ is understood to be present in the Lord's Supper or eucharist. In addition to these, other questions may be noted as being of importance, including the specific role of baptism, and the general question of what the sacraments actually do.

8.1 Clement of Alexandria on Faith as Feeding on Christ

In this second-century text, Clement explores the meaning of Paul's statement (1 Corinthians 3:2) "I fed you with milk, not meat, for you were not ready for meat." He interprets the text to refer to various types of nourishment for the soul. He then links the idea of spiritual food with the sacramental idea of feeding on Jesus Christ, he especially associates with John's Gospel. See also 8.2.

Source: *Paedagogus*, I.vi.38; in *Sources Chrétiennes*, vol. 70, ed. H.-I. Marroli (Paris: Cerf, 1960), p. 180.

* * *

We may understand "milk" (1 Corinthians 3:2) as meaning the preaching which has been spread far and wide, "meat" as the faith which as a result of instruction has been consolidated to form a foundation. In that faith is more solid than hearing, it is likened to "meat," since it provides analogous nourishment for the soul. In another place the Lord also expressed that by a different symbolism, when, in John's gospel, he says "Eat my flesh and drink my blood" (John 6:53–5). The metaphor of drinking, applied to faith and the promise, clearly means that the church, consisting (like a human being) of many members, is refreshed and grows, is consolidated and welded together, by both of these, faith being the body and hope the soul: just as the Lord was made of flesh and blood. In reality, hope is the blood of faith, as it gives cohesion to faith, as with the soul.

8.2 Clement of Alexandria on the Results of Baptism

Clement here develops a strongly physical and realistic understanding of the effects of baptism. Note especially the emphasis upon "enlightenment (*phōtisma*)." See also 8.1; 8.5; 8.10; 8.13.

Source: *Paedagogus*, I.vi.26; in *Sources Chrétiennes*, vol. 70, ed. H.-I. Marroli (Paris: Cerf, 1960), p. 158.

* * *

Being baptized, we are enlightened: being enlightened, we are adopted as sons: being adopted, we are made perfect; being made complete, we are made immortal. The Scripture says "I said, you are gods, and are all sons of the Highest" (Psalm 6:1). This operation has many names; gift of grace, enlightenment, perfection, and washing (*charisma kai phōtisma kai teleion kai loutron*). Washing, by which we are cleansed from the filth of our sins; gift of grace, by which the penalties of our sins are cancelled; enlightenment, through which that holy light which saves us is perceived, that is, by which our eyes are made alert to see the divine; perfection means the lack of nothing, for what is still lacking to anyone who has the knowledge of God? It would clearly be absurd to give the name of "grace" of God to a gift which is not complete. Being perfect, we may be assured that God will bestow perfect graces.

Cyprian of Carthage on Heretical Baptism 8.3

In this letter to his colleague Quintus, Cyprian argues that heretical baptism has no validity. To concede any validity to such baptisms would be to destory the distinctiveness and uniqueness of the Christian church. See also 7.3; 7.4; 8.7; 8.8.

Source: *Epistle LXXI*, 1; in *Saint Cyprien: Correspondence*, ed. Le Chanoine Bayard, 2nd edn (Paris: Société des Belles Lettres, 1961), pp. 256–7.

* * *

I do not know by what presumption some of our colleagues have been led to suppose that those who have been dipped (*tincti*) among the heretics ought not to be baptized when they join us; because, they say, there is "one baptism." Yes, but that one baptism is in the catholic church. And if there is one church, there can be no baptism outside it. There cannot be two baptisms: if heretics really baptize, then baptism belongs to them. And anyone who, asserting their own authority, grants them this privilege admits, by conceding their claim, that the enemy and adversary of Christ should appear to possess the power of washing, purifying, and sanctifying humanity (*abluendi et purificandi et sanctificandi hominis potestatem*). We declare that those who come to us out of heresy are not re-baptized by us; they are baptized. They do not receive anything there; there is nothing there for them to receive. They come to us so that they may receive here, where there is all grace and truth; for grace and truth are one.

Cyril of Jerusalem on the Meaning of Baptism 8.4

This is an extract from the first of a series of lectures given by Cyril in which he explains the significance of baptism. The lecture is of value in several respects, including its documentation of early Christian baptismal practices. The lecture is prefaced by the reading of 1 Peter 5:8–11. See also 8.2; 8.6.

Source: *First Address on the Mysteries*, 1–3; in *Sources Chrétiennes*, vol. 126, ed. A. Piédagnel and P. Paris (Paris: Cerf, 1966), 82.1–86.13.

* * *

For a long time I have wished, true born and long-desired children of the church, to speak to you about these spiritual and heavenly mysteries. However, knowing very well that seeing is believing, I waited until the present occasion, knowing that after what you have experienced you would be a more receptive audience, now that I am to lead you to the brighter and more fragrant meadows of this paradise. In particular, you are now able to understand the more divine mysteries of divine and life-giving baptism. So now that the time has come to prepare for you the table of more perfect instruction, let me explain what happened to you on the evening of your baptism.

First you entered the antechamber of the baptistery (*proaulios tou baptismatos oikon*), and turned westwards. When you were told to stretch out your hands, you renounced Satan as though he were there in person. Now you should know that ancient history provides a type of this. When Pharaoh, the harshest and most cruel of all tyrants, oppressed the free and noble people of the Hebrews, God sent Moses to deliver them from this harsh slavery which had been imposed on them by the Egyptians. They anointed their doorposts with the blood of a lamb, so that the destroyer might pass over the houses which bore the sign of this blood, and miraculously set the Hebrew people free from their bondage. After their liberation the enemy pursued them, and on seeing the sea open in front of them, they still continued to pursue them, only to be engulfed in the Red Sea.

Let us now pass from the old to the new, from the type to the reality. There Moses is sent by God to Egypt; here Christ is sent by the Father into the world. There, he was to lead an oppressed people from Egypt; here he was to deliver those who are under the tyranny of sin. There the blood of the lamb turned away the destoyer; here the blood of the unblemished lamb, Jesus Christ, puts the demons to flight. In the past, the tyrant pursued the Hebrew people right to the sea; in your case, the devil, the arch-evil one, followed each one of you up to the edge of the streams of salvation. This first [tyrant] was engulfed in the sea; this one disappears in the waters of salvation.

8.5 Cyril of Jerusalem on the Body and Blood of Christ

This address explains the meaning of the bread and wine to those who have recently been baptized. It is preceded by the reading of 1 Corinthians 11:23–5. Note especially the emphasis on the real change in the bread and wine as a result of their consecration. See also 8.1; 8.9; 8.10; 8.11; 8.12; 8.16; 8.18; 8.22; 8.23.

Source: *Fourth Address on the Mysteries*, 2–6; in *Sources Chrétiennes*, vol. 126, ed. A Piédagnel and P. Paris (Paris: Cerf, 1966), 136.1–138.6.

* * *

[Jesus Christ], by his own will, once changed water into wine at Cana in Galilee. So why should we not believe that he can change wine into blood? . . .

We should therefore have full assurance that we are sharing in the body and blood of Christ. For in the type of bread, his body is given to you, and in the type of wine, his blood is given to you, so that by partaking of the body and blood of Christ you may become of one body and one blood with him . . . In the words of Peter, "we are made to share in the divine nature" (2 Peter 1:4) . . .

So do not think of them just as bread and wine. As the Lord himself has declared, they are body and blood. And if your senses suggest otherwise, then let faith reassure you. Do not decide the question on the basis of taste, but on the basis of faith, and be assured beyond doubt that you have received the body and blood of Christ.

Hilary of Poitiers on the Effects of Baptism   8.6

In these comments on the baptism of Jesus, as recorded in the second chapter of Matthew's gospel, Hilary draws out the parallels between the work of the Father and Spirit in Jesus's baptism and that of ordinary believers. See also 8.3; 8.8.

Source: *in Matthaeum*, ii, 5; in *Sources Chrétiennes* vol. 254, ed. Jean Doignon (Paris: Cerf, 1978), 110.9–13.

   * * *

Everything that happened to Christ lets us know that, after the washing of water (*post aquae lavacrum*), the Holy Spirit descends upon us from the heights of heaven, and that we become sons of God, having been adopted by the voice of the Father.

Augustine on Donatist Approaches to the Sacraments   8.7

Augustine's view of the church accepts that congregations and priests will include sinners as well as saints. So does this invalidate the sacraments? Against the Donatist view, which declared that only the righteous can administer and profitably receive the sacraments (an *ex opere operantis* view of sacramental efficacy), Augustine argues that the efficacy of the sacraments rests on Christ himself, not on the merits of either the administrator or the recipient (an *ex opere operato* view of sacramental efficacy). See also 7.3; 7.4; 7.15; 8.3; 8.8.

Source: *de baptismo*, IV, 16, 18; in *Oeuvres de Saint Augustin*, vol. 29, ed. G. Finaert (Paris: Desclée, 1964), pp. 270–2; 280.

   * * *

Now as it is possible that the sacrament of Christ may be holy, even among those who are on the side of the devil . . . and even if they are such in heart when they received the sacrament . . . the sacrament is not to be readministered; . . . to my mind it is abundantly clear that in the matter of baptism we have to consider not who he is that gives it, but what it is that he gives; not who he is that receives, but what it is that he receives (*non esse cogitandum quis det sed quid det, aut quis accipiat sed quid accipiat, aut quis habeat sed quid habeat*) . . . wherefore, any one who is on the side of the devil cannot defile the sacrament, which is of Christ . . . When baptism is administered by the words of the gospel, however great the evil of either minister or recipient may be, the sacrament itself is holy on account of the one whose sacrament it is. In the case of people who receive baptism from an evil person (*per hominum perversum*), if they do not receive the perverseness of the minister but the holiness of the mystery, being united to the church in good faith and hope and charity, they will receive the forgiveness of their sins . . . But if the recipients themselves are evil, then that which is administered does not avail for their salvation while they remain in their errors. On the other hand, that which they receive remains holy in the recipients, and need not be repeated if they are subsequently corrected (*et sanctum tamen in eo permanet quod accipitur nec ei si correctus fuerit iteratur*).

8.8   Augustine on the "Right to Baptize"

Augustine lays down a fundamental distinction between an "irregular" and "invalid" administration of a sacrament. What makes a sacrament invalid is not sin on the part of the one who administers or receives it, but a deliberate breaking away from the body of Christ in schism. Augustine's view of the church as a "mixed body" recognizes that the church will include sinners as well as saints; however, he insists that schism leads to a break with the church and its sacraments, with the result that the latter are no longer of any benefit to their recipients. The sacrament are valid only within the church. See also 7.3; 7.4; 7.15; 8.3; 8.7.

Source: *contra Cresconium*, IV.xxi.26; in *Oeuvres de Saint Augustin*, vol. 31, ed. G. Finaert (Paris: Desclée, 1968), pp. 522–4.

* * *

We deal with these matters in case the unity of the harvest should be abandoned on account of evil dispensers of the sacraments – not their own, but the Lord's – who must, of necessity, be mixed among us, until the winnowing of the Lord's field (*ad tempus ventilationis areae dominicae*). Now to make a schism from the unity of Christ, or to be in schism, is indeed a great evil. And it is not possible in any way that Christ should give to the schismatics what is his own – not faith, that is, but a sacrilegious error; or that a schismatic should cleave, in Christ, to the root; or that Christ should be the fountain head to schismatics. And yet, if [a schismatic] gives the baptism of Christ, if it is given and if it is received, it will be received, not to eternal life but to eternal damnation of those who persevere in sacrilege, not by converting a good thing into evil but by having a good thing to their evil, so long as he receives evil.

John of Damascus on the Holy Spirit and Eucharist

8.9

In this important work, written in Greek in the first half of the eighth century, John of Damascus recognizes the central role of the Holy Spirit in bringing about the transformation of the bread into the body of Christ. The incarnation is seen as a further illustration of the same principle. See also 3.17; 4.18; 8.1.

Source: de fide orthodoxa, 86; in Patristische Texte und Studien, vol. 12, ed. P. Bonifatius Kotter O. S. B. (Berlin/New York: de Gruyter, 1973), 194.81–3; 195.97–9. Note that the division of this text varies between editions. The Migne edition [J. P. Migne, Patrologia Graeca, 94.1145A] designates this section as iv, 13.

* * *

And now you ask how the bread becomes the body of Christ, and the wine and the water become the blood of Christ. I shall tell you. The Holy Spirit comes upon them, and achieves things which surpass every word and thought . . . Let it be enough for you to understand that this takes place by the Holy Spirit, just as the Lord took flesh, in and through himself, of the Holy *Theotokos* and by the Holy Spirit.

Paschasius Radbertus on the Real Presence

8.10

The monastery of Corbie was the scene for some theological fireworks during the ninth century, focusing on the doctrine of predestination and the nature of the real presence. The two extracts which follow are from the writings of Paschasius Radbertus and Ratranmus of Corbie, who were both monks at Corbie during this period. Each wrote a work with the same title *De corpore et sanguine Christi*, yet developing very different understandings of the real presence. Radbertus, whose work was completed around 844, developed the idea that the bread and the wine become the body and blood of Christ in reality; Ratranmus, whose work was written shortly afterwards, defended the view that they were merely symbols of the body and blood (see 8.11). See also 8.12; 8.13.

Source: *De Corpore et sanguine Christi*, III.1; III.4; IV.1; in J. P. Migne, Patrologia Latina, 120.1275A; 1276D–1278A.

* * *

A sacrament is something which is passed down to us in any divine celebration as a pledge of salvation, when what is done visibly achieves something very different and holy inwardly . . .

We feed upon and drink the sacrament of the body and blood only during the journey through this life, so that, nourished by it, we may be made one in Christ, who sustains us this way so that we may be made ready for immortal and eternal things, while being nourished by angelic grace, we may be made alive spiritually. The holy Spirit who works in all these sacraments will do this . . . In baptism though water, we are all born again through him; afterwards, we daily feed upon Christ's body and drink his blood by his power. The same Spirit who created the human being Jesus Christ in the womb of the Virgin without any human seed daily creates the flesh and the blood of Christ by his invisible power through the consecration of this sacrament, even though this cannot be understood outwardly by either sight or taste ...

No one who believes the divine words of the Truth declaring "For my flesh is truly food, and my blood is truly drink" (John 6:55–6) can doubt that the body and blood are truly created by the consecration of the mystery ... Because it is not seemly to devour Christ with our teeth, he willed that, in this mystery, the bread and wine should truly be made his body and blood through their consecration by the power of the Holy Spirit, who daily creates them so that they might be sacrificed mystically for the life of the world. Just as through the Spirit true flesh was created without sexual union from the Virgin, so the same body and blood of Christ are created by mystical consecration out of the substance of bread and wine. It is clearly about this flesh and blood that Christ declares: "Truly, truly I say to you, unless you eat of the flesh of the Son of Man and drink his blood, you will not have eternal life within you" (John 6:53). There he is certainly speaking about nothing other than the true flesh and the true blood.

8.11 Ratranmus of Corbie on the Real Presence

See the comments to 8.10 for an introduction to this text. See also 8.10; 8.12; 8.13.

Source: *De corpore et sanguine Christi*, 2, 9–11, 16; in J. P. Migne, *Patrologia Latina*, 121.128A; 128D–129A; 131A–C; 132A; 135A.

* * *

Certain of the faithful say that [in the mystery] of the body and blood of Christ, which is celebrated daily in the church, nothing happens in the form of a figure or under a hidden symbol, but that it is an open manifestation of truth. Others, however, hold that these elements take the form of a mystery, so that it is one thing which appears to the physical senses, and something different which is discerned by faith ... There is no small difference between these two. And although the apostle writes to believers, telling them that they should all hold the same opinions and say the same things, and that no schism should appear among them, yet when they state such totally different views on the mystery of the body and blood of Christ, they are indeed divided by a schism ... The bread which, through the ministry of the priest, becomes the body of Christ exhibits one thing externally to human senses, and points to something different inwardly to the minds of believers. Externally, the bread has the same shape, colour and flavour as before; inwardly, however, something very different, something much more precious and excellent, is made known, because something heavenly and divine – that is, the body of Christ – is revealed. This is not perceived or received or consumed by the physical sense, but only in the sight of the believer. The wine also becomes the sacrament of the blood of Christ through priestly consecration. Superficially, it shows one thing; yet inwardly, it contains something else. What can be seen on the surface other than the substance of wine? Taste it, and it has the flavour of wine; smell it, and it has the aroma of wine; look at it, and see the colour of wine . . . Since nobody can deny that this is the case, it is clear that the bread and wine are the body and blood of Christ in a figurative sense. After the mystical consecration, when they are no longer called bread and wine, but the body and blood of Christ, as far as the external appearance is concerned, the likeness of flesh cannot be discerned in that bread, just as the actual liquid of blood cannot be seen . . . How then can they be called the body and blood of Christ when no change can be seen to have taken place? . . . As far as the physical appearance of both are concerned, they seem to be things which have been physically created. However, as far as their power is concerned, in that they have been created spiritually, they are the mysteries of the body and blood of Christ.

Candidus of Fulda on "This is My Body"   8.12

The monastery of Fulda, founded in 744, became a leading centre of theological reflection under Rabanus Maurus, who held the position of abbot during the period 822–42. One of the most noted theologians associated with the monastery during this period was Candidus, whose interpretation of the phrase "this is my body" (Matthew 26:26) is quite remarkable. Candidus understands this phrase to refer to the "body of Christ" – that is, the church. The purpose of the sacrament of the body and blood of Christ is to nourish and bring to perfection the church as the body of Christ. See also 8.10; 8.11.

Source: *de passione domini*, 5; in J. P. Migne, *Patrologia Latina*, 106.68D–69A.

* * *

"Take up and eat." That is, my people, make my body – which you now are. This is the body which was given for you. He took this body from the mass of humanity, broke it in the passion, and, having broken it, raised it again from the dead . . . What he took from us, he has now given to us. And you are to "eat" it. That is, you are to make perfect (*perficite*) the body of the church, so that it might become the entire, perfect one bread, whose head is Christ.

Lanfranc of Bec on the Mystery of the   8.13
Sacraments

Lanfranc of Bec, who preceded Anselm of Canterbury both as abbot of Bec and as archbishop of Canterbury, was outraged by what he regarded as totally improper logical explanations of the eucharist. Lanfranc directed his wrath particularly against Berengar of Tours, who had argued that it was ridiculous to suppose that the eucharistic bread could be the body of Christ. How could a piece of bread become the body of Christ, when that body had been in heaven for the last thousand years? In this treatise, written around 1070, Lanfranc vigorously defended the mystery of the sacraments, drawing a sharp distinction between the sacrament itself, and the thing which the sacrament signified. Without really providing an explanation of the point, Lanfranc insists that it is possible to eat "bits of Christ's flesh," while Christ's body remains intact in heaven. See also 8.11; 8.12.

Source: *de corpore et sanguine Christi*, in *Beati Lanfranci archiepiscopi Cantuarensis opera*, ed. J. A. Giles, vol. 2 (Oxford: Clarendon Press, 1844), p. 167.

* * * ──

On the one hand, there is the sacrament; on the other, there is the "thing of the sacrament (*res sacramenti*)." The "thing" (or the "reality") of the sacrament is the body of Christ. Yet Christ is risen from the dead. He does not die, and death has no more power over him (Romans 6:9). So, as the apostle Andrew says, while the bits of [Christ's] flesh (*carnes*) are really eaten and his blood is really drunk, he himself nevertheless continues in his totality (*integer*), living in the heavens at the right hand of the Father until such time as when all will be restored. If you ask me how this is possible, I can only reply briefly as follows: it is a mystery of faith. To believe it can be healthy; to investigate it cannot be of any use.

8.14 Hugh of St. Victor on the Definition of a Sacrament

In this comprehensive account of the theology of the sacraments, written in Latin at Paris in the first half of the twelfth century, Hugh of St. Victor set out a definition of a sacrament which included the need for a physical element which bore some resemblance to the grace it signified. This had the important consequence of excluding penance from the list of sacraments; it was only when Peter Lombard modified this definition (see 8.15) that the medieval formulation of the list of seven sacraments was standardized. See also 8.15; 8.17; 8.21.

Source: *de sacramentis*, IX, 2; in J. P. Migne, *Patrologia Latina*, 176.317C–318B.

* * * ──

Not every sign of a sacred thing can properly be called a sacrament (for the letters in sacred writings, or statues and pictures, are all "signs of sacred things," but cannot be called sacraments for that reason) . . . Anyone wanting a fuller and better definition of a sacrament can define it as follows: "a sacrament is a physical or material element set before the external senses, representing by likeness, signifying by its institution, and containing by sanctification, some invisible and spiritual grace." This definition is recognized as being so appropriate and perfect that it turns out to be appropriate in the case of every sacrament, yet only the sacraments. For everything that has these three elements is a sacrament; and everything that lacks these three cannot be considered as a sacrament. For every sacrament ought to have a kind of likeness to the thing of which it is the sacrament, according to which it is capable of representing the same thing. It ought also to have been instituted in such a way that it is ordained to signify this thing. And finally, it ought to have been sanctified in such a way that it contains that thing, and is efficacious in conferring the same on those who are to be sanctified.

Peter Lombard on the Definition of a Sacrament

8.15

In this major theological work, compiled at Paris during the years 1155–8, Peter Lombard set out a definition of a sacrament which differed from that offered by Hugh of St. Victor (see 8.14) by avoiding any reference to any physical element (such as bread, wine, or water). Using this definition, Peter was able to set out a list of seven sacraments, which became definitive for medieval catholic theology. See also 8.4.

Source: *Sententiarum libri quatuor*, IV.i.4; ii.1; in *Sententiae in IV Libris Distinctae* (Rome: Editiones Collegii S. Bonaventuri, 1981), vol. 2, 233.9–20; 239.18–240.8.

* * *

A sacrament bears a likeness to the thing of which it is a sign. "For if sacraments did no have a likeness of the things whose sacraments they are, they would not properly be called sacraments" (Augustine) . . . Something can properly be called a sacrament if it is a sign of the grace of God and a form of invisible grace, so that it bears its image and exists as its cause. Sacraments were therefore instituted for the sake of sanctifying, as well as of signifying . . . Those things which were instituted for the purpose of signifying alone are nothing more than signs, and are not sacraments, as in the case of the physical sacrifices and ceremonial observances of the Old Law, which were never able to make those who offered them righteous.

. . . Now let us consider the sacraments of the New Law, which are baptism, confirmation, the bread of blessing (that is, the eucharist), penance, extreme unction, ordination, and marriage. Some of these, such as baptism, provide a remedy against sin and confer the assistance of grace; others, such as marriage, are only a remedy; and others, such as the eucharist and ordination, strengthen us with grace and power . . . So why were these sacraments not instituted soon after the fall of humanity, since they convey righteousness and salvation? We reply that the sacraments of grace were not given before the coming of Christ, who is the giver of grace, in that they receive their virtue from his death and suffering.

8.16 Thomas Aquinas on Transubstantiation

The *Summa Theologiae* ("The Totality of Theology"), which Aquinas began to write in Latin in 1265 and left unfinished at the time of his death, is widely regarded as the greatest work of medieval theology. In this discussion of the doctrine of transubstantiation, Aquinas sets out an approach which would become normative for medieval catholic theology. See also 8.5; 8.10; 8.11; 8.12; 8.22; 8.23; 8.28.

Source: *Summa Theologiae*, IIIa, q. 75, aa. 2–5.

* * *

2. Whether the substance of bread and wine remain in this sacrament after consecration

... It has been held that the substance of bread and wine remain in this sacrament after consecration. But this position cannot be maintained, for in the first place it destroys the reality of this sacrament, which demands that in the sacrament there should be the true body of Christ, which was not there before consecration. Now a thing cannot be in a place where it was not before except either by change of position, or by the conversion of some other thing into it; as a fire begins to be in a house either because it is carried there or because it is kindled. But it is clear that the body of Christ does not begin to be in the sacrament through change of position... Therefore it remains that the body of Christ can only come to be in the sacrament by means of the conversion of the substance of bread into his body; and that which is converted into anything does not remain after the conversion... This position is therefore to be avoided as heretical.

3. Whether the substance of bread or wine is annihilated after the consecration of this sacrament

... As the substance of bread or wine does not remain in the sacrament, some have thought it impossible that their substance should be converted into that of the body or blood of Christ, and therefore have maintained that through the consecration the substance of bread or wine is either resolved into underlying matter (that is, the four elements) or annihilated... But this is impossible, because it is impossible to suppose the manner in which the true body of Christ begins to be in the sacrament, unless by conversion of the substance of bread; and this conversion is ruled out by the supposition of the annihilation of the substance of bread, or its resolution into underlying matter...

4. Whether bread can be changed into the body of Christ

... This conversion is not like natural conversions but is wholly supernatural, brought about only by the power of God... All conversion which takes place according to the laws of nature is formal... But God... can produce not only a formal conversion, that is, the replacement of one form by another in the same subject, but also the conversion of the whole being, that is, the conversion of the whole substance of A into the whole substance of B. And this is done in this sacrament by the power of God, for the whole substance of bread is converted into the whole substance of Christ's body ... Hence this conversion is properly called transubstantiation ...

5. Whether the accidents of bread and wine remain in the sacrament after this conversion

... It is obvious to our senses that after consecration all the accidents of bread and wine remain. And, by divine providence, there is a good reason for this. First, because it is not normal for people to eat human flesh and to drink human blood; in fact, they are revolted by this idea. Therefore Christ's flesh and blood are set before us to be taken under the appearances of those things which are of frequent use, namely bread and wine. Secondly, if we ate our Lord under his proper appearance, this sacrament would be ridiculed by unbelievers. Thirdly, in order that, while we take the Lord's body and blood invisibly, this fact may avail towards the merit of faith.

Martin Luther on the Number of Sacraments

8.17

In this opening part of the 1520 work entitled *The Babylonian Captivity of the Church*, Luther allowed that penance was a sacrament. By the end of the same work, he had changed his mind, and denied the sacramental character of penance, apparently on the basis of the fact that there was no sacramental sign associated with it. Luther here seems to base himself on the Vulgate version of 1 Timothy 3:16, which refers to Christ as a *sacramentum*. See also 8.18; 8.19; 8.26.

Source: *The Babylonian Captivity of the Church* (1520); in *D. Martin Luthers Werke: Kritische Ausgabe*, vol. 6 (Weimar: Böhlau, 1888), 509–12; 513–14.

* * *

To begin with, I must deny that there are seven sacraments, and for the present maintain that there are but three: baptism, penance, and the bread. All three have been subjected to a miserable captivity by the Roman curia, and the church has been robbed of all her liberty. Yet if I were to speak according to the usage of the Scriptures, I should have only one single sacrament, but with three sacramental signs.

8.18   Martin Luther on the Doctrine of Transubstantiation

In this 1520 criticism of the teachings of the medieval church concerning the sacraments, Luther argues that the concept of "transubstantiation" is untenable. While Luther maintains a doctrine of the real presence of Christ in the eucharist, he refuses to accept the specifically Aristotelian interpretation of it associated with transubstantiation. The "Cardinal of Cambrai" was Pierre d'Ailly, a noted late medieval theologian, who Luther studied while preparing for the priesthood.

Source: *The Babylonian Captivity of the Church* (1520); in *D. Martin Luthers Werke: Kritische Ausgabe*, vol. 6 (Weimar: Böhlau, 1888), 509.22–512.4. See also 8.16; 8.28.

* * *

Therefore it is an absurd and new imposition upon the words to understand "bread" to mean "the form or accidents" of bread, and "wine" to mean "the form or accidents of wine." Why do they not also understand all other things to mean their "forms or accident?" And even if this might be done with everything else, it would still not be right to weaken the words of God in this way, and to cause so much harm by depriving them of their signification.

But for more than twelve hundred years the church believed rightly, during which time the holy fathers never, at any time or place, mentioned this "transubstantiation" (a pretentious word and idea) until the pseudo-philosophy of Aristotle began to make its inroads into the church in these last three hundred years, in which many things have been incorrectly defined, as for example, that the divine essence is neither begotten nor begets; or that the soul is the substantial form of the human body. These and like assertions are made without any reason or cause, as the Cardinal of Cambrai himself admits.

They may want to argue that the danger of lapsing into idolatry demands that the bread and wine should not be truly present. This is ridiculous. The laity have never heard of their subtle philosophy of substance and accidents, and could not make sense of it even if they were taught about it. Anyway, the same danger is just as much present with the accidents which they can see, as with the substance which they cannot see. If they do not worship the accidents, but the Christ hidden under them, why should they worship the [substance of the] bread, which they do not see?

But why could not Christ include his body in the substance of the bread just as well as in the accidents? In red-hot iron, for example, the two substances, fire and iron, are so mingled that every part is both iron and fire. Why should it not be even more possible that the glorious body of Christ be contained in every part of the substance of the bread? . . . I rejoice greatly that the simple faith of this sacrament is still to be found, at least among ordinary people. For as they cannot understand the matter, neither do they dispute whether accidents are present without substance, but believe with a simple faith that Christ's body and blood are truly contained there, and leave the argument about what contains them to those who have nothing else to do with their time . . .

What is true concerning Christ is also true concerning the sacrament. In order for the divinity to dwell in a human body, it is not necessary for the human nature to be transubstantiated and the divinity contained under the accidents of the human nature. Both natures are simply there in their entirety, and it is true to say: "This man is God; this God is man." Even though philosophy is not capable of grasping this, faith is. And the authority of God's Word is greater than the capacity of our intellect to grasp it. In the same way, it is not necessary in the sacrament that the bread and wine be transubstantiated and that Christ be contained under their accidents in order that the real body and real blood may be present. But both remain there at the same time, and it is truly said: "This bread is my body; this wine is my blood," and vice versa. (I will understand it in this way for the time being on account of the honor of the holy words of God, to which I will allow no violence to be done by petty human arguments, nor will I allow them to be twisted into meanings which are foreign to them.)

Martin Luther on the Bread and Wine as a Testament   8.19

In this discussion of the function of the communion service, Luther argues that it acts like a "last will" or "testament," in which certain goods are promised to named heirs, once the testator has died. Note in particular how Luther insists that the incarnation means that it is perfectly proper to say that "God can die." The concept of a faith "which clings to the Word of the promising God" is characteristic of Luther. See also 6.27; 6.31.

Source: *The Babylonian Captivity of the Church* (1520); in *D. Martin Luthers Werke: Kritische Ausgabe*, vol. 6 (Weimar: Böhlau, 1888), 513.14–514.21.

* * *

Let this stand, therefore, as our first and infallible proposition: the mass or Sacrament of the Altar (*missam seu sacramentum altaris*) is Christ's testament (*testamentum Christi*), which, when he was dying, he left to be distributed among believers. For that is the meaning of his words, "This cup is the new testament in my blood" (Luke 22:20; 1 Corinthians 11:25). Let this truth stand, I say, as the immovable foundation on which we shall base all that we have to say. You will see that we are going to undermine every human impiety to have been brought into this most precious sacrament. Christ, who is the truth, truly says that this is the new testament in his blood, poured out for us (Luke 19:20). Not without reason do I dwell on this sentence; this is no minor matter, and it demands our full attention.

Were we to enquire what a testament is, we shall learn at the same time what the mass is, and what constitutes its use, benefits, and abuse.

A testament is, without doubt, a promise made by someone who is about to die, in which a bequest is identified and heirs are appointed. A testament, therefore, involves first, the death of the testator; and second, the promise of an inheritance and the identification of the heirs. Thus Paul discusses at length the nature of a testament in Romans 4, Galatians 3 and 4, and Hebrews 9. We see the same thing clearly also in these words of Christ. Christ testifies concerning his death when he says: "This is my body, which is given, this is my blood, which is poured out." (Luke 22:19–20). He names and designates the bequest when he says "for the forgiveness of sins" (Matthew 26:28). And he appoints the heirs when he says "For you (Luke 22:19–20; 1 Corinthians 11:24) and for many" (Matthew 26:28; Mark 14:24), that is, for those who accept and believe the promise of the testator. For it is faith that makes heirs, as we shall see.

So you see that what we call the mass is a promise of the forgiveness of sins, made to us by God, and such a promise as has been confirmed (*firma sit*) by the death of the Son of God. For a promise and a testament differ only in that a testament involves the death of the one who makes it. A testator is someone who promises and is about to die (*testator idem est quod moriturus promissor*), while someone who promises (if I may put it thus) is a testator who is not about to die. This testament of Christ is foreshadowed in all the promises of God from the beginning of the world; indeed, whatever value those ancient promises possessed derived totally from this new promise that was to come in Christ. Hence the words "compact," "covenant," and "testament of the Lord" (*pactum, foedus, testamentum domini*) occur so often in Scripture, by which it was signified that God would one day die. "For where there is a testament, the death of the testator must of necessity occur" (Hebrews 9:16). Now God made a testament; therefore, it was necessary that he should die. But God could not die unless he became a human. Thus the incarnation and the death of Christ are both to be understood as being in this one enormously rich word, "testament."

From this, it can be seen what constitutes the right and what is the wrong use of the mass, and what constitutes worthy and what the unworthy preparation for it. If the mass is a promise, as has been said, then access to it is to be gained, not with any works, or powers, or merits of one's own, but by faith alone. For where there is the Word of the promising God, there must necessarily be the faith of the accepting person (*Ubi enim est verbum promittendis dei, ibi necessaria est fides acceptantis hominis*), so that it is clear that the beginning of our salvation is a faith which clings to the Word of the promising God (*fides quae pendeat in verbo promittendis dei*), who, without any effort on our part, in free and unmerited mercy goes before us and offers us the word of his promise. "He sent forth his word, and thus healed them," (Psalm 107:20) not: "He accepted our work, and thus healed us." The Word of God is first of all. After it follows faith; after faith, love (*charitas*); then love does every good work, for it does no wrong, indeed, it is the fulfilling of the law (Romans 13:10). Humanity can only come to God or deal with him through faith.

Martin Luther on Baptism 8.20

This extract from Luther's *Small Catechism*, written in German in 1529, brings out the close relation between Word and Sacrament in Luther's thought. See also 6.27; 8.19.

Source: *The Small Catechism* (1529); in *D. Martin Luthers Werke: Kritische Gesamtausgabe*, vol. 30, part 1 (Weimar: Böhlaus, 1910), 255.20–257.24.

* * *

Q. What is baptism?

A. Baptism is not just water on its own, but it is water used according to God's command and linked with God's Word.

Q. What is this Word of God?

A. Our Lord Christ, as recorded in Matthew 28:19, said, "Go therefore and make disciples of all nations, baptizing them in the name of the Father and of the Son and of the Holy Spirit."

Q. What gifts or benefits does Baptism bring?

A. It brings about the forgiveness of sins, saves us from death and the devil, and grants eternal blessedness to all who believe, as the Word and promise of God declare.

Q. What is this Word and promise of God?

A. Our Lord Christ, as recorded in Mark 16:16, said, "Anyone who believes and is baptized will be saved; but those who do not believe will be condemned."

Q. How can water bring about such a great thing?

A. Water does not; but it is the Word of God with and through the water, and our faith which trusts in the Word of God in the water. For without the Word of God, that water is nothing but water, and there is no Baptism. But when it is linked with the Word of God, it is a Baptism, that is, a gracious water of life (*gnadenreych wasser desz lebens*) and a bath of new birth in the Holy Spirit (*ain bad der neuwen geburt im heyligen geyst*) . . .

Q. What does such washing with water mean?

A. It means that the old Adam in us should be drowned by daily sorrow and repentance, and put to death, along with all sins and evil lusts, and that a new person (*neuwermensch*) should come forth daily and rise up in righteousness and purity (*reynigkeyt*), to live forever before God.

Philip Melanchthon on Sacramental Signs 8.21

In this extract from the *Loci Communes* ("Commonplaces"), written in Latin in 1521, Melanchthon sets out his understanding of the relation of Word and Sacrament, and particularly between faith and the promises of God. Note the emphatic insistence that sacraments do not justify in themselves; they are merely signs of the justifying grace of God. Nevertheless, they serve the vital function of reassuring believers of God's grace and goodness. See also 6.27; 6.31; 8.19.

Source: *Loci Communes* (1521); in *Melanchthons Werke in Auswahl*, ed. H. Engelland (Gütersloh: Bertelsmann Verlag, 1953), vol. 2, 140.25–144.19.

* * *

We have said that the gospel is the promise of grace. The *locus* on signs is very closely related to promises. For in the Scriptures these signs are added to the promises as seals which remind us of the promises, and are certain witnesses to the divine will toward us, testifying that we shall certainly receive what God has promised. Major errors have resulted from the use of signs. For when the [medieval theological] schools dispute about the difference between the sacraments of the Old and New Testaments, they say that there is no power to justify in the sacraments of the Old Testament. They attribute the power to justify to the sacraments of the New Testament, which is clearly an error. For faith alone justifies. The nature of signs is best understood from Paul in Romans 4:10–12, where he speaks of circumcision. He says that Abraham was not justified *by* circumcision but *before* circumcision and without merit of circumcision. But afterward he received circumcision as a "seal of righteousness" – that is, a seal that God declared Abraham to be righteous, and declared that Abraham was righteous before God, so that his troubled conscience might not despair. And what can be more pleasing than this use of signs? It is not enough for signs to remind us of the divine promises. The great fact is that they are a testimony of God's will toward you. Thus Moses calls circumcision a "sign" in Genesis 17:11: "And it shall be a sign of the covenant between me and you." The fact that circumcision is a sign reminds Abraham and all who are circumcised of the divine promise. The fact that circumcision is a sign of the covenant, strengthens the conscience of Abraham so that he does not doubt at all that what has been promised will come to pass, that God will furnish what he promised. And what was it that God promised to Abraham? Was it not that he would be Abraham's God: that he would cherish, justify, and preserve him, and so one? Abraham did not doubt that these things were certain, since he had been strengthened by circumcision as by a seal . . .

Signs do not justify, as the apostle says: "circumcision counts for nothing" (1 Corinthian 7:19), so that baptism is nothing, and participation in the Lord's Supper (*mensa domini*) is nothing, but they are testimonies and "seals" of the divine will toward you which give assurance to your conscience if it doubts God's grace or benevolence toward you . . . You ought not to doubt that you have experienced mercy when you have heard the gospel and received the signs of the gospel, baptism, and the body and blood of the Lord. Hezekiah could have been restored without a sign if he had been willing to believe the bare promise of God, and Gideon would have overcome without a sign if he had believed. So you can be justified without a sign, provided you believe. Therefore, signs do not justify, but the faith of Hezekiah and Gideon had to be secured, strengthened, and confirmed by such signs. In the same way our weakness is strengthened by signs, lest it despair of the mercy of God amid so many attacks from sin. If God himself were to speak with you face to face or show you some special pledge of his mercy as, for example, a miracle, you would consider it nothing else than a sign of divine favor. As for these signs, then, you ought to believe with as much certainty that God is merciful to you when you receive baptism and participate in the Lord's Supper as you would if God himself were to speak with you or to show forth some other miracle that would relate directly to you. Signs are given for the purpose of stimulating faith. Those who call such things into question have lost both faith and the use of signs. The knowledge of signs is very healthful, and I have no idea whether there is anything else that consoles the conscience and strengthens it more effectively than this use of signs.

Those things which others call "sacraments" we call "signs," or, if you prefer, "sacramental signs." For Paul calls Christ himself a "sacrament" (Colossians 1:27; I Timothy 3:16). If you do not like the term "sign," you may call the sacraments "seals," for this term comes closer to the nature of the sacraments. Those who have compared these signs with symbols or military passwords are to be commended for doing so, because signs were only marks by which those to whom the divine promises pertained could be known. Although he had already been justified, Cornelius was baptized that he might be reckoned in the number of those to whom the promise of the Kingdom of God and eternal life pertained. I have given this instruction on the nature of signs that you may understand what a godly use of the sacraments is, lest anyone follow the Scholastics, who have attributed justification to the signs by a terrible error.

There are two signs, however, instituted by Christ in the gospel: baptism and participation in the Lord's Supper. For we judge that sacramental signs are only those which have been divinely handed down as signs of the grace of God. For we human beings can neither institute a sign of the divine will toward us nor can we adapt those signs which Scripture has employed in other ways as signifying that will. Therefore, we are all the more amazed at how it ever came into the minds of the Sophists to include among the sacraments things which the Scriptures do not mention by so much as a word, especially when they attributed justification to signs.

Kornelius Hendriks Hoen on "This is My Body"   8.22

In this letter, which circulated widely in 1525, this Dutch humanist writer argued for a symbolical or metaphorical interpretation of the Latin words *hoc est corpus meum* ("this is my body"). Although ignored by Luther, Hoen's letter was read with enthusiasm by Zwingli (8.23), whose own view of the matter subsequently came to strongly resemble Hoen's. See also 8.11.

Source: *Epistola christiana admodum* (published 1525); in *Corpus Reformatorum: Huldreich Zwinglis sämtliche Werke*, vol. 91 (Leipzig: Heinsius, 1927), 512.30–513.32.

* * *

For if we adore and worship this consecrated bread, honoring it in every way as if it were God, even though it is not God, how, I ask you, do we differ from those heathens who worshiped wood and stones? They believed that there was some divinity (*numen*) in them, which there was not, for they would not have wished to adore stones unless perhaps they had first believed that these stones were gods.

Now someone might say: "We have the Word of God which says, 'This is My Body'." That is true, you do have this Word of the Lord. In just the same way, you also have that word which encourages Roman tyranny: "Whatever you shall bind on earth is bound in heaven" (Matthew 16:19). But if you were to study this carefully, you will find it does not provide any basis at all for such tyranny. So let us examine these matters facing us, so that we may not be like those with blind guides, who fall together with them into a pit (Matthew 15:14). For the Lord prohibits us from believing anyone who says, "Here is Christ" or "There is Christ" (Matthew 24:23). For this reason, I should not have faith in those who say that Christ is in the bread: I could not excuse myself as having been deceived, since I have refused to listen to the warning voice of Christ. For now those dangerous times have come, during which he predicted this would happen.

Nor did the apostles speak of the sacrament in this way: they *broke* bread, and they *called* it bread: they were silent about this Roman belief. Nor is this contradicted by St. Paul who, although he says, "The bread which we break, is it not a sharing in the body of Christ?" (1 Corinthians 10:16), does not say that the bread *is* the body of Christ. It is therefore obvious that the word "is (*est*)" in this text should be interpreted as meaning "signifies (*significat*)" . . .

But let us first see on what foundation the Romanists build their doctrine, a teaching that is so singular and wonderful that nothing like it is found in Scripture. We read that Christ became flesh (*incarnatus*) – but that was once only, in the womb of the virgin. And this incarnation was predicted by many prophetic oracles; it was demonstrated in Christ's life, death, and whole way of life, and preached by the apostles. But that idea that Christ would daily become bread (*impanatus*), so to speak, in the hands of anyone conducting this sacrifice (*in manibus cuiusvis sacrificuli*) was neither foretold by the prophets nor preached by the apostles, but rests only on what Christ said: "This is my body; do this in remembrance of me."

8.23 Huldrych Zwingli on "This is My Body"

In this work, first published in Swiss-German on 23 February 1526 under the title *eine klare Unterrichtung vom nachtmal Christi*, Zwingli deals with the true meaning of the Latin phrase *hoc est corpus meum*, "this is my body" (Matthew 26:26). Using arguments which clearly reflect familiarity with Kornelius Hoen's letter on the subject (see 8.22), Zwingli argues that the only acceptable meaning of the word "is" in this phrase must be acknowledged to be "signifies." See also 8.10; 8.11; 8.27.

Source: *On the Lord's Supper* (1526); in *Corpus Reformatorum: Huldreich Zwinglis sämtliche Werke*, vol. 91 (Leipzig: Heinsius, 1927), 796.2–800.5.

* * *

But there are two clear flaws in the argument [that the words "this is my body" refer to the bread being the physical body of Christ]. The first is that we are not given any reason to believe that when the Pope or some other human person says: "This is my body," the body of Christ is necessarily present. It is useless to say that Christ himself said: "Do this in remembrance of me": therefore the body of Christ is there . . . The second flaw is a failure to see that before we use the Word of God to justify anything, we must first understand it correctly. For example, when Christ says: "I am the vine" (John 15:5), we have to consider that he is using figurative speech in the first place. In other words, he is *like* a vine, just as the branches are nourished by the vine and cannot bear fruit without it, so believers are in him, and without him they can do nothing. Now if you object against this interpretation of Christ's saying "I am the vine," and argue that therefore he must be a physical vine, you end up by making Christ into a piece of vine wood. In the same way, when you come to the words: "This is my body," you must first make sure that he intended to give his flesh and blood in physical form. Otherwise it is quite pointless to argue that he said it, and therefore it is so. For it is so only as he himself understood it to be so, and not as you misunderstand it . . . Let us consider the basis of the doctrine. If in Christ's saying: "This is my body," we take the little word "is" in a substantive manner, that is literally, then it necessarily follows that the substance of the body or the flesh of Christ is literally and essentially present. But this gives rise to two obvious mistakes.

The first is this: if he is literally and essentially present in the flesh, then he is actually torn apart by the teeth and tangibly masticated in human mouths. We cannot get round the issue by saying: "With God all things are possible." . . . It is evident, then, that the flesh is not present literally and corporally. For if it were, its mass and substance would be perceived, and it would be pressed with the teeth . . . Therefore, if the "is" is to be taken literally, the body of Christ must be visibly, essentially, physically and tangibly present (*so müßte der lychnam Christi sichtbar, wesenlich, lyplich, empfindlich da sin*). For that reason even in this erroneous teaching itself there is a proof that the words cannot possibly mean that we partake physically of flesh and blood: for if God says literally: "This is my body," then the body ought to be there literally and physically . . . And since we do not experience or perceive any such presence, it follows that the words of Christ cannot refer to physical flesh and blood. For if that were the meaning, we should constantly perceive them, for he cannot lie. You see, then, that the argument for a literal presence merely works against them.

The second error resulting from a literal interpretation corresponds to that second opinion which we mentioned alongside the first, namely, that we eat the body of Christ in or under the bread, the bread itself remaining bread. If we take the word "is" in a substantive way, that is literally, then it is an obvious mistake to say that the bread remains bread and to deny transubstantiation, the changing of the substance of bread into that of flesh. And for this reason: I apply the argument used in the first error. The Word of God is living. He said: "This is my body." Therefore it is his body. But if we take the word "is" literally, as the second error obstinately maintains, then necessarily the substance of bread has to be changed completely into that of flesh. But that means that the bread is no longer there. Therefore it is impossible to maintain that the bread remains, but that in or under the bread flesh is eaten. Notice how utterly unreasonable this position is. On no account will it allow that Christ's words: "This is my body," are figurative or symbolical. It insists that the word "is" must be taken literally. But it then proceeds to ignore that word and to say: "The body of Christ is eaten *in* the bread." Yet Christ did not say: "Take, eat, my body is eaten in the bread." He said: "This is my body." How dreadful a thing it is to get out of one's depth! If it were I who perverted the words of Christ in that way, surely the axe of judgment would strike me down. The second error is easily perceived, then, and we have only to compare the two and they cancel each other out. For the first maintains that the flesh and blood are present on account of the word "is." But if we take that word literally, it destroys the second, which tries to take it literally but still asserts that the bread remains bread. For if the word is taken literally, the bread is not bread but flesh. On the other hand, the second error at least recognizes that the substance of bread is not turned into the substance of flesh. It thus safeguards the truth that the word "is" cannot be taken literally. If it were literal, the flesh would be no less perceptible than the bread. For just as, before the consecration (as they term it), the bread is perceptible as bread, so from the moment of consecration (*wyhung*) it would have to be perceptible as flesh. Hence the first error is destroyed, and we may conclude that they are both obviously false. For when the second maintains that the "is" is to be taken literally, it is adopting a quite indefensible position, as we have seen: for there is no other way of avoiding a figurative interpretation. Yet when we forcibly expose this defect, pointing out that there is no foundation for such ideas, they simply cry: "We remain faithful to the simple words of Christ, trusting that those Christians who follow the simple words of Christ will not go astray." But what you call the simple meaning of those words is actually the most doubtful, the most obscure, the least intelligible of all. If the simple meaning of Scripture is that which we maintain through a misunderstanding of the letter, then Christ is a piece of vine wood, or a silly sheep, or a door, and Peter is the foundation-stone of the Church. The simple or natural sense of these words is that which obtains in all similar instances, that which the minds of all believers find the most natural and the most easily understood.

Huldrych Zwingli on the Nature of Sacraments

8.24

This work, published on 27 May 1525 in Swiss-German as *von dem touff*, opens with an important discussion of the nature of sacraments in general, before moving on to a more detailed analysis of baptism itself. Zwingli here develops an understanding of sacraments which focuses on their symbolic role, and particularly the way in which they function as signs of public commitment on the part of individuals to the church as a whole. He draws an analogy with the annual pilgrimage to the battleside of Nähenfels – the "Näfelser Fahrtfeier" – which commemorated a major Swiss victory over the Austrians in April 1388. Just as a loyal Swiss citizen would commemorate this great victory as a sign of loyalty to the nation, so the Christian celebrates Christ's death as a sign of loyalty to the church. See also 8.14; 8.15; 8.17; 8.19; 8.26.

Source: *On Baptism*; in *Corpus Reformatorum: Huldreich Zwinglis sämtliche Werke*, vol. 91 (Leipzig: Heinsius, 1927), 217.14–218.24.

* * *

Now [Christ] has left behind to us, his fellow members, two ceremonies, that is, two external things or sings: baptism and the thanksgiving or remembrance (*dancksagung oder widergedächtnus*), undoubtedly as a concession to our weakness . . . By the first of these signs, baptism, we are initially marked off to God, as we shall see later. In the other, the Lord's Supper or thanksgiving, we give thanks to God because he has redeemed us by his Son.

Before we speak about baptism, we must first identify the meaning of the word "sacrament." To us Germans, the word "sacrament" suggests something that has power to take away sin or to make us holy. But this is a serious error. For only Jesus Christ and no external thing can take away the sins of us Christians or make us holy . . . As used in this context the word "sacrament" means a sign of commitment (*pflichtszeichen*). If a man sews on a white cross, he proclaims that he is a [Swiss] Confederate (*Eydgnoß*). And if he makes the pilgrimage to Nähenfels and gives God praise and thanksgiving for the victory delivered to our forefathers, he testifies from his heart that he is a Confederate. Similarly the man who receives the mark of baptism is the one who is resolved to hear what God says to him, to learn the divine precepts and to live his life in accordance with them. And the man who, in the remembrance or supper, gives thanks to God in the congregation delcares that he heartily rejoices in the death of Christ and thanks him for it. So I ask these quibblers that they allow the sacraments to be real sacraments, and that they do not describe them as signs (*zeichen*) which are identical with the things which they represent. For if they are the things which they represent, they are no longer signs: for the sign and the thing which is represented cannot be the same thing. Sacraments – as even the papists maintain – are simply the signs of holy things. Baptism is a sign which pledges us to the Lord Jesus Christ. The remembrance shows us that Christ suffered death for our sake. they are the signs and pledges (*zeichen und verpflichtungen*) of these holy things. You will find ample proof of this if you consider the pledge of circumcision and the thanksgiving of the passover lamb.

8.25 The First Helvetic Confession on the Efficacy of the Sacraments

This important early statement of Reformed theology, formulated by Swiss theologians in 1536, sets out a view of the sacraments which regards them as efficacious signs. Note the emphatic assertion that the efficacy of these signs is totally due to God, rather than to anything which is inherent within those signs. The fact that they are able to bring about what they signify is due to the power of God, not to the power of the signs themselves. See also 8.18; 8.19; 8.26; 8.29.

Source: The First Helvetic Confession, article 20; in E. F. K. Müller (ed.), *Die Bekenntnisschriften der reformierten Kirche* (Leipzig: Böhme, 1903), 106.25–43.

* * *

The signs (*zeychen*), which are called sacraments, are two, namely, Baptism and the Lord's Supper. These sacraments are significant, holy signs of elevated and secret things (*hoher und heymlicher dingen*). However, they are not merely empty signs, but consist of both the sign and substance. For in baptism the water is the sign, but the substance and spiritual thing is rebirth and admission into the people of God. In the Lord's Supper the bread and wine are the signs, but the spiritual substance is the communion of the body and blood of Christ, the salvation acquired on the cross, and forgiveness of sins. As the signs are physically received, so these substantial, invisible and spiritual things are received in faith. In addition, the entire power, efficacy and fruit of the sacraments lies in these spiritual and substantial things. For this reason, we confess that the sacraments are not simply outward signs of Christian fellowship. On the contrary, we confess them to be signs of divine grace by which the ministers of the Church work with the Lord for the purpose and to the end which He Himself promises, offers, and efficaciously provides. We confess, however, that all sanctifying and saving power is to be ascribed to God, the Lord alone.

8.26 John Calvin on the Nature of Sacraments

In this section from the 1559 edition of the *Institutes of the Christian Religion*, Calvin explores the relation between a sacramental sign and the grace which it signifies. Notice the emphasis placed on God's deliberate accommodation to human weakness. See also 8.21; 8.25; 8.29.

Source: *Institutes*, IV.xiv.1, 3; in *Joannis Calvini: Opera Selecta*, ed. P. Barth and W. Niesel, vol. 5 (Munich: Kaiser Verlag, 1936), 259.1–261.3.

* * *

To start with, we must consider what a sacrament is. It seems to me that a simple and proper definition is that it is an outward sign by which the Lord seals on our consciences the promises of his good will towards us in order to sustain the weakness of our faith; and by which we in turn bear witness to our piety toward him in the presence of the Lord and of his angels, and before human beings. More briefly, it is a testimony of divine grace toward us, confirmed by an outward sign, with mutual attestation of our piety towards him (*cum mutua nostrae erga ipsum pietatis testificatione*). Whichever of these definitions is preferred, its sense does not differ from that given by Augustine, who teaches that a sacrament is "a visible sign of a sacred thing" or "a visible form of an invisible grace"; however, it explains the thing itself better and more clearly . . .

Now, from this definition we understand that a sacrament is never without a prior promise but is joined to it as a sort of appendix (*tanquam appendicem quandam adiungi*), with the objective of confirming and sealing the promise itself, and of making it clearer to us and, so to speak, ratifying it. God thus makes allowance first for our ignorance and slowness, then for our weakness. Yet, properly speaking, it is not so much needed to strengthen his holy Word as to support out faith in it. For God's truth is of itself firm and sure enough; nor can it receive better confirmation from any source other than from itself. But as our faith is slight and feeble unless it is supported at every point and sustained by every means, it trembles, wavers, totters, and finally falls down. So our merciful Lord, by his infinite kindness, adjusts himself to us in such a way that, since we are creatures who always creep on the ground, cleave to the flesh, and, do not think about or even conceive of anything spiritual, uses these earthly elements, and sets before us in the flesh a mirror of spiritual blessings. For if we were incorporeal (as Chrysostom says), he would give us these very things naked and incorporeal. Now, because we have souls inserted into our bodies, he imparts spiritual things under visible ones. This does not mean that the gifts set before us in the sacraments are bestowed with the natures of those things; rather, that they have been given this signification by God.

Martin Bucer on the Sacraments 8.27

In this work of Reformed pastoral theology, written during a period spent in England (1549–55), the German refomer Martin Bucer sets out his understanding of the place of sacraments in the life of a Reformed church. In the course of this analysis, Bucer brings out the pastoral function of the sacraments, particularly in relation to reassurance. See also 8.26.

Source: *De regno Christi*, I, 7; in *Martini Buceri Opera Latina: De regno Christi libri duo* (Paris: Presses Universitaires de France, 1955), pp. 66–8.

* * *

Another part of the sacred ministry is the administration of the sacraments. There are two sacraments explicitly instituted and commanded for us by

Christ. Moreover, the apostles so religiously used the sacrament of the imposition of hands in ordaining the ministry of the churches, as we read in Acts 13:3, the First Letter to Timothy, 4:14 and 5:22, and the Second Letter, 1:6, that it appears very likely that they did this at the command of the Lord. For Paul writes about the use of this sign to Timothy as if he was writing about a sacrament which was permanently established, in that he warns him not to lay hands on anyone as a matter of haste. But we have no explicit command of Christ to this effect in Scripture, as we do in the case of Baptism and the Eucharist.

We further read that the early churches used the sign of the laying on of hands in the reconciliation of penitents, as well as in the confirmation of the baptized in the faith of Christ. This the bishops normally did according to the example of the apostles, who by this sign bestowed the Holy Spirit on those who had been baptized (Acts 8:17–18). Those who desire that the Kingdom of Christ should be established correctly among them once more must therefore take special care to re-establish the legitimate administration of Baptism and the Eucharist.

But this involves the following matters. First, holy and blameless ministers should administer each sacrament, only to those whom they know to be holy and blameless according to the Word of the Lord.

For by Baptism people must be washed from sins, regenerated and renewed for eternal life, incorporated in Christ the Lord, and clothed with him, and all of these things are reserved only to those chosen for eternal life (Acts 22:16; Titus 3:5; 1 Corinthians 12:12–13; Galatians: 3:27). Concerning the baptizing of the infants of believers, the Word of the Lord is sufficient: "I will be your God, and of your seed" (Genesis 17:7), and "Your children are holy" (1 Corinthians 7:14). But adults, as has been said above, ought to be catechized before they are baptized and carefully examined as to whether they believe in their hearts what they profess with their lips ...

Secondly, since remission of sins and the holy communion of Christ are imparted through these sacraments, and the covenant of eternal salvation is thereby sealed and confirmed (*foedusque aeternae salutis obsignatur et confirmatur*), it is necessary that these mysteries be explained to those about to receive such sacraments in the presence of the whole church and that they be celebrated as reverently as possible. Hence the ancient churches spent an entire octave in celebrating the mysteries of Baptism. To accomplish this more effectively, they administered Baptism only at Easter and Pentecost, unless someone was in danger of death ...

At the administration of each of these sacraments, appropriate lessons from Holy Scripture should be read and expolained as reverently as possible, and then the people should be exhorted earnestly to a worthy reception of the sacraments. There ought also to be added most ardent prayers and thanksgivings to the Lord, and also devout offerings. For since people receive the supreme benefits of God through these sacraments – the forgiveness of sins and inheritance of eternal life – they should certainly not appear before God with empty hands (Exodus 23:15).

The Council of Trent on Transubstantiation 8.28

During the course of its thirteenth session, which ended on 11 October 1551, the Council of Trent set out a definitive statement on its understanding of the nature of the real presence of Christ in the eucharist, affirming that the term "transubstantiation" was appropriate to refer to the change in the substance of the bread and wine resulting from their consecration. See also 8.5; 8.9; 8.10; 8.11; 8.12; 8.16.

Source: Council of Trent, Session XIII, chapter 4; in H. Denzinger (ed.), *Enchiridion Symbolorum* 24–5 edn (Barcelona: Herder, 1948), p. 306.

* * *

Because Christ our Redeemer declared that it was truly his body that he was offering under the species of bread, it has always been the belief of the Church of God, which this sacred council reaffirms, that by the consecration of the bread and wine a change takes place in which the entire substance of the bread becomes the substance of the body of Christ our Lord, and the whole substance of the wine becomes the substance of his blood. This change the holy Catholic Church has fittingly and correctly called "transubstantiation."

Theodore Beza on Sacramental Signs 8.29

In this work, published in Latin in 1570, Beza set out a view of the nature and function of the sacraments which develops the views of Calvin. The most important feature of this discussion is its affirmation that sacramental signs are efficacious, in that they are able to bring about what they signify. Beza provides an illustration, based on a wax seal, which brings out the point at issue. See also 8.21; 8.24; 8.26.

Source: *Confessio Christianae Fidei*; in *Tractationes Theologicae*, 3 vols (Geneva: Jean Crispinus, 1570–82), vol. 1, pp. 26–7.

* * *

We use the word "sign" in explaining the sacraments, not to designate something ineffective, as if something were represented to us merely by a picture or memorial or figure, but to declare that the Lord, by his singular goodness, in order to help our weakness, uses external and physical things to represent to our external senses the greatest and most divine things, which he truly communicates to us internally through his Spirit. In this way, he does not give us the reality which is signified to any lesser extent than he gives us the external and physical signs . . . In the sacraments, therefore, neither the substance of the signs nor their natural qualities and quantities are changed, but they are changed with regard to the purpose and use for which they were given to the church of God. They now begin to signify truly heavenly and divine realities for us, not only on the basis of their own intrinsic nature, but also on the basis of their institution by the Son of God.

Therefore water, in terms of its natural use, may be used to wash away bodily stains, just as the bread and wine may be used to sustain life. But these things are applied in the sacraments for a very different purpose, namely to bring before our eyes the mystery of salvation ... To illustrate these very sacred matters, we may take an example from human affairs. The principle involved is like that which underlies the use of wax which is usually stamped with the seal of a prince or magistrate to confirm a public document. In this case, the nature or substance of the wax does not differ at all from any other wax. In terms of its use, however, it is very different ... The promises to which the sacraments are attached in this way in the manner of authentic seals concern Christ only. That is why it is first Jesus Christ himself and then all the riches which he has in himself, which are the only reality which the most compassionate Father gives us to bring us to eternal life. He signifies them to us truly and certainly by visible signs and by the word joined to the signs, so that faith, by which alone we can receive that offered treasure, is more and more increased and confirmed. And since this concerns our union with Christ as individual members of the Church, the sacraments have another purpose: to enhance that mutual union which the members of the same body should have with one another.

8.30 John Wesley on the Eucharist and Salvation

John and Charles Wesley were noted for their ability to express theology in the form of hymns, and for using these hymns as a means of educating their congregations theologically. In this important hymn, published in 1786, John Wesley stressed the connection between the actuality of salvation in Christ and its commemoration in the communion service. See also 5.19.

Source: *Hymns on the Lord's Supper*, 116; in John and Charles Wesley, *Hymns on the Lord's Supper* (London, 1786), pp. 86–7.

* * *

Victim divine, thy grace we claim,
While thus thy precious death we show,
Once offer'd up, a spotless Lamb,
In thy great temple here below,
Thou didst for all mankind atone,
And standest now before the throne.

Thou standest in the holiest place,
As now for guilty sinners slain,
Thy blood of sprinkling speaks and prays
All prevalent for helpless man;
Thy blood is still our ransom found,
And spreads salvation all around.

The smoke of thy atonement here,
Darken'd the sun, and rent the veil,
Made the new way to heaven appear
And show'd the great Invisible:

Well pleased in thee, our God looked down,
And called his rebels to a crown.

He still respects thy sacrifice,
Its savour sweet doth always please,
The offering smokes through earth and skies,
Diffusing life, and joy, and peace:
To these thy lower courts it comes,
And fills them with divine perfumes.

We need not now go up to heaven
To bring the long-sought Saviour down,
Thou art to all already given.
Thou dost e'en now thy banquet crown:
To every faithful soul appear,
And shew thy real presence here.

Study Questions to Chapter 8

What is the essential difference between the definitions of a sacrament offered by Hugh of St. Victor and Peter Lombard?

Name the seven sacraments recognized by the Catholic Church.

"This is my body" (Matthew 26:26). How was this understood in the ninth century? And in the sixteenth?

What was Luther's objection to transubstantiation? (Begin by outlining this doctrine from Thomas Aquinas, then deal with Luther's specific objections.)

Compare the views of Philip Melanchthon, Huldrych Zwingli and Theodore Beza on the relation of a sacramental sign and the spiritual reality to which it points.

9 Christianity and Other Religions

The issue of the relation of Christianity to other religions has become of particular importance in the twentieth century. However, as this set of readings will indicate, a debate was under way long before this. This chapter includes three major readings relating to the nature of religion itself. Ludwig Feuerbach regarded religion as an expression of human longing; Karl Marx, as the result of social and economic alienation: and Karl Barth, as an expression of human defiance in the face of God. Each of these views is influential, and worth wrestling with.

However, it is the issue of Christian theological responses to religious pluralism which is of chief importance in the modern situation. This chapter provides some extended readings relating to this theme, summarized in STUDY PANEL 23.

STUDY PANEL 23

Christian Approaches to Religious Pluralism

9.1 Justin Martyr on Christianity before Christ

Justin, writing in the second century, solved the problem of the relation between Christianity and other religions (and he had the Greek religions particularly in mind) by arguing that anyone who "lived according to the Logos" is a Christian. Justin regarded the Logos as having dispersed its seeds throughout the world (see 1.1), with the result that it is to be expected that peoples living in every culture and at every time could become Christians. See also 2.16; 2.17; 9.5; 9.6.

Source: *Apologia*, I.xlvi.1–3; in *Saint Justin: Apologies*, ed. A. Wartelle (Paris: Etudes Augustiniennes, 1987), 160.1–10.

* * *

It is unreasonable to argue, by way of refutation of our teachings, that we assert Christ was born a hundred and fifty years ago, under Cyrenius, and to have given his teaching somewhat later, under Pontius Pilate; and to accuse us of implying that everyone who was born before that time was not accountable. To refute this, I will dispose of the difficulty by anticipation. We are taught that Christ is the first-born of God, and we have explained above that he is the Word of whom all of humanity has a share, and those who lived according to the Logos (*hoi meta logou biōsantes*) are therefore Christians, even though they were regarded as atheists; among Greeks, Socrates, and Heraclitus; and among non-Greeks, Abraham, Ananias, Azanas, and Misad, and Elias, and many others.

9.2 Ludwig Feuerbach on the Origins of Religion

In his *Essence of Christianity*, published in 1841, Ludwig Feuerbach argued that the basic elements of religion were the projection of human longings and fears onto an imaginary transcendent place. The consciousness of God (a leading theme in the writings of F. D. E. Schleiermacher) is thus nothing more than human self-consciousness. See also 9.3.

Source: *The Essence of Christianity*; in *Gesammelte Werke*, ed. W. Schuffenhauer, vol. 5 (Berlin: Akademie Verlag, 1973), pp. 46–7.

* * *

Consciousness of God is human self-consciousness; knowledge of God is human self-knowledge. By the God you know the human, and conversely, by the human, you know the God. The two are one. What God is to a person that too is the spirit, the soul; and what the spirit, the soul, are to a person, that is the God. God is the revealed and explicit inner self of a human being. Religion is the ceremonial unveiling of the hidden treasures of humanity, the confession of its innermost thoughts, and the open recognition of its secrets of love.

However, to characterize the consciousness of God as human self-consciousness in this manner does not mean that religious people are themselves immediately aware of the fact that their consciousness of God is simply their own self-consciousness. In fact, the absence of such an awareness is the distinctive mark of religion. In order to avoid this misunderstanding, it should be said that religion is the *earliest* and *truly indirect* form of human *self-consciousness*. For this reason, religion precedes philosophy in the history of humanity in general, as well as in the history of individual human beings. Initially, people mistakenly locate their essential nature as if it were *outside* of themselves, before finally realizing that it is actually within them ... The historical progress of religion consists therefore in this: that what an earlier religion took to be objective, is later recognized to be subjective; what formerly was taken to be God, and worshipped as such, is now recognized to be something human. What was earlier religion is later taken to be idolatry: humans are seen to have adored their own nature. Humans objectified themselves but failed to recognize themselves as this object. The later religion takes this step; every consolidation in religion is therefore a deeper self-knowledge.

Karl Marx on Feuerbach's Views on Religion

9.3

In these eleven theses directed against Feuerbach's criticisms of Christianity (see 9.2), Marx argues that he has failed to go far enough. It is not enough to explain religion; the point is that social and economic changes must be introduced which will eliminate the causes of religion in the first place. Marx locates the human tendency to "invent" God in socio-economic alienation, and thus places an emphasis upon practical action in the world, rather than just theoretical reflection. This insight has subsequently been taken up once more within some sections of Latin American liberation theology. See also 1.26.

Source: *Theses on Feuerbach* (1845); in *Marx–Engels Gesamtausgabe*, vol. 1, part 5, ed. A Adoratskii (Berlin: Marx–Engels Verlag, 1932), 533.14–555.35.

* * *

1. The chief defect of all previous materialism (including Feuerbach's) is that things, reality, the sensible world are conceived only in the form of objects or observation, not as human sense activity (*sinnlich menschliche Tätigkeit*), not as practical activity; not subjectively ... In the *Essence of Christianity*, Feuerbach regards the theoretical attitude as the only genuine human attitude, while practical activity is apprehended only in its dirty Jewish manifestation. For this reason, he fails to grasp the significance of "revolutionary," "practical–critical," activity ...

4. Feuerbach sets out from the fact of religious self-alienation (*religiösen Selbstentfremdung*), the replication of the world in religious and secular forms. His achievement has therefore consisted in resolving the religious world into its secular foundation ...

6. Feuerbach resolves the essence of religion into the essence of *humanity*. But the essence of humanity is not an abstraction which inheres in each individual (*keim dem einzelnen Individuum inwohnendes Abstraktum*). Real human nature is a totality of social relations (*das ensemble der gesellschaftlichen Verhältnisse*). As Feuerbach does not deal with this point, he is obliged to:

(i) abstract from the historical process, to hypostatize religious feeling, and to postulate an abstract – *isolated* – human individual;

(ii) to conceive human nature only in terms of a "genus," as something inner and silent, which is the natural common link connecting many individuals.

7. Feuerbach therefore fails to see that "religious feeling" is itself a social product, and that the abstract individual who he is analysing belongs to a particular form of society (*einer bestimmten Gesellschaftsform*) . . .

11. The philosophers have only *interpreted* the world in different ways; the point is to change it (*Die Philosophen haben die Welt nur verschieden interpretiert, es kömmt drauf an sie zu verändern*).

9.4   Karl Barth on Christianity and Religion

Karl Barth addresses the question of the relation of Christianity and the religions by arguing that "religion" is basically a human invention, a category to which Christianity ought not to belong. Barth sets up a distinction between "religion" and "revelation," arguing that the former is a human attempt at self-justification, and the latter is God's contradiction of human ideas. See also 2.25; 3.28.

Source: Karl Barth, *Church Dogmatics*, I/2 (Edinburgh: T. & T. Clark, 1956), pp. 280, 297–300. Used with permission of the publisher.

* * *

A theological evaluation of religion and religions must be characterized primarily by the great cautiousness and charity of its assessment and judgments. It will observe and understand and take man in all seriousness as the subject of religion. But it will not be man apart from God, in a human *per se*. It will be man for whom (whether he knows it or not) Jesus Christ was born, died, and rose again. It will be man who (whether he has already heard it or not) is intended in the Word of God. It will be man who (whether he is aware of it or not) has in Christ his Lord. It will always understand religion as a vital utterance and activity of this man. It will not ascribe to this life-utterance and activity of his a unique "nature," the so-called "nature of religion." . . .

Revelation singles out the Church as the locus of true religion. But this does not mean that the Christian religion as such is the fulfilled nature of human religion. It does not mean that the Christian religion is the true religion, fundamentally superior to all other religions. We can never stress too much the connection between the truth of the Christian religion and the grace of revelation. We have to give particular emphasis to the fact that through grace the Church lives by grace, and to that extent it is the locus of true religion. And if this is so, the Church will as little boast of its "nature," i.e., the perfection in which it fulfils the "nature" of religion, as it can attribute that nature to other religions. We cannot differentiate and separate the Church from other religions on the basis of a general concept of the nature of religion . . .

We begin by stating that religion is unbelief. It is a concern, indeed, we must say that it is the one great concern, of godless man . . .

Where we want what is wanted in religion, i.e., justification and sanctification as our own work, we do not find ourselves – and it does not matter whether the thought and representation of God has a primary or only a secondary importance – on the direct way to God, who can then bring us to our goal at some higher stage on the way. On the contrary, we lock the door against God, we alienate ourselves from him, we come into direct opposition to him. God in his revelation will not allow man to try to come to terms with life, to justify and sanctify himself. God in his revelation, God in Jesus Christ, is the one who takes on himself the sin of the world, who wills that all our care should be cast upon him, because he careth for us . . .

Religion is never true in itself and as such. The revelation of God denies that any religion is true, i.e., that it is in truth the knowledge and worship of God and the reconciliation of man with God. For as the self-offering and self-manifestation of God, as the work of peace which God himself has concluded between himself and man, revelation is the truth beside which there is no other truth, over against which there is only lying and wrong. If by the concept of a "true religion" we mean truth which belongs to religion in itself and as such, it is just as unattainable as a "good man," if by goodness we mean something which man can achieve on his own initiative. No religion is true. It can only become true, i.e., according to that which it purports to be and for which it is upheld. And it can become true only in the way in which man is justified, from without; i.e., not of its own nature and being but only in virtue of a reckoning and adopting and separating which are foreign to its own nature and being, which are quite inconceivable from its own standpoint, which come to it quite apart from any qualifications or merits. Like justified man, true religion is a creature of grace. But grace is the revelation of God. No religion can stand before it as true religion. No man is righteous in its presence. It subjects us all to the judgment of death. But it can also call dead men to life and sinners to repentance. And similarly in the wider sphere where it shows all religion to be false, it can also create true religion. The abolishing of religion by revelation need not mean only its negation: the judgment that religion is unbelief. Religion can just as well be exalted in revelation, even though the judgment still stands. It can be upheld by it and concealed in it. It can be justified by it, and – we must at once add – sanctified. Revelation can adopt religion and mark it off as true religion. And it not only can. How do we come to assert that it can, if it has not already done so? There is a true religion: just as there are justified sinners. If we abide strictly by that analogy – and we are dealing not merely with an analogy, but in a comprehensive sense with the thing itself – we need have no hesitation in saying that the Christian religion is the true religion.

9.5   Karl Rahner on Christianity and the Non-Christian Religions

Karl Rahner devoted considerable attention to the relation between Christianity and other religions. In his analysis of the subject, Rahner maintains the distinctiveness of Christianity, while maintaining that the other religions are capable of offering their adherents genuine salvation. Rahner argues that the grace of God can be found in other religions, and suggests that their members may be regarded as "anonymous Christians." Note the four theses in which he summarizes his distinctive position. See also 9.6.

Source: Karl Rahner, *Theological Investigations*, vol. 5 (London: Darton, Longman and Todd, and New York: Crossroad, 1966), pp. 115–34. A translation of *Schriften zur Theologie*, V, published by Verlaganstalt Benziger AG, Einsiedeln. Reprinted by permission of the Crossroad Publishing Company, New York, and Darton, Longman and Todd, London.

* * *

1st Thesis

We must begin with the thesis which follows, because it certainly represents the basis in the Christian faith of the theological understanding of other religions. This thesis states that Christianity understands itself as the absolute religion, intended for all men, which cannot recognize any other religion beside itself as of equal right. This proposition is self-evident and basic for Christianity's understanding of itself. There is no need here to prove it or to develop its meaning. After all, Christianity does not take valid and lawful religion to mean primarily that relationship of man to God which man himself institutes on his own authority. Valid and lawful religion does not mean man's own interpretation of human existence. It is not the reflection and objectification of the experience which man has of himself and by himself. Valid and lawful religion for Christianity is rather God's action on men, God's free self-revelation by communicating himself to man. It is God's relationship to men, freely instituted by God himself and revealed by God in this institution. *This* relationship of God to man is basically the same for all men, because it rests on the Incarnation, death and resurrection of the one Word of God become flesh. Christianity is God's own interpretation in his Word of this relationship of God to man founded in Christ by God himself. And so Christianity can recognize itself as the true and lawful religion for all men only where and when it enters with existential power and demanding force into the realm of another religion and – judging it by itself – puts it in question. Since the time of Christ's coming – ever since he came in the flesh as the Word of God in absoluteness and reconciled, i.e. united the world with God by his death and resurrection, not merely theoretically but really – Christ and his continuing historical presence in the world (which we call "Church") is *the* religion which binds man to God. Already we must, however, make one point clear as regards this first thesis (which cannot be further developed and proved here). It is true that the Christian religion itself has its own pre-history which traces this religion back to the beginning of the history of humanity – even though it does this by many basic steps. It is also true that this fact of having a pre-history is of much greater importance, according to the evidence of the New Testament, for the theoretical and practical proof of the claim to absolute truth made by the Christian religion than our current fundamental theology is aware of. Nevertheless, the Christian religion as such has a beginning in history; it did not always exist but began at some point in time. It has not always and everywhere been *the* way of salvation for men – at least not in its historically tangible ecclesio-sociological constitution and in the reflex fruition of God's saving activity in, and in view of, Christ. As a historical quantity Christianity has, therefore, a temporal and spatial starting point in Jesus of Nazareth and in the saving event of the unique Cross and the empty tomb in Jerusalem. It follows from this, however, that this absolute religion – even when it begins to be this for practically all men – must come in a historical way to men, facing them as the only legitimate and demanding religion for them. It is therefore a question of whether this moment, when the existentially real demand is made by the absolute religion in its historically tangible form, takes place really at the same chronological moment for all men, or whether the occurrence of this moment has itself a history and thus is not chronologically simultaneous for all men, cultures and spaces of history . . .

2nd Thesis

Until the moment when the gospel really enters into the historical situation of an individual, a non-Christian religion (even outside the Mosaic religion) does not merely contain elements of a natural knowledge of God, elements, moreover, mixed up with human depravity which is the result of original sin and later aberrations. It contains also supernatural elements arising out of the grace which is given to men as a gratuitous gift on account of Christ. For this reason a non-Christian religion can be recognized as a *lawful* religion (although only in different degrees) without thereby denying the error and depravity contained in it. This thesis requires a more extensive explanation.

We must first of all note the point up to which this evaluation of the non-Christian religions is valid. This is the point in time when the Christian religion becomes a historically real factor for those who are of this religion. Whether this point is the same, theologically speaking, as the first Pentecost, or whether it is different in chronological time for individual peoples and religions, is something which even at this point will have to be left to a certain extent an open question. We have, however, chosen our formulation in such a way that it points more in the direction of the opinion which seems to us the more correct one in the matter although the *criteria* for a more exact determination of this moment in time must again be left an open question.

The thesis itself is divided into two parts. It means first of all that it is *a priori* quite possible to suppose that there are supernatural, grace-filled elements in non-Christian religions. Let us first of all deal with this statement. It does not mean, of course, that all the elements of a polytheistic conception of the divine, and all the other religious, ethical and metaphysical aberrations contained in the non-Christian religions, are to be or may be treated as harmless either in theory or in practice. There have been constant protests against such elements throughout the history of Christianity and throughout the history of the Christian interpretation of the non-Christian religions, starting with the Epistle to the Romans and following on the Old Testament polemics against the religion of the "heathens." Every one of these protests is still valid in what was really meant and expressed by them. Every such protest remains a part of the message which Christianity and the Church has to give to the peoples who profess such religions. Furthermore, we are not concerned here with an *a posteriori* history of religions. Consequently, we also cannot describe empirically what should not exist and what is opposed to God's will in these non-Christian religions, nor can we represent these things in their many forms and degrees. We are here concerned with dogmatic theology and so can merely repeat the universal and unqualified verdict as to the unlawfulness of the non-Christian religions right from the moment when they came into real and historically powerful contact with Christianity (and at first only thus!). It is clear, however, that this condemnation does not mean to deny the very basic differences within the non-Christian religions especially since the *pious*, God-pleasing pagan was already a theme of the Old testament, and especially since this God-pleasing pagan cannot simply be thought of as living absolutely outside the concrete socially constituted religion and constructing his own religion on his native foundations – just as St. Paul in his speech on the Areopagus did not simply exclude a positive and basic view of the pagan religion. The decisive reason for the first part of our thesis is basically a theological consideration. This consideration (prescinding from certain more precise qualifications) rests ultimately on the fact that, if we wish to be Christians, we must profess belief in the universal and serious salvific purpose of God towards all men which is true even within the post-paradisean phase of salvation dominated by original sin. We know, to be sure, that this proposition of faith does not say anything certain about the *individual* salvation man understood as something which has in fact been reached. But God desires the salvation of everyone. And this salvation willed by God is the salvation won by Christ . . .

3rd Thesis

If the second thesis is correct, then Christianity does not simply confront the member of an extra-Christian religion as a mere non-Christian but as someone who can and must already be regarded in this or that respect as an anonymous Christian. It would be wrong to regard the pagan as someone who has not yet been touched in any way by God's grace and truth. If, however, he has experienced the grace of God – if, in certain circumstances, he has already accepted this grace as the ultimate, unfathomable entelechy of his existence by accepting the immeasurableness of his dying existence as opening out into infinity – then he has already been given revelation in a true sense even before he has been affected by missionary preaching from without. For this grace, understood as the *a priori* horizon of all his spiritual acts, accompanies his consciousness subjectively, even though it is not known objectively. And the revelation which comes to him from without is not in such a case the proclamation of something as yet absolutely unknown, in the sense in which one tells a child here in Bavaria, for the first time in school, that there is a continent called Australia. Such a revelation is then the expression in objective concepts of something which this person has already attained or could already have attained in the depth of his rational existence. It is not possible here to prove more exactly that this *fides implicita* is something which dogmatically speaking can occur in a so-called pagan. We can do no more here than to state our thesis and to indicate the direction in which the proof of this thesis might be found. But if it is true that a person who becomes the object of the Church's missionary efforts is or may be already someone on the way towards his salvation, and someone who in certain circumstances finds it, without being reached by the proclamation of the Church's message – and if it is at the same time true that this salvation which reaches him in this way is Christ's salvation, since there is no other salvation – then it must be possible to be not only an anonymous theist but also an anonymous Christian . . .

4th Thesis

It is possibly too much to hope, on the one hand, that the religious pluralism which exists in the concrete situation of Christians will disappear in the foreseeable future. On the other hand, it is nevertheless absolutely permissible for the Christian himself to interpret this non-Christianity as Christianity of an anonymous kind which he does always still go out to meet as a missionary, seeing it as a world which is to be brought to the explicit consciousness of what already belongs to it as a divine offer or already pertains to it also over and above this as a divine gift of grace accepted unreflectedly and implicitly. If both these statements are true, then the Church will not so much regard herself today as the exclusive community of those who have a claim to salvation but rather as the historically tangible vanguard and the historically and socially constituted explicit expression of what the Christian hopes is present as a hidden reality even outside the visible Church. To begin with, however much we must always work, suffer and pray anew and indefatigably for the unification of the whole human race, in the one Church of Christ, we must nevertheless expect, for theological reasons and not merely by reason of a profane historical analysis, that the religious pluralism existing in the world and in our own historical sphere of existence will not disappear in the foreseeable future . . .

9.6   Vatican II on Non-Christian Religions

The Second Vatican Council issued its statement on the relation between Christianity and other religions on 28 October 1965. The statement affirms the distinctiveness of Christianity, while at the same time affirming that God can be known, to a limited extent, in other religious traditions. Note that the Council declined to follow Karl Rahner's suggestion that all religions should be regarded as having the ability to save their members (see 9.5).

Source: Vatican II, *Nostra Aetate*, 28 October 1965; in *Vatican II: Conciliar and Postconciliar Documents*, ed. Austin Flannery, OP (Northport, NY: Costello, and Dublin: Dominican Publications, 1975), pp. 738–42. Reprinted with the permission of the publishers.

* * *

1. In this age of ours, when men are drawing more closely together and the bonds of friendship between different peoples are being strengthened, the Church examines with greater care the relation which she has to non-Christian religions. Ever aware of her duty to foster unity and charity among individuals, and even among nations, she reflects at the outset on what men have in common and what tends to promote fellowship among them.

All men form but one community. This is so because all stem from the one stock which God created to people the entire earth (cf. Acts 17:26), and also because all share a common destiny, namely God. His providence, evident goodness, and saving designs extend to all men (cf. Wisdom 8:1; Acts 14:17; Romans 2:6–7; 1 Timothy 2:4) against the day when the elect are gathered together in the holy city which is illumined by the glory of God, and in whose splendor all peoples will walk (cf. Apocalypse 21:23ff).

Men look to their different religions for an answer to the unsolved riddles of human existence. The problems that weigh heavily on the hearts of men are the same today as in the ages past. What is man? What is the meaning and purpose of life? What is upright behavior, and what is sinful? Where does suffering originate, and what end does it serve? How can genuine happiness be found? What happens at death? What is judgment? What reward follows death? And finally, what is the ultimate mystery, beyond human explanation, which embraces our entire existence, from which we take our origin and towards which we tend?

2. Throughout history even to the present day, there is found among different peoples a certain awareness of a hidden power, which lies behind the course of nature and the events of human life. At times there is present even a recognition of a supreme being, or still more of a Father. This awareness and recognition results in a way of life that is imbued with a deep religious sense. The religions which are found in more advanced civilizations endeavor by way of well-defined concepts and exact language to answer these questions. Thus, in Hinduism men explore the divine mystery and express it both in the limitless riches of myth and the accurately defined insights of philosophy. They seek release from the trials of the present life by ascetical practices, profound meditation and recourse to God in confidence and love. Buddhism in its various forms testifies to the essential

inadequacy of this changing world. It proposes a way of life by which men can, with confidence and trust, attain a state of perfect liberation and reach supreme illumination either through their own efforts or by the aid of divine help. So, too, other religions which are found throughout the world attempt in their own ways to calm the hearts of men by outlining a program of life covering doctrines, moral precepts and sacred rites.

The Catholic Church rejects nothing of what is true and holy in these religions. She has a high regard for the manner of life and conduct, the precepts and doctrines which, although differing in many ways from her own teaching, nevertheless often reflect a ray of that truth which enlightens all men. Yet she proclaims and is in duty bound to proclaim without fail, Christ who is the way, the truth and the life (John 14:6). In him, in whom God reconciled all things to himself (2 Corinthians 5:18–19), men find the fulness of their religious life.

The Church, therefore, urges her sons to enter with prudence and charity into discussion and collaboration with members of other religions. Let Christians, while witnessing to their own faith and way of life, acknowledge, preserve and encourage the spiritual and moral truths found among non-Christians, also their social life and culture.

3. The Church has also a high regard for the Muslims. They worship God, who is one, living and subsistent, merciful and almighty, the Creator of heaven and earth, who has also spoken to men. They strive to submit themselves without reserve to the hidden decrees of God, just as Abraham submitted himself to God's plan, to whose faith Muslims eagerly link their own. Although not acknowledging him as God, they worship Jesus as a prophet, his virgin Mother they also honor, and even at times devoutly invoke. Further, they await the day of judgment and the reward of God following the resurrection of the dead. For this reason they highly esteem an upright life and worship God, especially by way of prayer, alms-deeds and fasting.

Over the centuries many quarrels and dissensions have arisen between Christians and Muslims. The sacred Council now pleads with all to forget the past, and urges that a sincere effort be made to achieve mutual understanding; for the benefit of all men, let them together preserve and promote peace, liberty, social justice and moral values.

4. Sounding the depths of the mystery which is the Church, this sacred Council remembers the spiritual ties which link the people of the New Covenant to the stock of Abraham.

The Church of Christ acknowledges that in God's plan of salvation the beginning of her faith and election is to be found in the patriarchs, Moses and the prophets. She professes that all Christ's faithful, who as men of faith are sons of Abraham (cf. Galatians 3:7), are included in the same patriarch's call and that the salvation of the Church is mystically prefigured in the exodus of God's chosen people from the land of bondage. On this account the Church cannot forget that she received the revelation of the Old Testament by way of that people with whom God in his inexpressible mercy established the ancient covenant. Nor can she forget that she draws nourishment from that good olive tree onto which the wild olive branches of the Gentiles have been grafted (cf. Romans 11:17–24). The Church believes that Christ who is our peace has through his cross reconciled Jews and Gentiles and made them one in himself (cf. Ephesians 2:14–16).

Likewise, the Church keeps ever before her mind the words of the apostle Paul about his kinsmen: "they are Israelites, and to them belong the sonship, the glory, the covenants, the giving of the law, the worship, and the promises; to them belong the patriarchs, and of their race according to the flesh, is the Christ" (Romans 9:4–5), the son of the virgin Mary. She is mindful, moreover, that the apostles, the pillars on which the Church stands, are of Jewish descent, as are many of those early disciples who proclaimed the Gospel of Christ to the world.

As holy Scripture testifies, Jerusalem did not recognize God's moment when it came (cf. Luke 19:42). Jews for the most part did not accept the Gospel; on the contrary, many opposed the spreading of it (cf. Romans 11:28). Even so, the apostle Paul maintains that the Jews remain very dear to God, for the sake of the patriarchs, since God does not take back the gifts he bestowed or the choice he made. Together with the prophets and that same apostle, the Church awaits the day, known to God alone, when all people will call on God with one voice and "serve him shoulder to shoulder" (Soph. 3:9; cf. Isaiah 66:23; Psalm 65:4; Romans 11:11–32).

Since Christians and Jews have such a common spiritual heritage, this sacred Council wishes to encourage and further mutual understanding and appreciation. This can be obtained, especially, by way of biblical and theological enquiry and through friendly discussions.

Even though the Jewish authorities and those who followed their lead pressed for the death of Christ (cf. John 19:6), neither all Jews indiscriminately at that time, nor Jews today, can be charged with the crimes committed during his passion. It is true that the Church is the new people of God, yet the Jews should not be spoken of as rejected or accursed as if this followed from holy Scripture. Consequently, all must take care, lest in catechizing or in preaching the Word of God, they teach anything which is not in accord with the truth of the Gospel message or the spirit of Christ.

Indeed, the Church reproves every form of persecution against whomsoever it may be directed. Remembering, then, her common heritage with the Jews and moved not by any political consideration, but solely by the religious motivation of Christian charity, she deplores all hatreds, persecutions, displays of antisemitism leveled at any time or from any source against the Jews.

The Church always held and continues to hold that Christ out of infinite love freely underwent suffering and death because of the sins of all men, so that all might attain salvation. It is the duty of the Church, therefore, in her preaching to proclaim the cross of Christ as the sign of God's universal love and the source of all grace.

5. We cannot truly pray to God the Father of all if we treat any people in other than brotherly fashion, for all men are created in God's image. Man's relation to God the Father and man's relation to his fellow-men are

so dependent on each other that the Scripture says "he who does not love, does not know God" (1 John 4:8).

There is no basis therefore, either in theory or in practice for any discrimination between individual and individual, or between people and people arising either from human dignity or from the rights which flow from it.

Therefore, the Church reproves, as foreign to the mind of Christ, any discrimination against people or any harassment of them on the basis of their race, color, condition in life or religion. Accordingly, following the footsteps of the holy apostles Peter and Paul, the sacred Council earnestly begs the Christian faithful to "conduct themselves well among the Gentiles" (1 Peter 2:12) and if possible, as far as depends on them, to be at peace with all men (cf. Romans 12:18) and in that way to be true sons of the Father who is in heaven (cf. Matthew 5:45).

Clark Pinnock on Pluralists and Christology

9.7

Clark Pinnock, a noted Canadian theologian, here argues that a commitment to religious pluralism generally leads to a weak Christology, in which Jesus is regarded as little more than one among many other religious personalities. He outlines the various strategies adopted by pluralists in dealing with this problem, and provides an assessment of their merits and deficiencies. See also 9.1; 9.5; 9.6.

Source: Clark H. Pinnock, *A Wideness in God's Mercy* (Grand Rapids: Zondervan, 1992), pp. 64–9. Taken from the book *A Wideness in God's Mercy*, by Clark Pinnock. Copyright © 1992 by Clark H. Pinnock. Used by permission of Zondervan Publishing House.

---

* * *

Theological pluralists have a problem with Christology. Were Jesus to be decisive for all nations, that would be unconducive to dialogue and cooperation among the religions. Therefore, ways must be found to reinterpret historical data so as to eliminate finality claims from Christology. They must be diminished so they do not constitute a barrier to interreligious peace. Pluralists hope there is a way to read the New Testament without coming up with a Christ who has to be normative for everybody in the world. They need a way for Jesus to be unique for his followers, but not necessarily for others. If his uniqueness could be relational, for example, this would create fewer problems. Pluralists think that belief in the finality of Jesus Christ stands in the way of our appreciating other religions and getting along smoothly with them. They intend to correct the problem.

Different solutions have been proposed. The least radical involves shifting the emphasis away from metaphysics in the direction of action/functional categories. The problem could be eased, in the minds of theological pluralists, if we would just learn to view Jesus as God's love in action and present him as one who assists people to find access to the grace of God. Why not put the emphasis on Christ's prophetic office, then stress the way he reveals the Father's character and will for humans in his own life and teachings? This would shift the emphasis away from Jesus as a metaphysical oddity and toward the impact he had on people, the way he shaped people's understanding of what God is like. Instead of repeating the idea that God entered history in Jesus from the outside in a miraculous way, we could explain how Jesus functions as a window into God's very nature . . . The late J. A. T. Robinson rook this tack. He claimed that it was God's love that was incarnate in Jesus of Nazareth, not the divine substance. Jesus was special because God was acting in and through him. He became the image for us of who God is. Incarnation imagery supplies an effective mythic expression of the way we relate to God through him. Jesus is the clue to the nature of God as personal love, not the absolutely unique embodiment of God's being. He is unique in degree but not in kind.

The idea of Jesus embodying God's love for us is true as far as it goes. But not going farther creates severe difficulties. First, unwanted claims of finality tend to attach themselves to action Christology, even though the claims are functional. Even when the Christ-event is taken only as disclosure, it is still viewed as decisive disclosure. But if decisive for us, why not for others? If it is decisive for us in our cultural setting, why not also in other people's settings? Second, functional Christology has a way of not remaining functional. Edward Schillebeeckx also places emphasis on Jesus' role in communicating God's love, but then he goes on to posit an ontological bond between Jesus and God his Father also. Substance and action categories are brought together in his final assessment. For, he reasons, if Jesus presents us with God most human, are we not also in the presence of unfathomable mystery? Third, there are texts that present ontological teaching about the person of Jesus elsewhere in the New Testament, so that moving to action Christology does not really get one off the hook. It cannot account for the entire biblical witness, even though it can account for some of it.

A second possible way to correct the "problem" of high Christology in the New Testament allows one to accept the higher-than-functional claims that are made for Jesus and still dispense with universal normativeness. With reference to the "once and for all" language of the New Testament for the decisive work of Jesus, Paul Knitter comments that, "To close one's eyes to such proclamation is either psychologically to repress or dishonestly to deny what one does not wish to face." We cannot prevent the biblical witnesses from saying what they meant to say.

Nevertheless, Knitter does try to evade the proclamation in another way. First, he explains the expressions in terms of the culture of the early Christians, saying it was natural for them to speak of their religious experiences in the ways that they did. Being a culturally conditioned way of speaking, their words tell us more about their social setting than about the actual person of Jesus. Second, their high praise of Jesus is more an expression of love and devotion to him than truth claims as such. It is rather like our saying, "My wife (or my husband) is the kindest and most loving person in the world." This is not a scientific statement based on research but rather love language. By looking at these claims in this way, Jesus can be relationally unique (like a spouse is relationally unique), unique in the way Christians experience God – but not unique in a universal sense, in the sense of being normative for other people who may experience God in different religious contexts. The confession, "Jesus is Lord," would express what Jesus means to us without carrying any implication that everybody in the world must worship him or come to God by way of him. This confession is our way to honor God, but need not be taken as a judgment on other confessions made by other people.

This approach allows one to admit that the New Testament witnesses make extraordinarily high claims for Jesus. Yet, one does not have to deny or excise them. The key is to reinterpret their significance in the experiential and confessional terms of love. Because they are culturally conditioned and psychologically rendered, the claims for Jesus turn out not to be truth claims in the ordinary sense, in which the church has understood them histor-ically. The problem of high Christology vanishes.

The approach is ingenious and possible, if not entirely plausible. But there are problems in the following areas. First, the New Testament writers appear to be stating, as far as one can tell, what they consider to be facts and truths. They are not only sharing religious feelings, but conveying what they took to be information as well . . . Second, there is also something of a justice issue involved here. What right does a modern interpreter have to alter what the biblical witnesses intend, so as to make it mean something else? What right has he or she to change and reduce the meaning in this way? To transmute claims about Jesus, as Savior of the world and risen from the dead, into a description of what was going on in their culturally conditioned psyches is illegitimate. Suppose one turned this same argu-ment on pluralists and reduced their claims in this same way? Are their claims for God similarly derivative from the psyche? Is it their love for God that makes them think there actually is a God? To argue in this way con-stitutes an unacceptable put-down. People have the right to make claims others do not like or accept without having others change and distort their meaning to suit themselves. New Testament claims for Jesus ought to be taken seriously, the same way Knitter's claim about God ought to be. It is inconsistent to apply a noncognitivist bias to claims for Jesus and not to claims for God.

Third, the suggestion is very dubious that Christians might confess a nonnormative Jesus without losing anything important in their faith. Knit-ter posits our living, and even dying, for Christ with the knowledge that the truth of the gospel is our truth, but not necessarily the truth for the world. It is as though we could confess that Jesus is Lord while harboring the reservation that maybe he is, and maybe he isn't. How can Christ's resur-rection be true for us and not for the world? The faith of Christians would be fatally damaged if it came to be accepted that the risen Lord were our myth of meaning and not more than that.

A more radical approach to the problem of high Christology in the New Testament is adopted by John Hick. First, he outright denies any uniqueness claims on the part of Jesus. He realizes that hesitating on this point would leave a thread of continuity between Jesus and the later developments, giving it a toehold of plausibility. This is certainly a wise move methodologically, if a risky one exegetically. Second, like Knitter he transposes all the uniqueness claims made on behalf of Jesus by the New Testament witnesses onto the level of noncognitive love language. Third, he attempts to locate the Christology of the Incarnation in a hypothetical context of the development of traditions. Using Buddhism as an example, he points to the process by which religious leaders are deified over time out of respect. Fourth, he adds that there are various insuperable logical problems with belief in Incarnation. This supplies a philosophical backup objection should all else fail.

Unfortunately, none of his points sticks firmly. First, one cannot deny Jesus' claims to uniqueness on the basis of critical exegesis. While granting his point about Jesus not making explicit claims to Incarnation, the implicit claims Jesus does make solidly ground the more-developed views of his person after the Resurrection. Not easily sidestepped, they entail the high view of Jesus which issued in the faith of the church. Second, transposing claims for Jesus' uniqueness made by the biblical witnesses onto the level of noncognitive love language is an unacceptable put-down of their sincerely held beliefs. It is rooted in hostile presuppositions against the truth of what they are declaring. Neither just nor fair, it refuses to take them seriously. Third, there is Christological development in early doctrine, and the Incarnation is noticeable in that development. But the Christology being developed there is already very high, with the event of Jesus' Resurrection, and constitutes an unpacking of what is implicit from the beginning. The centuries of development envisaged by the Buddhist analogy do not exist in this case. Fourth, as to whether belief in the Incarnation is rational or not, two things can be said. First, the problem of finality is much larger than belief in the Incarnation. In many other ways the biblical witnesses lift up Jesus as Lord of the universe. Second, not everyone is as impressed as Hick by the logical problems of believing in the Incarnation. A large number of thoughtful Christians find the belief coherent, even true and magnificent.

The New Testament quite effectively resists attempts of this type to rid it of the unwanted belief in the finality of Jesus Christ. Efforts to revise Christology downward are difficult to accept because they go against the evidence, and they appear to be based on special pleading and hostile presuppositions. It is impossible to bring it off in an exegetically convincing way. One cannot make the New Testament teach a non-normative Christology. There may be nothing wrong with trying – one learns a lot from conducting exegetical experiments. But in terms of results, the effort to rid the New Testament of the doctrine of the finality of Christ must be pronounced a failure.

John Hick on Complementary Pluralism   9.8

John Hick is the leading representative of a "pluralist" approach to the world's religions, seeing each as a distinctive and valid embodiment of "the infinite transcendent divine Reality." Note in particular the argument which leads to the conclusion that the religions "constitute different 'lenses' through which the divine Reality is differently perceived." See also 9.5; 9.6; 9.7.

Source: John Hick, *The Second Christianity* (London: SCM Press, 1983), pp. 82–7. Reprinted with the permission of the publisher.

* * *

Now it seems to many of us today that we need a Copernican revolution in our understanding of the religions. The traditional dogma has been that Christianity is the centre of the universe of faiths, with all the other religions seen as revolving at various removes around the revelation in Christ and being graded according to their nearness to or distance from it. But during the last hundred years or so we have been making new observations and have realized that there is deep devotion to God, true sainthood, and deep spiritual life within these other religions; and so we have created our epicycles of theory, such as the notions of anonymous Christianity and of implicit faith. But would it not be more realistic now to make the shift from Christianity at the centre to God at the centre, and to see both our own and the other great world religions as revolving around the same divine reality?

Indeed, if we are to understand the entire range of human awarenesses of the divine, including those enshrined in the Buddhist, Hindu and Taoist, as well as the Christian, Jewish and Muslim traditions, we shall need an even wider framework of thought. Such a framework can perhaps best be approached through a distinction which is found in one form or another within some strand of each of the great traditions. Its Christian form is the distinction between, on the one hand, God as he is in himself, in his infinite self-existing being, independently of and "before" creation, and on the other hand God in relation to and as experienced by his human creatures. In its Hindu form it is the distinction between Nirguna Brahman, i.e. the absolute Reality beyond the scope of human thought and language, and Saguna Brahman, i.e. Brahman humanly experienced as a personal God with describable characteristics. In Buddhism there is the distinction between the incarnate and the heavenly Buddhas (comprising the Nirmanakaya and the Sambhogakaya), and on the other hand the infinite and eternal Dharmakaya or cosmic-Buddha-nature. Again, the Taoist Scriptures begin by saying that "The Tao that can be expressed is not the eternal Tao." Within Jewish mysticism (in the *Zohar*) there is the distinction between En Soph, as the infinite divine ground, and the God of the Bible; and within Muslim mysticism (for example, in Ibn Arabi) between Al Haqq, the Real, and our concrete conceptions of God. Likewise, the Christian mystic Meister Eckhart distinguished between the Godhead (*deitas*) and God (*deus*) in a way which closely parallels the Nirguna–Saguna polarity in Hindu thought. And in the present century Paul Tillich has spoken of "the God above the God of theism." Contemporary process theology likewise distinguishes between the eternal and temporal natures of God. In all these ways we have a distinction between the infinite transcendent divine Reality *an sich*, or in its/his/her-self, and that same Reality as thought, imagined and experienced by finite human beings.

This distinction enables us to acknowledge both the one unlimited transcendent divine Reality and also a plurality of varying human concepts, images, and experiences of and response to that Reality. These different human awarenesses of and response to the Real are formed by and reciprocally inform the religious traditions of the earth. In them are reflected the different ways of thinking, feeling and experiencing which have developed within the world-wide human family. Indeed these cultural variations amount, on the large scale, to different ways of being human – for example, the Chinese, the Indian, the African, the Semitic, the Graeco-Roman way or ways, and the way of our contemporary technological Atlantic civilization. We do not know at all fully why the life of our species has taken these various forms, though geographical, climatic and economic factors have clearly played their parts.

However, given these various cultural ways of being human we can I think to some extent understand how it is that they constitute different "lenses" through which the divine Reality is differently perceived. For we know that all human awareness involves an indispensable contribution by the perceiver. The mind is active in perception, organizing the impacts of the environment in ways made possible both by the inherent structure of consciousness and by the particular sets of concepts embedded in particular consciousnesses. These concepts are the organizing and recognitional capacities by which we interpret and give meaning to the data which come to us from outside. And this general epistemological pattern, according to which conscious experience arises out of the interpretative activity of the mind, also applies to religious experience.

The wide range of the forms of human religious experience seems to be shaped by one or other of two basic concepts: the concept of God, or of the Real as personal, which presides over the theistic religions, and the concept of the Absolute, or of the Real as non-personal, which presides over the non-theistic religious hemisphere. These basic concepts do not, however, enter, in these general and abstract forms, into our actual religious experience. We do not experience the presence of God in general, or the reality of the Absolute in general. Each concept takes the range of specific concrete forms which are known in the actual thought and experience of the different religious traditions.

Thus the concept of deity is concretized as a range of divine *personae* – Yahweh, the Heavenly Father, Allah, Krishna, Shiva, etc. Each of these *personae* has arisen within human experience through the impact of the divine Reality upon some particular stream of human life. Thus Yahweh is the face of God turned towards and perceived by the Jewish people or, in more philosophical language, the concrete form in which the Jews have experienced the infinite divine Reality. As such, Yahweh exists essentially in relation to the Hebrews, the relationship being defined by the idea of covenant. He cannot be extracted from his role in Hebrew historic experience. He is part of the history of the Jews, and they are a part of his history. And as such Yahweh is a quite different divine *persona* from Krishna, who is God's face turned towards and perceived by hundreds of millions of people within the Vaishnavite tradition of India. Krishna is related to a different strand of human history from Yahweh, and lives within a different world of religious thought and experience. And each of these divine *personae*, formed at the interface between the divine Reality and some particular human faith community, has inevitably been influenced by human imaginative construction and sinful human distortion as well as by the all-important impact of the transcendent Reality; there is an element of human projection as well as of divine revelation. How otherwise can we account for the ways in which the various divine *personae* have sometimes validated cruel massacres, savage punishments, ruthless persecutions, oppressive and dehumanizing political regimes? God, as imaged and understood by the masses of believers within any of the great traditions, must be partly a human construction in order, for example, for God the Father to have been on both sides of the conflict in Europe in the Second World War, and for Allah to have been on both sides of the recent Iraq–Iran conflict. But it does not follow that the divine *personae* are purely human projections. On the contrary, the theory that I am outlining is that they constitute the concrete forms in which the transcendent divine Reality is known to us. Each *is* the Real as perceived and experienced (and partly misperceived and misexperienced) from within a particular strand of the human story.

And essentially the same is to be said concerning the various *impersonae* in terms of which the Real is known in the non-theistic religious traditions. Here the concept of the Absolute is made concrete as Brahman, Nirvana, the Dharma, the Dharmakaya, Sunyata, the Tao. And according as an individual's thoughts and practices are formed by the advaitic Hindu tradition, or the Theravada or Mahayana Buddhist tradition, he or she is likely to experience the Real in the distinctive way made possible by this conceptuality and meditational discipline.

But can the divine Reality possibly be such as to be authentically experienced by millions of people as a personal God, and also by millions of others as the impersonal Brahman or Tao or Sunyata? Perhaps there is a helpful analogy in the principle of complementarity in modern physics. Electromagnetic radiation, including light, is sometimes found to behave like waves and sometimes like particles. If we experiment upon it in one way we discover a wave-like radiation, whilst if we experiment upon it in another way we discover a procession of particles. The two observations have both had to be accepted as valid and hence as complementary. We have to say that the electromagnetic reality is such that, in relation to human observation, it is wave-like or particle-like according to how the observer acts upon it. Analogously, it seems to be the case that when humans "experiment" with the Real in one kind of way – the way of theistic thought and worship – they find the Real to be personal and when other humans approach the Real in a different kind of way – the way for example of Buddhist or Hindu thought and meditation – they find the real to be non-personal. This being so, we may well emulate the scientists in their realistic acceptance of the two sets of reports concerning the Real as complementary truths.

Such a theory has the merit that it does not lead us to play down the differences between the various forms of religious experience and thought. It does not generate any pressure to think that God the Father and Brahman, or Allah and the Dharmakaya, are phenomenologically, i.e., as experienced and described, identical; or that the human responses which they evoke, in spiritual practices, cultural forms, life-styles, types of society, etc., are the same. The theory – arrived at inductively by observation of the range of human religious experiences – is that the great world faiths embody different perceptions and conceptions of, and correspondingly different responses to, the Real or the Ultimate from within the major variant cultural ways of being human. Such a theory, I would suggest, does justice both to the fascinating differences between the religious traditions and to their basic complementarity as different human responses to the one limitless divine Reality.

This complementarity is connected with the fact that the great world traditions are fundamentally alike in exhibiting a soteriological structure. That is to say, they are all concerned with salvation/liberation/enlightenment/fulfilment. Each begins by declaring that our ordinary human life is profoundly lacking and distorted. It is a "fallen" life, immersed in the unreality of *maya*, or pervaded by *dukkha*, sorrow and unsatisfactoriness. But each then declares that there is another Reality, already there and already open to us, in relation to or in identity with which we can find a limitlessly better existence. And each proceeds to point out a path of life which leads to this salvation/liberation. Thus they are all concerned to bring about the transformation of human existence from self-centredness to Reality-centredness. Salvation/liberation occurs through a total self-giving in faith to God as he has revealed himself through Jesus Christ; or by the total self-surrender to God which is *islam*: or by transcending self-centredness and experiencing an underlying unity with Brahman; or by discovering the unreality of self and its desires and thus experiencing *nirvana*, or by becoming part of the flow of life which in its emptiness-fullness (*sunyata*) is found to be itself *nirvana*. Along each path the great transition is from the sin or error of self-enclosed existence to the liberation and bliss of Reality-centredness.

9.9   C. S. Song on the Cross and the Lotus

The Taiwanese theologian C. S. Song here reflects on the relation of Christianity and Buddhism, using the imagery of the cross and the lotus as a stimulus to his reflection. Note in particular the comparison between Jesus and the Buddha. See also 9.5.

Source: C. S. Song, *Third-Eye Theology: Theology in Formation in Asian Settings*, rev. edn (Maryknoll, NY: Orbis, 1990), pp. 109–13. Used with permission of the publisher.

* * *

The question we must now ask is: what has the cross to do with the lotus? As early as the third century, Tertullian raised this question in relation to Jerusalem and Athens: what has Jerusalem to do with Athens? His answer was negative. Jerusalem – the city of the holy temple, the place where Jesus was crucified, the symbol of salvation revealed to the world in Christ in Tertullian's mind – had nothing to do with Athens. Athens stood for reason whereas Jerusalem was the embodiment of the sacred. Athens was a "secular" city in contrast to Jerusalem, a "holy" city. Furthermore, with its many gods and shrines Athens was a center of paganism in the ancient Mediterranean world. There St. Paul had delivered his famous sermon on the unknown God before the Court of Areopagus. "Men of Athens," he declared:

> I see that in everything that concerns religion you are uncommonly scrupulous. For as I was going round looking at the objects of your worship, I noticed among other things an altar bearing the inscription "To an Unknown God." What you worship but do not know – this is what I now proclaim. (Acts 17:22–23)

Thus it was Paul who in his missionary zeal sought to penetrate the depth of Greek spirituality which had blossomed into art, literature, and philosophy on the one hand and worship of every conceivable deity on the other. Paul's effort in Athens was a dramatic demonstration of the fact that Jerusalem had much to do with Athens. It can even be said to have foreshadowed the Hellenization of Christianity by leaps and bounds in the subsequent history of the development of Christian thought in the West. Tertullian's verdict was wrong. The history of Christian thought was in a true sense a history of how Greek philosophy, especially that of Plato and Aristotle, became integrated into the mainstream of Christian faith. As has been pointed out, through the whole history of Christianity in the West there runs the dynamic of the Gospel's course from the Jew to the Greek, from the Greek to the barbarian.

However that may be, the cross and the lotus seem to have little in common, at first sight at any rate. The lotus springs from the surface of the water. When the wind blows and the water moves, the lotus also moves. It seems in perfect harmony with nature around it. In short, it gives the appearance of being at peace with itself. In contrast, the cross strikes out powerfully, painfully, and defiantly from the earth. It penetrates space and is incongruous with nature. The lotus appeals to our aesthetic feelings, whereas the cross is revolting to the eyes of the beholder. The lotus is soft in texture and graceful in shape, while the cross is hard and harsh. The lotus moves with nature, whereas the cross stands ruggedly and tragically out of the barren earth. The lotus distinguishes itself in gentleness, while the cross is the epitome of human brutality. The lotus beckons and the cross repels. Indeed, what has the cross to do with the lotus? They represent two entirely different spiritualities which seem to be totally incompatible. They seem to have nothing in common.

But the contrast between the cross and the lotus may be deceptive. Essentially, they are two different answers to some basic questions about life and death. They seek to unravel problems and difficulties that beset us in our earthly pilgrimage. They also try to point to the fulfillment of human destiny in the eternal and blissful presence of the divine. They are not primarily concerned with a metaphysical solution to these very important problems, but with practical, day-to-day struggles in the harsh reality of society. Neither the cross nor the lotus, fundamentally speaking, is a system of thought, a set of rituals, or an institution of devotion. Originally they sprang out of the midst of the daily life of the people. They are religions of the people, but theologians – both in Christianity and Buddhism – have taken them away from the people and turned them into theological systems and religious principles bearing little relationship to the genuine fears and aspirations of the people. It is thus not surprising that the cross and the lotus do not intersect in their theological systems or ecclesiastical structures. In fact, these systems and structures only pull the two spiritualities further apart. The place for the cross and the lotus to intersect and intercommunicate is the people – the people who have to fight both spiritual and physical fears, the people who have to live and die without knowing why. Then and only then can the cross and the lotus begin to intercommunicate; they can then begin to point to the mystery that surrounds human destiny. Thus intercommunication and inter-communion of different spiritualities should begin with the people, and with the ways in which they try to cope with the problems of life and the world in sociopolitical and religious terms.

This can be illustrated, first of all, by the way Jesus and Buddha tried to communicate their message through stories and parables. Jesus gave the following reason for using parables to his disciples: "It has been granted to you to know the secrets of the kingdom of Heaven; but to those others it has not been granted" (Matthew 13:11). Then he went on to explain the meaning of the parable of the sower. An abstruse mystery should not remain the monopoly of a few. Jesus mingled with the crowd and took pains to communicate the message of the Gospel to them. He definitely broke away from the religious elitism of his day and brought religion back to the people. In a sense he was the leader of a new religious movement around which the farmers and workers, the illiterate and the oppressed, could gather. He thus posed a threat to the official religion consolidated on hierarchical structures of religious orders and teachings not readily accessible or intelligible to outsiders.

In the rise of Buddhism in India we also see something of a religious reformation that returned religion from a religious elite to the people in the street. The religious and social situation of India at the time of Buddha in the sixth century BC was similar to that of the Jewish community in Palestine during the life of Jesus. "At the time of the Buddha," writes Kenneth Ch'en, "the dominant position in Indian society was held by the brahmans. They held the key to knowledge, and the power that went with that knowledge." Brahmanism, like Judaism in Jesus' day, was the privilege of the religious leaders and the burden of the masses. As a reformer who ended up by founding a new religion, Buddha repudiated the brahmanical claims that the *Vedas* were the sole and infallible source of religious truth. He also rejected correct performance of the rituals as means of salvation, and he disapproved of the Upanishadic emphasis on intellectual means to attain emancipation. He also protested against the iniquities of the caste system, especially the high pretensions of the brahman class, and welcomed among his followers members from not only the four castes but also from among the outcasts. Buddha was thus the first in the history of India to revolt against the caste system as the chief misfortune of Indian society.

It is therefore not surprising that Buddha tried to communicate a message of emancipation from the suffering of the world in plain language. We can hear him saying something like this:

> I have taught the truth which is excellent in the beginning, excellent in the middle, and excellent in the end; it is glorious in its spirit and glorious in its letter. *But* simple as it is, the people cannot understand it. I must speak to them in their own language. I must adapt my thoughts to their thoughts. They are like unto children and love to hear tales. Therefore, I will tell them stories to explain the glory of the dharma If they cannot grasp the truth in the abstract arguments by which I have reached it, they may nevertheless come to understand it, if it is illustrated in parables.

It is clear from this that Buddha fully grasped the dynamics of people in religion. As Buddhism spread to China, Japan, and Southeast Asia, it became a religion of the people that created popular culture and cultivated a sense of solidarity among ordinary men and women in all walks of life. To be sure, the teachings of Buddha in their high and lofty forms never filtered down to the people unadulterated. But what is important is that Buddha brought to common men and women a sense of well-being, security, and above all a sense of destiny.

In this way a religious faith can become alive and genuine if it casts aside ecclesiastical pretensions and formidable theological systems and touches the lives and hearts of the people. As previously mentioned, both Jesus and Buddha labored to bring the light of a new faith into the lives of the people. They were close to the people, used popular language, and told stories and parables that came right out of the everyday experiences of the people. No wonder that we find in the Sutra of the Lotus Flower of the Wonderful Law the story of the lost son that bears a remarkable resemblance to the parable of the prodigal son in Luke 15:32.

According to the Buddhist story of the lost son, a young man left his father and went to another city where he became extremely poor. He was reduced to begging for his food. In contrast, his father grew rich and moved to a big estate where he lived in great luxury. But all the time he grieved over his lost son and said to himself:

> I am old and well advanced in years, and though I have great possessions I have no son. Alas that time should do its work upon me, and that all this

wealth should perish unused ... It would be bliss indeed if my son might enjoy all my wealth.

One day the son wandered into his father's land, and the drama of the reunion of the father and son gradually unfolded:

> Then the poor man, in search of food and clothing, came to the rich man's home. And the rich man was sitting in great pomp at the gate of his house, surrounded by a large throng of attendants ... When he saw him the poor man was terrified ... for he thought that he had happened on a king or on some high officer of state, and had no business there ... So he quickly ran away. But the rich man ... recognized his son as soon as he saw him and he was full of joy ... and thought: "This is wonderful! I have found him who shall enjoy my riches. He of whom I thought of constantly has come back, now that I am old and full of years!" Then, longing for his son, he sent swift messengers, telling them to go and fetch him quickly.

The story goes on to describe how the father, who lived in a highly class-conscious society, was not able to disclose his identity to his own son and take him back into his household. The poor man had to go away without realizing that he had been in his own father's house. The father then contrived to have his son hired to work in his own household as a servant. Every day he watched with compassion as his son cleared away a refuse heap. Then one day the rich man came down, took off his wreath and jewels and rich clothes, put on dirty garments, covered his body with dust, and, taking a basket in his hand, went up to his son. And he greeted him at a distance and said, "Take this basket and clear away the dust at once!" By this means he managed to speak to his son.

In this way, the old man made every attempt to make his son feel at home but did not reveal his own identity. In the meantime, the son proved to be a frugal, honest, and industrious man. Finally, knowing that his end was near, the old man

> sent for the poor man again, presented him before a gathering of his relatives, and, in the presence of the king, his officers, and the people of town and country, he said: "Listen, gentlemen! This is my son, whom I begot ... To him I leave all my family revenues, and my private wealth he shall have as his own."

Consequently, through the father's painful and patient effort the son was reinstated in society and accepted into his father's blessing.

It goes without saying that the ethos of this Buddhist story is quite different from that of the biblical story of the prodigal son. It is Asian through and through in its emphasis on class distinctions that affect even family relations, on accumulation of wealth as a moral and social virtue, and on inheritance as a chief factor affecting the father–son relationship. These are the elements that are part and parcel of a traditional Asian society. For the people in the street such social factors provide a background against which a religious truth can be apprehended. There is in this story no reference to the son's repentance, no mention of the elder son's protest against the father's treatment of the lost son. Despite all these differences in ethos and details, the story points up the father's compassion for his son, the expression of which is very Asian in its reserve and its respect for social conventions. It stresses the acceptance of the son by the father through a ceremony in accordance with the father's social status. The resemblance of the Buddhist story of the lost son to the biblical story of the prodigal son may be accidental. But it is evidence of the fact that deep in people's spirituality is a reflection of God's love and compassion for the world. Jesus Christ, we must admit, is not merely a reflection of God's love. He is the embodiment of that love. In any case, the father's compassion for the son in the Buddhist story may be seen as a reflection, however imperfect, of God's passionate love in the parable of the prodigal son.

John B. Cobb Jr on Religious Pluralism 9.10

In this essay, John B. Cobb, who has developed a particular interest in the relation between Christianity and Buddhism, raises some penetrating questions concerning certain pluralist assumptions about the religions. In particular, he questions whether there is a universal category called "religion," and points to the way in which Buddhism and Confucianism coexisted in China, one relating to spirituality and the other to morality, as an illustration of the complexity of the issue. See also 9.4; 9.5; 9.6; 9.7; 9.8.

Source: John B. Cobb Jr, "Beyond Pluralism," in G. D'Costa (ed.), *Christian Uniqueness Reconsidered: The Myth of a Pluralistic Theology of Religions* (Maryknoll, NY: Orbis, 1990), pp. 81–95; quote at pp. 81–4. Cited with permission of the publisher.

* * *

How odd I find it to be writing for a collection of essays in criticism of theologies espousing religious pluralism! Yet I have agreed to do so because of the very narrow way – indeed an erroneous way, I think – in which pluralism has come to be defined. By *that* definition of pluralism, I am against pluralism. But I am against pluralism for the sake of a fuller and more genuine pluralism. Let me explain.

I declined to write a paper for the conference that led to the publication of the book, *The Myth of Christian Uniqueness*, because I did not share in the consensus that conference was supposed to express and promote. In the minds of the organizers, that consensus was to be around the view that the several major religions are, for practical purposes, equally valid ways of embodying what religion is all about. The uniqueness that is rejected is any claim that Christianity achieves something fundamentally different from other religions. From my point of view, the assumptions underlying these formulations are mistaken and have misled those who have accepted them.

Probably the most basic assumption is that there is an essence of religion. This essence is thought to be both a common characteristic of all "religions" and their central or normative feature. Hence, once it is decided that Buddhism, Confucianism, or Christianity is a religion, one knows what it is all about and how it is to be evaluated. The next step is then the one about which the consensus was to be formed. Given the common essence, let us agree to acknowledge that it is realized and expressed more or less equally well in all the great religions. It is hoped in this way to lay to rest once and for all Christian arrogance and offensive efforts to proselytize. Christians could then contribute to that peace among religions that is an indispensable part of the peace the world so badly needs.

If, as in my case, one rejects this whole view of religion, then it is very difficult to take part in the discussion as thus posed. I do believe there is a family of traits or characteristics that guides the use of the term *religion* for most people. But the term is used even when only some, not all, the traits are present. For example, most people in the sphere of dominance of the Abrahamic faiths think of worship of a Supreme Being or deity as a religious trait. Yet when they find this absent in most Buddhist traditions, they do not automatically deny that Buddhism is a religion. They notice that it is permeated by a spirit of deep reverence or piety, that it aims to transform the quality and character of experience in a direction that appears saintly, that it manifests itself in such institutions as temples and monasteries in which there are ritual observances, and so forth. The overlap of characteristics suffices for most people, so that Buddhism is almost always included among the world's religions.

If one turns to Confucianism one finds a different set of overlaps with Abrahamic assumptions about religion and a different set of discrepancies. By a certain stretch of terms one can find in it a worship of a Supreme Being, but the function this plays is far less central than in Judaism, Christianity and Islam. There is great concern for the right ordering of human behavior, but much less interest in transforming the quality and character of experience. So is Confucianism a religion? This question divided Jesuits and their opponents in the seventeenth century, and the vacillation by Rome prevented what might otherwise have been the conversion of the Chinese court to Catholicism.

In the twentieth century the more acute issue is whether communism is a religion. Those who take their cue from the Abrahamic faiths notice at once the denial of God, but such denial does not exclude Buddhism. They notice also the evangelistic fervor, the selfless devotion evoked, the totalistic claims, the interest in the transformation of the human being, the confidence that a new age is coming. And in all this they see religious characteristics. One might judge that communism actually resembles Christianity, at least in its Protestant form, more closely than does Buddhism, yet the features it omits or rejects seem the most "religious" aspects of Christianity. A popular solution is to call communism a *quasi-religion*, whatever that may mean.

It would be possible to draw up a long list of characteristics that one person or another associates with the word *religion*. A list drawn up by a Buddhist would be likely to overlap with, but differ from, a list drawn up by a Muslim. Does that mean that one list would be more accurate than the other? That would imply that there is some objective reality with which the lists more or less correspond. But there is no Platonic idea "Religion" to which the use of the term *ought* to conform. The term means what it has come to mean through use in varied contexts. Each user should be at some pains to clarify his or her meaning. But arguments as to what religion truly is are pointless. There is not such thing as religion. There are only traditions, movements, communities, people, beliefs, and practices that have features that are associated by many people with what they mean by religion.

One meaning of religion derived from its Latin root deserves special attention here. *Religion* can mean "a binding together"; it can be thought of as a way of ordering the whole of life. All the great traditions *are*, or can be, religions in this sense. So is communism. All are, or can be, ways of being in the world. In most instances they designate themselves, or are readily designated, as Ways. If this were all that were meant by calling them religions, I would have no objection to designating them as such. But we would need to recognize that this use does not capture all the meanings of religion that are important to people. In fact, we do not cease thinking of these traditions as religious when they fail to function as the overarching ways of life for people who identify themselves with them. In the case of Buddhism in China, most people who identified themselves as Buddhists also identified themselves as Confucianists. Neither constituted an inclusive way of being in the world. For many people, being Chinese provided the comprehensive unity of meaning, the basic way of being, in the context of which they could adopt Buddhism for certain purposes and Confucianism for others. When religion is taken to mean the most foundational way of being in the world, then being Chinese is the religion of most of the Chinese people. This meaning of religion needs to be kept in mind along with others, but in most discourse it functions more as one of the characteristics that may or may not be present than as the decisive basis of use of the term.

If one views the situation in this way, as I do, the question, so important to the editors of *The Myth of Christian Uniqueness*, can still arise as to whether all the great traditions are of roughly equal value and validity. But the requisite approach to an answer to this question is then much more complex than it is for those who assume that all these traditions have a common essence or purpose just because they are religions. The issue, in my view, is not whether they all accomplish the same goal equally well – however the goal may be defined. It is first of all whether their diverse goals are equally well-realized.

Consider the case of Buddhism and Confucianism in China. What of their relative value and validity? They coexisted there through many centuries, not primarily as alternate routes to the same goal, but as complementary. In crude oversimplification, Confucianism took care of public affairs, while Buddhism dealt with the inner life. Perhaps one might go on to say that they were about equally successful in fulfilling their respective roles, but that statement would be hard to support and does not seem especially important.

Questions about the relative value of the great religious traditions can all be asked, and asked with less confusion, if the category "religion" is dropped. Both Buddhism and Confucianism are traditions that are correctly characterized in a variety of ways. By most, but not all, definitions of "religious," both can be characterized as religious. But to move from the fact that they are, among other things, "religious," to calling them religions is misleading and has in fact misdirected most of the discussion. It is for this reason that I am belaboring what appears to me an all-too-obvious point. The horse I am beating is not dead. It is alive as an assumption of the editors of *The Myth of Christian Uniqueness*. The assumption is so strong that, so far as I can discover, no argument is given in its support, and arguments against it, such as mine, are systematically ignored rather than debated.

I oppose the "pluralism" of the editors of (and some of the contributors to) *The Myth of Christian Uniqueness*, not for the sake of claiming that only in Christianity is the end of all religion realized, but for the sake of affirming a much more fundamental pluralism. Confucianism, Buddhism, Hinduism, Islam, Judaism, and Christianity, among others, are religious traditions, but they are also many other things. Further, of the family of characteristics suggested by "religious," they do not all embody the same ones.

Few of the supporters of either "pluralism" or "anti-pluralism" deny the fact of diversity. Our difference is that they discern within and behind the diversity some self-identical element, perhaps an a priori, that they call religion. It is this that interests them and that functions normatively for them. The issue among the Christians who espouse this view is whether Christians should claim superiority.

What strikes the observer of this discussion is that among those who assume that religion has an essence there is no consensus as to what the essence may be. Even individual scholars often change their mind. The variation is still greater when the scholars represent diverse religious traditions. Yet among many of them the assumption that there is an essence continues unshaken in the midst of uncertainty as to what that essence is.

I see no a priori reason to assume that religion has an essence or that the great religious traditions are well understood as religions, that is, as traditions for which being religious is the central goal. I certainly see no empirical evidence in favor of this view. I see only scholarly habit and the power of language to mislead. I call for a pluralism that allows each religious tradition to define its own nature and purposes and the role of religious elements within it.

9.11   Lesslie Newbigin on the Gospel in a Pluralist Culture

In a series of lectures given at Glasgow University in 1988, the British theologian and missionary Lesslie Newbigin explored a number of major difficulties he detected in the pluralist approaches to religion associated with writers such as John Hick, Wilfrid Cantwell Smith, and Gordon Kaufman, and other contributors to the volume *The Myth of Christian Uniqueness*. The discussion opens with a response to the suggestion that acknowledging the equal validity of all religions would make the world a more peaceful place. See also 9.5; 9.7; 9.8.

Source: Lesslie Newbigin, *The Gospel in a Pluralist Society* (Grand Rapids: Eerdmans, 1989), pp. 159–61; 168–70. Reprinted with the permission of the publisher.

* * *

There is a longing for unity among all human beings, for unity offers the promise of peace. The problem is that we want unity on our terms, and it is our rival programs for unity which tear us apart. As Augustine said, all wars are fought for the sake of peace. The history of the world could be told as the story of successive efforts to bring unity to the world, and of course the name we give to these efforts is "imperialism." The Christian gospel has sometimes been made the tool of an imperialism, and of that we have to repent. But at its heart it is the denial of all imperialisms, for at its center there is the cross where all imperialisms are humbled and we are invited to find the center of human unity in the One who was made nothing so that all might be one. The very heart of the biblical vision for the unity of humankind is that its center is not an imperial power but the slain Lamb.

The truth, of course, is that every program for human unity has implicit in it some vision of the organizing principle which is to make this unity possible. As Andrew Dumas has pointed out, if this is not clearly recognized and stated, as it is in the Christian vision of the cross of Jesus as the place where all peoples may find reconciliation, then we shall find that the interests and intentions of the proposer are the hidden center. If there is no explicit statement of the center of unity, then the assumptions and interests of the proposer become the effective center. This becomes very clear in *The Myth of Christian Uniqueness*. Professor Gordon Kaufman of Harvard begins with the need for human unity, assumes without argument that the Christian gospel cannot furnish the center for such unity, and goes on to say that "modern historical consciousness" requires us to abandon the claim to Christ's uniqueness, and to recognize that the biblical view of things, like all other human views, is culturally conditioned. This same "modern historical consciousness" will enable us to enter into the mental worlds of the other religions without supposing that we can impose our Christian norms on them. But to a person living in another culture it is not obvious that the modern historical consciousness of twentieth-century Western intellectuals provides us with a vantage point which can displace the one provided by the Christian story, or that it can furnish a basis for human unity. It is true that modern historical studies enable us to see that people in other times and places were looking at the world through culturally conditioned lenses and that their claim to "see things as they really are" is relativized by our studies in the history of cultures. But to suppose that modern historical consciousness gives us a privileged standpoint where we really do see things as they are, is of course unsupported dogma. Modern historical consciousness is also the product of a particular culture and can claim no epistemological privilege. Kaufman's theology of religions is thus similar to that of the Christian in that it finally rests on an ultimate faith-commitment which does not and cannot seek validation from some more ultimate ground. In this case the ultimate faith-commitment is to the validity of the "modern historical consciousness."

The same is true for the often made claim that all religions are variants of one central human experience, namely that which has been explored most fully by the great mystics. It is indeed true that mystical experience has played a very important role in all the world's great religions, including Christianity. But in no religious tradition is it the only reality. There is much else in all religious traditions, much about the conduct of human life, about justice, freedom obedience, and mutual charity. To select the mystical element in religion as the core reality is a decision which can be questioned in the name of other elements in the religious life. And the claim that the mystical experience is that which provides the primary clue to what is real, and therefore the one road to salvation for all humanity, is – once again – to choose a particular faith-commitment among others which are possible. It does not enable one to evade the question: Why this, rather than that?

Wilfrid Cantwell Smith in the same volume restates his familiar view that all the religions have as their core some experience of the Transcendent; that whether we speak of images made of wood and stone or images made in the mind, or even of such an image as the man Jesus, all are equally the means used by the Transcendent to make himself, herself, or itself present to us humans. To claim uniqueness for one particular form or vehicle of this contact with the Transcendent is preposterous and even blasphemous. Much rather accept the truth so beautifully stated in the *Bhagavad Gita* and in the theology of Ramanuja, that God is so gracious that he (or she or it) accepts everyone who worships whatever be the form through which that worship is offered.

It is clear that in Smith's view "The Transcendent" is a purely formal category. He, she, or it may be conceived in any way that the worshipper may choose. There can therefore be no such thing as false or misdirected worship, since the reality to which it is directed is unknowable. Smith quotes as "one of the theologically most discerning remarks that I know" the words of the *Yogavasistha*: "Thou art formless. Thy only form is our knowledge of Thee." Any claim for uniqueness made for one concept of the Transcendent, for instance the Christian claim that the Transcendent is present in fullness in Jesus (Colossians 1:19), is to be regarded as wholly unacceptable. There are no criteria by which different concepts of the Transcendent may be tested. We are shut up to a total subjectivity: the Transcendent is unknowable. . . .

I venture to offer two concluding comments on the pluralist position as it is set out in *The Myth of Christian Uniqueness*. One is from the perspective of the sociology of knowledge. The culture in which this type of thinking has developed is one in which the most typical feature is the supermarket. In a society which has exalted the autonomous individual as the supreme reality, we are accustomed to the rich variety offered on the supermarket shelves and to the freedom we have to choose our favorite brands. It is very natural that this mentality should pervade our view of religion. One may stick to one's favorite brand and acclaim its merits in songs of praise; but to insist that everyone else should choose the same brand is unacceptable.

And that leads to a second point which is more fundamental. The *Myth* volume celebrated a decisive move beyond exclusivism, and beyond the inclusivism which acknowledges the saving work of Christ beyond Christianity, to a pluralism which denies any uniqueness to Jesus Christ. This move, the "crossing of the Rubicon," is the further development of what was described by John Hick as a Copernican revolution – the move from a christocentric view of reality to a theocentric one. The further move is described as "soteriocentric" – it has its center in the common quest for salvation. Even the word "God" excludes some concepts of the Transcendent Reality and is therefore exclusivist. But what is "salvation"? It is, according to Hick, "the transformation of human experience from self-centredness to God – or Reality – centredness". The Christian tradition affirms that this salvation has been made possible because God, the creator and sustainer of all that is, has acted in the historical person of the man Jesus to meet us, take our burden of sin and death, invite us to trust and love him, and so to come to a life centered in God and not in the self. The authors of the *Myth* deny this. "Reality" is not to be identified with any specific name or form or image or story. Reality "has no form except our knowledge of it." Reality is unknowable, and each of us has to form his or her own image of it. There is no objective reality which can confront the self and offer another center – as the concrete person of Jesus does. There is only the self and its need for salvation, a need which must be satisfied with whatever form of the unknown Transcendent the self may cherish. The movement, in other words, is exactly the reverse of the Copernican one. It is a move away from a center outside the self, to the self as the only center. It is a further development of the move which converted Christian theology from a concern with the reality of God's saving acts, to a concern with "religious experience," the move which converts theology into anthropology, the move about which perhaps the final word was spoken by Feuerbach who saw that the "God" so conceived was simply the blown-up image of the self thrown up against the sky. It is the final triumph of the self over reality. A "soteriocentric" view makes "reality" the servant of the self and its desires. It excludes the possibility that "reality" as personal might address the self with a call which requires an answer. It is the authentic product of a consumer society.

It is not easy to resist the contemporary tide of thinking and feeling which seems to sweep us irresistibly in the direction of an acceptance of religious pluralism, and away from any confident affirmation of the absolute sovereignty of Jesus Christ. It is not easy to challenge the reigning plausibility structure. It is much easier to conform. The overwhelming dominance of relativism in contemporary culture makes any firm confession of belief suspect. To the affirmation which Christians make about Jesus, the reply is, "Yes, but others make similar affirmations about the symbols of their faith; why Jesus and not someone or something else?"

Thus a reluctance to believe in something leads to a state of mind in which the *Zeitgeist* becomes the only ruling force. The true statement that none of us can grasp the whole truth is made an excuse for disqualifying any claim to have a valid clue for at least the beginnings of understanding. There is an appearance of humility in the protestation that the truth is much greater than any one of us can grasp, but if this is used to invalidate all claims to discern the truth it is in fact an arrogant claim to a kind of knowledge which is superior to the knowledge which is available to fallible human beings. We have to ask, "How do you know that the truth about God is greater than what is revealed to us in Jesus?" When Samartha and others ask us, "What grounds can you show for regarding the Bible as uniquely authoritative when other religions also have their sacred books?" we have to ask in turn, "What is the vantage ground from which you claim to be able to relativize all the absolute claims which these different scriptures make? What higher truth do you have which enables you to reconcile the diametrically opposite statements of the Bible and the Qur'an about Jesus? Or are you in effect advising that it is better not to believe in anything?" When the answer is, "We want the unity of humankind so that we may be saved from disaster," the answer must be, "We also want that unity, and therefore seek the truth by which alone humankind can become one." That truth is not a doctrine or a worldview or even a religious experience; it is certainly not to be found by repeating abstract nouns like justice and love; it is the man Jesus Christ in whom God was reconciling the world. The truth is personal, concrete, historical. To make that confession does not mean, as critics seem to assume, that we believe that God's saving mercy is limited to Christians and that the rest of the world is lost.

Study Questions to Chapter 9

Why does Justin Martyr regard Socrates as a Christian? What issues does this raise?

To what does Karl Marx attribute the origins of religion? And what does he mean when he declares: "The philosophers have only *interpreted* the world in different ways; the point is to change it."

Karl Rahner develops the idea of an "anonymous Christian." What does he mean by this? How does he arrive at this idea? What questions does this raise?

According to Clark Pinnock, what Christological issues are raised by an awareness of the world's religions? How would you assess the various approaches he notes?

John Hick is a noted exponent of "complementary pluralism." What are the basic features of this approach? And how do they explain the phenomenon of religious pluralism? What are the implications of the kinds of arguments developed by Lesslie Newbigin for this approach?

In his discussion of religious pluralism, John B. Cobb remarks that, in China, "most people who identified themselves as Buddhists also identified themselves as Confucianists." What significance does he attribute to this observation?

10 Last Things

This final chapter focuses on the Christian understanding of the last things, often referred to as "eschatology" (Greek *eschata*, last things). In the early church, discussion of eschatology often centered on the question of the nature of the millennium, and the way in which the final transformation of the creation, especially human nature itself, would come about. A discussion of particular importance in this connection focused on the nature of the resurrection body, and its relation to the existing physical bodies of believers.

Although these questions continued to be of importance in later periods, they were supplemented by other issues. The medieval period saw the emergence of highly developed doctrines of hell, purgatory and heaven. These doctrines had a considerable influence on popular piety, and were often presented in visual forms, including the "mystery plays" enacted at great medieval cathedrals such as York Minster in England. However much these doctrines may have influenced popular Christianity and theologians with strong popular roots, their influence over more academic theology waned considerably as a consequence of the Enlightenment, which regarded them as outmoded superstitions.

The twentieth century, however, has seen the rebirth of interest in eschatology. Rudolf Bultmann's existential interpretation of eschatological ideas showed that they continued to have considerable contemporary relevance. Perhaps more importantly, Jürgen Moltmann showed how a rediscovery of eschatology could lead to a rediscovery of an authentically Christian doctrine of hope, which contrasted with secular ideas of a hope grounded in technological or political progress. In addition, eschatological issues continue to be of importance within popular Christianity, as the recent debate over conditional immortality (a concept which has its roots in the patristic era) has made clear.

10.1 Irenaeus on the Final Restoration of Creation

In this passage, Irenaeus sets out his belief in a restored earthly realm, which will be set up at the second coming of Christ, and will last for a thousand years (the "millennium"). After this time, the final judgement will take place. This idea of a worldly millennium is, for Irenaeus, confirmed by a number of considerations, especially Christ's promise to drink wine again with his disciples. How can this happen, he asks, if they are disembodied spirits? The reference to the future drinking of wine is a sure indication that there will be a kingdom of God established upon earth before the final judgement. See also 10.4; 10.13.

Source: *adversus haereses* V. xxxii.1; V.xxxiii.1; in *Sources Chrétiennes*, vol. 153, ed. A. Rousseau, L. Doutreleau, and C. Mercier (Paris: Cerf, 1969), 396.1–398.20; 406.9–408.21.

* * *

For some people allow themselves to be induced into error by heretical writings, and are ignorant of the way in which God works and of the mystery of the resurrection of the righteous, and of the kingdom, which is the beginning of immortality (*principium incorruptelae*), the kingdom by which such as have proved worthy are gradually accustomed to receive God. For this reason it is necessary to say something on this matter, and to explain that in the restored creation the righteous must first rise at the appearing of the Lord to receive their promised inheritance, promised by God to the fathers, and to reign therein; after that the judgement will come. For it is only right that they should receive the reward of their endurance in that created order (*conditio*) in which they laboured or suffered affliction, and were tested by suffering in all kinds of ways; that they should be brought to life in that created order in which they were put to death for the love of God; and to reign where they had endured bondage. For God is "rich in all things" (Romans 10:12) and all things are his. Therefore this created order must be restored to its first condition and be made subject to the righteous without hindrance; and this the Apostle shows in the Epistle to the Romans, when he says, "The earnest expectation of the creation awaits the revelation of the sons of God" (Romans 8:19–21) . . .

[After citing the words of Jesus in Matthew 26:29, "I will no more drink the fruit of the vine until I drink it anew in my Father's kingdom," Irenaeus continues:] It is certain that he will drink it in the heritage of the earth, which he himself will renew and restore to the service of the glory of the sons of God. As David says, he "shall renew the face of the earth" (Psalm 104:30). He promised to "drink of the fruit of the vine" with his disciples (Matthew 26:39), and by doing this, he indicated two things: the inheritance of the earth in which the new fruit of the vine will be drunk, and the physical resurrection of his disciples. For it is the body which is raised in a new condition which receives the new drink. Now this should not be understood to mean that he will drink the fruit of the vine with his disciples in some higher region above the heavens (*in supercaelesti loco*). Nor does it mean that those who drink it are disembodied, as the drink from the vine is more proper to the body rather than to the spirit.

Theophilus of Antioch on Conditional Immortality   10.2

Theophilus of Antioch composed his treatise *ad Autolycum* shortly after 180. It represents a defense of Christianity against the objections of the pagan Autolycus. Theophilus, in common with other writers of this period, such as Justin Martyr and Irenaeus, argued that the immortality of the human soul was conditional, rather than intrinsic. In other words, the immortality of the soul was not an integral part of human nature; immortality was to be understood as being conditional upon total obedience to God. A similar assumption underlies the argument in Anselm of Canterbury's *Cur Deus homo*. See also 5.10; 10.18.

Source: *ad Autolycum*, II, 27; in *Sources Chrétiennes*, vol. 20, ed. G. Bardy (Paris: Editions du Cerf, 1948), p. 164.

* * *

Was humanity created merely mortal in nature? Certainly not. So is humanity therefore immortal? We do not accept this either. So maybe humanity is nothing? We do not say this either. What we do say is that humanity was by nature neither mortal nor immortal. If God had created humanity mortal, God would therefore be the author of human death. So God did not create humanity as either mortal or immortal, but, as we have said above, with the capacity for them both. If humanity inclined towards those things which relate to immortality by keeping the commandments of God, then it would receive immortality as a reward from God, and thus become divine. On the other hand, if humanity should incline towards those things which relate to death by disobeying God, then humanity would be the cause of its own death. For God created humanity free (*eleutheros*) and with power over itself (*autexousios*).

Tertullian on Hell and Heaven   10.3

The argument here is that pagan philosophers have no right to criticize Christian ideas of heaven and hell, in that these are already anticipated in pagan Greek writings. Tertullian implies that these pagan writings may have plagiarized Old Testament sources, a common view among Christian writers of this early period. The *Apologeticus* is one of Tertullian's earliest writings, and dates from around 197. See also 10.9; 10.10; 10.12; 10.16; 10.17.

Source: *Apologeticus*, XLVII, 12–14; in *Tertullian: Apology*, Loeb Classical Library, ed. T. R. Glover (Cambridge, Mass.: Harvard University Press, 1960), p. 210.

* * *

And so we are also ridiculed because we proclaim that God is going to judge the world. Yet even the poets and philosophers place a judgement seat in the underworld. In the same way if we threaten Gehenna, which is a store of hidden underground fire for purposes of punishment, we are received with howls of derision. Yet they likewise have the river Pyriphlegethon in the place of the dead. And if we mention paradise, a place of divine delight appointed to receive the spirits of the saints, cut off from the knowledge of this everyday world by a kind of barrier consisting of that zone of fire (*maceria quadam igneae illius zonae a notitia orbis communis segregatum*), then the Elysian Fields have anticipated the faith in this respect. So how, I ask you, do these resemblances to our doctrines on the part of the philosophers or poets come about? They are just taken from our mysteries. And our mysteries, being earlier, are more trustworthy, and more to be believed than these mere copies! If they invented these mysteries subsequently out of their senses, then our mysteries would have to be reckoned as copies (*imagines*) of what came later. For the shadow never preceded the body, nor the copy before the truth (*Nunquam enim corpus umbra aut veritatem imago praedecit*).

10.4 Tertullian on the Millennium

The "millennium" here refers to an earthly reign of God, lasting for a thousand years, in which evil is eliminated from the earth. After enjoying the pleasures of this earthly paradise, believers are then finally raised to heaven. Tertullian uses the word "resurrection" to refer to both the entry into this kingdom, and subsequently entry into heaven. The work from which this extract is taken is a polemic against the heretic Marcion, dating from 207–8. See also 10.17.

Source: *adversus Marcionem*, III.xxiv.3–6; in Oxford Early Christian Texts: *Adversus Marcionem*, ed. E. Evans (Oxford: Clarendon Press, 1972), pp. 246–8.

* * *

For we also hold that a kingdom has been promised to us on earth, but before heaven: but in another state than this, as being after the resurrection. This will last for a thousand years, in a city of God's own making, the Jerusalem which has been brought down from heaven which the Apostle also designates as "our mother from above" (Galatians 4:26). When he proclaims that "our *politeuma*," that is, citizenship, "is in heaven" (Philippians 3:20), he is surely referring to a heavenly city . . . We affirm that this is the city established by God for the reception of the saints at the resurrection, and for their refreshment with an abundance of all blessings, spiritual blessings to be sure, in compensation for the blessings we have despised or lost in this age. For indeed it is right and worthy of God that his servants should also rejoice in the place where they suffered hardship for his name. This is the purpose of that kingdom, which will last a thousand years, during which period the saints will rise sooner or later, according to their merit (*sanctorum resurrectio pro meritis maturius vel tardius resurgentium*). When the resurrection of the saints is completed, the destruction of the world and the conflagration of judgement will be effected; we shall be "changed in a moment" into the angelic substance, by the "putting on of incorruption" (1 Corinthians 15:52–3), and we shall be transferred to the heavenly kingdom.

Origen on the Resurrection Body   10.5

In this passage, dating from the first half of the third century, Origen sets out his distinctive view that the resurrection body is totally spiritual in character. See also 10.6.

Source: *de principiis*, II.x.3; in *Sources Chrétiennes*, vol. 252, ed. H. Crouzel and M. Simonetti (Paris: Cerf, 1978), 380.82–382.119.

* * *

Now we ask how can anyone imagine that our animal body is to be changed by the grace of the resurrection and become spiritual? . . . It is clearly absurd to say that it will be involved in the passions of flesh and blood . . . By the command of God the body which was earthly and animal will be replaced by a spiritual body, such as may be able to dwell in heaven; even on those who have been of lower worth, even of contemptible, almost negligible merit, the glory and worth of the body will be bestowed in proportion to the deserts of the life and soul of each. But even for those destined for eternal fire or for punishment there will be an incorruptible body through the change of the resurrection.

Methodius of Olympus on the Resurrection   10.6

This work, which was originally written in Greek around the year 300, takes the form of a discussion set in the house of the physician Aglaophon. The book is concerned to refute Origen's idea that the resurrection necessarily involves a spiritual body. Origen had argued that human flesh was simply a prison for the eternal spirit, which was liberated at death, and would be raised again in a purely spiritual manner. Methodius argues that the resurrection is like the recasting of a damaged metal statue. The Bonwetsch edition, used here, includes material which has been recovered from rediscovered Slav versions of this document; as a result, the numbering of the sections differs from that of older editions. In the edition provided by J. P. Migne, *Patrologia Graeca*, the section is numbered I.6. See also 10.5.

Source: *de resurrectione*, I.xlii.1–xliii.4; in *Methodius*, ed. G. N. Bonwetsch (Leipzig: J. C. Hinrichs' sche Buchhandlung, 1917), 289.12–291.10.

* * *

So it seems that it is as if some skilled artificer had made a noble image, cast in gold or other material, which was beautifully proportioned in all its features. Then the artificer suddenly notices that the image had been defaced by some envious person, who could not endure its beauty, and so decided to ruin it for the sake of the pointless pleasure of satisfying his jealousy. So the craftsman decides to recast this noble image. Now notice, most wise Aglaophon, that if he wants to ensure that this image, on which he has expended so much effort, care and work, will be totally free from any defect, he will be obliged to melt it down, and restore it to its former condition . . .

Now it seems to me that God's plan was much the same as this human example. He saw that humanity, his most wonderful creation, had been corrupted by envy and treachery. Such was his love for humanity that he could not allow it to continue in this condition, remaining faulty and deficient to eternity. For this reason, God dissolved humanity once more into its original materials, so that it could be remodelled in such a way that all its defects could be eliminated and disappear. Now the melting down of a statue corresponds to the death and dissolution of the human body, and the remolding of the material to the resurrection after death.

10.7 Cyril of Jerusalem on Prayers for the Dead

In the course of his explanation of aspects of Christian worship, Cyril turns to deal with a section of the liturgy which offers prayers for the dead in the eucharist. The argument is that offering such prayers in the presence of Christ lends them an efficacy which they might not possess in other contexts. See also 10.8; 10.9.

Source: *Fifth Address on the Mysteries*, 9–10; in *Sources Chrétiennes*, vol. 126, ed. Auguste Piédagnel (Paris: Cerf, 1966), 158.4–160.13.

* * *

Following this, we pray for the holy fathers and bishops who have fallen asleep, and in general for all those who have fallen asleep before us, in the belief that it is a great benefit to the souls for whom the prayers are offered, while the holy and magnificent victim himself is present . . . In the same way, by offering to God our prayers for those who have fallen asleep and who have sinned, we . . . offer Christ sacrificed for the sins of all, and by doing so, obtain the loving God's favour for them and for ourselves.

10.8 John Chrysostom on Prayers for the Dead

In this homily, one of a major series composed during the period 386–98, Chrystostom provides theoretical justification for the practice of praying for the dead, noting its important place in Christian liturgical practice at the time. See also 10.7; 10.9.

Source: *Homilia in 1 Corinthos* xli, 5; in *Interpretatio Omnium Epistolarum Paulinarum*, vol. 2 (Oxford: Oxford University Press, 1847), pp. 525–6.

* * *

Let us help and commemorate them. After all, if the children of Job were purified by the sacrifice of their father (Job 1:5), why should we doubt that

our offerings for the dead bring them any comfort? ... Let us not hesitate
to help those who have died, and to offer our prayers on their behalf.

Gregory the Great on Purgatory   10.9

This important early reference to the idea of "purgatory," dating from 593 or 594, is grounded
on Gregory's exposition of Matthew 12:31, especially its references to sins which can be
forgiven "in the age to come." Note especially the reference to the "purifying fire." See also
10.7; 10.8; 10.11.

Source: *Dialogia*, IV.xli.3; in *Sources Chrétiennes*, vol. 265, ed. Adalbert de Vogüé (Paris: Cerf, 1980),
148.12–18.

* * *

As for certain lesser faults, we must believe that, before the final judgement,
there is a purifying fire (*purgatorius ignis*), for he who is the truth declares
that "whoever utters blasphemy against the Holy Spirit will not be pardoned either in this age, or in the age which is to come" (Matthew 12:31).
From this statement, it is to be understood that certain offences can be
forgiven in this age, whereas certain others will be forgiven in the age
which is to come.

Benedict XII on the Hope of Heaven   10.10

In this document published on 29 January 1336, and also known as *De visione Dei beatifica*
("On the Beatific Vision of God"), Pope Benedict XII set out an authoritative statement of the
Christian hope, from which the following extract is taken. See also 10.1; 10.3; 10.17.

Source: *Benedictus Deus*, in H. Denzinger (ed.), *Enchiridion Symbolorum* 24–5 edn (Barcelona: Herder,
1948), p. 230.

* * *

By virtue of our apostolic authority, we define the following point. According to the general disposition of God, since the ascension of our Lord and
Savior Jesus Christ into heaven the souls of all the saints ... and other
believers who died after receiving Christ's holy baptism (provided that
they were not in need of purification when they died ... or, if they did
need, or will need, such purification, when they have been purified after
death) ... have been, are and will be in heaven, in the heavenly kingdom
and celestial paradise with Christ, and are joined with the company of the
angels, already before they take up their bodies once more and before the
general judgement. Since the passion and death of our Lord Jesus Christ,
these souls have seen and do see the divine essence with an intuitive vision,
and even face to face, without the mediation of any creature.

10.11 Catherine of Genoa on Purgatory

The date of composition of Catherine's *Treatise on Purgatory* is not known for certain, although it may date from the 1490s. In this work, written in Italian, Catherine outlines her influential understanding of the basis and purpose of purgatory. See also 10.9.

Source: *Treatise on Purgatory*, iii, v; in *Edizione Critica dei Manoscritti Cateriniani*, ed. Umile Bonzi da Genova, vol. 2 (Genoa: Marietti, 1960), pp. 327–32.

* * *

The basis of all the pains [of purgatory] is sin, whether original or actual. God created the soul pure, simple and clean from all stain of sin, with a beatific instinct towards the one from whom original sin, in which the soul presently finds itself, draws it away. When actual sin is added to this original sin, the soul is drawn still further from him ...

When a soul draws near to the pure and clear state in which it was at its first creation, its beatific instinct is rediscovered and grows continually stronger with such force that any obstacle preventing the soul from finally reaching its goal appears to be unbearable. The more it glimpses this vision, the greater its pain.

Because the souls in purgatory are without the guilt of sin, there is no obstacle between them and God except their pain, which holds them back so that they cannot reach perfection through this instinct. They can also see that this instinct is held back by a need for righteousness. For this reason, a fierce fire (*un tanto extreme foco*) comes into being, which is like that of Hell, with the exception of guilt. This is what makes evil the wills of those who are condemned to Hell, on whom God does not bestow his goodness; they therefore remain in their evil wills, and opposed to the will of God ...

The souls in purgatory have wills which are in all things in accord with the will of God himself. For this reason, God bestows upon them his goodness. As a result they are joyful and cleansed of all their sin.

And as for guilt, these souls are just as they were when they were originally created by God, in that God forgives immediately the guilt of those who have passed from this life distressed by their sins, and having confessed them and resolved not to commit them any more. Only the corrosion of sin is left, and they are cleansed from this by pain in the fire.

When they have been cleansed for all guilt, and united in their wills with God, they may see him clearly (to the extent that he makes himself known to them), and see also how much it means to enjoy him, which is the goal for which they have been created.

Jonathan Edwards on the Reality of Hell 10.12

In this famous sermon, originally preached during the Great Awakening in eighteenth-century Massachusetts, Edwards presents a vigorous defense of a traditional idea of Hell, designed to shock his audiences into repentance. See also 10.3; 10.17; 10.18.

Source: The sermon "Sinners in the Hands of an Angry God"; in *The Works of President Edwards*, ed. S. B. Wright, 10 vols (New Haven: Yale University Press, 1929–30), vol. 7, pp. 163–77.

* * *

There is no want of *power* in God to cast wicked men into hell at any moment. Men's hands cannot be strong when God rises up. The strongest have no power to resist him, nor can any deliver out of his hands. He is not only able to cast wicked men into hell, but he can most easily do it. Sometimes an earthly prince meets with a great deal of difficulty to subdue a rebel, who has found means to fortify himself, and has made himself strong by the numbers of his followers. But it is not so with God. There is no fortress that is any defence from the power of God. Though hand join in hand, and vast multitudes of God's enemies combine and associate themselves, they are easily broken in pieces. They are as great heaps of light chaff before the whirlwind; or large quantities of dry stubble before devouring flames. We find it easy to tread on and crush a worm that we see crawling on the earth; so it is easy for us to cut or singe a slender thread that any thing hangs by: thus easy is it for God, when he pleases, to cast his enemies down to hell. What are we, that we should think to stand before him, at whose rebuke the earth trembles, and before whom the rocks are thrown down?

They *deserve* to be cast into hell; so that divine justice never stands in the way, it makes no objection against God's using his power at any moment to destroy them. Yea, on the contrary, justice calls aloud for an infinite punishment of their sins. Divine justice says of the tree that brings forth such grapes of Sodom, "Cut it down, why cumbereth it the ground?" (Luke 13:7). The sword of divine justice is every moment brandished over their heads, and it is nothing but the hand of arbitrary mercy, and God's mere will, that holds it back.

They are already under a sentence of *condemnation* to hell. They do not only justly deserve to be cast down thither, but the sentence of the law of God, that eternal and immutable rule of righteousness that God has fixed between him and mankind, is gone out against them, and stands against them; so that they are bound over already to hell. John 3:18 "He that believeth not is condemned already." So that every unconverted man properly belongs to hell; that is his place; from thence he is, John 8:23 "Ye are from beneath." And thither he is bound; it is the place that justice, and God's word, and the sentence of his unchangeable law assign to him.

They are now the objects of that very same *anger* and wrath of God, that is expressed in the torments of hell. And the reason why they do not go down to hell at each moment, is not because God, in whose power they are, is not then very angry with them; as he is with many miserable creatures now tormented in hell, who there feel and bear the fierceness of his wrath. Yea, God is a great deal more angry with great numbers that are now on earth: yea, doubtless, with many that are now in this congregation, who it may be are at ease, than he is with many of those who are now in the flames of hell.

So that it is not because God is unmindful of their wickedness, and does not resent it, that he does not let loose his hand and cut them off. God is not altogether such an one as themselves, though they may imagine him to be so. The wrath of God burns against them, their damnation does not slumber; the pit is prepared, the fire is made ready, the furnace is now hot, ready to receive them; the flames do now rage and glow. The glittering sword is whet, and held over them, and the pit hath opened its mouth under them.

The *devil* stands ready to fall upon them, and seize them as his own, at what moment God shall permit him. They belong to him; he has their souls in his possession, and under his dominion. The scripture represents them as his goods (Luke 11:12). The devils watch them; they are ever by them at their right hand; they stand waiting for them, like greedy hungry lions that see their prey, and expect to have it, but are for the present kept back. If God should withdraw his hand, by which they are restrained, they would in one moment fly upon their poor souls. The old serpent is gaping for them; hell opens its mouth wide to receive them; and if God should permit it, they would be hastily swallowed up and lost . . .

All wicked men's pains and *contrivance* which they use to escape hell, while they continue to reject Christ, and so remain wicked men, do not secure them from hell one moment. Almost every natural man that hears of hell, flatters himself that he shall escape it; he depends upon himself for his own security; he flatters himself in what he has done, in what he is now doing, or what he intends to do. Every one lays out matters in his own mind how he shall avoid damnation, and flatters himself that he contrives well for himself, and that his schemes will not fail. They hear indeed that there are but few saved, and that the greater part of men that have died heretofore are gone to hell; but each one imagines that he lays out matters better for his own escape than others have done. He does not intend to come to that place of torment; he says within himself, that he intends to take effectual care, and to order matters so for himself as not to fail. But the foolish children of men miserably delude themselves in their own schemes, and in confidence in their own strength and wisdom; they trust to nothing but a shadow. The greater part of those who heretofore have lived under the same means of grace, and are now dead, are undoubtedly gone to hell; and it was not because they were not as wise as those who are now alive: it is not because they did not lay out matters as well for themselves to secure their own escape.

John Wesley on Universal Restoration   10.13

In this sermon, John Wesley sets out his vision of a universal final restoration of the creation, including the animal and plant worlds. Note Wesley's admission than he cannot justify any assertion that God holds humanity and the remainder of the creation in equal esteem. See also 10.1.

Source: Sermon LXV: "The Great Deliverance," sections III.1–5; in John Wesley, *Sermons on Several Occasions*, vol. 2 (London: Wesleyan Conference Office, 1874), pp. 61–3.

* * *

But will "the creature," will even the brute creation, always remain in this deplorable condition? God forbid that we should affirm this; yea, or even entertain such a thought. While "the whole creation groaneth together" (whether men attend or not), their groans are not dispersed in idle air, but enter the ears of Him that made them. While his creatures "travail together in pain,' he knoweth all their pain, and is bringing them nearer and nearer to the birth, which shall be accomplished in its season. He seeth the "earnest expectation" wherewith the whole animated creation "waiteth for" that final "manifestation of the sons of God," in which "they themselves also shall be delivered" (not by annihilation; annihilation is not deliverance) "from the present bondage of corruption into" a measure of "the glorious liberty of the children of God." ...

A general view of this is given us in the twenty-first chapter of the Revelation. When He that "sitteth on the great white throne" hath pronounced "Behold, I make all things new," when the word is fulfilled, "the tabernacle of God is with men, and they shall be his people, and God himself shall be with them, and be their God" – then the following blessing shall take place (not only on the children of men; there is no such restriction in the text; but) on every creature according to its capacity ...

To descend to a few particulars. The whole brute creation will then, undoubtedly, be restored, not only to the vigour, strength, and swiftness which they had at their creation, but to a far higher degree of each than they ever enjoyed. They will be restored, not only to that measure of understanding which they had in paradise, but to a degree of it as much higher than that, as the understanding of an elephant is beyond that of a worm. And whatever affections they had in the garden of God, will be restored with vast increase; being exalted and refined in a manner which we ourselves are not able to comprehend. The liberty they then had will be completely restored, and they will be free in all their motions. They will be delivered from all irregular appetites, from all unruly passions, from every disposition that is either evil in itself, or has any tendency to evil. No rage will be found in any creature, no fierceness, no cruelty, or thirst for blood. So far from it that "the wolf shall dwell with the lamb, the leopard shall lie down with the kid, the calf and the young lion together; and a little child shall lead them. The cow and the bear shall feed together, and the lion shall eat straw like an ox. They shall not hurt nor destroy in all my holy mountain" (Isaiah 11:6–7) ...

But though I doubt not that the Father of All has a tender regard for even his lowest creatures, and that, in consequence of this, he will make them large amends for all they suffer while under their present bondage; yet I dare not affirm that he has an *equal* regard for them and for the children of men.

10.14   Rudolf Bultmann on the Existential Interpretation of Eschatology

In this book, which represents the published form of the 1955 Gifford Lectures at Edinburgh University, Bultmann argues for an existentialist reinterpretation of the last things, in which the traditional understanding of judgment is understood in terms of a personal existential decision on the part of the believer in the present. See also 2.27.

Source: Rudolf Bultmann, *History and Eschatology* (Edinburgh: Edinburgh University Press, 1957), pp. 151–5. Reprinted by permission of the publisher.

* * * ──

[The gospel] message knows itself to be legitimated by the revelation of the grace of God in Jesus Christ. According to the New Testament, *Jesus Christ is the eschatological event*, the action of God by which God has set an end to the old world. In the preaching of the Christian Church the eschatological event will ever again become present and does become present ever and again in faith. The old world has reached its end for the believer; he is "a new creature in Christ." For the old world has reached its end with the fact that he himself as "the old man" has reached his end and is now "a new man," a free man.

It is the paradox of the Christian message that the eschatological event, according to Paul and John, is not to be understood as a dramatic cosmic catastrophe but as happening within history, beginning with the appearance of Jesus Christ and in continuity with this occurring again and again in history, but not as the kind of historical development which can be confirmed by any historian. It becomes an event repeatedly in preaching and faith. Jesus Christ is the eschatological event not as an established fact of past time but as repeatedly present, as addressing you and me here and now in preaching.

Preaching is address, and as address it demands answer, *decision*. This decision is obviously something other than the decisions in responsibility over against the future which are demanded in every present moment. For in the decision of faith I do not decide on a responsible action, but on a new understanding of myself as free from myself by the grace of God and as endowed with my new self, and this is at the same time the decision to accept a new life grounded in the grace of God. In making this decision I also decide on a new understanding of my responsible acting. This does not mean that the responsible decision demanded by the historical moment is taken away from me by faith, but it does mean that all responsible decisions are born of love. For love consists in unreservedly being for one's neighbour, and this is possible only for the man who has become free from himself.

It is the paradox of Christian being that the believer is taken out of the world and exists, so to speak, as unworldly and that at the same time he remains within the world, within his historicity. To be historical means to live from the future. The believer too lives from the future; first because his faith and his freedom can never be possession; as belonging to the eschatological event they can never become facts of past time but are reality only over and over again as event; secondly because the believer remains within history. In principle, the future always offers to man the gift of freedom; Christian faith is the power to grasp this gift. The freedom of man from himself is always realized in the freedom of historical decisions.

The paradox of Christ as the historical Jesus and the ever-present Lord and the paradox of the Christian as an eschatological and historical being is excellently described by Enrich Frank:

> ... to the Christians the advent of Christ was not an event in that temporal process which we mean by history today. It was an event in the history of salvation, in the realm of eternity, an eschatological moment in which rather this profane history of the world came to its end. And in an analogous way, history comes to its end in the religious experience of any Christian "who is in Christ." In his faith he is already above time and history. For although the advent of Christ is an historical event which happened "once" in the past, it is, at the same time, an eternal event which occurs again and again in the soul of any Christian in whose soul Christ is born, suffers, dies and is raised up to eternal life. In his faith the Christian is a contemporary of Christ, and time and the world's history are overcome. The advent of Christ is an event in the realm of eternity which is incommensurable with historical time. But it is the trial of the Christian that although in the spirit he is above time and world, in the flesh he remains in this world, subject to time; and the evils of history, in which he is engulfed, go on ... But the process of history has gained a new meaning as the pressure and friction operate under which the Christian has to refine his soul and under which, alone, he can fulfill his true destiny. History and the world do not change, but man's attitude to the world changes.

In the New Testament the eschatological character of the Christian existence is sometimes called "sonship." F. Gogarten says: "Sonship is not something like an habitus or a quality, but it must be grasped ever and again in the decisions of life. For it is that towards which the present temporal history tends, and therefore it happens within this history and nowhere else." Christian faith just "by reason of the radical eschatological character of the salvation believed in never takes man out of his concrete worldly existence. On the contrary, faith calls him into it with unique sobriety ... For the salvation of man happens only within it and nowhere else."

We have no time to describe how Reinhold Niebuhr in his stimulating book *Faith and History* (1949) endeavours to explain the relation between faith and history in a similar way. Nor have we time to dispute with H.

Butterfield's thought, developed in his book *Christianity and History*. Although I do not think he has clearly seen the problem of historicism and the nature of historicity, his book contains many important statements. And I agree with him when he says: "Every instant is eschatological." I would prefer, however, to say: every instant has the possibility of being an eschatological instant and in Christian faith this possibility is realized.

The paradox that Christian existence is at the same time an eschatological unworldly being and an historical being is analogous with the Lutheran statement *simul iustus, simul peccator*. In faith the Christian has the standpoint above history which Jaspers like many others has endeavoured to find, but without losing his historicity. His unworldliness is not a quality, but it may be called *aliena* (foreign), as his righteousness, his *iustitia* is called by Luther *aliena*.

We started our lectures with the question of meaning in history, raised by the problem of historicism. We have seen that man cannot answer this question as the question of the meaning in history in its totality. For man does not stand outside history. But now we can say: the meaning in *history* lies always in the present, and when the present is conceived as the eschatological present by Christian faith the meaning in history is realized. Man who complains: "I cannot see meaning in history, and therefore my life, interwoven in history, is meaningless," is to be admonished: do not look around yourself into universal history, you must look into your own personal history. Always in your present lies the meaning in history, and you cannot see it as a spectator, but only in your responsible decisions. In every moment slumbers the possibility of being the eschatological moment. You must awaken it.

10.15 Jürgen Moltmann on the Rediscovery of Eschatology

In this passage, which addresses and engages with the secular optimism characteristic of western culture in the mid-1960s, Moltmann argues that eschatology is of central importance to Christian thinking. Moltmann's attitude of orientation towards the future, defined and informed by the promises of God, is summarized in a slogans: *spes quaerens intellectum – spero, ut intellegam* ("hope seeking understanding – I hope, in order that I may understand"). Each of these represents a significant modification of the viewpoint of Anselm of Canterbury, who emphasized the importance of faith, and was summarized in the slogans: *fides quaerens intellectum – credo, ut intellegam* ("faith seeking understanding – I believe, in order that I may understand"). Moltmann sets out the way in which this orientation towards the future could transform both Christian thought and action, rather than remaining simply a piece of theological jargon.

Source: Jürgen Moltmann, *Theology of Hope: On the Grounds and Implications of a Christian Eschatology* (London: SCM Press, and New York: Harper & Row, 1968), pp. 32–6. English translation copyright © 1968 by SCM Press Ltd. Reprinted by permission of SCM Press Ltd and HarperCollins Publishers, Inc.

* * *

All that we have said so far of hope might be no more than a hymn in praise of a noble quality of the heart. And Christian eschatology could regain its leading role in theology as a whole, yet still remain a piece of sterile theologizing if we fail to attain to the new thought and action that are consequently necessary in our dealings with the things and conditions of this world. As long as hope does not embrace and transform human thought and action, it remains topsy-turvy and inactive. Hence Christian eschatology must make the attempt to introduce hope into worldly thinking, and thought into the believing hope.

In the Middle Ages, Anselm of Canterbury set up what has since been the standard basic principle of theology: – *fides quaerens intellectum* – *credo, ut intelligam*. This principle holds also in eschatology, and it could well be that it is of decisive importance for Christian theology today to follow the basic principle: *spes quaerens intellectum – spero, ut intellegam*. If it is hope that maintains and upholds faith and keeps it moving on, if it is hope that draws the believer into the life of love, then it will also be hope that is the mobilizing and driving force of faith's thinking, of its knowledge of and reflections on human nature, history, and society. Faith hopes in order to know what it believes. Hence all its knowledge will be an anticipatory, fragmentary knowledge forming a prelude to the promised future, and as such is committed to hope. Hence also *vice versa* the hope which arises from God reveals all thinking in history to be eschatologically orientated and eschatologically stamped as provisional. If hope draws faith into the realm of thought and of life, then it can no longer consider itself to be an eschatological hope as distinct from the minor hopes that are directed towards attainable goals and visible changes in human life, neither can it as a result dissociate itself from such hopes by relegating them to a different sphere while considering its own future to be supra-worldly and purely spiritual in character. The Christian hope is directed towards a *novum ultimum*, towards a new creation of all things by the God of the resurrection of Jesus Christ. It thereby opens a future outlook that embraces all things, including also death, and into this it can and must also take the limited hopes of a renewal of life, stimulating them, revitilizing them, giving them direction. It will destroy the *presumption* of these hopes of better human freedom, of successful life, of justice and dignity for our fellow human beings, of control of the possibilities of nature, because it does not find in these movements the salvation it awaits, because it refuses to let the entertaining and realizing of utopian ideas of this kind reconcile it with existence. It will thus outstrip these future visions of a better, more humane, more peaceable world – because of its own "better promises" (Hebrews 8:6), because it knows that nothing can be "very good" until "all things are become new."

10.16   Hans Urs von Balthasar on Hell

In this difficult passage, von Balthasar interacts with a traditional Roman Catholic understanding of Hell in assessing the significance of the doctrine of Christ's descent into Hell. Notice especially the distinction drawn between "Hades" as the place of the dead, and "Hell" as a place of divine judgement. Von Balthasar argues that the implicit identification of these two notions in earlier theology led to considerable confusion. See also 10.3.

Source: Hans Urs von Balthasar, *Mysterium Paschale* (Edinburgh: T. & T. Clark, 1990), pp. 176–7. Used with permission of the publisher.

* * *

As a Trinitarian event, the going to the dead is necessarily also an event of salvation. It is poor theology to limit this salvific happening in an a priori manner by affirming – in the context of a particular doctrine of predestination and the presumed identification of Hades (Gehenna) with Hell – that Christ was unable to bring any salvation to "Hell properly so called," *infernus damnatorum*. Following many of the Fathers, the great Scholastics set up just such a prioristic barriers. Once agreed that there were four subterranean "reception areas" – pre-Hell, Purgatory, the Hell of unbaptized infants, and the true Hell of fire – theologians went on to ask just how far Christ had descended and to just what point his redemptive influence extended, whether by his personal presence, *praesentia*, or merely by a simple effect, *effectus*. The most frequent reply was that he showed himself to the damned in order to demonstrate his own power, even in Hell; that in the Hell of infants he had nothing to achieve; that in Purgatory an amnesty could be promulgated, its precise scope a matter of discussion. The pre-Hell remained the proper field of play of the redemptive action . . . This whole construction must be laid to one side, since before Christ (and here the term "before" must be understood not in a chronological sense but in an ontological), there can be neither Hell nor Purgatory – as for a Hell for infants, of that we know nothing – but only that Hades (which at the most one might divine speculatively into an upper and a lower Hades, the inter-relationship of the two remaining obscure) whence Christ willed to deliver "us" by his solidarity with those who were (physically and spiritually) dead.

But the desire to conclude from this that all human beings, before and after Christ, are henceforth saved, that Christ by his experience of Hell has emptied Hell, so that all fear of damnation is now without object, is a surrender to the opposite extreme . . . Here the distinction between Hades and Hell acquires its theological significance. In rising from the dead, Christ leaves behind him Hades, that is, the state in which humanity is cut off from access to God. But, in virtue of his deepest Trinitarian experience, he takes "Hell" with him, as the expression of his power to dispose, as judge, the everlasting salvation or the everlasting loss of man.

Gabriel Fackre on the Last Things   10.17

In this discussion, Gabriel Fackre points out what he sees as being the dangers of over-precise speculation concerning the last things. He argues that it is possible to discern some basic themes lying beneath the complex network of images and terms used in Christian eschatological language, and enters a plea for moderation in relation to this kind of speculation. See also 10.1; 10.3; 10.4; 10.6; 10.11; 10.12.

Source: Gabriel Fackre, *The Christian Story: A Narrative Interpretation of Basic Christian Doctrine*, rev. edn (Grand Rapids: Eerdmans, 1984), pp. 223–5. Reprinted with the permission of the publisher.

* * *

What does the Christian message have to say about the end? First we must be clear about what it does *not* say. In periods of uncertainty and peril, there is a temptation to claim to know far more about the times and seasons than befits the modesty of classical Christian Faith (2 Thessalonians 5:1–2). The history of the Church is replete with movements that responded to crisis times or circumstances with detailed forecasts of the how, when, where, and who of the end. Thus eschatology becomes *apocalypticism* with its blue-print, timetable, map, and cast of characters, all in a soon arriving cataclys-mic conclusion. Most often, the lush imagery of contemporary apocalyptic takes the form of a *premillennialist* scenario in which identifiable pretribulationary events in the present move toward the "rapture" of be-lievers, a tribulation of holocaust proportions, the return of Christ to estab-lish a thousand-year kingdom in this world, succeeded by a final revolt of the powers of evil, their overthrow, the coming of a new heaven and a new earth, and the going of the damned to the everlasting fires. *Postmillennialist* views read the same texts differently forecasting the Kingdom within history before Christ's final return. And amillennialist conceptions less sanguine about both the postmillennialist possibilities of history and the premillennialist claims to a God's-eye view of the consummation construe the apocalyptic imagery symbolically and see sin and evil persisting to the End. Here we follow in the tradition of the latter while respecting the insights of the other views. "Travelogue eschatologies" (Hans Schwarz) do not re-present the mainstream of Christian teaching about the future, for Jesus' own counsel has been decisive: "About that day and hour no one knows" (Mark 13:32). Tellers of the Christian Story are at their best when they observe this counsel and acknowledge that "We see through a glass darkly" (1 Corinthians 13:12 KJV). The glass is not transparent, giving us a full and clear view, but translucent. We have enough light by which to see and to discern some of the shape of things to come.

While the Christian epic does not yield up encyclopedic knowledge about the *how, when, where,* and *who* of the Consummation, it does give us bold affirmations about the *that* and *what* of the matter. In this respect the doc-trine of the End is much like the doctrine of the Beginning. The factuality and form of creation and Consummation are the things of interest to the Storyteller. *That* God shall fulfill the divine Intention, *that* history moves toward its Omega is fundamental to the meaning of the Christian saga. *What* the dimensions of that fulfillment are is equally important. The latter is summarized in the classic creeds of the Church. The Storytelling community has sifted through the Storybook in its own struggle age after age with human questioning and has fixed upon certain biblical refrains: *the resurrection of the dead, the return of Christ, the last judgment, everlasting life.* These comprise the kernel of Christian teaching about the End. These are the last things.

The kernel is surrounded by a husk. The color and sheen of this covering have a way of attracting the seeker, sometimes causing him or her to settle too quickly for the surface instead of probing to the center. There is a range of rich metaphors and images – the Anti-Christ, a thousand-year reign of peace, golden streets and pearly gates, numerology, the conversion of Israel – in which the great affirmations are housed. Three things should be noted about them: (1) They are not dominant or ubiquitous New Testament motifs, but random assertions. (2) They rise out of particular historical circumstances (Nero, Rome, etc.) and are often calculated to shore up the faith of the early Christians faced with oppression and martyrdom. (3) Most of them fall short of being eschatological affirmations since they do not deal with the transfiguration *of* the world, but with events *in* the world. Christian eschatology is not secular forecasting but the futurology of the World to Come. While these exuberant scenarios provide material for the armchair speculations and sometimes frenzied imaginations so popular in periods of travail in human history, Christian thought about the End has in the main chosen to be reserved about the details, focusing rather on the centralities of resurrection, return, judgment, and eternal life.

10.18 Philip E. Hughes on Everlasting Death

In this passage from one of his final works, Philip E. Hughes raises a series of questions concerning the traditional idea of "everlasting death." He notes a number of difficulties with this traditional approach, before offering his own understanding of conditional immortality, which he regards as avoiding the difficulties of the traditional approach. See also 10.2; 10.12; 10.13.

Source: Philip E. Hughes, *The True Image: The Origin and Destiny of Man in Christ* (Grand Rapids: Eerdmans, 1989), pp. 404–7. Reprinted with the permission of the publisher.

* * *

The difficulty (if such it is) of equating everlasting death with everlasting existence was compounded in the case of Augustine by reason of the fact that he took the unquenchable flames of eternal fire to be meant in a literal sense. In facing the question how it would be possible for resurrected persons of body and soul to be kept from being consumed by these flames he invoked the support of scientific fact, as he thought it to be, that certain lower creatures, and in particular the salamander, "can live in the fire, in burning without being consumed, in pain without dying." It was decidedly shaky support, however, because the naturalists known to him of his own and earlier periods reported this competence of the salamander with scepticism as a traditional or legendary notion. But in any case the supposed ability of the salamander was irrelevant, because it is not a capacity shared by human beings with salamanders, and Augustine had perforce to resort to the hypothesis that in the flames of hell the wicked would in this respect become salamander-like: "Although it is true," he wrote, "that in this world there is no flesh which can suffer pain and yet cannot die, yet in the world to come there will be flesh such as there is not now, as there will also be death such as there is not now."

Augustine, in short, found it necessary to introduce a change in the meaning of *death* if his belief in the endlessness of the torments of hellfire was to be sustained; and this is a necessity for all who understand eternal destruction in this way, whether or not they consider the flames of hell to be intended in a literal sense. Such persons can indeed claim to be in good company; but they should be aware that their interpretation is open to serious questioning. Apart from the fact that it involves a drastic change in the meaning of death so that, in this eschatological perspective, it signifies being kept alive to suffer punishment without the power of dying, some other considerations must be taken into account.

First of all, because *life* and *death* are radically antithetical to each other, the qualifying adjective *eternal or everlasting* needs to be understood in a manner appropriate to each respectively. Everlasting life is existence that continues without end, and everlasting death is destruction without end, that is, destruction without recall, the destruction of obliteration. Both life and death hereafter will be everlasting in the sense that both will be *irreversible:* from that life there can be no relapse into death, and from that death there can be no return to life. The awful negation and the absolute finality of the second death are unmistakably conveyed by its description as "the punishment of eternal destruction and exclusion from the presence of the Lord" (2 Thessalonians 1:9).

Secondly, immortality or deathlessness, as we have said, is not inherent in the constitution of man as a corporeal–spiritual creature, though, formed in the image of God, the potential was there. That potential, which was forfeited through sin, has been restored and actualized by Christ, the incarnate Son, who has "abolished death and brought life and immortality to light through the gospel" (2 Timothy 1:10). Since inherent immortality is uniquely the possession and prerogative of God (1 Timothy 6:16), it will be by virtue of his grace and power that when Christ is manifested in glory our mortality, if we are then alive, will be superinvested with immortality and our corruption, if we are then in the grave, will be clothed with incorruption, so that death will at last be swallowed up in victory (1 Corinthians 15:51–57; 2 Corinthians 5:1–5). And thus at last we shall become truly and fully human as the destiny for which we were created becomes an everlasting reality in him who is the True Image and the True Life. At the same time those who have persisted in ungodliness will discover for themselves the dreadful truth of Christ's warning about fearing God, "who can destroy both body and soul in hell" (Matthew 10:28).

Thirdly, the everlasting existence side by side, so to speak, of heaven and hell would seem to be incompatible with the purpose and effect of the redemption achieved by Christ's coming. Sin with its consequences of suffering and death is foreign to the design of God's creation. The renewal of creation demands the elimination of sin and suffering and death. Accordingly, we are assured that Christ "has appeared once for all at the end of the ages to put away sin by the sacrifice of himself" (Hebrews 9:26; 1 John 3:5), that through his appearing death has been abolished (2 Timothy 1:10), and that in the new heaven and the new earth, that is, in the whole realm of the renewed order of creation, there will be no more weeping or suffering, "and death shall be no more" (Revelation 21:4). The conception of the endlessness of the suffering of torment and of the endurance of "living" death in hell stands in contradiction to this teaching. It leaves a part of creation which, unrenewed, everlastingly exists in alienation from the new heaven and the new earth. It means that suffering and death will never be totally abolished from the scene. The inescapable logic of this position was accepted, with shocking candor, by Augustine, who affirmed that "after the resurrection, when the final, universal judgment has been completed, there will be two kingdoms, each with its own distinct boundaries, the one Christ's, the other the devil's, the one consisting of good, the other of bad." To this it must be objected that with the restoration of all things in the new heaven and the new earth, which involves God's reconciliation to himself of *all things*, whether on earth or in heaven (Acts 3:21; Colossians 1:20), there will be no place for a second kingdom of darkness and death. Where all is light there can be no darkness; for "the night shall be no more" (Revelation 22:5). When Christ fills all in all and God is everything to everyone (Ephesians 1:23; 1 Corinthians 15:28), how is it conceivable that there can be a section or realm of creation that does not belong to this fulness and by its very presence contradicts it? The establishment of God's everlasting kingdom of peace and righteousness will see the setting free of the whole created order from its bondage to decay as it participates in the glorious liberty of the children of God (Romans 8:21).

Fourthly, the glorious appearing of Christ will herald the death of death. By his cross and resurrection Christ has already made the conquest of death, so that for the believer the fear and sting of death have been removed (Hebrews 2:14–15; 1 Corinthians 15:54–57), the passage from death to life is a present reality (John 5:24), and the resurrection power of Jesus is already at work within him, no matter how severely he may be afflicted and incommoded outwardly (2 Corinthians 4:11, 16). We do not yet see everything in subjection to the Son (Hebrews 2:8); but nothing is more sure than that every hostile rule and authority and power will finally be destroyed, including death itself. Hence the assurance that "the last enemy to be destroyed is death" (1 Corinthians 15:24–26). Without the abolition of death the triumph of life and immortality cannot be complete (2 Timothy 1:10). This is the significance of *the second death*: it will be the abolition not only of sin and the devil and his followers but also of death itself as, in the final judgment, not only will Death and Hades give up their dead for condemnation but Death and Hades themselves will be thrown with them into the lake of fire (Revelation 20:13–15). Hence the clear promise that "death shall be no more" (Revelation 21:4).

Though held by many, it is a hollow contention that if the death sentence pronounced at the final judgment against the unregenerate meant their annihilation the wicked would be getting off lightly and would be encouraged to regard the consequence of their sin without fear. (It may be interposed that far more does the expectation of the never-ending torment of finite creatures raise the question of the purpose that might be served by such retribution.) There is altogether no room for doubting that, first, at the last judgment God will mete out condign punishment in accordance with the absolute holiness of his being, and, second, the Scriptures allow no place whatsoever to the wicked for complacency as they approach that dreadful day when they will stand before the tribunal of their righteous Creator. This ultimate Day of the Lord is depicted as a day of indescribable terror for the ungodly, who will then be confronted with the truth of God's being which they had unrighteously suppressed and experience the divine wrath which previously they had derided . . .

The horror of everlasting destruction will be compounded, moreover, by the unbearable agony of *exclusion*. To be inexorably excluded from the presence of the Lord and from the glory of his kingdom, to see but to be shut out from the transcendental joy and bliss of the saints as in light eternal they glorify their resplendent Redeemer, to whose likeness they are now fully and forever conformed, to be plunged into the abyss of irreversible destruction, will cause the unregenerate of mankind the bitterest anguish of weeping and wailing and gnashing of teeth. In vain will they have pleaded, "Lord, Lord, open to us!" (Matthew 25:11–12.; cf. 7:21–23). Too late will they then wish they had lived and believed differently. The destiny they have fashioned for themselves will cast them without hope into the abyss of obliteration. Their lot, whose names are not written in the Lamb's book of life, is the destruction of the second death. Thus God's creation will be purged of all falsity and defilement, and the ancient promise will be fulfilled that "the former things shall not be remembered or come to mind" as the multitude of the redeemed are glad and rejoice forever in the perfection of the new heaven and the new earth (Isaiah 65:17–18; Revelation 21:14).

Study Questions to Chapter 10

On the basis of the writings of Irenaeus and Tertullian, what is to be understood by "the millennium"?

Why did Methodius of Olympus criticize Origen's views on the resurrection body?

What biblical justification does Gregory the Great offer for belief in purgatory? And what purpose does it serve, according to Catherine of Genoa?

What did Rudolf Bultmann mean by "demythologization"? And in what way does he apply this method to eschatology?

For what reasons does Philip E. Hughes express anxieties concerning the idea of "everlasting death"?

Details of Theologians

Abelard *see* Peter Abelard.

Alexander of Hales (*c*.1186–1245). An Englishman from Halesowen in the West Midlands, who took up a chair of theology at the University of Paris around 1220. He became a Franciscan in 1236, and did much to establish the distinctive features of Franciscan theology in the period of High Scholasticism. His *Summa Theologica* is a composite work, including material added after his death by writers such as William of Melitona. See 3.20.

Ambrose of Milan (*c*.339–97). A leading Roman civil servant who was ordained bishop of the northern Italian city of Milan in 374, despite being neither baptized nor ordained. He was a vigorous defender of orthodoxy, and made several fundamental contributions to the development of Latin theology. He was also instrumental in bringing about the conversion of Augustine of Hippo. See 6.8.

Ambrosiaster. An unknown writer, who was first given this unusual name in the sixteenth century by Erasmus of Rotterdam. Initially confused with Ambrose of Milan, the distinctive character of this fourth-century writer, who is best known for his commentaries on the Latin text of the letters of Paul, is now recognized. See 6.9.

Anselm of Canterbury (*c*.1033–1109). Born in Italy, Anselm migrated to Normandy in 1059, entering the famous monastery of Bec, becoming its prior in 1063, and abbot in 1078. In 1093 he was appointed archbishop of Canterbury. He is chiefly noted for his strong defense of the intellectual foundations of Christianity, and is especially associated with the "ontological argument" for the existence of God. See 1.7; 3.18; 5.10.

Apollinarius of Laodicea (*c*.310–*c*.390). A vigorous defender of orthodoxy against the Arian heresy, who was appointed bishop of Laodicea at some point around 360. He is chiefly remembered for his Christological views, which were regarded as an over-reaction to Arianism, and widely criticized at the Council of Constantinople (381).

Aquinas *see* Thomas Aquinas.

Arius (*c*.250–*c*.336). The originator of Arianism, a form of Christology which refused to concede the full divinity of Christ. Little is known of his life, and little has survived of his writings. With the exception of a letter to Eusebius of Nicomedia, his views are known mainly through the writings of his opponents. See 4.6.

Athanasius (*c*.296–373). One of the most significant defenders of orthodox Christology during the period of the Arian controversy. Elected as bishop of Alexandria in 328, he was forced to resign on account of his opposition to Arianism. Although he was widely supported in the west, his views were finally recognized as authoritative after his death, at the Council of Constantinople (381). See 4.7; 5.4; 5.5.

Athenagoras of Athens (second century). Little is known of this writer, who was one of the most able of the second-century apologists. See 3.1.

Augustine of Hippo (354–430). Widely regarded as the most influential Latin patristic writer, Augustine was converted to Christianity at the northern Italian city of Milan in the summer of 386. He returned to north Africa, and was made bishop of Hippo in 395. He was involved in two major controversies — the Donatist controversy, focusing on the church and sacraments, and the Pelagian controversy, focusing on grace and sin. He also made substantial contributions to the development of the doctrine of the Trinity, and the Christian understanding of history. See 1.4; 2.8; 3.12; 3.13; 3.14; 6.10; 6.11; 6.12; 6.13; 6.14; 6.15; 6.16; 6.17; 8.7; 8.8.

Aulén, Gustaf (1879–1978). A Swedish Lutheran writer who was appointed to a chair of systematic theology at the University of Lund in 1913, and became bishop of Strängnäs in 1933. He is chiefly remembered for his work on the doctrine of the Atonement, and particularly his rehabilitation of the *Christus Victor* approach to the death of Christ. See 5.24.

Balthasar, Hans Urs von (1905–88). A leading Swiss Roman Catholic theologian, who, despite never holding an academic teaching position, has had a major influence on twentieth-century theology. He is chiefly noted for his emphasis on the need to relate theology to human culture, and for the strongly spiritual aspects of his theological reflection. See 10.16.

Barth, Karl (1886–1968). Widely regarded as the most important Protestant theologian of the twentieth century. Originally inclined to support liberal Protestantism, Barth was moved to adopt a more theocentric position through his reflections on the First World War. His early emphasis on the "otherness" of God in his Romans commentary (1919) was continued and modified in his monumental *Church Dogmatics*. Barth's contribution to modern Christian theology has been immense. See 1.20; 2.25; 3.28; 6.42; 9.4.

Basil of Caesarea (*c*.330–79). Also known as "Basil the Great," this fourth-century writer was based in the region of Cappadocia, in modern Turkey. He is particularly remembered for his writings on the Trinity, especially the distinctive role of the Holy Spirit. He was elected bishop of Caesarea in 370. See 3.9.

Benedict XII (died 1342). Originally named Jacques Fournier, this writer and scholar was elected as third Avignon pope in 1334. Although he was a significant theologian, few of his writings have survived. His most important writing is the papal constitution "Benedictus Deus" (1336), which deals with the beatific vision. See 10.10.

Bernard of Clairvaux (1090–1153). This French writer entered the Cistercian monastery of Cîteaux in 1112. In 1115, he was given the task of establishing a new monastery. He chose to do this at Clairvaux, which soon became established as a major center for spirituality. His writings are characterized by a deep personal devotion and love of God. See 2.11.

Beza, Theodore (1519–1605). Also known as Theodore de Besze, this French nobleman was attracted to Geneva in 1548, where he became a leading exponent of the ideas of John Calvin. He was appointed a professor at the Genevan Academy in 1558, and after Calvin's death in 1564 was recognized as a leading exponent of Reformed theology. See 6.34; 8.29.

Bloesch, Donald G. (born 1928). Leading North American evangelical theologian, particularly noted for his contributions to discussions of the authority of Scripture. See 2.30.

Boff, Leonardo (born 1938). A Brazilian Roman Catholic theologian, chiefly noted for his contribution to the development of Latin American liberation theology, especially in relation to the Trinity as a model of society. Boff's views eventually led to his alienation from the Roman Catholic establishment. See 3.30; 7.21.

Bonhoeffer, Dietrich (1906–45). German Protestant theologian, active in the ecumenical movement in the 1930s, and heavily involved in the theological resistance to Nazism. His most notable writings focus on the future of Christianity in a "religionless world." He was arrested in 1943, and hanged in 1945. See 1.23.

Brunner, Emil (1889–1966). A Swiss theologian who, while being influenced by his fellow countryman Karl Barth, developed ideas on natural theology which distanced them during the later 1930s. He is particularly noted for his strongly personalist idea of revelation. See 2.26; 6.41; 6.43.

Bucer, Martin (1491–1551). Also known as "Butzer." A German catholic writer who was coverted to Lutheranism around 1518, and became the reformer of the city of Strasbourg. In 1549, he moved to England at the invitation of Edward VI. He is chiefly noted for his work on biblical exegesis, and his doctrine of the church. See 8.27.

Bultmann, Rudolf (1884–1976). A German Lutheran writer, who was appointed to a chair of theology at Marburg in 1921. He is chiefly noted for his program of "demythologization" of the New Testament, and his use of existential ideas in the exposition of the twentieth-century meaning of the gospel. See 2.27; 10.14.

Cabasilas, Nicholas (born c.1322). A leading Byzantine theologian, remembered especially for his "Concerning Life in Christ," which elaborates the way in which the believer achieves union with Christ. See 5.14.

Calvin, John (1509–64). Leading Protestant reformer, especially associated with the city of Geneva. His *Institutes of the Christian Religion* has become one of the most influential works of Protestant theology. See 1.12; 2.16; 2.17; 5.15; 6.30; 6.31; 6.32; 7.14; 8.26.

Candidus of Fulda (died c.845). A monastic theologian associated with the monastery of Fulda, which became a leading center of theological reflection during the period 822–42. See 8.12.

Carr, Anne. Currently professor of theology at the Divinity School of the University of Chicago, with a particular interest in the relation of feminism and the Christian tradition. See 3.35.

Catherine of Genoa (1447–1510). A mystical Italian writer, who underwent a conversion experience at the age of 26. Her "Treatize on Purgatory" remains a major exploration of this theme. See 10.11.

Chrysostom, John (c.347–407). A noted preacher and theologian, who was appointed patriarch of Constantinople in 398. Apart from his considerable gifts as a public speaker and preacher, he is remembered for his homilies on a number of biblical books, which were originally delivered at Constantinople during the period 396–8. See 10.8.

Clement of Alexandria (c.150–c.215). A leading Alexandrian writer, with a particular concern to explore the relation between Christian thought and Greek philosophy. See 1.2; 2.3; 5.3; 8.1; 8.2.

Cobb, John B. Jr (born 1925). North American theologian, particularly noted for his commitment to process theology, and the exploration of Christian–Buddhist dialogue. See 9.10.

Cyprian of Carthage (died 258). A Roman rhetorician of considerable skill who was converted to Christianity around 246, and elected bishop of the north African city of Carthage in 248. He was martyred in that city in 258. His writing focus particularly on the unity of the church, and the role of its bishops in maintaining orthodoxy and order. See 7.3; 8.3.

Cyril of Alexandria (died 444). A significant writer, who was appointed patriarch of Alexandria in 412. He became involved in the controversy over the Christological views of Nestorius, and produced major statements and defenses of the orthodox position on the two natures of Christ. See 3.16; 4.11; 4.12; 4.13.

Cyril of Jerusalem (*c*.315–86). A writer noted especially for his series of 24 catechetical lectures, given at some point around 350 to those preparing for baptism, which are an important witness to the ideas which prevailed in the Jerusalem church around this point. He was appointed bishop of Jerusalem at some point around 349. See 2.7; 7.5; 8.4; 8.5; 10.7.

Descartes, René (1596–1650). French philosopher noted for his emphasis on the role of systematic doubt, and the importance of "perfection" in discussion of the nature of God. See 1.15.

Donne, John (1571–1631). A leading English poet, who was appointed dean of St. Paul's Cathedral, London, in 1621. See 5.17.

Dulles, Avery (born 1918). A noted American Roman Catholic writer, with a distinguished record of writings. He is particularly noted for his writings on the doctrine of the church. See 7.22.

Edwards, Jonathan (1703–58). Leading American theologian in the Reformed tradition, noted especially for his metaphysical defense of Christianity in the light of the increasingly influential ideas of the Enlightenment, and his positive statements of traditional Reformed doctrines. See 2.22; 6.39; 10.12.

Ellul, Jacques (1912–94). A French Reformed theologian and sociologist, particularly noted for his analysis of the interaction between Christianity and culture. See 3.33.

Epiphanius of Constantia (*c*.315–403). Also known as "Epiphanius of Salamis." A vociferous defender of orthodoxy, particularly against Sabellianism. His "Panarion," also known as "The Refutation of All Heresies," is an important witness to the controversies affecting the church at this stage. See 3.15.

Eriugena, John Scotus (*c*.810–*c*.877). A significant Irish philosopher and theologian, especially noted for his *Periphyseon*, which develops ideas concerning the four categories of nature. This work is often regarded as pantheistic. See 6.23.

Fackre, Gabriel (born 1926). North American theologian with a particular interest in the relation of narrative and systematic theology. See 10.17.

Feuerbach, Ludwig (1804–72). German Hegelian writer, whose ideas concerning the origin of religion had considerable influence on Karl Marx. His *Wesen des Christentums* ("Essence of Christianity"), which argued that Christianity was basically a projection of human needs and hopes, had considerable impact on its western European readership. See 9.2.

Forsyth, Peter Taylor (1848–1921). An English Protestant theologian, with considerable interest in contemporary German theology, who abandoned his early theological liberalism. He is chiefly remembered for his *Person and Place of Jesus Christ* (1909), a vigorous criticism of liberal Protestant views of Christ. See 4.27.

Francis of Assisi (1181–1226). Although not a theologian, Francis had a considerable impact on the theology of High Scholasticism through his spirituality, particularly his emphasis on nature. See 6.24.

Franck, Sebastian (c.1499–c.1542). German radical reformer, noted for his commitment to the ideal of total freedom of thought in matters of religion. See 7.12.

Fulgentius of Ruspe (c.462–527). A Roman civil servant who became bishop of Ruspe in north Africa around 502. A strong supporter of the theology of Augustine of Hippo, his theology is representative of the thought of the period, rather than original. See 3.17.

Gaunilo. An eleventh-century Benedictine monk, who criticized Anselm's argument for the existence of God. Little is known of him. See 1.8.

Gerrish, Brian A. Professor of theology at the Divinity School, University of Chicago, with a particular interest in the history and contemporary exposition of the Reformed tradition. See 1.27.

Gore, Charles (1853–1932). A leading English theologian of the late nineteenth and early twentieth century, who was appointed bishop of Oxford in 1911. He is chiefly remembered for his Christological writings, including the 1891 Bampton Lectures, published as *The Incarnation of the Son of God*. See 5.22.

Gregory of Nazianzen (329–89). Also known as "Gregory of Nazianzus." He is particularly remembered for his "Five Theological Orations," written around 380, and a compilation of extracts from the writings of Origen, which he entitled the *Philokalia*. See 3.10; 4.9.

Gregory the Great (c.540–604). Also known as Gregory I. He was elected as pope in 590, and did much to establish the political power of the papacy, which reached its zenith in the Middle Ages. As a theologian, he is particularly noted for his pastoral and exegetical works. See 10.9.

Gregory Palamas (c.1296–1359). A major Greek writer of the Hesychastic school, placing emphasis upon inner mystical prayer. He was elected as archbishop of Thessalonica in 1347. See 4.19.

Gunton, Colin E. British theologian, particularly associated with the exploration of the contemporary relevance of Trinitarian theology. See 5.28.

Gutiérrez, Gustavo (born 1928). Leading Latin American liberation theologian. See 1.26.

Hampson, Daphne. One of the leading contemporary representatives of feminism in Great Britain. See 4.31; 6.45.

Hayter, Mary. An English writer concerned to explore the relation between traditional Christian thought and aspects of feminism. See 6.46.

Herbert, George (1593–1633). Leading English religious poet of the seventeenth century, noted especially for his collection of poems entitled *The Temple*. See 5.18.

Hick, John (born 1922). British philosopher of religion, based in the United States for the final stage of his career, noted for his commitment to a pluralist understanding of the relation of the world's religions. See 9.8.

Hilary of Poitiers (c.315–67). A noted Latin defender of orthodoxy, especially against Arianism, who was elected bishop of the southern French city of Poitiers around 353. See 3.11; 8.6.

Hippolytus (c.170–c.236). Widely regarded as the most important Roman theologian of the third century. Writing in Greek, he devoted particular attention to the theological role of the Logos, and the relation of philosophy and theology. See 2.4.

Hodge, Archibald Alexander (1823–86). The son of the noted American Presbyterian writer Charles Hodge, who established himself as a leading defender of the "Old Princeton Theology" in the middle of the nineteenth century. He was called to a chair of systematic theology at Princeton Theological Seminary in 1877, and is particularly noted for his views on biblical authority and inspiration. See 2.24.

Hoen, Kornelius Hendriks (died 1524). A Dutch lawyer, active in The Hague, who developed the idea of a purely symbolic presence of Christ in the eucharist. See 8.22.

Hooker, Richard (c.1554–1600). Leading theologian of the Church of England in the period of the Elizabethan Settlement. He is noted especially for his *Laws of Ecclesiastical Polity*, notable for its defense of an episcopal form of church government. See 7.15.

Hugh of St. Victor (died 1142). A theologian, of Flemish or German origin, who entered the Augustinian monastery of St. Victor in Paris around 1115. His most important work is *de sacramentis Christianae fidei* ("On the Sacraments of the Christian Faith"), which shows awareness of the new theological debates which were beginning to develop at this time. See 5.12; 8.14.

Hughes, Philip E. (1915–90). Anglo-American evangelical theologian, particularly remembered for his works of biblical exposition and systematic theology. See 10.18.

Hus, Jan (c.1372–1415). Also known as "Huss." A Bohemian theologian who was elected as dean of the faculty of Philosophy at the University of Prague in 1401. He became noted for his views on the need to reform the church, which were given substance in his major work *de ecclesia* ("On the church"), published in 1413. He was burned at the stake in July 1415. See 7.8.

Ignatius of Antioch (c.35–c.107). A major early Christian martyr, noted for his letters to Christian churches in Asia Minor. Of particular interest is his vigorous defence of the reality of Christ's human nature and sufferings, in the face of those who wished to maintain that they were simply an appearance. See 4.1.

Irenaeus of Lyons (c.130–c.200). Probably a native of Asia Minor, who was elected as bishop of the southern French city of Lyons around 178. He is chiefly noted for his major writing *adversus haereses* ("Against the heresies"), which defended the Christian faith against Gnostic misrepresentations and criticisms. See 2.2; 3.2; 3.3; 4.2; 5.1; 5.2; 6.1; 7.1; 10.1.

Jenson, Robert. North America's leading Lutheran theologian, noted for his major contributions to the doctrine of the Trinity. See 3.31.

Jerome (*c*.342–420). One of the most noted biblical scholars and translators of the early church, sometimes referred to as "Hieronymus." His most significant achievement was his translation of most of the Bible into Latin. However, he was also noted for his biblical commentaries and writings which discussed the place of the Bible in Christian thought and life. See 2.9.

Jewett, Paul. North American evangelical writer, with an interest in the restatement of evangelical ideas in a modern context. See 3.34.

John of Damascus (*c*.675–*c*.749). A major Greek theologian, whose work *de fide orthodoxa* ("On the Orthodox Faith") is of considerable importance in the consolidation of a distinctively eastern Christian theology. See 4.18; 8.9.

Julian of Norwich (*c*.1342–*c*.1415). Little is known of the life of this English mystic, apart from the details she herself provides in her *Sixteen Revelations of Divine Love*. For at least part of her active life, she lived a solitary life in the city of Norwich. See 3.22.

Jüngel, Eberhard (born 1934). A leading modern German Protestant theologian, who is currently professor of systematic theology at the University of Tübingen. His most significant work to date is *God as the Mystery of the World* (1977), which reclaims a distinctively Christian understanding of God in the face of its Cartesian rivals. See 3.32.

Justin Martyr (*c*.100–*c*.165). One of the most noted of the Christian apologists of the second century, with a concern to demonstrate the moral and intellectual credibility of Christianity in a pagan world. His *First Apology* stresses the manner in which Christianity brings to fulfilment the insights of classical philosophy. See 1.1; 9.1.

Kähler, Martin (1835–1912). A German Lutheran theologian with a particular concern for the theological aspects of New Testament criticism and interpretation. He was appointed to the chair of systematic theology at Halle in 1867. His most famous work is an essay of 1892, in which he subjected the theological assumptions of the "Life of Jesus Movement" to devastating criticism. See 4.24.

Kant, Immanuel (1724–1804). German philosopher, based at the University of Königsberg in East Prussia. His philosophical writings have been of major importance, especially to German Protestant theology. His critique of the "ontological argument" is generally regarded as being of decisive importance. See 1.18.

Lactantius (*c*.240–*c*.320). A Latin Christian apologist, especially noted for his *Divinae Institutiones* ("Divine Institutions"), which was intended to demonstrate the cultural and intellectual credibility of Christianity. See 6.7.

Lanfranc of Bec (c.1010–89). Leading eleventh-century theologian, who became prior of the Norman abbey of Bec around 1045, and archbishop of Canterbury in 1070. He was a noted controversialist, and is remembered particularly for his biblical commentaries and his polemic writings dealing with the real presence. See 8.13.

Leo the Great (died 461). Also known as "Leo I," who became pope in 440. He is remembered particularly for the "Tome of Leo" (449), a document which was intended to serve a diplomatic function in the midst of the fierce Christological disputes of the period. See 4.14; 7.6.

Lessing, Gotthold Ephraim (1729–81). A significant representative of the German Enlightenment, noted for his strongly rationalist approach to Christian theology. See 4.22.

Lindbeck, George. Leading North American theologian, noted for his contributions to ecumenical theology, and more recently, his discussion of the nature of Christian doctrine. See 1.28.

Locke, John (1632–1704). A noted English philosopher, particularly associated with the empiricist doctrine that all knowledge derives from sense experience. Locke insisted that knowledge of God also arose through the senses, in contrast to Descartes, who argued that the idea was inherent to humanity. See 1.14.

Lossky, Vladimir (1903–58). A leading Russian Orthodox theologian, who was expelled from his homeland in 1922 following the Bolshevik revolution. He settled in Paris, and became a leading exponent of the ideas of Russian Orthodoxy in the west. See 5.25.

Luther, Martin (1483–1546). Perhaps the greatest figure in the European Reformation, noted particularly for his doctrine of justification by faith alone, and his strongly Christocentric understanding of revelation. His "theology of the cross" has aroused much interest in the late twentieth century. Luther's posting of the Ninety-Five Theses in Ocober 1517 is generally regarded as marking the beginning of the Reformation. See 1.11; 2.14; 2.15; 4.20; 6.26; 6.27; 6.28; 7.9; 7.10; 8.17; 8.18; 8.19; 8.20.

Marx, Karl (1818–83). A highly influential left-wing Hegelian political thinker, whose ideas were developed in international Marxism, and found their embodiment, in various forms, in socialist states such as the Soviet Union during the twentieth century. Marx regarded religion of any kind as the result of social and economic alienation, and argued that the coming of the revolution would eliminate religion altogether. See 9.3.

McFague, Sallie. North American theologian, with a particular interest in the role of theological language and models in contemporary theological restatement. See 1.25.

Melanchthon, Philip (1497–1560). A noted early Lutheran theologian, and close personal associate of Martin Luther. He was responsible for the systematization of early Lutheran theology, particularly through his *Loci*

Communes (first edition published in 1521) and his "Apology for the Augsburg Confession." See 6.29; 7.11; 8.21.

Methodius of Olympus (died *c*.311). A noted critic of Origen's theology, particularly the doctrines of the transmigration of souls and a purely spiritual resurrection body. His treatise on the resurrection develops the thesis of the continuity between the pre- and post-resurrection bodies. See 10.6.

Möhler, Johann Adam (1796–1838). Leading German Catholic theologian, and founder of the Tübingen School within Catholic theology, and widely regarded as one of the most important Catholic theologians of the nineteenth century. Möhler's most famous writing is his *Symbolik* ("Symbolics," 1832), which sought to clarify the Catholic position in relation to the new Protestant theology of Schleiermacher. See 2.23.

Moltmann, Jürgen (born 1926). One of the most influential of modern German Protestant theologians, particularly noted for his rehabilitation of eschatology and his exploration of the doctrine of the Trinity. See 3.29; 10.15.

Nestorius (died *c*.451). A major representative of the Antiochene school of theology, who became patriarch of Constantinople in 428. His vigorous emphasis upon the humanity of Christ seemed to his critics to amount to a denial of his divinity. Nestorius's failure to endorse the term "Theotokos" led to him being openly charged with heresy. Although far more orthodox than his opponents allowed, the extent of Nestorius's orthodoxy remains unclear and disputed. See 4.10.

Newbigin, Lesslie (born 1909). British theologian, with substantial experience of the Church of South India, with a particular interest in the relation of Christianity and modernity, and the issue of religious pluralism. See 9.11.

Newman, John Henry (1801–90). Leading Roman Catholic theologian, who began his career as a member of the Church of England, and was initially involved in the reinvigoration of the catholic wing of that church. He is particularly associated with a theory of the development of doctrine. See 1.19.

Niebuhr, Reinhold (1892–1971). Leading North American theologian, whose early optimism concerning human nature gave way to a theology of human nature and society which is grounded in the doctrine of original sin. See 6.44.

Oetinger, Friedrich Christoph (1702–82). Noted German Pietist writer, who reacted against the rationalism of Christian Wolff, and came under the influence of the Pietist writer Johann Albrecht Bengel. His works emphasize the need for personal faith and renewal. See 6.38.

Origen (*c*.185–*c*.254). Leading representative of the Alexandrian school of theology, especially noted for his allegorical exposition of Scripture, and his use of Platonic ideas in theology, particularly Christology. The originals of many of his works, which were written in Greek, have been lost, with the result that some are known only in Latin translations of questionable reliability. See 2.6; 3.5; 3.6; 3.7; 3.8; 4.5; 6.5; 6.6; 7.2; 10.5

Owen, John (1616–83). A leading English Puritan writer, who was elevated to high office during the period of Oliver Cromwell's Commonwealth. He is particularly noted for his strong defense of a Reformed doctrine of grace against Arminianism. See 3.25; 7.17.

Packer, James I. (born 1926). Leading Anglo-American evangelical writer, particularly noted for his writings on the doctrine of God and the Reformed theological and spiritual heritage. See 2.31; 5.27.

Pannenberg, Wolfhart (born 1928). One of the most influential German Protestant theologians, whose writings on the relation of faith and history, and particularly the foundations of Christology, have had considerable influence. See 5.26.

Pascal, Blaise (1623–62). An influential French Roman Catholic writer, who gained a considerable reputation as a mathematician and theologian. After a religious conversion experience in 1646, he developed an approach to his faith which was strongly Christocentric and experiential. His most famous writing is the collection known as the *Pensées*, first gathered together in 1670, some years after his death. See 1.16; 1.17.

Paschasius Radbertus (*c.*790–865). A Benedictine writer, who entered the monastery at Corbie in 822, and was noted as a vigorous defender of the real physical presence of Christ in the eucharist. See 8.10.

Pelagius. A British theologian who was active at Rome in the final decade of the fourth and first decade of the fifth centuries. No reliable information exists concerning the date of his birth or death. Pelagius was a moral reformer, whose theology of grace and sin brought him into sharp conflict with Augustine, leading to the Pelagian controversy. Pelagius's ideas are known mostly through the writings of his opponents, especially Augustine. See 6.18; 6.19; 6.20.

Peter Abelard (1079–1142). French theologian, who achieved a considerable reputation as a teacher at the University of Paris. Among his many contributions to the development of medieval theology, his most noted is his emphasis upon the subjective aspects of the atonement. See 5.11.

Peter Lombard (*c.*1100–60). A noted medieval theologian, active at the University of Paris, who was appointed bishop of Paris in 1159. His most significant achievement was the compilation of the textbook known as the "Four Books of the Sentences," a collection of extracts from patristic writers. See 8.15.

Petilian of Citra (born *c.*365). Donatist bishop of Citra, and defender of a rigorist approach to the ministry. See 7.4.

Pinnock, Clark H. (born 1937). Leading Canadian evangelical theologian, noted as a contemporary exponent of Arminianism, and more recently, for his exploration of an inclusivist approach to religious pluralism. See 9.7.

Rahner, Karl (1904–84). One of the most influential of modern Roman Catholic theologians, whose *Theological Investigations* pioneered the use of the essay as a tool of theological construction and exploration. See 2.28; 9.5.

Rashdall, Hastings (1858–1924). Leading English modernist theologian, noted especially for his emphasis upon the moral influence of Christ's death, and his criticisms of classic Protestant understandings of the atonement. See 5.23.

Ratramnus of Corbie (died 868). A ninth-century theologian, based at the monastery of Corbie, who is noted chiefly for his doctrine of double predestination, and his rejection of any understanding of a real physical presence of Christ at the eucharist. See 8.11.

Richard of St. Victor (died 1173). A leading representative of the school of thought based at the Abbey of St. Victor, in Paris. His most important work is *de Trinitate* ("On the Trinity"), which sets out an influential understanding of God as a person. See 3.19.

Rufinus of Aquileia (*c*.345–410). Although born in Italy, this writer eventually settled in Egypt, and was responsible for the translation of many Greek theological writings, including those of Origen, into Latin. He was also an original thinker in his own right. See 5.7.

Sayers, Dorothy L. (1893–1957). English novelist and dramatist, with a strong interest in Christian theology. See 4.29.

Schleiermacher, F. D. E. (1768–1834). One of the most influential German Protestant writers since the Reformation, noted especially for his emphasis on the role of "feeling" in theology in reaction against the rationalism of the Enlightenment. His most important work is *Der christliche Glaube* ("The Christian Faith"). See 3.27; 4.23; 5.20; 5.21; 7.18.

Schweitzer, Albert (1875–1965). This leading German Protestant theologian was noted particularly for his work on the historical Jesus, which led to a series of influential publications calling its validity and presuppositions into question. In 1913, he gave up his theological career to undertake medical work in Africa. See 4.26.

Simeon the New Theologian (949–1022). A leading representative of Byzantine theology, who is widely regarded as one of the most influential writers within the movement. His writings develop characteristic Byzantine themes, such as redemption as deification, while laying the foundations of the movement known as Hesychasm. See 5.9.

Song, C. S. [Choan-Seng] (born 1920). Taiwanese theologian, with a particular interest in the relation of Christianity and Asian (especially Chinese) culture. See 9.9.

Spener, Philip Jakob (1635–1705). Widely regarded as the founder of German Pietism, Spener laid considerable emphasis upon the experiential and devotional aspects of faith, which he believed to be missing from contemporary Lutheran Orthodoxy. See 2.20.

Spinoza, Benedict de (1632–77). A Jewish philosopher, noted for his pantheism. Spinoza's most important work, the *Ethica* ("Ethics") was published posthumously in 1677. See 3.26.

Jacques Lefèvre d'Etaples (*c*.1455–1536). A noted humanist scholar, who acted as libarian at the Parisian monastery of St. Germain-des-Prés. His writings on biblical translation and interpretation had a significant influence on the development of the Reformation. Although best known by his French name, he is also often referred to by his Latin name: Jacobus Faber Stapulensis. See 2.13.

Stephen Langton (died 1228). An English theologian who achieved fame as one of the leading biblical scholars and interpreters of the University of Paris. He was noted particularly for his exegetical and homiletical works. In 1207, he was appointed archbishop of Canterbury. See 2.12.

Tertullian (*c*.160–*c*.225). A major figure in early Latin theology, who produced a series of significant controversial and apologetic writings. He is particularly noted for his ability to coin new Latin terms to translate the emerging theological vocabulary of the Greek-speaking Eastern church. See 1.3; 2.5; 3.4; 4.3; 4.4; 6.2; 6.3; 6.4; 10.3; 10.4.

Theophilus of Antioch. One of the more significant Christian apologists of the second century. Little is known of his life, including the dates of his birth and death. Of his writings, the most significant to survive is the apology addressed to Autolycus. See 10.2.

Thomas Aquinas (*c*.1225–74). Probably the most famous and influential theologian of the Middle Ages. Born in Italy, he achieved his fame through his teaching and writing at the University of Paris and other northern universities. His fame rests chiefly on his *Summa Theologiae*, composed towards the end of his life and not totally finished at the time of his death. However, he also wrote many other significant works, particularly the *Summa contra Gentiles*, which represents a major statement of the rationality of the Christian faith. See 1.9; 1.10; 3.21; 5.13; 6.25; 7.7; 8.16;

Thomas à Kempis (*c*.1380–1471). A leading representative of the *Devotio Moderna*, who is widely accepted to be the author of the classic work of spirituality known as the *Imitatio Christi* ("The Imitation of Christ"). See 3.24.

Tillich, Paul (1886–1965). A German Lutheran theologian who was forced to leave Germany during the Nazi period, and settled in the United States. He held teaching positions at Union Theological Seminary, New York; Harvard Divinity School; and the University of Chicago. His most significant theological writing is the three-volumed *Systematic Theology* (1951–64). See 1.24; 4.30.

Torrance, Thomas F. (born 1913). Leading Scottish theologian, particularly noted for his writings dealing with the relation of Christianity and the natural sciences, and the interpretation of Karl Barth. See 2.32.

Tribble, Phyllis. Noted North American feminist writer and biblical scholar. See 2.29.

Troeltsch, Ernst (1865–1923). A theologian and sociologist who was closely involved in the founding of the "History of Religions School," which placed an emphasis upon the historical continuity of the religions. His most important theological contributions are thought to lie in the field of Christology, especially his discussion of the relation between faith and history. See 4.28.

Turrettini, François (1623–87). A leading Reformed theologian, of Italian origin, who became professor of theology at the Genevan Academy in 1653. He is regarded as one of the leading representatives of Calvinist thought during this period. See 4.21.

Tyrrell, George (1861–1909). A leading representative of English Modernism, noted for his increasing hostility towards traditional Roman Catholic teachings, and his criticism of the liberal Protestantism of Adolf von Harnack. See 4.25.

Ussher, James (1581–1656). A noted Irish Anglican writer, who eventually became archbishop of Armagh. He was strongly Calvinist in his theology. See 6.35.

Vincent of Lérins (died before 450). A French theologian who settled on the island of Lérins. He is particularly noted for his emphasis on the role of tradition in guarding against innovations in the doctrine of the church, and is credited with the formulation of the so-called "Vincentian canon." See 2.10.

Wesley, Charles (1707–88). English writer of hymns and theologian, noted for his Pietist emphases and hostility to Calvinism. Along with his brother John, he contributed to a significant revival within eighteenth-century English Christianity. See 5.19.

Wesley, John (1703–91). English theologian, pastor and hymn-writer, remembered especially as the founder of Methodism. Like his brother Charles, he was deeply influenced by Pietism, which had a considerable impact on his early theology. His theology found its expression in hymns and sermons, rather than works of systematic theology. See 6.40; 8.30; 10.13.

William of Ockham (c.1285–1347). Also known as "William of Occam." An English scholastic writer who developed the teachings of his predecessor Johannes Duns Scotus, and is particularly associated with the development of "nominalism" or "terminism" as a philosophical system. See 3.23.

Wittgenstein, Ludwig (1889–1951). An Austrian philosopher, noted for his exploration of the relation of language and the structure of the world. See 1.21; 1.22.

Zeno (*c.*450–90). Emperor of the east from 474, noted for his attempt to resolve the Monophysite controversy through his *Henoticon* (482). The attempt misfired, leaving relations between Rome and Constantinople worse than they had been before. See 4.16.

Zinzendorf, Nicolas Ludwig von (1700–60). A German writer who reacted against the rationalism of the theology of his day, and emphasized the emotional and experiential aspects of Christian faith. There is a clear connection between Zinzendorf's ideas and those of Pietism. He is remembered especially as the founder of a religious community at Herrnhut. See 2.21; 6.37.

Zizoulas, John D. (born 1931). Leading contemporary exponent of the ideas of Greek Orthodoxy. See 7.20.

Zwingli, Huldrych (1484–1531). (Also known as "Ulrich Zwingli.") A leading Swiss reformer, particularly associated with the vigorous denial of the real presence of Christ at the eucharist, a view usually designated "Zwinglianism." He died in battle, as a result of his attempts to spread his reforming ideas in his native Switzerland. See 8.23; 8.24.

Details of Conciliar, Creedal, and Confessional Material

The Apostles' Creed

A short creed whose origins can be traced back to the baptismal creeds of the early church, and which was given its final form by the eighth century. See 1.6.

The Council of Carthage

A local council, meeting in the north African city of Carthage in 418, which condemned Pelagianism in the region. See 6.21.

The Council of Chalcedon

This council, which met in 451, was responsible for a definitive statement of the two natures of Christ. See 4.15.

The Council of Trent

A major gathering of Catholic bishops and theologians, which aimed to reform the church in the face of Protestant criticisms, and clarify and defend

Catholic doctrine. The Sixth Session, focusing on the doctrine of justification, concluded in 1547; the Thirteenth Session, dealing with the real presence, ended in 1551. See 6.33; 8.28.

The First Helvetic Confession

An early Reformed confession of faith, drawn up in 1536 by representatives of Swiss cities. See 7.13; 8.25.

The Formula of Concord

A Lutheran formula of faith, drawn up in 1577 to settle a series of damaging disputes within German Lutheranism. See 2.19.

The Gallic Confession of Faith

A confession of faith drawn up by French Reformed churches in 1559. See 2.18.

The Heidelberg Catechism

A German Reformed catechism, drawn up in 1563, which has been widely accepted within the international Reformed community. See 1.13.

The Nicene Creed

One of the most important ecumenical creeds, formulated at the Council of Nicea, which sets out the orthodox position on the two natures of Christ. See 1.5.

The Synod of Arles

A local council, meeting in southern Gaul at some point around 473, which issued further condemnations of Pelagianism. See 6.22.

The Synod of Barmen

A gathering of the Confessing Church in 1934, which aimed to define the beliefs and objectives of the German Protestant churches in the face of Nazism. See 7.19.

The Westminster Confession of Faith

A major Reformed confession of faith, formulated in 1643 during the period of the Puritan Commonwealth. See 6.36; 7.16

A Glossary of Theological Terms

What follows is a brief discussion of a series of terms that the reader is likely to encounter in the course of reading original sources, such as those included in the present volume, or the secondary literature relating to them. Where the meaning of terms can be appreciated further by consulting readings in this volume, reference is provided to those most suitable for this purpose.

Adiaphora

Literally, "matters of indifference." Beliefs or practices which the sixteenth-century Reformers regarded as being tolerable, in that they were neither explicitly rejected nor stipulated by Scripture.

Alexandrian School

A patristic school of thought, especially associated with the city of Alexandria in Egypt, noted for its Christology, which placed emphasis upon the divinity of Christ, and its method of biblical interpretation, which employed allegorical methods of exegesis. A rival approach in both areas was associated with Antioch. See 2.6; 4.5; 4.7.

Anabaptism

A term derived from the Greek word for "re-baptizer," and used to refer to the radical wing of the sixteenth-century Reformation, based on thinkers such as Menno Simons or Balthasar Hubmaier.

Analogy of faith (*analogia fidei*)

The theory, especially associated with Karl Barth, which holds that any correspondence between the created order and God is only established on the basis of the self-revelation of God.

Analogy of being (*analogia entis*)

The theory, especially associated with Thomas Aquinas, that there exists a correspondence or analogy between the created order and God, as a result of the divine creatorship. The idea gives theoretical justification to the practice of drawing conclusions from the known objects and relationships of the natural order concerning God. See 1.10.

Anthropomorphism

The tendency to ascribe human features (such as hands or arms) or other human characteristics to God. See 1.27.

Antiochene School

A patristic school of thought, especially associated with the city of Antioch in modern-day Turkey, noted for its Christology, which placed emphasis upon the humanity of Christ, and its method of biblical interpretation, which employed literal methods of exegesis. A rival approach in both areas was associated with Alexandria. See 4.10.

antiPelagian writings

The writings of Augustine relating to the Pelagian controversy, in which he defended his views on grace and justification. See "Pelagianism." See 6.10; 6.11; 6.12; 6.13; 6.14; 6.15; 6.16.

Apocalyptic

A type of writing or religious outlook in general which focuses on the last things and the end of the world, often taking the form of visions with complex symbolism. The book of Daniel (Old Testament) and Revelation (New Testament) are examples of this type of writing.

Apologetics

The area of Christian theology which focuses on the defense of the Christian faith, particularly through the rational justification of Christian belief and doctrines.

Apophatic

A term used to refer to a particular style of theology, which stressed that God cannot be known in terms of human categories. "Apophatic" (which derives from the Greek *apophasis*, "negation" or "denial") approaches to theology are especially associated with the monastic tradition of the Eastern Orthodox church.

Apostolic era

The period of the Christian church, regarded as definitive by many, bounded by the resurrection of Jesus Christ (*c.*AD 35) and the death of the last apostle (*c.*AD 90?). The ideas and practices of this period were widely regarded as normative, at least in some sense or to some degree, in many church circles.

Appropriation

A term relating to the doctrine of the Trinity, which affirms that while all three persons of the Trinity are active in all the outward actions of the Trinity, it is appropriate to think of those actions as being the particular work of one of the persons. Thus it is appropriate to think of creation as the work of the Father, or redemption as the work of the Son, despite the fact that all three persons are present and active in both these works. See 3.12; 3.14.

Arianism

A major early Christological heresy, which treated Jesus Christ as the supreme of God's creatures, and denied his divine status. The Arian controversy was of major importance in the development of Christology during the fourth century. See 1.5; 4.6.

Atonement

An English term originally coined by William Tyndale to translate the Latin term *reconciliatio*, which has since come to have the developed meaning of "the work of Christ" or "the benefits of Christ gained for believers by his death and resurrection."

Barthian

An adjective used to describe the theological outlook of the Swiss theologian Karl Barth (1886–1968), and noted chiefly for its emphasis upon the priority of revelation and its focus upon Jesus Christ. The terms "neo-Orthodoxy" and "dialectical theology" are also used in this connection.

Beatific Vision

A term used, especially in Roman Catholic theology, to refer to the full vision of God, which is allowed only to the elect after death. However, some writers, including Thomas Aquinas, taught that certain favored individuals – such as Moses and Paul – were allowed this vision in the present life.

Calvinism

An ambiguous term, used with two quite distinct meanings. First, it refers to the religious ideas of religious bodies (such as the Reformed church) and individuals (such as Theodore Beza) who were profoundly influenced by John Calvin, or by documents written by him. Second, it refers to the religious ideas of John Calvin himself. Although the first sense is by far the more common, there is a growing recognition that the term is misleading.

Cappadocian Fathers

A term used to refer collectively to three major Greek-speaking writers of the patristic period: Basil of Caesarea, Gregory of Nazianzen and Gregory of Nyssa, all of whom date from the late fourth century. "Cappadocia" designates an area in Asia Minor (modern-day Turkey), in which these writers were based.

Cartesianism

The philosophical outlook especially associated with René Descartes (1596–1650), particularly in relation to its emphasis on the separation of the knower from the known, and its insistence that the existence of the individual thinking self is the proper starting point for philosophical reflection.

Catechism

A popular manual of Christian doctrine, usually in the form of question and answer, intended for religious instruction.

Catholic

An adjective which is used to refer both to the universality of the church in space and time, and also to a particular church body (sometimes also known as the Roman Catholic Church) which lays emphasis upon this point. See STUDY PANEL 19.

Chalcedonian definition

The formal declaration at the Council of Chalcedon that Jesus Christ was to be regarded as having two natures, one human and one divine. See 4.15.

Charisma, charismatic

A set of terms especially associated with the gifts of the Holy Spirit. In medieval theology, the term "charisma" is used to designate a spiritual gift, conferred upon individuals by the grace of God. Since the early twentieth century, the term "charismatic" has come to refer to styles of theology and worship which place particular emphasis upon the immediate presence and experience of the Holy Spirit.

Christology

The section of Christian theology dealing with the identity of Jesus Christ, particularly the question of the relation of his human and divine natures. See the material presented in chapter 4.

Circumincession

See Perichoresis.

Conciliarism

An understanding of ecclesiastical or theological authority which places an emphasis on the role of ecumenical councils.

Confession

Although the term refers primarily to the admission to sin, it acquired a rather different technical sense in the sixteenth century – that of a document which embodies the principles of faith of a Protestant church, such as the Lutheran Augsburg Confession (1530), which embodies the ideas of early Lutheranism, and the Reformed First Helvetic Confession (1536).

Consubstantial

A Latin term, deriving from the Greek term *homoousios*, literally meaning "of the same substance." The term is used to affirm the full divinity of Jesus Christ, particularly in opposition to Arianism. For its use, see 1.5.

Consubstantiation

A term used to refer to the theory of the real presence, especially associated with Martin Luther, which holds that the substance of the eucharistic bread and wine are given together with the substance of the body and blood of Christ. See 8.18; 8.19.

Correlation, Method of

An approach to theology especially associated with Paul Tillich (1886–1965), which attempts to relate the questions of modern western culture to the answers of the Christian tradition. See 1.24.

Creed

A formal definition or summary of the Christian faith, held in common by all Christians. The most important are those generally known as the "Apostles' Creed" and the "Nicene Creed." See 1.5; 1.6.

Deism

A term used to refer to the views of a group of English writers, especially during the seventeenth century, the rationalism of which anticipated many of the ideas of the Enlightenment. The term is often used to refer to a view of God which recognizes the divine creatorship, yet which rejects the notion of a continuing divine involvement with the world.

Demythologization

An approach to theology especially associated with the German theologian Ruldolf Bultmann (1884–1976) and his followers, which rests upon the belief that the New Testament worldview is "mythological." In order for it to be understood within, or applied to, the modern situation, it is necessary that the mythological elements should be eliminated. See 2.27.

Dialectical Theology

A term used to refer to the early views of the Swiss theologian Karl Barth (1886–1968), which emphasized the "dialectic" between God and humanity. See 3.28.

Docetism

An early Christological heresy, which treated Jesus Christ as a purely divine being who only had the "appearance" of being human. See 4.1; 4.23.

Donatism

A movement, centering upon Roman North Africa in the fourth century, which developed a rigorist view of the church and sacraments. See 7.4; 8.7.

Doxology

A form of praise, usually especially associated with formal Christian worship. A "doxological" approach to theology stresses the importance of praise and worship in theological reflection.

Ebionitism

An early Christological heresy, which treated Jesus Christ as a purely human figure, although recognizing that he was endowed with particular charismatic gifts which distinguished him from other humans. See 4.23.

Ecclesiology

The section of Christian theology dealing with the theory of the church. See chapter 7.

Enlightenment, The

A term used since the nineteenth century to refer to the emphasis upon human reason and autonomy, characteristic of much of western European and North American thought during the eighteenth century.

Eschatology

The section of Christian theology dealing with the "end things," especially the ideas of resurrection, hell, and eternal life. See chapter 10.

Eucharist

The term used in the present volume to refer to the sacrament variously known as "the mass," "the Lord's Supper" and "holy communion."

Evangelical

A term initially used to refer to the nascent reforming movements, especially in Germany and Switzerland, in the 1510s and 1520s, but now used of a movement, especially in English-language theology, which places especial emphasis upon the supreme authority of Scripture and the atoning death of Christ. See 2.30; 2.31; 5.27 for illustrations.

Exegesis

The science of textual interpretation, usually referring specifically to the Bible. The term "biblical exegesis" basically means "the process of interpreting the Bible." The specific techniques employed in the exegesis of Scripture are usually referred to as "hermeneutics." See STUDY PANEL 5.

Exemplarism

A particular approach to the atonement, which stresses the moral or religious example set to believers by Jesus Christ. See 5.23.

Existentialism

A movement which places emphasis on the subjectivity of individual existence, and the way in which this is affected by one's environment. The theological development of this approach is especially associated with Rudolf Bultmann and Paul Tillich. See 1.24; 2.26; 4.30; 10.14.

Fathers

An alternative term for "patristic writers."

Feminism

A major movement in western theology since the 1960s, which lays particular emphasis upon the importance of "women's experience," and has directed criticism against the patriarchalism of Christianity. See 2.29; 3.35; 4.31; 6.45 for illustrations.

Fideism

An understanding of Christian theology which refuses to accept the need for (or sometimes the possibility of) criticism or evaluation from sources outside the Christian faith itself.

Five Ways, The

A standard term for the five "arguments for the existence of God" associated with Thomas Aquinas. See 1.9.

Fourth Gospel

A term used to refer to the Gospel according to John. The term highlights the distinctive literary and theological character of this gospel, which sets it apart from the common structures of the first three gospels, usually known as the "Synoptic Gospels."

Fundamentalism

A form of American Protestant Christianity, which lays especial emphasis upon the authority of an inerrant Bible.

Hermeneutics

The principles underlying the interpretation, or exegesis, of a text, particularly of Scripture, particularly in relation to its present-day application.

Hesychasm

A tradition, especially associated with the eastern church, which places considerable emphasis upon the idea of "inner quietness" (Greek: *hesychia*) as a means of achieving a vision of God. It is particularly associated with writers such as Simeon the New Theologian and Gregory Palamas. See 4.19; 5.9.

Historical Jesus

A term used, especially during the nineteenth century, to refer to the real historical person of Jesus of Nazareth, as opposed to the Christian interpretation of that person, especially as presented in the New Testament and the creeds. See STUDY PANEL 11.

Historico-Critical Method

An approach to historical texts, including the Bible, which argues that proper meaning must be determined only on the basis of the specific historical conditions under which it was written. See 4.24; 4.26; 4.28.

History of Religions School

The approach to religions history, and Christian origins in particular, which treats Old and New Testament developments as responses to encounters with other religions, such as Gnosticism.

Homoousion

A Greek term, literally meaning "of the same substance," which came to be used extensively during the fourth century to designate the mainline Christological belief that Jesus Christ was "of the same substance as God." The term was polemical, being directed against the Arian view that Christ was "of similar substance (*homoiousios*)" to God. See also "Consubstantial." For its use, see especially 1.5.

Humanism

In the strict sense of the word, an intellectual movement linked with the European Renaissance. At the heart of the movement lay, not (as the modern sense of the word might suggest) a set of secular or secularizing ideas, but a new interest in the cultural achievements of antiquity. These were seen as a major resource for the renewal of European culture and Christianity during the period of the Renaissance. See 2.13 for an example of a humanist writer.

Hypostatic union

The doctrine of the union of divine and human natures in Jesus Christ, without confusion of their respective substances.

Ideology

A group of beliefs and values, usually secular, which govern the actions and outlooks of a society or group of people.

Incarnation

A term used to refer to the assumption of human nature by God, in the person of Jesus Christ. See 1.5; 4.7; 4.12 for illustrations. The term "incarnationalism" is often used to refer to theological approaches which lay especial emphasis upon God's becoming human.

Justification by faith, doctrine of

The section of Christian theology dealing with how the individual sinner is able to enter into fellowship with God. The doctrine was to prove to be of major significance at the time of the Reformation. See 6.26 for a foundational text.

Kenoticism

A form of Christology which lays emphasis upon Christ's "laying aside" of certain divine attributes in the incarnation, or his "emptying himself" of at least some divine attributes, especially omniscience or omnipotence.

Kerygma

A term used, especially by Rudolf Bultmann (1884–1976) and his followers, to refer to the essential message or proclamation of the New Testament concerning the significance of Jesus Christ. For its use in the writings of Rudolf Bultmann, see 2.27; 10.14.

Liberal Protestantism

A movement, especially associated with nineteenth-century Germany, which stressed the continuity between religion and culture, flourishing between the time of F. D. E. Schleiermacher and Paul Tillich. The "method of correlation" provides a good illustration of its later approaches: see 1.24.

Liberation Theology

Although this term designates any theological movement laying emphasis upon the liberating impact of the gospel, the term has come to refer to a movement which developed in Latin America in the late 1960s, which stressed the role of political action and orientated itself towards the goal of political liberation from poverty and oppression. For illustrations, see 1.26; 3.30; 7.21.

Liturgy

The written text of public services, especially of the eucharist.

Logos

A Greek term meaning "word," which played a crucial role in the development of patristic Christology. Jesus Christ was recognized as the "word of God"; the question concerned the implications of this recognition, and especially the way in which the divine "logos" in Jesus Christ related to his human nature. See STUDY PANEL 10.

Lutheranism

The religious ideas associated with Martin Luther, particularly as expressed in the Lesser Catechism (1529) and the Augsburg Confession (1530). For specifically Lutheran confessional material, see 2.19; 8.20.

Manicheism

A strongly fatalist position associated with the Manichees, to which Augustine of Hippo attached himself during his early period. A distinction is drawn between two different divinities, one of which is regarded as evil, and the other good. Evil is thus seen as the direct result of the influence of the evil god.

Modalism

A Trinitarian heresy, which treats the three persons of the Trinity as different "modes" of the Godhead. A typical modalist approach is to regard God as active as Father in creation, as Son in redemption, and as Spirit in sanctification. See 3.15.

Monophysitism

The doctrine that there is only one nature in Christ, which is divine (from the Greek words *monos*, "only one," and *physis*, "nature"). This view differed from the orthodox view, upheld by the Council of Chalcedon (451), that Christ had two natures, one divine and one human. See 4.16; 4.17.

Neo-Orthodoxy

A term used to designate the general position of Karl Barth (1886–1968), especially the manner in which he drew upon the theological concerns of the period of Reformed Orthodoxy.

Ontological Argument

A term used to refer to the type of argument for the existence of God especially associated with the scholastic theologian Anselm of Canterbury. See 1.7; 1.8; 1.18.

Orthodoxy

A term used in a number of senses, of which the following are the most important: Orthodoxy in the sense of "right belief," as opposed to heresy; Orthodoxy in the sense of the forms of Christianity which are dominant in Russia and Greece; Orthodoxy in the sense of a movement within Protestantism, especially in the late sixteenth and early seventeenth century, which laid emphasis upon need for doctrinal definition.

Parousia

A Greek term, which literally means "coming" or "arrival," used to refer to the second coming of Christ. The notion of the *parousia* is an important aspect of Christian understandings of the "last things."

Patripassianism

A theological heresy, which arose during the third century, associated with writers such as Noetus, Praxeas and Sabellius, focusing on the belief that the Father suffered as the Son. In other words, the suffering of Christ on the cross is to be regarded as the suffering of the Father. According to these writers, the only distinction within the Godhead was a succession of modes or operations, so that Father, Son, and Spirit were just different modes of being, or expressions, of the same basic divine entity. See 4.3.

Patristic

An adjective used to refer to the first centuries in the history of the church, following the writing of the New Testament (the "patristic period"), or thinkers writing during this period (the "patristic writers"). For many writers, the period thus designated seems to be *c.*100–451 (in other words, the period between the completion of the last of the New Testament writings and the landmark Council of Chalcedon).

Pelagianism

An understanding of how humans are able to merit their salvation which is diametrically opposed to that of Augustine of Hippo, placing considerable emphasis upon the role of human works and playing down the idea of divine grace. See 6.18; 6.19; 6.20.

Perichoresis

A term relating to the doctrine of the Trinity, often also referred to by the Latin term *circumincessio*. The basic notion is that all three persons of the Trinity mutually share in the life of the others, so that none is isolated or detached from the actions of the others. See 3.12; 3.14.

Pietism

An approach to Christianity, especially associated with German writers in the seventeenth century, which places an emphasis upon the personal appropriation of faith, and the need for holiness in Christian living. The movement is perhaps best known within the English-language world in the form of Methodism. For illustrations of its approach, see 2.20; 2.21; 5.19; 6.37; 6.38; 6.40.

Postliberalism

A theological movement, especially associated with Duke University and Yale Divinity School in the 1980s, which criticized the liberal reliance upon human experience, and reclaimed the notion of community tradition as a controlling influence in theology. For an illustration, see 1.28.

Postmodernism

A general cultural development, especially in North America, which resulted from the general collapse in confidence of the universal rational principles of the Enlightenment.

Praxis

A Greek term, literally meaning "action," adopted by Karl Marx to emphasize the importance of action in relation to thinking. This emphasis on "praxis" has had considerable impact within Latin American liberation theology. See 1.26; 9.3.

Protestantism

A term used in the aftermath of the Diet of Speyer (1529) to designate those who "protested" against the practices and beliefs of the Roman Catholic church. Prior to 1529, such individuals and groups had referred to themselves as "evangelicals."

Quadriga

The Latin term used to refer to the "fourfold" interpretation of Scripture according to its literal, allegorical, tropological moral, and analogical senses. See 2.3; 2.14.

Radical Reformation

A term used with increasing frequency to refer to the Anabaptist movement – in other words, the wing of the Reformation which went beyond what Luther and Zwingli envisaged, particularly in relation to the doctrine of the church. See 7.12.

Reformed

A term used to refer to a tradition of theology which draws inspiration from the writings of John Calvin (1510–64) and his successors. The term is now generally used in preference to "Calvinist." For examples of specifically Reformed material, see 1.13; 2.18; 6.36; 7.16; 8.25.

Sabellianism

An early trinitarian heresy, which treated the three persons of the Trinity as different historical manifestations of the one God. It is generally regarded as a form of modalism. See 3.15.

Sacrament

In purely historical terms, a church service or rite which was held to have been instituted by Jesus Christ himself. Although Roman Catholic theology and church practice recognize seven such sacraments (baptism, confirmation, eucharist, marriage, ordination, penance, and unction), Protestant theologians generally argue that only two (baptism and eucharist) were to be found in the New Testament itself. See chapter 8 for details.

Schism

A deliberate break with the unity of the church, condemned vigorously by influential writers of the early church, such as Cyprian and Augustine. See 7.3.

Scholasticism

A particular approach to Christian theology, associated especially with the Middle Ages, which lays emphasis upon the rational justification and systematic presentation of Christian theology. For examples of its approach, see 1.9; 1.10; 3.20; 3.23; 5.13.

Scripture Principle

The theory, especially associated with Reformed theologians, that the practices and beliefs of the church should be grounded in Scripture. Nothing that could not be demonstrated to be grounded in Scripture could be regarded as binding upon the believer. The phrase *sola scriptura*, "by Scripture alone," summarizes this principle. For its application, see 2.19.

Soteriology

The section of Christian theology dealing with the doctrine of salvation (Greek: *sōteria*). See chapter 5.

Synoptic Problem

The scholarly question of how the three Synoptic Gospels relate to each other. Perhaps the most common approach to the relation of the three Synoptic Gospels is the "Two Source" theory, which claims that Matthew and Luke used Mark as a source, while also drawing upon a second source (usually known as "Q"). Other possibilities exist: for example, the Grisebach hypothesis, which treats Matthew as having been written first, followed by Luke and then Mark.

Synoptic Gospels

A term used to refer to the first three gospels (Matthew, Mark, and Luke). The term (derived from the Greek word *synopsis*, "summary") refers to the way in which the three gospels can be seen as providing similar "summaries" of the life, death, and resurrection of Jesus Christ.

Theodicy

A term coined by Leibnitz to refer to a theoretical justification of the goodness of God in the face of the presence of evil in the world.

Theopaschitism

A disputed teaching, regarded by some as a heresy, which arose during the sixth century, associated with writers such as John Maxentius and the slogan "one of the Trinity was crucified." The formula can be interpreted in a perfectly orthodox sense and was defended as such by Leontius of Byzantium. However, it was regarded as potentially misleading and confusing by more cautious writers, including Pope Hormisdas (died 523), and the formula gradually fell into disuse.

Theotokos

Literally, "the bearer of God." A Greek term used to refer to Mary, the mother of Jesus Christ, with the intention of reinforcing the central insight of the doctrine of the incarnation – that is, that Jesus Christ is none other than God. The term was extensively used by writers of the eastern church, especially around the time of the Nestorian controversy, to articulate both the divinity of Christ and the reality of the incarnation. See 4.10; 4.13.

Transubstantiation

The doctrine according to which the bread and the wine are transformed into the body and blood of Christ in the eucharist, while retaining their outward appearance. See 8.16; 8.28.

Trinity

The distinctively Christian doctrine of God, which reflects the complexity of the Christian experience of God. The doctrine is usually summarized in maxims such as "three persons, one God." See STUDY PANEL 9.

Two Natures, doctrine of

A term generally used to refer to the doctrine of the two natures, human and divine, of Jesus Christ. Related terms include "Chalcedonian definition" and "hypostatic union."

Vulgate

The Latin translation of the Bible, largely deriving from Jerome, upon which medieval theology was largely based.

Zwinglianism

The term is used generally to refer to the thought of Huldrych Zwingli, but is often used refer specifically to his views on the sacraments, especially on the "real presence" (which for Zwingli was more of a "real absence"). See 8.23; 8.24.

Suggestions for Further Reading

Readers

The readings presented in this work represent only a very small sample of the enormous selection of material available. Further specialist readers dealing with specific writers, themes or schools of thought are readily available, for those wishing to follow up particular issues in more detail. Examples of schools of thought which are surveyed in this way include:

Feminist Theology

Ann Loades, *Feminist Theology: A Reader* (London: SPCK, 1990).

Narrative theology

Stanley Hauerwas and Gregory L. Jones, *Why Narrative? Readings in Narrative Theology* (Grand Rapids: Eerdmans, 1989).

Specific themes surveyed in specialist readers include:

Philosophical Theology

B. A. Brody, *Readings in the Philosophy of Religion* (Englewood Cliffs, NY: Prentice-Hall, 1974).
William L. Rowe and William J. Wainwright, *Philosophy of Religion: Selected Readings* (New York: Harcourt Brace Jovanovich, 1973).

Individual theologians surveyed through specialist readers include:

Thomas Aquinas

Mary T. Clark, *An Aquinas Reader* (London: Hodder & Stoughton, 1974).

Martin Luther

Timothy F. Lull, *Martin Luther's Basic Theological Writings* (Minneapolis: Fortress Press, 1989).

In view of its likely readership, the present volume has a strongly western orientation. However, Christian theology is now expanding strongly in other parts of the world, such as Africa and Asia. As a result, users of this work should be aware of the existence of readers specially devoted to regional theological developments. Examples include:
J. Parratt (ed.), *A Reader in African Christian Theology* (London: SPCK, 1987).
R. S. Sugirtharajah and C. Hargreaves (eds), *Readings in Indian Christian Theology* (London: SPCK, 1993).

The History of Theology

The following work is especially recommended as an introduction to the various aspects of the history of Christian Theology:
Jaroslav Pelikan, *The Christian Tradition: A History of the Development of Doctrine*, 5 vols (Chicago: University of Chicago Press, 1989). The five volumes of this excellent study are arranged as follows:
1. The Emergence of the Catholic Tradition (100–600)
2. The Spirit of Eastern Christendom (600–1700)
3. The Growth of Medieval Theology (600–1300)
4. Reformation of Church and Dogma (1300–1700)
5. Christian Doctrine and Modern Culture (since 1700).

On the patristic period, the following are especially useful: W. H. C. Frend, *The Rise of Christianity* (Philadelphia: Fortress Press, 1984).
Ian Hazlett (ed.), *Early Christianity: Origins and Evolution to A.D. 600* (London: SPCK, 1991).
Herbert Jedin and John Dolan (eds), *A Handbook of Church History*, vol. 1 (London: Burns & Oates, 1965).
J. N. D. Kelly, *Early Christian Doctrines*, 4th edn (London: A. & C. Black, 1968).

On the medieval and renaissance periods, the following should be consulted: Peter Burke, *The Italian Renaissance: Culture and Society in Italy*, revised edition (Oxford: Polity Press, 1986).
B. B. Price, *Medieval Thought: An Introduction* (Oxford/Cambridge, Mass.: Blackwell, 1992).

On the Reformation period, see:
Euan Cameron, *The European Reformation* (Oxford: Oxford University Press, 1991).
Timothy George, *The Theology of the Reformers* (Nashville, Tenn.: Abingdon, 1988).
Alister E. McGrath, *Reformation Thought: An Introduction*, 2nd edn (Oxford/Cambridge, Mass.: Blackwell, 1993).

On the modern period, there are a number of major resources available. For a survey of Christian thought since the Enlightenment, see Alister E. McGrath (ed.), *Blackwell Encyclopaedia of Modern Christian Thought* (Oxford/Cambridge, Mass.: Blackwell, 1993).

For specialist studies of nineteenth-century Christian theology, see: Ninian Smart, John Clayton, Patrick Sherry and Steven T. Katz (eds), *Nineteenth-Century Religious Thought in the West*, 3 vols (Cambridge: Cambridge University Press, 1985).

Claude Welch, *Protestant Thought in the Nineteenth Century*, 2 vols (New Haven: Yale University Press, 1972–85).

For a valuable survey of twentieth-century writers, see:

David F. Ford (ed.), *The Modern Theologians*, 2 vols (Oxford/Cambridge, Mass.: Blackwell Publishing, 1990).

Stanley J. Grenz and Roger E. Olson, *Twentieth-Century Theology: God and the World in a Transitional Age* (Downers Grove, Ill.: InterVarsity Press, 1992).

For further details of many theologians active in the nineteenth and twentieth centuries, see Martin E. Marty and Dean G. Peerman, *A Handbook of Christian Theologians* (Nashville: Abingdon Press, 1984).

Specific Topics

Figures in bold type placed against each chapter number indicate the chapters of the companion volume *Christian Theology: An Introduction*, which are of direct relevance to this material. Works from which readings are reprinted should also be consulted, and are not noted in this section.

Chapter 1 (5)

Carl E. Braaten, "Prolegomena to Christian Dogmatics," in C. E. Braaten and R. W. Jenson (eds), *Christian Dogmatics*, 2 vols (Philadelphia: Fortress Press, 1984), vol. 1, pp. 5–78.

C. Stephen Evans, *Philosophy of Religion: Thinking about Faith* (Downers Grove, Ill.: InterVarsity Press, 1982).

Basil Mitchell, *The Justification of Religious Belief* (Oxford: Oxford University Press, 1981).

Wolfhart Pannenberg, *Theology and the Philosophy of Science* (London: Darton, Longman and Todd, 1976), pp. 3–22.

Richard G. Swinburne, *Faith and Reason* (Oxford: Clarendon Press, 1981).

Nicolas Wolterstorff, *Reason within the Bounds of Religion*, 2nd edn (Grand Rapids: Eerdmans, 1984).

Chapter 2 (6)

R. J. Coggins and J. L. Houlden, *A Dictionary of Biblical Interpretation* (London: SCM Press, 1990).

Avery Dulles, *Models of Revelation* (Dublin: Gill & Macmillan, 1983).

Edward Farley and Peter Hodgson, "Scripture and Tradition," in P. Hodgson

and R. King (eds), *Christian Theology* (Philadelphia: Fortress Press, 1982), pp. 35–61.
Bruce M. Metzger, *The New Testament Canon* (Oxford: Oxford University Press, 1987).
Robert Morgan, *Biblical Interpretation* (Oxford: Oxford University Press, 1988).
Anthony C. Thiselton, *New Horizons in Hermeneutics* (Grand Rapids: Zondervan, 1992).
K. R. Tremblath, *Evangelical Theories of Biblical Inspiration* (Oxford: Oxford University Press, 1988).

Chapter 3 (7, 8)

Vincent Brümmer, *Speaking of A Personal God: An Essay in Philosophical Theology* (Cambridge: Cambridge University Press, 1992).
Martin Buber, *I and Thou* (New York: Scribners, 1970).
Langdon Gilkey, "God," in P. Hodgson and R. King (eds), *Christian Theology* (Philadelphia: Fortress Press, 1982), pp. 62–87.
Colin E. Gunton, *The Promise of Trinitarian Theology* (Edinburgh: Clark, 1991).
Sallie McFague, *Models of God* (Philadelphia: Fortress Press, 1987), pp. 91–180.
Ronald H. Nash, *The Concept of God* (Grand Rapids: Zondervan, 1983).
A. W. Wainwright, *The Trinity in the New Testament* (London: SPCK, 1969).

Chapter 4 (9, 10)

Colin Brown, *Jesus in European Thought 1778–1860* (Durham, NC: Labyrinth Press, 1985).
Peter Carnley, *The Structure of Resurrection Belief* (Oxford: Clarendon Press, 1987).
J. D. G. Dunn, *Christology in the Making* (London: SCM Press, 1980).
Aloys Grillmeier, *Christ in Christian Tradition*, 2nd edn (London: Mowbrays, 1975).
Alister E. McGrath, *The Making of Modern German Christology*, 2nd edn (Grand Rapids: Zondervan, and Leicester, UK: Inter-Varsity Press, 1993).
John Macquarrie, *Jesus Christ in Modern Thought* (London: SCM Press and Philadelphia: Trinity Press International, 1990).
I. H. Marshall, *The Origins of New Testament Christology*, 2nd edn (Leicester: Inter-Varsity Press, 1992).
G. E. Michalson, *Lessing's Ugly Ditch: A Study of Theology and History* (University Park: Pennsylvania State University Press, 1985).
C. F. D. Moule, *The Origin of Christology* (Cambridge: Cambridge University Press, 1977).
Rowan Williams, *Arius: Heresy and Tradition* (London: Darton, Longman and Todd, 1987).

Chapter 5 (11)

D. M. Baillie, *God was in Christ: An Essay in Incarnation and Atonement* (London: Faber & Faber, 1956).

F. W. Dillistone, *The Christian Understanding of Atonement* (London: SCM Press, 1984).

R. S. Franks, *The Work of Christ: A Historical Study* (London/New York: Nelson, 1962).

Leon Morris, *The Apostolic Preaching of the Cross* (Leicester: Inter-Varsity Press, 1965).

S. W. Sykes (ed.), *Sacrifice and Redemption* (Cambridge: Cambridge University Press, 1991).

Dietrich Wiederkehr, *Belief in Redemption: Concepts of the Salvation from the New Testament to the Present Time* (London: SPCK, 1979).

Chapter 6 (12)

Julian N. Hartt, "Creation and Providence," in P. Hodgson and R. King (eds), *Christian Theology* (Philadelphia: Fortress Press, 1982), pp. 115–40.

Philip J. Hefner, "Creation," in C. E. Braaten and R. W. Jenson (eds), *Christian Dogmatics*, 2 vols (Philadelphia: Fortress Press, 1984), vol. 1, pp. 269–357.

David H. Kelsey, "Human Being", in P. Hodgson and R. King (eds), *Christian Theology* (Philadelphia: Fortress Press, 1982), pp. 141–67.

Alister E. McGrath, *Iustitia Dei: A History of the Christian Doctrine of Justification*, 2 vols (Cambridge: Cambridge University Press, 1986).

Paul R. Sponheim, "Sin and Evil," in C. E. Braaten and R. W. Jenson (eds), *Christian Dogmatics*, 2 vols (Philadelphia: Fortress Press, 1984), vol. 1, pp. 363–463.

N. P. Williams, *The Ideas of the Fall and Original Sin* (London: Longman, 1927).

R. R. Williams, "Sin and Evil," in P. Hodgson and R. King (eds), *Christian Theology* (Philadelphia: Fortress Press, 1982), pp. 168–95.

Chapter 7 (13)

Avery Dulles, *Models of the Church* (Dublin: Gill & Macmillan, 1976).

Philip J. Hefner, "The Church," in C. E. Braaten and R. W. Jenson (eds), *Christian Dogmatics* 2 vols (Philadelphia: Fortress Press, 1984), vol. 2, pp. 183–247.

Peter Hodgson, "The Church," in P. Hodgson and R. King (eds), *Christian Theology* (Philadelphia: Fortress Press, 1982), pp. 223–47.

Hans Küng, *The Church* (New York/London: Sheed & Ward, 1968).

Juan Luis Segundo, *The Community Called Church* (Maryknoll, NY: Orbis Books, 1978).

G. G. Willis, *Saint Augustine and the Donatist Controversy* (London: SPCK, 1950).

Chapter 8 (14)

Francis Clark, *Eucharistic Sacrifice and the Reformation* (London: Darton, Longman and Todd, 1960).

Robert W. Jenson, *Visible Words* (Philadelphia: Fortress Press, 1978).

Aidan Kavanagh, *The Shape of Baptism* (New York: Pueblo Publishing Co., 1978).

Bernard Leeming, *Principles of Sacramental Theology* (Westminster, MD: Newman Press, 1960).

David N. Power, *The Sacrifice We Offer: The Tridentine Dogma and its Reinterpretation* (Edinburgh: T. & T. Clark, 1987).

Hugh M. Riley, *Christian Initiation* (Washington, DC: Catholic University of America Press, 1974).

Alexander Schmemann, *The Eucharist* (Crestwood, NY: St. Vladimir's Seminary Press, 1988).

Herbert Vorgrimler, *Sacramental Theology* (Collegeville, MN: Liturgical Press, 1992).

World Council of Churches, *Baptism, Eucharist and Ministry* (Geneva: World Council of Churches, 1982).

Chapter 9 *(15)*

John B. Cobb, *Christ in a Pluralistic Age* (Philadelphia: Westminster Press, 1975).

——, "The Religions," in P. Hodgson and R. King (eds), *Christian Theology* (Philadelphia: Fortress Press, 1982), pp. 299–322.

Gavin D'Costa, *Theology and Religious Pluralism* (Oxford: Blackwell, 1986).

—— (ed.), *Christian Uniqueness Reconsidered: The Myth of a Pluralistic Theology of Religions* (Maryknoll, NY: Orbis Books, 1990).

John Hick, *An Interpretation of Religion* (London: Macmillan, 1989).

——, and Paul Knitter (eds), *The Myth of Christian Uniqueness* (Maryknoll, NY: Orbis Books, 1987).

Hendrik Kraemer, *The Christian Message in a Non-Christian World* (London: Harpers, 1938).

Harold A. Netland, *Dissonant Voices: Religious Pluralism and the Question of Truth* (Grand Rapids: Eerdmans, 1991).

Wilfrid Cantwell Smith, *Towards a World Theology* (London: Macmillan, 1981).

Chapter 10 *(16)*

John M. Baillie, *And the Life Everlasting* (London: Oxford University Press, 1934).

Carl E. Braaten, "The Kingdom of God and the Life Everlasting," in P. Hodgson and R. King (eds), *Christian Theology* (Philadelphia: Fortress Press, 1982), pp. 274–98.

J. A. MacCulloch, *The Harrowing of Hell* (Edinburgh: Clark, 1930).

James Martin, *The Last Judgement in Protestant Theology* (Edinburgh: Oliver & Boyd, 1963).

Paul Minear, *Christian Hope and the Second Coming* (Philadelphia: Fortress Press, 1974).

H. Richard Niebuhr, *The Kingdom of God in America* (New York: Harper & Row, 1959).

J. A. T. Robinson, *In the End God* (London: Collins, 1968).

John Sanders, *No Other Name: An Investigation into the Destiny of the Unevangelized* (Grand Rapids: Eerdmans, 1992).

Hans Schwarz, *On the Way to the Future: A Christian View of Eschatology* (Minneapolis: Augsburg Publishing House, 1979).

Krister Stendahl (ed.), *Immortality and Resurrection* (New York: Macmillan, 1965).

Theological Timeline

This chart aims to allow readers to survey the chronological development of Christian theology, by indicating the approximate dates of the readings set out in this volume. Note that some of the dates given in the earlier sections of this chart are uncertain. Also note that a number of writers, such as Augustine and Karl Barth, wrote over an extended period of time, making their precise location on the chart difficult to indicate.

	Year
Ignatius of Antioch	100
Justin Martyr	
Athenagoras of Athens	
Theophilus of Antioch	
Irenaeus	
Muratorian Fragment (*c.*190)	
Hippolytus	
	200
Clement of Alexandria	
Tertullian	
Origen	
Cyprian of Carthage	
Methodius of Olympus	
	300
Cyril of Jerusalem	
Arius	
Athanasius	

Council of Nicea (325)
Basil of Caesarea
Gregory of Nazianzen
Lactantius
Hilary of Poitiers
Ambrose
Ambrosiaster
Petilian of Citra
John Chrysostom
Epiphanius of Constantia

400

Augustine
Pelagius
Jerome
Rufinus of Aquileia
Council of Carthage (418)
Nestorius
Cyril of Alexandria
Leo the Great
Council of Chalcedon (451)
Vincent of Lérins
Fulgentius of Ruspe
Synod of Arles (c.473)

500

Gregory the Great

600

Apostles' Creed (final form)
John of Damascus

800

Paschasius Radbertus
Ratranmus of Corbie
Candidus of Fulda
John Scotus Eriugena

900

Simeon the New Theologian

1000

Lanfranc of Bec
Anselm of Canterbury
Gaunilo

1100

Peter Abelard
Bernard of Clairvaux
Hugh of St. Victor
Richard of St. Victor
Peter Lombard
Francis of Assisi

1200

Stephen Langton
Alexander of Hales
Thomas Aquinas

1300

William of Ockham
Benedict XII
Nicholas Cabasilas
Gregory Palamas
Julian of Norwich

1400

Jan Hus
Thomas à Kempis
Catherine of Genoa

1500

Jacques Lefèvre d'Etaples
Martin Luther
Philip Melanchthon
Kornelius Hendriks Hoen
Huldrych Zwingli
First Helvetic Confession (1536)
Sebastian Franck
John Calvin
Martin Bucer
Gallic Confession (1559)
Council of Trent
Heidelberg Catechism (1563)
Theodore Beza
Formula of Concord (1577)
Richard Hooker

1600

James Ussher
Racovian Catechism (1605)
George Herbert
John Donne
René Descartes

Westminster Confession of Faith (1643)
Blaise Pascal
John Owen
François Turrettini
Philip Jakob Spener
Benedict Spinoza
John Locke

1700

Friedrich Christoph Oetinger
Jonathan Edwards
Nicolas Ludwig von Zinzendorf
John Wesley
Gotthold Ephraim Lessing
Immanuel Kant

1800

F. D. E. Schleiermacher
Johann Adam Möhler
Ludwig Feuerbach
Karl Marx
John Henry Newman
Alexander Archibald Hodge
Martin Kähler
Charles Gore
Hastings Rashdall

1900

George Tyrrell
Albert Schweitzer
Peter Taylor Forsyth
Ernst Troeltsch
Gustaf Aulén
Karl Barth
Barmen Declaration (1934)
Ludwig Wittgenstein
Rudolf Bultmann
Reinhold Niebuhr
Dorothy L. Sayers
Dietrich Bonhoeffer

1950

Paul Tillich
Emil Brunner
Vladimir Lossky
Second Vatican Council (1965)

James I. Packer
Jürgen Moltmann
Wolfhart Pannenberg
Karl Rahner
Leonardo Boff
Hans Urs von Balthasar
Sallie McFague
Phyllis Tribble
Gabriel Fackre
Gustavo Gutiérrez
Brian A. Gerrish
Robert Jenson
Jacques Ellul
John Hick
C. S. Song
John B. Cobb, Jr
Thomas F. Torrance
Colin E. Gunton
Donald G. Bloesch
Mary Hayter
Lesslie Newbigin
George Lindbeck
Daphne Hampson
Paul Jewett
Philip E. Hughes
Clark Pinnock
Anne Carr

Index